Microsoft® Office PowerPoint 2010
A Lesson Approach, Complete

Pat R. Graves

Amie Mayhall

Connect
Learn
Succeed™

MICROSOFT® OFFICE POWERPOINT 2010: A LESSON APPROACH, COMPLETE

Published by McGraw-Hill, a business unit of The McGraw-Hill Companies, Inc., 1221 Avenue of the Americas, New York, NY, 10020. Copyright © 2011 by The McGraw-Hill Companies, Inc. All rights reserved. No part of this publication may be reproduced or distributed in any form or by any means, or stored in a database or retrieval system, without the prior written consent of The McGraw-Hill Companies, Inc., including, but not limited to, in any network or other electronic storage or transmission, or broadcast for distance learning.

Some ancillaries, including electronic and print components, may not be available to customers outside the United States.

This book is printed on acid-free paper.

2 3 4 5 6 7 8 9 0 RMN/RMN 1 0 9 8 7 6 5 4 3 2

ISBN   978-0-07-733119-1
MHID   0-07-733119-2

Vice president/Editor in chief: *Elizabeth Haefele*
Vice president/Director of marketing: *John E. Biernat*
Executive editor: *Scott Davidson*
Developmental editor: *Alan Palmer*
Marketing manager: *Tiffany Wendt*
Lead digital product manager: *Damian Moshak*
Digital development editor: *Kevin White*
Director, Editing/Design/Production: *Jess Ann Kosic*
Lead project manager: *Rick Hecker*
Buyer II: *Sherry L. Kane*
Senior designer: *Marianna Kinigakis*
Media project manager: *Cathy L. Tepper*
Interior design: *Kay Lieberherr*
Typeface: *10.5/13 New Aster*
Compositor: *Aptara®, Inc.*
Printer: *R. R. Donnelley*

Library of Congress Cataloging-in-Publication Data

Graves, Pat R.
   Microsoft Office PowerPoint 2010 : a lesson approach, complete / Pat R. Graves,
Amie Mayhall.
      p. cm.
   Includes index.
   ISBN-13: 978-0-07-733119-1 (alk. paper)
   ISBN-10: 0-07-733119-2 (alk. paper)
      1. Presentation graphics software. 2. Microsoft PowerPoint (Computer file) I. Mayhall,
Amie. II. Title.
T385.G7374452 2011
005.5'8––dc22

                                                          2010016095

The Internet addresses listed in the text were accurate at the time of publication. The inclusion of a Web site does not indicate an endorsement by the authors or McGraw-Hill, and McGraw-Hill does not guarantee the accuracy of the information presented at these sites.

www.mhhe.com

CONTENTS

POWERPOINT 2010

Unit 1 *Basic Skills*

v

Unit 2 *Presentation Illustration*

Unit 3 *Visual Impact*

Unit 4 *Development and Distribution*

Microsoft® Office PowerPoint 2010: A Lesson Approach is written to help you master Microsoft PowerPoint. The text takes you step-by-step through the PowerPoint features that you're likely to use in both your professional and personal life.

Case Study

Learning about the features of PowerPoint is one thing, but applying what you learn is another. That's why a Case Study runs through the text. The Case Study offers the opportunity to learn PowerPoint in a realistic business context. Take the time to read the Case Study about Good 4 U, a fictional business located in New York City. All the documents for this course involve Good 4 U.

Organization of the Text

The text includes four units. Each unit is divided into smaller lessons. The 14 lessons are each self-contained, but they build on previously learned procedures. This building block approach, together with the Case Study and the features listed next, enables you to maximize the learning process.

Features of the Text

- Objectives are listed for each lesson.
- The estimated time required to complete each lesson up to the Lesson Applications section is stated.
- Within a lesson, each heading corresponds to an objective.
- Easy-to-follow exercises emphasize learning by doing.
- Key terms are italicized and defined as they are encountered.
- Extensive graphics display screen contents.
- Toolbar buttons and keyboard keys are shown in the text when used.
- Large toolbar buttons in the margins provide easy-to-see references.
- Lessons contain important Notes, useful Tips, and helpful Reviews.
- A Lesson Summary reviews the important concepts taught in the lesson.
- A Command Summary lists the commands taught in the lesson.
- Concepts Review includes true/false, short answer, and critical thinking questions that focus on lesson content.
- Skills Review provides skill reinforcement for each lesson.
- Lesson Applications ask you to apply your skills in a more challenging way.
- On Your Own exercises let you apply your skills creatively.
- Unit Applications give you the opportunity to use the skills you learn throughout a unit.
- A Glossary and an Index are included. An Appendix of Microsoft's certification standards is also available on the OLC at www.mhhe.com/lessonapproach2010.

Lesson Approach Web Site

Visit the Lesson Approach Web site at www.mhhe.com/lessonapproach2010 to access a wealth of additional materials.

Conventions Used in the Text

This text uses a number of conventions to help you learn the program and save your work.

- Text to be keyed appears either in **red** or as a separate figure.
- File names appear in **boldface.**
- Options that you choose from tabs and dialog boxes, but that aren't buttons, appear in green; for example, "Choose Print from the Office menu."
- You're asked to save each document with your initials followed by the exercise name. For example, an exercise might end with this instruction: "Save the document as *[your initials]*5-12." Your instructor may ask you to name your work with an identifier different from your initials.

If You Are Unfamiliar with Windows

If you're unfamiliar with Windows, review the next section "Windows Tutorial" before beginning Lesson 1. This tutorial provides a basic overview of Microsoft's operating system and shows you how to use the mouse. You might also want to review "File Management" to get more comfortable with files and folders.

Screen Differences

As you practice each concept, illustrations of the screens help you follow the instructions. Don't worry if your screen is different from the illustration. These differences are due to variations in system and computer configurations.

If you are not familiar with Windows, review this "Windows Tutorial" carefully. You will learn how to:

- Use a mouse.
- Start Windows and explore window features.
- Use the taskbar, menus, Ribbon, dialog boxes, and other important aspects of Windows.
- Practice using Search and Help.
- End a computer session.

If you are familiar with Windows but need help navigating Windows files and folders, refer to the "File Management" tutorial. There you will find information on how Windows stores information and how to use Windows Explorer, a tool for managing files and folders.

Computers differ in the ways they can be configured. In most cases, when you turn on your computer, Windows loads automatically and the Windows log-on screen appears. When you see the Windows log-on screen, you need to log on and key a password. In order to log on, you need to know how to use the mouse.

Using the Mouse

A *mouse* is a pointing device and is your access to the computer screen, allowing you to accomplish specific tasks. A mouse typically has two buttons—one on the left (primary) and one on the right (secondary). A mouse might also have a center button or a wheel. To use a mouse, place your right index finger over the left mouse button. Place your thumb on the left side of the mouse. (Left-handed users can switch mouse button functions by using the Control Panel.)

NOTE

Laptop computers typically use a touch pad to select or move objects rather than a mouse.

The mouse operates through a pointer, a screen object you use to point to objects on the computer screen. The normal shape for the mouse pointer is an arrow. To move the pointer arrow on the screen, you roll the mouse on any flat object, or on a mouse pad, which has a smooth surface designed for easy mouse rolling. Although you can use the keyboard with Windows, you will probably find yourself using the mouse most of the time.

To use the mouse to point to an object on the computer screen:

1. Turn on the computer (if it is not on already). Windows loads, and the log-on screen appears. The screen includes at least one log-on name and picture. If the computer has multiple users, you will see several names and pictures.

To log on, you need to move the mouse pointer to the log-on name that was assigned to you when your user account was created. The pointer on the computer screen mirrors the actions made by the mouse when you roll it. Place your hand over the mouse and roll it to the left. The pointer on the screen moves to the left.

2. Roll the mouse to the right, and watch the pointer on the screen move to the right.

3. Practice rolling the mouse in all directions.

4. Roll your mouse to the edge of the pad, and then lift it up and place it back in the middle of the pad. When you feel that you can control the mouse position on the screen, roll the mouse to the name you have been assigned.

To log on, you will need to click the name to select it. Mouse clicks are covered in the next section; instructions for logging on to Windows 7 are covered in succeeding sections.

Clicks and Double-Clicks

Pointing is a mouse action used to position the mouse pointer at a specific screen location. The tip of the mouse pointer should be touching the object on the screen. You may see a ScreenTip when you point to an object. A *ScreenTip* identifies or describes the object or command.

Figure 1
ScreenTip

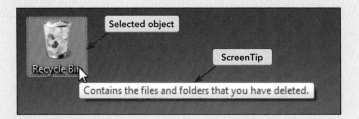

Single-click actions with the mouse are used to select objects or commands. To practice a single click:

1. Roll the mouse around on the mouse pad until the pointer on the screen is over the Recycle Bin icon. Remember that the direction in which you move the mouse on the pad represents the pointer's movement on the screen.

2. Press and release the left mouse button once. Pressing and releasing the mouse button is referred to as a *click*. The computer tells you that the action has been performed when the object you click is *highlighted* (typically, the color of the selected object changes) to indicate to you that it has been *selected*. In Windows, you often need to select an object before you can perform an action. For example, you usually need to select an object before you can copy it. Click a blank area of the computer screen to deselect the Recycle Bin icon.

Pressing and releasing the mouse button twice is referred to as a *double-click*. When you double-click an object on the screen, it is selected—the object is highlighted—and an action is performed. For example:

When you double-click a folder, it is highlighted and opens to a window showing the items the folder contains.

When you double-click a word in a text file, it is selected for a future action. In a text file, the pointer becomes an I-beam for selecting text in the document.

1. Point to and double-click the Recycle Bin icon. The Recycle Bin window displays.

Figure 2
Recycle Bin window

2. Locate and point to the red button in the upper-right corner of the Recycle Bin window. A ScreenTip identifies the Close button.
3. Click the Close button 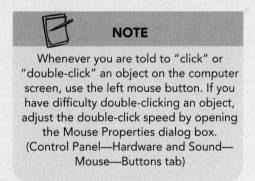 one time to close the Recycle Bin window.

NOTE

Whenever you are told to "click" or "double-click" an object on the computer screen, use the left mouse button. If you have difficulty double-clicking an object, adjust the double-click speed by opening the Mouse Properties dialog box. (Control Panel—Hardware and Sound— Mouse—Buttons tab)

Selecting and Highlighting

You can also select a larger object such as a picture or a block of text by using the mouse. Position the pointer on one side of the object, and hold down the left mouse button. Roll the mouse until the pointer reaches the other side of the object. Release the mouse button. The selected object is highlighted.

Drag and Drop—Moving an Object Using the Mouse

You can use the mouse to move an object on the screen to another screen location. In this operation, you select an object and drag the mouse to move the selected object, such as an icon. The operation is known as *drag and drop*. Follow the steps listed below to drag and drop objects.

1. Using the mouse, move the pointer over the object you want to drag.
2. Press the left mouse button but keep it pressed down. The selected object will be highlighted.
3. With the left mouse button still depressed, roll the mouse until the pointer and selected object are placed at the desired new location.
4. Release the mouse button to drop the object. The object is now positioned at the new location.

Using the Right Mouse Button

Pressing and quickly releasing the right mouse button is referred to as a *right-click*. Although the right mouse button is used less frequently, using it can be a real time-saver. When you right-click an icon, a *shortcut menu* appears with a list of commands. The list of commands displayed varies for each icon or object.

Figure 3
Shortcut menu

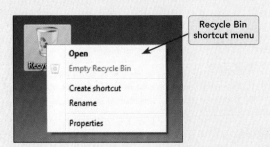

As you progress in this tutorial, you will become familiar with the terms in Table 1, describing the actions you can take with a mouse.

TABLE 1 Mouse Terms

TERM	DESCRIPTION
Point	Roll the mouse until the tip of the pointer is touching the desired object on the computer screen.
Click	Quickly press and release the left mouse button. Single-clicking selects objects.
Double-click	Quickly press and release the left mouse button twice. Double-clicking selects an object and performs an action such as opening a folder.
Drag	Point to an object on-screen, hold down the left mouse button, and roll the mouse until the pointer is in position. Then release the mouse button (drag and drop).
Right-click	Quickly press and release the right mouse button. A shortcut menu appears.
Select	When working in Windows, you must first select an object in order to work with it. Many objects are selected with a single click. However, depending on the size and type of object to be selected, you may need to roll the mouse to include an entire area: Holding down the left mouse button, roll the mouse so that the pointer moves from one side of an object to another. Then release the mouse button.

Pointer Shapes

As you perform actions on screen using the mouse, the mouse pointer changes its shape, depending on where it is located and what operation you are performing. Table 2 shows the most common types of mouse pointers.

TABLE 2 Frequently Used Mouse Pointers

SHAPE	NAME	DESCRIPTION
⬉	Pointer	Used to point to objects.
I	I-Beam	Used in keying text, inserting text, and selecting text.
⬌	Two-headed arrow	Used to change the size of objects or windows.
✥	Four-headed arrow	Used to move objects.
◎	Busy	Indicates the computer is processing a command. While the busy or working in background pointer is displayed, it is best to wait rather than try to continue working. Note: Some of the working in background actions will not allow you to perform other procedures until processing is completed.
⬉◌	Working in background	
👆	Link Select	Used to select a *link* in Windows' Help or other programs.

Starting Windows: The Log-on Screen

The Windows 7 log-on screen allows several people to use the same computer at different times. Each person is assigned a user account that determines which files and folders can be accessed and personal preferences, such as your desktop background. Each person's files are hidden from other users. However, users may share selected files using the Public folder. The log-on screen lists each user allocated to the computer by name.

If the administrator has added your name to a given computer, the log-on screen will include your name. If the computers are not assigned to specific individuals, you may find a box for Guest or for a generic user. If your computer is on a network, your instructor might need to provide you with special start-up instructions.

After you have logged on to Windows 7, the *desktop* is the first screen you will see. It is your on-screen work area. All the elements you need to start working with Windows appear on the desktop.

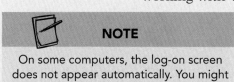

NOTE

On some computers, the log-on screen does not appear automatically. You might have to press the following keys, all at once, and then quickly release them: Ctrl + Alt + Delete .

1. If you have not already turned on the computer, do so now to begin the Windows 7 loading process. The Windows log-on screen appears.

2. Click your name to select it. The Password box appears with an I-beam in position ready for you to key your password.

3. Key your password.

4. Click the arrow icon to the right of the box. If you have entered the password correctly, the Windows desktop appears. If you made an error, the Password box returns for you to key the correct password.

The Windows Desktop

The Windows Desktop includes the Start button, taskbar, and Notification area. You may also see icons on the desktop that represent folders, programs, or other objects. You can add and delete icons from the desktop as well as change the desktop background. The Start button is your entry into Windows 7 functions.

Figure 4
Windows 7 Desktop

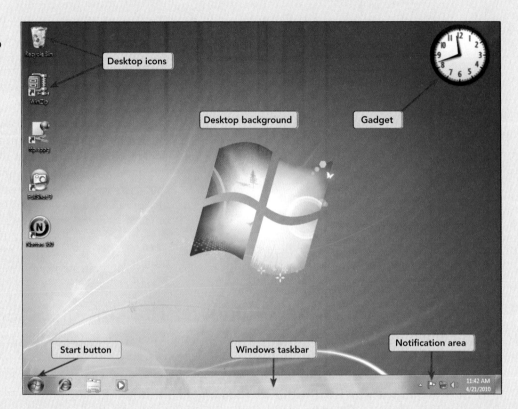

Using the Start Menu

Click the Start button on the Windows taskbar to open the Start menu. You can also press the Windows logo key on the keyboard or press Ctrl+Esc to open the Start menu. Use the Start menu to launch programs, adjust computer settings, search for files and folders, and turn off the computer. If this is a computer assigned to you for log-on, your Start menu may contain items that differ from those of another user assigned to the same computer.

1. To open and learn about the Start menu, first click the Start button on the Windows taskbar. The Start menu appears.

Figure 5
Start menu

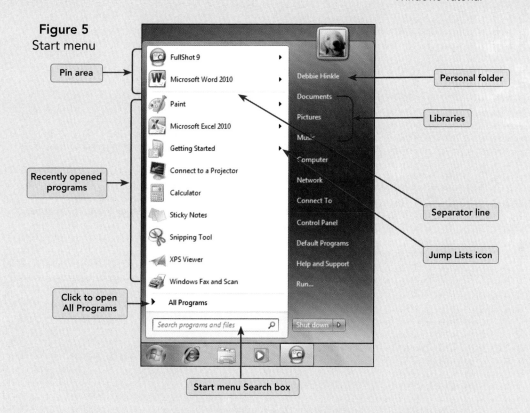

Pin area →

Recently opened programs →

Click to open All Programs →

Personal folder →

Libraries →

Separator line →

Jump Lists icon →

Start menu Search box

The left pane consists of three sections divided by separator lines. The top section, called the *pin area*, lists programs that are always available for you to open. These programs can include your Internet browser, e-mail program, your word processor, and so forth. You can remove programs you do not want listed, rearrange them, and add those you prefer.

Below the separator line are shortcuts to programs you use most often, placed there automatically by Windows. You can remove programs you do not want listed, rearrange them, but not add any manually. The Recently opened programs list displays up to ten programs. Use the Jump Lists icon  for quick access to documents, files, or tasks. Simply click the Jump Lists icon , and a submenu appears to the right of the Start menu program. *All Programs* displays a list of programs on your computer and is used to launch programs not listed on the Start menu.

Below the left pane is the *Search box,* which is used to locate programs and files on your computer.

The right pane is also divided into three sections. It is used to select folders, files, and commands and to change settings. Use the Shut down button at the bottom of the right pane to end the computer session.

2. Close the Start menu by clicking a blank area of the desktop.

NOTE

The list of programs in your Start menu is dynamic. Installing new programs adds new items to the Start menu. Frequently used programs are placed in the left pane of the Start menu automatically.

Table 3 describes the typical components of the Start menu.

TABLE 3 Typical Components of the Start Menu

COMMAND	USE
Left Pane	
Pin area	Lists programs that are always available. You can add and delete items to the pin area.
Below the First Separator Line	
Programs	Lists programs that you use most often. You can add to and rearrange the programs listed.
Below the Second Separator Line	
All Programs	Click to display a list of programs in alphabetical order and a list of folders. Click to open a program.
Search	Use to search programs and folders. Key text and results appear.
Right Pane	
Personal folder	Opens the User folder.
Documents	Opens the Documents library.
Pictures	Opens the Pictures library.
Music	Opens the Music library.
Games	Opens the Games library.
Computer	Opens a window where you can access disk drives and other hardware devices.
Network	Opens the Network window where you can access computers and other devices on your network.
Connect To	Displays networks and other connections that you can access.
Control Panel	Opens the Control Panel.
Devices and Printers	Opens a window where you can view devices installed on your computer.
Default Programs	Opens the Default Programs window where you can define default programs and settings.
Help and Support	Opens the Windows Help and Support window. Help offers instructions on how to perform tasks in the Windows environment.
Run	Opens a program, folder, document, or Web site.
Shut down button	Turns off the computer.

Using the All Programs Command

Most programs on your computer can be started from the All Programs command on the Start menu. This is the easiest way to open a program not listed directly on the Start menu.

1. To open the All Programs menu, click the Start button 🌐. The Start menu appears.

2. Click **All Programs** or the triangle to the left near the bottom of the left pane. The All Programs menu appears, listing the programs installed on your computer. Every computer has a different list of programs. Notice that some menu entries have an icon to the left of the name and others display a folder. Click a folder, and a list of programs stored in that folder appears. Point to a program to see a short description of the program. Click a program to open it.

Figure 6
All Programs

Program icons

Folder containing programs

Click arrow to return to opening Start menu

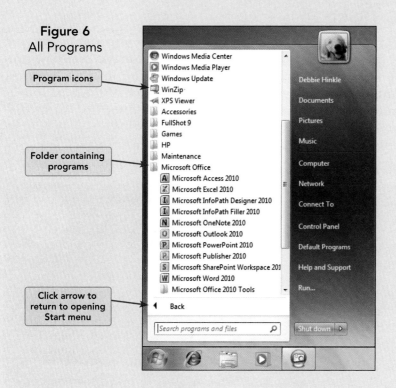

3. Click **Microsoft Office** to open a list of programs in the Microsoft Office folder. Click **Microsoft Word 2010**. (See Figure 6.) In a few seconds, the Word program you selected loads and the Word window appears. Notice that a button for the Word program 🅦 appears on the taskbar. Press Alt+F4 to close the window.

Customizing the Start Menu

Both the Start menu and the desktop can be customized. You can add short-cuts to the desktop if you prefer, and you can add and delete items from the Start menu. However, if your computer is used by others, the administrator may limit some customization functions.

To add a program to the pin area of the Start menu:

1. Point to the program you want to add to the pin list from the All Programs menu, and right-click it. A shortcut menu appears.

2. Click **Pin To Start Menu** on the shortcut menu. The program will be added to the pin list in the left pane above the first separator line.

To remove a program from the pin area of the Start menu:

1. Point to the program you want to remove from the pin list, and right-click. A shortcut menu appears.
2. Click Unpin From Start Menu. The program will be removed from the pin list.

To change the order in which programs are listed in the pin area:

1. Point to the program icon.
2. Drag the icon to the desired position.

Using the Taskbar

The taskbar at the bottom of your screen is one of the most important features in Windows 7. The taskbar is divided into several segments, each dedicated to a different use. The taskbar displays a button for launching Internet Explorer, Windows Explorer, and Windows Media Player, and each of these buttons is pinned to the taskbar. Point to each button to display a ScreenTip. The taskbar shows programs that are running, and you can use the taskbar to switch between open programs and between open documents within a program. A thumbnail preview appears when you move the mouse over a button on the taskbar.

Figure 7
The desktop and the taskbar

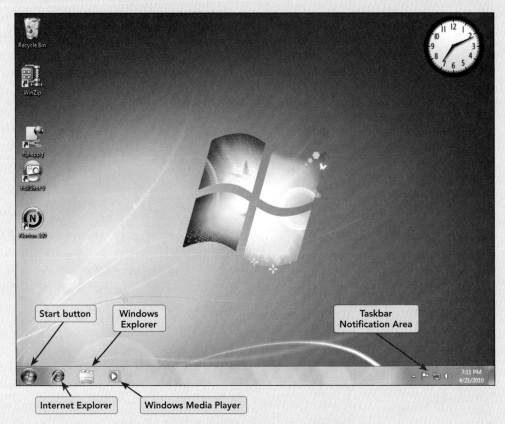

Taskbar Notification Area

The *notification area* is on the right side of the taskbar, where the current time is usually displayed. Along with displaying the time, tiny icons notify you as to the status of your browser connection, virus protection, and so forth. In the interest of removing clutter, the notification area hides most of the icons. Clicking the Show Hidden Icons button ▲ "hides" or "unhides" the icons in the notification area. Point to an icon to see a ScreenTip. Click an icon to open the control or program.

The Taskbar Notification area also includes the Show Desktop button ▯. The Show Desktop button appears at the right side of the taskbar. When you point to the Show Desktop button, the open program windows become transparent, and the desktop displays. The Show Desktop button is a toggle button. Click the Show Desktop button one time to minimize all open programs. Click again to display the programs. The *minimize* command temporarily removes a window from the desktop.

Figure 8
Taskbar Notification area

Show Hidden Icons button

Notification Area icons

Show Desktop button

The Active Window

The window in which you are working is called the *active window*. The title bar for the active window is highlighted, and its taskbar button is also highlighted.

1. Click the Start button and then click All Programs, Microsoft Office, Microsoft Word 2010 from the Start menu. The Word window displays.

2. Click the Start button and then click All Programs, Microsoft Office, Microsoft Excel 2010 from the Start menu. The Excel window displays. Notice how the Excel window covers the Word window, indicating that the window containing Excel is now active. Notice, too, that a new button for Excel has been added to the taskbar ▣.

Figure 9
Excel (the active window) covering the Word window

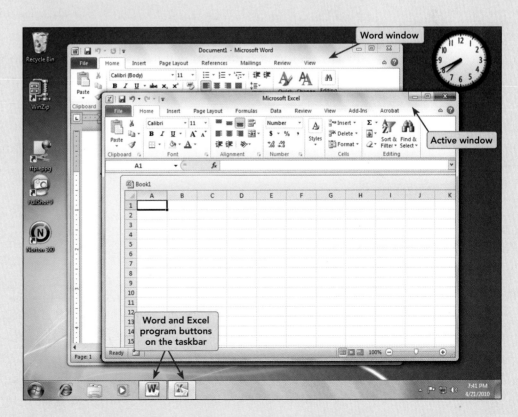

Word window

Active window

Word and Excel program buttons on the taskbar

3. Click the button on the taskbar for Word, the first program you opened. Word reappears in front of Excel. Notice the change in the appearance of the title bar for each program.

4. Click the button on the taskbar for Excel. Notice that you switch back to Excel.

5. Click the Word button on the taskbar to return to Word

Changing the Size of the Taskbar

You can change the size of the taskbar using your mouse if your toolbar is crowded. It is usually not necessary, because of the multiple document style buttons and other hide/unhide arrows on the taskbar. Before you can change the size of the taskbar, it may be necessary for you to unlock it. To unlock the taskbar, right-click an open area of the taskbar and click **Lock the Taskbar** to remove the checkmark. A checkmark is a toggle command. Click to turn it off, and click a second time to turn it on.

1. Move the pointer to the top edge of the taskbar until it changes from a pointer to a two-headed arrow ↕. Using the two-headed arrow, you can change the size of the taskbar.

2. With the pointer displayed as a two-headed arrow, hold down the left mouse button and move the arrow up until the taskbar enlarges upward.

3. Move the pointer to the top edge of the taskbar once again until the two-headed arrow displays. Hold down the left mouse button, and move the arrow down to the bottom of the screen. The taskbar is restored to its original size.

4. Close the Word and Excel programs by clicking the Close button ✖ for each program.

Parts of a Windows

Windows 7 displays programs and files in windows. When multiple windows display on the desktop, you will notice several common features in their appearance. Study the following windows and notice the similarities.

Figure 10
Notepad window

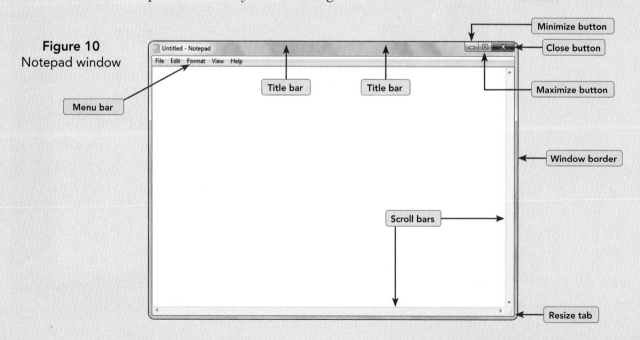

Figure 11
Microsoft Word
window

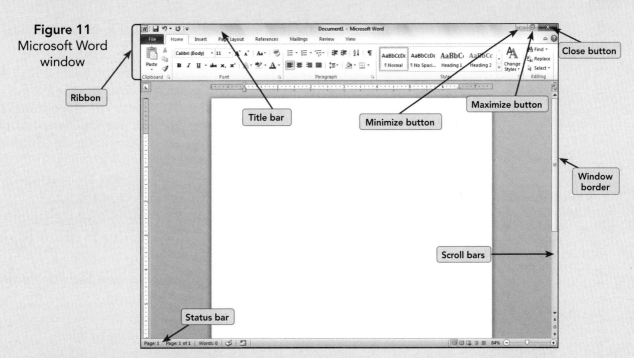

Ribbon

Title bar

Minimize button

Maximize button

Close button

Window border

Scroll bars

Status bar

Changing the Size of a Window

You can change the size of any window using either the mouse or the sizing buttons. Sizing buttons are the small buttons on the right side of the title bar that allow you to minimize or maximize the window (see Figures 10 and 11). This can be especially useful when you would like to display several open windows on your desktop and see them simultaneously.

NOTE

Notice that the window occupies the entire desktop, and the Maximize button has changed to a Restore Down button. This type of function is known as a toggle: When a button representing one state (Maximize) is clicked, an action is performed, the button toggles to the alternate state, and the other button (Restore Down) appears. A number of actions in Windows operate this way.

1. Open the Word and Excel programs if necessary. Click the Maximize button 🔲 on the Excel title bar if the Excel window does not fill the entire desktop.

Table 4 describes the sizing buttons.

TABLE 4 Sizing Buttons

BUTTON	USE
Minimize	Reduces the window to a button on the taskbar.
Maximize	Enlarges the window to fill the entire desktop (appears only when a window is reduced).
Restore Down	Returns the window to its previous size and desktop position (appears only when a window is maximized).

To practice changing the size of a window using the sizing buttons, follow these steps:

NOTE

You can double-click a window title bar to maximize or restore the window or right-click the program button on the taskbar and choose minimize, maximize, restore, or close. You can also use the *Shake* command to minimize every open window except the window you are "shaking." To use the shake feature, drag the title bar back and forth with your mouse until the other windows are minimized. You can also use the *Snap* feature to maximize a window. Point to the window's title bar and drag the window to the top of the screen. When the window's outline fills the screen, release the mouse.

2. Click the Restore Down button 🔲 on the Excel title bar. The Excel window reduces in size, and the Word window appears behind it. The Restore Down button has now changed to a Maximize button 🔲. Notice that the highlighted title bar of the Excel window indicates it is the active window.

3. Click the Excel Minimize button 🔲. The Excel window disappears, and its button appears on the taskbar.

4. Maximize the Word window by double-clicking the title bar. Double-click the title bar again to restore the window.

To practice resizing a window using the mouse, follow these steps:

5. Point to the lower right corner of the window. The mouse pointer changes to a two-headed arrow 🡢. Drag the window border toward the center of the screen. Drag the window border down and to the right to enlarge the window.

Figure 12
Sizing a window using the mouse

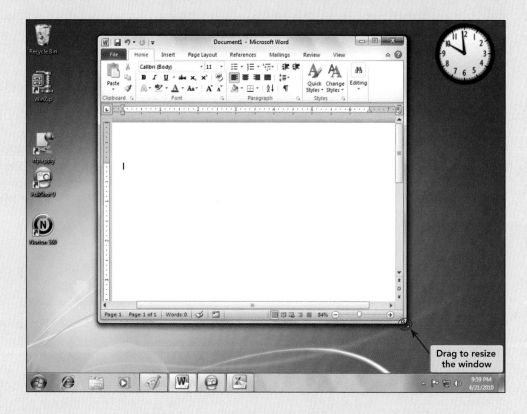

NOTE

You can place the pointer on any part of the window border to change its size. To change both the height and width of the window, move the pointer to the bottom right corner of the window. The double-headed arrow changes its orientation to a 45-degree angle (see Figure 12). Dragging this arrow resizes a window vertically and horizontally. Dragging a window border (top, bottom, left, or right) changes the vertical or horizontal size of the window. Sometimes the borders of a window can move off the computer screen. If you are having trouble with one border of a window, try another border or drag the entire window onto the screen by using the title bar.

6. Point to the top border of the window. Drag the border down to reduce the height of the window.
7. Point to the right border of the window. Drag the border to the left to reduce the width of the window.
8. Drag the window to the top of the screen. When the window outline expands to fill the screen, release the mouse.

Moving a Window

To move a window, point to the title bar and drag the window to a new location. You cannot move a maximized window.

1. Click the Word Restore Down button if necessary, and point to the Word title bar.
2. Drag the window to the lower left corner of the screen. Release the mouse.

Switch between Windows

When more than one program is open, you can switch between windows by using the sizing buttons or the taskbar. You can also press Alt+Tab to switch to the previous window.

1. If necessary, open Word and Excel, and maximize both windows.
2. Minimize the Excel window. The Word window displays.
3. Point to the Excel button [icon] on the taskbar. A thumbnail preview of the Excel window displays. If you point to the thumbnail, the thumbnail enlarges so that you can preview the window. This feature is called *Aero Peek*.

Figure 13
Taskbar buttons and thumbnail preview

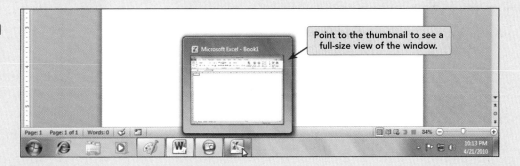

Point to the thumbnail to see a full-size view of the window.

NOTE

To display thumbnail preview, your computer must support the Windows Aero feature.

4. Click the Excel button to display the Excel window and to make it the active window.
5. Press Alt+Tab to switch to Word. You can switch to the previous window by pressing this shortcut, or you can continue to press Tab to switch to an open window on the desktop.

Display Two Program Windows Simultaneously

When multiple programs are open, you can arrange the windows using the following commands from the taskbar. You can also use the *Snap* feature to display two windows side by side on the desktop. To position two windows side by side, drag the title bar of one window to the left side of the screen until the window snaps to the left side. Release the mouse. Drag the second window to the right side of the screen until it snaps into place.

- Cascade windows
- Show windows stacked
- Show windows side by side
- Show the desktop

1. Open the Start menu, and display Excel and Word if necessary.
2. Right-click the taskbar, and click Show windows side by side. The windows display vertically.
3. Right-click the taskbar, and click Cascade windows. The windows display on top of each other. The title bar for each window is visible.
4. Click the Show Desktop button ⬚ located on the right side of the taskbar to see the desktop. The Word and Excel programs are minimized.
5. Click the Show Desktop button ⬚ again to restore the programs.
6. Right-click the taskbar, and click Show windows stacked. The windows are stacked vertically.
7. Click the Close button on the title bars of each of the two program windows to close them and to show the desktop.

Using Menus

When you open a window you may see a row of descriptive names just below the title bar. A menu bar contains a list of options for working with programs and documents. These operations are either mouse or keyboard driven. They are called commands because they "command" the computer to perform functions needed to complete the task you, the user, initiate at the menu level.

Executing a Command from a Menu

You open a menu by clicking the menu name listed in the menu bar. When a menu is opened, a list of command options appears. To execute a particular command from an open menu, press the left mouse button and then drag down and release the mouse (click and drag). You can also click the command once the menu is open.

Other Menu Symbols

Three dots following a menu option (an ellipsis . . .) indicate that a dialog box is displayed when that menu option is chosen. (Dialog boxes, discussed later, are small windows requesting and receiving input from a user.) Menus may also include a triangular arrow. Clicking the arrow displays a submenu with additional choices. If a menu command has a keyboard shortcut, the key or the combination of keys you press to activate the option appear on the right side of the menu. Commands that appear gray or dimmed are currently not available.

Figure 14
Notepad menu bar

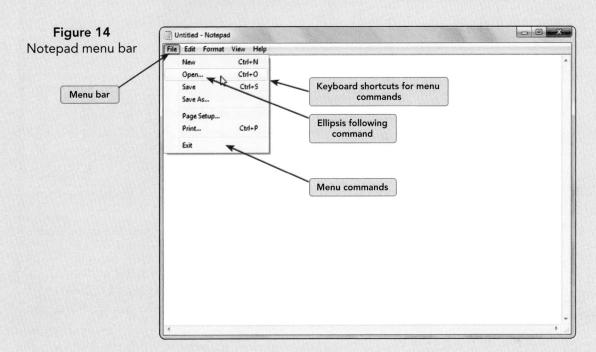

Perform the following steps for using menus:

1. Open the Start menu, click All Programs, and click the Accessories folder. Click Notepad. The Notepad program opens, and a button appears on the Windows taskbar.

2. Locate the menu bar, and click File. The File menu displays. Notice the keyboard shortcuts listed on the right side of the menu.

3. Locate the Open command and notice that three dots follow the command. Click the Open command. The Open dialog box displays. Click Cancel to close the Open dialog box.

4. Click File on the menu bar. Click Exit to close the Notepad window.

5. Click the Windows Explorer button 🖳 on the taskbar. The Windows Explorer window displays.

6. Locate the Organize command ⌈ Organize ▾ ⌋, and click the button. A menu of options appears below the command button.

Figure 15
Windows Explorer
window

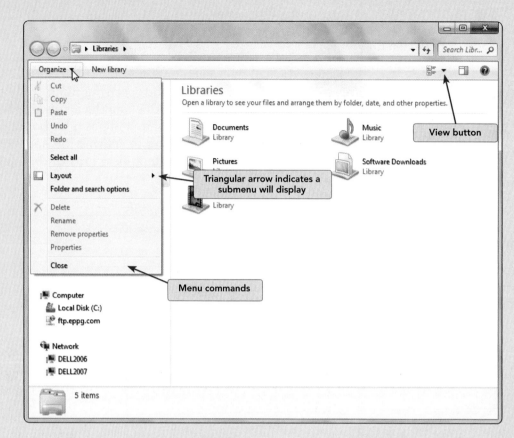

7. Click the Layout command, and a submenu displays with additional options. Notice that several of the options appear with a checkmark. The checkmark option ✓ indicates that the option is selected. Click the option again to turn off the checkmark.

8. Locate the View button 🔲▼, and click the arrow beside the button. Drag the slider to Medium Icons and notice the change in the appearance of the icons in the Windows Explorer window.

9. Press the Alt key, and a traditional-looking menu bar appears. Press Alt again to hide the menu bar.

10. Press Alt+F4 to close the Windows Explorer window.

Displaying a Shortcut Menu

When the mouse pointer is on an object or an area of the Windows desktop and you right-click, a shortcut menu appears. A shortcut menu typically contains commands that are useful in working with the object or area of the desktop to which you are currently pointing.

1. Position the mouse pointer on a blank area of the desktop, and right-click. A shortcut menu appears with commands that relate to the desktop, including view and sort options.

2. Click outside the shortcut menu to close it.

3. Right-click the time in the bottom right corner of the taskbar. A shortcut menu appears.

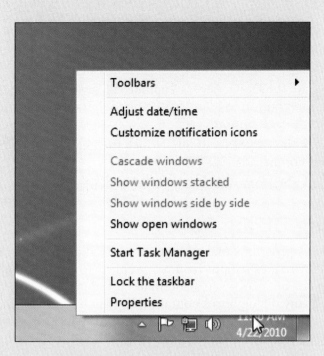

4. Click Adjust date/time on the shortcut menu. The Date and Time dialog box appears. You can use this dialog box to adjust your computer's date and time.

5. Click Cancel.

6. Right-click an icon on the desktop to display its shortcut menu, and then close the shortcut menu.

Using the Ribbon and Quick Access Toolbar

Microsoft Office 2010 applications include a Quick Access Toolbar and a Ribbon to access commands. The *Quick Access Toolbar* contains frequently used commands and is positioned above the Ribbon. The *Ribbon* consists of tabs, and each tab contains a group of related commands. The number of commands for each tab varies. A command can be one of several formats. The most popular formats include buttons and drop-down lists. The *File tab* displays a menu which lists the commands to create, open, save, and print a document.

1. Open the Word program. The Quick Access Toolbar arrow should point to the Save button.

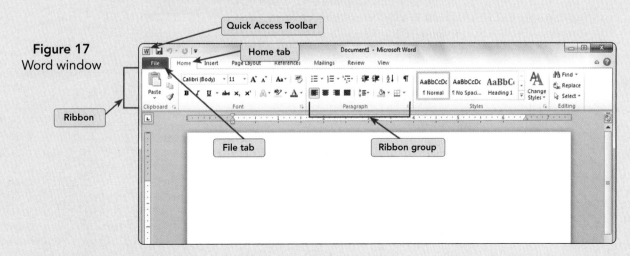

2. Point to and click the File tab. Notice the commands in the left pane.

3. Click the Home tab, and locate the groups of commands on the Home tab (Clipboard, Font, Paragraph, Styles, and Editing).

4. Locate the Quick Access Toolbar ⎸🖫 ↻ ⟳ ⎹ above the Ribbon. Point to each button to identify it. Notice that a keyboard shortcut displays beside each button.

5. Click the Page Layout tab. Notice the change in the number of groups and commands.

6. Click the Home tab.

Using Dialog Boxes

Windows programs make frequent use of dialog boxes. A *dialog box* is a window that requests input from you related to a command you have chosen. A dialog box appears when a command listed in a menu is followed by an ellipsis (. . .). Many dialog boxes contain tabs which resemble file folder tabs. Click a tab to select it and to display its options. All Windows programs use a common dialog box structure. Table 5 lists several options you will see in dialog boxes.

TABLE 5 Dialog Box Options

Check boxes are square in shape. Click a box to turn on (check) or turn off (uncheck) the option. You can select as many check box options as needed.	☑ Small caps ☐ All caps ☐ Hidden
A *Combo* or *List box* displays a list of choices. Use the scroll bar to display hidden choices. Use scroll arrows to move up or down in small increments. Drag the scroll box up or down to move quickly through the list of options. Click an item to select it, or key information in the text box.	Font: +Body +Body +Headings Agency FB Aharoni Albertus
Command buttons are rectangles with rounded corners, and they initiate an immediate action. If followed by an ellipsis (. . .) another dialog box opens.	OK Cancel Text Effects...
A *Drop-down list box* is rectangular in shape and displays the current selection in the rectangle. Click the arrow at the right of the box for a list of available options.	Font color: ▼
Option buttons are round in shape. Only one option may be selected from within a group of options. If selected, the option contains a dot.	Alignment ⊙ Left ○ Center ○ Right ○ Decimal ○ Bar
A *Slider* represents a range of values for a particular setting. Drag the slider left or right or click an arrow to change the current setting.	Brightness and Contrast Presets: ☼ ▼ Brightness: ──⬡── 14% ⇕ Contrast: ──⬡── -34% ⇕

(continues)

TABLE 5 Dialog Box Options   (*continued*)

Spin Box/Spinner includes two arrows. Click the up arrow to increase value. Click the down arrow to decrease value. Changes usually occur in an increment of one. You can also select the current value, and key a new number.

Text boxes are rectangular in shape and are used to enter data. An insertion point appears at the left side of the box, and text will be entered at the position of the insertion point. Press Delete or Backspace to delete or edit existing text. Double-click or drag over existing text to select it. Use the Home, End, or arrow keys to move the insertion point.

Margins

Top: 1"

Left: 1"

Gutter: 0"

File name:

Practice using dialog box options by completing the following instructions.

1. Open Word if necessary, and click the Home tab.

2. Locate the Font group, and notice the arrow in the lower right corner. Click the arrow (Font Dialog Box Launcher), and the Font dialog box displays.

Figure 18
Font dialog box

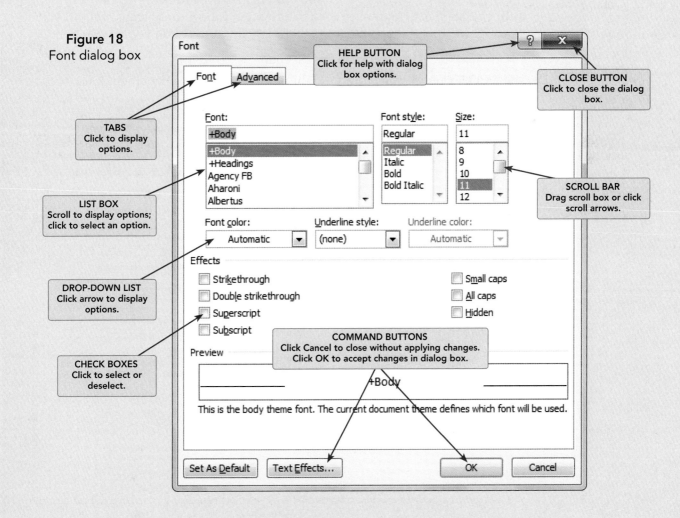

3. Click the Advanced tab, and notice the options in the dialog box. Click the Font tab.

4. Locate the Font group. The Font group displays a list box with several fonts available for formatting a document. Drag the scroll box to the bottom to view a list of available fonts. Click to select the Tahoma font. You can also click the up or down arrows to locate a font.

5. Locate the Font color group, and click the down arrow [▾] to the right of the box. Locate the Standard Colors, and point to the colors to view a ScreenTip. Click Blue. Notice the change in the Font color drop-down list.

6. Locate the Effects section. Click to select the check box for Small caps. A checkmark appears in the box.

7. Locate the command buttons at the bottom of the dialog box. Click Cancel [Cancel].

8. Close the Word program by clicking the Close button [X].

Changing the Desktop

Use the Control Panel to change the way Windows looks and works. Because your computer in school is used by other students, you should be very careful when changing settings. Others might expect Windows to look and work the standard way. Having Windows look or work in a nonstandard way could easily confuse other users. (Table 6 describes how to access other settings.) To change the appearance of your computer, follow these steps. Talk to your instructor first, however, before changing any settings on your computer.

1. Click the Start button on the taskbar.

2. Click Control Panel on the right pane. The Control Panel window displays.

Figure 19
Control Panel
window

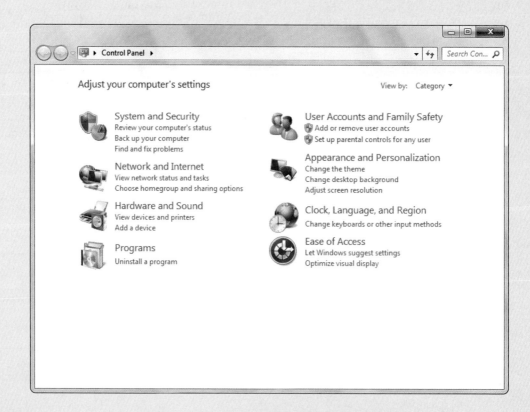

3. Click the Appearance and Personalization link. The Appearance and Personalization window displays.
4. Click Personalization and click the Window Color icon near the bottom of the window. Click a color from the color palette.
5. Click Save Changes.
6. Click the Desktop Background icon at the bottom of the Personalization window. Scroll through the list of pictures, and click to select a picture. Click Save Changes.
7. Close the Personalization window.

TABLE 6 Settings Options

OPTION	USE
Control Panel	Displays the Control Panel window, which lets you change background color, add or remove programs, change the date and time, and change other settings for your hardware and software. The items listed below are accessed from the Control Panel.
Network and Internet	Includes options to view the network status, connect to a network, set up file sharing, change Internet options, and so on.
Hardware and Sound	Includes options to add a printer, change default settings for AutoPlay, sound, mouse settings, keyboard, and so on.
Appearance and Personalization	Includes options to change the desktop background, adjust screen resolution, customize the Start menu and icons on the taskbar, and change sidebar properties.

Using the Search Command

If you do not know where a file or folder is located, you can use the Search command on the Start menu to help you find and open it. You can also use the Search box in Windows Explorer to locate an item.

1. Click the Start button on the taskbar. Notice the blinking insertion point in the Start Search box. You can start keying the name of a program, folder, or file immediately.
2. Key **calculator**. The Start menu is replaced with a list of options including programs, Control Panel items, files, and documents containing the characters you keyed in the Search box.
3. Click the Calculator option. The Calculator window displays.
4. Close the Calculator window.
5. Click the Windows Explorer button ⬚ on the taskbar. The Windows Explorer window displays.

Figure 20
Windows Explorer
window

6. Locate the Search box in the upper right corner of the Windows Explorer window.

7. Click in the Search box, and key **penguins**. A picture of penguins appears in the window.

8. Close the Windows Explorer window.

Using the Run Command

Windows allows you to start a program by using the Run command and keying the program name. This command is often employed to run a "setup" or "install" program that installs a new program on your computer. It is best to use this command after you have become more familiar with Windows 7.

1. Click the Start button on the taskbar.

2. Click All Programs, and click the Accessories folder.

3. Click Run.

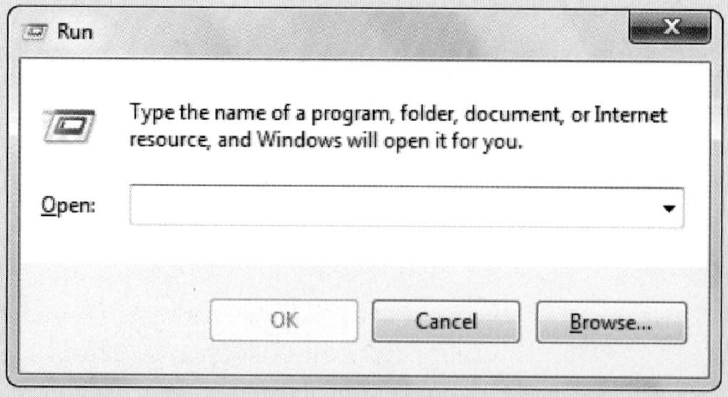

Figure 21
Run dialog box

4. If you know the name of a program you want to run, type the name in the Open text box. Often you will need to click Browse to open a drop-down list of the disk drives, folders, and files available to you.

5. Click Cancel to close the Run dialog box.

6. Open the Start menu, and locate the Start Search box.

7. Key **run**, and notice that the Run program displays under Programs.

8. Click the program name, and the Run dialog box displays.

9. Close the Run dialog box.

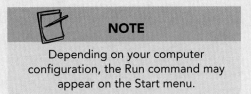

NOTE

Depending on your computer configuration, the Run command may appear on the Start menu.

Deleting Files Using the Recycle Bin

The *Recycle Bin* is the trash can icon on your desktop. To delete a file, click the file icon, and drag it to the Recycle Bin.

1. Double-click the Recycle Bin icon on the desktop. A window opens listing files you have deleted.

Figure 22
Recycle Bin window

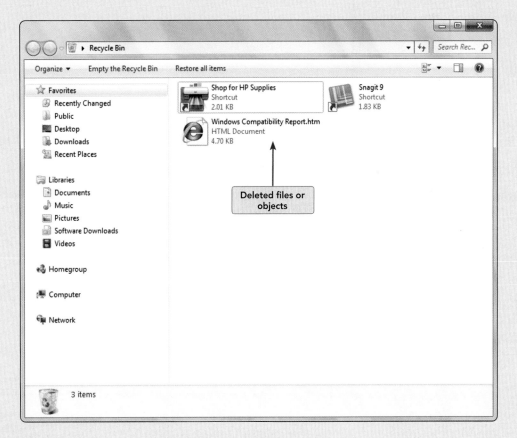

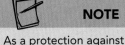

NOTE

As a protection against deleting a file unintentionally, any file you have placed in the Recycle Bin can be undeleted and used again.

2. To undelete a file, merely drag it out of the Recycle Bin window and place it on the desktop or right-click the file and click Restore.

3. To empty the Recycle Bin and permanently delete files, click Empty the Recycle Bin in the Recycle Bin window, or right-click the Recycle Bin icon on the desktop. The shortcut menu appears. Click Empty Recycle Bin.

Help and Support

Windows Help and Support is available to you as you work. Use the Help feature to answer questions, to provide instructions on how to do a procedure, or to troubleshoot problems you are experiencing.

1. Press the Windows logo key on the keyboard or click the Start button to display the Start menu.

2. Locate the Help and Support feature on the right side of the Start menu, and click to open the Windows Help and Support window.

Figure 23
Windows Help and
Support Window

3. Key **gadget** in the Search Help text box, and press Enter. A list of results for gadget appears in the Windows Help and Support window.

Figure 24
Search results for gadget

4. Point to the topic entitled "**Desktop gadgets (overview)**." Notice the shape of the mouse pointer 🖑. Click the topic, and the Windows Help and Support window displays information about gadgets. Read the information on Desktop gadgets.

5. Click the Back button ⬅ located in the upper left corner. You return to the list of gadget topics. Notice that the "Desktop gadgets (overview)" topic is a different color. When you visit a topic, the color of the topic (link) changes.

6. Click the topic entitled "**Desktop gadgets: frequently asked questions**."

7. Locate the **Show all** link in the upper right corner of the window. Click **Show all** to expand the text.

8. Key the text **keyboard shortcuts** in the Search text box, and press ⌅Enter. Click the link **Keyboard shortcuts**, then click the link **Windows logo key keyboard shortcuts**. Review the list. (You may want to print this list for future reference.)

9. Click the Browse Help button 📖 at the top of the Windows Help and Support window. Click the **All Help** link. A list of subject headings displays. Click a heading to view related categories.

10. Locate the Help button ❓ on the taskbar. Right-click the button, and choose Close window.

Exiting Windows

You should always exit any open programs and Windows before turning off the computer. This is the best way to be sure your work is saved. Windows also performs other "housekeeping" routines that ensure everything is ready for you when you next turn on your computer. Failure to shut down properly will often force Windows to perform time-consuming system checks the next time it is loaded. You can either log off the computer to make it available for another user, or shut it down entirely.

To Log Off

1. Click the Start button on the taskbar.
2. Click the arrow to the right of the Shut down button [Shut down ▷], and click Log Off.

To Shut Down

To exit Windows, use the Shut down command on the Start menu. This command has two important shut-down options which are accessed by clicking the arrow beside the Shut down button.

- *Restart:* Restarts the computer without shutting off the power. This is sometimes necessary when you add new software.

- *Sleep:* Puts the computer in a low-activity state. It appears to be turned off but will restart when the mouse is moved. Press the computer power button to resume work.

To shut down completely, click the Shut down button [Shut down ▷]. *Shut down* closes all open programs and makes it safe to turn off the computer. Some computers will turn off the power automatically.

1. Click the Start button on the taskbar.
2. Click the Shut down button [Shut down ▷].
3. Windows prompts you to save changes in any open documents. It then prepares the computer to be shut down.

Microsoft PowerPoint 2010 is a powerful and persuasive tool that can be used in many creative ways. It is the industry standard for business presentations. The possibilities for how you combine color, text, and graphics to illustrate your presentation are almost endless. However, making good choices requires more than just understanding how the program works. You need knowledge of your presentation situation and your audience to design your slides in an effective way. Also, speaking with the computer support of a slide show can be more demanding than speaking impromptu. You can appear very professional when you deliver your presentation with confidence and handle your software and equipment well.

To better understand the context of how PowerPoint is used in business, all the lessons in this text relate to everyday business tasks. Imagine yourself working as an intern for Good 4 U, a fictional New York restaurant. Through your work in this position you will develop design skills to prepare slides that are attractive and contribute to audience understanding.

Good 4 U Restaurant

The Good 4 U restaurant has been in business for only a little over three years, but it's been a success from the time it served its first veggie burger. The restaurant—which features healthy food and has a theme based on "everyday active life"—seems to have found an award-winning recipe for success. (Figure CS-1 shows the interior of the largest dining room in the restaurant. It features plants and a wide expanse of windows looking out over Central Park South, a tree-lined avenue on the south side of New York's Central Park.)

All the food at Good 4 U is low-fat and contains low sodium. The menu features a variety of vegetables (all organic, of course!), as well as fish and chicken. The restaurant doesn't serve alcohol, offering instead fruit juices and sparkling water. Good 4 U's theme of "everyday active life" is reflected on the restaurant's walls with running, tennis, and bicycling memorabilia. This theme really reflects the interests of the two co-owners: Julie Wolfe, who led the New York Flash to two Women's Professional Basketball Association championships in her 10 years with the team, and Gus Irvinelli, who is an avid tennis player and was selected for the U.S. Amateur team. Even the chef, Michele Jenkins, leads an active everyday life—she rides her bicycle 10 miles a day in and around Central Park.

Two years ago, Roy Olafsen was a marketing manager for a large hotel chain. He was overweight and out of shape. In the same week that his doctor

Figure CS-1 Interior of Good 4 U restaurant and a sampling of the fresh food prepared daily.

told him to eat better and exercise regularly, Roy received a job offer from Good 4 U. "It was too good to pass up," he said. "It was my chance to combine work and a healthy lifestyle." As you work through the text, you'll discover that Good 4 U is often involved in health-oriented products, as well as events that focus on athletics. Since Roy has been hired, he has worked to expand opportunities outside the restaurant walls and educate others about the healthy food available at Good 4 U. He has encouraged the restaurant to sponsor workshops, classes, marathons, and other health- and activity-based events. Roy has also encouraged Julie and Gus to expand their business by adding a catering component and by opening restaurants in two other cities.

As an intern at Good 4 U, you will work with the four key people shown in Figure CS-2 to help them develop presentations for potential customers, new hires, and community members. Each lesson will describe who will be presenting the material, the purpose of the presentation, and the intended audience. As you work with these presentations, notice the following things:

- The types of presentations needed in a small business to carry on day-to-day operations.

- The design of presentations. Real businesses must often focus on designing eye-catching, informative presentations for customers. The business's success is often influenced by the compelling presentations that sell its services to customers.

- The "Tips for Designing Presentations" at the end of this Case Study. Good presentations generally follow these basic guidelines.

Figure CS-2 Key employees

Julie Wolfe
Co-Owner

Gus Irvinelli
Co-Owner

Michele Jenkins
Head Chef

Roy Olafsen
Marketing Manager

As you use this text and become more experienced with Microsoft PowerPoint 2010, you will gain experience in creating, editing, and designing presentations for business that you can apply to your classes and work situations.

In your first meeting with Roy Olafsen, he gave you the following tips for designing presentations. These tips can be applied to any presentation.

Tips for Designing Presentations

- Prepare a distinctive title slide. Make sure the title identifies the presentation content.

- Maintain a consistent color scheme throughout the presentation for a sense of unity.

- Keep the background simple, and modify it to help create a unique theme for your presentation.

- Choose colors carefully so that all text can be seen clearly. You must have a high contrast between background colors and text colors for easy reading.

- Write lists with parallel wording, and be concise. Limit bulleted text to no more than seven words on a line and no more than seven lines on a slide.

- Avoid small text. Body text on slides, such as that for first-level bulleted lists, should be no smaller than 24 points. Text for second-level bulleted text or annotations may be slightly smaller, but not less than 20 points. Establish a hierarchy for text sizes based on text importance, and then use those sizes consistently.

- Think and design visually to express your message. Use graphics such as boxes, lines, circles, and other shapes to highlight text or to create SmartArt diagrams that show processes and relationships. Illustrate with pictures and other images as appropriate.

- Select all images carefully to make your presentation content more understandable. They should not detract from the message. Avoid the temptation to "jazz up" a slide show with too much clip art.

- Keep charts simple. The most effective charts are pie charts with three or four slices and column charts with three or four columns. Label charts carefully for easy interpretation.

- Provide some form of handout so that your audience can keep track of the presentation or make notes while you are talking.

- Include multimedia elements of animation, transitions, audio, and video if these elements strengthen your message, engage your audience, aid understanding, or make your presentation more compelling.

- Your final slide should provide a recommendation or summary to help you conclude your presentation effectively.

Unit 1

BASIC SKILLS

Lesson 1
Getting Started in PowerPoint

OBJECTIVES   *After completing this lesson, you will be able to:*

1. Explore Microsoft PowerPoint.
2. View a presentation.
3. Add text using placeholders.
4. Prepare presentation supplements.
5. Name, save, and close a presentation.

> Estimated Time: 2 hours

Microsoft PowerPoint is a presentation program widely used in business and in education. It enables you to show your presentation content in a visual way through on-screen slides that are displayed in a slide show. For example, a hotel manager may develop a presentation to help market the hotel at conferences and meetings, or an instructor may display notes for a lecture to help students keep focused. A financial analyst may present investment information to prospective clients, or a builder may present construction plans to an urban development commission for approval. Also, PowerPoint is an effective tool for creating flyers and other printed products because of its versatile drawing and layout tools.

In this lesson, you will be working as an intern with Roy Olafsen, Good 4 U marketing manager, to make revisions to a presentation he has developed. This lesson provides an overview of PowerPoint features so that you will become accustomed to the application screen and to the way slides move within a slide show. You will also see examples of graphics you will learn to create later in this text.

Exploring PowerPoint

NOTE

The presentations in this text relate to the case study about Good 4 U, a fictional restaurant.

To become familiar with PowerPoint, identify parts of the window such as the Ribbon, tabs, and command buttons shown in Figure 1-1. Several tabs are unique to PowerPoint, while others are very similar to tabs used in Word and Excel. The Quick Access Toolbar is located above the Ribbon.

TABLE 1-1 The PowerPoint Window

Part of Window	Purpose
Command buttons	Buttons designed to perform a function or display a gallery of options.
Groups	Logical sets of related commands and options.
Notes pane	The area where you can add speaker notes for the presenter.
Quick Access Toolbar	Located by default at the top of the PowerPoint window and provides quick access to commands that you use frequently.
Ribbon	Consists of task-oriented tabs with commands organized in groups.
Scroll bars	Used with the pointer to move a slide or outline text right or left and up or down. You can also use the vertical scroll bar to move from slide to slide.
Slide pane	The area where you create, edit, and display presentation slides.
Slides and Outline pane	The area that can display either an outline of the presentation's text or thumbnails—miniature pictures—of the presentation's slides. You choose either Outline or Slides by clicking the appropriate tab. (If this pane is not displayed, click the Normal view button.)
Status bar	Displays information about the current presentation.
Tabs	Task-oriented collections of commands. In addition to the standard tabs, contextual tabs appear relevant to the selected object.
Title bar	Contains the name of the presentation.
View buttons	Buttons used to switch between Normal view, Slide Sorter view, and Slide Show view.

Figure 1-1
PowerPoint window
in Normal view

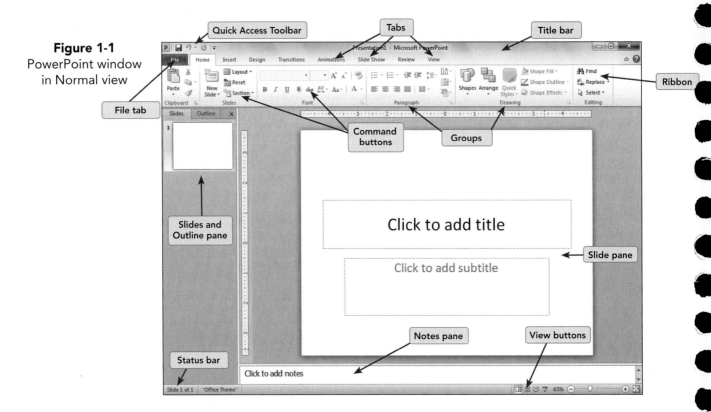

Exercise 1-1 IDENTIFY PARTS OF THE POWERPOINT WINDOW AND QUICK ACCESS TOOLBAR

The PowerPoint *Ribbon* contains nine task-oriented tabs: File, Home, Insert, Design, Transitions, Animations, Slide Show, Review, and View. Commands on each tab are organized in logical groups. A *ScreenTip* is the box displaying a command or object name that pops up when you point to it; sometimes a brief description will also appear. Within the Ribbon groups you will find drop-down galleries that easily present formatting options, graphics choices, layouts, and more.

The *Quick Access Toolbar* is a customizable toolbar located above the Ribbon. It contains common commands that function independently of the tab currently displayed. It can be moved under the Ribbon, but that location requires more space.

1.   Open PowerPoint. Using Figure 1-1 as a guide, move your pointer over items in the PowerPoint window to identify them by name using ScreenTips similar to Figure 1-2.

Figure 1-2
ScreenTip over the
New Slide command
button

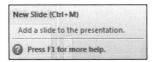

2.   Click the drop-down arrow at the end of the Quick Access Toolbar.

3.   Choose Show Below the Ribbon.

4.   Click the drop-down arrow again, and choose Show Above the Ribbon to return to the default position.

Exercise 1-2 OPEN AN EXISTING PRESENTATION

When you first open PowerPoint, you will often start a new blank presentation. However, in this exercise you open an existing PowerPoint presentation that Roy Olafsen developed for a local business organization to explain the background of the Good 4 U restaurant. You will make several revisions to this presentation.

1. Click the File tab to open Backstage view which displays quick commands.
2. Click Open.
3. In the Open dialog box, navigate to the appropriate drive and folder for your student files according to your instructor's directions.
4. When you locate the student files, click the arrow next to the Views button 📋 (see Figure 1-3) in the Open dialog box to display a menu of view options.

Figure 1-3
Folders listed in the Open dialog box

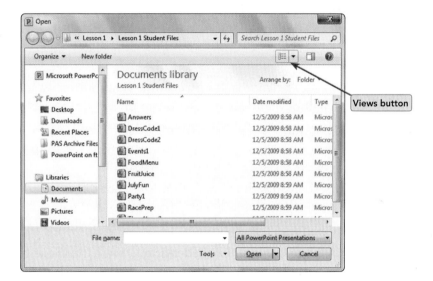

5. Choose Small Icons to list all files by name.
6. Click the Views button 📋 again, and choose Details to see the type of file and the date on which it was last modified.
7. Locate the file **ThreeYears2** (use the scroll bar if necessary), and click once to select the file.
8. Click Open. (You can also double-click the file's name to open it.) PowerPoint opens the file in Normal view.

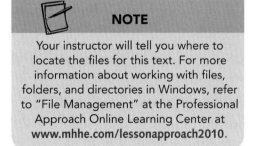

NOTE

Your instructor will tell you where to locate the files for this text. For more information about working with files, folders, and directories in Windows, refer to "File Management" at the Professional Approach Online Learning Center at **www.mhhe.com/lessonapproach2010**.

Exercise 1-3 WORK WITH RIBBONS, TABS, GROUPS, AND COMMAND BUTTONS

On the Ribbon, tabs reflect tasks you commonly perform, and they provide easy access to the commands organized in related groups of buttons and other controls. *Live Preview* is a feature that shows what your changes will look like before clicking or selecting an effect. Sometimes the group of available effects is presented in a *gallery* that displays thumbnails of different options you can choose.

1. Click the Insert tab.
2. Identify each of the groups located on the Insert tab: Tables, Images, Illustrations, Links, Text, Symbols, and Media. These groups contain command buttons that provide options through dialog boxes or galleries of options.

Exercise 1-4 USE MICROSOFT POWERPOINT HELP

Microsoft Office provides a *Help* feature that is an excellent reference tool for finding more information on any PowerPoint feature.

1. Click the Microsoft PowerPoint Help button 🔘 located on the upper right of the Ribbon, or you can press [F1]. The Help window will appear on top of your open PowerPoint presentation.
2. Key **Ribbon** in the search box located on the Help window, and press [Enter] (or click the Search button 🔍 Search ▾).
3. Scroll through the list of options that display, and click Familiarize yourself with the fluent Office user interface.
4. Read and scroll through the entire Help window.
5. When you have finished reading, click the Close button [✕] in the upper right corner of the Help window to close it and return to PowerPoint.

Viewing a Presentation

PowerPoint provides multiple views for working with your presentations based on what you need to do.

*   *Normal view.* Enter information directly on a slide or in outline format.
*   *Slide Sorter view.* Display multiple slides as thumbnails, or miniature slides, for a presentation overview, to rearrange slides, and to add special transition effects for the movements between slides.

- *Notes Page view.* Add speaker notes to accompany a slide.
- *Reading view.* Browse through your slides in sequence.
- *Slide Show view.* Display your presentation to an audience.

Views can be changed by using the View tab or by using the status bar at the bottom of the PowerPoint window.

Exercise 1-5 USE NORMAL AND SLIDE SORTER VIEWS

Normal view is the default view when PowerPoint opens and is the best view for writing text directly on a slide and designing your presentation. In this exercise, you will change to *Slide Sorter view* and rearrange slides by dragging.

1. Your PowerPoint window should be in Normal view. From the View tab, in the Presentation Views group, choose the Slide Sorter button 🖼. You may also use the Slide Sorter button 🖼 on the status bar.

2. Click slide 7 and hold down your left mouse button and drag until you see a vertical line before slide 6, then release the mouse button. This change creates a better sequence.

3. From the View tab, in the Presentation Views group, click the Normal view button 🖼 to return to Normal view. You may also click the Normal view button 🖼 on the status bar.

Exercise 1-6 USE THE SLIDES AND OUTLINE PANE

In Normal view, the *Slides and Outline pane* is at the left of the Slide pane. The Outline tab allows you to quickly enter text in an outline format because it shows only slide titles and listed text with *bullets,* small circular shapes, in front of each listing. The Slides tab provides thumbnails so that you can see or rearrange slides; it is similar to the Slide Sorter view.

1. Click the Outline tab at the top of the Slides and Outline pane to see only the presentation's text.

2. Point to the right border of the Slides and Outline pane. When the splitter 🔀 appears, drag the border about an inch to the right to increase the size of the Slides and Outline pane.

3. Scroll in the outline text until you see the text for slide 4.

Figure 1-4
Working with the
Slides and Outline
pane

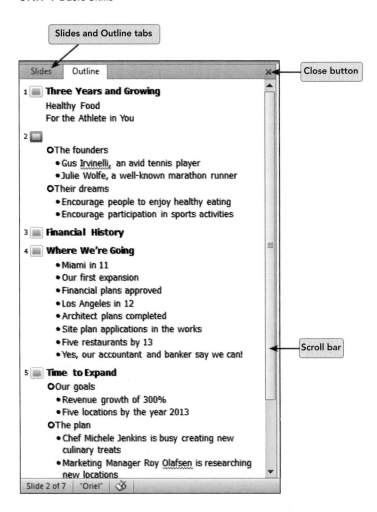

4. Working in the Outline tab, change each of the years (11, 12, and 13) to **2011, 2012**, and **2013**. The first line, for example, should read "Miami in 2011." Notice that, as you work, your changes are reflected in the Slide pane.

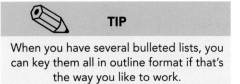

TIP

When you have several bulleted lists, you can key them all in outline format if that's the way you like to work.

5. Click in front of "Miami"; then from the Home tab, in the Paragraph group, click the Decrease List Level button ⊞ to promote the item by moving it to the left. Apply this same treatment to "Los Angeles in 2012" and "Five Restaurants by 2013." This distinguishes the main items in the list from the more detailed items under them.

6. Click the Close button ⊠ on the Slides and Outline pane to hide it. The Slide pane expands to fill the space.

7. From the View tab, in the Presentation Views group, click the Normal view button ⊞. The Slides and Outline pane is displayed again.

8. Click the Slides tab at the top of the Slides and Outline pane. The Slides and Outline pane becomes smaller and the size of the Slide pane increases.

Exercise 1-7 MOVE FROM SLIDE TO SLIDE

PowerPoint provides several ways to move from slide to slide when using Normal view:

- Drag the vertical scroll box, or click on the vertical bar above and below the box.
- Click the Previous Slide ▲ or Next Slide ▼ button located below the vertical scroll bar.
- Press PageUp and PageDown.

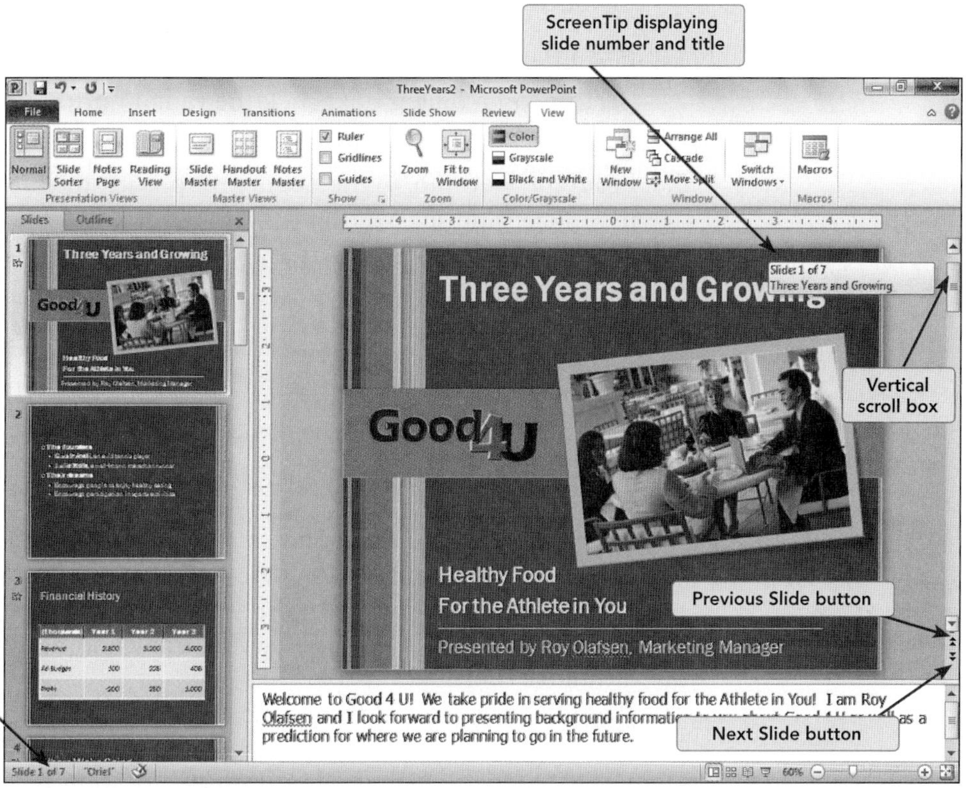

Figure 1-5
Moving from slide
to slide

1. At the right of the Slide pane, drag the box on the vertical scroll bar. Notice the pop-up box that displays slide numbers and slide titles as you drag. When you drag the box to the bottom of the scroll bar and release the mouse button, slide 7 appears in your window. Notice that slide 7 has a highlighted border around it in the Slides and Outline pane. This identifies it as the current slide.

2. Drag the scroll box up to display slide 6. Notice that "Slide 6 of 7" appears on the left side of the status bar to also identify the current slide.

3. Click the Previous Slide button ▲ at the bottom of the vertical scroll bar several times to move back in the presentation. Use the Next Slide button ▼ to move forward.

4. Press PageDown and PageUp on your keyboard several times to move to different slides. Use this method to move to slide 2. Check the status bar for the slide number.

Exercise 1-8   USE ZOOM AND FIT TO WINDOW

PowerPoint provides two different ways to change the size of the current slide in both Normal view and Slide Sorter view. The *Zoom* command can magnify your slide so that you can see small details for precise alignment and corrections. The *Fit to Window* command will change from the current zoom settings to fit your slide in the window that is open.

- From the View tab, in the Zoom group, click the Zoom or Fit to Window command button.
- Use the Zoom slider or Fit slide to current window button on the right end of the status bar.

1. From the View tab, in the Zoom group, click the Zoom button 🔍.
2. On the Zoom dialog box, click the radial button beside "200%" and click OK.
3. From the View tab, in the Zoom group, click the Fit to Window button 🔲 to reduce slide size so that the slide is viewable in the window.
4. On the right end of the status bar, click the Zoom In button (a plus) ⊕ until you reach "170%."
5. On the right end of the status bar, click the Fit slide to current window button 🔲 so that the entire slide is viewable again.

Exercise 1-9   USE READING AND SLIDE SHOW VIEWS

Both *Reading view* and *Slide Show view* display your slides at full-screen size beginning on the current slide. The Reading view command is on the View tab. From the Slide Show tab, you can start a slide show from the beginning or from the current slide. The Reading View and Slide Show commands are also available on the status bar.

Reading view is used to browse through your presentation with the title bar showing. The status bar is displayed with navigation tools to move from slide to slide. Slide Show view is used to show your presentation to an audience because only the slide is displayed. Navigation tools are available if you point to them.

In both views, slides can be changed by pressing the ⎵Spacebar, ⎙PageUp, ⎙PageDown, N, or P key or the arrow keys or by clicking the left mouse button.

1. Move to slide 1. From the View tab, in Presentation Views, click the Reading view button 🔲. The first slide in the presentation fills the screen, with the title bar at the top and status bar at the bottom.
2. On the status bar, click the right arrow to move to slide 2.
3. Press N on the keyboard to move to the next slide, slide 3.
4. Press P twice to return to slide 1. Press Esc to exit Reading view.

5. On slide 1, click the Slide Show button 🖵 located on the status bar to the left of the Zoom slider. The first slide in the presentation fills the screen.

6. Click the left mouse button to move to slide 2, and repeat to move to slide 3.

Exercise 1-10 OBSERVE ANIMATION AND TRANSITION EFFECTS

Animation effects are the special visual or sound effects that appear as objects are displayed on the screen or removed from view. *Transition effects* are the visual and sound effects that appear when changing slides. When developing this slide show, Roy Olafsen placed several different effects in the show to feature items on the slides and to control the way text appears on a slide while he is talking.

1. In Slide Show view and with slide 3 "Financial History" displayed, Press N to move to slide 4, which is titled "Where We're Going."

2. Using the left mouse button, click anywhere to see a sample of a PowerPoint text animation.

3. Press N again to move to slide 5 "Time to Expand." Notice the Box transition effect between slides 4 and 5.

4. Click the left mouse button two times to bring in the text on slide 5.

5. Press N to move to slide 6 "We've Come a Long Way." Press N three more times to bring in the text for slide 6. Notice the Entrance and Emphasis effects placed on this text. If your sound is on, you should also hear sound effects with each text item.

6. Press N to move to slide 7 and N again to finish the presentation.

7. Press Esc or – (minus) to end the slide show.

Adding Text Using Placeholders

Adding and editing text in PowerPoint is very similar to editing text in Word. When you point to an object on your screen that contains text, an *I-beam*, a vertical blinking bar in the shape of an uppercase "I," will appear and you can click in the position where you want to insert text. You can also drag the I-beam to select existing text. The Enter key moves the insertion point to the next line or bullet. The Delete key removes the character to the right of the insertion point. The Backspace key removes the character to the left of the insertion point.

Exercise 1-11 KEY PLACEHOLDER TEXT

Text *placeholders* are used for *title text* (the text that usually appears at the top of a slide), *body text* (text in the body of a slide such as a list), and other objects, such as picture captions. When you click inside a text placeholder, you *activate* it so that it is ready for editing or for inserting new text.

Placeholders help keep slide layout and formatting consistent within a presentation.

Body text often contains *bullets* (small dots, squares, or other symbols) to indicate the beginning of each item in a list; therefore, this text is called bulleted text. Bullets can also be decorative for an attention-getting effect.

NOTE

Notice that the pointer changes from an I-beam inside the border to an arrow pointer outside the border. When the pointer rests on top of the border, it becomes a four-pointed arrow, which can be used to move the text placeholder. When the pointer rests on top of a sizing handle, a two-pointed arrow appears for changing the placeholder size.

1. Move to slide 2, and click in the title text placeholder to activate the placeholder. Notice the border, a dashed line, that surrounds the placeholder, indicating that the placeholder is activated and you can edit or insert text. Sizing handles appear on the corners and edges.

2. Key the text **Where We Came From**.

3. In the body text placeholder, click anywhere on the line of text that begins "Gus Irvinelli."

4. Without clicking, move the pointer outside the placeholder border to the right and then back inside.

5. Drag the I-beam across the text "an avid" to select it, as shown in Figure 1-6. (Click to the left of "an avid," hold down the left mouse button, drag the I-beam across the two words, and then release the mouse button.)

Figure 1-6
Selecting text to edit

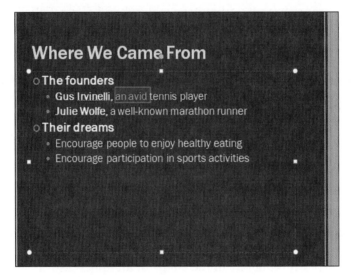

6. Key **a professional** to replace the selected text. (New text will automatically replace the selected text.)

7. Click the I-beam after the words "healthy eating," and press Enter to insert a new bulleted line. The new bullet is dimmed until you key text.

NOTE

Bulleted text lists the points being made in a slide presentation. This presentation uses open-circle and solid-dot bullets. Bullets can be changed to fit your presentation needs.

8. Key **Make their financial investments grow** after the new bullet.

9. Deactivate the placeholder by clicking a blank area of the slide. Be sure your pointer is a simple arrow, not an I-beam or a four-pointed arrow.

Exercise 1-12 CHANGE AND RESET PLACEHOLDER LAYOUT

Placeholders can be moved, resized, and rearranged on your slide. The *Layout* command of PowerPoint provides different slide layouts or can reset the placeholder to the original layout.

1.   Still working on slide 2, click in the title placeholder to activate it.

2.   Move your pointer to the outer border of the title placeholder.

3.   When your pointer turns to a four-pointed arrow (see Figure 1-7), click and drag the title placeholder to the bottom of the slide.

Figure 1-7
Selecting a
placeholder

4.   From the Home tab, in the Slides group, click the Reset button 🖼 to reposition the title placeholder in its original position.

Preparing Presentation Supplements

Although the primary way of viewing a presentation is as a slide show, you can also print PowerPoint slides in several different ways to create materials you will use as a speaker or to create documents for your audience. You should carefully review the way your document will look before printing and select settings appropriate for each presentation situation.

> **NOTE**
>
> Throughout this text you will be instructed to submit your work. Your instructor may require that you submit your files to an electronic drop box or that you print slides. To conserve paper and speed up printing, you may print a *handout* instead of full-size slides.

- *Slides.* Individual slides are printed in full size on separate pages.

- *Notes pages.* Individual slides are printed at the top of a page with speaker notes printed below.

- *Outline.* Only the slide titles and bulleted text are printed.

- *Handouts.* Multiple scaled-down slide images are printed on each page (one, two, three, four, six, or nine to a page) and are often given to an audience during a presentation. Printing several slides on a single page is also a good way to review your work away from your computer and a convenient way to print class assignments.

Exercise 1-13　PRINT FULL-PAGE SLIDES

You can start the printing process in one of the following ways:

- From the File tab, choose **Print**. The area that appears is called *Print Backstage* view. It displays PowerPoint's default print settings and indicates the designated printer. A preview of the current slide is shown with navigation and zoom controls on the bottom. A scroll bar is on the right.

- Press [Ctrl]+[P] to open the File tab with Print Backstage view displayed.

- From the Quick Access Toolbar, click the Quick Print button . You must first customize the Quick Access Toolbar to make this button available. Use it with caution. This feature does not allow you to control print options. It prints with the most recently used print options and could result in printing your entire presentation with one slide on each page.

1. To print the first slide in your presentation, display slide 1 and then, from the File tab, choose **Print**. The Print Backstage view appears, as shown in Figure 1-8. Some of the settings may appear differently on your computer depending on how PowerPoint was installed.

Figure 1-8
Print Backstage view

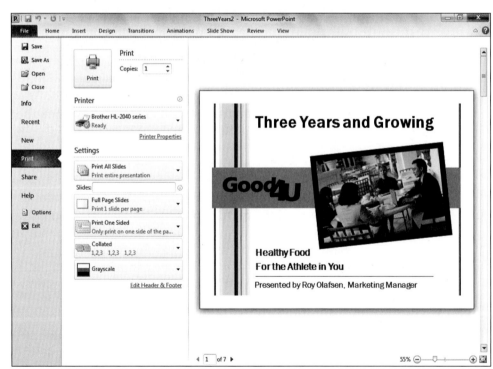

2. Notice that Print has the number of copies set for "1".

3. For Printer, the current printer is displayed. Click the down arrow to see the list of available printers. Follow your instructor's directions to choose an appropriate printer from the list.

4. Under Settings, look at the categories that are arranged as buttons with down arrows that display all your options. The option displayed on each button will change on the basis of the previous setting used. Make these changes:

    *   Click the down arrow for Print All Slides and choose Print Current Slide. This controls which slides will print.

        *   If Full Page Slides is displayed, it requires no change. This controls what you print, such as slides, notes pages, outlines, or handouts in a variety of layouts in both horizontal and vertical orientations.

        *   If Collated is displayed, it requires no change. This controls the printing order by choosing collated or uncollated.

        *   Color or Grayscale may be displayed depending on whether you are sending to a color printer or not; no change is required.

5. Click the Print button to print the current slide.

>
> **TIP**
>
> You can create a presentation that uses overhead transparencies by printing your slides on transparency film. Before printing, insert transparency sheets directly into your printer (choosing the correct type of transparency for a laser or ink-jet printer).

Exercise 1-14 PRINT NOTES PAGES AND OUTLINES

Roy Olafsen has written some notes on two slides of this presentation to remind himself about what he needs to say when those slides are displayed for his audience. In this exercise you will print those pages, review outline printing, and print a handout page.

In addition to the print settings covered previously, you will learn about printing in black and white. The *Grayscale* option converts the presentation colors to shades of gray. The *Pure Black and White* option converts all colors to either black or white, eliminating shades of gray.

1. On slide 1, press [Ctrl]+[P].

2. Under Settings, make these changes to prepare an outline:

    *   Click the down arrow for Print Current Slide, and choose Print All Slides.

    *   Click the down arrow for Full Page Slides, and choose Outline. Notice the text-only page that appears in the preview area. If you wanted to study the text of your presentation away from your computer, then printing this page would be convenient. To save paper, we will not print this view.

3. Notes pages provide a slide image at the top of a page with speaker notes below. Since Roy Olafsen made notes on slides 1 and 2, you need to print only those notes pages.

> **TIP**
>
> To print consecutive slides, you can use a hyphen. For example, key **2-4** to print slides 2 through 4. To print a combination of slides, you can key the range **1, 3, 5-9, 12** to print slides 1, 3, 5 through 9, and 12.

4. Under Settings, make these changes to prepare notes pages:

   - Click the down arrow for Outline, and choose Notes Pages.
   - Click the down arrow for Print All Slides, and choose Custom Range.
   - In the Slides text box, key **1,2** to print only slides 1 and 2.
   - Click the down arrow for Notes Pages, and choose the option Scale to fit paper to expand items to the full width of the page (or check the box beside Scale to fit paper).

5. If Color is displayed, click the list box down arrow and then Grayscale. If you have a color printer, you can choose Color from the list box but the grayscale setting will conserve your color ink or toner.

6. Click the Print button 🖨.

Exercise 1-15   PRINT HANDOUTS

For handouts, the number of slide images on a page can range from one to nine. You can use either landscape or portrait orientation, and the slides will be slightly larger if you choose Fit to Paper. Placing a line around the slides will make them more distinct on the page, especially if the slides have a light-colored background. You can choose to arrange the slides vertically or horizontally.

Roy Olafsen has seven slides in this presentation, and he has requested that you prepare a handout with all the slides on one page.

1. On slide 1, press Ctrl+P.

2. Under Settings, make these changes to prepare handouts:

   - Click the down arrow for Custom Range, and choose Print All Slides.
   - Click the down arrow for Notes Pages, and choose 9 Slides Horizontal to print the entire presentation on one page.
   - Click the down arrow for 9 Slides Horizontal, and select Scale to fit paper and Frame Slides (or check the box beside Scale to fit paper and Frame Slides).
   - Click the down arrow for Portrait Orientation. Click the list box down arrow and then Landscape Orientation so that the slides will be larger on the page. (If Landscape Orientation appears, it requires no change.)

3. For Print, change the Number of copies to **2**. The Collated list box by default is set to print the slide show from beginning to end two times.

4. For Color, click the list box down arrow and examine the options: Color, Black and White, or Grayscale. Click Grayscale. (If Grayscale appears, it requires no change.)

5. Click the Print button 🖨.

Naming, Saving, and Closing a Presentation

When you create a new presentation or make changes to an existing one, you must save the presentation to make your changes permanent. Until your changes are saved, they can be lost if you have a power failure or a computer problem; therefore, it is a good idea to save frequently.

The first step in saving a document is to give it a *file name*. File names can be up to 255 characters long, but short file names are generally preferred. You can use uppercase letters, lowercase letters, hyphens, underlines, and spaces. For example, you can use "Good 4 U Sales Report" as a file name. File names cannot include these characters: / \ < > * ? " : |

Throughout this text, your document file names will consist of **your initials** or an identifier your instructor asks you to use, such as **rst**, followed by the number of the exercise, such as **1-15**. PowerPoint assigns the file extension pptx, but you may not see this extension when you look at file names on your computer, depending on how the software is installed.

To save your presentation, you can use either the Save command or the Save As command.

- Use Save to update an existing document. The current file replaces the previously saved file. To save, click the Save button 🖫 on the Quick Access Toolbar; from the File tab, choose **Save**; or press Ctrl+S.

- Use Save As to name your presentation for the first time or to save your presentation using a different file name. In the latter case, the original presentation remains unchanged, and a second presentation with a new name is saved as well. To use Save As, from the File tab, choose **Save As**.

Exercise 1-16   CREATE A FOLDER AND SAVE YOUR PRESENTATION

NOTE

Your instructor will advise you on the proper drive or folder to use when creating your lesson folders.

Before saving a presentation file, decide where you want to save it: in a folder on your computer's hard drive, on a network drive, or on a removable drive. It's a good idea to create separate folders for specific categories to help keep your work organized. For example, you might want to create folders for different projects or different customers.

In this text, you will follow these steps to create a new folder for each lesson's work before you begin the lesson.

1. From the File tab, choose **Save As**. The Save As dialog box appears.

2. Using the list box at the top or folders on the left, follow your instructor's directions to navigate to the location where you should create your folder.

3. Click the New Folder button New folder on the Save As dialog box toolbar, as shown in Figure 1-9.

Figure 1-9
Save As dialog box

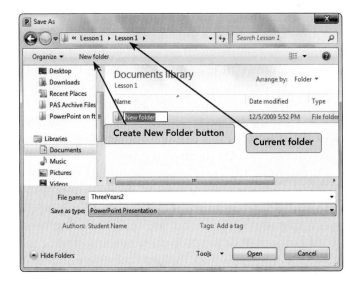

4. With the words "New folder" selected, key **Lesson 1** and click off the folder. A yellow folder icon appears with the name "Lesson 1."

NOTE

When saving presentations in the future, remember to navigate to the appropriate folder before saving your file.

5. Double-click the Lesson 1 folder to open it.

6. In the File name text box, key *[your initials]*1-16.

7. Click Save. Your document is saved for future use. Notice that the title bar displays the new file name.

Exercise 1-17 REVIEW PRESENTATION PROPERTIES AND PERMISSIONS

When a presentation is saved, PowerPoint automatically saves information about it such as the date created, file size, author name, and other information.

1. With your presentation still open, from the File tab, the Info group of quick commands will be automatically highlighted.

2. Notice the information on the right of the Backstage view.

3. Click the Properties button Properties ▾, and then click Advanced Properties. The General tab displays basic information about the file.

4. Click the Statistics tab. This tab shows precise information about the dates the file was created, modified, and accessed as well as the number of slides and other statistics.

5. Click the Summary tab. Here you can change existing information or add new information. Key *[your name]* as the author.

6. Click OK.

7. In the middle of the Backstage view, notice the Permissions category. The current setting indicates that the presentation is not restricted and anyone can open, copy, and change it.

8. Click the File tab again to close Backstage view.

9. Press Ctrl+S to save your changes to the properties of the document.

Exercise 1-18 CLOSE A PRESENTATION AND EXIT POWERPOINT

After you finish a presentation and save it, you can close it and open another presentation or you can close it and exit the program. Use one of these methods:

• From the File tab, choose Close or Exit PowerPoint.

• Use keyboard shortcuts. Ctrl+W closes a presentation, and Alt+F4 exits PowerPoint.

• Use the Close button ⊠ in the upper right corner of the window.

1. From the File tab, choose Close to exit the presentation.

2. Click the Close button ⊠ in the upper right corner of the window to exit PowerPoint.

Lesson 1 Summary

• Microsoft PowerPoint is a powerful graphics program used to create professional-quality presentations for a variety of settings.

• Identify items in the PowerPoint window by pointing to them and waiting for their ScreenTips to appear.

• PowerPoint command buttons are arranged in groups that can be accessed by clicking on the Ribbon tabs.

• The Quick Access Toolbar contains a set of commands independent of the tab that is currently displayed. The toolbar includes commonly used commands such as save, undo, redo, and print.

• The PowerPoint Help window is a great place to look for additional information on a topic or for steps in completing a task.

• Key and edit text on a slide in the same way as you would in Word.

• Use the Slide Show button to run a slide show. A slide show always starts with the slide that is currently selected.

- The Print Navigation pane provides a variety of ways to print your presentation: as slides, handouts, notes pages, and outlines.
- To print handouts that contain more than one slide on a page, use the Print Navigation pane to select from the Print Settings options.

LESSON 1		Command Summary	
Feature	Button	Ribbon	Keyboard
Close a presentation		File tab, Close	Ctrl + W or Ctrl + F4
Display Slides and Outline pane		View tab, Presentation Views group, Normal	
Document Properties		File tab, Document Properties	
End a slide show		Right-click, End Show	Esc or –
Exit PowerPoint		File tab, Exit PowerPoint	Alt + F4
Help		Help Button	F1
Next Slide			Page Down
Next Slide (Slide Show view)		Right-click, Next	N , Page Down
Normal view		View tab, Presentation Views group, Normal	
Open a presentation		File tab, Open	Ctrl + O
Permissions		File tab	
Previous Slide			Page Up
Previous Slide (Slide Show view)		Right-click, Previous	P , Page Up , Backspace
Print		File tab, Print; Quick Access Toolbar, Print button	Ctrl + P
Reading view		View tab, Presentation Views group, Reading view	
Reset		Home tab, Slides group, Reset	
Save		File tab, Save; Quick Access Toolbar, Save button	Ctrl + S
Save with a different name		File tab, Save As	
Slide Show		Slide Show tab, Start Slide Show group, From Beginning or From Current Slide buttons or View buttons, Slide Show	F5
Slide Sorter view		View tab, Presentation Views group, Slide Sorter	
Zoom		View tab, Zoom group, Zoom	

Concepts Review

True/False Questions

Each of the following statements is either true or false. Select your choice by indicating T or F.

T F 1. When you start PowerPoint, it automatically displays a blank presentation.

T F 2. Editing text in PowerPoint is similar to editing text in Word.

T F 3. ScreenTips identify command buttons by name only.

T F 4. In the Slides and Outline pane, you can display either slide thumbnails or outline text but not both at the same time.

T F 5. Using Normal view, you can edit text on the slide or in the Outline tab.

T F 6. You can display multiple slides as thumbnails in Slide Sorter view.

T F 7. When viewing a slide show, pressing the plus sign moves to the next slide.

T F 8. If you click the Quick Print button 🖶 on the Quick Access Toolbar, you can choose exactly which slides to print.

Short Answer Questions

Write the correct answer in the space provided.

1. What shape is the pointer when you move it over text?

_____

2. What is the purpose of using Zoom?

_____

3. Where on the PowerPoint window are the presentation view buttons always displayed?

_____

4. If the Slides and Outline pane is not displayed, what button can you click to make it appear?

_____

5. How would you save a copy of your presentation under a different file name?

_____

6. Name four ways to use the keyboard for moving to the previous slide during a slide show.

_____

7. Which keys can you press to stop a slide show?

_____

8. What is the maximum number of slides you can print on a handout page?

_____

Critical Thinking

Answer these questions on a separate page. Support your answers with examples from your own experience, if possible.

1. In this lesson you learned how to display slide thumbnails in the Slides and Outline pane and also in Slide Sorter view. Which way do you prefer to view thumbnails and why?

2. You can produce slide shows, printouts, overhead transparencies, and other presentation media with PowerPoint. Why might you choose one medium over another? What factors would influence your decision?

Skills Review

Exercise 1-19

Open a file, identify parts of the PowerPoint window, key text, print a handout, and save and close a presentation.

1. Open a presentation by following these steps:
    a. Open PowerPoint.
    b. From the File tab, choose Open.
    c. Choose the appropriate drive and folder, according to your instructor's directions.
    d. Double-click the file **Answers**.

2. Click anywhere on the text "Click to add subtitle," and key *[your name]*.

3. Select the two question marks in the text "Exercise 1-??" by dragging the I-beam across them. Key **19**.

4. To move to slide 2, click the Next Slide button ⬇ at the bottom of the vertical scroll bar.

5. Key your answers to the four questions on slide 2 by following these steps:
    a. Click to position the insertion point after the word "Answer:" and press [Spacebar].
    b. Key the answer to the question. Explore PowerPoint, and remember to use ScreenTips to help you answer the questions.

6. Print slides 1 and 2 by following these steps:

a. From the File tab, choose Print.

b. For Settings, choose:

- Print All Slides
- Handout with 2 slides on a page; check Frame Slides and Scale to Fit Paper.
- Grayscale.

c. Be sure the number of copies is 1 and then click the Print button .

7. From the File tab, choose Save As. Navigate to your Lesson 1 folder, and name the presentation as *[your initials]*1-19.

8. Close the presentation by clicking the Close button ⬛**X** in the upper-right corner of the PowerPoint window.

9. Close the presentation and submit your work.

Exercise 1-20

Edit text, save a presentation, run a slide show, print slides, and close a presentation.

> **NOTE**
>
> Before making the changes indicated in Figure 1-10, refer to "Proofreaders' Marks" at the Professional Approach Online Learning Center at **www.mhhe .com/lessonapproach2010**. Proofreaders' marks are special notations used to mark up a printed draft with changes to be made before final printing. Some proofreaders' marks might be confusing if you are unfamiliar with them. For example, a handwritten "=" indicates that a hyphen is to be inserted.

1. Open the file **FoodMenu.**

2. Notice on the status bar and by viewing the thumbnails in the Slides and Outline pane that this is a three-slide presentation (slide 1 of 3 now appears). Move to slide 3 by dragging the box on the vertical scroll bar.

3. Make corrections to the slide's text as shown in Figure 1-10.

Figure 1-10
Slide 3 corrections

```
Just Sweet Enough

     Carob Pecan Yogurt Cream Pie

This light and fluffy deŝert has an all-natural grâhm cracker crust,
great flavor, and very little sugar.

     Key Lime Soufflé

        intense
The  s̶t̶r̶i̶k̶i̶n̶g̶  lime flavor is Michelle's secret. Made from organic key
limes, sweetened with white grape juice, and thickened with organic
egg whites.
```

4. Move to slide 2, and notice that two items show the name of a dish and two items show the descriptions. The descriptions should be indented to distinguish them from the name of each dish; therefore, place your insertion point before each description and press Tab to indent those lines.

5. Run the presentation as a slide show by following these steps:

   a. Display slide 1. Click the Slide Show button .

   b. After slide 1 appears, click the left mouse button to advance to the next slide.

   c. Click the left mouse button three more times to return to Normal view.

> **TIP**
>
> If you are trying to insert text, but the text to the right of your insertion point is disappearing, click your Insert button once on your keyboard. This will take your computer out of Overtype mode.

6. Save the presentation as *[your initials]*1-20 in your Lesson 1 folder.

7. Print only slides 1 and 3 by following these steps:

   a. From the File tab, choose Print.

   b. In the Print range area, click Slides and key **1,3** in the text box.

   c. Choose Full Page Slides and Grayscale.

   d. Click the Print button.

8. Close the presentation by clicking the Close button   x .

9. Close the presentation and submit your work.

Exercise 1-21

Work with views, edit text, run a slide show, save, and close a presentation.

1. Open the file **DressCode1**.

2. View the presentation's text in outline format by following these steps:

   a. If the Slides and Outline pane is not displayed, click the Normal view button.

   b. Click the Outline tab.

   c. Point to the Slides and Outline pane's right vertical border, and drag the splitter bar to the right to increase the size of this tab. Move the splitter bar back to its original position.

3. Click the Slide Sorter view button, and move slide 3 before slide 2 by selecting slide 3 and dragging it before slide 2.

4. Double-click slide 1 to change back to Normal view.

5. Create a subtitle on slide 1 by following these steps:

   a. Click the text placeholder containing the text "Click to add subtitle."

   b. Key *[your name]*.

   c. Press Enter to start a new line; then key *[today's date]*.

6. Run a slide show and navigate within the show by following these steps:
   a. Click the Slide Show button 🖵.
   b. Advance through the slides by pressing [PageDown] several times.

7. Save the presentation as *[your initials]*1-21 in your Lesson 1 folder.

8. Close the presentation and submit your work.

Exercise 1-22

Key text, save, print a handout, and close a presentation.

1. Open the file **Events1**.

2. Display slide 2.

3. Insert a new line of bulleted text by following these steps:
   a. Click the I-beam after the text "National In-Line Skate demo team."
   b. Press [Enter] to start a new line with an automatic bullet.
   c. Key **Autograph session with Marsha Miles**.

4. Edit the text you keyed by following these steps:
   a. Click the I-beam between the words "with" and "Marsha" to position the insertion point.
   b. Key **aerobic video star**, and insert any necessary spaces.

5. Save the presentation as *[your initials]*1-22 in your Lesson 1 folder.

6. Print the slides full size by following these steps:
   a. From the File tab, choose Print.
   b. For Settings, choose:
      - Print All Slides.
      - Handouts, 6 Slides Horizontal, Frame Slides, Scale to Fit Paper.
      - Grayscale.
   c. Click the Print button 🖨.

7. Close the presentation and submit your work.

Lesson Applications

Exercise 1-23

Edit text, change presentation views, save, and close a presentation.

1. Open the file **Party1**.

2. Using the Outline tab, make the changes to slides 2 and 3 that are shown in Figure 1-11.

Figure 1-11
Slide 2 and 3
corrections

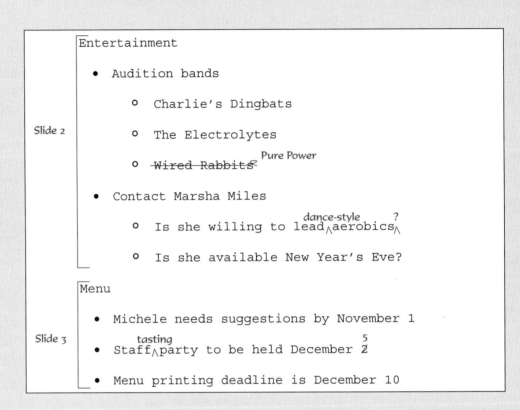

3. Save the presentation as *[your initials]*1-23 in your Lesson 1 folder.

4. View each slide in the presentation.

5. Print handouts three slides per page, grayscale, and framed.

6. Close the presentation and submit your work.

Exercise 1-24

Edit text, run a slide show, save, and close a presentation.

1. Open the file **JulyFun**.

2. Move to slide 2. Change "am" in the first and second bulleted text to **a.m.** Change the date in the last bulleted text to **June 25**.

3. Click the Outline tab, and drag the Outline pane's right border to make it wider.

4. Working on slide 3 in the outline area, change the age in the second bulleted item from "21" to **18**. Save the presentation as *[your initials]***1-24** in your Lesson 1 folder.

5. Click the Slides tab, and display slide 1. View the presentation as a slide show, clicking to display each new slide and text animation.

6. Close the presentation and submit your work.

Exercise 1-25

Edit text, print a handout, save, and close a presentation.

1. Open the file **DressCode2**.

2. On slide 1, key the word **Personnel** at the left of "Training" so that the second line of the title reads "Personnel Training Session."

3. Click to position the insertion point at the end of the last line of text on slide 2 (which begins "Under no circumstances") and key **while on the job**.

4. On slide 3, click to position the insertion point on the last line of text between "Good 4 U" and "test"; then key **proficiency** (the phrase should read "Good 4 U proficiency test").

5. Click the Outline tab, and make the Outline pane wide enough to work comfortably. Scroll down to display the outline text for slide 4.

6. Working on slide 4 in the Outline pane, delete the periods at the ends of the two sentences that begin "Guests" to have consistent formatting.

7. On the last bulleted text, change "Shirts are" to **T-shirts will be**.

8. Save the presentation as *[your initials]***1-25** in your Lesson 1 folder.

9. Print the presentation as a handout—four slides per page, grayscale, framed.

10. Close the presentation and submit your work.

Exercise 1-26 ◆ Challenge Yourself

Edit text, print a slide and handouts, and close a presentation.

1. Open the file **RacePrep**.

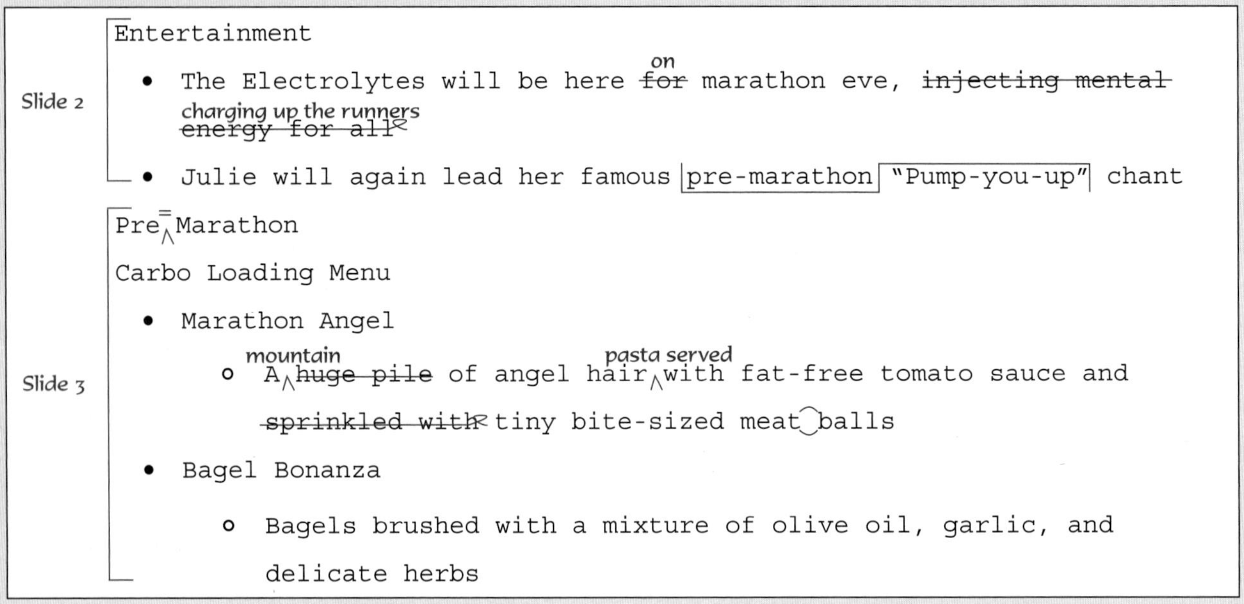

Figure 1-12
Slide 2 and 3
corrections

2. Using whichever view you choose, edit slide 2 and slide 3 as shown in Figure 1-12.

Slide 2

Entertainment

- The Electrolytes will be here ~~for~~ *on* marathon eve, ~~injecting mental~~ *charging up the runners* ~~energy for all~~

- Julie will again lead her famous pre-marathon "Pump-you-up" chant

Slide 3

Pre-Marathon

Carbo Loading Menu

- Marathon Angel
    - A *mountain* ~~huge pile~~ of angel hair *pasta served* with fat-free tomato sauce and ~~sprinkled with~~ tiny bite-sized meatballs

- Bagel Bonanza
    - Bagels brushed with a mixture of olive oil, garlic, and delicate herbs

3. View the presentation in Slide Sorter view.

4. Run a slide show of the presentation, beginning with slide 1.

5. Change the Properties to add your name as the author on the Summary tab in Advanced Properties.

6. Save the presentation in your Lesson 1 folder as *[your initials]*1-26.

7. Close the presentation and submit your work.

On Your Own

In these exercises you work on your own, as you would in a real-life work environment. Use the skills you've learned to accomplish the task—and be creative.

Exercise 1-27

Open the file **Events1**. Change the title on slide 2 to **Summer Events**. Edit the slide's bullets for June and July by changing the events to swimming, softball, sand volleyball, or other summer activities. Save the presentation as *[your initials]***1-27**. Preview and then print the presentation as handouts, two slides per page. Close the presentation and submit your work.

Exercise 1-28

Open the file **FoodMenu**. On slide 2, replace the text describing the pasta dishes with pasta creations from your imagination. On slide 3, replace the text describing the desserts with your own combination of sweet indulgences. The descriptions of food should be shown as bulleted text, indented beneath the name of the food item. Be sure the desserts you describe use healthy ingredients.

Save the presentation as *[your initials]***1-28**. Preview and then print the presentation as handouts, three slides per page. Close the presentation and submit your work.

Exercise 1-29

Open the file **FruitJuice**. On slide 1, add your name in the subtitle placeholder. On slide 2, decrease each of the list levels that begin with the word "variations." After the word "variations" under each type of juice, key your own creation of juice combinations that could create new juice titles. Get creative since the Good 4 U restaurant prides itself on serving healthy food and drinks. Save the presentation as *[your initials]***1-29**. Preview and then print the presentation as handouts, with landscape orientation, two slides per page. Close the presentation and submit your work.

Lesson 2
Developing Presentation Text

OBJECTIVES   *After completing this lesson, you will be able to:*

1. Create a new blank presentation.
2. Use the font group commands.
3. Adjust text placeholders.
4. Work with bullets and numbering.
5. Work with text boxes.

Estimated Time: 1¾ hours

You can add interest to a PowerPoint presentation by varying the appearance of text—this includes changing the font, text style, bullet shape, or position of text. You can change text appearance before or after you key it. Always strive for readability and continuity within your presentation.

In this lesson, you will learn how to change text attributes such as color, font, font style, and font size. You will also work with bullets and numbering for easy-to-read lists and modify paragraph indents. Several keystrokes you will use to quickly move around on slides or within your presentation are shown in Table 2-1.

As an intern at Good 4 U, you are developing content for a promotional presentation. Co-owner Julie Wolfe will be using this presentation when speaking to large corporations in the area to persuade them to get healthy and choose Good 4 U for their upcoming events.

NOTE

The documents you create in this course relate to the case study about Good 4 U, a fictional restaurant business (see frontmatter).

Creating a New Blank Presentation

PowerPoint provides several ways to begin a presentation. With any method, as you add new slides for your content, you choose an appropriate slide layout and key slide text.

TABLE 2-1 Using the Keyboard to Navigate on a Slide and in a Presentation

Keystrokes	Result
Ctrl + Enter	Selects and activates the next text placeholder on a slide. If the last placeholder (subtitle or body text) is selected or activated, pressing Ctrl + Enter inserts a new slide after the current slide. Pressing Ctrl + Enter never selects any objects on a slide (including text boxes) that are not placeholders.
Ctrl + M	Inserts a new slide after the current slide.
Enter	If a text box or text placeholder is activated so that the text can be edited, inserts a new paragraph, including a bullet if in a body text placeholder. If a text box or text placeholder is selected but not activated, selects all the text in the object.
Esc	Deactivates the currently activated text placeholder or text box and selects the entire text box instead. If a text box is selected but not activated, pressing Esc deselects the text box.
Esc, Tab	Moves to the next object on a slide, regardless of whether a text box is activated. It never inserts a new slide.
Shift + Enter	If a text box or text placeholder is activated, inserts a new line (but not a new paragraph) at the insertion point.
Shift + Tab	If a text box or text placeholder is not activated, selects the previous object on a slide. If the insertion point is between a bullet and the first text character on the line, promotes the bulleted text.
Tab	If a text placeholder or text box is activated, inserts a tab character at the insertion point; if not activated, selects the next object on the slide. If the insertion point is between a bullet and the first text character on a line, pressing Tab demotes the bulleted text. Pressing Tab repeatedly when no objects are activated cycles through all the objects on a slide but never moves to another slide.

- *Blank presentation*. Provides a plain background with simple text treatments and minimal color use. The very basic theme called Office is applied.
- *Theme*. Adds coordinated colors, font styles, background designs, and placeholder positioning to fit the background for an entire presentation. Themes give a unified and professional appearance.
- *Templates*. Provide a theme plus sample content as a guide in developing a presentation.

Since you will be learning how to create slides and key text in different ways, you will start this lesson with a blank presentation. Templates and Themes will be used in a different lesson.

Exercise 2-1 START A NEW BLANK PRESENTATION

Julie Wolfe would like to see the content for this presentation put together before deciding on colors and a design theme. Therefore, you will begin this exercise with a blank presentation.

1. Start PowerPoint. A blank title slide appears, ready for your text input, as shown in Figure 2-1.

Figure 2-1
Title slide

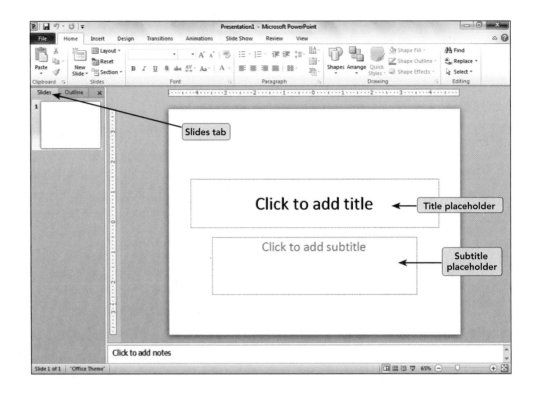

2. Click the title placeholder to activate it, and key **For the Pleasure of Your Company**.

3. Click the subtitle placeholder, and key **Plan Your Next Event with Good 4 U**.

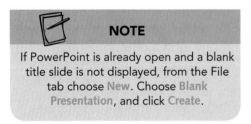

NOTE

If PowerPoint is already open and a blank title slide is not displayed, from the File tab choose New. Choose Blank Presentation, and click Create.

4. Position the insertion point after the word "Event" in the subtitle; then press Shift+Enter to insert a new line in the same paragraph. The subtitle is now split into two lines. Delete the space before "with" on the second line of the subtitle.

5. Using the same procedure, split the title text into two lines so that "Your Company" appears on the second line.

Exercise 2-2 ADD NEW SLIDES AND USE SLIDE LAYOUTS

To add a new slide after the current slide in a presentation, you can do one of the following:

- From the Home tab, in the Slides group, click the New Slide button.
- Press Ctrl+M.
- When a placeholder is selected, press Ctrl+Enter one or more times until a new slide appears.

When a new slide first appears on your PowerPoint window, you don't need to activate a placeholder to start keying text. When no placeholder is selected, as long as your slide pane is active, the text you key automatically goes into the title text placeholder. Knowing this can speed up the process of inserting new slides.

1. From the Home tab, in the Slides group, click the top of the New Slide button 🗒. A new slide appears, containing a title text placeholder and a body text placeholder.

2. Key **Excellent Service**. The text appears automatically in the title placeholder.

Figure 2-2
Keying text on a slide

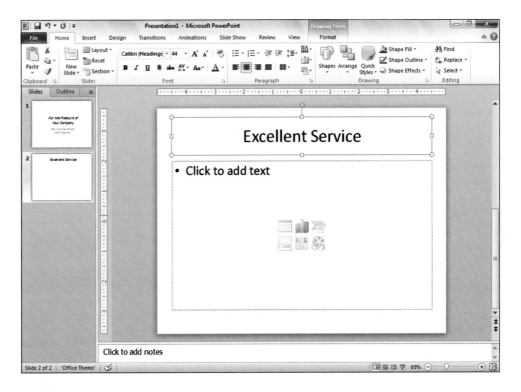

3. Press Ctrl + Enter or click the body text placeholder to activate it, and key the following text, pressing Enter at the end of each bulleted line:

   • We put your employees and guests at ease

   • We make your company look good

   • We adhere to promised schedules

   • We provide a professional and courteous staff

   • We guarantee customer satisfaction

4. Press Ctrl + M to create a new text slide.

5. Key **A Delightful Menu** as the title, and then key the following text in the body text placeholder:

   • High-quality, healthy food

   • Variety to appeal to a broad range of tastes

TIP

When you insert a new slide, it uses the same layout as the previous slide (unless the previous slide was the title slide).

6. From the Home tab, in the Slides group, click the down arrow on the New Slide button  to see thumbnail *slide layouts* with their names, as shown in Figure 2-3. Layouts contain placeholders for slide content such as titles, bulleted lists, charts, and shapes.

Figure 2-3
Inserting a new slide by using the slide layouts

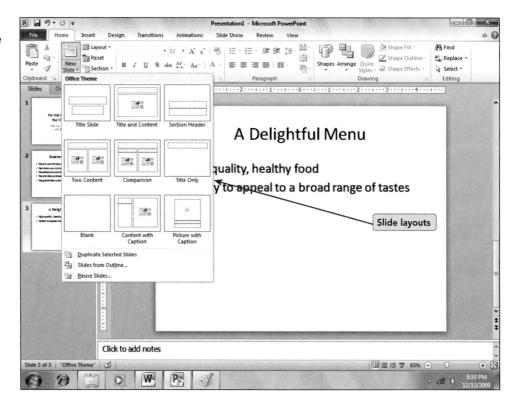

7. Click the Title and Content slide layout.

8. Key **High-Energy Fun** as the title, and then key the following body text. Notice that PowerPoint's AutoCorrect feature automatically adds an accent mark to the word "décor."

   • **Athletic decor**

   • **Sports promotions**

> **TIP**
>
> PowerPoint's *AutoCorrect* feature automatically corrects common spelling and other errors as you key text. It can be turned on or off, and you can customize it so that it will find errors that you frequently make.

9. Press [Ctrl]+[M] to insert another slide; then key **A Healthy Atmosphere** as the title, and key the following body text:

   • **Smoke-free**

   • **Alcohol optional**

   • **We sell none**

   • **We'll gladly serve your own**

10. Notice how each slide is numbered in the Slides and Outline pane.

11. Move to slide 4 "High-Energy Fun" by clicking on the slide 4 thumbnail, and from the Home tab, in the Slides group, click the down arrow on the New Slide button . Click the Two Content slide layout.

12. Key **Events That Are Good 4 U** as the title, and then key the following bulleted text in the left body text placeholder:
    - **High-energy meetings**
    - **Productive lunches**
    - **Company celebrations**
    - **Celebrity promotions**

13. Key the following bulleted text in the right body text placeholder:
    - **Entertaining customers**
    - **Demonstrating products**

14. Create a new folder for Lesson 2, and save the presentation *[your initials]***2-2** in your new Lesson 2 folder.

15. Close the presentation.

Using the Font Group Commands

One way to change the appearance of text in your presentation is by changing the font. A font is a set of characters with a specific design. You can change the *font face* (such as Times New Roman or Arial) and the *font size*. Fonts are measured in *points* (with 72 points in an inch), indicating how tall a font is.

Different fonts can take up different amounts of horizontal space, even though they are the same size. For example, a word formatted as 20-point Arial will be wider than a word formatted as 20-point Garamond, as shown in Figure 2-4.

Figure 2-4
Comparing fonts

20 point Arial: **Formatting**

20 point Garamond: Formatting

Another way to change the appearance of text is by applying text attributes. For example, you can apply a text style (such as bold or italic) and effect (such as underline or shadow). You use the Font group commands, shown in Figure 2-5 and described in Table 2-2, to change selected text.

Figure 2-5
The Font group on
the Home tab

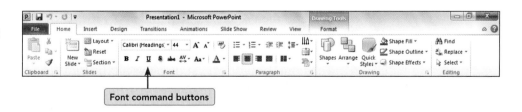

Font command buttons

TABLE 2-2 The Font Group Formatting Command Buttons

Button		Purpose
B	Bold	Applies the bold attribute to text.
Aa	Change Case	Applies different capitalizations such as uppercase, lowercase, or sentence case.
AV ↔	Character Spacing	Increases or decreases the space between characters.
Aa	Clear All Formatting	Removes all formatting from the selected text.
A▾	Decrease Font Size	Decreases the size of selected text by one font size.
Verdana ▾	Font	Enables you to choose a font face for selected text or for text to be keyed at the insertion point.
A	Font Color	Changes text color.
28 ▾	Font Size	Enables you to choose a font size for selected text or for text to be keyed at the insertion point.
A▴	Increase Font Size	Increases the size of selected text by one font size.
I	Italic	Applies the italic attribute to text.
S	Shadow	Applies a text shadow.
a̶b̶c̶	Strikethrough	Draws a line through selected text.
U	Underline	Applies the underline attribute to text.

Exercise 2-3 CHANGE THE FONT FACE AND FONT SIZE

One convenient way to apply text formatting is to first key the text, focusing on content, and then select the text and apply formatting, such as by changing the size or font. Keep in mind that no more than two or three fonts should be used in a presentation. The font you use influences the tone of your presentation.

The Font drop-down list displays all the fonts available for your computer. On the left side of each font name is a symbol indicating the font type; most of them are *TrueType* fonts **T**, while others are *OpenType* fonts **O**. These fonts work well in most situations and remain very readable when scaled to different sizes. OpenType fonts provide more detailed letter shapes and more variations of character sets. If you plan to show your presentation on a different computer or print it with a different printer, it is best to choose a TrueType font.

The font size should be large enough for easy reading when the presentation is displayed on a large projection screen. The Increase Font Size **A**▴ and Decrease

Font Size $\boxed{A^\vee}$ buttons change the size of all the text in a selected placeholder by one font-size increment. If several sizes of text are used in the placeholder, each size is changed proportionately. For example, if a text placeholder contains both 24-point text and 20-point text, clicking the Increase Font Size button $\boxed{A^\wedge}$ will change the respective text sizes to 28 and 24 points at the same time.

Figure 2-6
Font drop-down list

Many of the buttons used to format text are toggle buttons. A *toggle button* switches between on and off when you click it. The Shadow button $\boxed{S}$ is an example of a toggle button: Click it once to apply a shadow and once again to remove it. Other examples of toggle buttons are Bold $\boxed{B}$, Italic $\boxed{I}$, and Underline $\boxed{U}$.

The presentation that you will be working on throughout the rest of this lesson promotes heart smart living through a diet and exercise plan. You will be representing the Good 4 U restaurant by appearing at an annual community event. The goal of your presentation is to encourage customers to get healthy and think about joining the Good 4 U team.

Figure 2-7
Font size drop-down
list

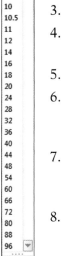

1. Open the file **Health**. Examine the Font group, and locate the command buttons listed in Table 2-2.

2. On slide 1, click the title placeholder to activate it, and key **Heart**.

3. Double-click on the word "Heart" to select this text.

4. In the Font group, click the down arrow next to the Font box. A drop-down list of available fonts appears, as shown in Figure 2-6.

5. From the drop-down list, choose Arial.

6. With "Heart" still selected, click the down arrow next to the Font Size box, as shown in Figure 2-7. Choose 66. The text size increases to 66 points.

7. Click the Decrease Font Size button $\boxed{A^\vee}$. The font size decreases by one size increment. Notice the number "60" displayed in the Font Size box.

8. Click the Increase Font Size button $\boxed{A^\wedge}$ twice. The font size increases by two size increments, to 72 points (the equivalent of 1 inch tall).

Exercise 2-4 APPLY BOLD, ITALIC, COLOR, AND SHADOW

It can be convenient to apply basic text formatting as you key. This is particularly true with bold, italic, underline, and shadow if you use the following keyboard shortcuts:

* $\boxed{\text{Ctrl}}+\boxed{B}$ for bold
* $\boxed{\text{Ctrl}}+\boxed{I}$ for italic
* $\boxed{\text{Ctrl}}+\boxed{U}$ for underline
* $\boxed{\text{Ctrl}}+\boxed{S}$ for shadow

The color drop-down gallery is composed of theme and standard colors. Theme colors span the top of the gallery, with variations of those colors, which represent shades (percentages) of the theme colors, below. Standard colors are arranged much like a rainbow at the bottom of the gallery. When you move the mouse over a color or a variation of a theme color, a ScreenTip is provided that identifies which theme or standard color it is and the percentage of variation.

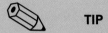
TIP

Theme colors are preselected groups of colors that provide variations suitable for many presentation needs. However, font colors or other graphic colors may need more emphasis than the theme colors provide.

1. Position the insertion point to the right of "Heart," and press ⌞Spacebar⌟. Click the Bold button **B** (or press ⌞Ctrl⌟+⌞B⌟), and then the Italic button *I* (or press ⌞Ctrl⌟+⌞I⌟) to turn on these attributes.

2. Key **Smart!** The word is formatted in bold italic as you key. Notice that this word is also 72-point Arial, like the previous word.

3. Double-click the word "Heart" to select it; then press ⌞Ctrl⌟+⌞B⌟ to make it bold.

Figure 2-8
Font Color gallery

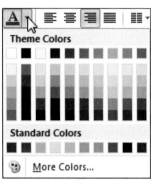

4. With "Heart" still selected, from the Home tab, in the Font group, click the Font Color button **A** down arrow to open the Font Color gallery showing Theme Colors and Standard Colors, as shown in Figure 2-8.

5. Drag your pointer over the row of standard colors, and you will see a live preview of that color before it is applied. Click the red box to apply a red font color.

6. Click in the word "Smart" to deselect "Heart." "Heart" is now red.

TIP

A shadow can help make the shapes of characters more distinctive. Be sure you always have a high contrast in color between your text colors and your background colors (light on dark or dark on light) for easy reading. Apply a shadow when it helps to make your text stand out from the background color, and apply the same type of shadow in a similar way for unity of design in your presentation.

7. Select both words in your title placeholder. From the Home tab, in the Font group, click the Shadow button **S**. Now the text appears to "float" above the slide background with a soft shadow behind it.

Exercise 2-5   CHANGE THE CASE OF SELECTED TEXT

Figure 2-9
Change Case
drop-down list

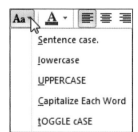

If you find that you keyed text in uppercase and want to change it, you don't have to rekey the text. By using the Change Case button **Aa**, as shown in Figure 2-9, you can change any text to Sentence case, lowercase, UPPERCASE, Capitalize Each Word, or tOGGLE cASE. You can also cycle through uppercase, lowercase, and either title case or sentence case (depending on what is selected) by selecting text and pressing ⌞Shift⌟+⌞F3⌟ one or more times.

1. Move to slide 3.

2. Select "walk to good health" which has no letters capitalized.

3. From the Home tab, in the Font group, click the Change Case button Aa down arrow, and choose Capitalize Each Word so that each word begins with a capital letter (uppercase).

4. Select the word "To" in the title. Press Shift+F3 two times to change it to lowercase.

5. Select the first bulleted item by clicking its bullet. This text was keyed with Caps Lock accidentally turned on.

6. From the Home tab, in the Font group, click the Change Case button Aa, and choose tOGGLE cASE. This option reverses the current case, changing uppercase letters to lowercase and lowercase letters to uppercase.

7. Select the two bulleted items under "Walking" (beginning with "reduces" and "lowers").

8. From Home tab, in the Font group, click the Change Case button Aa, and choose Sentence case. Now only the first word in each item is capitalized.

Exercise 2-6 CHANGE LINE SPACING WITHIN PARAGRAPHS

Line spacing can add space between the lines in a paragraph or space between paragraphs. Increased line spacing can make your text layout easier to read and enhance the overall design of a slide.

To change spacing between lines within a paragraph, you can use the Line Spacing button. Line spacing is changed in increments of .5 lines.

Figure 2-10
Line spacing sizes

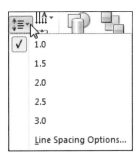

1. Move to slide 2. Click within the first bulleted item, which is considered a paragraph in the placeholder.

2. From the Home tab, in the Paragraph group, click the Line Spacing button, and a drop-down list of sizes appears, as shown in Figure 2-10.

3. Click 2.0, and the line spacing of the first paragraph increases.

4. Usually you will want to change the line spacing for an entire text placeholder. Click the placeholder border to select it.

5. From the Home tab, in the Paragraph group, click the Line Spacing button, and change the line spacing to 1.5 lines.

Exercise 2-7 CHANGE LINE SPACING BETWEEN PARAGRAPHS

The default paragraph line-spacing measurement is single. Using the Paragraph dialog box, you can add space by inserting points before or after paragraphs to expand the space between them. In PowerPoint, each bulleted item in a list is treated as a paragraph.

1. Still working on slide 2, click within the second bulleted item (a paragraph); then in the Paragraph group, click the Dialog Box Launcher ⬜ to open the Paragraph dialog box, as shown in Figure 2-11.

Figure 2-11
Paragraph dialog box

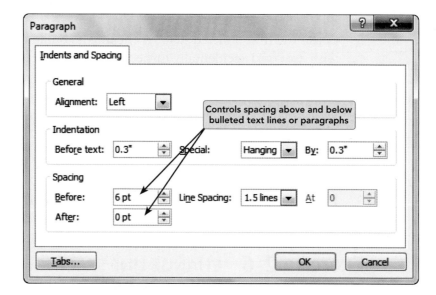

2. In the Spacing section, change the **Before** setting by clicking the spin-box up arrow twice to 18 points. Click **OK**.

3. To make all paragraph spacing uniform, select the entire text placeholder by clicking the placeholder border and open the Paragraph dialog box. Change the **Before** spacing to 12 points and the **After** spacing to 12. Change the Line spacing setting to **Single**. Click **OK**. The text is now evenly spaced in the placeholder.

Exercise 2-8 USE THE FONT DIALOG BOX TO MAKE MULTIPLE CHANGES

The Font dialog box is a convenient place to apply several font attributes all at one time. In addition to choosing a font, font style, and font size, this dialog box enables you to choose various effects, such as underline or shadow, and a font color.

1. Go to slide 1 and select the words "Diet and Exercise" in the subtitle. Notice that handles appear around the entire subtitle placeholder, but the colored area showing selection appears only around the text. This has happened because the placeholder is much bigger than the three words that are keyed in it.

2. Right-click the selected text to display the shortcut menu. Choose **Font** to open the Font dialog box, as shown in Figure 2-12.

TIP

Underlining is not the best way to emphasize text. Underlining can cut through the bottom of letters (the descenders) causing the text to be more difficult to read. And because underlining is used so much for hyperlinks on the Internet, underlining seems to have the connotation of a hyperlink. So emphasize your text in different ways, such as by using a larger font size, more dramatic color, or bold.

3. Choose the following options in the Font dialog box:
   - From the Latin text font list box, choose Arial.
   - From the Font style list box, choose Bold Italic.
   - From the Size list box, key **48**.
   - For Underline style, choose Wavy heavy line.
   - For Underline color, choose Dark red from the standard colors.
   - Notice the additional options available in this dialog box.

Figure 2-12
Font dialog box

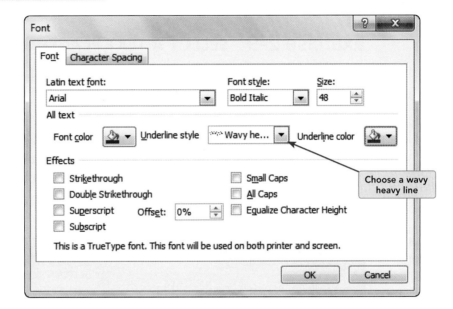

4. Click OK to close this dialog box.
5. Double-click the word "Heart" to select it, and then from the Home tab, in the Font group, click the Underline button $\underline{U}$ to turn on underlining. After looking at this underline feature, you decide that you would prefer it not be applied. Click the Underline button again to turn off this attribute.

TIP

You can change text attributes in the Outline tab in the same way as in the Slide pane.

6. With the word "Heart" still selected, change the size to 80 points.
7. Save the presentation as *[your initials]*2-8 in your Lesson 2 folder.

Adjusting Text Placeholders

The formatting for an entire placeholder, such as text size, color, or font, can be changed by first selecting the placeholder and then choosing the formatting. The placeholder border looks different depending on whether the placeholder is selected or text within the placeholder is selected.

You can select placeholders in several ways:

- Click the border of an active placeholder with the four-pointed arrow 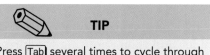.
- Press [Esc] while a placeholder is active (when the insertion point is in the text).
- Press [Tab] to select the next placeholder on a slide (only when a text box or text placeholder is not active).

You can deselect placeholders in several ways:

- Press [Esc] to deselect a placeholder or other object. (Press [Esc] twice if a text placeholder or text box is active.)
- Click an area on the slide where there is no object.

Exercise 2-9   SELECT A TEXT PLACEHOLDER

Selecting and applying formatting to an entire placeholder can save time in editing.

1. On slide 3, click anywhere in the title text to make the placeholder active. Notice that the placeholder is outlined with small dashes to create a border showing the size of the rectangle. Circles are positioned on the corners and squares are positioned at the midpoint of all four sides, as shown in Figure 2-13. When the placeholder looks like this, the insertion point is active and you are ready to edit the text within the placeholder.

Figure 2-13
Selecting a text placeholder

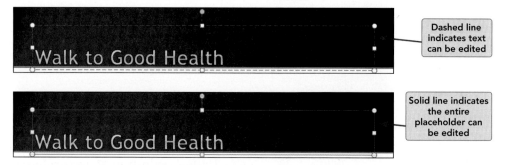

Dashed line indicates text can be edited

Solid line indicates the entire placeholder can be edited

Walk to Good Health

Walk to Good Health

2. Point to any place on the dashed-line border but not on a circle or square. When you see the four-pointed arrow, click the border. Notice that the insertion point is no longer active and the border's appearance has changed to a solid line. This indicates that the placeholder is selected. You can make changes to all the text within it, the fill color of the placeholder, the size of the placeholder, or the position of the placeholder.

TIP

Press [Tab] several times to cycle through the selection of all objects on a slide—text placeholders or other objects.

3. Press [Tab]. Now the body text placeholder is selected.
4. Press [Esc] to deselect the body text placeholder. Now nothing on the slide is selected.
5. Still working on slide 3, click inside the title placeholder text and then press [Esc]. This is another way to select an active placeholder.

6. Click the Increase Font Size button $\boxed{\mathbf{A^{\cdot}}}$ five times. The font size increases to 60 points.

7. Click the Decrease Font Size button $\boxed{\mathbf{A^{\cdot}}}$ two times until the font size is 48 points.

8. Press $\boxed{\text{Tab}}$ to select the body text placeholder. Notice the 23+ in the Font Size box. This indicates that there is more than one font size in the placeholder, and the smallest size is 23 points.

9. Click any text in the first bullet. Notice that its font size is 26 points. Notice also that when you click text inside a placeholder, its border is no longer selected. (The dashed line returns to the border, showing that you are editing the text.)

10. Click the first sub-bullet text below it, which is 23 points.

11. Press $\boxed{\text{Esc}}$ to reselect the entire placeholder.

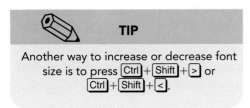

TIP

Another way to increase or decrease font size is to press $\boxed{\text{Ctrl}}$+$\boxed{\text{Shift}}$+$\boxed{>}$ or $\boxed{\text{Ctrl}}$+$\boxed{\text{Shift}}$+$\boxed{<}$.

12. Click the Increase Font Size button $\boxed{\mathbf{A^{\cdot}}}$ twice so that 28+ appears in the Font Size box.

13. From the Home tab, in the Font group, click the down arrow on the Font Color button $\boxed{\mathbf{A}}$, and choose Standard color Dark Blue (the color sample second from the right), making all the body text on this slide dark blue.

14. Still working in the Font group, click the Shadow button $\boxed{\mathbf{S}}$ to test that effect. Now all the text has a shadow, but with the colors being used, the text looks blurred. Remove the Shadow by clicking the Shadow button $\boxed{\mathbf{S}}$ again.

Exercise 2-10   CHANGE TEXT HORIZONTAL ALIGNMENT

Bulleted items, titles, and subtitles are all considered paragraphs in PowerPoint. Just as in a word-processing program, when you press $\boxed{\text{Enter}}$, a new paragraph begins. You can align paragraphs with either the left or right placeholder borders, center them within the placeholder, or justify long paragraphs so that both margins are even. However, the last alignment option should be reserved for longer documents such as reports, for which you want a formal appearance. Fully justified text is not appropriate for presentation slides.

You can change text alignment for all the text in a placeholder or for just one line, depending on what is selected.

1. Move to slide 5.

2. Position the insertion point in the first bulleted line, "Earn Good 4 U discounts."

3. From the Home tab, in the Paragraph group, click the Align Text Right button $\boxed{\equiv}$. The text in the first line aligns on the right.

4. Click the Align Text Left button $\boxed{\equiv}$, and the paragraph aligns on the left.

5.   Select the placeholder border, and click the Center button ▤ . Both lines are centered horizontally within the placeholder.

6.   Click the Bold button **B** .

Exercise 2-11   RESIZE A PLACEHOLDER

You may need to make a text placeholder narrower or wider to control how text wraps to a new line, or you might want to move all the text up or down on a slide. You can change the size and position of a selected text placeholder in several ways:

- Drag a *sizing handle* to change the size and shape of a text placeholder. Sizing handles are the four small circles on the corners and the squares on the border of a selected text placeholder or another object.

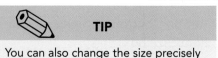

TIP

You can also change the size precisely using the Drawing Tools Format tab.

- Drag the placeholder border to move the text to a new position.

- Change placeholder size and position settings by using the Format Shape dialog box that is available from the shortcut menu when you right-click the placeholder.

By dragging a corner sizing handle, you can change both the height and the width of a placeholder at the same time.

1.   Still working on slide 5, select the body text placeholder. Notice the small white circles and squares on the border. These are the sizing handles, as shown in Figure 2-14.

2.   Position the pointer over the bottom center sizing handle.

3.   When the pointer changes to a two-pointed vertical arrow ⬍ , hold down your left mouse button and drag the bottom border up until it is just below the second line of text.

4.   As you drag, the border moves and the pointer turns into a crosshair ✛ . When you release the mouse, the border adjusts to the new position.

Figure 2-14
Resizing a placeholder

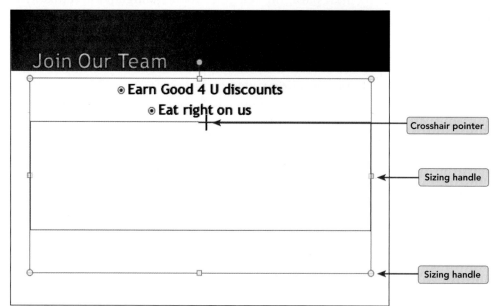

5. Position your pointer over the lower-left-corner sizing handle; then drag it toward the center of the text. Both the height and the width of the placeholder change.

6. Click the Undo button 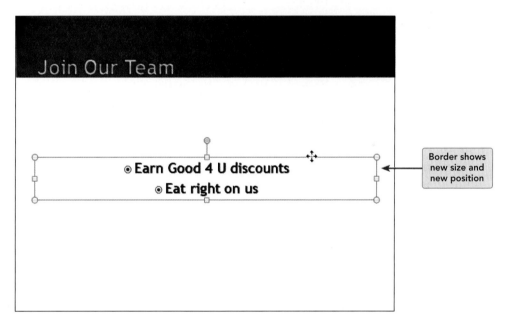 once to restore the placeholder to its previous size.

Exercise 2-12   MOVE A PLACEHOLDER

To change a placeholder's position, select it and point to any part of the placeholder border except the sizing handles. With your pointer showing the four-pointed arrow, drag to move the placeholder.

1. On slide 5, select the body text placeholder if it is not still selected.

2. Position the pointer over the placeholder border anywhere except on a sizing handle. The pointer changes to the four-pointed arrow ⊕.

3. Drag the four-pointed arrow ⊕ down until the placeholder appears approximately vertically centered on the white area of the slide, as shown in Figure 2-15.

Figure 2-15
Moving a placeholder

> Join Our Team
>
> ⊙ **Earn Good 4 U discounts**
> ⊙ **Eat right on us**
>
> Border shows new size and new position

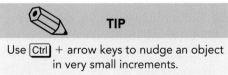

TIP
Use `Ctrl` + arrow keys to nudge an object in very small increments.

4. Deselect the placeholder. The text is now attractively placed on the slide.

5. Move to slide 1, and save the presentation as *[your initials]2-12*. Leave the presentation open for the next exercise.

Working with Bullets and Numbering

When you work with body text placeholders, each line automatically starts with a bullet. However, you can turn bullets off when the slide would look better without them. You can remove bullets, add new ones, change the shape and color of bullets, and create your own bullets from pictures. The Bullets and Numbering buttons are both found in the Paragraph group.

Exercise 2-13 REMOVE BULLETS

The Bullets button ⊞ is used to turn bullets off and on. Depending on how your text is selected, you can affect a single bullet or all the bulleted lines in a body placeholder when you use the Bullets button. The Bullets button is another example of a toggle button.

1. Display slide 2. Click within the body text to activate the placeholder. Press Esc to select the entire placeholder.

2. From the Home tab, in the Paragraph group, click the Bullets button ⊞. This turns bullets off for the entire placeholder and moves the text to the left.

3. Click the Bullets button ⊞ again to reapply the bullets.

4. Click within the first bulleted item, "Exercise regularly," and click the Bullets button ⊞ to turn off the bullet. This technique could be used to make the first line in the list serve as a heading for the list.

5. Click the Bullets button ⊞ again to reapply the bullet.

6. On slide 5, activate the body text placeholder and click the Bullets button ⊞. When text is centered, bullets are unnecessary.

Exercise 2-14 INCREASE AND DECREASE LIST LEVEL OF BULLETED TEXT

As you create bulleted items, a new bullet is inserted when you press Enter to start a new line. When you want to expand on a slide's main points, you can insert indented bulleted text below a main point. This supplemental text is sometimes referred to as a sub-bullet or a level 2 bullet. PowerPoint body text placeholders can have up to five levels of indented text, but you will usually want to limit your slides to two levels.

Increasing an item's list level moves the bulleted item to the right. Decreasing its list level moves the bulleted item to the left. These changes can be made by moving the insertion point before the text and pressing Tab to increase the list level or Shift+Tab to decrease the list level or by using the Increase List Level ⊞ or Decrease List Level ⊞ buttons found on the Home tab, in the Paragraph group.

1. With slide 2 displayed, move your insertion point after "regularly"; then press Enter to create a new bulleted line.

2. Press Tab to increase the list level to the second-level bullet, and key **Walk 30 minutes daily**; then press Enter.

3. Notice that the text is now indented automatically to the second-level bullet.

4. Key **Alternate aerobic and weight training**; then press Enter.

5. To return to the first-level bullet, press Shift+Tab.

6. Key **Get sufficient rest**.

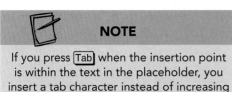

NOTE

If you press Tab when the insertion point is within the text in the placeholder, you insert a tab character instead of increasing the list level of the text.

Exercise 2-15 CHANGE THE COLOR AND SHAPE OF A BULLET

The Bullets gallery provides a few choices to change the shape of a bullet. The Bullets dialog box provides many more choices to change the bullet shape by choosing a character from another font. Fonts that contain potential bullet characters include Symbol, Wingdings, and Webdings. Another source of bullet characters is the Geometric Shapes subset available for most other fonts.

1. On slide 2, select the body text placeholder.

2. From the Home tab, in the Paragraph group, click the down arrow on the Bullets button to see the gallery options, as shown in Figure 2-16.

3. Click the checkmark bullet option.

Figure 2-16
Bullets and
Numbering gallery

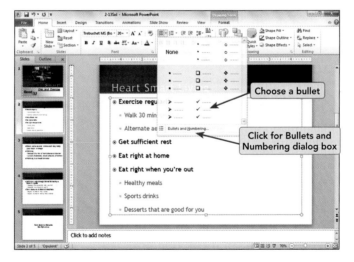

4. With the body text placeholder still selected, click the Bullets button again, and then choose Bullets and Numbering at the bottom.

Figure 2-17
Bullets and
Numbering dialog
box

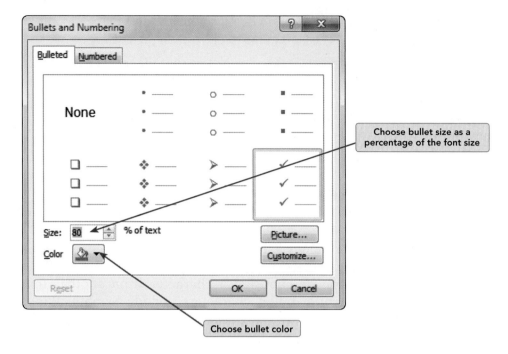

5. In the Bullets and Numbering dialog box, click the Color drop-down arrow, and choose a Standard Red, as shown in Figure 2-17.

6. In the Size box, click the down arrow several times until 80 is displayed. Click OK. All bullets on slide 2 are now red checkmarks, sized at 80 percent of the font size.

7. Select the first line of bulleted text; then press Ctrl while you use your I-beam pointer to select the text of the three remaining level-one bulleted text lines. Pressing Ctrl enables you to make multiple selections of non-adjacent text.

8. From the Home tab, in the Paragraph group, click the Bullets button down arrow ≔; then choose Bullets and Numbering.

9. Click Customize to open the Symbol dialog box, shown in Figure 2-18.

10. In the Font drop-down list (upper left corner of the dialog box), scroll to the top and choose Monotype Corsiva if it is not displayed.

11. In the Subset drop-down list (upper right corner), choose Geometric Shapes (near the bottom of the list). Several characters suitable for bullets appear in the dialog box grid.

Figure 2-18
Symbol dialog box

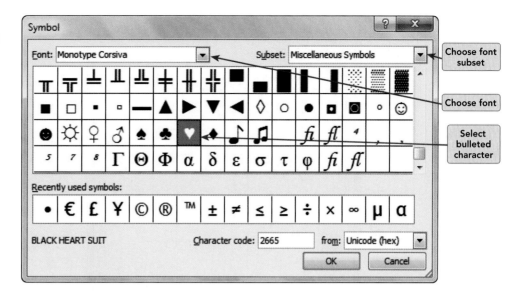

12. Click the heart bullet to select it; then click OK. The Symbol dialog box closes, and the Bullets and Numbering dialog box reappears.

13. Change the Size to 110%, and leave the Color on a Standard Red. Click OK. The selected four bullets on the slide change to red hearts. While the percentage you use is related to the size of the font for that bulleted item, symbols vary in size. You may need to try more than one adjustment before you accept a size that is pleasing to you.

Exercise 2-16 CREATE A BULLET FROM A PICTURE

A picture bullet can add a unique or creative accent to your presentation. A picture bullet is made from a graphics file and can be a company logo, a special picture, or any image you create with a graphics program or capture with a scanner or digital camera.

1. Display slide 3, and select the first two bullets (but not the sub-bullets).

2. From the Home tab, in the Paragraph group, click the Bullets button down arrow ▤; then choose Bullets and Numbering.

3. Click Picture to open the Picture Bullet dialog box. The Picture Bullet dialog box displays a variety of colorful bullets. You can choose from one of these bullets, or you can import a picture file of your own.

4. Click Import, and navigate to your student files and select **Walker.gif.** Choose Add.

5. Click the picture of a person walking to select it, and then click OK. The bullets are replaced with picture bullets, but they are too small.

Figure 2-19
Inserting a picture
bullet

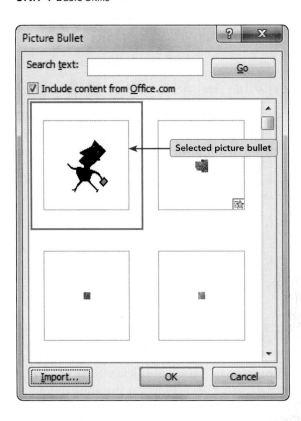

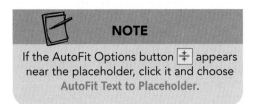

NOTE

If the AutoFit Options button ⬍ appears near the placeholder, click it and choose **AutoFit Text to Placeholder**.

6. With the two bullet items still selected, reopen the Bullets and Numbering dialog box. In the Size box, change the size to **175%**. Click **OK**.

7. Using the steps outlined above, change the bullet for the last bulleted item "Walking is a mood elevator" to the picture of the walker and size it to match the other bullets.

Exercise 2-17 CREATE NUMBERED PARAGRAPHS

Instead of using bullet characters, you can number listed items. A numbered list is useful to indicate the order in which steps should be taken or to indicate the importance of the items in a list.

Using the **Numbered** tab in the Bullets and Numbering dialog box, you can apply a variety of numbering styles, including numbers, letters, and Roman numerals. You can also create a numbered list automatically while you key body text.

1. Display slide 5, and select the body text placeholder.

2. From the Home tab, in the Paragraph group, click the Align Text Left button ▤.

3. Select all the text in the placeholder, and delete it.

4. With the placeholder activated, key **1.** and press Spacebar. Key **Walk with us**.

5. Press Enter. The second line is automatically numbered "2."

6. Key **Eat with us**, and press Enter.

7. Key **Do what's Good 4 U**. The slide now has three items, automatically numbered 1 through 3. Since AutoFit is on, your items can all be viewed even though you previously sized this text box for only two lines.

8. Press Esc to select the active placeholder.

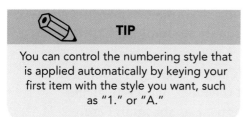

TIP

You can control the numbering style that is applied automatically by keying your first item with the style you want, such as "1." or "A."

9. From the Home tab, in the Paragraph group, click the down arrow on the Numbering button to see several different numbering styles. Then click Bullets and Numbering to open the Bullets and Numbering dialog box.

10. Click the first numbered option with the ScreenTip text 1.2.3. In the Color box, choose the Standard Red, and change the size to 100% of text. Click OK.

Exercise 2-18 USE THE RULER TO ADJUST PARAGRAPH INDENTS

A text placeholder will have one of three types of paragraph indents that affect all text in a placeholder. These paragraph indents are:

- *Normal indent.* All the lines of the paragraph are indented the same amount from the left margin.

- *Hanging indent.* The first line of the paragraph extends farther to the left than the rest of the paragraph.

- *First-line indent.* Only the first line of the paragraph is indented.

Paragraph indents are controlled by the Paragraph dialog box, shown in Figure 2-20, that is accessed through the Paragraph Dialog Box Launcher.

Figure 2-20
Paragraph dialog box

Paragraph		
Indents and Spacing		
General		
Alignment:	Left	
Indentation		Paragraph indent types
Before text:	0.56"	Special: Hanging By: 0.56"
Spacing		
Before:	6 pt	Line Spacing: Multiple At 0.8
After:	0 pt	
Tabs...		OK Cancel

You can also set indents by using the ruler. If the ruler is displayed, you can see and manipulate *indent markers* when you activate a text object for editing. Indent markers are the two small triangles and the small rectangle that appear on the left side of the ruler.

At times you might want to change the distance between the bullets and text in a text placeholder. For example, when you use a large bullet (as you did in Exercise 2-16), the space that it requires may cause the text that follows it to word-wrap unevenly. You can easily adjust this spacing by dragging the indent markers. The following steps will guide you through this process.

NOTE

The Ruler is a toggle command. Choose it once to display the rulers; choose it again to hide them.

1. Display slide 3. Notice how the text does not align correctly and the square second-level bullets are not indented enough.

2. From the View tab, in the Show group, click the checkbox to select the **Ruler**. The vertical and horizontal rulers appear, as shown in Figure 2-21.

Figure 2-21
Horizontal and vertical rulers

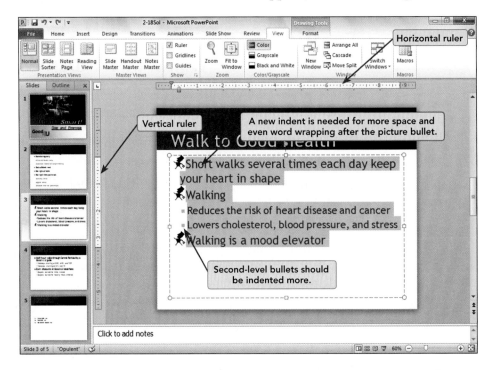

NOTE

You must have an insertion point somewhere inside a text box to change settings on the ruler. The appearance of the ruler reflects whether the entire placeholder is selected or the insertion point is active within the placeholder. If text is already in the placeholder, it must be selected for any ruler changes to apply to the text.

3. Click anywhere within the placeholder as if you were planning to edit some text. Notice the indent markers that appear on the horizontal ruler. Also notice that the white portion of the ruler indicates the width of the text placeholder.

4. Select all of the text in the placeholder.

5. Point to the first-line indent marker on the ruler (triangle at the top of the horizontal ruler, shown in Figure 2-22), and drag it to the right, to the 1-inch mark. The first line of each bulleted item is now indented the same way.

Figure 2-22
Indent markers

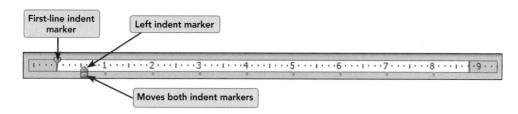

6. Drag the small rectangle (below the triangle on the bottom of the ruler) to the .5-inch mark on the ruler. Notice that both triangles move when you drag the rectangle.

7. Drag the left indent marker (triangle at the bottom of the ruler) to the right to the 1-inch mark on the ruler, and the text will word-wrap with even alignment after the picture bullet.

8. Select the text in the lines beginning with square bullets. Drag the first-line indent marker to the 1.5-inch mark on the ruler. Drag the left indent marker to the 2-inch mark on the ruler. Now the text has much better alignment.

9. Save the presentation as *[your initials]*2-18 in your Lesson 2 folder. Leave the presentation open for the next exercise.

Working with Text Boxes

Until now, you have worked with text placeholders that automatically appear when you insert a new slide. Sometimes you'll want to use *text boxes* so that you can put text outside the text placeholders or create free-form text boxes on a blank slide.

You create text boxes by clicking the Text Box button found on the Insert tab, in the Text group, and then dragging the pointer to define the width of the text box. You can also just click the pointer, and the text box adjusts its width to the size of your text. You can change the size and position of text boxes the same way you change text placeholders.

Exercise 2-19 CREATE A TEXT BOX

 TIP

You can also click and drag the text tool pointer to create a text box in a specific width. The text you key will wrap within the box if it does not fit on one text line. You can use the resizing handles to increase or decrease the text box width. You can practice making other text boxes on this slide and then click Undo as needed to return to just the first text box.

When you use the Text Box button to create a single line of text, you are free to place that text anywhere on a slide, change its color and font, and rotate it. This type of text is sometimes called floating text.

Since the goal of this presentation is to encourage others to join the Good 4 U team, you decide to emphasize this idea by adding a text box and visually enhancing the text.

1. Display slide 5.

2. From the Insert tab, shown in Figure 2-23, in the Text group, click the Text Box button.

Figure 2-23
Insert tab

Text Box button

Figure 2-24
Creating floating text

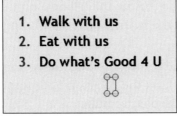

3. Place the pointer below the "G" in "Good 4 U," and click. A small text box containing an insertion point appears, as shown in Figure 2-24.

4. Key **Join Our Team Today!** Notice how the text box widens as you key text.

Exercise 2-20   CHANGE THE FONT AND FONT COLOR

You can select the text box and change the font and font color using the same methods as you did with text placeholders.

1. Click the text box border to select it. Change the text to 44 points, bold, shadowed.

2. With the text box selected, choose an attractive script font such as Monotype Corsiva or Script MT Bold.

3. Click the Font color button **A**, and change the text color to Red.

4. Using the four-pointed arrow ✥, move the floating text box to the bottom right corner of the slide. See Figure 2-25 for placement.

5. Increase the size of the placeholder surrounding the numbered list as needed to match Figure 2-25. Notice that AutoFit increases the size of the font as you increase the size of the placeholder up to 26-point font size.

Figure 2-25
Placement for floating text

Exercise 2-21 ROTATE AND CHANGE TEXT DIRECTION

You can *rotate* almost any PowerPoint object—including text boxes, placeholders, and clip art—by dragging the green rotation handle that appears at the top of a selected object. You can also control rotation of text boxes and placeholders by using the Format Shape dialog box.

To *constrain* the rotation of an object to 15-degree increments, hold down Shift while rotating.

1. On slide 5, click "Join Our Team Today!" and drag the text box up slightly so that you will have enough space to angle it on the slide.

2. Point to the green rotation handle at the top of the text box, and drag it to the left. Notice the circling arrow pointer that appears while you drag.

Figure 2-26
Rotating a text box

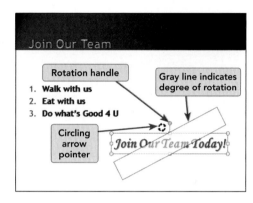

3. Position the text box as shown in Figure 2-26.

4. With the "Join Our Team Today!" text box selected, press Ctrl+C to copy.

5. Move to slide 4, and press Ctrl+V to paste.

6. Rotate the copied text box to make it straight again; then change the text to read **Offered Daily!**. The text box should resize itself to fit this text.

TIP

You can key a precise angle of rotation measurement on the 3-D Rotation tab of the Format Shape dialog box in the Z area.

---

7. With the text box selected, from the Home tab, in the Paragraph group, click Text Direction; then choose Rotate All Text 270° to make the text read from the bottom up.

8. Reposition this rotated text on the right of the slide.

Exercise 2-22 WRAP TEXT AND CHANGE ALIGNMENT

When you drag the pointer to define the width of a text box, *word wrapping* is automatically turned on. As you key, your insertion point automatically jumps to a new line when it gets to the right side of the box. The height of the box automatically adjusts to accommodate additional text lines.

1. Move to slide 2, "Heart Smart Living."

2. From the Insert tab, in the Text group, click the Text Box button.

3. Position your pointer to the right of "Exercise regularly"; then drag to the right to create a rectangle that is about 4 inches wide (use the ruler as a guide).

4. In the text box, key **Be consistent wherever you are!**

Figure 2-27
Text wrapped in a
text box

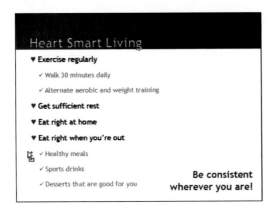

5. Click the text box border to select it; then increase the font size to 28 points, and make the text bold and red; and then right-align the text. Resize the text box if necessary to match Figure 2-27, and position the text box as shown.

6. Save the presentation as *[your initials]* 2-22 in your Lesson 2 folder.

7. Close the presentation and submit your work.

Lesson 2   Summary

- Creating a presentation by starting with a blank presentation lets you concentrate on textual content. Anytime during the process, you can choose a design theme and theme colors.

- Keyboard shortcuts are a big time-saver when creating a presentation. For example, Ctrl + Enter moves to the next text placeholder; Ctrl + M inserts a new slide.

- When you add a new slide, you can choose a slide layout. Slide layouts can be either text layouts or content layouts containing different arrangements of placeholders.

- After a slide is added, you can change the layout of the current slide or of a group of selected slide thumbnails.

- Before keying text in a placeholder, activate the placeholder by clicking inside it.

- A font is a set of characters with a specific design, for example, Arial or Times New Roman.

- Font size (the height of a font) is measured in points, with 72 points to an inch. Fonts of the same size can vary in width, some taking up more horizontal space than others.

- Many formatting buttons are toggle buttons, meaning that the same button is clicked to turn an effect on and clicked again to turn it off.

- Change text attributes and effects such as bold, italic, and text color by first selecting the text and then clicking the appropriate buttons on the Home tab in the Font group. Or apply formatting before you key text.

- The Font dialog box, accessible through the Font Dialog Box Launcher, enables you to apply multiple formatting styles and effects all at one time.

- When a text placeholder is selected, formatting that you apply affects all the text in the placeholder.

- Text in placeholders can be aligned with the left or right side of the placeholder, centered, or justified.

- Body text placeholders are preformatted to have bulleted paragraphs. Bullets for selected paragraphs or placeholders are turned on or off by clicking the Bullets button.
- Use the Bullets and Numbering dialog box to change the shape, size, and color of bullets or numbers.
- Graphic files can be used as picture bullets.
- Paragraph indents can be adjusted in text placeholders and text boxes by dragging indent markers on the ruler when a text object is selected.
- To display the ruler for a text object, from the View tab, in the Show group, choose Ruler, and then activate the text object as if to edit the text.
- Bulleted text always uses a hanging indent. Changing the distance between the first-line indent marker (top triangle) and the left indent marker (bottom triangle) on the ruler controls the amount of space between a bullet and its text.
- Indent settings apply only to the selected text object and all the text in the text box.
- Line spacing and the amount of space between paragraphs are controlled using the Line Spacing button and dialog box. Line and paragraph spacing can be applied to one or more paragraphs in a text object or to the entire object.
- Text boxes enable you to place text anywhere on a slide. From the Insert tab, in the Text group, click the Text Box button; then click anywhere on a slide or draw a box and then start keying text.
- Text in a text box can be formatted by using options in the Font group. Change the width of a text box to control how the text will word-wrap.
- When you select a text box on a slide, a green rotation handle appears slightly above the top-center sizing handle. Drag the rotation handle left or right to rotate the object.

LESSON 2		Command Summary	
Feature	Button	Menu	Keyboard
Activate placeholder			Ctrl + Enter
Align Text Left	≣	Home tab, Paragraph group, Align Text Left	Ctrl + L
Align Text Right	≣	Home tab, Paragraph group, Align Text Right	Ctrl + R
Apply a font	Verdana	Home tab, Font group, Font	Ctrl + Shift + F
Bold	**B**	Home tab, Font group, Bold	Ctrl + B
Center	≣	Home tab, Paragraph group, Center	Ctrl + E

continues

LESSON 2		Command Summary *continued*	
Feature	Button	Menu	Keyboard
Change case	Aa	Home tab, Font group, Change Case	Shift + F3
Change font size	28 ▾	Home tab, Font group, Font Size	Ctrl + Shift + P
Change paragraph spacing		Home tab, Paragraph group, Line Spacing	
Change text box options		Drawing Tools Format tab	
Create new presentation		File tab, New	Ctrl + N
Deactivate placeholder			Esc
Decrease Font Size	A▾	Home tab, Font group, Decrease Font Size	Ctrl + Shift + <
Decrease List Level			Shift + Tab or Alt + Shift + ←
Font Color	A	Home tab, Font group, Font Color	
Increase Font Size	A▴	Home tab, Font group, Increase Font Size	Ctrl + Shift + >
Increase List Level			Tab
Insert line break			Shift + Enter
Insert new slide		Home tab, Slides group, New Slide	Ctrl + M
Italic	*I*	Home tab, Font group, Italic	Ctrl + I
Justify	≡	Home tab, Paragraph group, Justify	Ctrl + J
Move to next placeholder			Ctrl + Enter
Shadow	S	Home tab, Font group, Shadow	Ctrl + S
Text Box	A	Insert Tab, Text group, Text Box	
Turn bullets on or off		Home tab, Paragraph group, Bullets	
Turn numbering on or off		Home tab, Paragraph group, Numbering	
Underline	U	Home tab, Font group, Underline	Ctrl + U

Concepts Review

True/False Questions

Each of the following statements is either true or false. Indicate your choice by circling T or F.

T F 1. A new presentation can begin as a blank presentation.

T F 2. A new slide is added by pressing Ctrl+Y.

T F 3. Pressing Esc while a text box is activated selects the entire text box.

T F 4. You can use Ctrl+Enter to activate the next slide placeholder and to insert a new slide.

T F 5. The Shift+F3 keyboard shortcut will change selected text from uppercase to lowercase.

T F 6. Sentence case capitalizes the initial letter of all words in a paragraph.

T F 7. Dragging a sizing handle repositions a placeholder.

T F 8. To move a text placeholder, the pointer must remain on the border and not touch a sizing handle.

Short Answer Questions

Write the correct answer in the space provided.

1. Name two ways to insert a new slide.

_____

2. Which key do you press to insert another bullet at the same level?

_____

3. Which command buttons change font size by incremental sizes?

_____

4. What must you do before you can change an attribute for existing text?

_____

5. How do you change the distance between bullets and text?

_____

6. What is the difference between line spacing and paragraph spacing?

_____

7. How do you create a text box that adjusts its width to the width of the text you key?

_____

8. How can you rotate a text box in 15-degree increments?

_____

Critical Thinking

Answer these questions on a separate page. Support your answers with examples from your own experience, if possible.

1. Explain how font faces can affect a presentation. Can you use too many fonts in a presentation? Explain your answer.

2. Under what circumstances might you choose to use a text box instead of a text placeholder?

Skills Review

Exercise 2-23

Create a new presentation, add new slides, and insert a new slide with a different layout.

1. Start a new, blank presentation.

2. Complete the title slide by following these steps:
    a. Key **Healthy Eating** as the first line of the title (you don't have to click the text "Click to add title" to begin keying the title slide text).
    b. Press Enter to start a new title line.
    c. Key **for Young Athletes** to complete the title.
    d. Press Ctrl+Enter.
    e. Key the subtitle **A Good 4 U Seminar**.

3. Add a new slide with the Title and Content layout by following these steps:
    a. Press Ctrl+M.
    b. Key **Basic Food Groups** as the title.
    c. Key the following bulleted text:
    - **Fats, oils, and sweets**
    - **Dairy products**
    - **Meat, poultry, fish, eggs, beans, and nuts**
    - **Fruits and vegetables**
    - **Rice, bread, and pasta**

4. From the Home tab, in the Slides group, click the top of the New Slide button ▣ to insert a third slide.

5. Key **Elements of a Healthy Diet** as the title of the slide and the following bulleted text:
   - **Choose a variety of foods**
   - **Eat moderate amounts**
   - **Choose low-fat foods**
   - **Choose fresh, unprocessed foods**
   - **Avoid candy and junk foods**

6. Move to slide 1 and save the presentation as *[your initials]2-23* in your Lesson 2 folder.

7. Close the presentation and submit your work.

Exercise 2-24

Change the font size, apply text attributes to selected text, and change the case of selected text.

1. Open the file **Walking**.

2. On slide 1, change the font size and color and apply bold and shadow effects for the title by following these steps:
   a. Select the title text "Power Walking" by dragging the I-beam pointer across the text.
   b. From the Home tab, in the Font group, change the font size to **36** points.
   c. From the Home tab, in the Font group, click the Font Color button **A** drop-down list and choose **Red**.
   d. Still working in the Font group, click the Bold button **B** and the Shadow button **S**.

3. On slide 3, increase the font size for the title by following these steps:
   a. Move to slide 3, and select the title text.
   b. From the Home tab, in the Font group, click the Increase Font Size button **28 ▾** several times until "36" appears in the Font Size box.

4. On slide 5, use the Font dialog box to change the title text formatting by following these steps:
   a. Select the title text.
   b. From the Home tab, in the Font group, click the Font Dialog Box Launcher ▣.
   c. Choose the font style **Bold**, and change the font color to **Red**.
   d. In the Size box, choose **36** points.
   e. Click **OK**.

5. Change the case of the text on slide 5 by following these steps:

a. Select the last bulleted item by clicking its bullet.

b. From the Home tab, in the Font group, click the Change Case button Aa.

c. Choose tOGGLE cASE.

6. Using step 4 above as a guide, change the title text formatting on slides 2, 3, 4, and 6 to match that on slide 5.

7. Move to slide 1, and save the presentation as *[your initials]*2-24 in your Lesson 2 folder.

8. Close the presentation and submit your work.

Exercise 2-25

Adjust indents using the ruler.

1. Open the file **EmpAward**.

2. Move to slide 2.

3. Create first-line indents by following these steps:

a. Click within the text box to activate the ruler.

b. Select the bulleted text.

c. From the Home tab, in the Paragraph group, click the Bullets button ☰ to remove the bullets from the body text placeholder.

d. If the ruler is not displayed, click the View tab, in the Show group, and choose Ruler.

e. Drag the first-line indent marker (top triangle) to the right, to the 1-inch mark on the ruler.

4. Move to slide 3, and change the spacing before the bullets by following these steps:

a. Select all the text in the body text placeholder.

b. Drag the left indent marker (bottom triangle) to the right one tick mark, to the 0.5-inch position on the ruler.

5. Move to slide 4, and select all the text. Increase the space between the bullets and the text by one tick mark on the ruler. Move the oval shapes that emphasize the words "week" and "paid" up slightly to the right. (Remember an easy way to select objects is to start with no object selected and press Tab until you cycle to the object you want to select.)

6. Move to slide 6, and modify the line spacing by following these steps:

a. Select both paragraphs (the quotation and hobbies).

b. From the Home tab, in the Paragraph group, choose the Dialog Box Launcher, and change the Before paragraph spacing to 0. Now the text will fit better on the slide.

7. Save the presentation as *[your initials]2-25* in your Lesson 2 folder.

8. Close the presentation and submit your work.

Exercise 2-26

Change text box settings and page setup options.

1. Open the file **Upgrade**.

2. On the title slide, make these changes:

   a. *Title placeholder.* Change to 66 points, shadow, and Orange, Accent 1 color.

   b. *Subtitle placeholder.* Change to 40 points and left alignment. Resize the placeholder to fit the text, and then position the placeholder on the lower right of the slide.

3. On slide 2, make the following changes to the body text placeholder:

   a. Remove the bullet, and indent the first line of the paragraph to the 1.5-inch mark on the ruler.

   b. Move the placeholder slightly to the left so that the left paragraph edge aligns with the word "Why" in the slide title.

4. On slide 3, from the Insert tab, in the Text group, click the Text Box button ⌨, and create three text boxes—one under each picture—to identify the equipment categories. For all three text boxes, use the font Corbel, 24 points, bold, and the Orange, Accent 1 color.

   Kitchen Equipment
   Tableware
   Computer Equipment

5. Center-align the text in each text box, and then center the text boxes below each of the three pictures as shown in Figure 2-28.

Figure 2-28
Text box alignment

6. Move to slide 6, and move the picture of the computer up and to the left, level with the rainbow-colored line under the slide title.

7. Save the presentation as *[your initials]2-26* in your Lesson 2 folder.

8. Close the presentation and submit your work.

Lesson Applications

Exercise 2-27

Create a new blank presentation, and add slides using different slide layouts.

1. Start a blank presentation.

2. Create a title slide with the text **First in Food Safety** as the title and **Good 4 U Employee Training** as the subtitle.

3. Using the text in Figure 2-29, create three slides. For slides 2 and 3, use the Title and Content layout. For slide 4, use the Two Content layout, and key the first three bulleted items in the left placeholder and the last three bulleted items in the right placeholder.

Figure 2-29
Slides 2, 3, and 4

Slide 2

Our Food Safety Programs
- Food handler training
- Management inspections
- Safety supervisors on-site
- Reports to USDA

Slide 3

Safe Food-Handling Practices
- Wear gloves, hair nets, and beard nets
- Wash hands before and after handling food
- Wear clean uniforms
- No smoking

Slide 4

Food Procurement ———— Use Two Content layout
- Know your suppliers
- Prefer local growers
- Prefer organic food
- Insist on freshness
- Insist on cleanliness
- Test for pesticides

4. Check both body text placeholders for extra blank lines, and remove them if necessary.

5. Move to slide 1, and save the presentation as *[your initials]*2-27 in your Lesson 2 folder.

6. Close the presentation and submit your work.

Exercise 2-28

Work with indents, tabs, line spacing, and page setup options.

1. Open the file **Inventory**.

2. Move to slide 2, and apply the following formatting changes:
   - Change the first-level bullet to a large solid square from the Wingdings 2 font.
   - Use the ruler to increase the space between the bullet and the text for a pleasing distance and correct word wrapping of the text.
   - Change the after-paragraph spacing to 12 points.

3. On slide 3, make the following changes to the body text placeholder:
   - Change the bullets to a numbered list, formatting the numbering at 100% of text size.
   - Reduce the width of the text placeholder to approximately 7 inches, making the line endings more even.
   - Change the after-paragraph spacing to 12 points.

4. On slide 4, select the three first-level bulleted items, and make these changes:
   - Change the bullets to a numbered list, formatting the numbering at 100% of text size.
   - Change the indent on the second-level bullets so that the bullet is indented 1.25 inches and the text is indented 1.5 inches.
   - Select the second-level bullets, and change the after-paragraph spacing to 12 points.

5. On slide 5, do the following:
   - Remove the bullets.
   - Press Tab after "Miami" so that the dates are aligned.
   - Select the text, and change the line spacing to 2.
   - Adjust the size of the placeholder to fit the text.
   - Center the placeholder horizontally so that you have even spacing on both sides of the text.

6. On slide 6, do the following:
   - Increase the size of the placeholder on the right so that no lines word-wrap.
   - Change the line spacing to 2.

7. Save the presentation as *[your initials]*2-28 in your Lesson 2 folder.

8. Close the presentation and submit your work.

Exercise 2-29

Add slides, modify fonts, and customize bullets.

1. Open the file **Marketing**.

2. On slide 1, increase the size of the title to 60 points, and move the placeholder to the left slightly so that the text aligns evenly with the picture on the left.

3. Select the subtitle placeholder; then make the text right-aligned and bold.

4. On slide 2, key the title **Our Products**, and make it bold.

5. Still working on slide 2, move the picture to the left of the slide. Insert a text box, and key the following items. Press Enter after each item.
   - **Merchandise**
   - **Food services**
   - **Honeys and confections**
   - **T-shirts**
   - **Caps**

6. Select the text box, and change the font size to 28 and the paragraph line spacing to 1.5.

7. Add bullets to the list, and then customize them—choose Arrow Bullets in a brown color that works well with the design theme colors.

8. Resize the text box as needed so that the lines do not word-wrap.

9. Align the bulleted list beside the picture as shown in Figure 2-30.

Figure 2-30
Slide 2

Our Products

> Merchandise

> Food services

> Honeys and confections

> T-shirts

> Caps

10. Move to slide 1, and save the presentation as *[your initials]*2-29 in your Lesson 2 folder.

11. Close the presentation and submit your work.

Exercise 2-30 ◆ Challenge Yourself

Work with indents, line spacing, and text box settings.

1. Open the file **PartyPlanning**.

2. On slide 1, change the text in the subtitle placeholder to today's date.

3. On slide 2, remove all the bullets from both body text placeholders. Resize the left placeholder, and move it under the slide title so that it is aligned on the left.

4. Resize the "Creative Services" text placeholder, and position it as shown in Figure 2-31. Modify the text "Creative Services" by applying bold and changing the font color to Pink, Text 2.

Figure 2-31
Slide 2

> **Decisions, Decisions, Decisions**
>
> Planning menus
> Selecting beverages
> Choosing draping and decorations
> Staffing support
>
> **Creative Services**
> Good 4 U has built a reputation for excellence in event services and customer care.

5. Move to slide 4, and create text boxes to key the text shown in Figure 2-32. Center-align all the text, and use the Arial Black font. Use 20 points for the text and 24 points for the heading in each section. Add spacing of 12 points after the heading in each section.

Figure 2-32
Slide 4

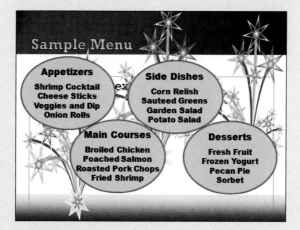

6. Save the presentation as *[your initials]***2-30** in your Lesson 2 folder.

7. Close the presentation and submit your work.

 TIP

A quick way to create these boxes is to make the first one, adjust all formatting settings, then select the text box, and press Ctrl + D three times to duplicate that text box for the other boxes. Then reposition and change the text in each one.

On Your Own

In these exercises you work on your own, as you would in a real-life work environment. Use the skills you've learned to accomplish the task—and be creative.

Exercise 2-31

You are on the marketing team for a local pizza parlor. Develop a proposal for a sales promotion to entice customers to frequent the parlor during the lunch hours. Organize your strategy, and create a PowerPoint presentation with a title slide. The intended audience of the presentation is the management at the pizza parlor. Save the presentation as *[your initials]***2-31**. Close the presentation and submit your work.

Exercise 2-32

Assume you are on a planning committee for a student organization or for your employer that has the responsibility of planning a holiday banquet. Create a slide show to guide discussion at your first meeting as your group starts planning this project. Identify all the tasks that must be accomplished before the event, and plan for the various courses of the meal, such as salad, main dish, side items, and dessert. Using the skills that you have learned up to this point, format the text attractively. Save the presentation as *[your initials]***2-32**. Close the presentation and submit your work.

Exercise 2-33

Imagine that you work at a car dealership where the computer system needs to be replaced. Research computer systems online, and create a presentation for your boss recommending the brand and options that would be appropriate. Be sure to include a slide presenting the costs and a slide describing the benefits of choosing this system. Provide the URL addresses for the sites on which you found the information. Create at least six slides using different slide layouts. Save the presentation as *[your initials]*2-33. Close the presentation and submit your work.

Lesson 3
Revising Presentation Text

OBJECTIVES   *After completing this lesson, you will be able to:*

1. Select slides, rearrange slides, add sections, and delete slides.
2. Use the Clipboard.
3. Check spelling and word usage.
4. Insert headers and footers.
5. Apply a consistent background and theme colors.
6. Add movement effects.

Estimated Time: 1½ hours

Loyal customers who enjoy dining at Good 4 U have asked Michele Jenkins, head chef, if she would consider catering meals for their businesses and meeting facilities. She is eager to try out this concept because of the success she had with catering in her previous job. Michele has set up a meeting with Julie Wolfe and Gus Irvinelli, co-owners of Good 4 U, to discuss some options she has in mind. She has developed a simple, text-based presentation to help her share these ideas in an organized way. She has asked you to help her rearrange some of the content and then apply a background with an attractive color scheme and interesting transitions. Because she put the presentation together quickly, she knows it has errors that must be fixed.

When using PowerPoint, it is important to review your presentation to ensure that it flows logically, is free of errors in spelling and grammar, and is consistent in its visual representation. Many PowerPoint tools will help with this important task.

Selecting Slides, Rearranging Slides, Adding Sections, and Deleting Slides

Just as you frequently rearrange paragraphs or sentences in a word-processing document, you will often need to rearrange or delete slides in a PowerPoint presentation. To change the arrangement of slides, you can drag them to a new position in the Slides tab, in the Outline tab, or in Slide Sorter view. You can also use sections to organize and rearrange content in the presentation.

You can delete selected slide thumbnails by pressing ⌊Delete⌋ on your keyboard.

Figure 3-1
Selecting contiguous slides

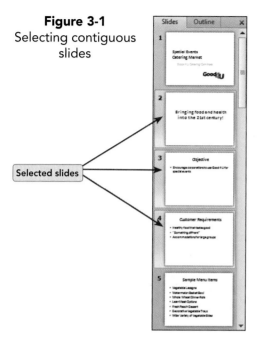

Selected slides

Exercise 3-1 SELECT MULTIPLE SLIDES

If you select multiple slides, you can move them to a new position or delete them all at one time. You can also apply transitions, animation schemes, and other effects to a group of selected slides.

Select multiple slides in one of these ways:

- To select *contiguous slides* (slides that follow one after another), click the first slide in the selection and then hold down ⌊Shift⌋ while you click the last slide in the selection.

- To select *noncontiguous slides* (slides that do not follow one after another), click the first slide and then hold down ⌊Ctrl⌋ while you click each slide you want to add to the selection, one at a time.

1. Open the file **Catering**.

2. Working in the Slides tab of the Slides and Outline pane, without clicking, point to each thumbnail one at a time and notice that a ScreenTip appears displaying the title of the slide.

3. Click the thumbnail for slide 2 "Bringing food and health . . ." to select it.

Figure 3-2
Selecting noncontiguous slides

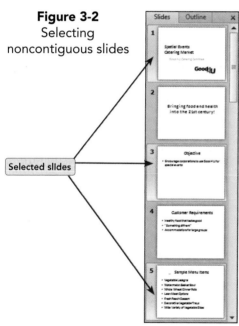

Selected slides

4. Hold down ⌊Shift⌋, and click the slide 4 thumbnail "Customer Requirements". Release ⌊Shift⌋.

   The heavy border around the slide 2, 3, and 4 thumbnails, as shown in Figure 3-1, indicates that they are selected. This is a contiguous selection.

5. With ⌊Shift⌋ released, click slide 3. Now it is the only slide selected.

6. Hold down ⌊Ctrl⌋, and click slide 1. Slide 1 and slide 3 are both selected. This is a noncontiguous selection.

7. While holding down ⌊Ctrl⌋, click slide 5. Now three noncontiguous slides are selected, as shown in Figure 3-2. You can add as many slides as you want to the selection if you hold down ⌊Ctrl⌋ while clicking each slide thumbnail.

 TIP

You can change the number and size of slides displayed in the Slides tab by dragging its border to the right or to the left.

Exercise 3-2 REARRANGE SLIDE ORDER

The Slides tab is a convenient place to rearrange slides. You simply drag selected slide thumbnails to a new position. *Slide Sorter view* enables you to see more thumbnails at one time and is convenient if your presentation contains a large number of slides. You select slides in Slide Sorter view in the same way as you do in the Slides tab.

1. Click the Slide Sorter view button ⊞.
2. Click the slide 2 thumbnail to select it.

Figure 3-3
Moving a slide in the
Slide Sorter view

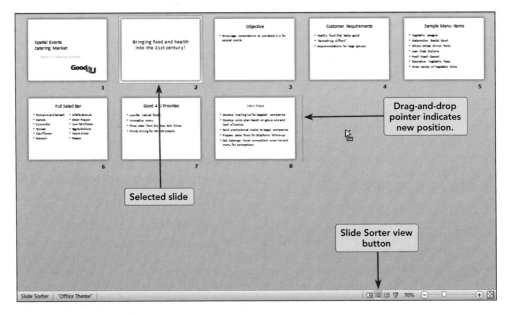

3. Click the slide 2 thumbnail, and drag the slide after the eighth slide, as shown in Figure 3-3. Notice the vertical line and the drag-and-drop pointer that shows where the slide will go.
4. Release the mouse button. Slide 2 "Bringing food and health . . ." becomes slide 8.
5. Using Ctrl, make a noncontiguous selection of slides 3 "Customer Requirements" and 6 "Good 4 U Provides".

> **NOTE**
>
> While you are dragging, be sure not to release the left mouse button until the drag-and-drop pointer is in the position where you want the selection to go. Otherwise, you might either cancel the selection or drop the slide in the wrong place.

6. Point to either slide in the selection, and drag the selection after the first slide. Both slides move to the new position.
7. Check to make sure your slides are in the following order. If they are not, rearrange your slides to match this order.

    Slide 1: Special Events Catering Market (This slide has a spelling error that you will correct later.)

    Slide 2: Customer Requirements

    Slide 3: Good 4 U Provides

Slide 4: Objective

Slide 5: Sample Menu Items

Slide 6: Full Salad Bar

Slide 7: Next Steps

Slide 8: Bringing food and health into the 21st century!

8. Double-click slide 1 to display it in Normal view.

Exercise 3-3 INSERT SECTIONS

By creating sections, you can easily organize the content of a presentation into groups by topic. On the Home tab, in the Slides group, click the Section button to open the drop-down list of available options. You can also right-click a slide thumbnail in the Slides tab to access this feature.

1. Working in Normal view on the Slides tab in the Slides and Outline pane, click the slide 1 thumbnail to select it.

2. From the Home tab, in the Slides group, click the Section button, and choose **Add Section**. Notice in the Slides tab that a line is added that says "Untitled Section" and all slides in the presentation are selected, as shown in Figure 3-4.

Figure 3-4
Adding a section

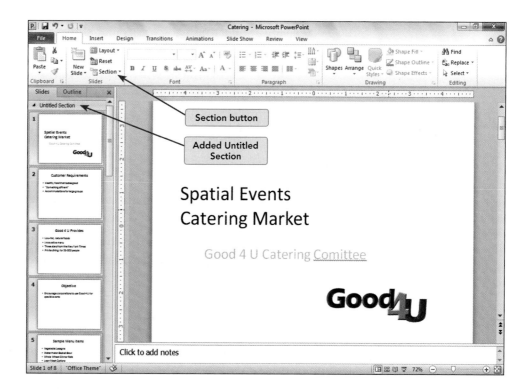

3. From the Home tab, in the Slides group, click the Section button, and choose **Rename Section**.

4. Key **Presentation Opening** in the Rename Section dialog box, and click Rename. Notice the section title changes in the Slides tab.

5. Still working in the Slides tab, select the slide 5 thumbnail, "Sample Menu Items."

6. Right-click the slide 5 thumbnail, and choose Add Section.

7. Right-click the line "Untitled Section," and choose Rename Section. Key **Menu Details**, and click Rename.

8. Add a section to slide 7 "Next Steps", and rename the section **Closing**.

TIP

Working with sections makes it easy to rearrange slide content by topic for reuse at different functions and makes a large amount of content in a presentation more manageable. The options of moving and removing sections can speed up the editing process.

9. Working in the Slides and Outline pane, click the "Presentation Opening" section title to select it and the slides below it.

10. From the Home tab, in the Slides group, click the Section button, and choose Collapse All. Notice that only the section titles are now showing in the Slides tab.

11. Right-click a section title, and notice the options for editing sections. Choose Expand All to expand the sections so that you can view the individual slides.

Exercise 3-4   DELETE SLIDES

When you want to delete slides, you first select them (in the Slides tab or in Slide Sorter view) the same way you select slides you want to move. Delete them by pressing [Delete] on your keyboard.

REVIEW

To advance through a slide show, click the left mouse button or press the [Spacebar], [PageDown], [→], or [N].

1. Working in Normal view on the Slides tab, click the slide 4 "Objective" thumbnail to select it.

2. Press [Delete] on your keyboard. Slide 4 is deleted, and the new slide 4 becomes selected.

3. Move to slide 1, and click the Slide Show button to view the presentation as a slide show.

4. Advance through the slides (using any method), reading the text and observing the built-in animation effects.

5. Create a new folder for Lesson 3. Save the presentation as *[your initials]*3-4 in the Lesson 3 folder. Leave the presentation open for the next exercise.

Using the Clipboard

The *Cut, Copy, Paste,* and *Duplicate* commands are almost universally available in computer programs. These commands work in the background using a temporary storage space called the *Clipboard* that can hold up to 24 items at a time.

*   *Cut.* The selected text or object is removed and stored on the Clipboard.

*   *Copy.* The selected text or object remains in its original place, and a copy is placed on the Clipboard.

- *Paste.* A copy of the item is placed at the location of the insertion point, and the item remains on the Clipboard.
- *Duplicate.* A copy of the item is made on the same slide, and a copy is placed on the Clipboard.

Items affected by these actions can be viewed and managed by using the Clipboard task pane. Duplicate works well when you need to create a second copy of something on the same slide; if you need to copy something and paste it on a different slide, then copy and paste is the best method to use. Unlike the Cut command, Delete does not save items to the Clipboard.

The following keyboard shortcuts are big time-savers when you do extensive editing:

- Ctrl+C   Copy
- Ctrl+X   Cut
- Ctrl+V   Paste
- Ctrl+D   Duplicate

Exercise 3-5 USE CUT, COPY, PASTE, AND DUPLICATE TO REARRANGE SLIDES

In the previous objective, you learned how to rearrange slides by dragging their thumbnails. This exercise presents another way to arrange slides: by using the clipboard. On the Home tab, in the Clipboard group, you can open the Clipboard task pane by clicking the Dialog Box Launcher.

Figure 3-5
Using the Clipboard task pane

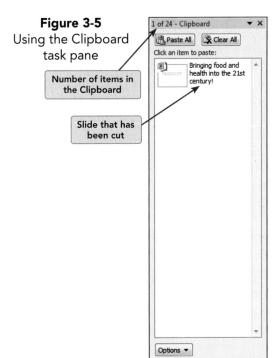

Number of items in the Clipboard

Slide that has been cut

1. With the *[your initials]*3-4 presentation open, from the Home tab, in the Clipboard group, click the Dialog Box Launcher ⬚ to display the Clipboard task pane, as shown in Figure 3-5.

2. On the Slides tab, click the thumbnail of slide 7 "Bringing food and health into the 21st century!".

3. From the Home tab, in the Clipboard group, click the Cut button ✄. This removes the slide and stores it on the Clipboard.

4. Select the thumbnail for slide 1 "Spatial Events Catering Market". Later you will change the spelling of the first word and the subtitle text.

5. From the Home tab, in the Clipboard group, click the Paste button 📋. The cut slide (on the Clipboard) is inserted (or pasted) after slide 1. This accomplishes the same thing as does moving the slide by dragging its thumbnail.

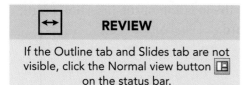

REVIEW

If the Outline tab and Slides tab are not visible, click the Normal view button on the status bar.

6. Select the thumbnail for slide 2 "Bringing food and health . . .". From the Home tab, in the Clipboard group, click the down arrow on the Copy button ; then click **Duplicate**. The duplicated slide appears immediately after the original slide but does not appear on the Clipboard.

7. Press Delete to remove the duplicate slide.

8. Select the slide 1 thumbnail "Spatial Events Catering Market". From the Home tab, in the Clipboard group, click the Copy button . Notice that two slides are stored on the Clipboard task pane.

9. Move to slide 7 "Next Steps". From the Home tab, in the Clipboard group, click the Paste button to paste the slide "Spatial Events Catering Market". A copy of the slide is inserted at the end of the presentation to use for making a concluding comment.

10. Move to slide 8, the copied slide.

11. Delete the subtitle text, and key the following text in its place on four lines:

    Catering Market Slogan:
    Make Your Event Special
    Call Good 4 U at
    800-555-1234

Exercise 3-6 USE CUT, COPY, AND PASTE TO REARRANGE TEXT

Figure 3-6
Text and slides stored on the Office Clipboard

The Cut, Copy, Paste, and Duplicate commands can be used for text, but some things are different when changing text compared to changing objects. The Paste Options button appears near a pasted item if the item's *source* formatting is different from the formatting of similar elements in its *destination* presentation. A Clipboard item's source is the presentation or other document from which text was cut or copied. Its destination is the presentation or other document in which it is pasted.

1. Display slide 7 "Next Steps".

2. Activate the body text placeholder; then click the second bullet to select all its text.

3. Press Ctrl+X to cut the text from the slide. It appears on the Clipboard task pane. Notice the difference between text and slides on the Clipboard, as shown in Figure 3-6.

4. Click in front of the text in the first bulleted item.

5. Click the first item on the Clipboard task pane (Develop price plan . . .) to insert that text as the first bulleted item.

6. Move to slide 6 "Full Salad Bar".

7. Select the title text "Full Salad Bar," and press Ctrl+C to copy the text from the slide.

8. Move to slide 5, and click after the text "Wide Variety of Vegetable Sides"; press Enter to create a new bullet, and press Ctrl+V. Notice that a Paste Options button appears each time you paste.

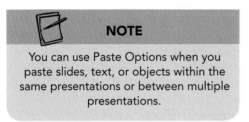

NOTE

You can use Paste Options when you paste slides, text, or objects within the same presentations or between multiple presentations.

9. Click the Paste Options button that appears underneath the new bulleted item, as shown in Figure 3-7, and choose the Keep Source Formatting button from the four choices. Notice that the new bulleted item font size does not match the size of the other bullets.

Figure 3-7
Viewing the Paste
Options button

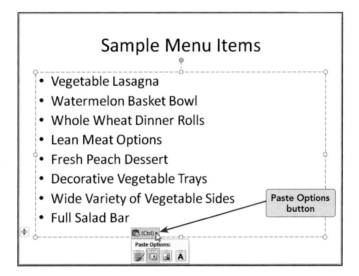

10. Click the Paste Options button again. This time, choose the Keep Text Only button. The bullet changes to match the size of the other bulleted items.

Exercise 3-7 CLEAR THE CLIPBOARD TASK PANE

The Clipboard task pane conveniently shows a series of items that have been cut or copied. The advantage of using the Clipboard to paste items is that you can have several items available and choose which ones you want to paste instead of having to paste immediately after copying or cutting. If you have copied a lot of items, you may find it beneficial to clear the Clipboard task pane.

The Clipboard Options button 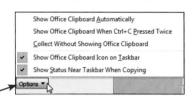 allows you to control the settings of the Clipboard task pane.

Figure 3-8
Viewing the
Clipboard task pane
options

Clipboard
Options button

1. If the Clipboard task pane is not open, click the Clipboard Dialog Box Launcher ⌐.

2. Click the Clipboard Options button [Options ▾] at the bottom of the task pane, as shown in Figure 3-8.

3. If it is not already selected, choose Show Office Clipboard Automatically to enable the Clipboard to automatically open when you use the Cut or Copy commands.

4. At the top of the Clipboard task pane, click the Clear All button [✗ Clear All] to clear all of the contents held on the Clipboard.

5. Click Close [✗] on the Clipboard task pane.

Exercise 3-8   USE UNDO, REPEAT, AND REDO

When a presentation opens, the Undo button 🔄 and the Repeat button 🔄 appear on the Quick Access Toolbar. The Repeat button duplicates any action taken. The Undo button 🔄 reverses the last action taken. You can undo a series of editing actions, including keying or deleting text, promoting or demoting items, or deleting slides. By using Undo more than once, you can undo multiple actions.

Once Undo is used, the Redo button 🔄 appears. It reapplies editing commands in the order you undid them.

TIP

By default, PowerPoint can undo the last 20 actions. You can increase or decrease this number by choosing File, Options, Advanced and changing the maximum number of undos. Increasing the number uses up more RAM memory on your computer.

1. Move to slide 7 "Next Steps". Click at the end of the second bulleted line, and press [Enter].

2. Click the Undo button 🔄. Notice that the new bullet is removed and your insertion point is back at the end of the second bulleted line.

3. Click the Redo button 🔄. The bullet is back and ready to accept text beside it.

4. On the new bulleted line, key the text below:

Fully develop a menu choices plan

TIP

It's fairly common to make unintentional deletions and unintentional text moves. The [Ctrl]+[Z] key combination is very handy to use when the unexpected happens.

5. Press [Ctrl]+[Z], the keyboard shortcut for Undo. Part of your text will go away.

6. Press [Ctrl]+[Y], the keyboard shortcut for Redo. The text that was taken away in step 5 is now back on your screen.

7. In the Slides and Outline pane, click slide 6, and press [Delete] on your keyboard. Notice that the slide is deleted.

8. Press [Ctrl]+[Z] to undo this deletion and put the slide back into place.

Exercise 3-9 USE FORMAT PAINTER

Format Painter makes it easy to copy formatting such as the font size, color, and font face from one object to another object on the same slide or within a presentation. When you copy the format of an object, many default settings associated with that object are copied as well.

1. On slide 6, select the title "Full Salad Bar."
2. From the Home tab, in the Clipboard group, click the Format Painter button 🖌. The Format Painter picks up the font formatting of this title.
3. Click within the word "cucumber" on the same slide. The text appears with the same formatting as the title. Click the Undo button ↺.
4. Select the title "Full Salad Bar" once again, and double-click the Format Painter button 🖌. Double-clicking keeps the Format Painter active, so you can copy the formatting to more than one object.
5. Move to slide 7, and click "Next" in the title. Notice that when you click just a word, it changes only that single word.
6. Click the word "Steps" to format it the same way.
7. Click the Format Painter button 🖌 again or press [Esc] to restore the standard pointer.
8. Save the presentation as *[your initials]*3-9 in the Lesson 3 folder. Leave the presentation open for the next exercise.

Checking Spelling and Word Usage

PowerPoint provides many tools to edit and revise text and improve the overall appearance of a presentation:

- *Spelling Checker,* which corrects spelling by comparing words to an internal dictionary file.
- *Research,* which allows you to search through reference materials such as dictionaries, encyclopedias, and translation services to find the information you need.
- *Thesaurus,* which offers new words with similar meanings to the word you are looking up.
- *Find* and *Replace,* which allows you to find a certain word or phrase and replace it with a different word or phrase.

Exercise 3-10 CHECK SPELLING

The *Spelling Checker* flags misspelled words with a red wavy underline as you key text. It can also check an entire presentation at once. The Spelling Checker is an excellent proofreading tool, but it should be used in combination with your own careful proofreading and editing.

In your internship position at Good 4 U, you have been asked to spell-check every presentation and document you create. This should be completed to ensure that no spelling errors appear because they will reflect badly on the image of Good 4 U.

1. In slide 1, a word in the subtitle has a red wavy underline indicating a spelling error. Right-click the word. Choose the correct spelling (Committee) from the shortcut menu, and click to accept it.

2. Notice the spelling of "Spatial" in the title. This is an example of a word that is correctly spelled but incorrectly used. The Spelling Checker can't help you with this kind of mistake. Change the spelling to **Special**. Do this on slide 8 also.

3. Move to slide 1, and run the Spelling Checker for the entire presentation. From the Review tab, in the Proofing Group, click the Spelling button 🔤, or press F7.

4. PowerPoint highlights "diffrent," the first word it doesn't find in its dictionary. It displays the word in the Spelling dialog box and suggests a corrected spelling, as shown in Figure 3-9.

Figure 3-9
Using the Spelling
Checker

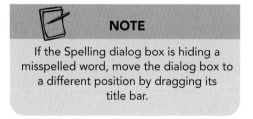

NOTE

If the Spelling dialog box is hiding a misspelled word, move the dialog box to a different position by dragging its title bar.

5. Click Change to apply the correct spelling, "different."

6. When the Spelling Checker locates "Privite," click Change on the correct spelling, "Private."

7. At the next spelling error "Caterngo," click Ignore because this is the correct spelling of the company name.

8. Click OK when the spelling check is complete.

Figure 3-10
Research task pane
with definitions

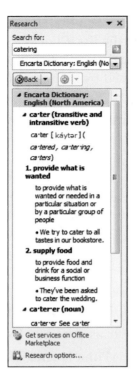

Exercise 3-11 USE RESEARCH

Research is a handy reference tool for looking up many facets of a word. For example, when you research the word "catering," you find information about the definition of the word from the dictionary, synonyms in the thesaurus, and an area where you can translate this word into another language.

1. From the Review tab, in the Proofing group, click the Research button.

2. On the Research task pane in the Search for box, type **catering**.

3. Click the down arrow in the Live Search list box, and choose Encarta Dictionary.

4. Definition 2, as shown in Figure 3-10, is the correct one for how the word "catering" is used.

5. On the Research pane, click the Close button ☒.

Exercise 3-12 USE THE THESAURUS

The *Thesaurus* is used to find words with similar meanings. This tool is extremely helpful when the same word becomes repetitious and you would like to use a similar word or when you are looking for a more appropriate word with a similar meaning.

1. On slide 6, put your insertion point in the word "Full." From the Review tab, in the Proofing group, click the Thesaurus button. In the Research task pane, the word "Full" is automatically placed in the Search for box, a search has already been performed, and the results displayed, as shown in Figure 3-11.

Figure 3-11
Highlighted search
word in Thesaurus
task pane

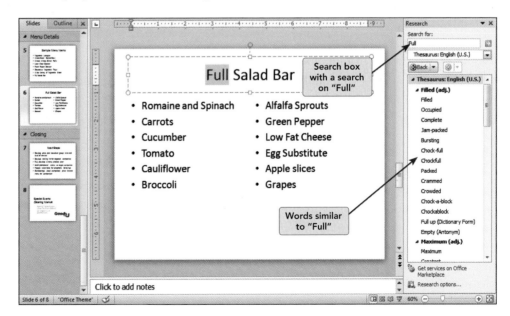

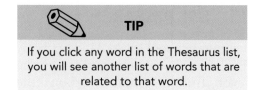

TIP

If you click any word in the Thesaurus list, you will see another list of words that are related to that word.

2. Scroll down until you find the word "Extensive" toward the bottom of the list. Click the down arrow beside "Extensive," and choose Insert. Notice that the word "Full" is replaced by the word "Extensive," and the slide now reads "Extensive Salad Bar."

3. On the Thesaurus task pane, click the Close button ☒.

Exercise 3-13   USE FIND AND REPLACE

When you create presentations—especially long presentations—you often need to review or change text. In PowerPoint, you can do this quickly by using the Find and Replace commands. The *Find* command locates specified text in a presentation. The *Replace* command finds the text and replaces it with a specified alternative.

1. Move to slide 1. From the Home tab, in the Editing group, click the Find button 🔍 (or press Ctrl+F) to open the Find dialog box.

2. In the Find what text box, key **Full**, as shown in Figure 3-12.

3. Click the Find Next button. PowerPoint locates and selects the text.

Figure 3-12
Find dialog box with text selected

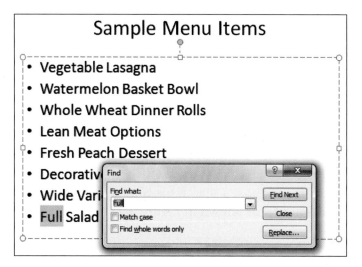

4. Click the Close button ☒ to close the Find dialog box.

5. Move to slide 1. From the Home tab, in the Editing group, click the Replace button (or press Ctrl+H) to open the Replace dialog box.

6. In the Find what text box, key **Full** if it is not displayed already. In the Replace with text box, key **Extensive**, as shown in Figure 3-13.

7. Check Match case and Find whole words only to ensure that you find only the text "Full" and not words that contain these letters (such as "fuller" or "fullest").

Figure 3-13
Replace dialog box

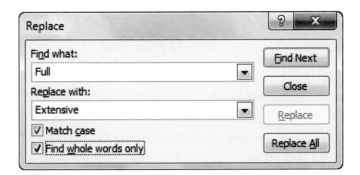

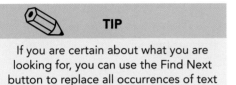

TIP

If you are certain about what you are looking for, you can use the Find Next button to replace all occurrences of text in one step.

8. Click the Find Next button Find Next , and PowerPoint finds the first occurrence of "Full." Click the Replace button and "Extensive" replaces "Full." A dialog box appears to tell you the search is completed. Click OK.

9. In the Replace dialog box, click Close.

10. Return to slide 1, and save the presentation as *[your initials]*3-13 in your Lesson 3 folder. Leave the presentation open for the next exercise.

Inserting Headers and Footers

You can add identifying information to your presentation using the Header and Footer dialog box. In PowerPoint, the information appears in placeholders on slides, notes pages, and handout pages for the following:

- *Date and time.* Current date and time updated automatically or keyed as a fixed date.

- *Header.* Descriptive text printed at the top of the page on note and handout pages only.

- *Page number.* Number placed in the lower right corner of note and handout pages by default.

- *Slide number.* Number placed on slides, usually in the lower right corner.

- *Footer.* Descriptive text printed at the bottom of slides, notes pages, and handout pages.

The Header & Footer button is on the Insert tab in the Text group. This command opens the Header and Footer dialog box, which has two tabs: the Slide tab and the Notes and Handouts tab.

Exercise 3-14 ADD SLIDE DATE, PAGE NUMBER, AND FOOTER

Using the Slide tab in the Header and Footer dialog box, you can add information to the footer of all slides in a presentation by clicking Apply to All, or you can add footer information to only the current slide by clicking Apply.

1. Working on the presentation *[your initials]*3-13, from the Insert tab, in the Text group, click the Header & Footer button 📄. Notice the two tabs in the Header and Footer dialog box, one for adding information to slides and one for adding information to notes and handouts, as shown in Figure 3-14. Click the Slide tab.

Figure 3-14
Header and Footer
dialog box, Slide tab

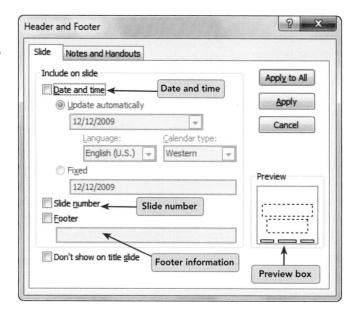

2. In the Preview box, notice the positions for the elements you can place on a slide. As you enable each element by selecting its check box, PowerPoint indicates where the element will print with a bold outline.

3. Click the Slide number check box to select it.

4. Click the check box labeled Don't show on title slide. When this box is checked, footer and page number information does not appear on the slides using the title slide layout.

5. Leave the Date and time check box unchecked.

6. Click the Footer check box, and key **Special Events Catering Market**.

7. Click Apply to All.

8. Move to slide 1, and click the Slide Show button 🖵 on the status bar to view the presentation as a slide show. Notice the footer information and slide number that appear at the bottom of the slide when you get to slide 3. Slides 1 and 2 do not contain this information since the slides are in the Title Slide layout.

9. Press Esc to exit the slide show.

Exercise 3-15 ADD HANDOUT DATE, PAGE NUMBER, AND HEADER

Using the Notes and Handouts tab, you can insert both header and footer information on notes pages and handouts.

1. From the Insert tab, in the Text group, click the Header and Footer button 📄. In the Header and Footer dialog box, click the Notes and Handouts tab, as shown in Figure 3-15.

2. Click the Date and time check box, and choose Update automatically to add today's date if it is not selected already. Each time you print the presentation handout, it will include the current date. You can choose different date and time formats from the drop-down list.

Figure 3-15
Header and Footer
dialog box, Notes
and Handouts tab

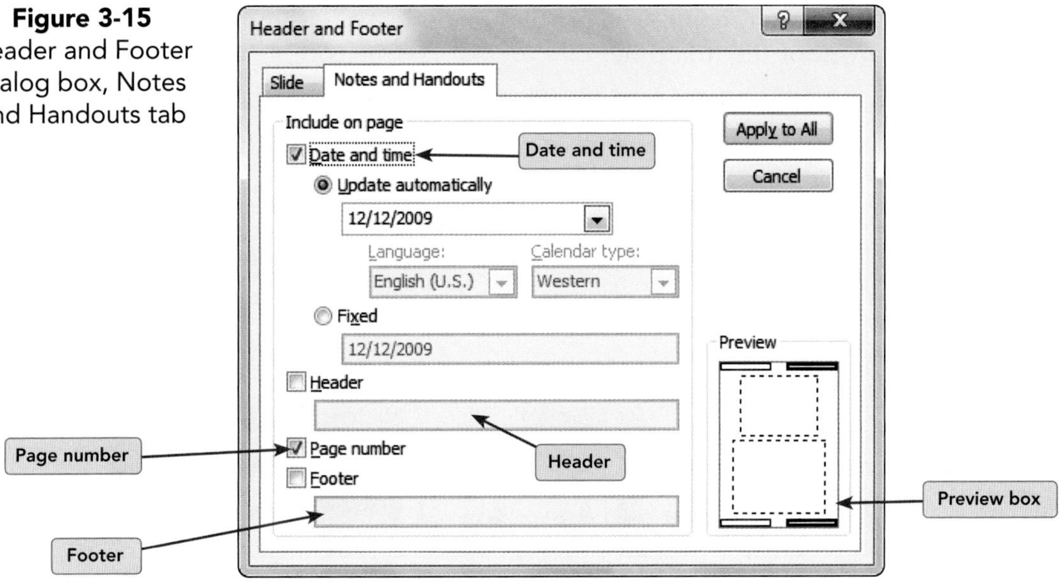

3. Click the Header check box to activate that feature, and key *[your name]* in the Header text box. The header is printed in the upper left corner of a note or handout page.

4. Leave the Page number check box checked. Page numbers are printed at the bottom right of the page.

5. Click the Footer check box to activate that feature, and key the file name *[your initials]*3-15 in the Footer text box.

6. Click Apply to All to add this information to all handout pages you print (but not to individual slides).

7. Save the presentation as *[your initials]*3-15 in your Lesson 3 folder. Leave the presentation open for the next exercise.

Applying a Consistent Background and Theme Colors

When you create a new blank presentation, the presentation contains no special formatting, colors, or graphics. Sometimes it's convenient to work without design elements so that you can focus all your attention on the presentation's text. Before the presentation is completed, however, you will usually want to apply a *design theme* to add visual interest. You can apply a design theme or change to a different one at any time while you are developing your presentation.

Exercise 3-16   SELECT A DESIGN THEME

The presentation that you have been working on in this lesson contains no theme. To select a design theme, from the Design tab, in the Themes group, click a design theme. The process to change a design theme is the same as to apply it for the first time.

1.   On the Design tab, in the Themes group, click the More button ⟱ to display the theme choices shown in a gallery as thumbnails.

Figure 3-16
Applying a design theme

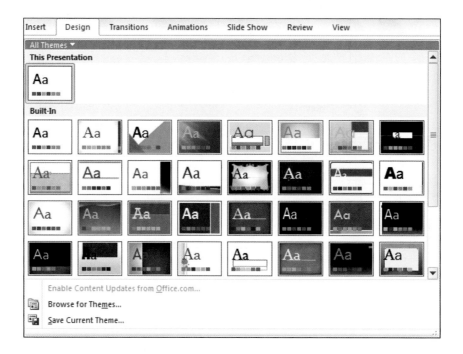

2.   Use the vertical scroll bar in the All Themes window to view the design thumbnails. The window is divided by "This Presentation," "Built-In" (listed in alphabetical order by name), and "From Office.com." Links are available for "Browse for Themes" and "Save Current Theme," as shown in Figure 3-16.

3.   Point to one of the design theme thumbnails, and notice the live preview that automatically shows what that design theme will look like when applied to your presentation. A ScreenTip also appears to indicate the name of the theme you are previewing or choosing.

4. Point to several design themes to sample what your presentation will look like with them applied.

5. Right-click any design theme thumbnail. Notice that you can apply the slide design to matching slides, all slides, or selected slides.

6. Click Apply to All Slides. The design theme that you selected is applied to all the slides in your presentation.

7. Locate the Austin design theme thumbnail, and click it. All the slides are automatically changed.

8. Notice that each thumbnail on the Slides tab shows the new theme design. The theme name appears on the status bar.

9. Move to slide 1, and view the presentation as a slide show; then return to slide 1 in Normal view.

Exercise 3-17   CHANGE THEME COLORS

You can apply different built-in colors to the current design theme by changing the *theme colors*. Live preview displays the theme colors on your slide as you point to each different theme.

Figure 3-17
Theme Colors drop-down list

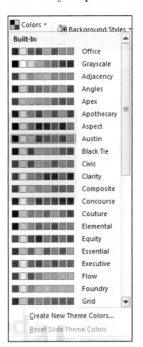

1. From the Design tab, in the Themes group, click the Colors button ▮. Theme colors are listed alphabetically by name, as shown in Figure 3-17. Scroll through the whole list.

2. Point to any theme color set to see a preview of what it will look like when applied to your presentation.

3. Click any theme color to apply it to your presentation.

4. Click the Equity theme color to apply it to your presentation.

5. Sometimes, theme colors or other changes do not update automatically, and you must reset layouts to ensure that all of the slide content has been changed. Click the slide 1 thumbnail on the Slides tab.

6. Press Ctrl+A to select all the slides.

7. From the Home tab, in the Slides group, click the Reset button 📄. The colors will all be updated to match the Equity theme colors.

8. View the presentation as a slide show; then return to Normal view. Notice that on slide 8 the logo overlaps the subtitle text. Press Esc to exit the slide show.

9. Move to slide 8. Move the title and subtitle placeholders up so that you can read the text.

10. Still working on slide 8, from the Design tab, in the Themes group, click the Colors button ▨.

11. Right-click the Civic theme color, and choose Apply to Selected Slides. Notice that the color of only slide 8 changes to make this closing slide contrast with the other slides.

Exercise 3-18 CHANGE THEME FONTS

You can apply different built-in fonts to the current design theme by changing the *theme font*. The built-in theme fonts include a heading and body font.

Figure 3-18
Theme Fonts
drop-down list

1. From the Design tab, in the Themes group, click the Fonts button [A]. Several choices for theme fonts are available, as shown in Figure 3-18.

2. Point to any theme font to see a preview of what it will look like applied to your presentation. A ScreenTip will pop up showing the name of the theme font.

3. Click any theme font to apply it to your presentation.

4. Point to the Fonts button [A] again and click the Grid theme font (Franklin Gothic Medium) to apply it to your presentation.

5. Move to slide 1, view the presentation as a slide show, and then return to Normal view.

Exercise 3-19 CHANGE THEME EFFECTS

You can apply different built-in effects to the current design theme by changing the *theme effects*.

Figure 3-19
Theme Effects
drop-down list

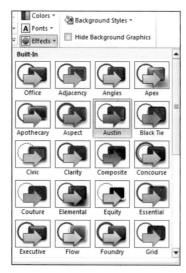

1. From the Design tab, in the Themes group, click the Effects button ◉. Several choices for theme effects are available, as shown in Figure 3-19.

2. Click any theme effect to apply it to your presentation. Right now you may not see any changes because these effects are most noticeable when applied to graphics you will use in later lessons.

3. Click the Module theme effect to apply it to your presentation.

4. View the presentation as a slide show; then return to Normal view.

Exercise 3-20 CREATE NEW THEME FONTS

Although there is a wide variety of built-in theme fonts, it is sometimes better to choose your own. You can accomplish this by creating new theme fonts.

1. From the Design tab, in the Themes group, click the Fonts button A.
2. Click Create New Theme Fonts at the bottom of the Font Theme drop-down list.
3. Click the drop-down arrow beside Heading font, and choose Gloucester MT Extra Condensed, as shown in Figure 3-20.
4. Click the drop-down arrow beside Body font, and choose Goudy Old Style.
5. In the Name box, key **Special Event Fonts**.

Figure 3-20
Create New Theme
Fonts dialog box

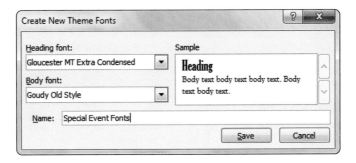

6. Click Save. Notice the change in the fonts of your presentation.
7. Save the presentation as *[your initials]*3-20 in your Lesson 3 folder. Leave the presentation open for the next exercise.

Adding Movement Effects

A *slide transition* is a movement effect that appears as slides change during a slide show. You can choose to make one slide blend into the next in a checker-board pattern or fade pattern, or you can choose from many other effects as slides enter and exit display on the screen. Transitions can have an effect like turning pages of a book. Movement can be applied to all slides in a presenta-tion or only to selected slides.

Exercise 3-21 APPLY SLIDE TRANSITIONS

Transitions can be applied to individual slides, to a group of slides, or to an entire slide show. To apply transitions, from the Transitions tab, in the Transition to This Slide group, click the More button ⇩ to display the gallery of transition options organized in groups: Subtle, Exciting, and Dynamic

Content. Click the transition to apply it. The Effect Options feature allows you to modify the chosen transition to fit your presentation needs.

1.   Move to slide 1.

2.   From the Transitions tab, in the Transition to This Slide group, click the More button ⊽ to view all the transition options as thumbnails.

3.   Point to several transitions, and notice the preview of how each transition effect will look applied to your slide.

4.   Choose Glitter from the gallery of transitions, as shown in Figure 3-21. This applies the transition to slide 1 only.

Figure 3-21
Choosing the Glitter transition

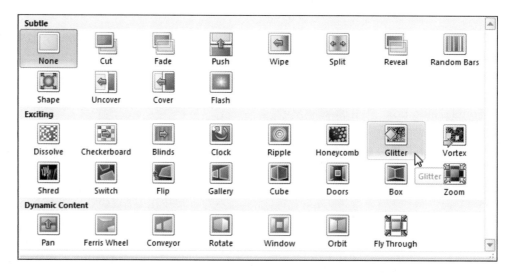

5.   From the Transitions tab, in the Transitions to This Slide group, click the Effect Options button 🖳, and choose Diamonds from Top so that the slide redraws from the top down using diamond shapes.

6.   From the Transitions tab, in the Timing group, click the Apply to All button 🗗. This applies the transition to all slides in the presentation.

7.   View the presentation as a slide show, and notice the transition you have applied.

Exercise 3-22   ADJUST SOUNDS AND DURATION

Transitions also have the option of including sounds during the transition, and you can adjust the speed at which the transition occurs.

1.   Move to slide 1. From the Transitions tab, in the Timing group, click the down arrow in the Duration box until you get to "02:00," which indicates a two-second duration time for the transition. This speeds up the transition time slightly.

2.   From the Transitions tab, in the Timing group, click Apply to All 🗗. This applies the duration changes to all slides in the presentation.

3. Click the drop-down arrow in the Sounds list box, and point to several sounds to listen to the possibilities for transition sounds.

4. Move to slide 1, and click **Applause** to apply the applause sound.

5. Still working in the Timing group, for **Advance slide** notice that **On mouse click** is selected. This option ensures that the transition from slide to slide occurs on a mouse click.

6. View the presentation as a slide show to hear this sound as slide 1 appears.

7. Save the presentation as *[your initials]*3-22 in your Lesson 3 folder.

8. Close the presentation and submit your work.

TIP

Try not to apply transition effects randomly. You might choose one transition for most of your presentation and then select one or two other effects to better emphasize the slide content as it appears. Be careful when using sounds, too, because they may detract from your presentation unless specifically suited to your content.

Lesson 3   Summary

- To change the order of slides in a presentation, use either the Slides tab on the Slides and Outline pane or the Slide Sorter view. Select the slides you want to move; then drag them to a new location. You can also delete selected slides.

- Sections can be used to organize and rearrange presentation content.

- The Clipboard can store up to 24 items that you cut or copy from a presentation. The items can be text, entire slides, or other objects. Insert a Clipboard item at the current location in your presentation by clicking the item.

- Text can be moved or copied by using the Cut, Copy, Paste, and Duplicate commands. Slides can also be rearranged by using these commands.

- The Paste Options button enables you to choose between a pasted item's source formatting and its destination formatting. The source is the slide or placeholder from which the item was cut or copied, and the destination is the location where it will be pasted.

- PowerPoint enables you to undo and—if you change your mind—redo multiple editing actions. The default number of available undos is 20.

- The Format Painter button enables you to copy formatting from one object to another.

- Double-clicking the Format Painter button keeps it active so that multiple objects can receive the copied format. Click the Format Painter button again to turn it off.

- Right-clicking a word flagged with a red wavy line provides a shortcut list of suggested spelling corrections. You can spell-check an entire presentation at one time by using the Spelling dialog box.

- Use the Research task pane to research items in the dictionary, thesaurus, and translator all at once.

- Use the Thesaurus task pane to find words with similar meanings.

- The Find command and the Replace command search your entire presentation for specified text. The Replace feature enables you to automatically make changes to matching text that is found.

- Headers and Footers can appear at the top and bottom of notes and handouts pages. Footers can appear at the bottom of slides. They are commonly used to provide page numbers, dates, and other identifying information common to an entire presentation.

- Design themes apply consistent color, design, fonts, and effects all at once.

- Built-in theme colors, theme fonts, and theme effects can be accessed from the Design tab, in the Themes group.

- Design themes, theme colors, theme fonts, and theme effects can be applied to individual slides, to a group of selected slides, or to an entire presentation.

- Slide transitions add visual interest to slide shows. They can be applied to individual slides, a group of slides, or an entire slide presentation.

- Effect options change the way a transition appears. They can be used to modify the direction of movement and sometimes the shape of the transition.

- Transition sounds and duration can be adjusted to add interest in a presentation.

LESSON 3		Command Summary	
Feature	**Button**	**Ribbon**	**Keyboard**
Add sections		Home, Slides, Section, Add Section	
Apply design theme		Design, Themes group, More	
Change list levels	or	Home, Font group, Decrease List Level or Increase List Level	
Choose theme colors		Design, Themes group, Colors	
Choose theme effects		Design, Themes group, Effects	
Choose theme fonts	A	Design, Themes group, Fonts	
Clear the Clipboard task pane	Clear All	Clipboard task pane, Clear All	
Copy formatting of an object		Home, Clipboard group, Format Painter	

continues

LESSON 3		Command Summary *continued*	
Feature	Button	Ribbon	Keyboard
Copy selected object or text		Home, Clipboard group, Copy	Ctrl + C
Cut selected object or text		Home, Clipboard group, Cut	Ctrl + X
Display Clipboard task pane		Home, Clipboard group, Dialog Box Launcher	
Duplicate		Home, Clipboard group, Copy, Duplicate	Ctrl + D
Find		Home, Editing group, Find	Ctrl + F
Header and footer		Insert, Text group, Header and Footer	
Modify section view (expand/collapse)		Home, Slides, Section, Expand All/Collapse All	
Paste (insert) cut or copied object or text		Home, Clipboard group, Paste	Ctrl + V
Paste options			
Redo		Quick Access Toolbar, Redo	Ctrl + Y
Rename Section		Home, Slides, Section, Rename	
Repeat		Quick Access Toolbar, Repeat	
Replace		Home, Editing group, Replace	Ctrl + H
Research definitions		Review, Proofing group, Research	
Select contiguous slides			Shift + click left mouse button
Select noncontiguous slides			Ctrl + click left mouse button
Slide transition		Transitions, Transition to This Slide group, More	
Spelling Checker		Review, Proofing group, Spelling	F7
Thesaurus		Review, Proofing group, Thesaurus	Shift + F7
Undo		Quick Access Toolbar, Undo	Ctrl + Z

Concepts Review

True/False Questions

Each of the following statements is either true or false. Indicate your choice by circling T or F.

T F 1. The only way to change the order of slides is to drag them to a new position in Slide Sorter view.

T F 2. The Clipboard can store up to 24 items that you cut or copy from a presentation.

T F 3. The keyboard shortcut for undoing a task is Ctrl+Z.

T F 4. The Format Painter tool can copy formatting from one slide to another.

T F 5. Slides can have headers, but handouts cannot have headers.

T F 6. The Spelling Checker is activated by pressing F1.

T F 7. The Find command is located on the Review tab.

T F 8. Slide transitions appear when you move from one slide to the next while presenting a slide show.

Short Answer Questions

Write the correct answer in the space provided.

1. How do you select two noncontiguous slides at the same time?

2. How do you change the theme colors of just one slide in a presentation?

3. Name two ways to copy a selection of text.

4. What is the default number of actions that you can undo using the undo feature in PowerPoint?

5. How do you use the thesaurus?

6. When you use the Header and Footer dialog box to add slide numbers to a presentation, where do the numbers usually appear on the slides?

_____

7. How would you apply a transition to all the slides in a presentation?

_____

8. What feature can you use to copy the formatting of selected text to new text?

_____

Critical Thinking

Answer these questions on a separate page. Support your answers with examples from your own experience, if possible.

1. PowerPoint enables the user to choose a different design theme, color, font, effect, transition, and animation for each slide. How can these effects be applied consistently, and why is it important to portray consistency throughout the presentation?

2. What information is important to include on slide footers? What information is important to include on handout and notes page headers and footers? Why?

Skills Review

Exercise 3-23

Add text, rearrange slides, add sections, and delete slides.

1. Open the file **Resort**.

2. On slide 1, replace "Student Name" with *[your name]*.

3. On slide 2, change the title "Customer Requirements" to **Vacationer's Expectations**.

4. On slide 3, insert a new bulleted line after the first bullet point, and key **Our name associated with gourmet dining**.

5. On slide 4, key the following text into the blank body text placeholder:

   Miami Beach
   Palm Springs
   Niagara Falls

6. Reverse the position of slides 2 and 3 by following these steps:

   a. On the Slides and Outline pane, click the Slides tab.

   b. Position your pointer on the right border of the Slides tab, and drag the splitter bar to the right to enlarge the slide thumbnails.

   c. Click the slide 3 thumbnail to select it.

   d. Drag slide 3 up so it is between slides 1 and 2.

   e. Release your mouse button.

7. Reverse the position of slides 5 and 6.

8. Add and rename a section by following these steps:

   a. Select slide 1 on the Slides tab.

   b. From the Home tab, in the Slides group, click the Section button 🔳, and choose Add Section.

   c. Right-click the section title "Untitled Section," and choose Rename Section.

   d. Key **Resort Presence**, and click Rename.

9. On slide 6, add another section called **Strengths**.

10. Delete slide 7 "Key Benefits".

11. Move to slide 1, and save the presentation as *[your initials]*3-23 in your Lesson 3 folder.

12. Close the presentation and submit your work.

Exercise 3-24

Rearrange slides; use cut, copy, duplicate, and paste; use undo; and check spelling.

1. Open the file **EatingGuide**.

2. Duplicate slide 1 by following these steps:

   a. Select slide 1 on the Slides tab.

   b. From the Home tab, in the Clipboard group, click the down arrow on the Copy button 📋, and choose Duplicate.

3. Press Ctrl+Z, the keyboard shortcut for Undo, to remove this duplicated slide.

4. On slide 3 "Basic Food Groups" select the text "Use sparingly," and from the Home tab, in the Clipboard group, click the Cut button ✂.

5. Move to slide 7, and paste the copied text by using the following steps:

   a. Click the I-beam pointer in the body text placeholder after "Sweets."

   b. Press Enter two times.

   c. From the Home tab, in the Clipboard group, click the Paste button 📋.

6. On the Home tab, in the Paragraph group, click the Decrease List Level button ⯇ so that "Use Sparingly" is even with the word "Examples."

7. On the Slide tab, drag slide 10 below slide 3.

8. Check spelling in the presentation using the following steps:

   a. Move to slide 1. From the Review tab, in the Proofing group, click the Spelling button 🗹.

   b. Make corrections as needed, and click OK when the spelling check is complete.

   c. Move to slide 1, and save the presentation as *[your initials]*3-24 in your Lesson 3 folder.

9. Close the presentation and submit your work.

Exercise 3-25

Use the Undo command, apply a design theme, change theme colors, and add a handout footer.

1. Start a new blank presentation.

2. Apply a design theme by using the following steps:

   a. From the Design tab, in the Themes group, click the More button ⊽.

   b. Click the Verve design theme to apply it to the presentation.

3. On slide 1, key **Smart Diet Options** for the presentation title. Key **Choosing Low-Fat Foods** for the subtitle.

4. Insert a new slide with the Two Content layout.

5. Key the title for slide 2 (on two lines) and bulleted text for slide 2 that are shown in Figure 3-22, increasing the list level for bulleted text below "Under" and "Over" as shown.

6. Repeat steps 4 and 5 to create slide 3.

Figure 3-22
Content for slides 2 and 3

Slide 2	Calories from Fat: Bread, Cereal, Rice, Pasta
	• Under 30% • Over 30%
	○ Bagels ○ Muffins
	○ Corn tortillas ○ Biscuits
	○ Pita bread ○ Taco shells
Slide 3	Calories from Fat: Vegetables
	• Under 30% • Over 30%
	○ Raw ○ French fries
	○ Steamed ○ Hash browns
	○ Vegetable juice ○ Onion rings

7. View the presentation as a slide show, starting on slide 1. Return to Normal view when you're finished.

8. Change the design theme: From the Design tab, in the Themes group, click the More button ⊽; then click the Concourse theme.

9. Change theme colors: From the Design tab, in the Themes group, click the Colors button ◼; then click Opulent.

10. Click the Undo button ↰ to compare the new color scheme with the previous one.

11. Click the Redo button ↱ to reapply the color change.

12. Check spelling in the presentation.

13. Create a Notes and Handouts footer: From the Insert tab, in the Text group, click the Header and Footer button 📄. On the Notes and Handouts tab, make these adjustments:

    a. Check Date and time, and choose Update automatically.

    b. Check Footer, and key *[your initials]*3-25 in the Footer text box.

    c. Make sure Page number is checked.

    d. Click Apply to All.

14. Move to slide 1, and save the presentation as *[your initials]*3-25 in your Lesson 3 folder.

15. Close the presentation and submit your work.

Exercise 3-26

Add headers and footers, change the theme colors, apply a slide transition, and modify effect settings.

1. Open the file **Takeout**.

2. On slide 1, replace "Student Name" with your name.

3. Add a transition effect by following these steps:

    a. From the Transitions tab, in the Transition to This Slide group, click the More button ⊽. In the Exciting category, select Dissolve.

    b. From the Transitions tab, in the Timing group, click the Sound list arrow, and choose Cash Register.

    c. Click the up arrow on the Duration box to increase the time of the transition by one .05-second increment to 01:25 seconds.

    d. From the Transitions tab, in the Timing group, click the Apply to All button 🔲.

4. Add a slide footer and numbers: From the Insert tab, in the Text group, click the Header and Footer button 🖹. On the Slide tab, make these adjustments:

   a. Check Slide number.

   b. Check Footer, and key your name.

   c. Click Don't show on title slide so that the footer and slide number do not print on slide 1.

   d. Click Apply to All.

5. Move to slide 2, and notice that with this theme the footer shows at the top of the slide.

6. Create a handout header and footer; include the date, your name as the header, the page number, and *[your initials]*3-26 as the footer.

7. Save the presentation as *[your initials]*3-26 in your Lesson 3 folder.

8. View all the slides as a slide show.

9. Close the presentation and submit your work.

Lesson Applications

Exercise 3-27

Rearrange slides, add sections, cut and paste text, and check spelling.

1. Open the file **FoodSafety**.

2. On slide 4, cut the bulleted items in column 2, and paste them at the bottom of column 1. Ignore the Paste Options button 📋 that appears; the text is formatted correctly.

3. Change the layout of slide 4 to Title and Content.

4. Edit text and increase the list level for the bulleted items as shown in Figure 3-23.

Figure 3-23
Completed slide

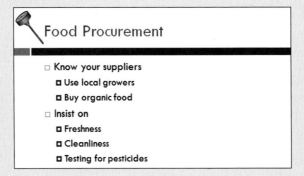

5. Add a new slide 5 using the Text and Content layout and the text shown in Figure 3-24.

Figure 3-24
Slide 5 content

```
Inspections
    •   Training inspections
        o   Scheduled
        o   Cooperative
    •   Internal evaluation inspections
    •   USDA inspections
```

6. Add two new sections to the presentation. Add one on slide 3 titled "Food Handling and Procurement" and one on slide 5 titled "Inspection."

7. Check spelling in the presentation.

8. Move to slide 1, and save the presentation as *[your initials]*3-27 in your Lesson 3 folder.

9. View the presentation as a slide show.

10. Close the presentation and submit your work.

Exercise 3-28

Delete and reorder slides, check spelling, find and replace text, and add a header and footer.

1. Open the file **Premium**.

2. On slide 1, change the subtitle text to the following:

   Item 1: Water bottle
   Item 2: Visor
   Item 3: Knee pads

3. Select the thumbnails for slides 2 "Introduction", 7 "Real Life", and 8 "What This Means".

4. Delete the selected slides.

5. Use the Replace command to replace each occurrence of the word "Topic" with the word "Item." Use the Match case and Find whole words only options so that you replace only "Topic" and not "Topics" or "topic."

6. Edit slides 2 "Topics of Discussion" through 6 "Next Steps" so that they contain only the text shown in Figure 3-25.

Figure 3-25
Content for slides 2
through 6

Slide 2
Topics of Discussion————Title
- Introduce new premium items to give away at special events
- All premium items will contain the Good 4 U logo

Slide 3
Item 1: Water Bottle————Title
- Made of durable plastic
- Excellent for outdoor sports and indoor workouts

Slide 4
Item 2: Knee Pads ————Title
- Made of durable vinyl/foam
- Essential protection for skaters

Slide 5
Item 3: Visor ————Title
- Made of white cotton blend
- Adjustable, one size fits all
- Ideal for tennis, running, walking

Slide 6
Next Steps ————Title
- Create designs
- Produce prototype items
- Analyze production costs

7. Move slide 5 "Item 3: Visor" above slide 4 "Item 2: Knee Pads", and renumber the titles of the slides to be in order by item number.

8. Check spelling in the presentation.

9. View the presentation as a slide show.

10. Add your name to the handout header and the file name *[your initials]*3-28 to the handout footer, and set the date and time to update automatically.

11. Move to slide 1, and save the presentation as *[your initials]*3-28 in your Lesson 3 folder.

12. Close the presentation and submit your work.

Exercise 3-29

Check spelling, add a header and footer, apply a design theme, change the theme colors, and add transitions.

1. Create a new presentation using the text shown in Figure 3-26.

Figure 3-26
Presentation content

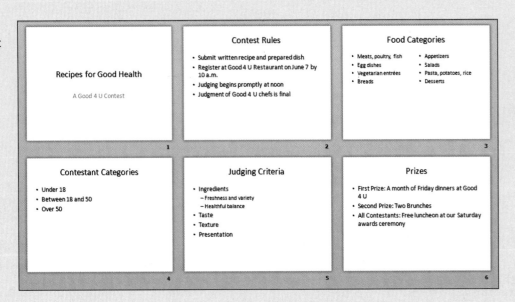

2. Apply the design theme Foundry.

3. Apply the theme color Median.

4. Check spelling in the presentation.

5. Add the Clock slide transition and apply the Wedge transition effect option to all slides.

6. Add slide numbers to all slides.

7. Create a handout header and footer; include the date, your name as the header, the page number, and *[your initials]*3-29 as the footer.

8. Move to slide 1, and save the presentation as *[your initials]*3-29 in your Lesson 3 folder.

9. Close the presentation and submit your work.

Exercise 3-30 ◆ Challenge Yourself

Rearrange and delete slides, cut and paste text, check spelling, add a handout header and footer, and add transition effects.

1. Open the file **Contest1**.

2. On slide 1, key the subtitle **Rules, Judging, and Prizes**.

3. Add a new slide with a Title and Text layout after the title slide. Key the text shown in Figure 3-27.

Figure 3-27
Slide 2 content

```
Contest Rules

•  Submit an original written recipe and dish

    o  Good 4 U Restaurant, Saturday, June 7

    o  10 a.m. to noon

•  Judging is from noon to 2 p.m.

•  Judges' decisions are final

•  Anyone may enter except Good 4 U employees and their
   families
```

4. Change slide 5 "Ingredients to Use" to a Two Content layout; then cut the body text from slide 3, and paste it in the second column of slide 5.

5. Change the title of slide 5 to **Recipe Ingredients**. Insert a new bulleted line at the top of the first column, and key **Use**. Increase the list level for all the text below it. Insert **Avoid** at the top of the second column, and increase the list level for all the text below it.

6. Delete slide 3 "Ingredients to Avoid"; then rearrange the remaining slides where needed so that they appear in the following order:

Slide 1: Recipe Contest   Slide 4: Awards

Slide 2: Contest Rules   Slide 5: Judging Criteria

Slide 3: Recipe Ingredients

7. Check spelling in the presentation.

8. Review the presentation as a slide show.

9. Add the Ripple transition with the Center effect option, and increase the duration to 01:75 seconds; apply to all slides in the presentation.

10. Create a handout header and footer; include the date updated automatically, your name as the header, the page number, and *[your initials]*3-30 as the footer.

11. Move to slide 1 and save the presentation as *[your initials]*3-30 in your Lesson 3 folder.

12. Close the presentation and submit your work.

On Your Own

In these exercises you work on your own, as you would in a real-life work environment. Use the skills you've learned to accomplish the task—and be creative.

Exercise 3-31

Imagine that you are organizing a fund-raiser for your local community college to raise money for an updated technology for the business department. Local businesses have donated interesting products, and business students will sell tickets for a drawing to determine who will receive the products. Decide how you might organize such an event, and prepare a slide show to promote it. Rearrange slides and copy and paste text as necessary to get them in a logical order. Add sections to organize the content of your presentation. Apply a design theme of your choice. Add a handout footer with your name and the file name in it. Check spelling in the presentation. Save the presentation as *[your initials]*3-31. Close the presentation and submit your work.

Exercise 3-32

You have decided to turn a personal interest or hobby into a business. Develop a presentation briefly describing your personal interest or hobby, i.e., scrapbooking, building guitars, quilting, riding motorcycles, cooking. Describe how you plan to generate income. Create at least six slides using a design theme, theme colors, theme effects, and slide transitions. Copy and paste as necessary to put the text in a logical sequence. Rearrange or delete slides as necessary to finalize your presentation. Check spelling in the presentation. Add page numbers to the slides. Save the presentation as *[your initials]*3-32. Close the presentation and submit your work.

Exercise 3-33

The owner of a bookstore has decided to increase traffic by hosting a book-reading or author-signing day based on a children's story. Choose a children's story, for example, a Dr. Seuss classic, Berenstain Bears, or Frog and Toad's adventures. Create a presentation that promotes the event. This presentation will be given at school reading nights to encourage parents to bring their children to the event. Include the title of the book and the author's name. Describe the event, and include small details of the story to increase interest. Rearrange slides as necessary to get them in a logical order. Choose a design theme and theme colors that convey the mood of the book and event. Add transition effects. Add page numbers to the slides. Check the spelling in the presentation. Save the presentation as *[your initials]*3-33. Close the presentation and submit your work.

Unit 1 Applications

Unit Application 1-1

Copy and delete slides, edit slide text, add sections, check spelling, add header and footer information to handouts and slides, modify bullet color, use the Format Painter, and choose print options.

1. Open the file **ThreeYears2**.

2. Use the Slide Sorter view to move slide 2 "Projected Revenue Growth" after slide 7.

3. Delete the newly numbered slide 2 "Presenting Good 4 U".

4. Move slide 4 "Financial History" after slide 5.

5. On slide 2, add the title **Who We Are**, and delete the text "Their dreams" and the subtext below it.

6. Move to slide 3, which contains blank placeholders; add the title **What We Want**, and key these bulleted items:

   - **To encourage healthy eating**

   - **To promote participation in sports activities**

   - **To expand our market base**

7. Change the bullets on slide 3 to a new color that matches the theme color in the presentation.

8. Using Format Painter, change the bullets on slide 7 to the square bullets used throughout the presentation.

9. Add a section for "Where We're Going" and a section for "Financial History" on their respective slides.

10. Check spelling in the presentation (assume that all proper names are spelled correctly).

11. View the presentation as a slide show, starting on slide 1.

12. Using the Header and Footer dialog box, add a slide number to all slides except the title slide. For handouts, include today's date as a fixed date, your name as the header, and the file name *[your initials]*U1-1 as the footer.

13. Move to the first slide, and save the file as *[your initials]*U1-1 in a new folder for Unit 1 Applications.

14. Preview the presentation, and then print it as handouts, four slides per page with landscape orientation, pure black and white framed.

15. Close the presentation and submit your work.

Unit Application 1-2

Rearrange slides, edit text, change bullet color, find and replace text, check spelling and style, add slide transitions, add slide numbers, and add handout headers and footers.

1. Open the file **NewFood**.

2. Find the word "desert," and replace it with **dessert**.

3. On slide 5 "Just Sweet Enough", delete the sentence that begins "The striking lime flavor."

4. On slide 3 (the first Pasta Delights slide), change the title to **Salad Delights**.

5. Select all the bulleted text on slide 3, and delete it, leaving a blank body text placeholder. In the placeholder, key the text shown in Figure U1-1.

Figure U1-1
Slide 3 content

```
•  Julie's Spin‸ᵃch Salad

•  Grilled Chicken Salad
        Michelle's
•  M̶i̶c̶h̶a̶e̶l̶'̶s̶ Cobb Salad

•  Wild Rice and Smoked Turkey Salad
        Southwestern
•  C̶o̶r̶n̶,̶ ̶B̶l̶a̶c̶k̶ ̶B̶e̶a̶n̶,̶ ̶a̶n̶d̶ ̶M̶a̶n̶g̶o̶ Salad
```

6. Change the color of the bullets in slide 3 to a new color that matches the current theme color.

7. Move slide 2 with the subtitle text "A New Dining Event" to the end of the presentation. (It will become slide 6.)

8. Move the new slide 5, "Appetizer Specials", after slide 1 so that it becomes slide 2. Increase the size of the body text placeholder slightly so that the size of the text will match that in the other body text placeholders.

9. Check spelling in the presentation.

10. Use the Thesaurus to replace the word "Event" on slide 6. Choose "experience" to replace it from the Thesaurus window. Use cut and paste and insert words as needed to get the text on slide 6 to read **A New Experience in Dining**. Resize the placeholder on the right so that the text remains on one line.

11. Add the Shape slide transition, modify the effect to be Diamond, and apply it to all slides.

12. Add a Drum Roll transition sound to only the first slide.

13. Add slide numbers to all slides except the title slide layouts. Add a handout header that contains your name, and add a handout footer that contains the file name *[your initials]*U1-2; do not add page numbers or a date.

14. Save the presentation as *[your initials]*U1-2 in your Unit 1 Applications folder.

15. Close the presentation and submit your work.

Unit Application 1-3

Create slides, change theme colors, change slide layout, apply text formatting, change text alignment, replace text, and change bullets.

1. Open the presentation **PowerWalk**.

2. Change the theme color to Metro.

3. On slide 1, change the slide title font to Arial Black, and change the font case to capitalize each word instead of using uppercase.

4. Make the subtitle stand out more:

   - Make "Good 4 U" bold.

   - Increase the font size of "4" by one font-size increment.

   - Move the placeholder up slightly so that all text fits in the green rectangle.

   - Right-align the subtitle text.

5. Working in either the Slide tab or the Outline tab, create slides 2 through 4 using the text shown in Figure U1-2. Use the Title and Content layout.

Figure U1-2
Slides 3, 4, and 5

Slide 2
```
Objectives
  • Encourage morning power walkers to breakfast at G4U
  • Make G4U a social center for power walkers
```

Slide 3
```
Strategies
  • Guided walks
  • Seminars
  • G4U merchandise
  • Advertising
```

Slide 4
```
Cost/Benefits Analysis
  • Costs
      - Walk guides' salaries
      - Seminar leaders' salaries
      - Merchandise costs
      - Advertising costs
  • Benefits
      - Increase breakfasts served
      - Increase repeat business
      - Increase merchandise sales
      - Increase general sales
```

6. Use the Replace command to change all instances of "G4U" to Good 4 U.

7. On slide 2, change the title text font to Arial Black, and increase the size by one increment.

8. Double-click the Format Painter; then apply this new formatting to the title on slides 3 and 4.

9. On slide 4, make the following changes:

   • Change the slide layout to Comparison.

   • Move the "Benefits" bullet and all its second-level bullets into the right column by cutting and pasting the text.

   • Cut "Costs" and "Benefits" and put them into their respective comparison heading boxes.

   • Increase the size of "Costs" to 32 points. Use the Format Painter to give "Benefits" the same treatment.

   • Decrease the list level for the bullets in both columns.

   • Change the color of the bullets in both columns to Green, Accent 1.

10. Change the color of all bullets in the presentation to match the ones on slide 4. (*Hint:* Do not use Format Painter, since the font size of this slide is different from that of the destination slides.)

11. Check spelling in the presentation.

12. View the presentation as a slide show.

13. Create a handout header and footer; include the date, your name as the header, the page number, and *[your initials]*U1-3 as the footer.

14. Move to slide 1, and save the presentation as *[your initials]*U1-3 in your Unit 1 Applications folder.

15. Close the presentation and submit your work.

Unit Application 1-4 ◆ Using the Internet

Research a topic, create a presentation, use cut and paste, rearrange slides, apply a design theme, change theme color, change theme font, add sections, add slide and handout headers and footers, check spelling, modify bullets, add a text box, and add transition effects.

Use the Internet to research a self-help topic. Choose something that interests you, such as weight loss, anti-aging, body toning, exercise, quitting smoking, spirituality, or personality improvement. Imagine that you work for a nonprofit organization that specializes in helping people with the topic you have chosen (e.g., Smokefree America or Shape Up America). The following is a list of suggested information to gather:

• Background on the topic.

• Who might be interested in this topic.

- Main points on beginning the process of self-help in this area.
- Any other information that you think would be useful for a presentation.
- Basic information about the nonprofit organization.
- Where interested parties should call or go for help.
- Where you found the information.

This material that you have researched will be used in a regional promotion by the nonprofit organization to get individuals in the area to seek help. Be sure to include at least six slides in the presentation. Choose any design theme, a new theme color, a new theme font, and new theme effects. Format the presentation attractively. Add a transition to all slides in the presentation.

Use cut and paste and rearrange slides as necessary to get presentation information into a logical sequence. Add at least two sections to organize the content of the presentation.

Change the bullets in the presentation to a new shape and color. Add at least one text box within the presentation.

In the slide footer, include the text **Prepared by** followed by your name. Include the slide number on all slides but not the date. In the handout footer, include *[your initials]*U1-4. In the handout header, key **Presented to**, and then identify to whom you will be giving this presentation (instructor or class). Include in the handout the date (as a fixed date) on which you will be delivering the presentation.

Check spelling in the presentation, and save it with the file name *[your initials]*U1-4 in your Unit 1 Applications folder. Practice delivering the presentation. Submit your work.

Unit 2

PRESENTATION ILLUSTRATION

Lesson 4
Working with Images

OBJECTIVES   *After completing this lesson, you will be able to:*

1. Work with shapes.
2. Insert and adjust clip art images.
3. Insert and enhance a picture.
4. Create WordArt.
5. Create a photo album.

Estimated Time: 2 hours

An effective presentation slide show consists of more than text alone. Although text may carry most of the information, you can use several types of objects to help communicate your message or draw attention to key points. For example, you can add shapes, free-floating text objects, clip art images, and photographs to help illustrate your presentation.

After you add an object to a slide, you can change its size, position, and appearance. In this lesson, you will concentrate on some basic drawing skills and begin to explore some of the many special effects made possible in PowerPoint 2010. You will utilize these skills to add interest to a presentation, **Opening1**, that Gus Irvinelli has started and will use to unveil the plans for the new Good 4 U location in Miami Beach, Florida. Gus is counting on you to improve the appearance of this presentation to help make a great first impression about the new location. On some slides, you will show him comparison images that he may choose from for the final presentation.

Working with Shapes

PowerPoint provides a variety of tools for drawing on the Home, Insert, and Drawing Tools Format tabs. In this lesson, you will learn basic drawing techniques. In later lessons, you will learn to create more complex drawings.

When you are drawing shapes, the ruler helps you to judge size and positioning. When the ruler is displayed, it appears in two parts: The horizontal measurement is across the top of the slide, and the vertical measurement is on the left. By default, the ruler measures in inches; the center of the slide (vertically and horizontally) appears as zero. A dotted line on each ruler indicates the horizontal and vertical position of your pointer.

Gus Irvinelli has requested that you become familiar with fundamental drawing concepts because he wants to use a lot of images with a variety of effects in his presentation. Therefore, the first seven exercises in this chapter will help you become familiar with PowerPoint's drawing tools.

NOTE

The presentations you create in this course relate to the case study about Good 4 U, a fictional restaurant (see frontmatter).

TABLE 4-1 Tools for Basic Drawing

Button	Name	Purpose
	Arrow	Draws an arrow.
	Clip Art	Inserts a clip art object, which could be a drawing, sound, movie, or stock photograph.
	Line	Draws a straight line.
	Oval	Draws an oval or circle.
	Photo Album	Creates a presentation made of pictures with one, two, or four pictures on a separate slide.
	Picture	Inserts a bitmap or photo image from a file.
	Rectangle	Draws a rectangle or square.
	Select	Selects an object. This tool is automatically in effect when no other tool is in use.
	Shape Effects	Adds a visual effect such as shadow, glow, or bevel.
	Shape Fill	Fills a shape with colors, patterns, or textures.
	Shape Outline	Changes the color of a shape's outline or the color of a line.
	Shapes	Opens the Shapes gallery, which contains tools for drawing a variety of predefined shapes.
	Text Box	Inserts text anywhere on a slide.
	WordArt	Creates Microsoft WordArt text on a slide.

Exercise 4-1 DRAW SHAPES—RECTANGLES, OVALS, AND LINES

In this exercise, you practice drawing several *shapes* on a blank slide. To draw a shape, click the appropriate drawing tool button (such as the Line $\diagdown$, Rectangle $\square$, or Oval $\bigcirc$); then drag the *crosshair pointer* $+$ on your slide until the shape is the size you want.

You can draw multiple shapes with the same drawing tool by using the *Lock Drawing Mode* option. This keeps the button activated, so you can draw as many of the same shapes as you want without the need to reclick the button. This feature is deactivated when you click another button. If you decide not to keep a shape, you can easily remove it by selecting it and pressing [Delete].

As you draw with different tools, the ones you have used appear at the top of the Shapes gallery in the Recently Used Shapes category; however, each tool is also shown in a related group when you access the entire Shapes gallery.

Gridlines and guides are useful for positioning objects on a slide while you are developing a presentation. *Gridlines* are evenly spaced vertical and horizontal lines. The space between the lines can be modified by using the Grid and Guides dialog box available on the View tab, in the Show group, by clicking the Dialog Box Launcher. *Guides* are lines that are shown at the vertical and horizontal center of the slide, and their positioning can be adjusted by dragging the lines. Gridlines and guides do not show when slides are printed or during a slide show.

NOTE

Three of the slides in this presentation were created by using the Blank slide layout. The Blank slide layout contains no text placeholders. Any text that appears on the slides is placed in text boxes.

NOTE

If you are using a computer screen resolution higher than 1024 × 768 or a wide-screen monitor, the Shapes gallery will be displayed in the Drawing group without clicking the Shapes button.

1. Open the presentation started by Gus Irvinelli, **Opening1**.

2. Insert a new slide after slide 2, and use the **Blank** layout. You will use this slide to practice drawing.

3. If the rulers are not showing, right-click the blank slide and choose **Ruler** from the shortcut menu. Notice that zero is placed at the midpoint of the slide on both the vertical ruler and the horizontal ruler.

4. From the View tab, in the Show group, click the check box beside **Gridlines** and the check box beside **Guides** to select them.

5. While watching the horizontal ruler at the top of the slide, move your pointer back and forth, observing the dotted line on the ruler indicating the pointer's position. While moving your pointer up and down, observe the dotted line on the vertical ruler.

6. From the Home tab, in the Drawing group, click the Shapes button $\boxed{\text{P}}$; then click the Rectangle button $\square$. The pointer changes to a crosshair pointer $+$.

7. Move the crosshair pointer $+$ to the 3-inch mark to the left of the zero on the horizontal ruler and to the 2-inch mark above the zero on the vertical ruler.

NOTE

Your shapes may appear in a gallery if there is room on your screen. If they do, you can pick a shape directly from the gallery or click the More button ⊽ and choose a shape.

8. Click and hold the left mouse button. Drag diagonally down and to the right until you reach the 2-inch mark below the zero on the vertical ruler and the 3-inch mark to the right of the zero on the horizontal ruler. Release your mouse button. A blue rectangle with a white outline appears. See Figure 4-1 to compare the size and placement of the completed rectangle.

Figure 4-1
Completed rectangle shape

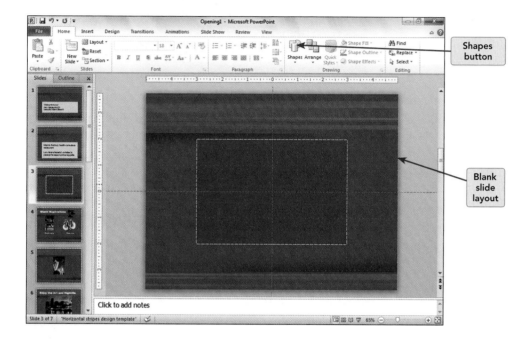

9. From the Home tab, in the Drawing group, click the Shapes button 🗗, and then choose the Oval button ⬭.

10. Draw a small oval (approximately 1 inch wide) on the inside of the rectangle that you previously drew, using the same method that you used to draw the rectangle.

REVIEW

The green handle just above the rectangle is a *rotation handle*. It can be used to make shapes angle.

11. From the Home tab, in the Drawing group, click the Shapes button 🗗, and then right-click the Line button ◸ and choose **Lock Drawing Mode**. Drag your pointer diagonally to draw a line from the left corner of the rectangle to the outline of the oval.

NOTE

The red handles that appear when you begin drawing lines to your oval are called connection sites. Connection points allow you to easily connect the lines to the oval that you have drawn.

12. Because the drawing mode is locked, notice that the pointer is still the crosshair pointer ➕ showing that the Line button ◸ is still selected. Draw three more lines from each corner of the rectangle to the outline of the oval.

13. Your screen should look similar to the back of an envelope with a seal, as shown in Figure 4-2.

Figure 4-2
An oval and lines

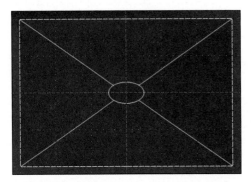

14. Click the Line button again to deactivate it.

15. Hold [Shift] down while you click to select all four lines and the oval; then press [Delete] to remove them all at once. The slide should now contain the original rectangle only.

Exercise 4-2   DRAW HORIZONTAL CONSTRAINED LINES

Pressing [Shift] while you draw shapes will *constrain* them. For lines, constraining enables you to make perfectly straight horizontal or vertical lines. If you press [Shift] while you rotate to angle a line, the lines move in increments of 45 degrees.

When using [Shift] to constrain a shape, it's important to release your mouse button before releasing [Shift]. Otherwise, you might accidentally move the pointer when [Shift] is no longer in effect, resulting in a shape that is no longer constrained.

1.   Still working on slide 3, from the View tab, in the Zoom group, click the Zoom button [🔍]. In the Zoom dialog box, key **110** percent, and click **OK**. Scroll as needed to display the rectangle. Zooming in on the area will make it easier to see what you're doing when you work on detailed objects.

> **NOTE**
>
> Depending on the settings of your computer and the size of your screen, you may need to use a different percent so that you can focus on the rectangle and not the entire slide.

2.   From the Home tab, in the Drawing group, click the Shapes button [🔲], and then right-click the Line button [＼]; then choose **Lock Drawing Mode** so that you can draw several constrained lines without needing to reclick the Line button each time you draw.

3.   Position the crosshair pointer [＋] on the left side of the rectangle on the vertical ruler's zero marker, hold down [Shift], and drag straight across to the right side of the rectangle. (As you drag, notice that the line remains straight, even if you move the pointer up or down a little.)

4.   When you reach the right side of the rectangle, release the mouse button first and then release [Shift].

Figure 4-3
Horizontal lines

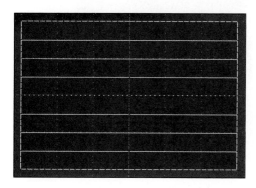

5. With the Line button ◻ still activated, position the crosshair pointer ⊞ at the left end of the rectangle again, about a half inch above where you drew the last line. Hold down ⬚Shift, and drag to the right edge of the rectangle. Release the mouse button, and then release ⬚Shift. Continue this process until the rectangle is full of horizontal lines a half inch apart, as shown in Figure 4-3.

6. Press ⬚Esc to release Lock Drawing Mode.

7. From the View tab, in the Zoom group, click the Fit to Window button ▦ to display the entire slide.

Exercise 4-3 CONNECT SHAPES WITH ELBOW LINES, CURVED LINES, AND ARROWHEADS

Sometimes two or more shapes need to be connected with a line; therefore, PowerPoint provides a variety of *connector lines* for this purpose. These lines are either straight connectors, elbow connectors (with 90-degree angles), or curved connector lines. Some lines have arrowheads on one or both ends to show a relationship or movement between the shapes when creating a diagram.

1. Insert a new slide after slide 3 using the Blank layout.

2. On the new slide 4, from the Home tab, in the Drawing group, click the Shapes button 🔲, and then choose the Rounded Rectangle button ▢. Notice that a ScreenTip will appear that labels each drawing tool button.

3. Position the crosshair pointer ⊞ on the left of your slide; then click and drag to create a rectangle as shown in Figure 4-4.

4. Repeat this process to create a similar rectangle on the right of the slide.

5. Still working with the Shapes tools, select the Elbow Connector button ⌐. Point to the left rectangle, and you will see a red square appear on all four sides of this rectangle. These are *connection sites* where the line and rectangle can be joined.

6. Click the red square at the bottom. This step connects the beginning portion of your line and the square changes to a red circle.

7. Notice this line has a white circle at the right end. Click and drag the white circle to the right until you connect to the red square on the left side of the second rectangle. When the connector line is selected, the connection sites at both ends show as red circles.

8. Notice that the connector line has two yellow diamond shapes. These are *adjustment handles* that enable you to change the horizontal or vertical portions of the line. Click and drag the bottom adjustment handle down to adjust the line as shown in Figure 4-4.

Figure 4-4
Elbow connector
line

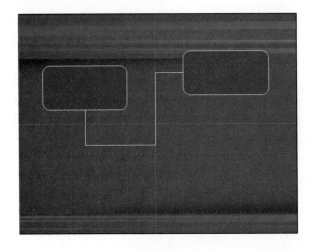

9. With the connector line still selected, press Delete to remove the connector line.

10. Now add a different connector line. Click the Curved Double-Arrow Connector button ↰, and repeat the process of connecting the bottom of the left rectangle with the left side of the rectangle on the right.

11. Notice how the adjustment handles affect the curve of the line as you move them horizontally or vertically. Adjust the line as shown in Figure 4-5.

Figure 4-5
Curved double-
arrow connector
line

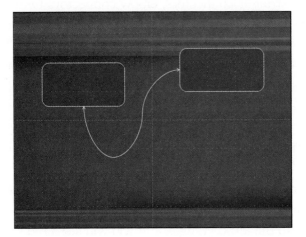

Exercise 4-4   CREATE SQUARES AND CIRCLES

When you constrain other shapes, such as rectangles or ovals, they grow at an equal rate horizontally and vertically as you draw, creating symmetrical objects such as squares and circles.

1. Insert a new slide after slide 4 using the Blank layout.

2. On the new slide 5, from the Home tab, in the Drawing group, click the Shapes button 🗗, and then choose the Rectangle button ▢.

NOTE

Your square might look more like a rectangle if your monitor's horizontal size and vertical size are not perfectly synchronized. Your square will print correctly, even if it is distorted on your screen.

3. Position the crosshair pointer ⊞ on the left of your slide.

4. Press and hold ⦵Shift⦵; then drag diagonally down and to the right, ending near the horizontal center of the slide. Release the mouse button first, and then release ⦵Shift⦵. See Figure 4-6 for the approximate size and placement of the completed square.

Figure 4-6
Square and circle

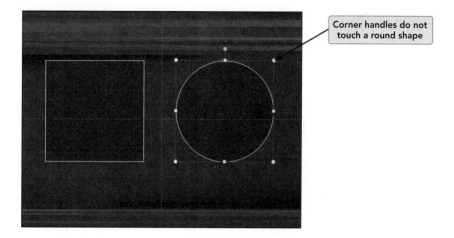

5. From the Home tab, in the Drawing group, click the Shapes button, and choose the Oval button.

6. Position your pointer to the right of the square.

TIP

To quickly verify the exact size of your object, click the Drawing Tools Format tab and check the Height and Width dimensions in the Size group.

7. While pressing ⦵Shift⦵, drag diagonally down and to the right to create a circle the same size as the square. Your screen should resemble Figure 4-6. Both the square and the circle in this example have a Height and Width measurement of **3.5″**.

8. Notice that with a circular shape, the corner handles do not touch the shape.

Exercise 4-5 RESIZE AND MOVE SHAPES

A shape that you draw is resized in the same way as resizing a text placeholder: Select it, and then drag one of its sizing handles. Holding down ⦵Shift⦵ and/or ⦵Ctrl⦵ while dragging a sizing handle has the following effects on an object:

- ⦵Shift⦵ preserves a shape's *proportions,* meaning that its height grows or shrinks at the same rate as its width, preventing shapes from becoming too tall and skinny or too short and wide.

- ⦵Ctrl⦵ causes a shape to grow or shrink from the center of the shape, rather than from the edge that's being dragged.

- ⦵Ctrl⦵+⦵Shift⦵ together cause a shape to grow or shrink proportionately from its center.

To move a shape, point anywhere in the shape, and when you see the four-pointed arrow 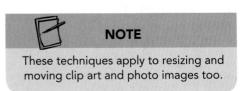, drag the shape to another place on your slide.

1. Still working on slide 5, select the circle by clicking anywhere inside it, and then point to its bottom center sizing handle. Your pointer changes to a two-pointed vertical arrow ⬍.

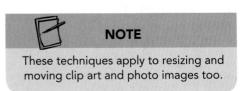

NOTE

These techniques apply to resizing and moving clip art and photo images too.

2. Drag the handle down. As you drag, the pointer changes to a crosshair ✛. The circle has changed into an oval and is now larger.

3. Drag the bottom-left-corner handle diagonally up and to the left. The oval is now wider and flattened, taking on an entirely new shape.

4. Click the Undo button ↩ twice to restore the circle to its original size and shape.

5. Point to the circle's lower-left-corner sizing handle. While holding down Shift, drag diagonally out from the circle's center, making it larger. (Don't worry if the circle overlaps the rectangle.) The circle retains its original shape. Press Ctrl+Z to undo this action and revert the circle to its original size.

6. While holding down both Ctrl and Shift, drag the lower-left-corner sizing handle toward the center of the circle. The circle becomes smaller, shrinking evenly from all edges. With this technique, all expanding and contracting of the size occurs from the shape's center, as shown in Figure 4-7.

Figure 4-7
Resizing a shape from its center

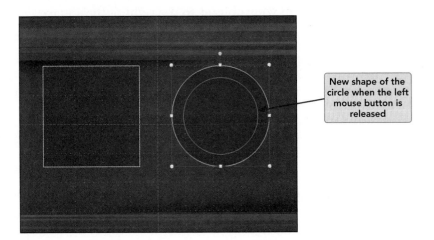

New shape of the circle when the left mouse button is released

7. Select the circle, and press Delete to remove it.

8. Select the square shape, and then from the Drawing Tools Format tab, in the Size group, key **4.5"** in both the Height and Width boxes.

9. Point in the square so that you see the four-pointed arrow ✥; then drag the square to the middle of the slide.

10. To control precise sizing and positioning, from the Drawing Tools Format tab, in the Size group, click the Dialog Box Launcher.

TIP

If you like working with ruler measurements, you can precisely size and position objects without the need to open the Format Shape dialog box, but keep in mind that the rulers measure distances from the center of the slide. So, if you point to the 2-inch mark at the right of the zero mark on the horizontal ruler, you need to do some math to figure out how far you are from either edge of the slide. The Position option on the Format Shape dialog box, however, lets you choose to measure either from the center of the slide or from its top left corner.

11. In the Format Shape dialog box, click the Size option. Select the Lock aspect ratio option to keep the vertical and horizontal sizing in the same ratio as a shape (or some other object) is resized. This can be very important when working with photographs.

12. Click the Position option; then change the Horizontal position of the square to 2.75" from the top left corner and the Vertical position to 1.75" down from the top left corner.

13. Click the Close button [Close].

14. Create a new folder for Lesson 4. Save the presentation as *[your initials]*4-5 in your Lesson 4 folder. Keep the file open for the next exercise.

Exercise 4-6 USE ADJUSTMENT HANDLES TO MODIFY SHAPES

The rectangles, ovals, and lines that you have created are very simple shapes. Many additional shapes are available, as shown in Figure 4-8.

Figure 4-8
Additional shapes in the Shapes gallery

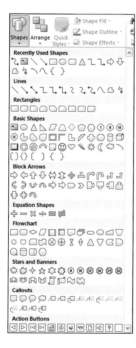

Shape tools are arranged in 10 different categories, including the Recently Used Shapes category, as shown in Figure 4-8. All of these shapes can be resized in the same way. Some shapes include one or more adjustment handles that enable you to change the shape dimensions, such as the tip of an arrow, after the shape is drawn.

1. You no longer need slides 3 and 4, on which you practiced making shapes. Click each of these slide thumbnails on the Slides tab, and press [Delete] to remove them.

2. Now working on slide 3, from the Home tab, in the Drawing group, click the Shapes button 🔲 to display the Shapes gallery.

3. In the Stars and Banners category, point to the various shape buttons and read their ScreenTips to see what each one is called.

4. Right-click the 5-Point Star button ☆, and choose Lock Drawing Mode. Draw several stars in different sizes, positioned randomly on the slide with some stars overlapping. Place stars on the rectangle and on the blank area of the slide.

5. Press [Esc] to exit the locked drawing mode.

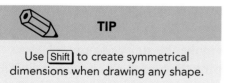

TIP

Use [Shift] to create symmetrical dimensions when drawing any shape.

6.   Select one of the stars, and drag its yellow diamond-shaped adjustment handle ◆ toward the center to make the points more narrow, as shown in Figure 4-9. Adjust each of the stars to look different from the others.

Figure 4-9
Dragging an
adjustment handle

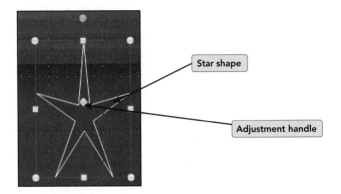

7.   Press Ctrl+Z several times to remove the stars so that only a square is left on the slide.

8.   From the **Basic Shapes** category, click the Sun button ☼. Draw a sun, about 2 inches in diameter, in the upper right corner of the slide.

9.   Drag the adjustment handle ◆ toward the center of the Sun shape to make the center circle smaller and the points longer.

Exercise 4-7   PLACE TEXT IN A SHAPE AND ROTATE

You can easily transform a shape into an attention-getting background for text. Simply select the shape and key text (or paste it from the Clipboard). You can format and edit the text in the same way as you do in a text placeholder.

1.   Select the Sun shape on slide 3, and press Delete.

2.   From the Home tab, in the Drawing group, click the Shapes button to display the Shapes gallery.

3.   In the **Stars and Banners** category, choose the 16-Point Star button ⚙; then click and drag to draw this shape in the upper right of the slide. It should slightly overlap the large square.

4.   Key **Grand Opening!** The text automatically appears in the center of the star in the same color as the star's outline.

5.   Click the star's border anywhere between two sizing handles to select it.

6.   From the Home tab, in the Font group, change the size from 18 points to 28 points, center the text, and apply bold. The text becomes too large for the star.

7.   Drag the left-center sizing handle to make the star wide enough to contain the text without word wrapping. Part of the star shape will be over the square shape.

8.   Drag the top-center sizing handle down to flatten the star, as shown in Figure 4-10.

Figure 4-10
Inserting text in a
shape

9. Click the green rotation handle (the green circle at the top of the shape), and drag it slightly to the left to rotate the star.

10. Drag the star up and to the left until it just slightly overlaps the upper left corner of the square, as shown in Figure 4-11.

Figure 4-11
Rotating a shape
with text

11. Compare slide 3 with Figure 4-11, and make any necessary adjustments.

12. Create a handout header and footer: Include the date, your name as the header, the page number, and *[your initials]*4-7 as the footer.

13. Move to slide 1, and save the presentation as *[your initials]*4-7 in your Lesson 4 folder. Keep the file open for the next exercise.

Inserting and Adjusting Clip Art Images

Included with Microsoft Office is a collection of ready-to-use images known as clip art, also called *clips,* that you can insert on PowerPoint slides. The *clip art* collection includes *vector drawings*—images made up of lines, curves, and shapes that are usually filled with solid colors. It also includes *bitmap pictures*—photographs made up of tiny colored dots that are made from scanned photographs or a digital camera. The Clip Art pane enables you to search for these clips by keyword. You can access this pane in two ways:

- From the Insert tab, in the Images group, click the Clip Art button 🔳.
- On a new slide content placeholder, click the Clip Art button 🔳.

Exercise 4-8 FIND CLIP ART AND MODIFY A SEARCH

Each clip art image that Microsoft provides has *keywords* associated with it that describe the subject matter of the picture. You use keywords to find the art you need for your presentation.

Clip art images (and other media such as photographs, sound, and movie files) are organized into collections and media types. You can choose to search all collections and types or to select a particular type. If you know that you want a photograph only, be sure to select only that type of media to make the search more efficient.

Figure 4-12
Clip Art pane

If you search for a keyword and don't find any images, or you don't find one you like, you can modify your search and try again.

1. If you have Internet access but are not connected, make a connection now (unless your instructor tells you otherwise).

2. Move to slide 2, and then from the Insert tab, in the Images group, click the Clip Art button 🔳. The Clip Art pane, as shown in Figure 4-12, is displayed on the right.

3. In the Clip Art pane, in the **Search for** box, key **food**.

4. Click the **Results should be** list box arrow. In this list box, you can choose to search all media types or limit your search to specific types. These options are helpful if you have a large number of media files stored on your computer or you are searching on the Internet. Check only the **Illustrations** category, and remove all other checks.

Figure 4-13
Search results

5. Notice that **Include Office.com content** is checked, meaning that all categories in the Microsoft Clip Organizer will be searched and, if you are connected to the Internet, the Microsoft Office Online collection will be searched too.

6. Click **Go**. Thumbnails of clips that match the search word will appear in the Clip Art pane, as shown in Figure 4-13.

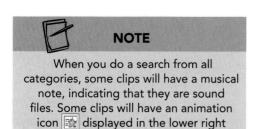

NOTE

When you do a search from all categories, some clips will have a musical note, indicating that they are sound files. Some clips will have an animation icon displayed in the lower right corner, indicating that they are videos.

7. Use the scroll bar to review some of the thumbnails.

8. In the Search for box, key **fruit**, and then click Go. Thumbnails of pictures with various types of fruit should appear in the pane. If you do not find a picture you like, modify the search using a different keyword.

Exercise 4-9 PREVIEW AND INSERT IMAGES

You can preview images in a larger format so that you can see more detail before choosing one of them.

1. Without clicking, point to a thumbnail in the Clip Art pane. As your pointer is over an image, a ScreenTip showing keywords, image dimensions, size, and file format appears. A gray bar with a downward-pointing triangle appears on the right side of the thumbnail. This bar changes to blue when you point to it.

2. Choose an image you would like to insert.

3. Click the gray bar beside the image you have chosen to display a list box of options. You can also display this list by right-clicking a thumbnail.

4. Choose Preview/Properties. In addition to displaying an enlarged picture, this dialog box also shows you the file name and more detailed information about the image, as shown in Figure 4-14.

Figure 4-14
Preview/Properties
dialog box

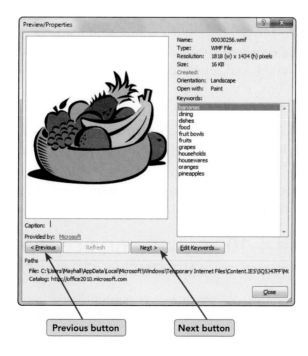

Previous button   Next button

5. Click the Next button [Next >] below the picture. The next picture in the pane is displayed.

6. Click the Next button [Next >] several times more; then click the Previous button [< Previous]. Gus has requested that you choose a professional-looking image to insert. When you find an appropriate picture of healthful food, such as the one in Figure 4-14 or Figure 4-15, click Close on the Preview/Properties dialog box. Notice that the last image you previewed has a blue selection box around it.

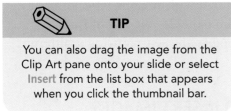

TIP

You can also drag the image from the Clip Art pane onto your slide or select Insert from the list box that appears when you click the thumbnail bar.

7. Click the image thumbnail to insert the image on the current slide.

Figure 4-15
Positioning of an illustrated image

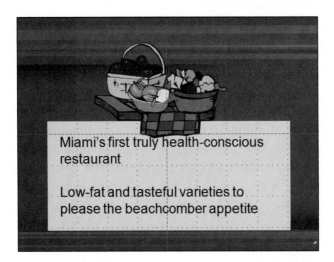

8. Drag the image above the text box, and resize or rotate it as necessary for a pleasing appearance. The image in Figure 4-15 was increased in size, rotated, and centered horizontally, and it overlaps the top edge of the text box. If you used a different image, then decide how to position it attractively on the slide.

9. Move to slide 1, and find another image that would be appropriate for Miami Beach. In the Search for box, key **palm tree**, and in the Results should be box, choose Photographs. Click Go.

10. When you find a photograph of a palm tree similar to the one in Figure 4-16, insert it on slide 1 and close the Clip Art pane.

Exercise 4-10 REARRANGE, DELETE, COPY, PASTE, AND DUPLICATE IMAGES

When developing a presentation, you might insert an image on one slide and later decide to move it to a different slide. You can rearrange, delete, copy, paste, and duplicate clip art images.

1. Still working on slide 1, click the photograph to select it. When you see the four-pointed arrow ⬚, drag the photograph down to center it vertically on the right edge of the text box.

2. Move to slide 4. This slide has four illustrations that were previously inserted. On the left, select the sunset beach scene, and notice the green rotation handle at the top. Practice dragging this handle to rotate the illustration.

3. Press [Delete] to remove the sunset beach scene from this slide.

4. On the right, select the palm tree image on the top, and press [Ctrl]+[C] to copy it and then [Delete] to remove it from this slide. The image is still on your Clipboard.

5. Insert a new slide after slide 4 using the Blank layout. Press [Ctrl]+[V] to insert the palm tree on the new slide 5.

6. When this image first appears, the size is 1.84 inches for both the height and the width. From the Picture Tools Format tab, in the Size group, change both Height and Width to 1.5".

7. Drag the palm tree to the upper left of the slide, aligning the bottom of the image with the darkest blue color on the background and the left edge of the image even with the left of the slide, as shown in Figure 4-16.

NOTE

When moving objects on the screen that need precise positioning, you can use the directional arrow keys on the keyboard to *nudge* the image gradually. If you press [Ctrl]+the arrow keys, the image will be nudged in very small increments.

Figure 4-16
Duplicated images

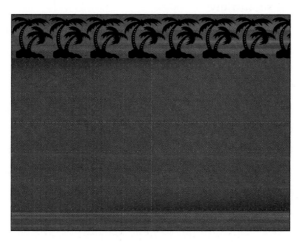

8. Press [Ctrl]+[D] to *duplicate* this image. Move the second image over to align with the bottom of the first image and position it so that the branches almost touch.

9. With the second image selected, press [Ctrl]+[D]. Because the positioning information from your first duplication is remembered by PowerPoint, this image should go into the same alignment.

10. Press [Ctrl]+[D] five more times to create a row of palm trees across the top of the slide as shown in Figure 4-16. Your final palm tree may extend past the end of the slide. This row of trees will create a nice top border for a night scene added later in the lesson.

NOTE

Using the Duplicate command is faster than using Copy and Paste when you want a second image on the same slide. Copy and Paste works best when you want to copy an image from one slide and paste it on another slide.

Exercise 4-11   GROUP AND UNGROUP IMAGES AND TEXT

When you *group* objects, you combine two or more shapes or images so that they behave as one. If you then move one object of the group, all the other objects move with it. Grouping ensures that objects meant to stay together don't accidentally get moved individually or deleted. When you apply formatting to a group, all the objects in the group receive the same formatting. If you need to work on the objects separately, then you can *ungroup* them. *Regrouping* can combine the objects again.

1. Move to slide 4. Press [Shift] while you click both the beach scene image and the text below it. Now selection handles appear on both images.

2. From the Picture Tools Format tab, in the Arrange group, click Group 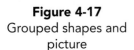; then select Group. Now the clip art image and the text are combined as one object.

3. Resize the group by stretching the corner sizing handle on the top right to make the image about as large as the palm tree on the right.

4. In resizing the group, the text has moved and is not in the best position. From the Picture Tools Format tab, in the Arrange group, click the Group button ⌗▾; then choose Ungroup. Now you can move the image and text separately.

5. Arrange the beach scene image on the left so that the bottom aligns evenly with the palm tree on the right. Move the beach scene text so that it is centered under the image and aligned with the palm tree text. You may need to resize the beach scene text box.

6. Now select the beach image. From the Picture Tools Format tab, in the Arrange group, click the Group button ⌗▾, and choose Regroup.

7. Select the palm tree image and the palm tree text, and group them.

8. Move to slide 6. Select the picture of Miami buildings, and press [Ctrl]+[C].

9. Move to slide 3, and press [Ctrl]+[V]. Position the picture so that it is in the center of the square shape.

10. Resize the square shape to change it to a rectangle that evenly frames the picture.

11. If necessary, select the 16-Point Star shape and move it up slightly so that the picture is not overlapping it.

Figure 4-17
Grouped shapes and picture

12. With the star selected, press Shift while you click the picture and the rectangle to select all three objects.

13. From the Drawing Tools Format tab, in the Arrange group, click the Group button 📑▾, and choose Group.

14. From the View tab, in the Show group, uncheck the boxes for Gridlines and Guides since we are finished aligning objects.

15. Move to slide 1, and save the presentation as *[your initials]*4-11 in your Lesson 4 folder. Keep the file open for the next exercise.

Inserting and Enhancing a Picture

More than any other graphic element, pictures can add a sense of realism to a presentation. Microsoft's online collection offers an abundance of photograph images that you can search for using the Clip Art pane. Pictures that you take with a digital camera also can be inserted. Or pictures that are already printed can be turned into an appropriate digital format by scanning.

Once the picture is inserted into PowerPoint, you have many options for improving its appearance using the commands on the Picture Tools Format tab shown in Figure 4-18 and defined in Table 4-2. In the next exercises, you will learn to crop to remove unwanted details, adjust brightness and contrast, and apply many different styles and special effects.

Figure 4-18
Picture Tools Format ribbon

TABLE 4-2 Picture Tools Format Tab Commands

Button	Name	Purpose
📑▾	Align	Evenly spaces multiple objects.
🖼	Artistic Effects	Adds interesting effects to pictures, including effects such as blur, pastels, light screen, cement, and painting.
🖼	Bring Forward	Adjusts stacking order of pictures and other objects.
🖼	Change Picture	Changes the selected picture to a different picture in the same size and format as a selected picture.
🖼	Color	Enables you to change the color saturation and tone of a picture and select different monotone variations based on theme colors.
🖼	Compress Pictures	Reduces resolution and removes unwanted information from a picture to make the presentation file size smaller.

continues

TABLE 4-2 Picture Tools Format Tab Commands *continued*

Button	Name	Purpose
	Corrections	Increases or decreases a picture's brightness, contrast, or sharpness.
	Crop	Enables you to trim away the edges of a picture, crop to shape, and adjust the aspect ratio of images.
	Group	Fastens multiple objects together to act as one object.
	Height	Adjusts the vertical size dimension.
	Picture Border	Places an outline around a picture in different colors, weights, or line styles.
	Picture Effects	Provides the effects of shadow, reflection, glow, soft edges, bevel, or 3-D rotation.
	Picture Layout	Converts the picture to a SmartArt graphic.
	Picture Quick Styles	Provides a gallery of preset effects to add interest. Displays when the Ribbon is not expanded to its full size.
	Remove Background	Removes unwanted portions of the picture background.
	Reset Picture	Restores a picture's original attributes if changes were made by using the Picture Adjustment tools.
	Rotate	Angles pictures and other objects.
	Selection Pane	Enables you to select individual pictures and other objects and change the visibility or order.
	Send Backward	Adjusts the stacking order of pictures and other objects.
	Width	Adjusts the horizontal size dimension.

Exercise 4-12 INSERT PHOTOGRAPH IMAGES

To search for a photograph image, use the same steps as you did for searching for illustrated images except choose Photographs instead of Illustrations under the Results should be list box.

1. Delete slide 6, since the photo is now used on slide 3.

2. Move to slide 5, and from the Insert tab, in the Images group, click the Clip Art button ▦.

3. In the Clip Art pane, in the Results should be list box, check only Photographs and remove other checks. Be sure Include Office.com content is checked.

4. In the Search for box, key **Miami**, and then click Go. The pane shows thumbnails (miniature images) of clips that match the search word.

Figure 4-19
Photograph inserted
from search

5. Double-click the Miami night image. Drag the corner sizing handle to increase the picture height to about 4 inches. Notice that the width automatically adjusts to keep the image in proportion.

6. Position the image as shown in Figure 4-19. Close the Clip Art pane.

Exercise 4-13 CROP A PICTURE

When a picture (photograph) is selected and you click the Picture Tools Format tab, many options become available to you for adjusting the picture or applying picture styles and effects. You can also *crop* (trim) parts of a picture, just as you might do with a page from a magazine by using a pair of scissors to reduce its size or remove unwanted details around the edge.

When you click the cropping tool, a picture's sizing handles change to *cropping handles*—short black markers that you drag to trim a picture.

1. On slide 5, select the night scene picture. The colors of the lighted buildings and water reflections can be featured more if the picture is trimmed across the top and bottom.

2. From the Picture Tools Format tab, in the Size group, click the Crop button 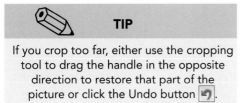. The cropping handles appear around the edges of the picture, and your pointer changes to a cropping tool.

TIP

If you crop too far, either use the cropping tool to drag the handle in the opposite direction to restore that part of the picture or click the Undo button.

3. Position the cropping pointer on the top-center handle, and drag the handle down until the cropping line is positioned a little closer to the top of the tallest building, as shown in Figure 4-20. Notice the dark area showing what portion of the image will be removed.

4. Repeat this process to crop from the bottom so that the picture ends just below the reflection.

Figure 4-20
Cropping a picture

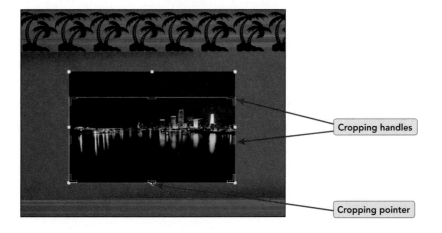

Cropping handles

Cropping pointer

5.   Click a blank area of the slide to turn off the crop function and to remove the dark areas indicating the cropped part of the image.

Exercise 4-14   MODIFY COLORS

The appearance of a photograph can be changed in many ways using color settings. These effects might be used, for example, to improve the clarity of an image, make an image look aged, or create a subtle image to be placed behind other slide objects.

1.   Move to slide 1, select the palm tree picture, and copy it. Insert a new slide Blank layout, and paste the picture.

2.   Select the picture on slide 2; then from the Picture Tools Format tab, in the Adjust group, click the Color button. A gallery of color options will appear, as shown in Figure 4-21.

Figure 4-21
Color gallery

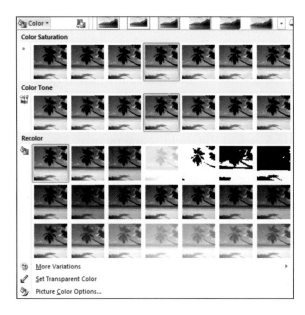

3.   In the gallery, slowly drag your pointer over each of the options to see a preview on the picture.

   • *Color Saturation.* Controls the intensity of the colors, making the image less or more vivid as the percentage changes from 100%.

   • *Color Tone.* Creates cool or warm tones by changing the temperature of the image on a scale of 4,700 to 11,200. The low end of this scale has cool tones, and the high end has warm tones.

   • *Recolor.* Provides options for grayscale, black and white, or different light and dark monotone variations of the presentation's theme colors.

4.   In the Recolor category in the last row, click Dark Blue, Accent color 1 Light to select this color change.

5.   Move the picture to the upper left of the slide. Use the lower right sizing handle, and drag down to reach the bottom of the slide.

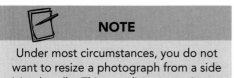

NOTE

Under most circumstances, you do not want to resize a photograph from a side sizing handle. This can distort your image. In this case, the tree is elongated, but the image looks best filling the entire slide.

6. Drag the right sizing handle to the right of the slide so that the picture completely fills the slide (dimensions: 7.5 inches by 10 inches).

7. Move to slide 1, press Ctrl+A to select all objects on the slide, and then press Ctrl+C to copy them.

8. On slide 2, press Ctrl+V to paste all objects over the recolored palm tree picture.

9. Move back to slide 1, and press Delete to remove the original slide 1.

Exercise 4-15 APPLY A PICTURE STYLE

Many different *picture styles* are available to display your pictures in beautiful and interesting ways. As with any of the creative techniques you are using, be careful that the styles and other treatments you apply to your pictures add to the appearance of the picture and do not distort it or diminish its effectiveness.

1. On the new slide 1, select the smaller color picture of the palm tree. From the Picture Tools Format tab, in the Picture Styles group, slowly drag your pointer over each of the Picture Styles options, and the results of that option will be displayed on the picture.

2. Click the More button ⊽ to see additional styles that are available, as shown in Figure 4-22.

Figure 4-22
Picture styles

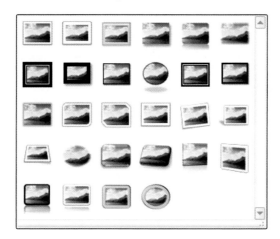

3. Now click the Picture Style Rounded Diagonal Corner, White, as shown in Figure 4-23.

Figure 4-23
Picture with Rounded Diagonal Corner, White effect

4. On slide 5, select the picture, and apply the same Picture Style, Rounded Diagonal Corner, White.

5. From the Insert tab, in the Text group, click the Text Box button [A], and draw a text box at the bottom of the picture. In the text box, key **Beautiful Miami Skyline**. Change the font to Bauhaus 93 in font size 36, apply italics, and right-align the text. The title should fit nicely in the black water area of the image.

Exercise 4-16 INSERT A PICTURE FROM A FILE

When you begin to acquire a collection of digital images, you need to keep them organized in some logical way in folders on your computer that are appropriately named to identify the folder's contents. These folders might be saved in the Pictures folder that is automatically created on your computer when Microsoft Office is installed.

However, for this exercise you have a picture file stored in the same folder as all the other files for this lesson.

1. Display slide 5; then, from the Home tab, in the Slides group, click the New Slide button [▣] to add a new slide with a Title Only layout. Key **Outdoor Dining** as the slide title.

2. From the Insert tab, in the Images group, click the Picture button [▣].

3. In the Insert Picture dialog box, locate where your student data files for this lesson are stored, and select the file **Restaurant.jpg**. Click Insert.

4. With the picture selected, click the Picture Tools Format tab. In the Size group, change the height to 5", and the width will automatically change to 3.7".

5. Move the picture to the left of the slide, under the title.

Exercise 4-17 USE CORRECTIONS TO SHARPEN OR SOFTEN AND ADJUST CONTRAST AND BRIGHTNESS

Sometimes a picture may be too dark to show needed details, or colors are washed out from too much sunshine when the picture was taken. PowerPoint's *Corrections* feature can fix these problems. Adjusting the brightness changes the picture's overall lightness, while adjusting contrast affects the difference between the picture's lightest and darkest areas. Modifying the sharpness makes objects look more or less precise.

1. On slide 6, select the picture, and press [Ctrl]+[D] to duplicate it. Position the second image on the right of the slide. Use it to make the color adjustments in this exercise so that you can compare your changes to the original.

2. With the second picture selected, from the Picture Tools Format tab, in the Adjust group, click the Corrections button [☀]. A gallery of thumbnails appears showing the current picture selected and the effect of adjustments in 20 percent increments, as shown in Figure 4-24, that increase or decrease the brightness and contrast of the picture.

Figure 4-24
Corrections gallery

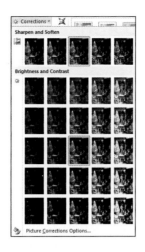

3. Drag your pointer over the thumbnails, and notice the effect on the picture and the ScreenTips that show brightness and contrast amounts. Click Brightness: +20% and Contrast: +20% (column 4, row 4) to increase the brightness and contrast by 20%.

4. Click the Corrections button ⚙. The same gallery appears showing adjustments in the Sharpen and Soften category in 25 percent increments that increase or decrease the sharpness of the picture. Drag your pointer over the thumbnails, and study the effect on the picture. Click Sharpen: 25% (column 4) to increase the sharpness.

5. Now click the Reset Picture button 🖼 to restore the picture's original colors.

6. Sometimes these 20 and 25 percent increments change a picture's colors too much, so you might need to adjust them more gradually to get good results. On the Picture Tools Format tab, in the Adjust group, click the Corrections button ⚙; then choose Picture Corrections Options to open the Format Picture dialog box. Move this dialog box away from the picture so that you can see the results of your changes as you make them.

7. Both the brightness and the contrast can be adjusted by dragging the slider to the left or right. You can also enter numbers in the spin boxes or click up or down to change in 1 percent increments.

8. Adjust the brightness to a positive 14% and the Contrast to a positive 24%. Modify the Sharpen setting to a positive 15%. Click Close.

9. The picture appears a little clearer now when you compare the one changed on the right with the original version on the left, as shown in Figure 4-25. You will leave both images in the presentation, so Gus can decide which image he prefers to use.

Figure 4-25
Picture with corrections

10. Save the presentation as *[your initials]*4-17 in your Lesson 4 folder. Leave the presentation open for the next exercise.

Exercise 4-18 CROP TO A SHAPE

Any picture that is inserted on a slide can be cropped to fill a shape for an unusual and creative treatment.

1. On slide 6, from the Home tab, in the Slides group, click the New Slide button to add a new slide with a Blank layout.

2. On slide 7, insert another picture from your Clip Art pane. If the search from earlier in the lesson is not displayed, then search again for Miami photograph images.

3. Insert the image that is angled showing a beach and buildings.

4. With this image selected, from the Picture Tools Format tab, in the Size group, click the down arrow on the Crop button, and choose Crop to Shape. Try several of these shapes by clicking on the buttons in any of the categories. The image becomes the fill for that particular shape.

5. In the Basic Shapes category, select the Heart shape.

Exercise 4-19 ADD A BORDER TO A PICTURE

The line that surrounds shapes and pictures is referred to as a Picture Border. This line can be shown in different colors and *line weights* (thicknesses) or in different styles (solid lines or dashes) to create a border around a picture just as you have used an outline on other shapes.

1. With the heart-shaped picture selected, from the Picture Tools Format tab, in the Picture Styles group, click the Picture Border button. As you drag your pointer over the colors, you can see how the color will look if selected.

2. From the colors that appear, in the Theme Colors group, click the White, Text 1 color.

3. Click the Picture Border button again, and click Weight. Choose 4 ½ pt for a thicker white line, as shown in Figure 4-26.

4. Continue to the next exercise.

Figure 4-26
Picture in a shape
with a border

Exercise 4-20 APPLY PICTURE EFFECTS

Special effects can be applied to pictures as well as other shapes you create using the Picture Effects button on the Picture Tools Format tab. Many different customized settings are possible. Picture effects are available in seven categories:

- *Preset.* Consists of a collection of images with several different settings already applied.

- *Shadow.* Displays a shadow behind the picture that can be adjusted in different ways to change direction, thickness, and blurring effect.

- *Reflection.* Causes a portion of the image to be displayed below the image as though it were reflecting in a mirror or on water.

- *Glow.* Adds a soft color around the picture edges that makes the picture stand out from the background.

- *Soft Edges.* Changes a picture's normal hard edges to a soft, feathered appearance that gradually fades into the background color.

- *Bevel.* Makes the picture look dimensional through several different options that can create a buttonlike effect.

- *3-D Rotation.* Enables the picture to be angled in different ways through perspective settings that change the illusion of depth.

Figure 4-27
Picture Effects

Preset	▶
Shadow	▶
Reflection	▶
Glow	▶
Soft Edges	▶
Bevel	▶
3-D Rotation	▶

1. On slide 7, select the heart-shaped picture. From the Picture Tools Format tab, in the Picture Styles group, click the Picture Effects button 🖼.

2. The drop-down list of effects appears, as shown in Figure 4-27. Each of these effects has several variations that you can see on your image as you drag your pointer over the effect thumbnail.

3. Click Shadow, and then Outer. Choose the shadow named Offset Diagonal Bottom Right to apply a soft shadow.

4. Adjustments can be made to the way the shadow appears. Click the Picture Effects button 🖼, click Shadow, and then choose the Shadow Options at the bottom of this gallery.

5. From the dialog box that appears as shown in Figure 4-28, key these numbers for each of the following settings:

   - Transparency   **20%**
   - Size   **100%**
   - Blur   **10 pt**
   - Angle   **40°**
   - Distance   **15 pt**

6. Click Close to accept these settings.

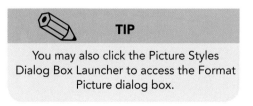

TIP

You may also click the Picture Styles Dialog Box Launcher to access the Format Picture dialog box.

Figure 4-28
Format Picture,
Shadow settings

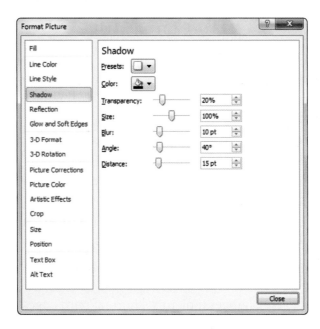

Exercise 4-21 APPLY ARTISTIC EFFECTS

Artistic Effects is a new feature in PowerPoint 2010 that applies photo filters to pictures. Previously, creating these interesting and unusual effects required photo editing software. The best way to become familiar with the Artistic Effects feature is to insert a picture image and apply different effects to observe how the image is modified. Artistic Effects include 23 different filters that can be adjusted in transparency or intensity. These include effects such as *Painting, Blur, Cement, Light Screen, Plastic Wrap, and Pastels.*

1. On slide 8, key **Innovative Dishes** as the slide title.

2. Use the Clip Art pane to search for and insert a photograph of a healthy salad or entrée similar to the one shown in Figure 4-29. Resize the picture to a height of 5″, and position it on the right beside the waiter image.

3. With this image selected, from the Picture Tools Format tab, in the Adjust group, click the Artistic Effects button 🖼. Point to the options to preview the effect that each has on the image.

4. Since the image displays food, choose the Plastic Wrap effect. This effect might be appropriate to illustrate how take-home food could be packaged.

Figure 4-29
Artistic Effects

Exercise 4-22   REMOVE A PICTURE BACKGROUND

The *Background Removal* feature is new in PowerPoint 2010. It allows you to remove the background of an image to help the audience focus on the important part of that picture.

You will work with two images in this exercise. The first one has a solid-color background, so you will see how the Background Removal feature works really well with pictures like this to remove areas that may be distracting or that do not blend with your slide background. The second image has a little more color and details, so you will see how the Mark to Remove and Mark to Include options are used to control which parts of the picture are retained.

1. On slide 8, increase the waiter image size to 6″, and position it attractively to the left of the salad image.

2. Because this image shows a person with a single-color background, the original background in the photo has probably been removed and replaced with white.

3. With the image selected, from the Picture Tools Format tab, in the Adjust group, click Remove Background. The background becomes pink as shown in Figure 4-30, indicating the area that is marked for removal, and handles appear on the area of the image to keep.

4. Resize the handles so that all of the waiter is within the rectangular shape.

5. On the Background Removal tab, in the Close group, click the Keep Changes button ✓, and the area marked in pink is removed. Now the waiter image looks more pleasing on the slide background.

Figure 4-30
Background
Removal, solid color

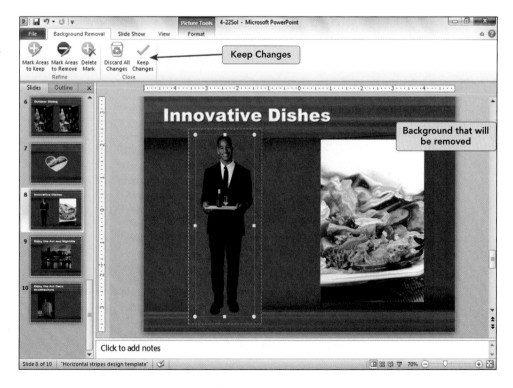

6. On slide 9, key **Enjoy the Art Deco Architecture** as the slide title.

7. Resize the image to a height of 6″, and position it on the left with the bottom of the picture aligned with the bottom of the slide. Press Ctrl+D, and position the duplicated image on the right. Make your changes on this second image, and use the first one for comparison.

8. Use the Zoom slider on the status bar to increase the slide size to 90% so that you can better see the details of the image.

9. With this image selected, from the Picture Tools Format tab, in the Adjust group, click the Remove Background button 🔳. The background becomes pink, indicating the area that is marked for removal, and handles appear on the area of the image to keep.

10. Resize the center handle on the bottom to extend the selected area to the bottom of the image.

11. On the Background Removal tab, in the Refine group, click the Mark Areas to Keep button 🔳, and your pointer becomes a pencil tool.

12. Very carefully click the edges of the building that should not be removed, and small plus marks will appear, indicating that this area is being added to the selected area. Include the palm tree on the right too.

13. If you mark the wrong area, click the Delete Mark button 🔳 to again remove an area marked for removal from the selection. If areas that are not marked should be removed, click the Mark Areas to Remove button 🔳.

14. When finished, click the Keep Changes button 🔳. As shown in Figure 4-31, the final image now focuses on the one building, and surrounding buildings no longer appear.

15. Use the Fit to Window button 🔳 on the status bar so that the slide fits in the available space of your monitor and you can compare this altered image to the original on the left.

Figure 4-31
Background Removal,
Mark Areas to Keep
and to Remove

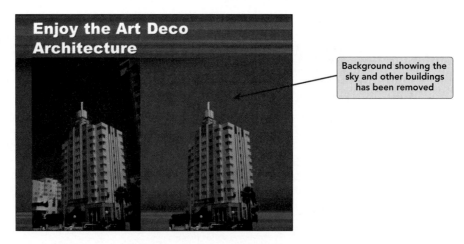

16. Move to slide 10 to make modifications to the final presentation slide. Apply the Rotated, White picture style, and resize the image so that the edges of the picture style touch the top and the bottom of the slide.

17. Apply the Artistic Effect Paint Brush.

18. Select the title text placeholder, and change the font to Bauhaus 93, bold, centered, with a font color of Light Blue, Background 1.

19. Resize the title text placeholder to fit the image, and rotate and reposition so that the title appears level with the bottom of the image.

20. Save the presentation as *[your initials]*4-22 in your Lesson 4 folder. Leave the presentation open for the next exercise.

Creating WordArt

WordArt provides special effects for text that are not possible with standard text-formatting tools. You can stretch or curve text and add special shading, 3-D effects, and much more to make text more readable or more decorative.

Exercise 4-23   CREATE AND MODIFY WORDART TEXT

In this exercise, you create WordArt text and then modify it by changing its shape and size.

Figure 4-32
WordArt Styles gallery

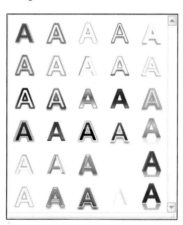

1. Display slide 3 with the building photograph.

2. From the Insert tab, in the Text group, click the WordArt button ④. The WordArt Styles gallery appears, as shown in Figure 4-32.

3. Point to the blue WordArt style Fill – Blue, Accent 2, Warm Matte Bevel (fifth row, third effect) and click to select it. WordArt appears in the middle of your slide with sample text as shown in Figure 4-33.

Figure 4-33
WordArt as it first appears

4. With the WordArt text selected, replace the text by keying **Good For You**.

TIP

Many different styles are displayed in the WordArt gallery using the colors of your current theme. When applied, some of the styles may need color adjustments so that the text is easily readable on the background color.

5. Click anywhere on the blank part of the slide to accept these changes, and the bevel effect of this style becomes more evident.

6. To edit WordArt text, simply select the text and change it. In this case, change the wording to **Good 4 U**.

7. Move the WordArt text to the lower left as shown in Figure 4-34.

Figure 4-34
WordArt positioning

8. Save the presentation as *[your initials]***4-23** in your Lesson 4 folder. Leave the presentation open for the next exercise.

Exercise 4-24 APPLY WORDART EFFECTS

Many of the same effects you applied to pictures can be applied to WordArt. From the Drawing Tools Format tab, in the WordArt Styles group, click the Text Effects [A]. A drop-down list displays the effects, as shown in Figure 4-35. In Exercise 4-20 you were introduced to most of these effects when applying them to a picture: Shadow, Reflection, Glow, Bevel, and 3-D Rotation. But the last category, *Transform,* is unique to WordArt because it enables you to change your text into different shapes.

Figure 4-35
Transform effects

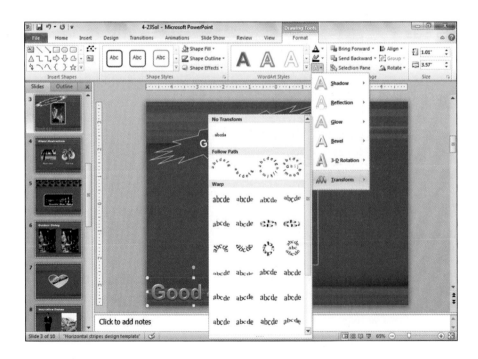

1. Still working on slide 3, with the Good 4 U WordArt selected, click the Drawing Tools Format tab; in the WordArt Styles group, click the Text Effects button Ⓐ, and choose Transform.

2. The default for WordArt text is No Transform because text will appear straight. When you drag your pointer over the various effects shown in this gallery, you will see a live preview showing that effect applied to your text. The text sample on each of the buttons gives you an indication of the particular effect.

3. From the Warp category, choose the effect Deflate Top (column 2, row 7), which causes the text in the middle of the WordArt to become smaller.

4. Move the WordArt to the bottom of the picture so that the letters "G" and "U" just slightly overlap with the blue rectangle, as shown in Figure 4-36.

Figure 4-36
Using Transform to apply the Deflate Top Warp effect

Exercise 4-25 EDIT WORDART FILL AND OUTLINE COLORS

The *Text Fill* color of WordArt text can be changed as well as the *Text Outline* color and the weight of the outline. The outline goes around the edge of each letter. Making it thick emphasizes the outline; making it thin provides less emphasis but still makes the text look quite different from the way it looks without an outline.

1. Move to slide 7.

2. From the Insert tab, in the Text group, click the WordArt button ④. For the style, click the white WordArt style that is called Fill – White, Warm Matte Bevel, and click to select it.

3. Key **We Love Miami Beach!** Select the text, and from the Home tab, in the Font group, change the font size to 44 points.

4. Move the WordArt text above the heart, centered horizontally on the slide.

5. With the WordArt selected, from the Drawing Tools Format tab, in the WordArt Styles group, click the Text Fill button 🅐. From the theme colors, choose Gray-25%, Accent 4.

6. With the WordArt selected, from the Drawing Tools Format tab, in the WordArt Styles group, click the Text Outline button and choose White, Text 1.

7. Click the Text Outline button , click Weight, and choose 4½ pt.

8. Now change the shadow effect so that it better matches the heart shape. From the Drawing Tools Format tab, in the WordArt Styles group, click the Dialog Box Launcher button .

9. From the Format Text Effects dialog box, choose Shadow. Change to these settings: Transparency 20%, Size 100%, Blur 4 pt, Angle 45°, Distance 2 pt. Click Close.

10. From the Drawing Tools Format tab, in the WordArt Styles group, click the Text Effects button , click Transform, and from the Warp category, select Wave 2.

11. Resize and adjust any necessary spacing so that your slide resembles Figure 4-37.

Figure 4-37
Completed WordArt
text

12. Update the handout footer to show *[your initials]*4-25. View the presentation as a slide show.

13. Save the presentation as *[your initials]*4-25 in your Lesson 4 folder. The presentation is now ready for Gus's review. Close the presentation and submit your work.

Creating a Photo Album

A presentation consisting of mostly pictures can be created quickly using PowerPoint's *Photo Album* feature. Picture files can be inserted from different locations on your computer and will be displayed with one, two, or four pictures on a slide. The pictures can be displayed at full screen size or framed in different shapes. Also, text can accompany each picture at the time you create the photo album, or text can be added to the individual slides. When complete, your saved photo album can be displayed just as any other presentation.

While this feature can be important for business situations, it could also be very helpful for creating a display for open-house functions or even wedding or birthday celebrations.

As an intern at Good 4 U, you are to create a photo album showcasing the most popular salad choices. The images have been taken by Chef Michele and are included in your student files. She will later add more content to this slide show for the purpose of explaining menu options to people she talks to about catered events.

Exercise 4-26 CREATE ALBUM CONTENT BY INSERTING NEW PICTURES

In your Lesson 4 student data files you have a folder named **Salads** containing five pictures for this exercise. Copy the **Salads** folder to your storage location.

1. Open PowerPoint if necessary, and start a new blank presentation.
2. From the Insert tab, in the Images group, click the top of the Photo Album button 🖼️. The Photo Album dialog box appears, as shown in Figure 4-38.

Figure 4-38
Photo Album dialog box

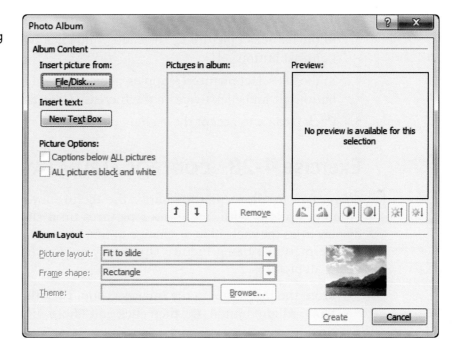

3. Click the File/Disk button File/Disk... ; then choose the storage location where you have the Salads folder. Select the folder name, and then click Insert.
4. Select all the picture files (using contiguous selection methods), and click Insert.
5. At the bottom of the dialog box, notice the Album Layout options. By default, the Picture layout is Fit to slide. This option will expand each picture to fill your computer's screen. Click Create.
6. Each picture appears on a separate slide, and a title slide has been created.

Exercise 4-27 ADJUST PICTURE ORDER, BRIGHTNESS, AND CONTRAST

Using the Format Photo Album dialog box, you can easily reorder pictures by selecting the picture name and clicking the up or down arrow. Pictures can be rotated if their orientation needs to change, and even the brightness and contrast can be adjusted. These changes can be made at the time you create the Photo Album or later by editing the pictures individually.

1. From the Insert tab, in the Images group, click the lower half of the Photo Album button ; then click Edit Photo Album.
2. Reorder the images using the up and down arrows below the image list to match the following order:
   1. apples
   2. avocado
   3. tuna
   4. chicken
   5. soup_salad
3. In the list select picture 2, "avocado," and click twice on the Increase Contrast button .
4. In the list select picture 1, "apples"; click once on the Increase Brightness button , and click twice on the Increase Contrast button .
5. Click Update to accept these changes.

Exercise 4-28 CONTROL ALBUM LAYOUT

Album Layout allows you to change the Picture layout from Fit to slide to different options with one to four pictures on a slide. You can choose to display titles for each slide or change to one of seven different Frame shapes for the pictures. Using Picture Options, you can choose to place captions below all pictures.

1. From the Insert tab, in the Images group, click the lower half of the Photo Album button ; then click Edit Photo Album.
2. For Picture Layout, change to 1 picture.
3. Now Picture Options are available. Click to place a check beside Captions below ALL Pictures.
4. For Frame shape, select several of the available options, and notice how the effect is displayed in the thumbnail area on the right. Select Simple Frame, White.
5. Now apply a background theme that will provide soft coloring on the background behind the pictures. For the theme, click Browse Browse... , and choose Apex; then click Select. (You may have to navigate to your themes for Office 2010.)
6. Be sure the options on your Edit Photo Album dialog box match those in Figure 4-39. Click Update.

Figure 4-39
Edit Photo Album
options

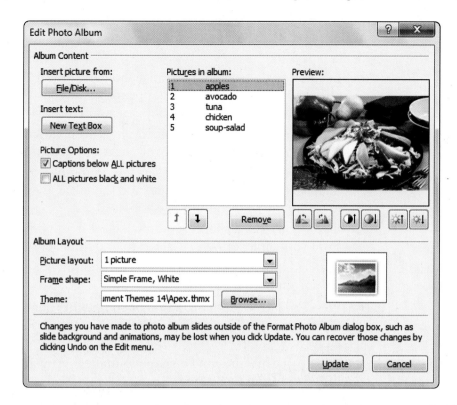

7. Now the pictures appear a little smaller on the slide and have a white frame with a subtle shadow effect, as shown in Figure 4-40. The Apex theme provides a soft background that is subtle and does not detract from the pictures.

Figure 4-40
Slide with framed
picture

8. Notice that the file name for each picture now appears in a text box below the picture. Chef Michele will later change this text to a more descriptive title for each salad.

9. On slide 1, key **New Salads** for the presentation title, and key **Good 4 U** for the subtitle. Change the subtitle text size to 36 points, and apply bold.

10. Add a header on the handout page with *[your initials]*4-28 in the header, remove the date, and put nothing in the footer.

11. Save the presentation as *[your initials]*4-28 in your Lesson 4 folder.

12. Close the presentation and submit your work.

Lesson 4   Summary

- In addition to providing text placeholders, PowerPoint offers a variety of objects to enhance the visual appearance of your slides. These include shapes, text boxes, clip art, pictures, and WordArt.

- PowerPoint has drawing tools for creating a variety of shapes including squares, circles, rectangles, ovals, and straight lines.

- To draw a shape, from the Insert tab, in the Illustrations group, click the Shapes button, choose a shape, and then drag diagonally on your slide to create the shape in the size you need.

- If you don't like a shape you drew, select it and press [Delete] to remove it from your slide, or press [Ctrl]+[Z] to undo the action.

- Use gridlines and guides to help with alignment and placement of objects on the slide.

- Press [Shift] while drawing a line or some other shape to constrain it. Constraining a shape makes it perfectly symmetrical, for example, a circle or a square, or it can make a line perfectly straight.

- Press [Ctrl] while drawing a shape to make it grow in size from the center instead of from one edge.

- Change the size of a drawn object by dragging one of its sizing handles (small white circles on its border) with a two-pointed arrow.

- To preserve an object's proportions when resizing it, hold down [Shift] while dragging a corner sizing handle.

- Move a drawn object by pointing to it and, when the four-pointed arrow appears, dragging the object to a new position.

- The Shapes gallery has many predefined shapes that are organized into several categories.

- When a shape is selected, text that you key appears inside the shape.

- Use the Clip Art pane to search for illustrations and photograph images. If you are connected to the Internet, Microsoft's Office.com content will automatically be searched.

- To see the file properties of an illustration or photograph in the Clip Art pane, point to a thumbnail and then click the vertical bar that appears on the right side of it (or right-click the thumbnail).

- Using the Cut, Copy, and Paste commands, you can easily move or copy objects from one slide to another or from one presentation to another.

- Using the Duplicate command is the quickest way to create a copy of an object on the same slide.

- Resize an image by dragging one of its sizing handles. If you want to preserve proportions, drag a corner handle. If you want to distort the proportions, drag one of the side handles.

- From the Picture Tools Format tab, in the Adjust group, use tools to change a picture's brightness, contrast, and colors.

- Illustrations and photograph images (vectors, bitmaps, or scanned images) can be cropped. Cropping is trimming away edges of a picture, much like using scissors to cut out a picture from a newspaper or magazine. Images can even be cropped to a shape.

- Artistic Effects enable you to alter a picture in some way, such as by making it look like a watercolor or oil painting.

- Picture Effects allow you to add shadows, reflection, glow, soft edges, bevel, and 3-D rotation effects. All of these can be customized.

- Remove Background enables you to take away unwanted portions of picture images.

- WordArt enables you to create special effects with text that are not possible with standard text-formatting tools.

- WordArt text is modified by using WordArt Styles and Text Effects to change its appearance in many different ways. These options are available on the Drawing Tools Format tab when WordArt text is selected.

- PowerPoint's Photo Album feature can be used to quickly create a presentation consisting mostly of pictures. One or more pictures can be placed on each slide, with a choice of different framing techniques.

- Once a photo album is created, it can be modified by choosing the Edit Photo Album option to rearrange pictures, request captions, and add a theme. A photo album is saved in the same way as any other presentation.

LESSON 4		Command Summary
Feature	**Button**	**Ribbon**
Adjust Picture Brightness, Contrast, and Sharpness	☼	Picture Tools Format tab, Adjust group, Corrections
Adjust Picture Color		Picture Tools Format tab, Adjust group, Color
Apply Artistic Effects		Picture Tools Format tab, Adjust group, Artistic Effects
Apply Picture Border		Picture Tools Format tab, Picture Styles group, Picture Border
Apply Picture Effects		Picture Tools Format tab, Picture Styles group, Picture Effects
Apply WordArt Styles		Drawing Tools Format tab, WordArt Styles group, More

continues

LESSON 4		Command Summary *continued*
Feature	**Button**	**Ribbon**
Apply WordArt Text Effects		Drawing Tools Format tab, WordArt Styles group, Text Effects
Change WordArt Color		Drawing Tools Format tab, WordArt Styles group, Text Fill
Change WordArt Outline		Drawing Tools Format tab, WordArt Styles group, Text Outline
Crop a Picture		Picture Tools Format tab, Size group, Crop
Crop a Picture to a Shape		Picture Tools Format tab, Size group, Crop down arrow, Crop to Shape
Insert Pictures		Insert tab, Images group, Picture
Insert Shapes		Home tab, Drawing group, Shapes or Insert tab, Illustrations group, Shapes
Insert WordArt		Insert tab, Text group, WordArt
Remove Background		Picture Tools Format tab, Adjust group, Remove Background
Search for Clip Art and Photographs		Insert, Images group, Clip Art, Clip Art pane, Search

Concepts Review

True/False Questions

Each of the following statements is either true or false. Indicate your choice by circling T or F.

T F   1.   You can key text only in an existing placeholder.

T F   2.   Use Shift with ☐ to create a square.

T F   3.   Every shape includes an adjustment handle.

T F   4.   A green handle on a PowerPoint object indicates that the object can be rotated.

T F   5.   The Insert Picture command is the quickest way to create a presentation with multiple images.

T F   6.   When you want to change the height of an object, but not the width, press Shift while dragging a corner sizing handle.

T F   7.   To apply a frame or shadow effect to a picture, choose a Picture Style.

T F   8.   WordArt enables you to create special effects with text.

Short Answer Questions

Write the correct answer in the space provided.

1.   How do you draw a perfect circle?

_____

2.   What kind of handle is the yellow diamond?

_____

3.   How can you make a picture have a different shape?

_____

4.   Describe the appearance of a bevel effect when applied to a picture or shape.

_____

5.   If Insert Picture is not used to add a photograph from a file, which pane would be used to search for a photograph?

_____

6.   What setting on the Format Picture dialog box will cause a shadow to appear from a particular direction?

_____

7. List three Artistic Effects available from the Picture Tools Format tab.

_____

8. How do you change the shape of WordArt text?

_____

Critical Thinking

Answer these questions on a separate page. There are no right or wrong answers. Support your answers with examples from your own experience, if possible.

1. Consider the Shapes gallery, and explain how three different shapes could help you illustrate or draw attention to a concept you need to explain.

2. Describe how Picture Styles can enhance the appearance of a photograph.

Skills Review

Exercise 4-29

Create shapes, use gridlines and guides, key text in a shape, and use the Format Shape dialog box.

1. Open the file **Seminar1**. Move to slide 3.

2. From the View tab, in the Show group, click to turn on the Gridlines and Guides.

3. Use the drawing tools to create the shapes shown in Figure 4-41. First, create the wide rectangle that appears on top of the triangle by following these steps:

Figure 4-41
Drawing shapes

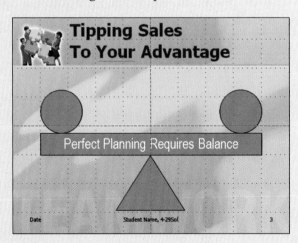

   a. From the Insert tab, in the Illustrations group, click the Shapes button 🔲 and then the Rectangle button ▢.

   b. Position the crosshair pointer ✛ on the left of the slide.

   c. Drag the pointer diagonally down and to the right, creating a wide rectangle, like the one shown in Figure 4-41. Release the mouse button. (Don't worry about the exact size or position of the rectangle because you will size and place it in the next step.)

4. Precisely size and position the rectangle by following these steps:

   a. Select the rectangle, and from the Drawing Tools Format tab, in the Size group, click the Dialog Box Launcher.

   b. In the Size category, change **Height** to **0.75"** and **Width** to **8"**.

   c. In the Position category, change Horizontal to **1"** and Vertical to **4"**. Click **Close**.

5. Key text in the rectangle by following these steps:

   a. Select the rectangle.

   b. Key **Perfect Planning Requires Balance**.

   c. From the Home tab, change the font to Arial Narrow, the size of the text to 36 points, the text color to white, and the alignment to center.

6. Create the triangle shown in Figure 4-41 by following these steps:

   a. From the Insert tab, in the Illustrations group, click the Shapes button 🔲; then from the **Basic Shapes** category, click the Isosceles Triangle button △.

   b. Position the pointer at the bottom center of the new rectangle.

   c. Drag diagonally down and to the right to create a triangle; then center it under the rectangle.

7. Draw a circle by following these steps:

   a. From the Insert tab, in the Illustrations group, click the Shapes button 🔲; then from the **Basic Shapes** category, click the Oval button ⚪.

   b. Position the crosshair pointer ✛ above the left end of the rectangle, hold down (Shift), and drag diagonally to draw a circle approximately the same size as the one in Figure 4-41.

   c. Hold down (Ctrl) while using the arrow keys on your keyboard to fine-tune the circle's position.

8. Select the circle, and then press (Ctrl)+(D) to duplicate it. Drag the second circle to the other end of the rectangle, positioning it appropriately.

9. Create a horizontal line on slide 3 by following these steps:

   a. From the Insert tab, in the Illustrations group, click the Shapes button 🔲; then from the **Lines** category, click the Line button ◥.

   b. Position the pointer below the "Y" in the word "Your."

   c. Hold down (Shift), and drag to the right to draw a straight line below the word. Release the mouse button first, and then release (Shift).

    d. From the Drawing Tools Format tab, in the Shape Styles group, click the Dialog Box Launcher to access the Format Shape dialog box. Change the Line Width to 3 pt., and then on the Line Color tab change the Line color to Turquoise, Accent 1.

    e. Adjust the position of the line, if necessary.

10. Check spelling in the presentation.

11. Create a footer for slide 3 only: Include the slide number, date, and your name, followed by a comma and *[your initials]*4-29.

12. Create a handout header and footer: Include the date, your name as the header, the page number, and *[your initials]*4-29 as the footer.

13. Move to slide 1, and save the presentation as *[your initials]*4-29 in your Lesson 4 folder.

14. Close the presentation and submit your work.

Exercise 4-30

Insert a picture from a file, crop a clip art image, search for and insert a clip art image, and place text on a shape.

1. Open the file **Seminar2**.

2. On slide 1, insert the picture file **Logo** (from your student data disk) by following these steps:

    a. From the Insert tab, in the Illustrations group, click the Picture button 🖼.

    b. Browse to find the student data files for Lesson 4, and click **Logo.**

    c. Click Insert.

3. Remove the white color in the image by following these steps:

    a. From the Picture Tools Format tab, in the Adjust group, click the Remove Background button 🖼. The white area of the image is marked for removal, and a rectangle with handles marks the area to be retained.

    b. Because the word "Good" is not selected, click the Mark Areas to Keep button 🖉 and then click each letter about three times until the entire letter appears. Because the letters have a beveled appearance, you may want to zoom in to see better the detail of each letter. Click the flat part of the letter and the highlighted areas will automatically be selected.

    c. Click the Keep Changes button ✓.

4. Resize the logo to make it slightly smaller.

5. Position the logo at the bottom of the slide, below the white graphic shape that is on the background.

6. Move to slide 2. In the content placeholder, click the Clip Art button 🖼. The Clip Art pane will appear.

    a. In the Search for box, key **refrigerator**, and then click Go.

    b. Look for an image that most closely resembles a commercial-grade refrigerator with stainless steel finish, and then insert it by clicking its thumbnail.

7. Resize the image proportionately from the center by following these steps:

   a. Select the image.

   b. Hold down Ctrl while dragging a corner handle.

   c. When the image is the size you want, release the mouse button first; then release Ctrl.

8. Crop an image by following these steps:

   a. Move to slide 3. Select the image on the right side of the slide.

   b. From the Picture Tools Format tab, in the Size group, click the Crop button ▣.

   c. Drag the top cropping handle down to just above the shape containing the chef's hat.

   d. Drag each of the side cropping handles in so that only the shapes containing the chef's hat and the rolling pin remain.

   e. Click a blank area on the slide to deactivate the Crop button ▣.

   f. Increase the size of the cropped image, and position it beside the list with balanced spacing above and below the image.

9. On slides 4 and 6, search for and insert images appropriate to the slide text content and the overall presentation design. Crop and/or resize the images if necessary.

10. On slide 2, at the bottom, insert a text box, key **Ask for our list of wholesale appliance dealers**, and change the font to 24-point Arial Narrow, italic. Position the text box on the lower left.

11. Check spelling in the presentation.

12. Create a handout header and footer: Include the date, your name as the header, the page number, and *[your initials]***4-30** as the footer.

13. Move to slide 1, and save the presentation as *[your initials]***4-30** in your Lesson 4 folder.

14. Close the presentation and submit your work.

Exercise 4-31

Insert and size a picture from a file, and create and edit WordArt.

1. Open the file **Seminar3**.

2. On slide 1, apply WordArt effects to the title by following these steps:

   a. Select the title text.

   b. From the Drawing Tools Format tab, in the WordArt Styles group, click the Quick Styles More button ⤓, and choose Fill – Orange, Accent 2, Matte Bevel (on the last row).

   c. Change the text fill color to Rose, Accent 5, Darker 50%.

3. Change the shape of WordArt text by following these steps:

   a. Select the WordArt text.

   b. From the Drawing Tools Format tab, in the WordArt Styles group, click the Text Effects button Ⓐ and then Transform.

c. From the Warp category, select the Chevron Up effect, and the text will increase in size when this effect is applied.

d. Hold down [Ctrl], and drag the bottom-center sizing handle up slightly to decrease the height of the WordArt shape. The height measurement should be about 1.5 inches.

4. Add the Good 4 U logo to the title slide by following these steps:

a. Delete the subtitle placeholder.

b. From the Insert tab, in the Images group, click the Picture button [icon].

c. Navigate to the drive and directory where your Lesson 4 student data files are stored, and select the file **Logo**. Click Insert.

d. Drag the logo to the bottom of the subtitle placeholder in the center of the slide, as shown in Figure 4-42.

Figure 4-42
WordArt effect

5. Create a handout header and footer: Include the date, your name as the header, the page number, and *[your initials]*4-31 as the footer.

6. Move to slide 1, and save the presentation as *[your initials]*4-31 in your Lesson 4 folder.

7. Close the presentation and submit your work.

Exercise 4-32

Create shapes and rotate, add text, insert a picture from a file, apply artistic effects, and adjust corrections settings.

1. Open the file **Seminar4**. Replace the word "Date" on slide 1 with today's date in a numeric format such as 09/12/10.

2. Create a left-arrow shape and position it by following these steps:

a. Move to slide 3, and from the Insert tab, in the Illustrations group, click the Shapes button [icon]. In the Block Arrows category, click Left Arrow (the second shape in the first row).

b. Position the crosshair pointer ⊞ at the top of the tallest bar in the fourth-quarter section of the chart, and then click and drag to create an arrow.

c. Select the arrow; then drag the green rotation handle above the arrow to the left until the arrow points down at about a 45-degree angle.

d. Reposition the arrow so that it points to the top of the tallest bar, as shown in Figure 4-43.

3. Draw a text box in the space at the right of the chart. Change the font to 20-point Arial, bold, and left-align the text. Key **Los Angeles division sales expected to double in the 4th quarter**.

Figure 4-43
Adding a text box to clarify an important point

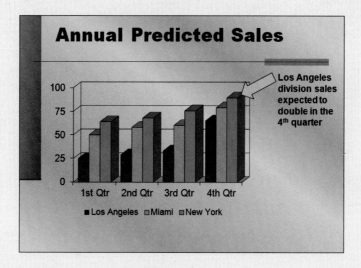

4. On slide 2, insert the **Restaurant** picture from your student data files.

a. Resize the picture to make it slightly smaller.

b. From the Picture Tools Format tab, in the Adjust group, click the Corrections button ⚙; access the Picture Correction Options dialog box, and adjust the Contrast and Brightness by +5 percent.

c. From the Picture Tools Format tab, in the Picture Styles group, apply the Reflected Bevel, Black picture style.

5. On slide 4, the picture that is already positioned on this slide is very dark.

a. Adjust the contrast and brightness to improve the image.

b. Apply the Reflected Bevel, Black picture style to match the style used on slide 2.

6. On slide 1, resize the date placeholder to fit the text, and change it to left alignment. Move the date to the upper left of the slide. Resize the title placeholder so that it fits the text, and move it above the horizontal line at the top of the slide.

7. Insert an image and add an Artistic Effect by following these steps:

   a. On slide 1, insert the **Soup-salad** picture from your student data files.

   b. Increase the height of the picture to 5.9 inches, and position it to be even with the bottom and right side of the slide.

   c. From the Picture Tools Format tab, in the Adjust group, click the Artistic Effects button ⊞, and choose the Cutout effect (bottom row).

8. On slide 1, change the title text placeholder fill color to Gold, Accent 2, and resize the placeholder to fit across the slide. Position it above the picture, as shown in Figure 4-44.

Figure 4-44
Completed title slide with artistic effect applied

9. Below the picture on slide 4, insert a text box with the words **Only the finest produce!**

   a. Format the text in a size, font, and color that match slide 3 (Arial, 20 point, bold).

   b. Position the text centered below the picture.

10. On slide 5, from the Insert tab, in the Illustrations group, click the Shapes button ⬚; then in the Stars and Banners subcategory click the 5-Point Star. Position and size the star so that it covers the gold rectangle on the right side of the horizontal line.

11. Place text in the star by following these steps:

   a. Select the star.

   b. Key **Star**, press Enter, and key **Team**. Make the text Arial Black in 32 points.

   c. Adjust the size of the star, if necessary, to fit the text.

12. Check spelling in the presentation.

13. Create a handout header and footer: Include the date, your name as the header, the page number, and *[your initials]*4-32 as the footer.

14. Move to slide 1, and save the presentation as *[your initials]*4-32 in your Lesson 4 folder.

15. Close the presentation and submit your work.

Lesson Applications

Exercise 4-33

Work with lines, text effects, shapes, and clip art.

1. Open the file **Market1**.

2. On slide 1, select the title text. From the Drawing Tools Format tab, apply the Text Effects of Bevel, Circle, and then apply Shadow, Outer category, Offset Bottom effect.

3. Draw a thin horizontal rectangle below the text in the title placeholder that extends under the title to the right edge of the slide.

4. Delete the subtitle placeholder. Draw a rectangle, approximately 3 inches wide. Position it on the lower right side of the slide.

5. Use the Clip Art pane to search for a photograph image by using the search word **meeting**. Choose a picture that has a horizontal orientation and is appropriate in style, content, and color for this slide.

6. Resize and crop the picture, if necessary, to make it fit on the solid-color area on the lower right of the slide, using the rectangle as a border for the picture. Apply a Shape effect of Shadow, Outer, Offset Bottom Shadow to the rectangle serving as a border for the picture so that it matches the title treatment, as shown in Figure 4-45.

Figure 4-45
Drop shadow effect

7. On slide 2, resize the body text placeholder to allow space on the right half of the slide for a picture.

8. Find another picture using the **meeting** search criteria in portrait orientation. Size and/or crop it as needed; then add the same shadow effect. Position it beside the bulleted list.

9. Check spelling in the presentation.

10. Create a handout header and footer: Include the date, your name as the header, the page number, and *[your initials]*4-33 as the footer.

11. Move to slide 1, and save the presentation as *[your initials]*4-33 in your Lesson 4 folder.

12. Close the presentation and submit your work.

Exercise 4-34

Insert pictures, apply effects, rotate, and insert WordArt.

1. Open the file **Orientation**.

2. On the title slide, select the illustrated image, copy it, and delete it from this slide.

3. Move to slide 3, and add a slide with a blank layout to create slide 4. Paste the illustrated image from slide 1 on slide 4.

4. On the title slide, increase the title text placeholder font size to 54 pt. Increase the size of this placeholder so that the text fits on two lines. Adjust the horizontal position so that the left edge of the text aligns with the left edge of the horizontal blue shape.

5. On the title slide, in the subtitle placeholder, key *[Your Name]*, press Enter, and key the *[Current Date]*.

6. Search for photograph images using the word **dining**. Insert three photographs. You may need to crop them to reduce the image size and feature the most appropriate part of the pictures. Adjust the size of these images so that each is 2.5" wide.

7. Add a Picture Style to all three of the photographs using Drop Shadow Rectangle.

8. Position and rotate these pictures with even vertical spacing on the left side of the slide, as shown in Figure 4-46. (Your pictures may be different ones.)

Figure 4-46
Positioning of pictures

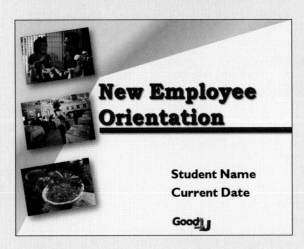

9. On slide 2, change the second bulleted item into two bulleted items, and revise the wording:

   • **Company History**
   • **Company Vision**

10. Insert two new slides after slide 3; use the Title and Content slide layout. Key the following on slides 4 and 5:

    Who's Who
    • **Julie Wolfe and Gus Irvinelli are the co-owners of the restaurant**
    • **Michele Jenkins is the head chef**
    • **Roy Olafsen is the marketing manager**
    Summary
    • **Good 4 U is growing rapidly with our new franchising opportunities**
    • **Our healthy living message has worldwide appeal**
    • **We are relying on you, our new employees, to help us grow**

11. On slide 6, insert WordArt for the words **Welcome to Good 4 U**, and make it fit on two text lines, left aligned. Adjust WordArt colors and effects to be appropriate for the presentation color scheme. Use the same Bookman Old Style font that is used in the slide titles.

12. Position the image and the WordArt text for a pleasing arrangement.

13. Check spelling in the presentation.

14. Scroll through the presentation, and check each slide to make sure the images and text are positioned appropriately.

15. Create a handout header and footer: Include the date, your name as the header, the page number, and *[your initials]*4-34 as the footer.

16. Move to slide 1, and save the presentation as *[your initials]*4-34 in your Lesson 4 folder.

17. Close the presentation and submit your work.

Exercise 4-35

Create shapes, insert and resize pictures, apply artistic effects, and insert WordArt.

1. Open the file **Investors**.

2. On slide 1, select the title text, and apply the WordArt Style Gradient Fill – Orange, Accent 1 (third row, fourth column).

3. With the title selected, use the Text Effect of Transform to change the text shape to Deflate Bottom.

4. Resize the WordArt to stretch across the slide with a width of 9.0" and height of approximately 2.5". Move it up to be centered in the black area of the slide.

5. Key the following bulleted text on slides 2 through 5, using the left content placeholder for slides 2 through 4. Slide 5 has only one content placeholder for the text.

Objectives
- **Obtain investors to establish Good 4 U as a franchise**
- **Revisit the current business plan**
- **Hire a marketing consulting firm**

Our Specialties
- **Organic fruit and vegetables**
- **Fresh juices**
- **Innovative cuisine**

What Investors Want
- **High-profile location**
- **Hotel or storefront**
- **City with tourism, such as Miami or New York**
- **"Curb Appeal"**

Next Steps
- **Target health-conscious areas**
- **Target high-profile areas**
- **Study traffic patterns in selected areas**

6. On slide 2, on the shape on the right, key **Investors are our building blocks** with a font size of 36 points and bold. Resize the shape with a height of 3" and a width of 3" so that the text word-wraps on four lines. Adjust the shape's position so that it is even with the bulleted list on the left.

7. On slide 3, remove the bullets from the body text placeholder, and center its text. Adjust the size of the placeholder so that the text fits on three lines, and move it to the bottom of the slide to make room for two pictures above it. Center the placeholder horizontally.

8. Insert two landscape-oriented pictures: a picture of fruit and a picture of vegetables. Find pictures that will complement each other on the slide. Adjust their size if necessary, and position them side by side above the text. Apply the Picture Style Simple Frame, White.

9. On slide 4, search for a picture of New York that coordinates with the color scheme of the presentation, and insert it. Resize the picture so that it fits on top of the shape on the right of the slide. The picture should be approximately 3" wide. Apply the same Picture Style, Simple Frame, White, and then resize the shape so that it fits evenly behind the picture.

10. On slide 5, remove the bullets from the list, and resize the placeholder to fit the text on three lines. Change the shape fill to Gray-50%, Text 2, Lighter 40%, and move the text to the lower right of the slide.

11. On slide 5, search for a photograph of a target, apply the same Picture Style, Simple Frame, White, and position the photograph under the slide title as shown in Figure 4-47. Apply the Artistic Effect of Glow Diffused (column 4, row 2).

12. On slide 5, draw a **Right Arrow** shape, and rotate it so that it points up slightly. Change the shape fill and shape outline to **Red**, and resize if necessary. Duplicate this arrow by pressing Ctrl+D, and position the second arrow above the first one. Repeat for two more arrows. The arrows should angle up, as shown in Figure 4-47.

Figure 4-47
Completed slide

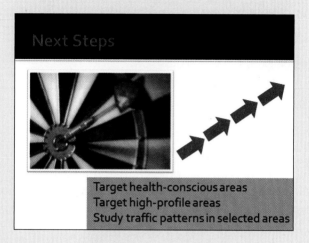

13. Review each slide, and make changes to the size and position of any objects you think should be adjusted for good alignment and spacing.

14. Check spelling in the presentation.

15. Create a handout header and footer: Include the date, your name as the header, the page number, and *[your initials]*4-35 as the footer.

16. Move to slide 1, and save the presentation as *[your initials]*4-35 in your Lesson 4 folder.

17. Close the presentation and submit your work.

Exercise 4-36 ◆ Challenge Yourself

Create a photo album presentation, insert WordArt, and adjust Text Effects.

1. Start a new blank presentation.

2. Create a photo album using the five pictures from the Cooking Classes folder.

3. Rearrange the picture order to put **Chopping** first, followed by **Slicing**, **Sauce making**, **Pastry baking**, and **Bread baking**.

4. For the Album layout, choose the Picture Layout of **1 picture**.

5. For Frame shape, choose **Simple Frame, Black**.

6. For Theme, click **Browse**, and then choose **Foundry**.

7. Click **Create**. Once the slides appear, choose the Design tab, Colors, and **Office** theme colors.

8. On slide 1, for the title text key **Cooking Classes**; for the subtitle key **by Michele Jenkins, Head Chef**, and make it bold.

9. Insert WordArt with the text **Back by Popular Demand**, using the Style of Fill – Red, Accent 2, Matte Bevel. Change the font size to 40 points, and resize the WordArt so that the text fits on two lines.

10. Rotate the WordArt text, and position it on the upper left of the slide.

11. Insert a text box below the subtitle to show the class dates:

    October 17 and 18, 9-10:30 a.m.

    November 7 and 8, 2-3:30 p.m.

    Registration required

12. Use right alignment for the text box so that it matches the title and subtitle positioning.

13. On slide 2, insert a text box, change the font size to 28 points, and key **Efficient food handling methods**. Change the fill color to Red, Accent 2, Darker 25%, and resize the box so that the text fits on one line. Position this text box near the bottom of the picture on the right.

14. Press Ctrl+C to copy the text box, and paste it on slide 3. Edit the text to be **Fresh fruits and vegetables**. Position this text box at the bottom of the picture on the left.

15. Repeat this process for slides 4, 5, and 6, using separate text boxes placed in different positions on each slide, as shown in Figure 4-48:

    | Slide 4 | **Savory sauces** |
    | Slide 5 | **Pastry for a crowd** |
    | Slide 6 | **Breads like Grandma made** |

Figure 4-48
Completed Photo
Album slides

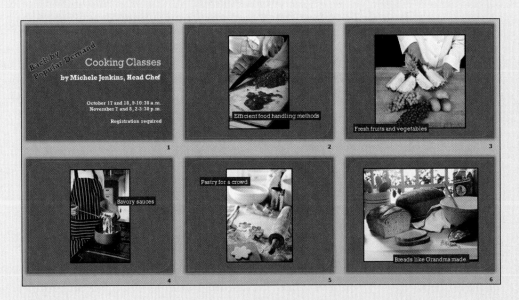

16. Move to slide 1, and save the presentation as *[your initials]*4-36.

17. Close the presentation and submit your work.

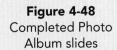

On Your Own

In these exercises you work on your own, as you would in a real-life work environment. Use the skills you've learned to accomplish the task—and be creative.

Exercise 4-37

Imagine that you are about to open a new retail store or restaurant. Using the content and layout of the Miami Beach presentation from this lesson as a general guide, create a presentation with at least five slides announcing the opening of your business. Use images, text boxes, shapes, WordArt, and, if possible, scanned photos to illustrate your presentation. Include a transition effect. Save the presentation as *[your initials]*4-37. Close the presentation and submit your work.

Exercise 4-38

Personal shoppers are responsible for suggesting ideas on gifts that their clients can give to others. Imagine you are a personal shopper, and create a presentation entitled "Gift Suggestions for *[choose occasion or person]*." Select five or more suitable items from mail-order catalogs, and create a separate slide describing each item, including the price and why you selected it. If you have access to a scanner, scan each item's picture from the catalog and insert it on the appropriate slide. If a scanner is not available, insert a suitable clip art image on each slide. Use your own creativity and the techniques learned in this and previous lessons to add interest to the slides. Save the presentation as *[your initials]*4-38. Close the presentation and submit your work.

Exercise 4-39

You are the owner of an electronic scrapbook preparation service. You have a friend or family member who has requested that you create a photo album presentation to commemorate a special occasion on which several pictures were taken. Locate appropriate pictures, or use your own digital photos. Create an appropriate theme for your presentation based on the background design and colors that you choose. Add images, text boxes, shapes, and WordArt to illustrate your presentation like a scrapbook. Save the presentation as *[your initials]*4-39. Close the presentation and submit your work.

Lesson 5
Creating Tables

OBJECTIVES *After completing this lesson, you will be able to:*

1. Create a table.
2. Draw a table.
3. Modify a table structure.
4. Align text and numbers.
5. Enhance the table.
6. Create a tabbed table.

Estimated Time: 2 hours

Julie Wolfe will soon be speaking to an economic development group about employee opportunities that Good 4 U provides to the community. So that this audience can easily compare the data she is presenting, she has asked you to prepare tables showing the number of employees in various positions and how the number of employees has changed in the last year.

Tables display information organized in rows and columns. Once a table is created, you can modify its structure by adding columns or rows, plus you can merge and split cells to modify your table's design. Table content can be aligned in different ways, and color can be applied to highlight selected table cells or to add table borders. In this lesson you will learn many different ways to make these changes that, ultimately, make a table easy to read.

Creating a Table

A *table* consists of rows, columns, and cells. *Rows* consist of individual cells across the table horizontally. *Columns* consist of individual cells aligned vertically down the table. The *cell* is the intersection between the column and a row.

PowerPoint provides several convenient ways to create a table. With each method listed below, you specify the number of columns and rows that you need.

- Insert a new slide, choose the Title and Content layout, and click the Insert Table button ▦.
- From the Insert tab, in the Tables group, click the Table button ▦, and choose Insert Table.
- From the Insert tab, in the Tables group, click the Table button ▦, and drag the mouse to select the correct number of columns and rows.
- From the Insert tab, in the Tables group, click the Table button ▦, and then click Draw Table. Using the pencil pointer, click and drag to create the size of the table, and then divide it into columns and rows.
- Create a table using tab settings.

When you insert a table into your presentation, your Ribbon will change to show the Table Tools Design and Layout tabs. These tabs contain many options for formatting and modifying tables.

Exercise 5-1 INSERT A TABLE

When you use the Table button ▦ on the Insert tab, you may define a table's dimensions by dragging down and across a grid to determine the number of columns and rows.

1. Open the file **Briefing**. Insert a new slide after slide 1 that uses the Title Only slide layout. Julie Wolfe will show the number of employees for the previous year; therefore, key the title **Employment Levels 2009**.

2. From the Insert tab, in the Tables group, click the Table button ▦. A grid appears for defining the size of the table.

3. Drag your pointer down three squares and across four squares to define a 4 by 3 table (four columns by three rows), as shown in Figure 5-1. A table is automatically placed on your slide.

Figure 5-1
Defining a table

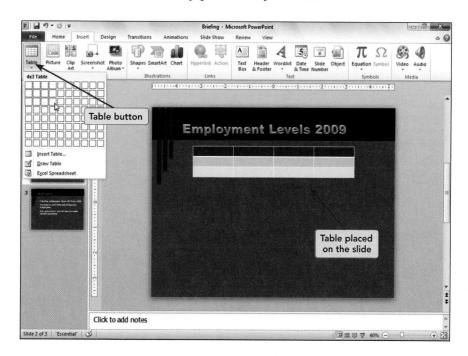

4.   Point to the table's border so that the four-pointed arrow ⊕ appears; then drag the table down about a half inch.

5.   Key the text shown in Figure 5-2. Use your pointer to click in the first cell of the table, and then press Tab to move from cell to cell. Numbers will be right aligned later in the lesson.

Figure 5-2
Table with text

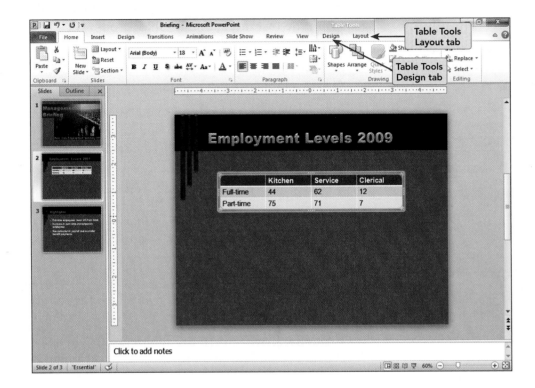

Exercise 5-2   NAVIGATE IN A TABLE

Use these methods to navigate in a table:

*   Click the cell with the I-beam.
*   Use the arrow keys: ←, →, ↑, and ↓.
*   Press Tab to move forward or Shift+Tab to move backward.

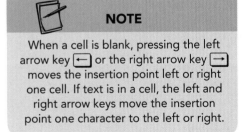

NOTE

When a cell is blank, pressing the left arrow key ← or the right arrow key → moves the insertion point left or right one cell. If text is in a cell, the left and right arrow keys move the insertion point one character to the left or right.

1.   Click in the first table cell to put your insertion point there.

2.   Press Tab several times. The insertion point moves through cells from left to right. When you reach the last cell in the last row, pressing Tab adds a new row with the insertion point in the first cell.

3.   Since you do not need another row, click the Undo button ↩ to reverse this action.

4.   Press Shift+Tab several times. The insertion point moves through cells from right to left.

5.   Press each arrow key several times, and observe the movement of the insertion point.

Exercise 5-3 SELECT TABLE STYLES

A *table style* is a combination of formatting options based on your theme colors. A table style is applied automatically to any table that you add through the Insert Table command. These styles are applied using the Table Tools Design tab shown in Figure 5-3. When your pointer is over any thumbnail in the Table Styles gallery, you will see a preview of what your table will look like if you apply that style.

1. Right-click in any of the table cells, and choose Select Table from the shortcut menu.

2. From the Table Tools Design tab, in the Table Styles group, choose the More button ⬇ to open the Table Styles Gallery.

Figure 5-3
Table Tools
Design tab

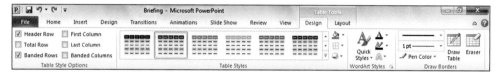

3. Point to several thumbnails to see the ScreenTip with the name of the style and preview the effect on your table.

4. From the Best Match for Document category, choose Themed Style 1, Accent 1 by clicking on the thumbnail. Notice how this table style blends well with the background.

Exercise 5-4 APPLY TABLE STYLE OPTIONS

The *Table Style Options* feature is used to modify specific parts of your table. The options include:

- *Header Row*. Emphasizes the first row of the table.
- *Total Row*. Emphasizes the last row of the table.
- *Banded Rows*. Provides rows in alternating colors.
- *First Column*. Emphasizes the first column of the table.
- *Last Column*. Emphasizes the last column of the table.
- *Banded Columns*. Provides columns in alternating colors.

1. With the table selected, from the Table Tools Design tab, in the Table Style Options group, click the First Column check box. Notice that the text in the first column now appears bold.

2. Click the Header Row check box to uncheck the box. Notice that the dark red disappears and the banded rows alternate starting with the first row.

3. Click the Undo button to reapply the Header Row formatting.

4. Click the Banded Rows check box to uncheck the box. Notice that the row alternating colors are removed.

5. Click the Banded Columns check box to apply alternating colors to the columns.

✏️ **TIP**

If you were comparing the number of kitchen staff versus the number of clerical staff, the Banded Columns format would make the table easier to interpret because it emphasizes the staff categories. However, if you were comparing the number of full-time versus the number of part-time employees, the Banded Rows format would be a better choice.

Drawing a Table

The *Draw Table* command in PowerPoint allows you to control the exact size of the table and how it is divided by specifying where horizontal and vertical lines are placed. Once the table is created, all other table features can be applied.

Exercise 5-5   USE THE PENCIL POINTER TO DRAW A TABLE

To draw a table, you first drag the *pencil pointer* ✐ diagonally down and across to create a rectangle for the table's outside border. Then you draw horizontal and vertical lines within the table to divide it into rows and columns.

1. Insert a new slide after slide 3 that uses the Title Only slide layout. Julie Wolfe will show how employment numbers have increased from the previous year; therefore, key the title **Employment Levels 2010**.

2. From the Insert tab, in the Tables group, click the Table button ▦, and then choose Draw Table.

3. Using the pencil pointer, drag from under the left edge of the title (down and to the right) to create a rectangle that fills the available space. See Figure 5-4 for size and placement. At this point, you have a one-cell table.

Figure 5-4
Using the pencil
pointer

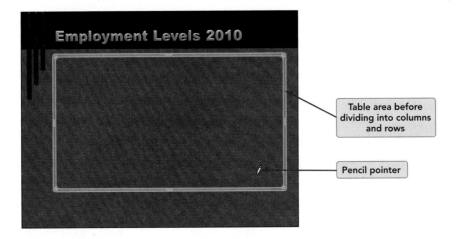

Employment Levels 2010

Table area before
dividing into columns
and rows

Pencil pointer

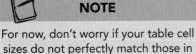

NOTE

For now, don't worry if your table cell sizes do not perfectly match those in Figure 5-5 or if your text wraps within the cell. You will learn how to adjust cell sizes later in this lesson.

4. The pencil pointer creates rows and columns when you draw lines within the table area to create inside borders. Be sure the pointer is inside the table before you start drawing so that the lines you draw divide the table space. If the pointer touches the outside table border, a new table will be created. (If this happens, press [Ctrl]+[Z] to undo the action and try again.)

5. With the table selected, from the Table Tools Design tab, in the Draw Borders group, click the Draw Table button ▨, and draw a horizontal line through the middle of the table area. Each time you draw a line, one cell is

split into two cells. Because you are drawing horizontal lines now, the cells you are splitting create table rows. Draw two more horizontal lines to create four rows in the table, as shown in Figure 5-5.

6. Now split the table with four vertical lines to create five columns.

7. From the Table Tools Design tab, in the Draw Borders group, click Draw Table to turn off the pencil pointer.

8. Key the table text shown in Figure 5-5.

9. Right-click the table, and choose Select Table. From the Home tab, in the Font group, change Font Size to 24.

Figure 5-5
Table text

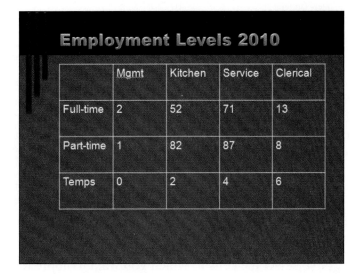

Exercise 5-6 CHANGE TABLE TEXT DIRECTION

Text direction changes can affect the appearance of a table and how it fits within a given space. If a column title is the only long text in the column, changing the column title text direction allows you to fit more columns in a given area. However, use this feature with caution because the text will not be as easy to read as horizontal text.

Text direction in a table can be changed using the Text Direction button ▥ available from the Home tab or the Table Tools Layout tab (see Figure 5-6).

Figure 5-6
Table Tools Layout tab

1. Click in the cell that reads Mgmt.

2. From the Table Tools Layout tab, in the Alignment group, click the Text Direction button ▥.

Figure 5-7
Text Direction drop-
down list

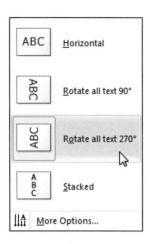

3. From the drop-down list, choose Rotate all text 270°, as shown in Figure 5-7.

4. Notice how the text reads going up in the cell. Change the text direction in the same manner for Kitchen, Service, and Clerical.

5. Select the entire first row of text by pointing to the left of the first table row and clicking when your pointer changes to a dark black arrow. From the Table Tools Layout tab, in the Cell Size group, change the Table Row Height to 1.3".

Exercise 5-7   APPLY SHADING AND BORDERS

When you first draw a table, the table cells contain no shading, allowing the slide's background to show. You can apply a shading color or other shading effects (such as a gradient or a picture effect) to one or more selected cells in your table. All the shading options are available from the Table Tools Design tab, in the Table Styles group, in the Shading button 🖌 gallery. This button works the same as the Shape Fill button 🖌.

Table borders are the lines forming the edges of cells, columns, and rows and the outline of the table. You can apply borders to all the cells in a selection, to just an outside border, or to just the inside borders separating one cell from another. Applying table borders is a three-step process:

- First, select the cells to which you want to apply the border effect.
- Second, select the border style, border width, and pen color you want.
- Third, click the Borders button ⊞, and choose an option from the drop-down list to control where the border appears.

1. On slide 4, with the table active, select all the cells in the top row by moving your pointer to the left of row 1 until you get a solid black arrow pointing at the row. Click to select the whole row.

2. From the Table Tools Design tab, in the Table Styles group, click the Shading button 🖌, and choose Dark Red, Accent 5, Darker 25% (column 9, row 5).

3. Change the font color for the selected row to Light Yellow, Text 2.

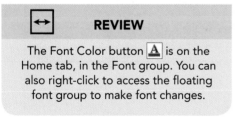

REVIEW

The Font Color button 🅰 is on the Home tab, in the Font group. You can also right-click to access the floating font group to make font changes.

4. Select the first column in the table by pointing to the top of the first column and clicking when you get a solid black arrow pointing down at the column. Apply the same Dark Red, Accent 5, Darker 25%, and change the font color to Light Yellow, Text 2.

5. Select all the cells that contain numbers by clicking in the first number cell and dragging your pointer down and to the right to the last number cell.

6. From the Table Tools Design tab, in the Table Styles group, click the Shading button 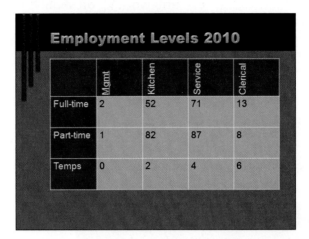, and apply Brown, Background 2, Lighter 40%. With these cells still selected, change the font color to Black, Background 1.

7. Click outside the table to observe the effect. Now the table has an appearance that distinguishes it from the slide background. Compare your table to Figure 5-8.

Figure 5-8
Shading applied to a table

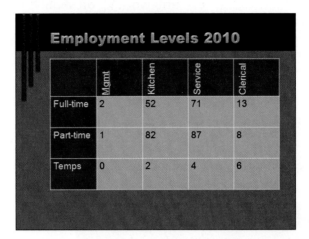

8. Select the whole table by right-clicking any cell within the table and choosing Select Table from the shortcut menu.

9. From the Table Tools Design tab, in the Draw Borders group, click the Pen Weight button ⌐1 pt————⌐, and change to 2¼ pt.

10. Still working in the Draw Borders group, click the Pen Color button, and choose Brown, Background 2, Darker 50%.

11. Click the Borders button ⊞ in the Table Styles group, and choose Top Border. Repeat this step for Bottom Border, Left Border, and Right Border. Click outside the table to deselect it, and notice the difference in the table with the borders in a different color.

Exercise 5-8   CHANGE BORDER AND SHADING COLORS

Table Border and Shading styles can be changed at any point while creating your presentation.

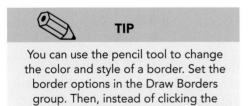

TIP

You can use the pencil tool to change the color and style of a border. Set the border options in the Draw Borders group. Then, instead of clicking the Borders button, use the pencil to click the borders you want to change.

1. Select any cell in your table. From the Table Tools Design tab, in the Draw Borders group, click Pen Style ⌐————⌐, and from the list box choose the dashed line (second style).

2. Click the Pen Weight button ⌐1 pt————⌐, and choose 1½ pt.

Figure 5-9
Borders button
drop-down list

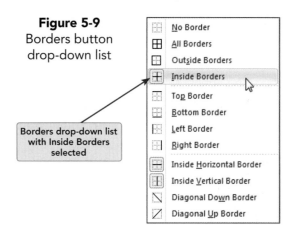

Borders drop-down list
with Inside Borders
selected

3. Click the Pen Color button 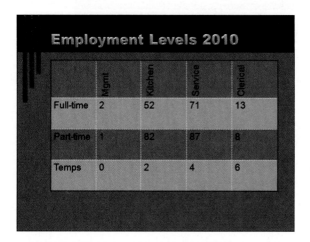, and choose Brown, Background 2, Lighter 80%.

4. Right-click in the table, and choose Select Table.

5. Click the Borders button ⊞ list box arrow; then click Inside Borders, as shown in Figure 5-9. The inside borders of the table are now dashed lines.

6. Still working on slide 4, select row 3 of the table. From the Table Tools Design tab, in the Table Styles group, click the Shading button, and choose Orange, Accent 2, Darker 25%.

7. Repeat this process for row 1 of the table, using the same Orange, Accent 2, Darker 25%.

8. Repeat this process for rows 2 and 4 but apply the shading color Brown, Background 2, Lighter 40%, as shown in Figure 5-10.

9. Select the table, and change the font color to Black, Background 1.

Figure 5-10
Table with shaded
rows

Exercise 5-9   ERASE CELL BORDERS

The *Eraser* can be used to delete borders between cells.

1. Click in the last cell of the table on slide 4. Click Tab one time. Notice that PowerPoint automatically inserts another row below the last row in the table. If this row causes your table to extend below the slide, resize the table from the bottom so it fits on the slide.

2. From the Table Tools Design tab, in the Draw Borders group, choose the Eraser button.

3. Click each of the four borders that divide the last row of the table into five cells. Notice that as you click each border, it disappears. When all four are removed, the last row has only one cell.

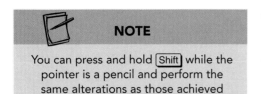

NOTE

You can press and hold Shift while the pointer is a pencil and perform the same alterations as those achieved with the Eraser.

4. Press Esc to turn off the Eraser. Click in the last row, and key **Estimated Projection**.

5. Create a new folder for Lesson 5, and save the presentation as *[your initials]***5-9** in your new Lesson 5 folder. Leave the presentation open for the next exercise.

Modifying a Table Structure

When creating a table, you decide how many rows and columns the table should have. After entering some data, you might discover that you have too many columns or perhaps too few rows. Or you might want one row or column to have more or fewer cells than the others. You can modify your table structure by inserting or deleting columns, merging a group of cells, or splitting an individual cell into two or more cells.

Exercise 5-10 INSERT AND DELETE ROWS AND COLUMNS

When you are inserting columns and rows, it is important to recognize which cell is active. Columns can be inserted either to the right or to the left of the column that contains the active cell. The column formatting of the active column is copied to the new column, or the table style is applied. Rows can be inserted above or below the row that contains the active cell. The row formatting of the active row is copied, or the table style is applied to the new row.

Insert columns and rows using one of these methods:

• From the Table Tools Layout tab, in the Rows & Columns group, choose which option you would like to insert.

• Right-click a cell in the table, and use commands on the shortcut menu.

• Insert a row at the bottom of the table by pressing Tab if you're in the last cell of the last table row. This is convenient if you run out of rows while you're entering data.

1. Move to slide 2, and click in the "Kitchen" cell.

2. Right-click, and from the shortcut menu, as shown in Figure 5-11, choose Insert and then Insert Columns to the Left. A new column appears to the left of "Kitchen." It is the same size as the "Kitchen" column and has the formatting of the table style applied. The table is wider to accommodate the extra column.

Figure 5-11
Inserting a column through the shortcut menu

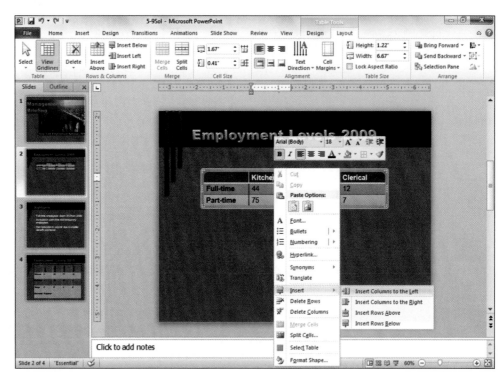

3. Click the blank cell in the upper-left corner of the table.

4. From the Table Tools Layout tab, in the Rows & Columns group, click the Insert Right button. A new column appears to the right of the selected cell, and it is the same size and is formatted with the selected table style.

5. Click any cell in this new column.

6. From the Table Tools Layout tab, in the Rows & Columns group, click the Delete button; then choose **Delete Columns**. The new column is deleted, and the table is resized. Your table should now have one blank column located to the left of the "Kitchen" column, and some of your titles may be wrapped to two lines. This will be fixed later.

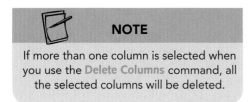

NOTE

If more than one column is selected when you use the **Delete Columns** command, all the selected columns will be deleted.

7. Click a cell in the second table row; then, from the Table Tools Layout tab, in the Rows & Columns group, click the Insert Below button.

8. Click the last cell in the last row, containing the number "7." Press Tab. A new row is inserted at the bottom of the table.

9. Click in the blank row below the text "Full-time," right-click, and choose **Delete Rows** from the shortcut menu.

10. Complete the table by keying the information shown in Figure 5-12 into the blank row and blank column.

and the width of columns individually by dragging cell borders. You can also choose the exact height and width of the cells by using the Cell Size group on the Table Tools Layout tab.

From the Table Tools Layout tab, in the Cell Size group, use the *Distribute Columns* button to easily adjust several columns to be the same width. The *Distribute Rows* button works in a similar way.

1. Move to slide 2, and move your pointer over the right border of the first column until the pointer changes to a resizing arrow.

2. Using this pointer, click and drag the column border to the right, making the column wide enough for the text "Part-time" to appear on one line, as shown in Figure 5-14. The column width increases, and the adjacent column becomes smaller. Now the second column might be too narrow for the word "Mgmt."

3. Use the resizing arrow to double-click the right border of the "Mgmt" column. Double-clicking a right border makes the column wide enough to accommodate the widest text line in the column.

4. Double-click the right border of each of the remaining columns to allow the widest text to be all on one line.

Figure 5-14
Resizing column width

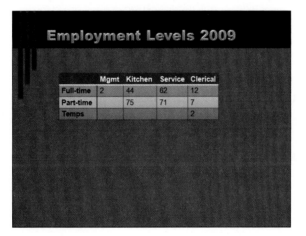

	Mgmt	Kitchen	Service	Clerical
Full-time	2	44	62	12
Part-time		75	71	7
Temps				2

Employment Levels 2009

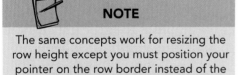

NOTE

The same concepts work for resizing the row height except you must position your pointer on the row border instead of the column border.

5. Move to slide 4. Select the "Mgmt," "Kitchen," "Service," and "Clerical" columns by dragging across the second, third, fourth, and fifth cells in any row (or drag the small, black, down-facing arrow ↓ just above the top border of the four columns).

6. From the Table Tools Layout tab, in the Cell Size group, click the Distribute Columns button. The four selected columns are now all the same width.

7. Select the second through fourth cells in the first column.

8. Click the Distribute Rows button. Now the second through fourth rows are exactly the same height.

9. Create a handout header and footer: Include the date and your name as the header, and the page number and *[your initials]*5-13 as the footer.

10. Save the presentation as *[your initials]*5-13 in your Lesson 5 folder. Leave the presentation open for the next exercise.

Aligning Text and Numbers

Table cell content can be aligned vertically at the top, middle, or bottom. The cell content can be aligned horizontally at the left, center, or right. You can use *Cell Margins* to refine even further the position of text and numbers in a cell. A cell margin is the space between cell borders and the contents of the cell.

Exercise 5-14   ALIGN TEXT AND NUMBERS HORIZONTALLY

Text is aligned horizontally within cells by using the alignment buttons on the Table Tools Layout tab, in the Alignment group, or on the Home tab, in the Paragraph group. You can also right-click to access the floating font group.

1. On slide 2, select the cells in the first row that contain the text "Mgmt," "Kitchen," "Service," and "Clerical."

2. From the Table Tools Layout tab, in the Alignment group, click the Center button ☰. The text is horizontally centered in each cell.

3. Select all the cells that contain numbers, and from the Table Tools Layout tab, in the Alignment group, click the Align Text Right button ☰.

4. Move to slide 4. In the last row of the table, select the text "Revised Figures." From the Home tab, in the Paragraph group, click the Align Text Right button ☰. This text arrangement helps to make the cell look split instead of just having a border in it.

Exercise 5-15   CHANGE THE VERTICAL POSITION OF TEXT IN A CELL

The appearance of a table can be affected by changing the vertical alignment of text or objects within cells. This change can improve the appearance when the cell is much larger than the text.

1. On slide 4, select the cells in the first row that contain the text "Mgmt," "Kitchen," "Service," and "Clerical."

2. From the Table Tools Layout tab, in the Alignment group, choose the Center Vertically button ▤. The text in the selected cells is now in the center of the cells.

3. Select all the cells in the second, third, and fourth rows.

4. Click the Align Bottom button ▤. The text moves to the bottom edge of the cells.

Exercise 5-16   USE MARGIN SETTINGS TO ADJUST THE POSITION OF TEXT IN A CELL

Sometimes, the horizontal and vertical alignment settings do not place text precisely where you want it in a cell. You might be tempted to use Spacebar to indent the text, but that usually doesn't work well.

You can precisely control where text is placed in a cell by using the cell margin settings, combined with horizontal and vertical alignment, as shown in Figure 5-15. For example, you can right-align a column of numbers and also have them appear centered in the column.

1. Move to slide 2. Select all the cells that contain numbers (include the blank cells too).

2. From the Table Tools Layout tab, in the Alignment group, click Cell Margins. From the drop-down list, click **Custom Margins**.

Figure 5-15
Using the Cell Text
Layout dialog box to
control cell margins

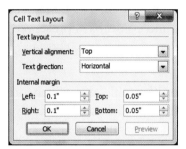

TIP

When table contents fit on one row, then the middle vertical alignment usually provides the best appearance. When table contents vary, with some cells having only a little text while others have several lines of text, then the top vertical alignment will give the best results.

3. Click the **Vertical alignment** list box arrow to see the other settings. Choose **Middle**.

4. Under Internal margin, change the **Right** setting to **0.5"**, and then click **OK**. The numbers are still right-aligned, but some space is between the cell border and the numbers, as shown in Figure 5-16.

5. Select all the cells in the first column that contain text, and change the left margin to **0.2"**. Resize the column as needed to position each label on one line.

Figure 5-16
Table with improved
alignment

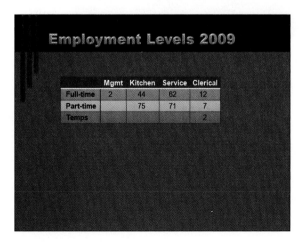

Exercise 5-17   RESIZE A TABLE

To resize an entire table, drag one of the sizing handles. When you drag, make sure the pointer is one of these object resizing arrows: ⬍, ⬌, ⬈; it should not be the resizing arrow used for changing column width ◄║► or row height ═╪═.

If you hold down Shift while dragging a corner sizing handle, the table will resize proportionately. Whenever possible, depending on how large or small you make the table, the relative proportions of row heights and column widths are preserved.

1. Move to slide 4, and click anywhere inside the table. Notice the eight sizing handles (shown as three or four dots) on the outside border (one in each corner and one in the middle of each side). They work just like sizing handles on other PowerPoint objects.

2. Using the diagonal two-pointed arrow ⬈, drag the lower right corner up and to the left about a half inch. The table becomes smaller, and the relative size of the rows and columns is preserved.

3. Resize the rows and columns as necessary so that text does not word-wrap.

4. Position the table attractively on the slide by using the method that you use to move text boxes or other objects (see Figure 5-17).

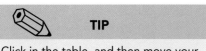
TIP

Click in the table, and then move your pointer to an outside border. When you get a four-pointed arrow, you may click and drag the table to position it.

Figure 5-17
Resized table

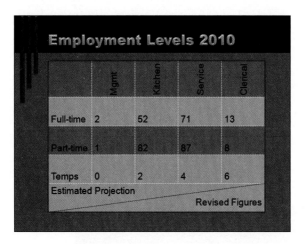

Enhancing the Table

You can enhance a table by adding one of the many three-dimensional effects available in PowerPoint 2010 or by inserting images. Images or special effects can be added to single cells or applied to an entire table.

Exercise 5-18 APPLY AND MODIFY A CELL BEVEL EFFECT

The *Cell Bevel* effect is a dimensional effect that makes cells look raised and rounded or pressed in, as shown in Figure 5-18. The Cell Bevel effect is found on the Table Tools Design tab, in the Table Styles group, under the Effects button ⊡.

1. On Slide 4, select the whole table. From the Table Tools Design tab, in the Table Styles group, click the Effects button ⊡.

2. Choose Cell Bevel; then choose Riblet. Notice the effect that is applied to the table.

3. With the table still selected, click the Effects button ⊡, choose Cell Bevel and then No Bevel to remove the bevel effect.

4. Click the Effects button ⊡ again, choose Cell Bevel, and then choose Relaxed Inset.

Figure 5-18
Bevel effect applied to a table

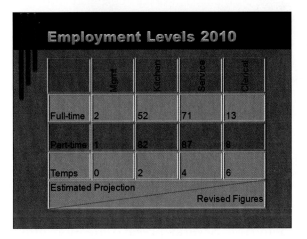

Exercise 5-19 APPLY AND MODIFY A SHADOW EFFECT

Another dimensional effect is the *Shadow* effect. Just as you do when working with other objects, you can modify the shadow direction, its color, and many other settings. The Shadow effect can be applied from the Table Tools Design tab, in the Table Styles group, under the Effects button ⊡.

1. Still working on slide 4, select the table. From the Table Tools Design tab, in the Table Styles group, click the Effects button ⊡.

2. Choose Shadow, and move your pointer over several of the options. Notice the effect that the shadow has on the table.

3. Without selecting a shadow, choose Shadow Options at the bottom of the gallery. The Format Shape dialog box appears and allows you to control every aspect of the shadow.

4. For Presets, in the Outer group, choose Offset Diagonal Bottom Right.

5. For Color, choose Dark Red, Accent 1, Darker 50%.

6. Change the other settings as follows:

- Transparency   **35%**
- Size   **100%**
- Blur   **5 pt**
- Angle   **50°**
- Distance   **15 pt**

7. Click Close on the dialog box to return to your presentation. Deselect your table, and notice the shadow applied to the table, as shown in Figure 5-19.

Figure 5-19
Shadow effect
applied to a table

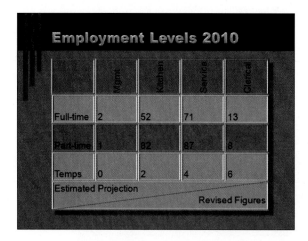

Exercise 5-20 APPLY AND MODIFY A REFLECTION EFFECT

The *Reflection* effect makes the table appear to be reflecting on a body of water or a mirror. Several preset reflection effects are available. The Reflection effect is found on the Table Tools Design tab, in the Table Styles group, under the Effects button.

1. Move to slide 2, and select the table.
2. From the Table Tools Design tab, in the Table Styles group, click the Effects button.

Figure 5-20
Reflection effect
applied to a table

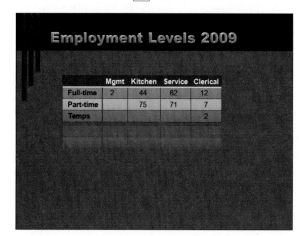

3. Choose Reflection, and move your pointer over several of the options, noticing the effect that each reflection has on the table.

4. Choose Half Reflection, 8 pt offset. The lower half of the table is reflected slightly below the table, as shown in Figure 5-20.

Exercise 5-21   INSERT A PICTURE AND APPLY GRADIENT SHADING

Pictures within a table can help viewers understand the context of the data in the table. A picture can be inserted in one cell, a selection of cells, or an entire table. Gradient shading on rows or columns can add interest or perhaps make text easier to read.

1. On slide 4, click in the first cell of the table.

2. From the Table Tools Design tab, in the Table Styles group, click the Shading button 🖌, and choose Picture.

3. Locate your student files for Lesson 5, and double-click **Employees** to insert the picture into the table.

4. Select the last four cells in the first row in the table, and change their color and effects following these steps:

   a. From the Table Tools Design tab, in the Table Styles group, click the Shading button 🖌, and choose Gradient.

   b. In the Dark Variations category, choose From Bottom Right Corner, which shows the blending of colors in a particular direction.

5. Repeat this process for all the cells on row 3.

6. Select row 5. From the Table Tools Design tab, in the Table Styles group, click the Shading button 🖌, and choose Orange, Accent 2, Darker 25%. Next, apply the same gradient fill as the one you applied to rows 1 and 3.

7. Click outside the table to observe the effects. Compare your table to Figure 5-21.

Figure 5-21
Gradient shading effects applied to a table

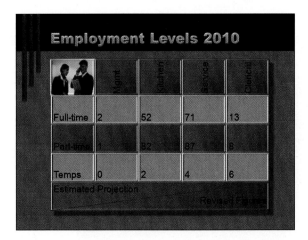

8. Update the handout footer to include the text *[your initials]*5-21.

9. Save the presentation as *[your initials]*5-21 in your Lesson 5 folder. Leave the presentation open for the next exercise.

Creating a Tabbed Table

In this lesson, you have learned several ways to create tables using Power-Point's table tools. You can also create tables through tab settings using the *Ruler* feature. Sometimes information can be effectively displayed with just a very simple table.

Exercise 5-22   SET AND EDIT TABS

In PowerPoint you set tabs on the ruler the same way you set tabs in Word, and they are left-aligned by default. However, PowerPoint's default tabs are set at 1-inch intervals. To set your own tabs, click the Tab Alignment button 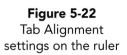 (above the vertical ruler) to choose the alignment type and then click the position on the horizontal ruler to set a tab.

1. Insert a new slide after slide 4 that uses the Title Only slide layout.
2. From the View tab, in the Show group, check the Ruler if it is not already checked.
3. Key the title **Full-time Employment Change**.
4. Draw a text box starting an inch below the slide title and extend it to the right (approximately 8 inches wide), as shown in Figure 5-22.
5. Key the following, pressing Tab where indicated: Tab **Department**, Tab **2009**, Tab **2010**, Tab **% Change**.
6. Select the text box, apply bold, and change the font color to Brown, Background 2, Darker 50%.
7. Click anywhere within the text box to activate the text box ruler.

Figure 5-22
Tab Alignment
settings on the ruler

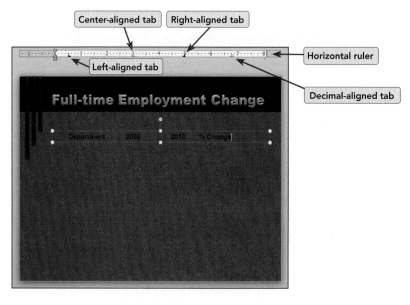

NOTE

Tabs are set when the Tab Alignment symbol appears on the ruler. The tabs you set override the default tabs, and the default tabs are removed. It might take some practice before you are comfortable with tab selection and placement.

8. Click the Tab Alignment button ⌊ above the vertical ruler. Each time you click the button, the alignment changes, enabling you to cycle through the four Tab Alignment choices, as shown in Table 5-1 and Figure 5-22.

TABLE 5-1 Tab Alignment Types

Tab	Purpose
⌊	Left-aligns text at the tab setting
⊥	Centers text at the tab setting
⌟	Right-aligns text at the tab setting
⊥	Aligns decimal points at the tab setting

9. Click the Tab Alignment button ⌊ one or more times until the left-aligned tab symbol ⌊ appears. Click the ruler at the 0.5-inch position to set a left tab.

10. Repeat this process for each of these tab settings:

   a. Center-aligned tab ⊥. Click the ruler at the 3-inch position. The text "2009" moves so that it is centered under the tab.

TIP

When setting tabs, you might want to increase the zoom setting for an enlarged view of the ruler. After tabs are set, tabbed text that you key will automatically align under the tab symbols you placed on the ruler.

   b. Left-aligned tab ⌊. Click the ruler at the 3.5-inch mark to set a left tab.

   c. Right-aligned tab ⌟. Click the ruler at the 5-inch mark to set a right-aligned tab.

   d. Decimal-aligned tab ⊥. Click the ruler at the 6.75-inch mark to set a decimal-aligned tab.

11. Click the tab setting at the 3.5-inch mark, a left-aligned tab symbol, and click and drag it down and off the ruler. This removes the tab from the slide. The final tab settings are show in Figure 5-22.

Exercise 5-23   CREATE A TABBED TABLE

Once the tabs are set for a tabbed table, the text can be entered by pressing Tab between each item. Tab spacing can be adjusted after the text is entered if necessary.

1. Working in the text box you created on slide 5, position the insertion point at the end of the text and press Enter to start a new text line.

2. Key the table text, shown in Figure 5-23, pressing [Tab] at the beginning of each line and between columns and pressing [Enter] at the end of each text line. The text box will increase in size as the text is keyed.

3. Select the entire text box by clicking its border. Increase the font size to 20 points.

4. With the text box still selected, from the Drawing Tools Format tab, in the Shape Styles group, click the Shape Fill button ⬛, and add the shape fill Brown, Background 2, Lighter 80%. Now the text is easier to read.

5. From the Drawing Tools Format tab, in the Shape Styles group, click the Shape Outline button ⬛, and add the shape outline Brown, Background 2, Darker 50%.

6. Select the text in the table, and from the Home tab, in the Paragraph group, change the line spacing to 1.5.

7. Highlight the text in the text box. Drag the decimal-aligned tab symbol from the 6.75-inch position on the ruler to 7.5 inches. The entire column moves to the left.

Figure 5-23
Creating a tabbed table

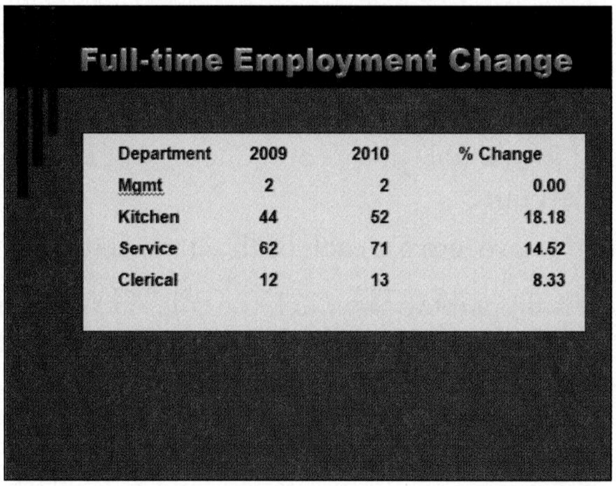

Full-time Employment Change			
Department	2009	2010	% Change
Mgmt	2	2	0.00
Kitchen	44	52	18.18
Service	62	71	14.52
Clerical	12	13	8.33

8. Drag the center-aligned marker (at 3 inches) down and off the ruler to remove it. The table realigns in an unattractive way that does not make sense.

9. Click the Undo button ↩ once to restore the table's appearance.

10. Update the handout footer to include *[your initials]*5-23.

11. View the presentation as a slide show to be sure all tables are appropriately positioned, and make any necessary adjustments.

12. Save the presentation as *[your initials]*5-23 in your Lesson 5 folder.

13. Close the presentation and submit your work.

Lesson 5 Summary

- Tables offer a convenient way to quickly organize material on a slide. From the Insert tab, in the Table group, you can use the Table button to insert a table. You can insert a table by choosing a content slide layout. You can "draw" a table directly on a slide by using the Draw Table button, or you can create a tabbed table through setting tabs.

- Before you can apply special formatting to table cells, you must first select the cells. You can select individual cells, groups of cells, rows, columns, or the entire table.

- Use the buttons on the Table Tools Design tab, in the Table Styles group, to apply fill effects and border effects to individual cells, a group of cells, or the entire table.

- Change the overall size of a table by dragging one of its sizing handles with a two-pointed arrow.

- Change the width of a column by dragging or double-clicking its border. Change the height of a row by dragging its border.

- Rows and columns can be easily inserted or deleted as you develop a table. Select at least one cell in the row or column where you want to insert or delete; then use buttons on the Table Tools Layout tab.

- While you are keying text in a table, a quick way to insert a new row at the bottom is to press Tab when you reach the last table cell.

- Occasionally, you might want one row or column to have more or fewer cells than the others. You can make this happen by merging a group of cells or splitting an individual cell into two or more cells.

- A diagonal line can be added to a cell to make it appear to be split into two cells. Careful placement of text within the cell completes this illusion.

- Applying and removing shading effects is similar to applying shading effects to other PowerPoint objects. Table and cell fills can be gradients, textures, or pictures.

- Before applying a border to cells or the entire table, choose the border style, border width, and border color from the Table Tools Design tab, in the Draw Borders group. Then select cells, and choose an option from the Borders button drop-down list or use the pencil pointer to apply it to the borders you want to change.

- Use the text alignment buttons on the Home tab, in the Paragraph group, to control the horizontal position of text in a cell.

- Use the Align Top, Center Vertically, and Align Bottom buttons on the Table Tools Layout tab in the Alignment group to control the vertical position of text in a cell.

- To fine-tune the horizontal or vertical position of text, change a cell's margin settings by using the Cell Margins button on the Table Tools Layout tab, in the Alignment group.

- Add and modify 3-D effects by selecting the table and clicking the Effects button on the Table Tools Design tab.

- Click the Tab Type button on the left edge of the ruler to change the type of tab. The button cycles through four tab types: left-aligned, centered, right-aligned, and decimal.
- Create a tabbed table by using a text box and setting tabs to control how the information is indented. Remove tabs or move tabs as needed by clicking and dragging.
- If table text has been entered in a tabbed table, then text must be highlighted before changes in tab settings will affect the text.

LESSON 5		Command Summary	
Feature	Button	Ribbon	Keyboard
Add Header Row		Table Tools Design tab, Table Style Options group, check Header Row	
Align Table Text vertically	⬒, ⬓, or ⬓	Table Tools Layout tab, Alignment group	
Apply Bevel, Shadow, or Reflection effects	◇	Table Tools Design tab, Table Styles group, Effects	
Apply Borders	⊞	Table Tools Design tab, Table Styles group, Borders	
Apply Shading effect to cells	⬧	Table Tools Design tab, Table Styles group, Shading	
Change table style		Table Tools Design tab, Table Styles group, More	
Change Text Direction	‖A	Table Tools Layout tab, Alignment group, Text Direction	
Delete table columns	⊠	Table Tools Layout tab, Rows & Columns group, Delete	
Distribute Columns evenly	⊞	Table Tools Layout tab, Cell Size group, Distribute Columns	
Distribute Rows evenly	⊟	Table Tools Layout tab, Cell Size group, Distribute Rows	
Draw Table	✎	Tables Tools Design tab, Draw Borders group, Draw Table	
Erase cell borders	✐	Table Tools Design tab, Draw Table group, Eraser	
Insert Table	▦	Insert tab, Tables group, Table	

continues

LESSON 5		Command Summary *continued*	
Feature	**Button**	**Ribbon**	**Keyboard**
Insert table columns		Table Tools Layout tab, Rows & Columns group, Insert Left or Insert Right	
Insert table rows		Table Tools Layout tab, Rows & Columns group, Insert Above or Insert Below	
Merge table cells		Table Tools Layout tab, Merge group, Merge Cells	
Navigate in a table			Tab; Shift+Tab; ↓; ↑; ←; →
Select column, row, or table		Table Tools Layout tab, Table group, Select	
Select table style		Table Tools Design tab, Table Styles group, More	
Set table cell margins		Table Tools Layout tab, Alignment group, Cell Margins	
Split a table cell		Table Tools Layout tab, Merge group, Split Cells	

Concepts Review

True/False Questions

Each of the following statements is either true or false. Indicate your choice by circling T or F.

T F 1. You can adjust the width of individual columns in a table, but row heights must all be the same.

T F 2. Effects can be used to give the table a dimensional look.

T F 3. You don't need to be exact when you define the size of a table because it's easy to insert rows and columns later.

T F 4. Borders are available in only one width.

T F 5. Text in a table cell can have its vertical position adjusted independently of other cells.

T F 6. When you insert a new column, it is always inserted to the left of the currently selected column.

T F 7. Cell margins provide a space between cell borders and the contents of the cell.

T F 8. After setting ruler tabs, you can remove one of these tabs by dragging it off the ruler.

Short Answer Questions

Write the correct answer in the space provided.

1. What do you call the intersection between a column and a row?

_____

2. Other than dragging down all the cells or using a button on the Ribbon, how can you select a column in a table?

_____

3. What tab contains the Center Vertically button?

_____

4. What method can be used to select the entire table?

_____

5. What three types of 3-D effects are available to apply to a table?

_____

6. What are the three methods of merging cells in a table?

_____

7. What is different about splitting a cell diagonally compared to splitting it horizontally or vertically?

_____

8. What's the quickest way to make a group of selected columns of varying widths all the same width?

_____

Critical Thinking

Answer these questions on a separate page. Support your answers with examples from your own experience, if possible.

1. Why might you choose to put information in a table instead of in a bulleted placeholder?

2. Tables can be created in three ways: inserting, drawing, or tabbing. Why would you choose one method over another? What criteria would affect which method you use?

Skills Review

Exercise 5-24

Create a table, key text, and apply table styles.

1. Open the file **CookOff**, and move to slide 4, "The Winning Fare."

2. Insert a new table by following these steps:
   a. Click the Table button ▦ in the content placeholder.
   b. In the dialog box that appears, choose two columns by four rows.

3. Key text in the table by following these steps:
   a. Click the upper left cell to select it, and then key **Name**.
   b. Press ⟨Tab⟩ to move to the next cell, and then key **Recipe Description**.

4. Key the text shown in Figure 5-24 for the remaining cells.

UNIT 2 LESSON 5

Figure 5-24
Table text

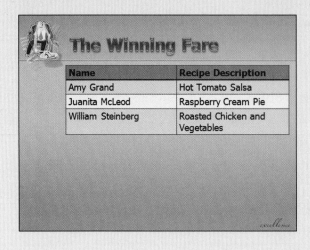

5. Apply a table style from the Best Match for Document category by following these steps:

   a. Select the table by right-clicking within the table and choosing Select Table from the shortcut menu.

   b. From the Table Tools Design tab, in the Table Styles group, click the More button ⏷.

   c. From the Best Match for Document category, choose Themed Style 1, Accent 1.

6. Create a slide footer for the current slide (slide 4 only) containing today's date, your name, and *[your initials]*5-24.

7. Move to slide 1, and save the presentation as *[your initials]*5-24 in your Lesson 5 folder.

8. View the presentation as a slide show from slide 1.

9. If your instructor requires a printout, print slide 4 only. If you have a color printer, print it in color.

10. Close the presentation and submit your work.

Exercise 5-25

Draw a table, and apply border and shading options.

1. Open the file **Operations1**.

2. Insert a new slide after slide 3 that uses the Title Only layout. Key the title **Capital Equipment 2012**.

3. Draw a new table by following these steps:

   a. From the Insert tab, in the Tables group, click the Table button ▦, and choose Draw Table.

   b. Use the pencil pointer to draw a table from under "Capital" to under "2012" and down about 3.5 inches on the ruler.

   c. From the Table Tools Design tab, in the Draw Borders group, click the Draw Table button ✎.

d. Click and drag two vertical borders to create three columns.

e. Click and drag four horizontal borders to create five rows.

f. Press Esc to turn off the pencil pointer.

4. For the table text, key the information shown in Figure 5-25.

Figure 5-25
Table text in
completed table

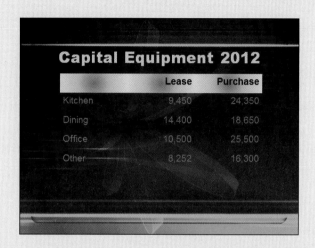

Capital Equipment 2012		
	Lease	Purchase
Kitchen	9,450	24,350
Dining	14,400	18,650
Office	10,500	25,500
Other	8,252	16,300

5. Apply shading effects to table cells by following these steps:

a. Move the pointer to the outside of the table beside row 1; when you get a right-facing arrow, click to select all the cells in the first row.

b. From the Table Tools Design tab, in the Table Styles group, click the Shading button ⬛.

c. Choose Aqua, Text 2, Lighter 40%.

d. Click the list box arrow on the Shading button again, and choose Gradient.

e. In the Variations category, choose From Center.

f. With the first row still selected, change the font color to a deep blue: Indigo, Accent 6, Darker 50%. Apply bold to the first row.

g. Horizontally center the first row of text.

6. Make all the columns the same width and all the rows the same height by following these steps:

a. Select the entire table by right-clicking within the table and choosing Select Table.

b. From the Table Tools Layout tab, in the Cell Size group, click the Distribute Columns button ⊞.

c. From the Table Tools Layout tab, in the Cell Size group, click the Distribute Rows button ⊟.

d. With the table still selected, change the font size of the entire table to 24 points.

7. Remove all the table's borders by following these steps:

a. Select the entire table.

b. From the Table Tools Design tab, in the Table Styles group, click the Borders button ⊞, and choose No Border.

8. Select all cells with numbers and the column heading cells; then make them right-aligned.

9. Create a handout header and footer: Include the date, your name as the header, the page number, and *[your initials]*5-25 as the footer.

10. View the presentation as a slide show.

11. Move to slide 1, and save the presentation as *[your initials]*5-25 in your Lesson 5 folder.

12. Close the presentation and submit your work.

Exercise 5-26

Draw a table, insert and delete rows and columns, adjust column and row width, and apply formatting for text, shading, and borders.

1. Open the file **Operations2**.

2. Display slide 5, titled "Reservation Requests."

3. Draw a table on slide 5 by following these steps:

   a. From the Insert tab, in the Tables group, click the Table button ▦, and choose Draw Table.

   b. Use the pencil pointer to draw a table from under the "v" in "Average" to the right edge of the slide and down about 3.5 inches on the ruler.

   c. From the Table Tools Design tab, in the Draw Borders group, click the Pen Color button ✐, and choose Light Blue, Accent 6, Darker 50%.

   d. Within the table, draw four vertical lines (to create five columns) and three horizontal lines (to create four rows). They don't need to be the same size.

   e. Press Esc to turn off the pencil pointer.

4. For the table's text, key the data in Figure 5-26. Adjust the size of the table as needed to match the figure.

Figure 5-26
Table text

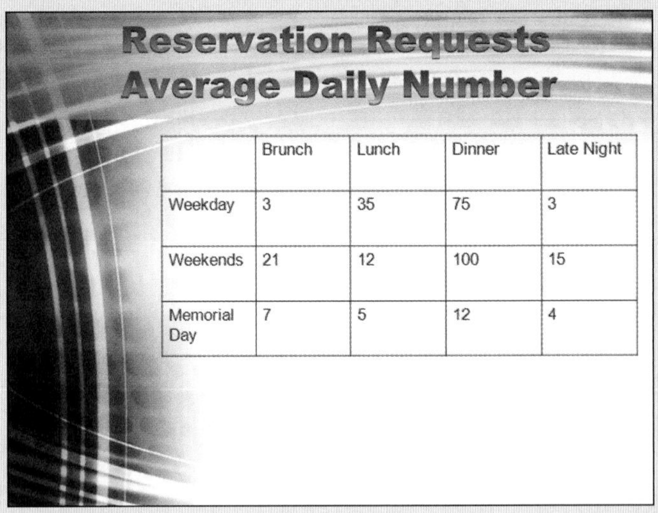

Reservation Requests
Average Daily Number

	Brunch	Lunch	Dinner	Late Night
Weekday	3	35	75	3
Weekends	21	12	100	15
Memorial Day	7	5	12	4

5. Select the table, and make the text bold. Make all the numbers Light Blue, Accent 6, Darker 50%.

6. Insert a new row between "Weekends" and "Memorial Day" by following these steps:

   a. Right-click "Memorial Day."

   b. Choose Insert from the shortcut menu, and choose Insert Row Above.

7. Insert a new column to the left of "Brunch" by following these steps:

   a. Click anywhere in the "Brunch" column.

   b. Click the Table Tools Layout tab, in the Rows & Columns group, and choose Insert Left.

8. Delete a column and a row by following these steps:

   a. Select the entire "Late Night" column.

   b. Right-click the selection, and choose Delete Columns from the shortcut menu.

   c. Select the "Memorial Day" row. Right-click the selection, and choose Delete Rows from the shortcut menu.

9. In the second column, key **Breakfast** for the column heading. Key **5** for "Weekday" and **18** for "Weekends." Change the "Weekday" cell to **Weekdays**.

10. Key the following information in the new row:

    Holidays, [Tab] **6,** [Tab] **9,** [Tab] **15,** [Tab] **94**

11. Move the table to a new position, and change its size by following these steps:

    a. Right-click anywhere inside the table, and choose Select Table from the shortcut menu.

    b. Move your pointer over the table's border until you see the four-pointed arrow [⊕]. If necessary, drag the table to position it on the white area of the slide so that all the numbers are easy to read.

    c. Make the table wider by dragging the right-center sizing handle to the right until all text and numbers are on one line. Before you drag, make sure the pointer appears as [⟷].

12. Make all the columns the same width and all the rows the same height. Then adjust the first column size as needed to fit all the text on one line.

13. Align the text horizontally by following these steps:

    a. Select the first row by clicking the first cell and dragging down to the last cell.

    b. From the Home tab, in the Paragraph group, click the Center button [≡] (or press [Ctrl]+[E]).

    c. Select all the cells that contain numbers by dragging diagonally across the cells.

    d. Click the Align Text Right button [≡] (or press [Ctrl]+[R]) to right-align the numbers.

14. Change the cell margin settings by following these steps:

    a. Make sure all the cells that contain numbers are selected.

b. From the Table Tools Layout tab, in the Alignment group, choose the Cell Margins button, and choose Custom Margins.

c. In the Internal margin section, key **0.5"** in the Right text box. Click OK.

15. Change the vertical alignment of text and numbers in their cells by following these steps:

a. Select the entire table from the Table Tools Layout tab, in the Table group, by clicking the Select button and Select Table.

b. Still working on the Table Tools Layout tab, in the Alignment group, click the Center Vertically button.

16. Create a handout header and footer: Include the date, your name as the header, the page number, and *[your initials]***5-26** as the footer.

17. Move to slide 1, and save the presentation as *[your initials]***5-26** in your Lesson 5 folder.

18. View the presentation as a slide show. Close the presentation and submit your work.

Exercise 5-27

Insert a table, merge cells, and work with tabbed tables.

1. Open the file **Miami Beach**.

2. Insert a new slide after slide 2, and use the Title and Content layout. Key **Appetizers** as the title.

3. Set a decimal tab at the 4.5-inch position on the ruler by following these steps:

a Click in the body text placeholder.

b. Click the Tab Alignment button L until the Decimal Tab appears.

c. Click the ruler at the 4.5-inch position.

4. Key the following in the body text placeholder, pressing Tab before each price:

Wild Rice Soup	Tab	**6.25**
Dill Cucumber Salad	Tab	**5.50**
Four Bean Salad	Tab	**5.25**

5. Insert a new slide after slide 3, and use the Title Only layout. Key **Entrée Selections** as the title.

6. Insert a table with three columns and seven rows.

7. Merge the cells in rows 3, 5, and 7 using the following steps:

a. Select the cells in row 3.

b. From the Table Tools Layout tab, in the Merge group, choose the Merge Cells button.

c. Repeat the process for row 5 and row 7.

TIP

You can use right tabs instead of decimal tabs to align numbers if all the numbers in the list have the same number of decimal places.

8. Key the text shown in Figure 5-27 into your table.

Figure 5-27
Completed table
with table text

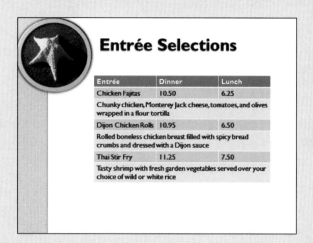

9. Move the table down and to the right, and resize as necessary the table, columns, and rows.

10. Center the text vertically in the table rows.

11. Create a handout header and footer: Include the date, your name as the header, the page number, and *[your initials]*5-27 as the footer.

12. Save the presentation as *[your initials]*5-27 in your Lesson 5 folder.

13. Review the presentation as a slide show.

14. Close the presentation and submit your work.

Lesson Applications

Exercise 5-28

Create a presentation with a table slide, apply table styles, arrange and format text, and change column widths and table size.

1. Open the file **Print**.

2. Insert three slides after slide 1. Use the Title and Content layout for all three slides.

3. Key the text shown in Figure 5-28.

4. On slide 4, select the Table button 🔲 from the content placeholder, and select the correct number of columns and rows before keying the information. Select the entire table, and change the font to Dark Red, Text 1. In the first row, press Enter to divide the text in each cell into two lines of text as shown in Figure 5-28.

Figure 5-28
Presentation content

Print Advertising 2011

Slide 2
- Campaigns use a variety of print media
- Each medium targets a specific market segment
- Every campaign must meet specific sales objectives

Coupon Redemption

Slide 3
- Effective measure of return on investment
- Used for promotional purposes in a variety of print media

Coupons Redeemed 2010

	Column 1	Column 2	Column 3	Column 4
Row 1	Newspaper and Magazine	Coupons Redeemed	Average Check	Cost of One Ad
Row 2	NY Times	414	$31.50	$6,800
Row 3	NY Magazine	476	$25.00	$2,850
Row 4	NY Runner	1,063	$23.50	$975
Row 5	NY Health	125	$16.25	$650

Slide 4

5. On slide 4, change the Table style to Themed Style 2, Accent 4 in the Best Match for Documents category.

6. For the entire table, change all right and left cell margins to 0.2". Using the resize column arrow ↔, double-click each column border so that each column self-adjusts to fit the widest text in the column.

7. Center the headings for the columns containing numbers.

8. Right-align all numbers.

9. Vertically center all text and numbers in the table.

10. Adjust the overall size and position of the table for attractive positioning on the slide, as shown in Figure 5-29.

Figure 5-29
Completed table
slide

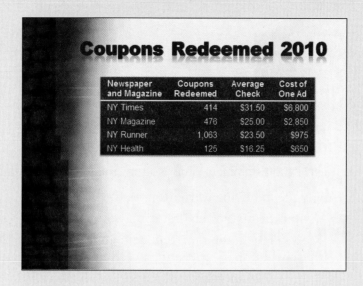

11. Create a slide footer for the current slide (slide 4) containing today's date, your name, and *[your initials]*5-28.

12. Create a handout header and footer: Include the date, your name as the header, the page number, and *[your initials]*5-28 as the footer.

13. Save the presentation as *[your initials]*5-28 in your Lesson 5 folder.

14. View the presentation as a slide show.

15. Close the presentation and submit your work.

Exercise 5-29

Insert a table slide; insert rows; change row height, column width, alignment, and cell margins; and apply a 3-D effect.

1. Open the file **Ads**.

2. On slide 1, change "Student Name" to your name.

3. Insert a table on a new slide after slide 1 using the Title and Content layout, and key the text shown in Figure 5-30.

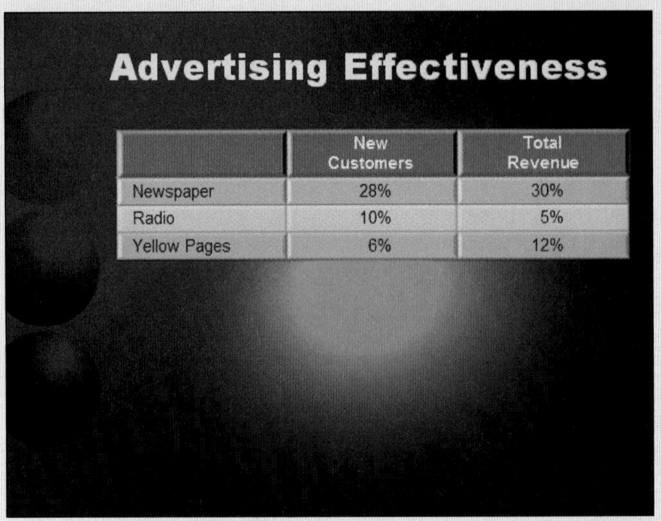

Figure 5-30
Table text

4. Resize the title placeholder so that the text fits on one line.

5. Apply the following formatting to the table's text:
   - Center the text in the first row.
   - Right-align all the numbers, and apply a 1-inch right cell margin so that the numbers appear centered under their headings.
   - Apply a 0.25-inch left cell margin to all the cells in the first column.
   - If necessary, adjust the column width of the first row so that "Yellow Pages" is on one line.

6. Insert a row above "Yellow Pages" with the following text:
   Mailers   12%   18%

7. Make the table easy to read by adjusting the column widths, row heights, and vertical alignment of cells, as necessary. Resize and reposition the table appropriately on the slide.

8. Change the table style to Themed style 1, Accent 1.

9. Select all the text in the table except the first row, and change the font to Gray-50%, Background 2, Darker 50%.

10. Add a Convex cell bevel to the entire table. Compare your slide with the table in Figure 5-30, and make any necessary changes.

11. Create a slide footer for the current slide (slide 2) containing today's date, your name, and *[your initials]*5-29.

12. Create a handout header and footer: Include the date, your name as the header, the page number, and *[your initials]*5-29 as the footer.

13. Check spelling, and change any words that need to be corrected.

14. Save the presentation as *[your initials]*5-29 in your Lesson 5 folder.

15. View the presentation as a slide show.

16. Close the presentation and submit your work.

Exercise 5-30

Create a tabbed table.

1. Start a new blank presentation. Use the Concourse design theme with the Equity color theme.

2. On slide 1, key a two-line title with the text **Good 4 U** and **Softball Schedule**.

3. Key **Spring/Summer 2012** for the subtitle.

4. Find a softball clip art image, and insert it on the title slide in the color bar at the bottom. Duplicate the softball several times, and resize the images and arrange them so that they get progressively smaller. If an image is unavailable, use **Softball.gif** from the student files. See Figure 5-31 for an example.

Figure 5-31
Slide 1

5. Using the Title Only layout, create slide 2 as shown in Figure 5-32. Key the table and its heading all in one text box, and format the table as follows:

   - Set appropriate tabs (approximately 2.5-inch center tab, 5-inch center tab, 8-inch right tab).
   - Add bold to the headings.
   - Change the font size of the table to 24 points.
   - Apply 1.5 spacing to the table.
   - Position the table appropriately on the slide.

6. Add the same softball used in slide 1 to the bottom left corner of slide 2.

Figure 5-32
Slide 2

7. Using the Title and Content layout, create slide 3 as shown in Figure 5-33.

8. Copy and paste the softball from slide 2 onto slide 3, and insert a softball image recolored to match the theme colors on the right of the slide.

Figure 5-33
Slide 3

9. Check spelling in the presentation. The names of team members are spelled correctly; do not make any changes.

10. Create a handout header and footer: Include the date, your name as the header, the page number, and *[your initials]*5-30 as the footer.

11. Save the presentation as *[your initials]*5-30 in your Lesson 5 folder.

12. Close the presentation and submit your work.

Exercise 5-31 ◆ Challenge Yourself

Edit and format a presentation including a table slide, add data, change alignment, change table colors, and merge cells.

1. Open the file **MarketSummary**.

2. Create a table on a new slide after slide 3 using the layout Title Only. Key the title **Marketing Expenses 2010**.

3. Draw a table using the pencil pointer; then use Figure 5-34 as an example as you create the table. For the column heading font, use 24 points, brown, and bold; for the remaining text, use 18 points, white, and bold.

Figure 5-34
Table slide

4. Use appropriate alignment techniques, fill colors, and border treatments. Use a preset gradient color for the heading row fill for a gold appearance. (This option is found under More Gradients.)

5. Distribute the columns and rows evenly.

6. Using the Title and Content layout, insert a new slide after slide 4 with the title **Estimated Budget 2011**. Use Figure 5-35 as an example as you create the table. Choose an appropriate table style to coordinate with the theme.

7. Adjust the size of the columns, rows, and table as necessary. Use wide cell margins.

8. Select the table, and choose the Reflection effect Half Reflection, 4 pt offset.

Figure 5-35
Table slide

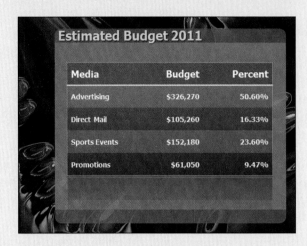

9. Create a handout header and footer: Include the date, your name as the header, the page number, and *[your initials]*5-31as the footer.

10. Check spelling in the presentation.

11. Save the presentation as *[your initials]*5-31 in your Lesson 5 folder.

12. Close the presentation and submit your work.

On Your Own

In these exercises you work on your own, as you would in a real-life work environment. Use the skills you've learned to accomplish the task—and be creative.

Exercise 5-32

Chef Michele will soon be giving a cooking class. She wants to use a slide show to display the finished dish, share the recipe, and feature the preparation steps as she demonstrates how to prepare the dish. Find a recipe that you can use for this purpose (one of your own or one you like from http://allrecipes.com). Create a title slide with the name of the food dish, where the recipe came from, and, if possible, a picture of the finished dish. Add one or two slides describing in general terms what the dish contains and why it is a healthy choice. Create a series of slides containing tables that present the ingredients and the steps in creating the dish. Design your own table structures to present the information in a way that you think is easy to understand; use inserted tables with table styles applied consistently throughout the presentation. Format your presentation attractively, picking up colors, fonts, and other style features that accent the recipe you have chosen. Save your presentation as *[your initials]*5-32. Close the presentation and submit your work.

Exercise 5-33

Find a schedule of events from your local newspaper or other source, for example, a movie schedule, your class schedule, the TV listings, or a schedule of community or school events. Create a presentation containing a table that lists those events in a way you think is easy to understand. Create a second table listing the three events or classes you think are the most interesting in one column and a description of those events in a second column. The presentation should include a title slide, two table slides, and any other slides you think will enhance your presentation. Use your creativity to make the tables interesting and fun to view. Be sure to resize the table and cells as needed and add borders, shading, and effects to add interest. Save the presentation as *[your initials]*5-33. Close the presentation and submit your work.

Exercise 5-34

Assume that you are the manager of a movie rental business and you need to promote sales of previously viewed movie DVDs to reduce your inventory. Prepare a single-slide presentation that you can print as a flyer and display for customers to see when they visit the store. Create columns based on categories that would help describe the movie in a concise way, such as the movie title, lead actors, rating, and cost. Apply a table style to make this flyer attractive and eye-catching. Use WordArt to create a bold title. Save the presentation as *[your initials]*5-34. Close the presentation and submit your work.

Lesson 6
Creating Charts

OBJECTIVES   *After completing this lesson, you will be able to:*

1. Create a chart.
2. Format a column chart.
3. Use different chart types.
4. Work with pie charts.
5. Enhance chart elements.

> Estimated Time: 1½ hours

Charts, sometimes called *graphs,* are diagrams that display numbers for visual comparison. Charts illustrate quantitative relationships and can help people understand the significance of numeric information more easily than viewing the same information as a table or a list of numbers. Charts are well suited for making comparisons or examining the changes in data over time.

Creating a Chart

PowerPoint provides several ways to start a new chart. You can add a chart to an existing slide, or you can select a slide layout with a chart placeholder at the time you create a new slide. Microsoft Excel is opened using either of these methods. Excel then holds the chart data in a *worksheet,* and these data are linked to PowerPoint where the chart is displayed. If changes are made to the data in Excel, the chart is automatically updated in PowerPoint.

If Excel is not installed on your computer when you start a new chart, Microsoft Graph will open with a sample *datasheet.* A datasheet provides rows and columns in which you key the numbers and labels used to create a chart. Advanced features of charting with Excel are not available with Graph.

Gus Irvinelli has requested that you create a presentation. The audience will be the general managers at each Good 4 U location. The presentation will include a progress report and a forecast for the future of Good 4 U. Gus prefers that the data be displayed in charts for an easy-to-understand visual representation.

Exercise 6-1 CHOOSE A SLIDE LAYOUT FOR A CHART

Several slide layouts are suitable for charts. Title and Content features one chart on a slide, while Two Content layouts make it easy to combine a chart and body text on the same slide.

1. Open the file **Finance1**.

2. Insert a new slide after slide 1 that uses the Title and Content slide layout, as shown in Figure 6-1. Key the slide title **Sales Forecast**. This layout contains a placeholder suitable for one chart.

Figure 6-1
Choosing a slide layout for a chart

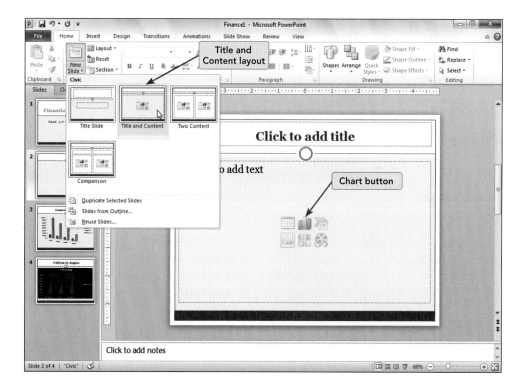

3. Click the Chart button 📊 in the center of the content placeholder.

4. On the Insert Chart dialog box, click the different chart categories on the left and notice the chart types that are displayed. From the Column category, click the 3-D Clustered Column Chart, and click OK. Excel opens, displaying a worksheet with sample data, and a chart is inserted into PowerPoint. Chart-related tabs appear on the Ribbon.

Exercise 6-2 EDIT THE DATA SOURCE

The worksheet contains rows and columns. Each number or label is in a separate *cell*—the rectangle formed by the intersection of a row and a column.

As you enter data, you can monitor the results on the sample chart. You key new information by overwriting the sample data or by deleting the sample data and keying your own data.

Figure 6-2
Creating a chart

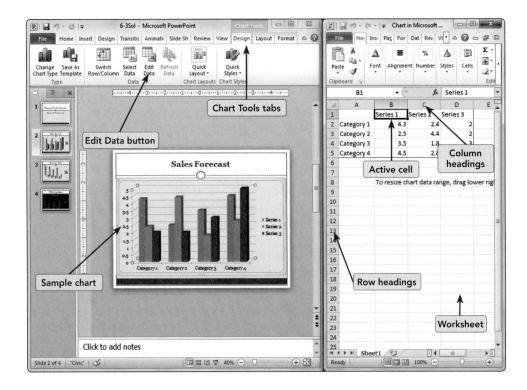

NOTE

If Excel is not installed on your computer, Microsoft Graph will open a datasheet that contains gray column headings and row headings with a buttonlike appearance that indicate column letters and row numbers. If you like, you can move the datasheet by dragging its title bar, and you can resize it by dragging its borders.

1. On the worksheet, click Series 1. A heavy black border, which indicates that this is the active cell, surrounds the cell that contains "Series 1," as shown in Figure 6-2. Notice that, when you are working on the worksheet, your pointer is a white cross ✛, called a *cell pointer*.

2. Move around the worksheet by clicking on individual cells. Then try pressing Enter, Tab, Shift + Enter, Shift + Tab, and the arrow keys to explore other ways to navigate in a worksheet.

3. Click cell B2 (the cell in column B, row 2, that contains the value 4.3); then key 10, and press Enter. The chart data will automatically update in PowerPoint.

4. Click cell B2 with the value "10," which represents Category 1 of Series 1.

5. Press Delete to remove the contents of cell B2, and press Enter. Notice that the first column in the chart is no longer displayed.

6. Click and drag the pointer from cell B3 to cell B5 to select the rest of the numbers in the Series 1 column.

7. Press Delete, and then for Series 1 no columns are displayed in the chart. Because the Series 1 column is still included on the worksheet, however, space still remains on the chart where the columns were removed and Series 1 shows in the legend.

8. Click the box in the upper left corner of the worksheet where the row headings meet the column headings, as shown in Figure 6-3. The entire worksheet is selected.

NOTE

If you leave gaps between columns or rows as you enter data, your chart will not display correctly.

Figure 6-3
Editing the worksheet

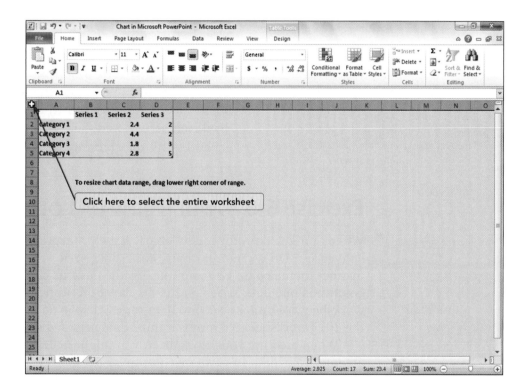

NOTE

If PowerPoint does not recognize your data from Excel, from the Chart Tools Design tab, in the Data group, click the Select Data button 📊 and then click the red arrow at the end of the Chart data range box. In Excel select the range of data you wish to use on the chart, click the red arrow again, and click OK.

9. Press Delete. The worksheet is now blank and ready for you to key new data. Notice that the columns in the chart have been removed.

10. Click the first cell in the upper left corner. All the cells in the worksheet are deselected.

11. Close Excel. The worksheet is not visible. The worksheet can be closed at any point and accessed when you wish.

12. From the Chart Tools Design tab, in the Data group, choose the Edit Data button . This reopens the worksheet, and you can now enter new data.

13. Key the numbers and labels shown in Figure 6-4. Be sure to put the labels in the top row and left-most column. Notice how the chart gets larger as you key data.

Figure 6-4
Worksheet with new data

	A	B	C	D	E
1		2011	2012	2013	
2	New York	920	1130	1450	
3	Miami	500	850	1210	
4	Los Angeles	350	760	990	
5	Row heading				

TIP

You do not need to be concerned about number formatting in the worksheet. If any of the labels or numbers do not fit in a cell, move to the right of the column heading for the cell until you get the two-pointed arrow and double-click. This will adjust the column to fit the longest line of text.

14. Notice on the chart in PowerPoint that there is a blank area. In the sample chart, there were four categories. To fix this, row 5 must be deleted. Click the row heading number for row 5. Right-click, and choose Delete. This will update the chart by removing the blank space where the fourth-category columns were displayed before, and the remaining columns will expand to fill the chart area.

Exercise 6-3   SWITCH ROW OR COLUMN DATA

When you key data for a new chart, Excel interprets each row of data as a *data series*. On a column chart, each data series is usually displayed in a distinct theme color. For example, on the current chart, the 2011 worksheet column is one data series and is displayed in orange on the chart; the 2012 worksheet column is a second data series, displayed in blue on the chart; and the 2013 worksheet column is a third data series, displayed in a dark red.

When creating your worksheet, you might not know whether it is best to arrange your data in rows or columns. Fortunately, you can enter the data and easily change the way it is displayed on the chart.

1. In PowerPoint, click the slide 2 chart area to continue modifying this chart.

2. From the Chart Tools Design tab, click the Switch Row/Column button. The chart columns are now grouped by year instead of by city. The years are displayed below each group of columns.

3. Click the Switch Row/Column button again to group the chart columns by city. Your chart should look like the one shown in Figure 6-5.

4. Close Excel, but continue working in PowerPoint on the chart.

5. Create a slide footer for the current slide (slide 2 only) containing today's date, your name, and *[your initials]*6-3.

6. Create a new folder for Lesson 6. Save the presentation as *[your initials]*6-3 in your Lesson 6 folder.

Figure 6-5
Chart with new data

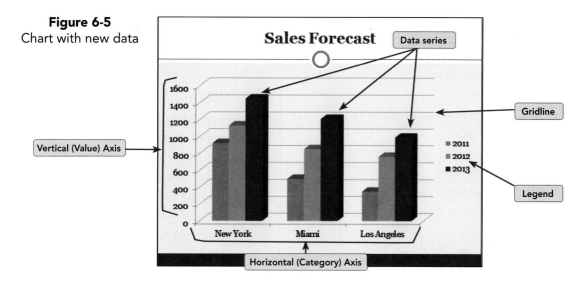

Formatting a Column Chart

You can apply a wide variety of format options to charts by changing the colors, gradients, fonts, and number formats of a chart. Some of these options are appropriate on the basis of the particular chart type being used. In this lesson you have been working with a 3-D Clustered Column chart.

You can alter the appearance of your chart's axes by changing text color, size, font, and number formatting. You can also change scale and tick mark settings. The *scale* indicates the values that are displayed on the value axis and the intervals between those values. *Tick marks* are small measurement marks, similar to those found on a ruler, that show increments on the *Vertical (Value) Axis* (on the left for column charts) and the *Horizontal (Category) Axis* (on the bottom for column charts).

To make these changes, use the Format Axis dialog box, which you display in one of the following ways:

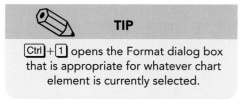

TIP

Ctrl+1 opens the Format dialog box that is appropriate for whatever chart element is currently selected.

- From the Chart Tools Format tab, in the Current Selection group, choose the area you want to format, and click the Format Selection button 🐝.
- Right-click an axis, and choose Format Axis from the shortcut menu.

Exercise 6-4 EXPLORE PARTS OF A CHART

PowerPoint provides several tools that help you navigate around the chart and ScreenTips that help you select the part of the chart on which you want to work.

1. Click the chart to select it.
2. Move the pointer over the words "New York." The ScreenTip identifies this part of the chart as the Horizontal (Category) Axis.

Figure 6-6
Chart Elements list

3. Point to one of the horizontal gray lines (gridlines) within the chart. The ScreenTip identifies these lines as Vertical (Value) Axis Major Gridlines.

4. Move the pointer around other parts of the chart to find the Plot Area, Chart Area, and Legend Entries. Each of these areas can be formatted with fill colors, border colors, and font attributes.

5. From the Chart Tools Format tab, in the Current Selection group, the chart element that is currently selected is displayed. Click the Chart Elements down arrow to see a list of the various chart elements as shown in Figure 6-6.

6. Choose Floor from the list to select the chart floor. Sometimes it's easier to select the chart's smaller elements this way.

Exercise 6-5   CHANGE CHART STYLES

PowerPoint provides preset *Chart Styles* that can be applied to a chart to enhance its appearance. Chart Styles are sets of formatting combinations that can be applied to a chart as a group in one click.

1. On slide 2, click anywhere inside the chart to select it.

2. From the Chart Tools Design tab, in the Chart Styles group, click the More button ⬇.

3. Move your pointer over several of the style samples. Click the Style 4 chart style, as shown in Figure 6-7.

Figure 6-7
Chart Styles gallery

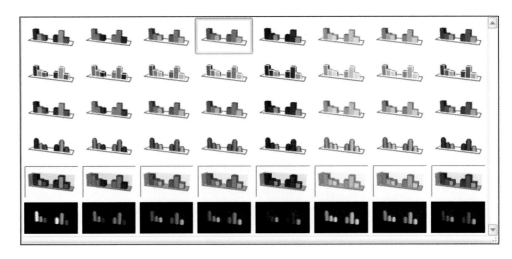

4. Notice the effect that applying a style has on the selected chart. The chart still coordinates with theme colors, but it has three blue colors applied.

Exercise 6-6 FORMAT THE VERTICAL (VALUE) AND HORIZONTAL (CATEGORY) AXES

The Vertical (Value) Axis and the Horizontal (Category) Axis are formatted through the Format Axis dialog box to change fonts, scales, units, and more options.

1. On slide 2, point to one of the numbers on the left side of the chart. When you see the Vertical (Value) Axis ScreenTip, right-click to open the shortcut menu.

2. Using the floating font group, change the font to Arial, **Bold**.

3. Right-click the Value Axis again to reopen the shortcut menu, and choose Format Axis. Click the Number option at the left of the dialog box; then, in the Category box, choose Currency. Change the decimal places to **0** because all numbers in the worksheet are even numbers. Change the symbol to **$ English (U.S.)**.

4. At the left of the dialog box, click Axis Options. In the Maximum box, choose Fixed, and key **1500** to set the largest number on the Value Axis.

5. In the Major unit box, choose Fixed, and key **500** to set wider intervals between the numbers on the Value Axis.

6. Click Close. The chart now shows fewer horizontal gridlines, and each value is formatted as currency with a dollar sign, as shown in Figure 6-8.

Figure 6-8
Formatting the Value Axis

7. Right-click the text New York on the Horizontal (Category) Axis.

8. Using the floating font group, change the font to Arial, Bold.

Exercise 6-7   APPLY DIFFERENT CHART LAYOUTS

The *Chart Layouts* feature controls the position where different chart elements appear. PowerPoint provides many different preset layouts.

1. Move to slide 3, and click anywhere within the chart area.

2. From the Chart Tools Design tab, in the Chart Styles group, click the More button 🔽, and choose Style 2.

3. From the Chart Tools Design tab, in the Chart Layouts group, click the More button 🔽. (Click the Quick Layout button 🖼 if your Layout Styles are not displayed.)

4. Select Layout 2. Notice the new position of several chart elements. Also, the Vertical (Value) Axis is gone, and it has been replaced with data labels showing the values on the columns, as shown in Figure 6-9.

Figure 6-9
Choosing a Chart Layout

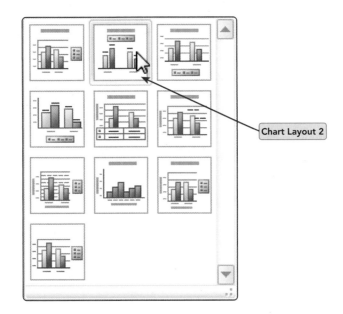

Chart Layout 2

5. Select the "Chart Title" text box, and press ⎣Delete⎦ to remove it.

Exercise 6-8   CHANGE OR REMOVE THE LEGEND

A *legend* is a box showing the colors assigned to the data series. You can customize a chart's legend by changing the border, background colors, and font attributes.

1. Move to slide 2, and right-click the legend box.

2. Using the floating font group, change the font to Arial, Bold.

3. Right-click the legend box again, and choose Format Legend so that you can make several changes at once. Click the Fill option at the left of the dialog box, choose Solid Fill, and select the Gold, Accent 4 color to change the legend fill color.

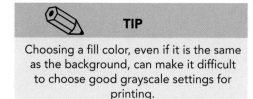

TIP

Choosing a fill color, even if it is the same as the background, can make it difficult to choose good grayscale settings for printing.

4. At the left of the dialog box, click Legend Options, and choose Top. Click Close. The legend appears above the chart, and the fill color is changed. Note that sizing handles surround the legend.

5. Using a right or left sizing handle, resize the legend to make it wider (approximately 5 inches) so that there is more space between the legend items and all three items are still visible.

6. Select the legend, and drag it down so that it fits below the top gridline and above the columns, as shown in Figure 6-10. Adjust the width of the legend if it overlaps any columns.

Figure 6-10
Legend repositioned

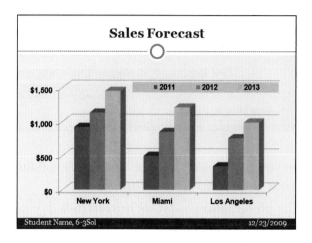

Exercise 6-9   APPLY OR REMOVE GRIDLINES

Gridlines are the thin lines that can be displayed for major and minor units on vertical or horizontal axes. They align with major and minor tick marks on the axes when those are displayed. Gridlines make quantities easier to understand. In situations where numbers are displayed within the chart, gridlines may not be needed. The chart style you used on slide 3 did not display gridlines.

1. Still working on slide 2, click anywhere within the chart area.

2. From the Chart Tools Layout tab, in the Axes group, click the Gridlines button.

3. Choose Primary Horizontal Gridlines and Minor Gridlines. Notice that there are many horizontal gridlines now, as shown in Figure 6-11, instead of only gridlines on the major units.

Figure 6-11
Gridlines options

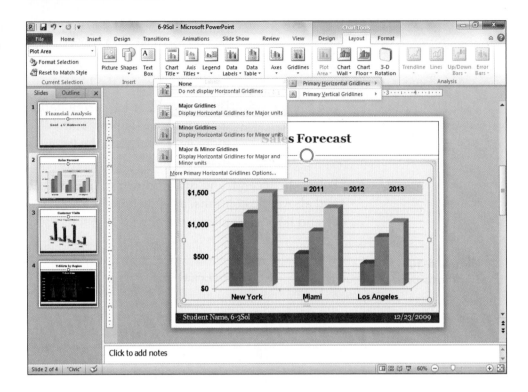

4. Update your slide footer for the current slide (slide 2 only) with today's date, your name, and *[your initials]*6-9.

5. Save the presentation as *[your initials]*6-9 in your Lesson 6 folder.

Using Different Chart Types

In addition to providing the 3-D Clustered Column chart, PowerPoint offers a wide variety of chart types, such as bar, area, line, pie, and surface, in both two- and three-dimensional layouts. In addition, you can include more than one chart type on a single chart, such as a combination of lines and columns.

If you are working on a two-dimensional (2-D) chart, you can add a secondary axis so that you can plot data against two different scales. For example, air temperature could be compared to wind speed, or number of customers could be compared to dollar sales. A secondary axis is also a good choice if you need to display numbers that vary greatly in magnitude; for example, sales generated by a small local brand could be compared with national sales trends.

Exercise 6-10 SWITCH TO OTHER CHART TYPES

Sometimes a different chart type can make data easier to understand. You can change chart types in the following ways:

- From the Chart Tools Design tab, in the Type group, click the Change Chart Type button 📊 to open the Change Chart Type dialog box.

- Right-click the chart area; then choose Change Chart Type from the shortcut menu.

1. Move to slide 3, and click the chart area to activate the chart. This chart compares dollar sales to number of customer visits. Because of the different types of data, the sales figures are not easy to understand.

2. Right-click the chart, and choose Change Chart Type from the shortcut menu. In the Change Chart Type dialog box, chart types are organized by category, as shown in Figure 6-12.

3. At the left of the dialog box, click Bar. Point to different thumbnails, and notice the description that appears in the ScreenTip. Choose Clustered Bar in 3-D, and click OK. The chart's vertical columns change to horizontal bars.

Figure 6-12
Changing to a
different chart type

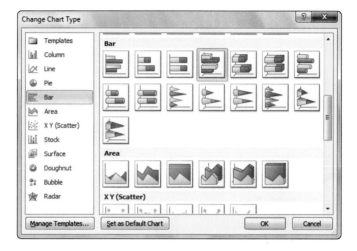

4. From the Chart Tools Design tab, in the Type group, click the Change Chart Type button [icon]. The Change Chart Type dialog box opens again.

5. At the left of the dialog box, click Column. Point to different thumbnails, and notice the description that appears in the ScreenTip. Click the Clustered Column type in the upper left of this category. Click OK. The chart changes to a two-dimensional column chart.

Exercise 6-11 ADD A SECONDARY CHART AXIS

The chart on slide 3 (Customer Visits) contains dollar values for apparel and food sales and also unit values for number of customer visits. Plotting customer visits on a secondary axis will improve the chart by making it easier to interpret.

If you are working with a 3-D chart, you must change it to a 2-D chart (as you did in the previous exercise), before you can add a secondary axis.

1. Select the chart on slide 3.

2. From the Chart Tools Design tab, in the Chart Layouts group, choose Layout 1, and delete the chart title text box.

3. Right-click one of the "Customers" columns, and choose **Format Data Series** from the shortcut menu. Click **Series Options** at the left of the dialog box.

4. In the **Plot Series On** area of the dialog box, select **Secondary axis**. Click **Close**. Now the orange and blue columns have become taller, and a new scale has been added on the right, as shown in Figure 6-13. In the following exercises you will improve the appearance of this chart.

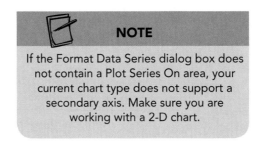

NOTE

If the Format Data Series dialog box does not contain a Plot Series On area, your current chart type does not support a secondary axis. Make sure you are working with a 2-D chart.

Figure 6-13
Adding a secondary axis

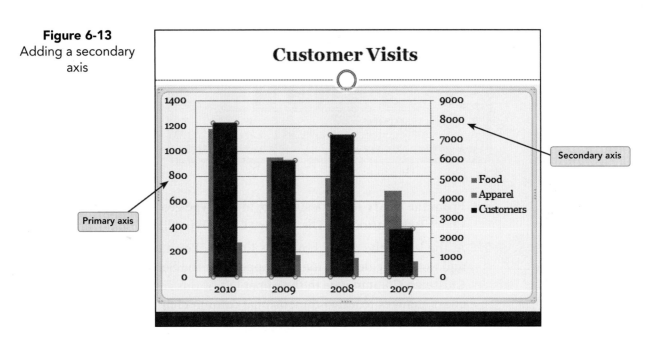

Exercise 6-12 COMBINE CHART TYPES

A good way to distinguish between different data types on a single chart is to assign different chart types. For example, with the current chart, the "Customers" data series can be shown as a line or an area, while the sales data can remain as columns, as shown in Figure 6-14.

1. On slide 3 select the "Customers" data series if not already selected.

2. Right-click the data series, and choose **Change Series Chart Type** from the shortcut menu. Click the **Area** category at the left of the dialog box, and choose the **Area** chart type. Click **OK**.

Figure 6-14
Area and Column
combination chart

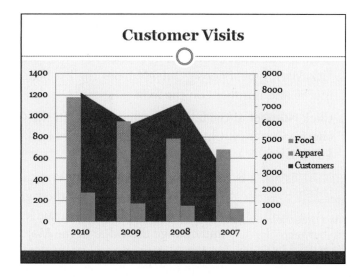

3. Click the "Customers" area to select it; then right-click, and choose Change Series Chart Type from the shortcut menu. Choose the Line category at the left of the dialog box, and click the Line chart type. Click OK.

4. Right-click the red line representing "Customers," and choose Format Data Series from the shortcut menu.

5. At the left of the dialog box, click Line Style, and change the Width to 3 points.

6. At the left of the dialog box, click Line Color, and change the Color to Red, Accent 3, Darker 50%. Click Close.

Exercise 6-13 FORMAT PRIMARY AND SECONDARY AXES

Proper formatting and labeling on a chart is always important to ensure that viewers understand the information you want to convey. This is even more important when you have both primary and secondary axis scales on the chart.

1. On slide 3, click the chart area to select it.

2. From the Chart Tools Layout tab, in the Labels group, click the Axis Titles button [icon], and choose Primary Vertical Axis Title and Rotated Title.

3. In the Vertical (Value) Axis Title text box located on the primary vertical axis, delete the text and key **Sales (thousands)**. The size of the text box will adjust automatically. Figure 6-15 indicates the position of the text on the chart.

4. From the Chart Tools Layout tab, in the Labels group, click the Axis Titles button [icon], and choose Secondary Vertical Axis Title and Rotated Title. An Vertical (Value) Axis Title text box appears beside the secondary axis scale on the left.

5. In the Vertical (Value) Axis Title text box, delete the text and key **Customer Visits (hundreds)**. Descriptive titles now appear next to both the primary and the secondary axes.

6. Right-click the Vertical (Value) Axis (the "Sales" numbers on the left), and choose Format Axis. Click Axis Options at the left of the dialog box; then, in the Major unit text box, choose Fixed, and key **500**. Under Major Tick Mark Type, choose Outside from the list box. This will insert tick marks and numbers on the axis.

7. Click Number at the left of the dialog box. In the Category list box, choose Currency. Change the Decimal places to **0**. Under symbol, choose $ English (U.S.). Click Close.

TIP

It is best to avoid using red and green in the same chart to distinguish between data sets. Some individuals have difficulty distinguishing between those two colors, so they would have difficulty comparing columns, bars, or pie slices.

8. Right-click the Secondary Vertical (Value) Axis (the "Customers" numbers on the right), and choose Format Axis. Click Axis Options at the left of the dialog box, and change the value in the Major unit text box to Fixed and **1500** to reduce some of the number labels. Click Number at the left of the dialog box. In the Category list box, choose Number. Change the Decimal places to **0**. The Use 1000 Separator should be checked. Click Close.

9. Click outside the chart area to view your changes.

10. Click the legend; then right-click, and choose Format Legend. For the Legend Position choose Top. Click Close. Now the chart appears more balanced, with the scales evenly spaced on each side.

Figure 6-15
Completed combination chart

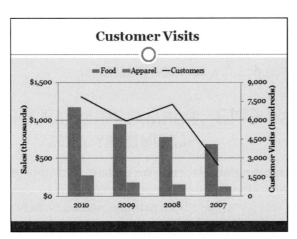

11. Create a slide footer for only slide 3 that includes the date, your name, and *[your initials]*6-13. Save the presentation as *[your initials]*6-13 in your Lesson 6 folder.

Working with Pie Charts

A *pie chart* is a simple, yet highly effective, presentation tool that shows individual values in relation to the sum of all the values—a pie chart makes it easy to judge "parts of a whole." Each value is displayed as a slice of the pie.

A pie chart can show only one data series. To show more than one data series, use more than one pie chart.

Exercise 6-14   CREATE A PIE CHART

In this exercise, you create a pie chart to display the breakdown of the restaurant's sales by category.

    If your worksheet contains more than one data series, a pie chart uses the first column of numbers. You can change to a different row or column if you like.

1. Insert a new slide after slide 3 that uses the Title Only layout. This layout provides a white background.

2. Key the title **2010 Sales Categories**.

3. From the Insert tab, in the Illustrations group, click the Chart button.

Figure 6-16
Worksheet for pie chart

	A	B
1		2010 Sales
2	Food	3339
3	Beverage	2933
4	Apparel	1529
5	Other	906

4. Click the Pie category, and choose the first chart type that appears in the pie chart category: Pie. Click OK. Excel opens and displays a sample worksheet, and in PowerPoint you will see a sample pie chart reflecting that data.

5. Replace the sample data with the data shown in Figure 6-16.

6. Close the Excel worksheet, and leave the presentation open for the next exercise.

Exercise 6-15   ADD PIE SLICE LABELS

You can add labels to the chart's data series and edit those labels individually. Labels help identify the categories being charted more easily than legends or datasheets.

1. Click one of the pie slices to select the Chart Series data.

2. From the Chart Tools Layout tab, in the Labels group, click the Data Labels button, and click More Data Label Options.

3. Click Label Options at the left of the dialog box, and make several changes under the Label Contains heading:

   a. Select both Category Name and Percentage.

   b. Deselect Value and Show Leader Lines.

   c. Click Close.

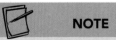

NOTE

Depending on the pie chart, sometimes parts of the data labels might be hidden by the edges of the chart placeholder. In this case, you need to resize the pie by using the plot area sizing handles.

4. Data labels now appear on the pie slices. With the addition of the data labels, the pie is now smaller; however, the legend is no longer needed since the slices are each labeled, as shown in Figure 6-17.

5. Because the slide title identifies what the pie contains, the pie chart title for 2010 sales can be removed. Select this text box, and press Delete. The pie will expand to fill the available space.

6. Right-click the legend box, and choose Delete from the shortcut menu. The pie chart becomes a little larger.

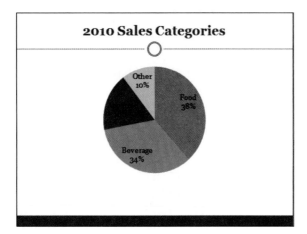

7. Click any data label. All the data labels are selected. Right-click one of the labels, and use the floating font group to change the font to Arial, 16 points, bold, and italic. Click outside the pie to turn off this selection.

8. Click the data label "Other 10%" twice to select just that label. As with columns, click once to select all labels, and click again to select just one. You can now edit the selected label's text.

9. Click within the text to display an insertion point. Delete the word "Other" (but not "10%"), and key in its place **Take-out**.

10. Click the "Take-out 10%" label two times to select just that label. Right-click, and choose Format Data Label. Under the Label Position heading, choose Inside End. Click Close. Now the label is positioned on the slice. This will ensure that the new label stays on the pie.

Exercise 6-16   APPLY 3-D ROTATION

You can enhance the appearance of your pie chart with additional effects, such as changing to a 3-D appearance and rotating the angle of the pie or *exploding* a slice (dragging it out from the center of the pie) for emphasis.

1. Click to select the chart. From the Chart Tools Design tab, in the Type group, click the Change Chart Type button ▥, and select Pie in 3-D. The pie now has a perspective treatment. Click OK.

2. From the Chart Tools Layout tab, in the Background group, click the 3-D Rotation button ▣. At the bottom of the Format Chart Area dialog box, click Default Rotation, and the pie becomes more dimensional but almost flat.

3. In the Perspective box, key **0.1°**.

4. Under the Rotation heading, change the X degree to **35°** to move the "Take-out 10%" slice to the right. Click Close.

5. Click the center of the pie once to select all the slices. Notice that each slice has selection handles where the slices join.

6. Click the "Food 38%" slice so that you have handles on that slice only (be careful not to select the label), and drag it slightly away from the center of the pie. This is called *exploding a slice,* as shown in Figure 6-18.

Figure 6-18
Pie chart with 3-D rotation and exploded slice

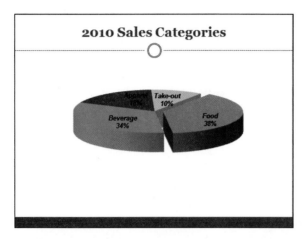

7. In Normal view, select the chart area, and use the corner sizing handles to make the pie chart larger to fill the slide.

8. Create a slide footer for slide 4 that includes the date, your name, and *[your initials]***6-16**.

9. Save the presentation as *[your initials]***6-16** in your Lesson 6 folder. Keep the presentation open for the next exercise.

Enhancing Chart Elements

You can add many interesting effects to charts. In addition to changing colors, you can add shapes or pictures that help you make a particular point or highlight one aspect of the data. You can also annotate your charts with text to clarify or call attention to important concepts.

Exercise 6-17   ADD SHAPES FOR EMPHASIS

Shapes can be combined with text or layered to emphasize the point you need to make. For this exercise, you will combine an arrow and text.

1. Move to slide 5, titled "T-Shirts by Region."

2. Because this chart reflects only one data series, the legend at the side is not needed. Select the legend, and press [Delete].

3. Because the slide title identifies the content of this chart, the chart title is redundant; therefore, select the chart title, and press [Delete].

4. From the Insert tab, in the Text group, click the Text Box button , and click and drag above the Miami column to create a space to enter text. Change the font color to White, Background 1, and key **L.A. may top Miami in 2011**.

5. Select the text inside the text box, right-click, and use the floating font group to change the text to Arial, bold, italic.

6. From the Insert tab, in the Illustrations group, click the Shapes button ; then, from the Block Arrow category, click the Left Arrow shape. Draw an arrow above the Los Angeles chart shape. Change the shape fill color to Gold, Accent 4, and remove the shape outline. Reposition and resize the arrow and text box as shown in Figure 6-19.

TIP

You may want to use Zoom to enlarge the slide so that you can more easily use the arrow's rotation handle.

Figure 6-19
Chart with arrow and text box

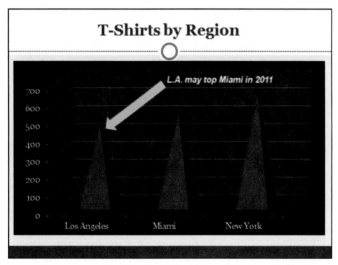

7. Create a slide footer for slide 5 that includes the date, your name, and *[your initials]*6-17.

8. Save the presentation as *[your initials]*6-17 in your Lesson 6 folder.

Exercise 6-18   CHANGE COLORS IN CHART AREAS

You can change the colors of individual chart areas, columns, or an entire data series. Shape fill effects, including textures and gradient fills, can be used the same way you use them for other PowerPoint shapes. You can also change the outline style of columns, bars, and other chart elements.

1. Move to slide 2, and point to one of the darkest blue columns, the 2011 series. Notice the ScreenTip that appears, identifying the data series.

2. Click any light-blue column, the 2013 series. All the light-blue columns are selected, as indicated by the box that is displayed around each selected column.

3. Click the light-blue column for Los Angeles. Now the Los Angeles column is the only one selected. Clicking once selects all the columns in a series; clicking a second time (not double-clicking) changes the selection to just one column.

4. Click one of the darkest blue columns to select all of the 2011 series.

5. From the Chart Tools Format tab, in the Shape Styles group, click the Shape Fill button . Choose Blue, Accent 2, Darker 50%.

> **TIP**
>
> You can change colors and fills on each part of the chart. Be sure to select the element that you would like to change before beginning to change colors or gradients or add a picture.

6. Click the darker blue column for Los Angeles, and then change the fill color to Orange, Accent 1. The Los Angeles column is now a different color from that of the other columns in its series. Click the Undo button 🔙 to return the column to the darker blue to match the other columns in the series.

7. Select the columns that contain the light-blue fill color, the 2013 series. Click the Shape Fill button, and choose the blue color Ice Blue, Accent 5. Click the Shape Fill button 🪣 again, and choose Gradient. Under the Light Variations category, select Linear Up so that the lightest color is at the top of the column.

Exercise 6-19   ADD A PICTURE FILL BEHIND A CHART

A picture can help communicate the meaning of the chart by illustrating the data in some way. For instance, if you are discussing T-shirts as in this exercise, it is appropriate to have a shirt picture in the chart background.

1. Move to slide 5. Change the font color of the text on both axes and in the text box font to Black, Text 1 to make it easier to read once a picture has been added.

2. From the Chart Tools Layout tab, in the Current Selection group, choose Chart Area from the Chart Elements drop-down list. Click the Format Selection button 🪣.

3. At the left of the dialog box, click Fill then choose Picture or texture fill. For Insert from:, click File.

4. Navigate to your student files, and click the file **t-shirt**. Click Insert. Click Close. The picture fills the background of your chart. You need to recolor other parts of the chart so that the T-shirt is visible in the background, as shown in Figure 6-20.

5. Click the dark area behind the chart shapes, the back and side walls. Right-click, and choose Format Walls. Choose No Fill, and click Close.

6. Right-click the Vertical (Value) Axis numbers, and change the font to Arial, Bold.

7. Right-click the Horizontal (Category) Axis numbers, and change the font to Arial, Bold.

8. Adjust the position of the text box or arrow if necessary.

9. Update the slide footer for slide 5 to include the text *[your initials]6-19*.

Figure 6-20
Chart with picture
background

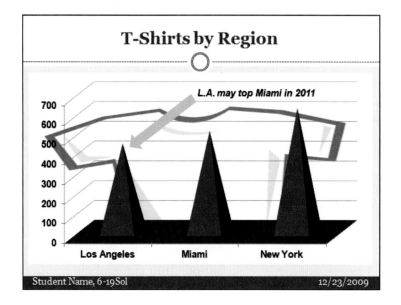

10. View the presentation as a slide show, starting with slide 1.

11. Create a handout header and footer: Include the date, your name as the header, the page number, and *[your initials]6-19* as the footer.

12. Move to slide 1, and save the presentation as *[your initials]6-19* in your Lesson 6 folder.

13. Close the presentation and submit your work.

Lesson 6   Summary

- Charts are diagrams that visually represent numeric information. Charts illustrate quantitative relationships and can help people understand the significance of numeric information more easily than viewing the same information as a list of numbers.

- When you start a new chart, a sample worksheet appears in Excel. On the worksheet, you key the numbers and labels that will be used to create a chart.

- The worksheet contains rows and columns. You key each number or label in a separate *cell*—the rectangle formed by the intersection of a row and a column.

- On the worksheet, key labels in the first row and column.

- A data series is a group of data that relate to a common object or category. Often, more than one data series is displayed on a single chart.

- Use the Switch Row/Column button to change how a data series is displayed on a chart.
- A wide variety of chart types are available, including column, bar, area, line, pie, and surface, with many different chart format options.
- Several content layouts are suitable for charts. Two Content layouts make it easy to combine a chart and body text on the same slide.
- Use the Chart Elements drop-down list to select specific parts of a chart, or use ScreenTips to identify parts as you point to them.
- Special fill and border effects, including textures and gradient fills, can be used in charts the same way you use them for other PowerPoint objects.
- Use the Format Axis dialog box to modify the units, font, and number format of the value axis or secondary value axis. Modify the unit settings to specify the range of numbers displayed and increments between numbers.
- Axis titles are an important part of charts. Careful labeling ensures that your charts will be interpreted correctly.
- A legend is a box showing the colors assigned to each data series. Customize a chart's legend by changing the border, background colors, and font attributes.
- Use a secondary axis when you need to plot two dissimilar types of data on the same chart. A secondary axis is available only for a 2-D chart type.
- Proper formatting and labeling on a chart is important when your chart has both a primary and a secondary axis.
- A good way to distinguish between different data types on a single chart is to assign different chart types. For example, use columns for one type of data and lines for the other type.
- A pie chart shows individual values in relation to the sum of all the values. Each value is displayed as a slice of the pie.
- A pie chart can show only one data series. To show more than one data series, use more than one pie chart.
- The plot area of a chart is the area containing the actual columns, bars, or pie slices. It can be formatted with or without a border and a fill effect.
- Exploding a pie slice (dragging it out from the center of the pie) emphasizes the slice.
- Use the Insert tab to add shapes and text boxes. Use text boxes wherever needed to annotate your chart to clarify its meaning.
- Charts can be enhanced by adding pictures, colors, and 3-D effects.

LESSON 6		Command Summary	
Feature	**Button**	**Ribbon**	**Keyboard**
Add a secondary axis		Chart Tools Format, Current Selection group, Format Selection (with data series selected)	
Add data labels		Chart Tools Layout, Labels group, Data Labels	
Add/remove gridlines		Chart Tools Layout, Axes group, Gridlines	
Apply different chart layouts		Chart Tools Design, Chart Layouts group, More	
Change chart style		Chart Tools Design, Chart Styles group, More	
Change chart type		Chart Tools Design, Type group, Change Chart Type	
Display worksheet		Chart Tools Design, Data group, Edit Data	
Format a chart object		Chart Tools Format, Current Selection group, Format Selection	Ctrl + 1
Insert a chart		Insert, Illustrations group, Chart	
Insert axis titles		Chart Tools Layout, Labels group, Axis Titles	
Insert or remove a legend		Chart Tools Layout, Labels group, Legend	
Switch data series between columns and rows		Chart Tools Design, Data group, Switch Row/Column	

Concepts Review

True/False Questions

Each of the following statements is either true or false. Indicate your choice by circling T or F.

T   F   1.   PowerPoint offers only one slide layout choice for slides with charts.

T   F   2.   The sample worksheet in Excel is always blank when you create a new chart.

T   F   3.   You cannot see the chart while you are working on the worksheet.

T   F   4.   You can change the colors and patterns of columns in a chart to whatever you find appealing.

T   F   5.   The units shown on the value axis are set by PowerPoint and cannot be changed.

T   F   6.   Every chart must include a legend.

T   F   7.   You must use a two-dimensional chart if you want to include a secondary axis.

T   F   8.   Double-clicking a pie slice or column enables you to change its size.

Short Answer Questions

Write the correct answer in the space provided.

1.   How can you delete all the sample data in the worksheet at one time?

_____

2.   How do you change the grouping of the data series on a chart from columns to rows?

_____

3.   While working on a chart, how do you display the worksheet if it is not visible?

_____

4.   What type of number formatting do you apply to values to display dollar signs?

_____

5.   What group found on the Chart Tools Format tab can you use to select different parts of a chart?

_____

6.   Which button can you click to change the color of a selected pie slice?

_____

7.   How can you change the font size for chart labels without opening a dialog box or using the Ribbon?

_____

8.   On a 2-D column chart, how can you change one of the data series so that it is displayed as an area chart?

_____

Critical Thinking

Answer these questions on a separate page. Support your answers with examples from your own experience, if possible.

1.   How do you decide whether a chart is needed in your presentation? Do you think a presentation can have too many charts? Explain your answers.

2.   Imagine that you are trying to explain to someone how you spend your waking hours during a typical day. Can you think of a chart that would break down your activities into different categories and show how much time you spend on each during the day? Describe the chart's appearance and the values that you would include.

Skills Review

Exercise 6-20

Create a new presentation that includes a simple column chart.

1.   Open the file **FinSummary**.

2.   Create a chart by following these steps:
     a. Insert a new slide after slide 2 that uses the Title and Content layout.
     b. Key **2010 Quarterly Earnings** for the title.
     c. Click the Chart button in the center of the content placeholder.
     d. Choose a 3-D Clustered Column chart, and click OK.
     e. Replace the sample data with the data shown in Figure 6-21.

3.   Click in any cell of row 5 that was used in the sample worksheet. Right-click, and then choose Delete from the shortcut menu. Choose Entire Row; then click OK. This step removes the unused row and the empty space from the chart.

Figure 6-21
Worksheet

◢	A	B	C	D	E
1		Q1	Q2	Q3	Q4
2	New York	1888	2008	2116	1543
3	Los Angeles	1743	1799	1844	1539
4	Miami	1634	1439	1783	1469

4. Close Excel.

5. Edit the chart by following these steps:

    a. Be sure the chart is selected; then, from the Chart Tools Design tab, in the Data Group, click Edit Data 🗎.

    b. Click cell E3 (Q4 for Los Angeles) to select it.

    c. Key **1849** to replace the value "1539." Press ⏎Enter.

    d. Still working on the Chart Tools Design tab, in the Data group, click the Switch Row/Column button 🗎.

    e. Close Excel.

6. Create a handout header and footer: Include the date, your name as the header, the page number, and *[your initials]*6-20 as the footer.

7. Move to slide 1, and save the presentation as *[your initials]*6-20 in your Lesson 6 folder. View the presentation.

8. Close the presentation and submit your work.

Exercise 6-21

Edit and format an existing chart, change chart style, and format the legend.

1. Open the file **Finance2**.

2. Edit the chart on slide 4 by following these steps:

    a. Click the chart to activate it.

    b. From the Chart Tools Design tab, in the Data group, click the Edit Data button 🗎 to open Excel.

    c. On the worksheet, click cell B2 containing the value "−2%," and key **2** to overwrite the negative value with a positive value. Press ⏎Enter.

    d. Close Microsoft Excel.

3. Change the style of the chart by following these steps:

    a. From the Chart Tools Design tab, in the Chart Styles Group, click the More button ⏷.

    b. Choose Style 25.

4. Change the font for the Horizontal (Category) Axis label by following these steps:

    a. Click the category axis label "2010" to select the category axis.

    b. Right-click the axis, and make the following changes from the floating font group: Choose Tahoma font, 20 points font size, and Brown, Background 2 font color.

5.   Format the Vertical (Value) Axis by following these steps:

   a. Right-click a number on the value axis, and choose Format Axis.

   b. For Major unit choose Fixed, and key .05. Click Close.

   c. Right-click the axis, and make the following changes from the floating font group: Choose Tahoma font, 20 points font size, and Brown, Background 2 font color.

6.   Format the legend by following these steps:

   a. Right-click the legend, and choose Format Legend from the shortcut menu.

   b. Under the Legend Position heading, choose Top Right, and click Close.

   c. Use the floating font group to change the legend font to the Tahoma font and a font size of 16 points.

7.   Create a handout header and footer: Include the date, your name as the header, the page number, and *[your initials]*6-21 as the footer.

8.   Move to slide 1, and save the presentation as *[your initials]*6-21 in your Lesson 6 folder.

9.   Close the presentation and submit your work.

Exercise 6-22

Add a chart, format chart axes, add a secondary axis, and combine chart types.

1.   Open the file **Finance3**.

2.   Add a slide after slide 3 with the Title and Content layout.

3.   Key the title **2010 Special Events Revenue**.

4.   Click the Chart button 📊. In the Column category, choose the Clustered Column chart. Replace the sample data with the information in Figure 6-22.

5.   Once the data are keyed, click the row 4 heading and drag down to select both rows 4 and 5. Right-click, and choose Delete.

Figure 6-22
Worksheet

	A	B	C	D	E
1		1st Quarter	2nd Quarter	3rd Quarter	4th Quarter
2	Special Events	71	141	118	149
3	Total Revenue	800	1076	1149	1207

6.   From the Chart Tools Design tab, in the Data group, click the Switch Row/Column button 📋.

7.   Close Microsoft Excel.

TIP

You started with a 2-D chart in this exercise since a 2-D chart is required to add a secondary axis.

8. Add a secondary axis to the chart by following these steps:

   a. Right-click one of the "Total Revenue" columns, and choose Format Data Series from the shortcut menu.

   b. In the Plot Series On area, click Secondary axis. Click Close.

9. Change the chart type for the "Total Revenue" columns by following these steps:

   a. Be sure the columns in this data series are still selected.

   b. From the Chart Tools Design tab, in the Type group, click the Change Chart Type button .

   c. In the Line category, choose the Line chart.

   d. Click OK.

10. Change the formatting of the line for the data series by following these steps:

   a. Select the line (being careful not to select the gridlines); then right-click, and choose Format Data Series from the shortcut menu.

   b. Click Line Style at the left of the dialog box, and change the Width to **8 points**.

   c. Click Marker Options at the left of the dialog box. Change the Marker Type to Built-In, choose the Diamond, and change the size to **15**.

   d. Click Marker Fill at the left of the dialog box. Change to a Solid Fill, and then make the color Tan, Text 2. Click Close.

11. Format the secondary value axis by following these steps:

   a. Right-click one of the numbers on the right side of the chart—on the Secondary Vertical (Value) Axis—and choose Format Axis.

   b. Change the Major unit to Fixed, and key **500**.

   c. Click Number at the left of the dialog box, and choose Currency. For Decimal places key **0**, and for Symbol choose $ English (United States). Click Close.

   d. Right-click the secondary axis again, and use the floating font group to change the font to Arial.

12. Apply the following formatting to the Vertical (Value) Axis (on the left side of the chart) using the same process as that for the secondary axis.

   a. Right-click the Vertical (Value) Axis, and choose Format Axis.

   b. Change the Maximum to **250** and the Major unit to Fixed and **50**.

   c. Click Number at the left of the dialog box, and choose Currency. For Decimal places key **0**, and for Symbol choose $ English (United States). Click Close.

   d. Change the font to Arial using the floating font group.

13. Change the formatting of the Horizontal (Category) Axis. Right-click the category axis, and change the font to Arial using the floating font group.

14. Add chart titles and a legend by following these steps:

   a. Click to activate the chart.

   b. From the Chart Tools Layout tab, in the Labels group, click the Axis Titles button 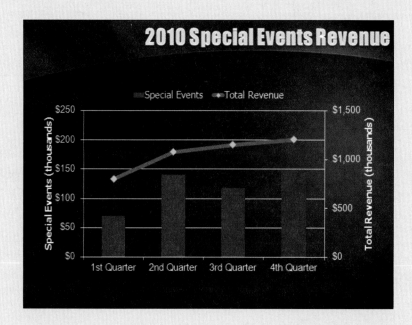.

   c. Choose Primary Vertical Axis Title and Rotated Title.

   d. Select the text that appears in the text box; delete it, and key **Special Events (thousands)**.

   e. Still working on the Chart Tools Layout tab, in the Labels group, click the Axis Titles button.

   f. Choose Secondary Vertical Axis Title and Rotated Title.

   g. Select the text that appears in the text box; delete it, and key **Total Revenue (thousands)**.

15. Right-click the legend, choose Format Legend from the shortcut menu, and change the legend position to Top. Click Close.

16. Check to be sure your elements and positioning match Figure 6-23.

Figure 6-23
Completed chart

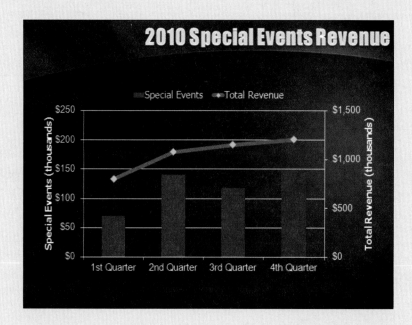

17. Create a handout header and footer: Include the date, your name as the header, the page number, and *[your initials]*6-22 as the footer.

18. Move to slide 1, and save the presentation as *[your initials]*6-22 in your Lesson 6 folder.

19. Close the presentation and submit your work.

Exercise 6-23

Create and format a pie chart; add shapes, text boxes, and color.

1. Open the file **Apparel**.

2. Insert a new slide after slide 2 that uses the Title and Content layout. Key the title **Apparel Mix—2010**.

3. Create a pie chart by following these steps:

   a. Click the Chart button in the center of the content placeholder.

   b. Click the Pie category, and choose the Pie in 3-D chart type. Click OK.

   c. On the worksheet, replace the sample information with the information shown in Figure 6-24.

4. Close Excel.

5. Format a pie slice by following these steps:

   a. Click the dark-blue pie slice (Bike Jerseys) once to select the entire pie.

   b. Click the dark-blue slice again to select the individual slice.

   c. From the Chart Tools Format tab, in the Shape Styles group, click the Shape Fill button, and choose Light Blue from the Standard Colors category. This sets the color apart from the other blues.

   d. Click these slices and change to the following standard colors: "T-Shirts," light green; "Visors," yellow; "Knee Pads," red; and "Elbow Pads," purple.

6. Right-click the pie's legend, and choose Delete from the shortcut menu.

7. Delete the chart title.

8. Add data labels by following these steps:

   a. Activate the chart.

   b. From the Chart Tools Layout tab, in the Labels group, click the Data Labels button, and choose More Data Label Options.

   c. In the Label Contains area, select the Category Name and the Percentage check boxes, and deselect the Value check box.

   d. In the Label Position area, choose Best Fit.

   e. Click Close.

9. Resize the chart to fill the available white space.

10. Explode a pie slice by following these steps:

    a. Select the red "Knee Pads" slice by clicking it twice.

    b. Drag the slice slightly away from the center of the pie.

    c. Center the chart area horizontally on the slide and enlarge it to fill the available space.

    d. Adjust label positions on or beside pie slices for easy reading.

TIP

To use an em dash (the long straight line in the title), key two hyphens with no space around them. Then space once after "2010" and the two hyphens will change to an em dash, a more contemporary punctuation mark. This adjustment is controlled with PowerPoint's AutoCorrect feature.

Figure 6-24
Worksheet

	A	B
1		Unit Sales
2	T-Shirts	4208
3	Bike Jerseys	1112
4	Visors	528
5	Knee Pads	663
6	Elbow Pads	967

11. Insert a text box and an arrow by following these steps:

    a. From the Insert tab, in the Text group, click the Text Box button 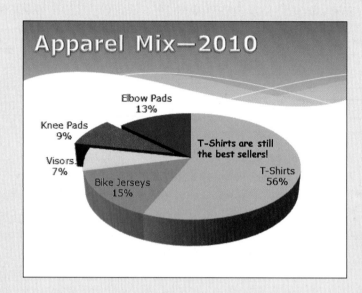.

    b. Click outside the chart area; draw the text box, and key **T-Shirts are still the best sellers!**

    c. Move the text box on top of the large, light-green T-Shirts pie slice. Change the text box font to Comic Sans MS and bold. Resize the box so that the text fits on two lines, as shown in Figure 6-25.

Figure 6-25
Exploded slice and text box

12. Create a handout header and footer: Include the date, your name as the header, the page number, and *[your initials]***6-23** as the footer.

13. Move to slide 1, and save the presentation as *[your initials]***6-23** in your Lesson 6 folder.

14. Close the presentation and submit your work.

Lesson Applications

Exercise 6-24

Create a presentation containing a column chart, and format the chart.

1. Start a new presentation using the Median design template and the Aspect theme color.

2. Using the text in Figure 6-26, create a three-slide presentation; use the Title Slide layout for slide 1 and the Title and Content layout for slides 2 and 3. The first line of each is the title for the slide.

Figure 6-26

Slide 1 Three Years of Phenomenal Sales

Slide 2 Highlights
- New York revenue still increasing
- Miami and Los Angeles meeting goals
- Revenues reach 120% of budget

Slide 3 Sales by Region—2008 to 2010

3. Right-align the title on slide 1.

4. On slide 3, create a 3-D Clustered Column chart by using the data shown in Figure 6-27. Delete row 5.

Figure 6-27
Worksheet

	A	B	C	D
1		New York	Los Angeles	Miami
2	2008	5650	4183	3843
3	2009	8753	5892	6388
4	2010	11332	9852	8487

5. Close Excel.

6. Change the Vertical (Value) Axis options to have a Maximum of **12,000** and a Major unit of **3,000**. Change its Number formatting to Currency, $ English (U.S.) with no decimals.

7. Change to Chart Style 3.

8. For the value and category axes and legend, change the font to 16 points, not bold.

9. Move the legend to the bottom.

10. Resize and reposition the chart to keep the spacing on both sides even.

11. Create a handout header and footer: Include the date, your name as the header, the page number, and *[your initials]*6-24 as the footer.

12. Move to slide 1, and save the presentation as *[your initials]*6-24 in your Lesson 6 folder.

13. Close the presentation and submit your work.

Exercise 6-25

Create and format a pie chart.

1. Open the file **Expense**.

Figure 6-28
Worksheet

◢	A	B
1		2010 Expenses
2	Food	2190
3	Payroll	1813
4	Depreciation	577
5	Lease	1737

2. Insert a new slide after slide 1 that uses the Title and Content layout. Key the title **Expense Breakdown**.

3. Create a 2-D pie chart on the new slide 2 by using the data from Figure 6-28.

4. Add Percentage data labels only to the chart. Change the font size to 32 points.

5. Increase the legend font to 20 points, bold.

6. Change the chart title size to 28 points, and move the title to the top left of the chart area.

7. Change the chart to a Pie in 3-D.

8. Explode the "Food" slice of the pie slightly.

9. If any of the percentage labels move off the slices, then right-click, choose Format Data Label, and choose the Label Position Inside End or click and drag the labels onto the slices of the pie.

10. Create a handout header and footer: Include the date, your name as the header, the page number, and *[your initials]*6-25 as the footer.

11. Move to slide 1, and save the presentation as *[your initials]*6-25 in your Lesson 6 folder.

12. Close the presentation and submit your work.

Exercise 6-26

Insert a chart; change the chart to a combination chart; format the chart text, data series, and legend; add a secondary axis; and add a shape.

1. Open the file **Earnings**, and apply the Oriel design template using the Concourse theme color.

2. Insert a new slide between slides 2 and 3 that uses the Title and Content layout. Key the title **Gross Income**.

3. Create a clustered column chart (2-D) on the new slide by using the data in Figure 6-29.

Figure 6-29
Worksheet

◢	A	B	C	D
1		2008	2009	2010
2	San Francisco	1246	2033	5432
3	Miami	2734	4630	6325
4	Los Angeles	2871	4126	7235
5	New York	3566	5135	7555
6	Year Total	10417	15924	26547

4. Switch Row/Column.

5. Close Excel.

6. Plot the "Year Total" data series on a secondary axis. Change the chart type for the series to **Line Chart**. Format the line in a matching color, and change the width to **10**.

7. Change the font for the Vertical (Value) Axis, Horizontal (Category) Axis, Secondary Vertical (Value) Axis, and Legend to 16-point Arial (not bold).

8. For the Vertical (Value) Axis (on the left), change the units to minimum **0** and maximum **8,000**, displayed fixed at major units of **2,000**, and change the number formatting to **Currency** with no decimal places.

9. Format the Secondary Vertical (Value) Axis (on the right) with the units to minimum **0** and maximum **30,000**, displayed fixed at major units of **5,000**, and change the number formatting to **Currency** with no decimal places.

10. Move the legend to the bottom of the chart.

11. Expand the width and height of the chart area to fill the open space.

12. Apply a **Blue, Accent 4, Lighter 80%** fill to the legend area to distinguish it from the slide background.

13. Apply a gradient fill to the columns in each data series. After the first data series has been changed, you will need to choose the fill color for each series selected and then apply the gradient coloring. Choose **Linear Up** in the Dark Variations category so that the lightest color is on top.

14. Click outside the chart area to deselect the chart.

15. Now work in the area at the top of the chart to create the following graphic elements, and then move them into position when complete. Use Zoom to increase the size of the slide so that you can work better in detail.

    a. Create a text box centered above the chart. Key **Impressive!** in the text box. Change the font to 24-point Arial.

    b. Draw a small **5-Point Star** with a yellow fill and red outline.

    c. Place the star on the top of the New York column for the year 2007.

    d. Place the text box above the columns near the star, as shown in Figure 6-30.

Figure 6-30
Completed chart

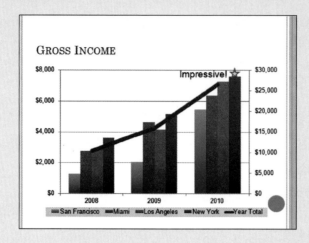

16. Create a handout header and footer: Include the date, your name as the header, the page number, and *[your initials]*6-26 as the footer.

17. Move to slide 1, and save the presentation as *[your initials]*6-26.

18. Close the presentation and submit your work.

Exercise 6-27 ◆ Challenge Yourself

Insert a chart; change the chart style; apply gridlines; format the chart text, data series, and legend; add a picture fill; and add a shape.

1. Open the file **Suppliers**.

2. On slide 1, key your name as the subtitle.

3. Insert a new slide after slide 2 that uses the Title and Content layout. For the slide title, key **Produce Cost Comparison**.

4. Create a 3-D Clustered Column chart on the new slide by using the data in Figure 6-31.

Figure 6-31
Worksheet

◢	A	B	C	D
1		Frankie's Food	Distributing by Dano	Patty's Produce
2	Apples (20 lb)	10.99	11.84	9.85
3	Lettuce (24 ct)	27.45	29.75	25.29
4	Cucumbers (bushel)	19.8	20.25	19.45
5	Tomatoes (case)	9.55	10.85	9.12

5. Change the chart style to Style 7.

6. Change the Floor color to the Orange, Background 1 theme color.

7. Select the legend, and change to a Top position.

8. Deselect the chart. Draw a rectangle shape over "Patty's Produce" in the legend area; then change the fill color to No Fill and the outline to Orange, Background 1.

9. Add a text box on the right, and key **Lowest Costs**. Change the fill color to Orange, Background 1 and the text color to Dark Red, Accent 6.

10. Add an arrow from the text box pointing to "Patty's Produce." Change the fill color and the outline color to Orange, Background 1, as shown in Figure 6-32.

Figure 6-32
Completed chart

11. Insert a new slide after slide 3 using the Title and Content layout. For the slide title, key **Lead Time Comparison**.

12. Insert a Line with Markers chart, and enter the data in Figure 6-33 into the chart.

13. Delete row 5 and columns C and D.

Figure 6-33
Worksheet

	A	B
1		Days from Order to Delivery
2	Frankie's Food	7
3	Distributing by Dano	10
4	Patty's Produce	4

14. Remove the legend.

15. Increase the width of the line to 8 points, and make the line Green, Accent 1. Increase the marker size to 28 points, and make the marker Orange, Background 1.

16. Reposition the chart to fit evenly on the dark area of the slide.

17. Draw a green 5-pointed star, and place it in front of the name of the supplier with the lowest lead time.

18. Change the font color of the value and category axes and the chart title to Dark Red, Accent 2.

19. Insert the picture **Apple** from your data files into the background of the chart.

20. Change the gridline color to Orange, Background 1, as shown in Figure 6-34.

Figure 6-34
Completed chart

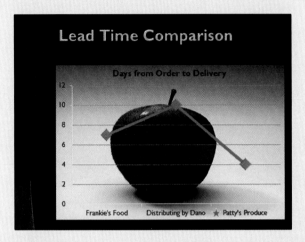

21. Create a handout header and footer: Include the date, your name as the header, the page number, and *[your initials]*6-27 as the footer.

22. Move to slide 1, and save the presentation as *[your initials]*6-27.

23. Close the presentation and submit your work.

On Your Own

In these exercises you work on your own, as you would in a real-life work environment. Use the skills you've learned to accomplish the task—and be creative.

Exercise 6-28

Obtain a list of stock quotes either online or from *The Wall Street Journal*. Create a chart listing at least five of your stock picks. Compare the prices of each stock visually through a chart. Create another chart showing the percentage change in stock value since closing the day before compared with the other stocks you have chosen. In addition, create a separate slide for each stock, giving details about the company. Format the presentation in a way that will hold a viewer's attention. Save your presentation as *[your initials]*6-28. Close the presentation and submit your work.

Exercise 6-29

Analyze your time management skills by making a list of your activities during a typical weekday, including the actual time you spend on each activity. Group your activities into no more than eight categories. Make sure the times add up to 24 hours. Add a second set of times listing the amount of time you should be spending on each activity, and add a third set of times listing the amount of time you would prefer to spend on each. Create a column or bar chart to depict these times, and then add three pie chart slides, one for each set of times (actual, should, prefer). Add a title slide and a conclusion slide. Use your creativity to make the charts interesting and fun to view—include colors, pictures, shapes, and 3-D rotation. Save the presentation as *[your initials]*6-29. Close the presentation and submit your work.

Exercise 6-30

Research information about your state of residence from the current census. Prepare slides to explain the facts that you find, using bulleted lists and charts. Find some statistics about diversity within your state, home ownership in your state compared to the national average, types of businesses, and so on, and create at least two charts to display the statistics. Add a title slide and a conclusion slide. Format your presentation attractively, save it as *[your initials]*6-30. Close the presentation and submit your work.

Lesson 7

Creating SmartArt Graphics

OBJECTIVES *After completing this lesson, you will be able to:*

1. Create SmartArt graphics.

2. Enhance SmartArt layouts.

3. Prepare an organization chart.

4. Create other diagrams with SmartArt.

5. Change SmartArt graphics.

Estimated Time: 1½ hours

Diagrams provide a very effective way to illustrate data and have been important in business communication for a long time. Diagrams show a visual representation of information that can help an audience understand a presenter's message. For example, diagrams can be used to show the steps of a process or the relationship between managers and subordinates. An audience can see the process or relationship because it is portrayed with shapes and connecting lines or layered in some way.

PowerPoint's SmartArt graphics make it easy to create diagrams and other graphical layouts with a very professional appearance. A wide range of predesigned layouts can be customized in many different ways.

The slide show in this lesson is being developed for Julie Wolfe and Gus Irvinelli, Good 4 U co-owners, for a presentation to all employees at the New York location. They are announcing a new organizational structure and their philosophy behind the changes, which emphasizes a customer focus and the need for ongoing improvements. As you help them work on this presentation, you will create a variety of SmartArt graphics.

Creating SmartArt Graphics

A *SmartArt graphic* can be inserted on your slide, and the shapes of the graphical layout it creates can be filled in with identifying text. Or if you have text in a bulleted list or in text shapes, the text items can be converted to a graphical layout. You will use both of these techniques in this lesson.

From the Insert tab, in the Illustrations group, click the SmartArt button ⊞ to display the Choose a SmartArt Graphic dialog box shown in Figure 7-1. You can display thumbnails of all possible layouts, or you can view them organized by the type of layout. On the right side of this dialog box, each layout is displayed in a larger size with a definition below to help you decide which layout best illustrates your communication needs. The white lines that you see on the sample diagram indicate where your text will appear when you label each part of the diagram.

Figure 7-1
Choose a SmartArt
Graphic dialog box

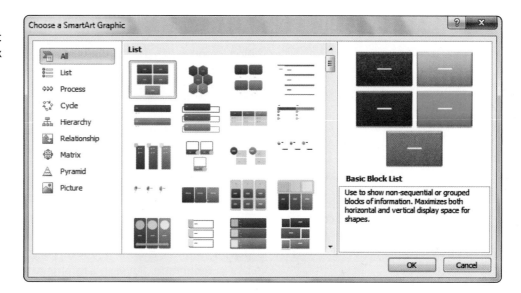

Preparing a few bulleted lists is a simple way to create a series of slides for a presentation. However, a presentation including only bulleted lists is not very appealing to an audience from a visual standpoint and may not be the best way to communicate the meaning of your message that an audience needs to understand.

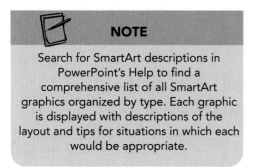

NOTE

Search for SmartArt descriptions in PowerPoint's Help to find a comprehensive list of all SmartArt graphics organized by type. Each graphic is displayed with descriptions of the layout and tips for situations in which each would be appropriate.

As you develop your presentation content, you should be considering your message from the viewpoint of the audience and not just thinking about what you need to say. To help your audience visualize the message concepts and remember them better, plan alternative ways to illustrate the concepts, such as by including pictures, charts, and shapes, to draw attention to key points. You can choose from an extensive array of SmartArt graphics. These graphics are diagrams that are arranged within eight types, as listed in Table 7-1.

TABLE 7-1 SmartArt Graphics Diagram Types

Diagram Type	Purpose
Cycle	Represents a continuous series of events such as an ongoing manufacturing or employee-review process. A cycle can be arranged in a circular pattern or with slices or gears to reflect interconnected parts. A radial cycle begins with a central part and then other parts extend from the center.
Hierarchy	Illustrates reporting relationships or lines of authority between employees in a company such as in an organization chart. These connections are sometimes called parent-child relationships. Hierarchy diagrams can be arranged vertically or horizontally such as in a decision tree used to show the outgrowth of options after choices are made.
List	Provides an alternative to listing text in bulleted lists. List diagrams can show groupings, labeled parts, and even directional concepts through the way the shapes are stacked. Several diagrams show main categories and then subtopics within those categories.
Matrix	Allows placement of concepts along two axes or in related quadrants. Emphasis can be on the whole or on individual parts.
Picture	Displays one or more pictures with a variety of other shapes to contain explanatory text or short captions.
Process	Shows a sequence of events or the progression of workflow such as in a flowchart. Process diagrams show connected parts of a process or even converging processes using a funnel technique. Several diagrams with arrows can portray conflict or opposing viewpoints.
Pyramid	Shows interconnected or proportional relationships building from one direction such as a foundational concept on which other concepts are built.
Relationship	Shows interconnected, hierarchical, proportional, or overlapping relationships. Some of these diagrams also appear in different categories too.

Exercise 7-1   USE GRAPHICAL LISTS TO SHOW GROUPS OF INFORMATION

In this exercise you will create a SmartArt graphic *list* in two different ways:

- Start with a Title and Content slide layout, click the SmartArt button 🖾, and key content using a Text pane.
- Start with an existing bulleted list, and convert it to a SmartArt graphic.

1. Open the file **Organize**. Julie and Gus started this presentation with a title slide and bulleted list on slide 2, but they have requested that you

Figure 7-2
Using the Text pane

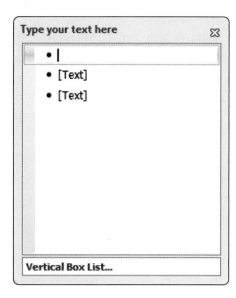

NOTE

If you added a fourth bulleted item, the shapes on the slide would become a little smaller so that four could be displayed.

update the presentation to show the bulleted information in a more visual way that better emphasizes the content.

2. Move to slide 1, and from the Home tab, in the Slides group, click the New Slide button and add a Title and Content slide. On the content placeholder, click the SmartArt button.

3. Click the List type. Click the Vertical Box List thumbnail; then click OK.

4. A Text pane appears on the left, as shown in Figure 7-2. When you key text here, it appears on shapes in the SmartArt layout.

5. For the three items in the list, key **New Procedure**, **New Philosophy**, and **New Department**. Use the arrow keys to move from bullet to bullet unless you want to add additional bullets.

6. Close the Text pane.

7. For the slide title, key **Organizational Changes**, as shown in Figure 7-3.

8. The Vertical Box List diagram works best when you have very concise information for first-level bulleted items. If you entered second-level items, they would appear in the white rectangle below each item. As you can see from the diagram, if you have three first-level items, very little space remains for second-level items.

Figure 7-3
Vertical Box List diagram

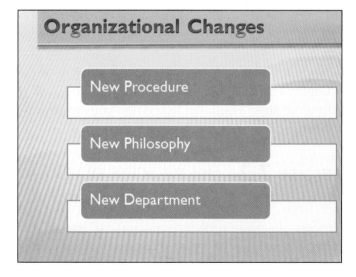

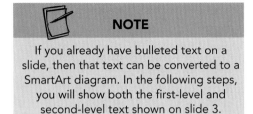

NOTE

If you already have bulleted text on a slide, then that text can be converted to a SmartArt diagram. In the following steps, you will show both the first-level and second-level text shown on slide 3.

9. In the Slides and Outline pane, click slide 3, and press Ctrl+D to duplicate the slide. Once your diagram is prepared on slide 4 and you have confirmed that all the text is appropriately displayed, you can delete slide 3 with the bulleted list. But for now, it is a good idea to leave one slide as originally prepared so that it is available for comparison.

10. Now highlight all the bulleted text on slide 4.

11. From the Home tab, in the Paragraph group, click the Convert to SmartArt button.

12. Click More SmartArt Graphics to access all the types, and choose the List type.

13. Double-click the Horizontal Bullet List thumbnail to insert it onto the slide.

14. The first-level bulleted items appear in the top rectangles, and the second-level bulleted items appear in the bottom rectangles with bullets. The color treatment is more dominant for first-level words than for second-level subpoints, as shown in Figure 7-4.

Figure 7-4
Horizontal Bullet List diagram

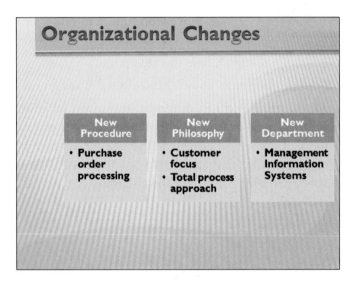

15. Confirm that the diagram on slide 4 includes all the text that is in the original slide 3 bulleted list. When you are sure that everything matches, delete slide 3.

Exercise 7-2 USE PROCESS DIAGRAMS TO SHOW SEQUENTIAL WORKFLOW STEPS

A *process diagram* reflects concepts or events that occur sequentially. Generally speaking, one part must be finished before the next part begins. Many variations for portraying these processes are available in SmartArt.

1. Move to slide 3. From the Home tab, in the Slides group, click the New Slide button.

2. On the slide 4 content area, click the SmartArt button 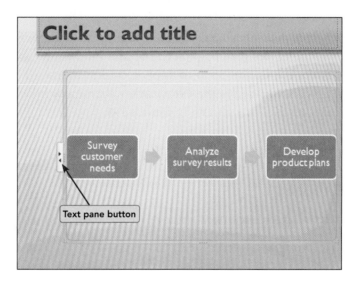; then choose the Process SmartArt type.

3. Examine the different options in this type. Double-click the Basic Process thumbnail. A three-part diagram appears, as shown in Figure 7-5. You can enter text by using the Text pane or keying directly in the diagram shapes. If the Text pane does not open automatically, click the Text pane border button on the left border to open it.

4. For this exercise, key directly in each of the shapes. As you key, the text will automatically word-wrap in the shape and become smaller to fit within that shape. Therefore, when using this method, be careful to keep wording very concise.

5. Click in the first rectangle shape, and key **Survey customer needs**.

6. Click in the second rectangle shape, and key **Analyze survey results**.

7. Click in the third rectangle shape, and key **Develop product plans**.

Figure 7-5
Basic Process
diagram

8. Because you need to include a fourth step in this process, you need to increase the size of the SmartArt area. Point to the top left corner of the SmartArt border, and drag it close to the left edge of the slide.

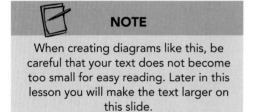

NOTE

When creating diagrams like this, be careful that your text does not become too small for easy reading. Later in this lesson you will make the text larger on this slide.

9. Select the third shape in the diagram; then click the Text pane button to open the Text pane. The third shape is the third bulleted item that is highlighted.

10. Click at the end of the word "plans" in the text pane, and press [Enter]. Key **Introduce new products**. A fourth shape is added, and the text size is automatically adjusted again.

11. Close the Text pane.

12. For the slide title, key the text **New Development Process**.

Exercise 7-3   USE CYCLE DIAGRAMS TO SHOW A CONTINUING SEQUENCE

A *cycle diagram* is used to communicate a continuing process. In this exercise you will use the same information as you did for slide 4 but will display it in a cycle. Instead of creating the diagram first, however, you will enter text using a bulleted list and then convert the list into a SmartArt graphic.

1. Insert a new slide with the Title and Content layout after slide 4. Key the title **New Development Cycle**.

2. In the content placeholder key four bulleted items:

    Survey customer needs
    Analyze survey results
    Develop product plan
    Introduce new products

3. Select the listed text, and right-click. From the shortcut menu, choose Convert to SmartArt; then click Basic Cycle.

4. Select the four shapes. From the SmartArt Tools Format tab, in the Shape Styles group, click the Shape Fill button 🔲, and choose Orange, Accent 1, Darker 25% to apply a darker theme fill color. Select the four arrows, and apply the even darker theme color Orange, Accent 1, Darker 50%, as shown in Figure 7-6.

Figure 7-6
Completed cycle diagram

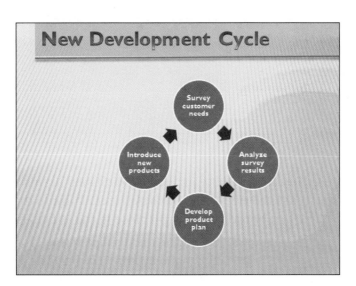

5. Create a handout header and footer: Include the date, your name as the header, the page number, and *[your initials]*7-3 as the footer.

6. Create a new folder for Lesson 7. Save the presentation as *[your initials]*7-3 in your new Lesson 7 folder.

Enhancing SmartArt Layouts

Once a SmartArt graphic is inserted on your slide, its appearance can be altered using the effects that you have learned to apply to shapes. However, additional options exist for customizing SmartArt layouts.

Exercise 7-4 APPLY SHAPE QUICK STYLES

One of the quickest ways to change the appearance of shapes within a diagram is to apply *Quick Styles*. These styles include more than one preset adjustment.

1. On slide 2, select the three rectangle shapes that contain text content.
2. From the Home tab, in the Drawing group, click the Quick Styles button 🔲 to see a gallery of styles in theme colors, as shown in Figure 7-7.

Figure 7-7
Shape Quick Styles

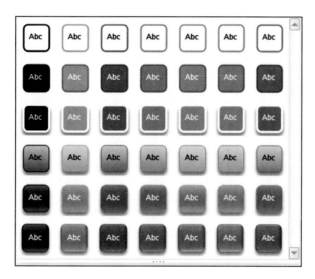

3. As you move your pointer horizontally, you will see different colors applied to the selected shapes. As you move your pointer vertically, you will see different effects such as outlines, beveling, and shadows.
4. To use a darker color and apply a shadow effect to the shapes, click Light 1 Outline, Colored Fill – Brown, Accent 2 (third row, third column).

Exercise 7-5 ADJUST 3-D FORMAT AND ROTATION

In the previous exercises, the shapes have a *2-D* orientation—you see the shapes in dimensions of height (up/down measurement) and width (left/right measurement). Three-dimensional (*3-D*) settings add a perspective dimension to create the illusion of depth. For example, a square can look like a cube. Rotation settings enable you to tilt shapes on the screen.

1. Move to slide 4, and select the four rectangles.

2. From the Home tab, in the Drawing group, click the Shape Effects button [◙]; then choose 3-D Rotation.

Figure 7-8
3-D Rotation effects

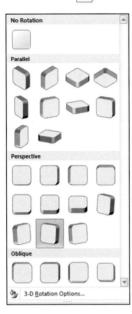

3. From the gallery of effects, choose Perspective Heroic Extreme Left, as shown in Figure 7-8.

4. Now add two more shape effects to customize this diagram. Select the rectangle shapes, and follow these steps on the Home tab, in the Drawing group:

   a. Click the Shape Effects button [◙], choose Bevel, and then click Circle.

   b. Click the Shape Effects button [◙], choose Shadow, and then from the Outer type, click Offset Diagonal Top Right.

   c. Click anywhere on the slide to turn off the selection.

5. Select the three arrows, and apply the same Bevel and Shadow effects.

Exercise 7-6 ADJUST THE OVERALL SIZE AND LAYOUT OF THE DIAGRAM

Diagrams can be resized like any other PowerPoint object. However, you must always be sure the text is still readable if the size of shapes is reduced. You may need to use only a single word on very small shapes. In this exercise, you will experiment with a couple of sizing techniques.

1. Duplicate slide 4; then make the following changes on the slide 5 diagram.

2. Notice that the four rectangles and connecting arrows extend across the complete slide, so you don't have any extra horizontal space unless the shapes become smaller. Resize the SmartArt area by dragging the right side about a half inch to the left. The text on the shapes becomes slightly smaller.

3. Resize the top and bottom of the SmartArt area so that it is just large enough to contain the shapes.

4. Drag this diagram up to fit directly under the slide title.

5. With the diagram selected, press [Ctrl]+[D] to duplicate the diagram. Position the second diagram evenly below the first one. Duplicating is a quick way to make a second diagram because you can simply edit the text on each shape for new wording without having to reset the Shape Effects.

6. On the second diagram, resize the bottom border of the SmartArt area to increase the available space for repositioning the shapes, as shown in Figure 7-9. Follow these steps:

   a. Select the first rectangle, and drag it to the upper left of the SmartArt area. Notice that the arrow between this rectangle and the second one automatically repositions itself.

   b. Select the second rectangle, and move it to the left.

   c. Select the third rectangle, and move it to the left and down slightly. Be careful that you allow enough space for the arrow.

   d. Select the fourth rectangle, and move it to the left and down slightly.

   e. Adjust rectangle positioning by nudging (using the arrow keys) so that the arrows remain approximately the same size.

7. Now you are still portraying the four-step process because of the connecting arrows that show the direction. However, with this curving arrangement, you will have enough room on the slide for a picture or some other graphic element to accompany the diagram.

Figure 7-9
A process diagram
arranged two ways

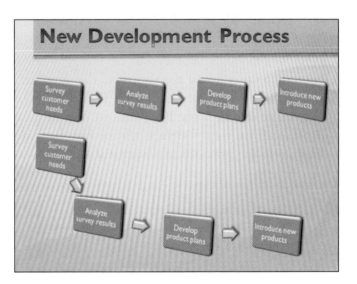

Exercise 7-7 ADD SHAPES

In Exercise 7-2 you added a shape, so you already have some experience in modifying the structure of a SmartArt graphic. While layouts add shapes in different places, the new shape is normally connected to the selected one in some way. Therefore, the shape that is selected when you add another shape is important.

1. Move to slide 6, and create a new slide with the Title and Content layout. Key **Adding SmartArt Shapes** as the slide title. Click the SmartArt button 📄 in the content placeholder.

2. From the List type, double-click the Stacked List thumbnail.

3. Now edit the text on each shape as follows:

    a. In the circle on the left, key **One**; then for the related text key **First item** and **Second item**.

    b. In the circle on the right, key **Two**; then for the related text key **First item** and **Second item**.

    c. Notice that the text automatically resizes and word-wraps for each shape.

4. Now under the left circle labeled "One," click the "First item" text to select that shape. From the SmartArt Tools Design tab, in the Create Graphic group, click the Add Shape button 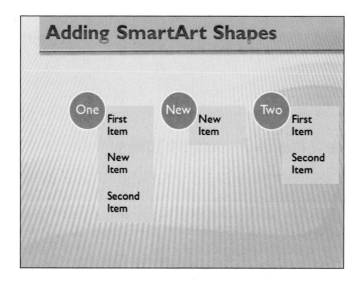 down arrow; then choose Add Shape After. A new shape appears below the first item, and the diagram has been resized. Key **New item** in this shape.

5. Now select the left circle labeled "One." Click the Add Shape button down arrow; then choose Add Shape After. This time a second circle with a related rectangle shape is added, as shown in Figure 7-10. Notice that you have the options of before and after as well as above and below when you are adding shapes, so it is very important that you choose where you want the shape to go.

6. In the added circle, key **New**; in the related shape, key **New item**.

7. Rearrange the order of the shapes in the diagram. Select the circle labeled "New." From the SmartArt Tools Design tab, in the Create Graphic group, click the Right to Left button, and the diagram is displayed from right to left. Click the button again to return the diagram to the previous arrangement.

Figure 7-10
Adding SmartArt shapes

Adding SmartArt Shapes

One First Item
New Item
Second Item

New New Item

Two First Item
Second Item

Exercise 7-8 CHANGE COLORS, APPLY SMARTART STYLES, AND RESET THE GRAPHIC

Using the Quick Styles feature is not the only way to change the appearance of a SmartArt layout. Many more options are available from the SmartArt Tools Design tab, in the SmartArt Styles group, as shown in Figure 7-11.

Figure 7-11
SmartArt Styles

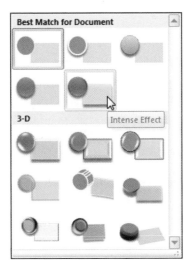

1. On slide 7 select the SmartArt layout. From the SmartArt Tools Design tab, in the SmartArt Styles group, click the More button ⬇ to see the gallery of SmartArt Styles arranged in two categories, Best Match for Document and 3-D. As you point to each thumbnail, you will see that effect applied to your diagram.

2. Choose Intense Effect.

3. With your SmartArt layout selected, from the SmartArt Tools Design tab, in the SmartArt Styles group, click the Change Colors button. Colors are arranged in eight categories: Primary Theme Colors, Colorful, and six Accent colors. The current color is selected, as shown in Figure 7-12.

Figure 7-12
Change Colors for a SmartArt layout

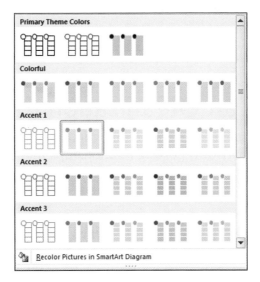

4. Point to different thumbnails in this gallery of colors, and consider the changes on your slide. Notice that, as you go down the list, colors change between the various accent colors in the presentation's design theme. Then as you go across, different line and shading treatments are used.

NOTE

As you work with diagrams, you will find the keyboard shortcuts listed in Table 7-2 helpful because they provide a quick way to move between shapes, select shapes, or select the text within the shapes.

5. Select the Gradient Loop – Accent 5 color.

6. If you are not pleased with your change, it is easy to remove it. On the SmartArt Tools Design tab, in the Reset group, click the Reset Graphic button 🔁, and the original style of your layout is restored.

7. Update the handout footer text to *[your initials]*7-8.

8. Move to slide 1, and save the presentation as *[your initials]*7-8 in your Lesson 7 folder.

TABLE 7-2 Using the Keyboard to Navigate in SmartArt Graphics

Key	Result
Enter	Activated shape: Inserts a new text line.
Esc	Deactivates a selected shape.
F2	Toggles the current shape between being selected and activated.
← or →	Selected shape: Nudges the position of the shape left or right.
Shift + Tab	Selected shape: Moves to the previous shape. Activated shape: Inserts a tab at the insertion point.
Tab	Selected shape: Moves to the next shape. Activated shape: Inserts a tab at the insertion point.
↑ or ↓	Selected shape: Nudges the position of the shape up or down.

Preparing an Organization Chart

Organization charts are most commonly used to show a hierarchy such as the lines of authority or reporting relationships in a business. You start an organization chart in the same way as you start other SmartArt graphics, but it is important to consider superior and subordinate relationships.

Exercise 7-9   CREATE AN ORGANIZATION CHART

When you start a new organization chart, you begin with a default arrangement of five rectangular shapes. Each shape is positioned on a *level* in the chart, which indicates its position in the hierarchy. The top shape indicates the highest level (such as the president of a company) and shows a direct line down to the second level (such as the managers who report to the president). The shape that branches from the central line reflects a supporting position (such as an assistant to the president).

1. Insert a new slide after slide 7 that uses the Title and Content layout. Key the title **New Management Structure**.

2. In the content placeholder click the SmartArt button 🖾.

3. Choose the Hierarchy type; then double-click Organization Chart. A chart with five shapes appears, with text placeholders that show text in a large size. The text size will become smaller as you key text into the shapes.

4. Click the top shape in the chart. Notice the dashed outline that indicates the shape is activated, so you can key text.

5. Key **Julie Wolfe &**, press Enter, and key **Gus Irvinelli** to position the names on two lines. You will later format this text to fit on one line.

6. Press Enter to start a new line, and key **Co-owners**.

7. Press Esc to deactivate text editing. The shape now has a solid outline.

8. Press Tab to move to the first lower-level shape.

9. Key the following three items on three lines:

   Administration
   Michael Peters
   Administration Mgr

10. The text becomes smaller to fit in the shape. Press F2 to deactivate text editing.

11. Press Tab to move to the second shape on the lower level. Key the following items on three lines:

    Sales & Marketing
    Roy Olafsen
    Marketing Mgr

12. Press F2; then press Tab to move to the third shape, and key the following items on three lines:

    Operations
    Michele Jenkins
    Head Chef

13. Press F2; then press Tab to move to the shape that branches from the central line, and press Delete.

14. Click outside the SmartArt area to deactivate the organization chart, as shown in Figure 7-13.

Figure 7-13
Organization chart

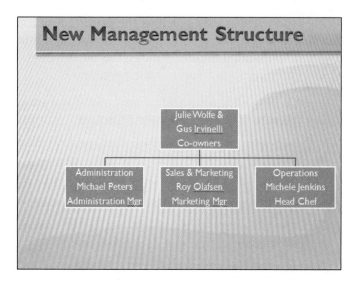

Exercise 7-10 INSERT SUBORDINATE SHAPES

The organization of many companies changes frequently. You might need to promote, demote, or move organization chart shapes as the reporting structure changes or becomes more complex.

To expand an organization chart (see Figure 7-14), you can insert additional shapes of the following types:

- *Subordinate shapes.* Shapes that are connected to a superior shape (a shape on a higher level).

- *Coworker shapes.* Shapes that are connected to the same superior shape as another shape.

- *Assistant shapes.* Shapes that are usually placed below a superior shape and above subordinate shapes.

Figure 7-14
Structure of an
organization chart

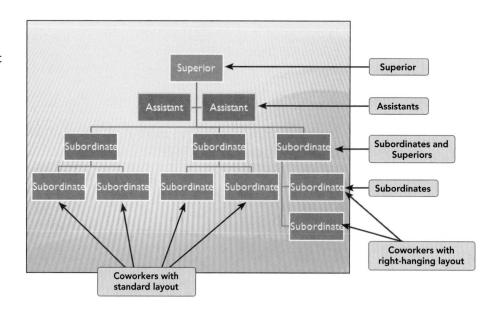

To add *subordinate shapes*, first select the shape that will be their superior and then, from the SmartArt Tools Design tab, in the Create Graphic group, click the Add Shape button [icon].

1. Still working on slide 8, select the first shape on the second level, with the name "Michael Peters."

Figure 7-15
Adding organization chart shapes

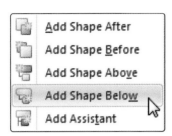

2. From the SmartArt Tools Design tab, in the Create Graphic group, click the Shape button [icon] down arrow; then click Add Shape Below, as shown in Figure 7-15. A shape appears below the selected shape with a connecting line, and now the new shape is selected.

3. Click the Add Shape button [icon] down arrow; then click Add Shape Before. Now two shapes show a reporting relationship to Michael Peters. They are currently shown with the Right-Hanging Layout. All the shapes automatically become smaller so that the chart will fit on the slide.

> **NOTE**
>
> Both Add Shape After and Add Shape Before insert new shapes at the same level. Add Shape Above inserts a new shape in the level above, which would be a superior position. Add Shape Below inserts a new shape in the level below, which would be a subordinate position. Add Assistant inserts a new shape between levels.

4. Repeat this process to add one shape under Roy Olafsen and three shapes under Michele Jenkins. Once again the shapes are resized to fit, but the text that has been entered is now too small to read. This will be corrected later.

Exercise 7-11 ADD ASSISTANT AND COWORKER SHAPES

Assistant shapes are used for positions that provide administrative assistance or other support. They are inserted below a selected shape but above the next-lower level.

Coworker shapes are inserted at the same level as the selected shape and report to the same superior as does the selected shape.

1. On slide 8, select the level 1 shape.

2. From the SmartArt Tools Design tab, in the Create Graphic group, click the Add Shape button [icon], and choose Add Assistant. A new shape is inserted between levels 1 and 2.

3. Select the shape below Michael Peters to add another shape at the same level. From the SmartArt Tools Design tab, in the Create Graphic group, click the Add Shape button [icon], and choose Add Shape Before. A new shape is inserted at the same level—it represents a coworker.

4. Repeat step 3 to add one more shape under Roy Olafsen.

5. Now increase the slide size so that you can more easily see the text. From the View tab, in the Zoom group, click the Zoom button 🔍, and check **90%**; then click **OK**.

6. Scroll on the enlarged slide to locate the assistant shape below the level 1 shape; key **Troy Scott**, press Enter, and then key **Assistant** so that this text fits on two text lines.

7. In the three shapes under Michael Peters, key the following employee information on two text lines in each shape. After the text is entered, press F2 or Esc to deactivate the shape and then press Tab to move to the next shape.

MIS	Billing	HR
Chuck Warden	Sarah Conners	Chris Davis

8. After keying the text in Chris Davis's shape, press Esc to deactivate the text shape. Press Tab one time to move to Roy Olafsen's shape, and press Tab to move to the first shape under Roy Olafsen.

9. In the two shapes under Roy Olafsen, key the following employee information:

Events	Marketing
Ian Mahoney	Evan Johnson

10. In the first two shapes under Michele Jenkins, key the following (leave the last shape blank):

Kitchen	Purchasing
Eric Dennis	Jessie Smith

11. From the View tab, in the Zoom group, click the Fit to Window button 🔲. Notice that the organization chart again adjusted the text to a smaller size, as shown in Figure 7-16. The text is too small to be readable when projected in a presentation. You will fix this with the changes you make in the next two exercises.

Figure 7-16
Organization chart
with small text

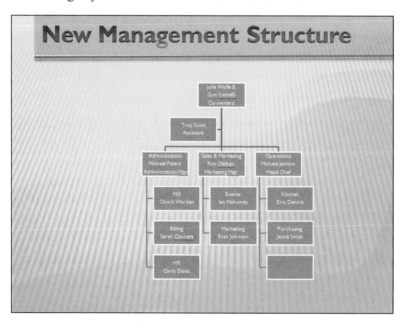

Exercise 7-12 CHANGE LAYOUT, DELETE SHAPES, AND REORDER SHAPES

The layout of the organization chart can be changed to show subordinates in a *standard* format or a *hanging indent* format. A shape can be repositioned to a higher level by promoting (moving up) or repositioned to a lower level by demoting (moving down). An entire group of connected shapes can be moved right or left. If you have more shapes than necessary, you can delete them at any time.

1. On slide 8, select the shape for Michael Peters. From the SmartArt Tools Design tab, in the Create Graphic group, click the Layout button ▦, and choose Standard. The subordinate shapes below Michael Peters (coworkers) are now arranged side by side instead of in a vertical, hanging arrangement.

2. Select the blank subordinate shape below Michele Jenkins, and press [Delete].

3. Select the shape for Eric Dennis, and click the Promote button ⬅. The shape moves up a level, and the connected shape moves with it. Click the Undo button ↺.

4. Select Roy Olafsen's shape, click the Layout button ▦, and choose Standard. Repeat this process to change the layout for Michele Jenkins's shape to Standard.

5. This arrangement communicates nicely the three levels of the organization, as shown in Figure 7-17; however, the text is very small. The next steps will rearrange the layout so that each shape can be a little larger.

Figure 7-17
Organization chart
with standard layout

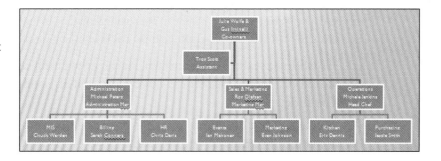

6. Select the shape for Michael Peters. From the SmartArt Tools Design tab, in the Create Graphic group, click the Layout button ▦, and choose Right Hanging. Repeat this process to apply the Right Hanging indent to the other two level 2 shapes.

7. Select the shape of Sarah Conners, and click the Demote button ➡. Now this shape is indented under Chuck Warden.

8. Select the shape of Evan Johnson, and click the Move Selection Up button ⬆ to move this shape above Ian Mahoney.

9. Select the shape of Eric Dennis, and click the Move Selection Down button ⬇ to move this shape below Jessie Smith.

10. Select the shape for Michael Peters, and click the Right to Left button ⇄. This entire branch of the chart is reordered to appear on the right, as shown in Figure 7-18.

Figure 7-18
Organization chart with hanging indent layout

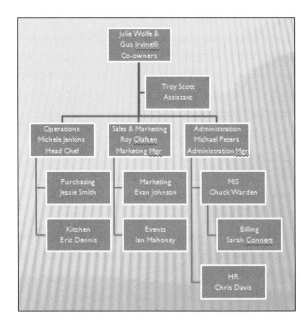

Exercise 7-13   CHANGE SHAPE SIZING AND STYLES

The entire SmartArt area can be made larger to accommodate charts with several levels. Selected shapes can be resized and connected shapes repositioned so that the text fits better. Text can be increased or decreased in size.

1. On slide 8, resize the SmartArt area by dragging its border to expand it horizontally on both sides as well as vertically to fill the open space on the slide.

2. Select the level 1 shape, resize it horizontally to make it wider, and then make both names fit on one line.

3. Select all three level 2 shapes, and resize horizontally and vertically to allow a little more room in each shape.

4. Select all of the chart's shapes, and increase the font size to 16 points and bold. Adjust the horizontal size of shapes if the text word-wraps.

5. Now spread apart the related shapes in the chart for easier reading. Select the Michael Peters shape and the related shapes below it. Hold Ctrl and press the right arrow → press about five times to move this branch to the right. The connecting lines automatically adjust.

6. Select the Michele Jenkins shape and the related shapes below it. Hold Ctrl and press the left arrow ← about five times to move this branch to the left.

7. With the SmartArt area selected, from the SmartArt Tools Design tab, in the SmartArt Styles group, click the Change Colors button 🎨, and select Colorful – Accent Colors.

8. You can also change the color of individual shapes. Select the Assistant shape; then from the SmartArt Tools Format tab, in the Shape Styles group, click the Shape Fill button 🖌, and choose a little lighter fill color but keep the text readable.

9. Select the entire SmartArt, and from the SmartArt Tools Design tab, in the SmartArt Styles group, examine the effect of different SmartArt Styles on the chart. Click the SmartArt Styles More button ⥥, and then choose the Inset Effect from the 3-D category, as shown in Figure 7-19.

10. Update the handout footer text to *[your initials]*7-13.

11. Save the presentation as *[your initials]*7-13 in your Lesson 7 folder.

Figure 7-19
Completed
organization chart

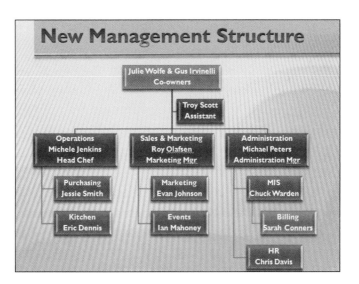

Creating Other SmartArt Graphics

The eight types of PowerPoint SmartArt graphics offer many options to illustrate your thoughts in a visual way. This exercise will focus on three diagrams in the relationship category.

Exercise 7-14 CREATE A RADIAL DIAGRAM

A *radial diagram* starts with a central circle (level 1) and four circles (level 2) connected to and surrounding the center circle. You can insert as many additional circles as you need to illustrate your message.

1. Insert a new slide after slide 8 that uses the Title and Content layout. Key the title **New Customer Philosophy**.

2. From the content placeholder click the SmartArt button .

3. Click the Relationship type; then double-click Basic Radial. A chart appears with four circle shapes that radiate from the center circle with text placeholders.

4. Click the center circle; then from the SmartArt Tools Design tab, in the Create Graphic group, click the Add Shape button, and a new circle is added to the diagram. It becomes the selected circle.

5. With the new circle selected, press Delete to remove this new shape.

6. Click the center circle, and key **Customer**.

7. Think about your diagram's positioning as though you were referring to the face of a round clock. Click the top outer circle (12 o'clock position), and key the information shown under "12 o'clock" in Figure 7-20. Press Enter after the individual words so that the information appears on three text lines. (Because AutoCorrect capitalizes the words, you must make a correction to change the second and third words in each shape to lowercase.)

8. Click the circle at the 3 o'clock position, and key the corresponding text.

9. Working in a clockwise direction, key the remaining text shown in Figure 7-20 in the remaining outer circles.

Figure 7-20
Radial diagram text

12 o'clock	3 o'clock	6 o'clock	9 o'clock
Satisfy	Provide	Provide	Resolve
customer	courteous	excellent	problems
needs	service	quality	promptly

NOTE

If PowerPoint automatically capitalizes the second and third word in each circle, change the letters to lowercase. Automatic capitalization is caused by AutoCorrect. You can turn off this feature, if you wish, by following these steps: Click the File tab, choose Options, then choose Proofing. Click AutoCorrect Options, deselect Capitalize first letter of sentences, click OK, and then click OK again.

10. From the SmartArt Tools Design tab, in the SmartArt Styles group, click the Change Colors button, and choose Colored Fill – Accent 6. Then click the SmartArt Styles More button, and look at the effect of different options as you point to them. Choose the Cartoon style.

11. Drag the borders of the SmartArt area to increase the size of the diagram so that it fills the open space.

12. Choose the center shape; then from the SmartArt Tools Format tab, in the Shape Styles group, click the Shape Fill button and choose a darker shade of the shape fill color to emphasize the center, as shown in Figure 7-21.

Figure 7-21
Radial diagram

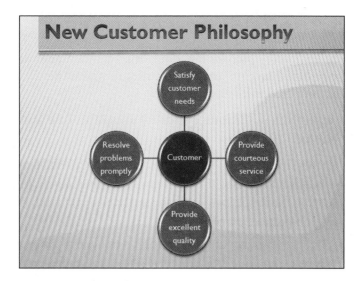

Exercise 7-15 CREATE A GEAR DIAGRAM

Gears have spokes that stick out from a round shape and lock with other gears to make them turn. The turning of each gear is dependent on the other gears. Therefore, the *gear diagram* communicates interlocking ideas that are each shown as shapes.

1. Insert a new slide after slide 9 that uses the **Title and Content** layout. Key the title **Interlocking Ideas**.

2. From the content placeholder, click the SmartArt button 📇.

3. Click the **Relationship** type, and then double-click **Gear**. A chart with three shapes and directional arrows appears. Key the text as shown in Figure 7-22.

4. From the SmartArt Tools Design tab, in the SmartArt Styles group, click the SmartArt Styles More button ⩔, and choose the **Sunset Scene** from the 3-D category.

5. Resize and reposition the SmartArt graphic so that it is balanced on the slide, with even spacing around the diagram.

Figure 7-22
Completed gear
diagram

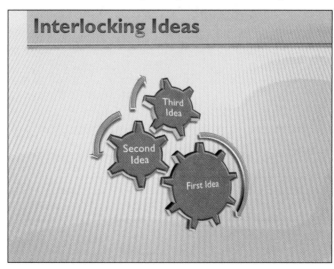

Exercise 7-16 INSERT A CONTINUOUS PICTURE LIST

The *continuous picture list* contains round placeholders for pictures and a horizontal arrow to communicate that the items shown represent interconnected information.

1. Insert a new slide after slide 10 using the Title and Content layout. Key the title **New Desserts**.

2. From the content placeholder click the SmartArt button .

3. Click the Relationship type, and then double-click Continuous Picture List. A chart appears with three shapes that each contain a small circle with a picture placeholder.

4. Click the first picture placeholder to access the Insert Picture dialog box. Navigate to your student files, select the **cake** picture, and click Insert. Or, if you prefer, you could double-click to insert the picture.

5. Repeat this process on the next two placeholders, inserting the **cookies** picture in the middle shape and the **strawberry** picture in the right shape.

6. Now key the following text below the pictures as shown in Figure 7-23, and the text will automatically resize:

   Fruit Cake Holiday Delight
   Oatmeal and Raisin Cookies
   Cream Cake and Strawberries

7. From the SmartArt Tools Design tab, in the SmartArt Styles group, click the More button ▾, and select the **3-D, Polished** style.

8. Resize and reposition the SmartArt graphic on the slide.

9. Update the handout footer text to *[your initials]*7-16.

10. Save the presentation as *[your initials]*7-16 in your Lesson 7 folder.

Figure 7-23
Continuous Picture
List

Changing SmartArt Graphics

Once a SmartArt graphic is created, the layout can easily be changed by selecting a different type of layout. However, the levels of your information may not translate well into some layouts. Shapes within the SmartArt area can also be repositioned by dragging them. SmartArt graphics can be converted to text or to shapes that can then be edited as drawing objects.

Exercise 7-17　CHANGE DIAGRAM LAYOUTS

At any time during the development of your SmartArt graphic, you can apply a different diagram layout. Level 1 information and level 2 information will be reformatted to fit the new layout, so the layout you choose must have matching levels to display all the text you entered.

1. Move to slide 3, and select it in the Slides and Outline pane. Press Ctrl+C to copy the slide; then move to slide 11, and press Ctrl+V to paste.

2. Now working on slide 12, select the SmartArt graphic; then from the SmartArt Tools Design tab, in the Layouts group, click on several different layouts to consider the different options that are available. Notice how the level 1 and level 2 information is arranged, and consider the emphasis that each level receives. The next three steps point out specific diagrams to try and what you should notice in each one.

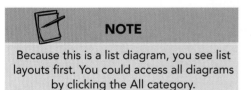

NOTE

Because this is a list diagram, you see list layouts first. You could access all diagrams by clicking the All category.

3. Click **Table Hierarchy**. This layout does not distinguish between the levels; level 1 information is placed above level 2, but no color or lines are used to show any connecting effect or relationship between the levels.

4. Click **Grouped List**. Now it is easy to see that certain items relate to other items because the shapes used for level 1 create a "container" for the shapes used for level 2 information. This layout emphasizes level 2 text.

5. Click **Vertical Arrow List**. This layout clearly distinguishes between the two levels, and it works well for bulleted lists of information. The arrows that display level 2 information communicate that the level 2 information is an outgrowth of level 1. Click to apply this layout.

6. The fill color on the arrows blends too much with the slide background to be easily visible, so change the colors and the style to make the arrows stand out more. On the SmartArt Tools Design tab, in the SmartArt Styles group, click the Change Colors button ; then choose **Colorful Range – Accent Colors 5 to 6**. Click the SmartArt Style More button , and choose **Flat Scene** in the 3-D category.

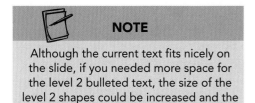

NOTE

Although the current text fits nicely on the slide, if you needed more space for the level 2 bulleted text, the size of the level 2 shapes could be increased and the size of the text on the level 2 shapes could be reduced.

7. Select the three arrows; then from the SmartArt Tools Format tab, in the Shape Styles group, click the Shape Fill button , and choose White, Background 1, Darker 15%. Now the arrows still blend with the theme design, but they are easier to see, as shown in Figure 7-24.

8. Resize the diagram to fill the slide.

Figure 7-24
Diagram with changed layout

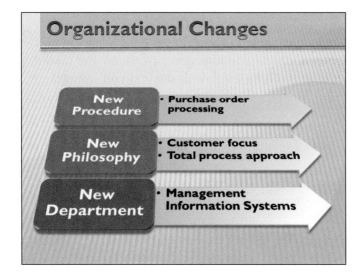

Exercise 7-18 CHANGE THE ORIENTATION OF DIAGRAMS

Because of the particular information a diagram must contain, the information may need to be displayed in a different orientation than the original SmartArt shape provides. For example, instead of a top-to-bottom orientation, it might need to be left to right.

1. From the Slides and Outline pane, select slide 8 and copy it. Move to the last slide in your presentation, and paste the slide.

2. Now on slide 13, select the SmartArt graphic. From the SmartArt Tools Design tab, in the Layouts group, click the More button , and choose the Horizontal Hierarchy layout. The shapes are now positioned horizontally as in a decision-tree diagram.

3. While the shapes are still connected, the sizes should be adjusted on some of them.

4. Select the three shapes for Michael Peters, Roy Olafsen, and Michele Jenkins. Resize them horizontally and vertically to increase the shape size so that all text prints on three lines and there is sufficient space above and below the text in each shape.

5. Select the MIS shape, all the ones below it, and the Billing shape. Resize these shapes horizontally so that each name fits on one text line, as shown in Figure 7-25.

6. Increase the vertical size of the Julie Wolfe & Gus Irvinelli shape.

Figure 7-25
Diagram with
different orientation

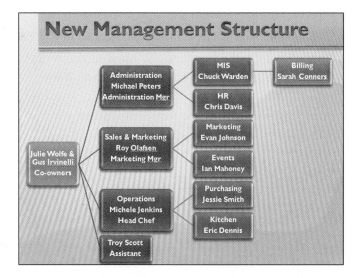

Exercise 7-19 CONVERT SMARTART GRAPHICS TO TEXT AND SHAPES

If you need to use only the text of a diagram, you can convert a SmartArt graphic to text and then a bulleted list will be created to replace the diagram. Some diagrams convert well to bulleted lists; others will require more editing to create usable lists.

If you convert to shapes, the diagram becomes a drawing object that can be ungrouped and edited just as any other shape can. Once the shape conversion is done, however, the diagram cannot be edited as a SmartArt graphic.

1. From the Slides and Outline pane, select slide 12 and copy it. Move to slide 13, and paste the slide.

2. Now on slide 14 select the SmartArt diagram. From the SmartArt Tools Design tab, in the Reset group, click the Convert button 🗐; then choose Convert to Text. The text is changed to a bulleted list showing two levels.

3. Click Undo 🔄 to return this text to the previous diagram.

4. With the diagram selected, from the SmartArt Tools Design tab, in the Reset group, click the Convert button 🗐 again, and then choose Convert to Shapes. Now the diagram is a grouped set of shapes.

5. From the Drawing Tools Format tab, in the Arrange group, click the Group button 🔲, and choose Ungroup. Now all the diagram parts are separate shapes.

6. Select the three shapes on the left. From the Drawing Tools Format tab, in the Shape Styles group, click the More button ⬇, and click Intense Effect – Orange, Accent 6.

7. Change the alignment on these shapes to left.

8. Reposition the three arrows by moving them under the rectangles so that the bullet does not show before each item.

Figure 7-26
Diagram with changed layout

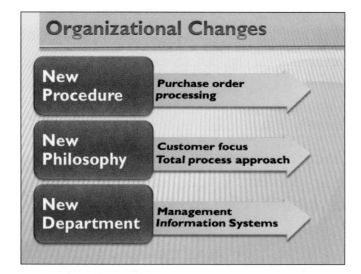

9. With the three arrows selected, from the Home tab, in the Paragraph group, click the Align Text button 🔲; then click Middle.

10. Check the positioning of all six parts for even spacing on the slide.

11. Update the handout footer text to *[your initials]*7-19.

12. Save the presentation as *[your initials]*7-19 in your Lesson 7 folder. Close the presentation and submit your work.

Lesson 7 Summary

- SmartArt graphics are used to present information in a visual manner.
- SmartArt graphics are organized by eight different types that include a wide variety of layouts such as organization charts, radial diagrams, list diagrams, and relationship diagrams.
- The SmartArt Design tab has command buttons for inserting shapes and modifying the predefined layouts. Shapes can be added and removed.
- List layouts provide an alternative to listing information in a bulleted list because concise text can be placed on shapes that help to graphically communicate topics and subtopics.
- Process diagrams show a sequence of events or the progression of workflow.
- Cycle diagrams communicate a continuous or ongoing process.
- Hierarchy diagrams are used to depict a hierarchical structure, showing who reports to whom and who is responsible for what function or task.
- Pyramid diagrams show interconnected or proportional relationships.
- Relationship diagrams contain interconnected shapes that reflect relationships in some way.
- Matrix diagrams display two axes in related quadrants that emphasize the whole or the individual parts.
- An organization chart is a type of hierarchy chart in a tree structure, branching out to multiple divisions in each lower level.
- When an organization chart shape is promoted, it moves up a level. When a chart shape is demoted, it moves down a level.
- The SmartArt Text pane provides a quick way to enter text that labels SmartArt shapes.
- List diagrams can show both level 1 and level 2 information, but text must be concise for easy reading.
- Text entered in SmartArt shapes automatically resizes to fit the shape; if shapes are increased in size, the text they contain is also increased in size.
- An existing bulleted list can be converted to a SmartArt graphic.
- Quick Styles provide choices for color and effect changes such as outlines, beveling, and shadows that can be applied to any selected shape.
- SmartArt Styles consist of predefined effects that work well together for diagrams.
- An illusion of depth is created with 3-D style options.
- Shapes can be resized and repositioned within the SmartArt area.
- The Change Colors option provides many possible variations of theme colors.

- If color changes made to a SmartArt graphic are unacceptable, the colors can be reset to their original colors.
- Several layouts in the List type have placeholders for pictures.

LESSON 7		Command Summary
Feature	**Button**	**Ribbon**
Change back to original formatting		SmartArt Tools Design, Reset group, Reset Graphic
Change organization chart layout		SmartArt Tools Design, Create Graphic group, Layout
Change SmartArt Style		SmartArt Tools Design, SmartArt Styles group, More
Change text from a bulleted list to a graphical layout		Home, Paragraph group, Convert to SmartArt
Change the color of a selected shape		SmartArt Tools Format, Shape Styles group, Shape Fill
Create a graphical list or diagram on a slide		Insert, Illustrations group, SmartArt Graphic
Create additional shapes within a diagram		SmartArt Tools Design, Create Graphic group, Add Shape
Decrease the level of a selected bulleted item or shape		SmartArt Tools Design, Create Graphic group, Demote
Increase the level of a selected bulleted item or shape		SmartArt Tools Design, Create Graphic group, Promote
Pick from choices for shape color and effects		Home, Drawing group, Quick Styles
Rearrange layout direction or sequencing of shapes		SmartArt Tools Design, Create Graphic group, Right to Left
Select from variations of theme colors		SmartArt Tools Design, SmartArt Styles group, Change Colors

Concepts Review

True/False Questions

Each of the following statements is either true or false. Indicate your choice by circling T or F.

T F 1. SmartArt contains a wide range of graphical layouts organized in eight different categories.

T F 2. All the shapes in a diagram must be the same color.

T F 3. An organization chart is an example of a hierarchy diagram.

T F 4. Graphical lists can show both level 1 and level 2 information as long as it is concisely written.

T F 5. If you add too many shapes to an organization chart, you can delete the extra shapes.

T F 6. Quick Styles provide color and effect choices for selected shapes.

T F 7. SmartArt Styles can be applied to individual shapes within a layout.

T F 8. The Change Colors option provides color options from the Standard colors.

Short Answer Questions

Write the correct answer in the space provided.

1. How do you create a SmartArt graphic?

_____

2. What feature enables you to quickly key text to create a SmartArt graphic?

_____

3. How can you convert an existing bulleted list to a diagram?

_____

4. If you have created a process diagram, how can you change it to a cycle diagram?

_____

5. Describe how to change the size of a SmartArt shape.

6. If you have six subordinates reporting to one superior, how do you change the six shapes so that they are stacked vertically in two columns?

7. Which types of SmartArt graphics provide picture placeholders?

8. What type of diagram is used to illustrate a continuous, ongoing relationship?

Critical Thinking

Answer these questions on a separate page. Support your answers with examples from your own experience, if possible.

1. When developing your presentation content and making decisions about which SmartArt graphic to use, why is it important to consider your audience's viewpoint?

2. Organization charts are by nature rather detail-oriented. On the basis of what you learned about designing presentations, how can you ensure that an organization chart is easy to interpret?

Skills Review

Exercise 7-20

Create a list diagram, and apply SmartArt styles.

1. Open the file **Retail**. Insert a new slide after slide 3 that uses the Title and Content layout. Key the title **New Retail Items**.

2. Insert a Trapezoid List SmartArt graphic by following these steps:
    a. Click the SmartArt button 🔳.
    b. From the List type, double-click Trapezoid List. A SmartArt graphic will appear with three trapezoid shapes with title and list placeholders.
    c. From the SmartArt Tools Design tab, in the Create Graphic group, click the Text Pane button 🔲 to open the Text pane on the left, as shown in Figure 7-27.

Figure 7-27
Trapezoid List
diagram

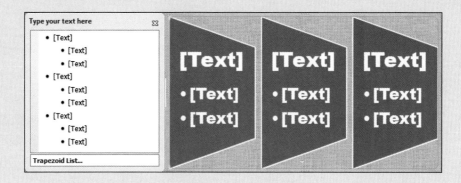

3. The first-level bullet will be the heading in each shape, and the second-level bullet will be the items listed in each shape. At first, two bulleted items appear, but if you add third and fourth items, the text will adjust its size to fit in the shape.

4. Working in the Text pane or directly on each shape, key the text to complete all three shapes as shown in Figure 7-28.

Figure 7-28
Completed
Trapezoid List
diagram

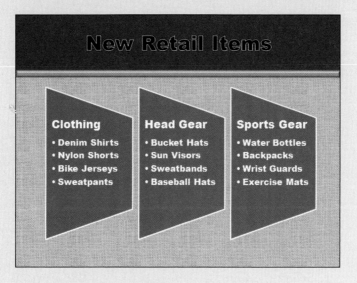

5. Close the Text pane.

6. Create a slide footer for only slide 4 that includes today's date, your name, and *[your initials]*7-20 as the footer.

7. Save the presentation as *[your initials]*7-20 in your Lesson 7 folder.

8. Close the presentation and submit your work.

Exercise 7-21

Create a simple organization chart, change theme colors, and format shapes.

1. Open the file **Kitchen1**. Insert a new slide after slide 3 that uses the Title and Content layout. Key the title **Operations**.

2. Start an organization chart by following these steps:

   a. From the content placeholder, click the SmartArt button 🖾.

   b. From the Hierarchy type, double-click Organization Chart.

   c. In the top shape, key:

   Michele Jenkins
   Head Chef & Operations Mgr

   d. Click the assistant shape, and press Delete.

   e. In the first shape on the second level, key:

   Eric Dennis
   Asst Chef & Kitchen Mgr

   f. Press Esc, press Tab to move to the next shape, and then key:

   Claudia Pell
   Maitre d' & Service Mgr

   g. Press Esc, press Tab to move to the right shape, and then press Delete.

3. Insert subordinate shapes by following these steps:

   a. Select the Eric Dennis shape.

   b. From the SmartArt Tools Design tab, in the Create Graphic group, click the Add Shape button 🖾; then choose Add Shape Below.

   c. Now the second shape is selected. To add a second shape at the same level, click the Add Shape button 🖾 and then choose Add Shape After.

   d. Key the following information in the two shapes:

First shape	Second shape
G. Robinson	S. Stefano
Sr. Cook	Sr. Cook, Weekends

   e. Select the Claudia Pell shape. Using the previous steps b and c, insert two shapes below Claudia Pell and key the following information:

First shape	Second shape
T. Domina	T. Conway
Banquets	Facilities & Maint

4. Change the layout:

   a. Click the shape for Eric Dennis. From the SmartArt Tools Design tab, in the Create Graphic group, click the Layout button 🖾, and choose Standard to make the shapes appear beside each other.

   b. Repeat this process for the Claudia Pell shape.

5. On all shapes, make the employee names (but not their titles) bold.

6. Change the font color for all text to Blue, Background 1.

7. From the SmartArt Tools Design tab, in the SmartArt Styles group:

   a. Click the Change Colors button 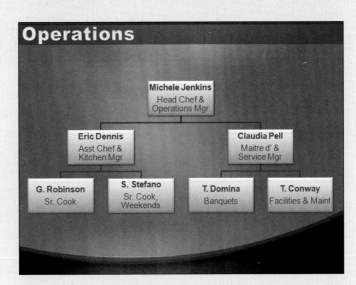; in the Primary Theme Colors group, select Dark 2 Outline.

   b. Click the More button ⬇, and choose Intense Effect.

8. Move the SmartArt graphic up and slightly to the left so that it is balanced better on the slide, as shown in Figure 7-29.

Figure 7-29
Completed slide

9. Create a slide footer for only slide 4 that contains today's date, your name, and *[your initials]*7-21 as the footer.

10. Move to slide 1, and save the presentation as *[your initials]*7-21 in your Lesson 7 folder.

11. Close the presentation and submit your work.

Exercise 7-22

Create cycle and process diagrams.

1. Open the file **Health**.

2. Insert a new slide after slide 1 that uses the Title and Content layout. Key the title **Heart Smart Living**.

3. Create a cycle diagram by following these steps:

   a. Click the SmartArt button 📧 in the content placeholder.

   b. In the Cycle type, double-click Block Cycle.

   c. With one of the shapes selected, press Delete so that you have four shapes in the diagram.

4. Working with the shapes as if they were a round clock, insert the following text in the shapes of the diagram:

12 o'clock	3 o'clock	6 o'clock	9 o'clock
Get enough sleep	Eat right when you're out	Eat right at home	Exercise regularly

5. Format the four text shapes. Press Ctrl while you click each of the four shapes to select them. Make the following changes:

   a. Make the text bold.

   b. Increase the font size to 20 points; then stretch the shapes horizontally so that the text in each shape fits on two text lines.

   c. Right-click one of the shapes; from the shortcut menu choose Change Shape, and then select an Oval. Resize the oval shapes if necessary.

6. Insert a new slide after slide 4 that uses the Title and Content layout. Key the title **Do What's Good 4 U**.

7. Create a process diagram by following these steps:

   a. Click the SmartArt button in the content placeholder.

   b. In the Process type, double-click the Continuous Block Process thumbnail.

   c. With one of the shapes selected, from the SmartArt Tools Design tab, in the Create Graphic group, click the Add Shape button, and then choose Add Shape After so that you have four shapes in the diagram.

8. In the first shape on the left, key **Join Our Team!!** Notice that in the small shapes of this diagram the text automatically word-wraps with one word on each line. Key the other text as follows:

   Second—**Eat With Us**
   Third—**Play With Us**
   Fourth—**Walk With Us**

9. Create a handout header and footer: Include the date, your name as the header, the page number, and *[your initials]*7-22 as the footer.

10. Move to slide 1, and save the presentation as *[your initials]*7-22 in your Lesson 7 folder.

11. Close the presentation and submit your work.

Exercise 7-23

Add, promote, demote, and reorder shapes in an existing organizational chart.

1. Open the file **Kitchen2**. Move to slide 3, and click the organization chart to make it active.

2. Add three subordinate shapes to the G. Robinson level 2 shape, and key the information shown below:

First shape	Second shape	Third shape
Pastry	Cooks	Banquets
G. Gordon	L. Tilson	T. Domina
J. Lemmer	S. Mason	J. Fulman

3. Adjust the format by following these steps:

a. Select the level 3 Banquets shape, and then from the SmartArt Tools Design tab, in the Create Graphic group, click the Promote button ◀ to move it up to level 2.

b. Select the level 2 Facilities shape; then from the SmartArt Tools Design tab, in the Create Graphic group, click the Layout button 🖼, and choose Left Hanging.

c. Using the sizing handles on the organization chart border, make the chart larger, as shown in Figure 7-30.

d. Make the text on all shapes bold.

e. Apply the Moderate Effect SmartArt Style.

f. In all shapes, change the first text line to 14 points and the color to Gray-80%, Text 2, Darker 25%.

Figure 7-30
Completed slide

4. Create a handout header and footer: Include the date, your name as the header, the page number, and *[your initials]*7-23 as the footer.

5. Move to slide 1, and save the presentation as *[your initials]*7-23 in your Lesson 7 folder.

6. Close the presentation and submit your work.

Lesson Applications

Exercise 7-24

Create a process diagram and a list diagram, and apply SmartArt styles.

1. Open the file **Market1**.

2. On slide 3, select the two bulleted items. From the Home tab, in the Paragraph group, click the Convert to SmartArt button 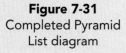. Choose More SmartArt Graphics.

3. Choose the Process type, and consider which diagrams would best show these two different media categories. Double-click Arrow Ribbon.

4. The two words are now positioned on a shape with arrows pointing in two directions.

5. Because this is such a simple shape and only two words are used, the SmartArt graphic is very large. Resize it to make the diagram smaller so that it does not overpower the slide.

6. Change the colors to Primary Theme Colors, Dark 2 Fill.

7. On slide 4, select the bulleted list; from the Home tab, in the Paragraph group, click the Convert to SmartArt button 🖹, and choose More SmartArt Graphics.

8. From the List type, double-click the Pyramid List. Now the text is positioned over a pyramid shape that can imply volume or levels of importance.

9. Change the colors to Primary Theme Colors, Dark 2 Outline.

10. For slide 3, apply the SmartArt Style Bird's Eye Scene.

11. Repeat steps 8 and 9 to convert the bulleted text on slide 5 to the same diagram. This time the height of the text shapes is smaller because six items are listed.

12. For slides 4 and 5, apply the SmartArt Style Polished, as shown in Figure 7-31.

Figure 7-31
Completed Pyramid
List diagram

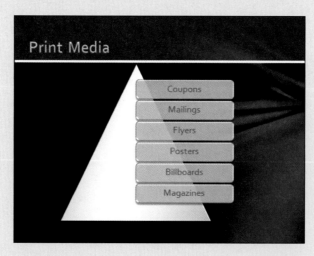

13. Create a handout header and footer: Include the date, your name as the header, the page number, and *[your initials]*7-24 as the footer.

14. Move to slide 1, and save the presentation as *[your initials]*7-24 in your Lesson 7 folder.

15. Close the presentation and submit your work.

Exercise 7-25

Create an organization chart, and adjust the layout.

1. Open the file **MISdept**.

2. Insert a new slide after slide 2 that uses the Title and Content layout. Key the title **MIS Department Organization**.

3. Create an organization chart using a horizontal hierarchy with the information shown in Figure 7-32.

Figure 7-32
Organization chart text

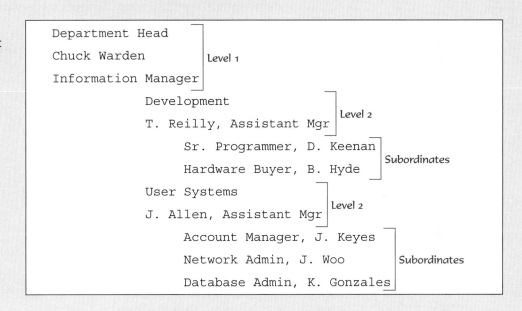

4. Change the font of all diagram text to 14 points, and apply bold.

5. Adjust the shape sizing to avoid word-wrapping of the job titles, but keep the size uniform at each level. When the names in the chart are shown below the job titles, no commas should follow the job titles.

6. Change the colors to Gradient Loop – Accent 1.

7. Adjust the position of other shapes to spread them out in the SmartArt area as shown in Figure 7-33.

UNIT 2 LESSON 7

Figure 7-33
Completed
organization chart

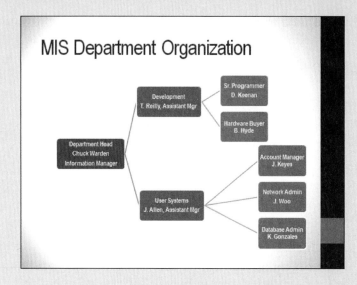

8. Create a slide footer for slide 3 that contains today's date, your name, and *[your initials]*7-25.

9. Move to slide 1, and save the presentation as *[your initials]*7-25 in your Lesson 7 folder.

10. Close the presentation and submit your work.

Exercise 7-26

Create a radial diagram on a promotional flyer.

1. Open the file **NewYear**. Create a SmartArt graphic in the content placeholder for this single-page flyer.

2. From the Cycle type, double-click Basic Radial.

3. Add five additional shapes (for a total of nine plus one in the center).

4. Key the text **Great Food** in the center circle; then key the text shown below in the outer circles, starting with the 12 o'clock position and moving in a clockwise direction.
   Poached Salmon
   Texan Tofu
   Fresh Fruit
   Pecan Pie
   Peanut Soup
   Veggies & Dip
   Green Beans
   Corn Relish
   Spring Rolls

5. Make these design changes:
   a. Change the colors to Colorful Accent Colors.
   b. Apply the SmartArt Style Polished.
   c. Apply bold to all text.

6. Make these changes to the center shape:

   a. Increase the size of the center shape, and press ⌈Shift⌋ while you resize to keep the current proportions.

   b. Change the shape to a 16-point star, and resize as needed so that the text fits on two lines, as shown in Figure 7-34.

Figure 7-34
Completed flyer

7. Save the presentation as *[your initials]*7-26 in your Lesson 7 folder.

8. Close the presentation and submit your work.

Exercise 7-27 ◆ Challenge Yourself

Convert bulleted lists to appropriate diagrams.

1. Open the file **Market3**, and examine the slide content.

2. For slide 2, convert the listed text to an Upward Arrow SmartArt graphic from the Process type.

3. Increase the text size to 20 points, and then resize the text boxes as necessary to avoid words being cut off in the middle. Change the colors to one of the colorful options, and apply the Moderate Effect SmartArt Style.

4. For slides 4 and 5, convert both lists to the Multidirectional Cycle SmartArt graphic. Change the colors to one of the accent colors, and apply a Cartoon Effect SmartArt Style. Change the text color to black.

5. Create a handout header and footer: Include the date, your name as the header, the page number, and *[your initials]*7-27 as the footer.

6. Move to slide 1, and save the presentation as *[your initials]*7-27 in your Lesson 7 folder.

7. Close the presentation and submit your work.

On Your Own

In these exercises you work on your own, as you would in a real-life work environment. Use the skills you've learned to accomplish the task—and be creative.

Exercise 7-28

Think of the steps in the job search process, and arrange the steps in a process diagram. Include no more than 10 steps, and use concise terms to label each diagram shape so that the text is easy to read. Add SmartArt styles and color changes to improve the design and make it attractive. Add a title slide and one or two additional slides giving information about the process. Save the presentation as *[your initials]*7-28. Close the presentation and submit your work.

Exercise 7-29

Create an organization chart of your place of employment; if you work in a large company, focus on your department. Include a title slide for your presentation and one or two slides describing something of interest or special accomplishments of one or more people on your chart. Use your own creativity to format the presentation and the chart attractively. Save the presentation as *[your initials]*7-29. Close the presentation and submit your work.

Exercise 7-30

Create a diagram to depict a relationship among several functions or departments at your school or workplace or in some other organization you are familiar with. For example, a drama club might have a director, stagehands, costume designer, actors, musicians, and a playwright. Choose any of the SmartArt diagram types except the organization chart. Add a title slide and one or two other slides describing some aspect of the relationship. Save the presentation as *[your initials]*7-30. Close the presentation and submit your work.

Unit 2 Applications

Unit Application 2-1

Work with WordArt, work with images, group objects, and create a table.

1. Open the file **Runner**.

2. On slide 1, key **Good 4 U** as the title and **Proud Sponsor of the Fall Festival Marathon** as the subtitle.

3. Find and insert an illustration of a runner. Position it in the upper right area of the slide.

4. Resize the image to about 4 inches wide so that it does not overlap any text, and color it a dark blue to match the theme.

5. Change the picture style to Drop Shadow Rectangle. Your completed slide 1 should look similar to Figure U2-1.

Figure U2-1
Completed title slide

6. Working in the Outline pane, key the text shown in Figure U2-2, inserting new slides where needed.

7. On slides 2 and 4, remove the bullets from the body text placeholders.

Figure U2-2
Presentation text

8. On slide 4, insert the **Fireworks** picture from your student data files, and position it in the bottom right corner of the slide. Apply the Glow Diffused artistic effect.

9. Insert the **Rocket** picture from your student data files, and rotate the image so that the rocket points at the title on the slide, as shown in Figure U2-3.

Figure U2-3
Finished slide with artistic effect

10. Insert a new slide after slide 4 that uses the Blank layout. Insert an illustration of a race. Resize the picture proportionately so that it almost fills the open space on the slide. If the picture is an odd size, crop it where necessary so that it is the same size and shape as the slide. Change the picture color to Brown, Accent color 4 light, and adjust the picture's brightness and contrast settings to soften the colors so that WordArt will be readable when placed over the image.

11. Create WordArt text by using Gradient Fill – Turquoise, Accent 1, Outline – White, Glow – Accent 2. Key the following text on three lines, and center this text over the image:

Award Ceremony
6 p.m.
Central Park

12. Increase the text size to 60 points, and apply a dark-blue shadow Offset Left with a distance of 8.

13. Check spelling in the presentation.

14. Create a handout header and footer: Include the date, your name as the header, the page number, and *[your initials]*U2-1 as the footer.

15. Create a new Unit 2 Applications folder. Move to slide 1, and save the presentation as *[your initials]*U2-1 in your Unit 2 Applications folder.

16. Close the presentation and submit your work.

Unit Application 2-2

Add a table, insert a chart, create a SmartArt cycle diagram, and add a shape and a text box to a chart.

1. Open the file **HeadCount**. Apply the Verve design theme, and use the Trek theme color.

2. Insert a new slide after slide 3 that uses the Title and Content layout, and key the title **Current Breakdown**.

3. Create a table with five columns and four rows, and key the data shown in Figure U2-4.

4. Merge two cells for "Kitchen" and two cells for "Service."

5. Change the Table Style to Dark Style 1 – Accent 6.

6. Adjust the column widths so that the text fits attractively, and align the text to match the figure. The overall table dimensions should be approximately 6.2 inches wide by 3 inches tall.

7. Vertically center all of the text in the table.

8. Position the table evenly on the slide.

Figure U2-4
Table data

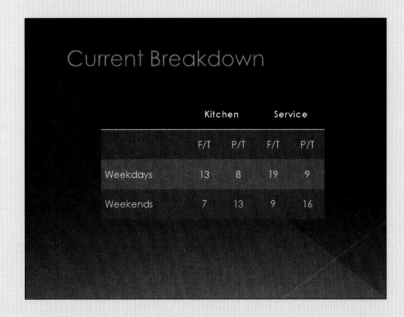

9. Increase the font size of the text in the table to 24 points.

10. Insert a new slide after slide 4 that uses the Title and Content layout, and key the title **Past, Current, Projected**. Create a Clustered column chart by using the data shown in Figure U2-5. Delete any extra rows or columns or select a new range of data to ensure that only the chart data are selected.

Figure U2-5
Chart worksheet data

	A	B	C
1		Full-time	Part-time
2	2009	41	30
3	2010	40	35
4	2011	48	46
5	2012	68	61

11. Apply a gradient fill to each series of columns, using theme colors of your choice. Move the legend to the bottom.

12. Draw a text box at the top of the chart; key the text **Projecting 61 P/T, 38 F/T!**. Change the text to 24 points, and make it bold. Resize the text box so that all the text fits on one line.

13. Draw an arrow from the text to the top of the 2012 columns.

14. Insert a new slide after slide 5. Use the Title and Content layout, and key the title **Plan for Increasing P/T Headcount**.

15. On the new slide 6, insert a Block Cycle SmartArt graphic showing the five steps in Figure U2-6, starting with the top shape in the 12 o'clock position and moving clockwise.

Figure U2-6
Data for Basic Cycle SmartArt graphic

Step 1	Advertise P/T positions
Step 2	T. Scott to schedule interviews
Step 3	M. Peters to interview and hire employees
Step 4	J. Farla to train
Step 5	L. Klein to assign schedules

16. Increase the size of the SmartArt to fill the open area of the slide. Increase the font size to 18 points, and make the font bold. Resize the shapes as necessary to fit text.

17. Apply the 3-D, Polished style.

18. Apply the Vortex, From Bottom transition to all the slides.

19. View the presentation as a slide show.

20. Create a slide footer for all slides, except the title slide, containing today's date, your name, and *[your initials]*U2-2.

21. Create a handout header and footer: Include the date, your name as the header, the page number, and *[your initials]*U2-2 as the footer.

22. Move to slide 1, and save the presentation as *[your initials]*U2-2 in your Unit 2 Applications folder.

23. Close the presentation and submit your work.

Unit Application 2-3

Create a presentation with an organization chart and a diagram.

1. Start a new presentation that uses the Solstice design theme and the Apex theme color.

2. Insert two additional slides, and key the text shown in Figure U2-7. Use the Two Content layout for the second slide and the Title and Content layout for the third slide.

Figure U2-7
Presentation text

Slide 1	Good 4 U Senior Management Current and Future Organization

Slide 2	Why Change What Works?
	
	  • Current structure—designed for a single-restaurant company
	
	  • Future structure—a national, multi-restaurant organization

Slide 3	Future Structure
	
	  • Reorganization planned for 2012
	
	  • Two functional areas
	
	  • Chef and Administration Managers—report to Julie Wolfe
	
	  • Marketing and Information Managers—report to Gus Irvinelli

3. Select all of the text on slide 3, and decrease the font size by one increment.

4. On slide 1, insert an appropriate illustration or picture showing managers, a business setting, or the like. Change the color to match the presentation theme color.

5. On slide 2, use the content placeholder to insert a SmartArt graphic, Cycle type, Radial Cycle layout.

6. Insert one additional shape on the radial diagram, making a total of five shapes in the outer circle plus a center shape.

7. Key **Good** [Enter] **4 U** in the center shape. For the other shapes, key the text shown in Figure U2-8, starting with "New York" in the 12 o'clock position and moving clockwise. The text with two words will appear on two lines.

```
New York

Miami

Los Angeles

San Francisco

More soon
```

8. Change the SmartArt Style to **3-D, Metallic Scene**, and change the colors to **Gradient Loop – Accent 6**.

9. Resize the bulleted text placeholder to reduce its width, and move it to the left slightly. Resize the diagram to make it as large as possible without overlapping the bulleted text placeholder.

10. Insert a new slide after slide 2 that uses the **Title and Content** layout. Key the title **Current Organization**.

11. On slide 3, create a SmartArt graphic for the Good 4 U restaurant by using the data in Figure U2-9. Choose the **Hierarchy** type and **Organization Chart** layout. Arrange the chart shapes in an attractive and functional way.

```
Julie Wolfe & Gus Irvinelli, Co-owners ——— Level 1
    Michele Jenkins, Head Chef ——————— Level 2
        Claudia Pell, Maitre d'
                                        Level 3
        Eric Dennis, Assistant Chef
    Roy Olafsen, Marketing Manager ——— Level 2
        Jerry Wayne, Sales
                                        Level 3
        Jane Kryler, Promotions
    Chuck Warden, Information Manager —— Level 2
        Tanya Reilly, Development
                                        Level 3
        Jerry Allen, User Systems
    Michael Peters, Administration Manager —— Level 2
        Robert Lee, Purchasing
        Carol Lynne, Personnel          Level 3
        Sharon Ray, Payroll
```

12. Resize the shapes to fit information on two lines, keeping all shapes on the same level the same size. Remove the commas after the name and before the title, since these are positioned on two lines. Add additional spaces if necessary to ensure that no titles are on the same lines as the names.

13. Increase the size of the chart, making it as large as possible.

14. Choose the SmartArt style Cartoon. Change the colors to Colorful - Accent Colors.

15. Insert a slide after slide 4 using the Title and Content layout. Key the title **What We Expect**. Create a table showing the positive effects that the restructuring will have on the business. See Figure U2-10 for the table data and alignment.

16. Apply Themed Style 1 – Accent 6 to the table.

17. Increase the font size of the text in the table to 20 points. Resize the table, and position it evenly on the slide.

Figure U2-10
Table data

Positive Effects of the Restructuring
Questions/Concerns to be handled in a more timely manner
Increase in responsiveness to customers
A more focused business ready to expand into new markets
Increase in adaptability of business if turnover takes place
Increase in job satisfaction by empowering employees
Tap into the skills and expertise of owners

18. Review all slides, adjusting the size and position of objects where needed.

19. View the presentation as a slide show.

20. Create a handout header and footer: Include the date, your name as the header, the page number, and *[your initials]*U2-3 as the footer.

21. Move to slide 1, and save the presentation as *[your initials]*U2-3 in your Unit 2 Applications folder.

22. Close the presentation and submit your work.

Unit Application 2-4 ◆ Using the Internet

Write and design a presentation that uses images, charts, tables, and SmartArt graphics.

Use the Internet to research a topic of current interest that would lend itself to a presentation including images, charts, tables, and SmartArt graphics such as an organization chart. You decide what your topic will be. Here are a few topics to give you ideas, but you are not limited to these topics:

- The impact of increased security for air travel.

- Enrollment information at your local college or university.

- How global warming is affecting weather patterns.

- How the financial health of Hollywood is affected by the overall economy.

- The problems caused by overuse of antibiotics.

- The growth of computer use in the general population.

Illustrate the information you gathered by using a variety of images, charts, tables, and SmartArt graphics. Be sure to include at least five slides, and format them in an attractive way. Prepare a slide listing the resources you used. When the presentation is complete, check spelling.

In the slide footer, include the text **Prepared by** followed by your name. Include the slide number, but not the date, on all slides. In the handout footer, include the completed filename *[your initials]*U2-4. In the handout header, key **Presented to**, and then identify to whom you would be giving this presentation. Include in the handout the date that you would be delivering the presentation.

Save the presentation as *[your initials]*U2-4 in your Unit 2 Applications folder. Practice delivering the presentation. Close the presentation and submit your work.

UNIT 3

VISUAL IMPACT

Customizing Colors and Effects

OBJECTIVES *After completing this lesson, you will be able to:*

1. Change the outline color and weight.
2. Work with solid and gradient colors.
3. Work with pictures and textures.
4. Apply shape effects.
5. Adjust presentation color settings.

Estimated Time: 1½ hours

Your presentation can be enhanced in many ways so that it is unique and customized for your content. The possibilities for how to apply color, patterns, pictures, shading, line styles, and shape effects are almost endless, but you need to use these effects skillfully. This lesson will guide you through some detailed settings that can make your work appear very professional.

Julie Wolfe has started a presentation about equipment needs and employee hiring practices for the new Good 4 U location in San Francisco. She has asked you to make improvements to this slide show to make it more interesting.

Changing the Outline Color and Weight

The outline of a shape, picture, placeholder, or object can be modified in many ways such as by adjusting the line color, line style and compound type, and transparency percentage.

Exercise 8-1   APPLY COLOR AND LINE STYLES

Shape outline refers to the border of a shape. Outlines can be any color, and the way you change an outline can make a subtle difference in the shape, such as by defining its edges, or can make a dramatic difference that emphasizes the shape. Outlines are solid, dashed, or compound (made up of more than one line). The *weight* of a line is its width or thickness, measured in points. A *dash type* a pattern of dashes and dots and includes a solid line, square dots, dashes, and combinations of dashes and dots. Outline settings also apply to lines and arrows drawn with the Line tool.

To modify a shape's outline, open the Format Shape dialog box in one of the following ways:

- Right-click the object; then choose Format Shape from the shortcut menu.

- From the Drawing Tools Format tab, in the Shape Styles group, click the Shape Outline button 🖉.

1. Open the file **SanFran**, and move to slide 2.

2. Select the body text placeholder, right-click, and choose Format Shape.

3. On the Format Shape dialog box, click Line Color on the left, and Solid Line should be selected.

4. Click the Color button 🖫, and choose Gold, Accent 2, Lighter 80% (column 6).

5. Click Line Style at the left of the Format Shape dialog box, and click the Width spin box down arrow to change the width to 5 pt.

6. Click the Compound type button ☰, and from the list box choose the second option Double, as shown in Figure 8-1. Notice the Join type is Round.

Figure 8-1
Line Style options in the Format Shape dialog box

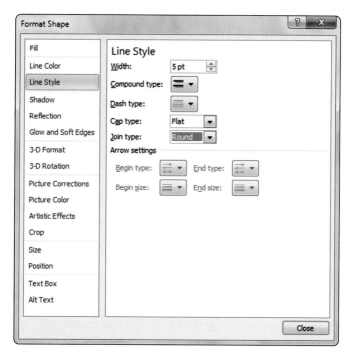

7. Click Close. You have now created an outline using colors from the current theme.

8. Deselect the text box, and change the Zoom to 100% to see the double line clearly.

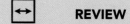

REVIEW

To change the zoom, you can use the Zoom slider and the Fit to Window button on the status bar or similar buttons on the View tab.

Figure 8-2
Finished shape
outline

9. Change the Zoom setting back to Fit to Window.

10. On slide 4, select the large oval shape.

11. From the Drawing Tools Format tab, in the Shape Styles group, click
    the Shape Outline button 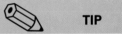 to make the following changes (you must
    click the button each time you make a change).

-   For Theme Colors, click Orange, Accent 5, Lighter 40% (second column
    from the right).

-   For Weight, click the 6 pt line weight to apply a thick outline on the
    star.

-   For Dashes, select the second type, titled Round Dot, as shown in
    Figure 8-3.

Figure 8-3
Dash type

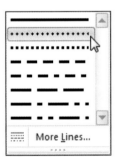

> **TIP**
>
> The outline is always present on a shape. If
> you do not want a contrasting color, then
> choose no line. If you want to emphasize
> the outline as a border, then choose a
> contrasting color that blends with your
> theme colors and make the line thicker so
> that it is easily visible on your slide.

Exercise 8-2   ADJUST LINE ARROWHEAD

Lines with attached *arrowheads* with preset arrow shapes can be customized
using the Format Shape dialog box. Line style options include different arrow
settings to change the tips on either end of the line to arrowheads, dots, or
diamonds.

1. Move to slide 3.

2. From the Insert tab, in the Illustrations group, click the Shapes button,
    and then click the Arrow button. Draw a diagonal line that slants down
    from the left, pointing toward the first step in the diagram.

3. From the Drawing Tools Format tab, in the Shape Styles group, click the Shape Outline button , choose Weight , and then choose 6 pt to increase the thickness of the arrow. Click the Shape Outline button  again, and change the color to White, Text 1 so that there is a contrast between the arrow and the slide background.

Figure 8-4
Arrow styles

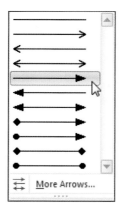

4. Deselect the line. Notice the small arrowhead on the end of the line.

5. Select the arrow. From the Drawing Tools Format tab, in the Shape Styles group, click the Shape Outline button , and choose Arrows and Arrow Style 3, a left-pointing arrow. The arrow points away from the diagram.

6. Click the Shape Outline button  again. Choose Arrows and Arrow Style 5, a right-pointing arrow, as shown in Figure 8-4.

7. Click the Shape Outline button  again, and choose Arrows and then More Arrows.

8. Under the End Size heading, choose Arrow R Size 9. This increases the arrowhead tip size. Click Close to close the dialog box and return to the presentation.

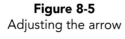

NOTE

The placement of the arrow head is determined by where you started drawing the line. The left arrowhead appears at the beginning of the line, and the right arrowhead appears at the end of the line.

9. Adjust the length and angle of the arrow by dragging the sizing handle on the end of the arrow so that it points to the word "Planning," as shown in Figure 8-5. No rotation handle is required to make lines angle on the slide.

Figure 8-5
Adjusting the arrow

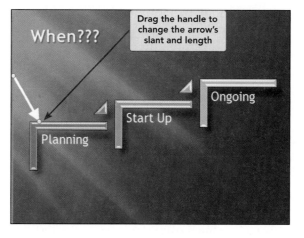

Exercise 8-3 ADJUST TRANSPARENCY AND ROTATE

When you increase the *transparency* of an outline or fill color, you allow more of the background slide color to show through the selected shape.

1. Still working on slide 3, select the arrow.

2. Right-click the arrow, and choose Format Shape from the shortcut menu.

3. In the Format Shape dialog box, click the **Line Color** option at the left of the dialog box.

4. Move the Transparency slider over to **30%**, as shown in Figure 8-6. Move the dialog box as necessary, and notice that the colors behind the arrow show slightly through the arrow.

Figure 8-6
Format Shape dialog box with 30% line transparency

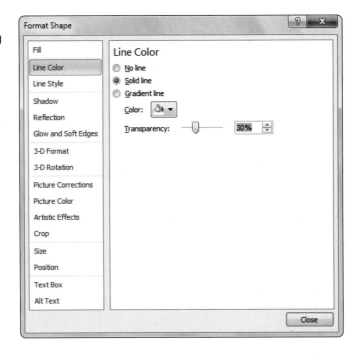

5. Click the **3-D Rotation** option at the left of the dialog box.

6. Scroll the X Rotation to **50%**. Notice how the appearance of the arrow changes.

7. Click **Close** on the Format Shape dialog box.

8. Move the arrow as necessary to ensure that it is still pointing at the first step.

9. Create a handout header and footer: Include the date, your name as the header, the page number, and *[your initials]***8-3** as the footer.

10. Create a new folder for Lesson 8. Save the presentation as *[your initials]***8-3** in the new Lesson 8 folder.

Working with Solid and Gradient Colors

Up to this point, you have used theme colors when applying color to objects. An infinite number of other colors are also available.

Theme colors are convenient to use because if you change to a different theme, the colors will automatically be adjusted. But you may want to use a different color in some cases, such as to present a company logo or to enhance the slide in some way. Be careful when choosing extra colors because too many colors can seem confusing. Also, remember that custom colors you add to a presentation will not be changed if you select a different theme.

Extra colors are available from the Colors dialog box. Standard colors are premixed colors that you choose by clicking a sample, and custom colors are colors that you mix yourself.

Exercise 8-4   ADD A SOLID FILL THEME COLOR TO A SHAPE

You change the fill color by using one of two options:

- Use the Shape Fill button on the Drawing Tools Format tab in the Shape Styles group.

- Right-click the shape, and choose Format Shape from the shortcut menu. The Format Shape dialog box will appear, so you can use the Fill option.

If you apply a fill to a shape and later decide you don't want it, it's easy to remove. Choose the Shape Fill option No Fill to remove the fill from the shape.

1. Move to slide 4, and right-click the oval. From the shortcut menu, choose Format Shape to open the Format Shape dialog box.

2. Click the Fill option at the left of the dialog box, and notice that Solid fill is selected. Click the Color list box arrow, and choose the Gold, Accent 2, Lighter 80% color.

3. Click Close. This color is too light because the white text is not readable.

4. With the oval still selected, from the Drawing Tools Format tab, in the Shape Styles group, click the Shape Fill button, which opens the gallery shown in Figure 8-7. Click the Black, Background 1, Lighter 15% (column 1) theme color.

Figure 8-7
Changing an object's fill color

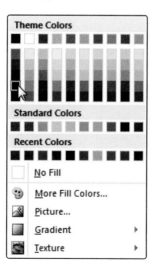

5. Still working on slide 4, select the rounded rectangle.

6. From the Drawing Tools Format tab, in the Shape Styles group, click the Shape Fill button, and choose No Fill. The color disappears, but the line remains.

7. With the rounded rectangle still selected, click the Shape Outline button, and choose No Outline. Now only the text is displayed.

8. Click the Shape Fill button again, and choose Orange, Accent 5, Darker 25% (column 9). The rounded rectangle is once again visible.

Exercise 8-5 CHOOSE A STANDARD COLOR
OR CUSTOM COLOR

You open the Colors dialog box by choosing More Fill Colors from the Shape Fill button's drop-down list or by choosing More Outline Colors from the Shape Outline button's drop-down list.

The Standard tab contains a honeycomb of preset color choices that you may apply to your presentation. However, these colors do not have ScreenTip names as shown for theme colors.

The Custom tab on the Colors dialog box enables you to create any color you desire. Drag a crosshair to choose the color you want; then use a scroll bar to choose the brightness level for the color. Remember these color terms for the RGB color model a computer uses to mix all colors that you see:

- *Hue.* The actual name of the color that you select.

- *Saturation.* The intensity of the color. Colors you select from the top of the Custom color palette are strong colors that are highly saturated; colors at the bottom seem muted because their saturation level is low.

- *Luminance.* The brightness of the color. When you drag the pointer up on the vertical bar, you are increasing the amount of white in a color; therefore, the luminance level has increased, and the color is brighter. When you drag the pointer down, you are decreasing the amount of white in the color and adding black. Therefore, the color has a lower luminance level and is less bright.

After you choose a custom color, it appears on the second line of the Shape Fill and Shape Outline buttons' drop-down lists, so you can use it again without having to re-create it.

1. On slide 4 select the oval. From the Drawing Tools Format tab, in the Shape Styles group, click the Shape Fill button.

Figure 8-8
Working with
Standard colors

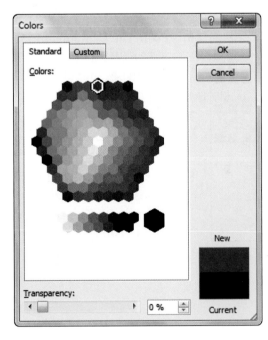

2. Select More Fill Colors to display the Colors dialog box.

3. Click the Standard tab. The honeycomb of colors is displayed.

4. Click the blue color in the top center edge of the honeycomb (no color names are displayed). Notice the color sample on the lower right of the dialog box, showing you the current color and the new color you just selected, as shown in Figure 8-8.

5. Click OK.

6. Still working on slide 4, select the rounded rectangle.

7. From the Drawing Tools Format tab, in the Shape Styles group, click the Shape Fill button ⬛, and choose More Fill Colors.

8. Click the Custom tab on the Colors dialog box. This dialog box contains a color palette and a vertical bar for choosing brightness, as shown in Figure 8-9.

Figure 8-9
Working with Custom colors

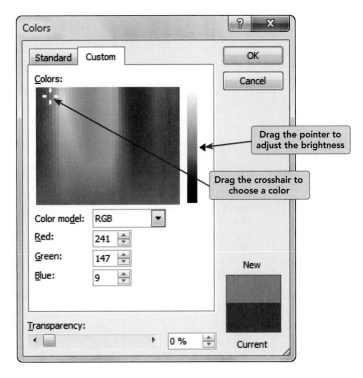

9. Drag the crosshair straight up. Notice in the sample on the lower right corner that the new color has a higher saturation level than the current color.

10. Drag the crosshair across the top of the palette. All the colors at the top have a high saturation, and the colors change horizontally like a rainbow.

11. Drag the crosshair across the bottom of the palette. The colors are muted due to low saturation.

12. Choose a saturated color; then drag the black pointer on the vertical bar up and down to see how the color brightness changes.

13. Experiment with the color palette and the brightness bar until you find a color that blends with the blue on the oval shape. Click OK.

Exercise 8-6 CHOOSE A GRADIENT FILL

A gradient fill can add interest and dimension to PowerPoint shapes, text placeholders, text boxes, and other objects. When you apply a *gradient fill*, blended colors are applied. A gradient fill can consist of one color blending to black, two colors that blend to each other, or a preset combination of multiple colors.

Besides choosing colors for gradient fills, you can specify the direction of the gradual color change, such as horizontal or diagonal.

1. Still working on slide 4, select the oval shape.

2. From the Drawing Tools Format tab, in the Shape Styles group, click the Shape Fill button ⬛. Choose Gradient at the bottom of the menu and then More Gradients. The Format Shape dialog box appears.

3. Click the Fill option at the left of the dialog box.

4. In the Fill option area, click Gradient fill. Click the Preset colors list box arrow, and choose Late Sunset. Move the dialog box over, and observe the effect that this has on the oval shape.

5. Click the Type drop-down list box arrow, and choose Path, as shown in Figure 8-10.

Figure 8-10
Format Shape dialog box showing Gradient stops

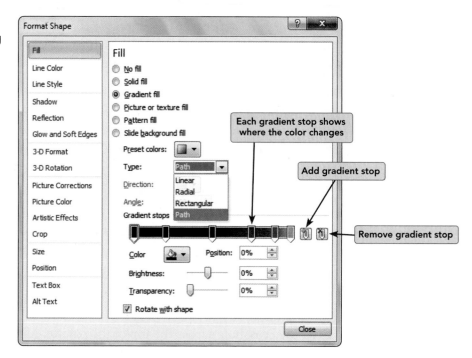

6. Click Close to view your new gradient fill.

7. Move to slide 2, and select the body text placeholder.

8. Right-click, and choose Format Shape from the shortcut menu to open the Format Shape dialog box.

9. Select the Fill option at the left of the dialog box, and choose Gradient fill.

10. Click Remove gradient stop several times to take out the previously set gradient stops until there are only two stops left on the slider.

11. Click Gradient Stop 1 on the slider, click the the Color list box arrow, and choose Tan, Text 2, Darker 50% (column 4). Drag the Position slider bar to 30%.

12. Click Gradient Stop 2, click the Color list box arrow, and choose Black, Background 1 (column 1). Drag the Position slider to 100% if it is not already there.

13. Click the Type list box arrow, and choose Linear. For Direction, choose Linear Diagonal - Top Left to Bottom Right, with the darker color in the lower right corner.

14. Click Close. Notice the color changes.

Exercise 8-7 ADJUST GRADIENT COLORS

You may need to adjust gradient colors after applying a shape's fill. To do this, reopen the Format Shape dialog box using either the Shape Fill button 🖌 or the shortcut menu and modify only the stops you wish to change.

1. Move to slide 4, and select the rounded rectangle.

2. From the Drawing Tools Format tab, in the Shape Styles group, click the Shape Fill button 🖌, and choose Gradient. The samples that are previewed under this gradient option show the current fill color combined with white or black in different blending directions of the two colors.

3. Select More Gradients to open the Format Shape dialog box and display the Fill option.

4. Choose Gradient fill, and choose Path. Click Add gradient stop or Remove gradient stop until you have four stops. Adjust the slider position and colors as follows (use More Fill Colors as needed):

Gradient Stop	Position	Standard Colors
1	0%	Red
2	33%	Dark red
3	67%	Brown
4	100%	Black

5. Click Close to view your gradient effects.

6. Update your handout footer to show the text *[your initials]*8-7. Save the presentation as *[your initials]*8-7 in the Lesson 8 folder.

Working with Pictures and Textures

Pictures and textures can be a great addition to your PowerPoint shapes. They can fill a shape to make the shape stand out on your slide. Many adjustments can be made to the picture and texture fills to modify the look of the shape.

Exercise 8-8 APPLY A PICTURE FILL

As you learned previously, pictures can be cropped to a shape. In this exercise, you will start with a shape and apply a picture fill. While the results will look the same, you may want to use this technique if the shape where the picture will be placed has already been planned, as in the three diamond shapes on slide 6. They are consistently sized, so each fill will occupy the same space.

1. Move to slide 6, and select the three diamonds.

2. From the Drawing Tools Format tab, in the Shape Styles group, click the Shape Outline button ☑, and change the outline color to Black, Background 1. Change the weight of the outline to 3 pt.

3. Select the bottom diamond. Still working on the Drawing Tools Format tab, in the Shape Styles group, click the Shape Fill button ⬛, and choose Picture.

4. Navigate to the folder in which your student files are stored.

5. Select the file **employee1**, and click Insert. The diamond shape is now filled with an employee picture, as shown in Figure 8-11.

Figure 8-11
Picture fill

6. Click the first diamond.
7. Click the Shape Fill button ⬛ again, and choose Picture.
8. Navigate to the folder in which your student files are stored.
9 Select the file **chef1**, and click Insert. The diamond shape is now filled with a chef picture.

Exercise 8-9 APPLY A TEXTURE AND PATTERN FILL

In addition to using gradient fills and pictures, you can apply textured fill effects, such as marble and wood grain, and patterned effects that use two colors. These are foreground and background colors. When they are similar in color, the pattern will be subtle; when the colors are very different, the pattern will be more defined.

1. Still working on slide 6, right-click the middle diamond; then choose Format Shape from the shortcut menu to open the Format Shape dialog box.

2. Click the Fill option at the left, and choose Picture or texture fill; then click the Texture drop-down list box arrow, as shown in Figure 8-12.

3. Point to several different textures, one at a time. Notice that the name of the texture appears as a ScreenTip.

4. Choose Granite.

TIP

You are not limited to the textures shown on the Textures tab. Use the Insert from File option to choose textures you have obtained from other sources.

Figure 8-12
Choosing a textured fill

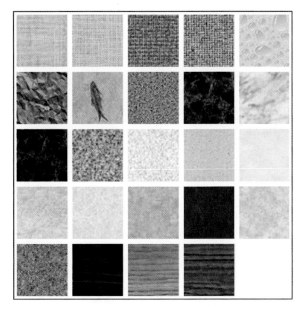

5. With the Format Shape dialog box still open, click slide 1 on the Slides tab.

6. On slide 1, select the rectangle. For Fill, click Pattern fill. A gallery of patterns appears with both the foreground and background colors displayed. Point to different patterns to see the ScreenTip identifying each one and the preview on your slide.

7. Click Light upward diagonal (column 3); then click Close to close the Format Shape dialog box.

Exercise 8-10   USE OFFSETS TO STRETCH OR REPOSITION A PICTURE

Offsets are used to scale the size of a picture within a shape or to reposition a picture within a shape. Positive numbers move the picture edge toward the center of the shape, and negative numbers move the picture edge away from the shape. Tiling options work similar to offsets but are used when a picture or texture is tiled to repeat itself.

1. On slide 6, select the first diamond shape with the chef picture fill.

2. Right-click the **chef1** picture, and select Format Picture from the shortcut menu. Drag the Format Picture dialog box to the right so that you can view the changes to the picture as you make them.

3. In the Format Picture dialog box, click Fill on the left of the dialog box.

4. Check the box Tile picture as texture. This allows you to adjust the picture within the shape. Make the following changes, as shown in Figure 8-13.

   Offset X   -3 pt
   Scale X   62%
   Offset Y   6 pt
   Scale Y   63%

Figure 8-13
Format Picture
dialog box

5. Click the drop-down arrow beside Alignment; choose several different options, and note what happens to the picture within the diamond when each option is chosen. Choose Top Left.

6. Notice how the chef, who is the main focus of the picture, is more centered within the shape.

7. Select the bottom diamond with the employee1 picture, click the Fill option at the left of the dialog box, and adjust the following Offsets under Stretch options, as shown in Figure 8-14:

   Left   -6%
   Right   -4%
   Top   3%
   Bottom   1%

Figure 8-14
Format Picture
dialog box stretch
options

8.   Click Close.

Exercise 8-11   ADJUST TRANSPARENCY AND PICTURE ROTATION

Adjusting the transparency of an object can make the shape or picture seem to blend into the background.

1.   Still working on slide 6, select the middle diamond shape that is filled with the granite texture.

2.   Right-click, and choose Format Picture from the shortcut menu.

3.   Working on the Fill option of the Format Picture dialog box, drag the Transparency slider to 50%. Notice the effect applied to the diamond shape on the slide.

4.   Click Close to accept the transparency setting and close the Format Picture dialog box.

5.   Move to slide 1. Select the picture of San Francisco.

6.   From the Picture Tools Format tab, in the Arrange group, click the Rotate button ⬗▾, and choose More Rotation Options.

7.   For Size and rotate, change the Rotation box to -10°. Negative numbers move the object counterclockwise; positive numbers move the object clockwise.

8.   Click Close. Notice the picture's rotation, as shown in Figure 8-15.

Figure 8-15
Changing picture
rotation

Exercise 8-12   USE PRECISE SIZE DIMENSIONS

Resizing stretches or shrinks the dimensions of any object. You can also resize to fit precise dimensions by using the Size and Position options on the Format Picture or Format Shapes dialog boxes. *Lock aspect ratio* keeps the vertical and horizontal dimensions in the same proportions when an object is resized.

1. Move to slide 2, and select the picture on the slide.

2. From the Picture Tools Format tab, in the Size group, click the Dialog Box Launcher ⌧.

3. Under the Size and rotate heading, decrease the Height to **3.5"**. Because the Lock aspect ratio is checked, as shown in Figure 8-16, the width changes automatically to keep the size proportional and not distort the picture.

Figure 8-16
Using precise
dimensions

Format Picture		?	✕

Fill
Line Color
Line Style
Shadow
Reflection
Glow and Soft Edges
3-D Format
3-D Rotation
Picture Corrections
Picture Color
Artistic Effects
Crop
Size
Position
Text Box
Alt Text

Size

Size and rotate

Height: 3.5"   Width: 2.34"

Rotation: 0°

Scale

Height: 117%   Width: 117%

☑ Lock aspect ratio
☑ Relative to original picture size
☐ Best scale for slide show

Resolution 640 x 480

Original size

Height: 2.99" Width: 2"

Reset

Close

4. Click the Position option at the left of the Format Picture dialog box.

5. Under Position on Slide, the dimensions shown are currently measured from the Top Left Corner. Decrease the Horizontal Position to **7″** and the Vertical Position to **3.3″** so that the picture is positioned better over the bottom right corner of the text placeholder.

6. Click Close. Notice the resized and repositioned picture.

7. Update the handout footer to show the text *[your initials]8-12*.

8. Move to slide 1, and save the presentation as *[your initials]8-12* in your Lesson 8 folder.

Applying Shape Effects

Effects can enhance the appearance of your PowerPoint objects. Effects may be applied to text, shapes, pictures, charts, tables, and more. The many options for shape effects include *Shadows, Glow, Bevel,* and *3-D Rotation.*

Exercise 8-13   ADD SHADOW AND REFLECTION

The Shadow and Reflection effects appear to create either a shadow of the selected object or a lighter transparent copy of the object appearing as a reflection. These effects are found on Format tabs for the corresponding object.

1. Move to slide 1, and select the picture of San Francisco.

2. From the Picture Tools Format tab, in the Picture Styles group, click the Picture Effects button .

3. Choose Shadow, and select Shadow Options.

4. Working in the Format Picture dialog box under Presets, choose Offset Diagonal Bottom Right.

5. Under the Color heading, choose Black, Background 1, Lighter 50%.

6. Change the following Shadow setting options, as shown in Figure 8-17:

Transparency	**60%**
Size	**103%**
Blur	**8.5 pt**
Angle	**40°**
Distance	**10 pt**

> **TIP**
>
> If you move your dialog box to the side of the picture, you can observe the changes that each item makes.

Figure 8-17
Changing Shadow
settings

7. Click Close. Notice how the shadow has changed.

8. Move to slide 6, and select the middle diamond shape with the granite fill.

9. From the Drawing Tools Format tab, in the Shape Styles group, click the Shape Effects button 🖳, and choose Reflection and then Half Reflection, 4 pt offset.

Exercise 8-14   ADD GLOW AND SOFT EDGES

The Glow and Soft Edges effects appear around the entire object that is selected. The *Glow* effect applies a color around the object that blends into the background. The *Soft Edges* effect makes the object's edges blend into the background and appear less distinct. Shape effects are found on the Format tab for the corresponding object.

1. Move to slide 4, and select the rounded rectangle.

2. From the Drawing Tools Format tab, in the Shape Styles group, click the Shape Effects button 🖳.

3. Choose Glow, and select Orange, 18 pt glow, Accent Color 5, as shown in Figure 8-18.

4. Select the oval. Click the Shape Effects button 🖳 again, choose Glow, and select Orange, 18 point glow, Accent Color 5.

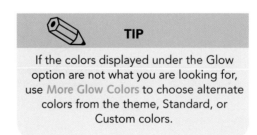

TIP

If the colors displayed under the Glow option are not what you are looking for, use More Glow Colors to choose alternate colors from the theme, Standard, or Custom colors.

Figure 8-18
Applying a Glow
effect

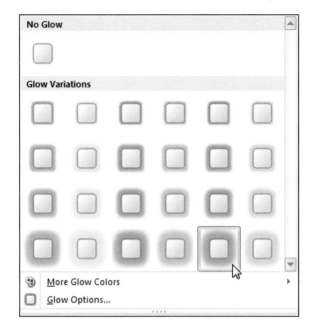

5. Select the rounded rectangle.

6. From the Drawing Tools Format tab, in the Shape Styles group, click the Shape Effects button.

7. Choose **Soft Edges** and **10 point**. Notice how the effect is applied to the shape. The shape's dark edges are softened, but the glow effect is still applied to the shape.

Exercise 8-15   ADD BEVEL EFFECTS

Bevel is a shape effect that gives an object the appearance of being three dimensional. Shape effects are found on the Format tab for the corresponding object.

1. Move to slide 5, and notice that the picture has a bevel effect applied.

2. Select the picture, and from the Picture Tools Format tab, in the Picture Styles group, click the Picture Effects button.

3. Choose **Bevel** and **3-D Options**.

4. Under Bevel in the Top section, choose **Art Deco**, and change the Width to **16 pt** and the Height to **15 pt**.

5. Under Contour, change the color to **White, Text 1, Darker 50%**, and change the size to **3.5 pt**.

6. Under Surface, change the material to **Special Effect, Dark Edge** and the Lighting to **Cool, Chilly**. Change the Angle to **80°**, as shown in Figure 8-19.

7. Click **Close**. Notice the bevel effect.

Figure 8-19
Applying a Bevel
effect

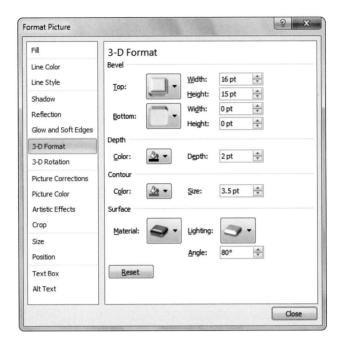

Exercise 8-16   ADJUST 3-D ROTATION

The *3-D Rotation* option allows you to change the way your three-dimensional object is viewed. Shape effects are found on the Format tab for the corresponding object.

1.   Move to slide 4, and select the oval. From the Drawing Tools Format tab, in the Shape Styles group, click the Shape Effects button 🔲.

2.   Choose 3-D Rotation and 3-D Rotation Options.

3.   Under Presets, in the Parallel group, choose Off Axis 1 Right.

4.   Change the X Rotation to 350° and the Z Rotation to 10°, as shown in Figure 8-20.

Figure 8-20
Adjust 3-D rotation

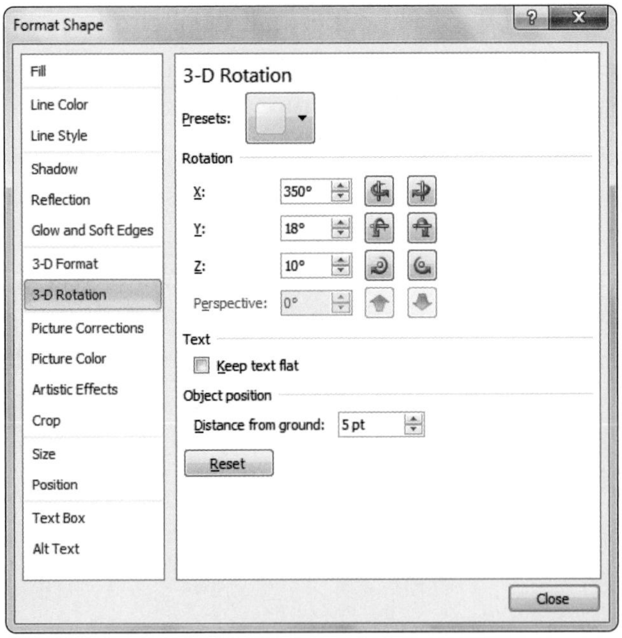

5. Change the Distance from Ground to **5 pt**.

6. Click **Close**. Notice the 3-D effect.

7. Use steps 1 to 6 to apply the same effects to the rounded rectangle on slide 4.

8. Update the handout footer to show the text *[your initials]*8-16.

9. Move to slide 1, and save the presentation as *[your initials]*8-16 in your Lesson 8 folder.

Adjusting Presentation Color Settings

In many cases, slides look great in color, but the text becomes difficult or impossible to read when you print in grayscale (shades of gray) with a black-and-white printer.

Fortunately, you can display the grayscale view of your presentation in the Slide pane. When the grayscale view is displayed, you can change grayscale settings without affecting the color version of your presentation.

Exercise 8-17 ADJUST GRAYSCALE SETTINGS

To adjust the grayscale colors in a presentation, display and adjust the grayscale version of your presentation by following these steps:

- From the View tab, in the Color/Grayscale group, click the Grayscale button ▣.

- When the grayscale version is in view, select an object on a slide and click a button in the Change Selected Object group on the Grayscale tab to choose one of the options.

1. Move to slide 1. From the View tab, in the Color/Grayscale group, click the Grayscale button ▣. The slide colors change to grayscale, and the Grayscale tab appears, as shown in Figure 8-21.

2. Select the large rectangle on slide 1.

3. From the Grayscale tab, in the Change Selected Object group, click the Light Grayscale button ▣.

Figure 8-21
Changing grayscale
settings

4. Move to slide 2, and select the body text placeholder. From the Grayscale tab, in the Change Selected Object group, click the Black with White Fill button ▢. This setting displays all lines in black and eliminates fills, but the white text does not display. Click Undo ↺; then click Light Grayscale ▣.

5. On slide 4, select the rounded rectangle, and click the Inverse Grayscale button ▣.

6. Select the oval, and click the Light Grayscale button ▣.

7. From the Grayscale tab, in the Close group, click the Back to Color View button ▣ to return to the normal color view.

Exercise 8-18 CHOOSE THE BLACK-AND-WHITE VERSION

The black-and-white version of a PowerPoint presentation is available from the View tab, in the Color/Grayscale group used in the previous exercise. The black-and-white option may save ink when printing and can be useful when preparing handouts that must photocopy clearly.

1. Move to slide 1. From the View tab, in the Color/Grayscale group, click the Black and White button ▣. The slide changes to show only black and white.

2. Notice that the Grayscale tab appears, as in the previous exercise. Select the large rectangle on slide 1. From the Grayscale tab, in the Change Selected Object group, click the Black button ▣. Notice that the rectangle is filled with black and the text is not visible. This could be used to show contrast, but will use too much ink in printing.

3. Click the Undo button ↰.

4. With the rectangle still selected, click the Black with White Fill button ▢, and the gray shading is removed. This treatment would work well for photocopied handouts.

5. Repeat step 4 to change the text placeholder on slide 2.

6. Click the Back to Color View button ▣. Notice that nothing has changed in the color view of the presentation.

7. Update the handout footer to show the text *[your initials]8-18*.

8. Move to slide 1, and save the presentation as *[your initials]8-18* in your Lesson 8 folder.

9. Close the presentation and submit your work.

Lesson 8   Summary

- All PowerPoint objects—shapes, text placeholders, text boxes, and WordArt—can be enhanced with the addition of shape outline, shape fill, and shape effects.

- Shape Outline options include solid lines, gradient lines, and dashed lines in any thickness (weight) or color you want.

- Apply Shape Outline options by using the Shape Outline button found on the Drawing Tools Format tab in the Shape Styles group. Alternatively, you can use the Format Shape dialog box.

- The Arrow button draws a line with an arrowhead at its end. You can add or remove an arrowhead from any drawn line by using the Shape Outline button and then selecting Arrows.

- The Line Style tab of the Format Shape dialog box offers additional ways to format an arrow, enabling you to choose the size and shape of the arrowhead and line formatting options.

- Shape Fill options include solid colors, gradients, textures, and pictures. In addition, solid colors and gradients can have varying degrees of transparency, enabling background objects and colors to show through.

- Remove an outline from an object by choosing the No Outline option from the Shape Outline button's drop-down list. Remove the shape fill from an object by choosing the No Fill option from the Shape Fill button's drop-down list.

- It is usually best to use the coordinating theme colors that are part of the slide design color theme, but, occasionally, a few additional colors can enhance a presentation.

- Additional colors are available by choosing More Fill Colors from the Shape Fill button's drop-down list, More Outline Colors from the Shape Outline button's drop-down list, or More Colors from the Font Color button's drop-down list.

- The Colors dialog box enables you to choose from a honeycomb of premixed colors on the Standard tab or to mix your own colors on the Custom tab.

- You have several options when using gradient fills—the blending of colors into each other—including the direction and transparency of the effect. You may choose a preset gradient or create your own.

- PowerPoint includes several textures that you can use for fill effects. In addition, you can use graphics files containing textures from other sources that are saved on your computer or network.

- Any picture—a scanned photograph or some other image—can be used to fill an object. When using a picture, you have the choice of distorting the picture to fill the space or preserving its aspect ratio.

- Picture borders and picture effects can be modified through the Picture Tools Format tab or through the Format Picture dialog box.

- PowerPoint objects can be resized, positioned, and rotated using precise dimensions for location and size.

- The Reflection effect creates a lighter transparent copy of the image that appears reflected from the original object.
- The Glow effects apply a color around an object.
- The Soft Edge effects blend an object's edges into the background.
- Bevel effects create the appearance of three-dimensional objects.
- The objects in 3-D can be rotated to increase the three-dimensional perspective.
- The grayscale version and the black-and-white version of a presentation can be adjusted for clearer printing on black-and-white printers. Adjusting the grayscale settings has no effect on the color version of the presentation.

LESSON 8		Command Summary
Feature	**Button**	**Ribbon**
Apply Picture Effects		Picture Tools Format, Picture Styles group, Picture Effects
Apply Shape Effects		Drawing Tools Format, Shape Styles group, Shape Effects
Format lines and outlines of shapes		Drawing Tools Format, Shape Styles group, Shape Outline
Format Shape Fill		Drawing Tools Format, Shape Styles group, Shape Fill
Switch from color to black and white		View, Color/Grayscale group, Black and White
Switch from color to grayscale		View, Color/Grayscale group, Grayscale

Concepts Review

True/False Questions

Each of the following statements is either true or false. Indicate your choice by circling T or F.

T F   1.   Transparency can be adjusted with solid fill colors only.

T F   2.   Effects can be used to give objects the appearance of being in 3-D.

T F   3.   A gradient fill can have only two colors.

T F   4.   Shape outlines are available in only one width.

T F   5.   Granite and marble are examples of texture fills.

T F   6.   Offsets can be used to reposition or stretch pictures within shapes.

T F   7.   You cannot create custom colors to use for shape fills and outlines.

T F   8.   You must be careful when making changes in Grayscale view because these changes affect the color view of your presentation also.

Short Answer Questions

Write the correct answer in the space provided.

1.   What dialog box can you use to change the size and shape of arrowheads?

_____

2.   What button should be used to apply gradient fill options?

_____

3.   How do you remove a shape outline from an object?

_____

4.   Which shape effect creates a lighter transparent copy of the image that appears below the original object?

_____

5.   How do you apply a custom color to a Shape Outline?

_____

6.   How do you create a custom gradient fill?

_____

7. How do you switch the screen display of your presentation from color to grayscale?

_____

8. How do you change grayscale settings for PowerPoint objects?

_____

Critical Thinking

Answer these questions on a separate page. Support your answers with examples from your own experience, if possible.

1. Think of the way you used a gradient fill using the path type to add dimension to an oval. What other objects could you change by using a gradient fill to add dimension?

2. Why is it necessary to be sure to modify the grayscale settings before printing handouts that will be photocopied for a presentation?

Skills Review

Exercise 8-19

Format outline colors and styles, and change fill colors.

1. Open the file **Funding**.

2. Add an outline to the title text placeholder on slide 1 of the presentation by following these steps:
   a. Select the title text placeholder.
   b. From the Drawing Tools Format tab, in the Shape Styles group, click the Shape Outline button ✎.
   c. Choose White, Background 1, Darker 50%.

3. Format the outline by following these steps:
   a. With the title text placeholder selected, from the Drawing Tools Format tab, in the Shape Styles group, click the Shape Outline button ✎.
   b. Choose Weight and 6 pt.
   c. Click the Shape Outline button ✎ again.
   d. Choose Dashes, and select the Round Dot style.

4. Apply a fill to the title text placeholder on slide 1 by following these steps:
   a. With the title text placeholder selected, from the Drawing Tools Format tab, in the Shape Styles group, click the Shape Fill button ⬧.
   b. Select White, Background 1, Darker 25%.

c. Click the Shape Fill button again, and select More Fill Colors. On the Custom Color tab, change the transparency to 40%, and click OK.

d. Apply the same outline and fill to all the body text placeholders in the presentation using the Format Painter.

5. Draw and format an arrow by following these steps:

a. Move to slide 3; from the Insert tab, in the Illustrations group, click the Shapes button 🔲, and then click the Arrow button ↘.

b. Drag the cross pointer from the word "Specialties" in the title to the word "fat" in the first line of the body text placeholder.

6. Use the Format Shape dialog box to format the arrow by following these steps:

a. Right-click the arrow, and choose Format Shape from the shortcut menu.

b. Click the Line Style option at the left of the dialog box.

c. In the Width section, scroll up to 6 pt.

d. For Dash type, choose Solid.

e. From the End type drop-down list, choose Stealth Arrow.

f. From the End size drop-down list, choose Arrow R Size 6.

g. Click the Line Color option at the left of the dialog box.

h. Click the Color drop-down list, and choose White, Background 1, Darker 50%. Click Close.

7. Check spelling in the presentation.

8. Create a handout header and footer: Include the date, your name as the header, the page number, and *[your initials]*8-19 as the footer.

9. Move to slide 1, and save the presentation as *[your initials]*8-19 in your Lesson 8 folder.

10. Close the presentation and submit your work.

Exercise 8-20

Apply gradient fills using theme and custom colors, and use a picture fill.

1. Open the file **Owners**.

2. Apply a gradient fill to an object by following these steps:

a. Move to slide 2, and select the body text placeholder.

b. From the Drawing Tools Format tab, in the Shape Styles group, click the Shape Fill button 🖌, and choose Gradient and More Gradients.

c. Click the Fill option at the left of the dialog box, and then select Gradient fill.

d. Click Remove to clear the extra previous setting.

TIP

PowerPoint remembers your gradient stops. If you want the same stops as the ones you used the last time you created a gradient fill, proceed with creating a gradient fill on your new object and the previous gradient stops will be there. This saves time by not having to adjust the numbers.

e. Set Stop 1 Color to Gold, Accent 2, Lighter 60% with Stop position at 40%.

f. Set Stop 2 Color to Tan, Background 2, Darker 25% with Stop position at 100% and Transparency at 40%.

g. Be sure Type is set to Linear. Under Direction, choose Linear Diagonal - Top Right to Bottom Left.

h. Click Close. Notice that the gradient fill blends nicely with the background design.

i. Apply the same gradient effect to the two body text placeholders on slide 3 and the body text placeholder on slide 4.

3. Add dimension to a circle by following these steps:

   a. Click the top circle on slide 1.

   b. From the Drawing Tools Format tab, in the Shape Styles group, click the Shape Fill button 🖌, and choose Gradient and More Gradients.

   c. Click the Fill option at the left of the dialog box, and then select Gradient fill.

   d. Set Stop 1 Color to Aqua, Accent 1 with Stop position at 20%.

   e. Set Stop 2 Color to Tan%, Background 2, Darker 50% with Stop position at 50%.

   f. Add another stop position, and set Stop 3 to Tan, Background 2, Darker 10% with Stop position at 70% and Transparency of 60%. Click Add.

   g. Add another stop position, and set Stop 4 to Aqua, Accent 1, Lighter 60% with Stop position at 100%.

   h. Under Type, choose Path. This makes the gradient pattern go in a circle inside your shape.

   i. Click Close to view your gradient fill.

4. Use the Format Painter button 🖋 to copy the formatting of the circle to the other circles in the presentation following these steps:

   a. Select the circle with the gradient applied.

   b. From the Home tab, in the Clipboard group, double-click the Format Painter button 🖋.

   c. Click each of the remaining circles in the presentation.

   d. Click the Format Painter button again to turn it off.

5. Apply a custom color fill to a placeholder by following these steps:

   a. Move to slide 1, and select the subtitle text placeholder.

   b. From the Drawing Tools Format tab, in the Shape Styles group, click the Shape Fill button 🖌, and choose More Fill Colors.

   c. In the Colors dialog box, click the Custom tab.

   d. On the Colors palette, drag the crosshair near the middle of the yellow section to create a tan color that blends with the theme.

   e. Drag the black pointer up the vertical bar to make the color a little lighter.

f. Add 30% transparency to the object so that you can still read the white text.

g. Compare the current and new colors in the sample box in the lower right corner of the dialog box. When you like the new color, click OK.

h. Click Close to close the Colors dialog box.

6. Make the "Good 4 U" text 44 points, bold, and shadowed.

7. Fill a shape with a picture by following these steps:

a. Select the second circle on slide 1.

b. From the Drawing Tools Format tab, in the Shape Styles group, click the Shape Fill button ⬛, and choose Picture.

c. Navigate to your student files for Lesson 8, and insert **food1**.

8. Check spelling in the presentation, and view it as a slide show.

9. Create a handout header and footer: Include the date, your name as the header, the page number, and *[your initials]*8-20 as the footer.

10. Move to slide 1, and save the presentation as *[your initials]*8-20 in your Lesson 8 folder.

11. Close the presentation and submit your work.

Exercise 8-21

Apply a gradient fill, use shape effects, and change grayscale settings.

1. Open the file **Opening2**.

2. On slide 2, select the title placeholder, and apply a gradient fill by following these steps:

a. From the Drawing Tools Format tab, in the Shape Styles group, click the Shape Fill button ⬛, and choose Gradient and More Gradients.

b. Select Gradient fill to activate the gradient options.

c. Under Preset, choose Ocean from the Preset colors list box.

d. Under Direction, choose Linear Diagonal - Bottom Right to Top Left.

e. Click Close.

f. Using the Format Painter, apply the same formatting to the title placeholders on slides 3 and 4.

3. Apply the Soft Edges shape effect by following these steps:

a. Move to slide 3, and select the picture.

b. From the Picture Tools Format tab, in the Picture Styles group, click the Picture Effects button ⬛.

c. Choose Soft Edges and 10 points.

4. From the View tab, in the Color/Grayscale group, click the Grayscale button ⬛. Scroll through the presentation.

5. Change the grayscale settings by following these steps:

   a. Select the picture on slide 1.

   b. From the Grayscale tab, in the Change to Selected Object group, click the Light Grayscale button 🔲.

   c. Repeat this setting for the title placeholders on slides 2 to 4. Do not use Format Painter for this change.

6. Scroll through all the slides to view the changes to grayscale settings.

7. From the Grayscale tab, in the Close group, click the Back to Color View button 🔳.

8. Check spelling in the presentation.

9. Create a handout header and footer: Include the date, your name as the header, the page number, and *[your initials]*8-21 as the footer.

10. Move to slide 1, and save the presentation as *[your initials]*8-21 in your Lesson 8 folder.

11. Close the presentation and submit your work.

Exercise 8-22

Apply a gradient fill, apply shape effects, and work with grayscale settings.

1. Open the file **Entertainment**.

2. On slide 1, apply a border by following these steps:

   a. Select the picture on slide 1; then right-click, and choose Format Picture from the shortcut menu.

   b. Click the Line Color option at the left of the dialog box, and choose Solid Line.

   c. Choose the color Black, Background 1.

   d. Set Transparency at 25%.

   e. Click the Line Style option at the left of the dialog box, and change the Width to 35 pt.

   f. Click Close.

3. Apply a gradient fill to an object by following these steps:

   a. On slide 1, select the title text placeholder.

   b. From the Drawing Tools Format tab, in the Shape Styles group, click the Shape Fill button 🎨, and select Gradient and More Gradients.

   c. Choose Gradient fill.

   d. Set the following stops for the gradient fill:

Stop	Color	Position	Transparency
1	Black, Background 1	0%	0%
2	Blue-Gray, Accent 1, Lighter 60%	87%	25%
3	White, Text 1	100%	75%

    e. Choose the Linear Right direction.

    f. Click Close.

4. Apply shape effects by following these steps:

    a. Move to slide 2, and select the body text placeholder. From the Drawing Tools Format tab, in the Shape Styles group, click the More button ⏷.

    b. Choose the shape style Intense Effect, Brown, Accent 2.

    c. Select the first star on slide 2.

    d. From the Drawing Tools Format tab, in the Shape Styles group, click the Shape Effects button ⬯, and choose Bevel.

    e. Choose Relaxed Inset from the Bevel options.

    f. Use the Format Painter to apply this shape effect to the other three stars on the slide, as shown in Figure 8-22.

Figure 8-22
Slide with shape effects

5. Adjust grayscale settings by following these steps:

    a. Move to slide 2.

    b. From the View tab, in the Color/Grayscale group, click the Grayscale button ▦.

    c. Select the first star on slide 2.

    d. From the Grayscale tab, in the Change Selected Object group, click the Light Grayscale button ▦.

    e. Apply the same settings to all the stars on the slide.

    f. From the Grayscale tab, in the Close group, click the Back to Color View button ▦.

6. Check spelling in the presentation.

7. Create a handout header and footer: Include the date, your name as the header, the page number, and *[your initials]*8-22 as the footer.

8. Move to slide 1, and save the presentation as *[your initials]*8-22 in your Lesson 8 folder.

9. Close the presentation and submit your work.

Lesson Applications

Exercise 8-23

Apply a custom gradient fill, apply a texture fill, and format an arrow.

1. Open the file **Recruit1**, and apply the design theme Urban. Use the theme color Trek.

2. Insert two new slides after slide 3 using the Title and Content layouts. Use the text in Figure 8-23 to create bulleted lists.

Figure 8-23
Slides 4 and 5

Slide 4
Who's Who
- Julie Wolfe, Co-owner
- Gus Irvinelli, Co-owner
- Michele Jenkins, Head Chef
- Roy Olafsen, Marketing Manager

Slide 5
Summary
- Six-month probation period
- Annual salary increases
- Quarterly stock purchase options
- Annual profit sharing

3. On slide 1, select the title text, and then from the Drawing Tools Format tab, in the WordArt Styles group, click the More button ⬚. Choose Fill - Orange, Accent 6, Warm Matte Bevel (column 2, row 6).

4. Using the Format Painter, copy the formatting of the title with text effects and paint onto the title text on the remaining slides. Move the title text on slide 1 up slightly, as needed, after the effects are applied.

5. On slide 1, select the subtitle text placeholder, and create a two-stop gradient fill using White, Background 1 (column 1, row 1) with the stop position of 50% and Brown, Accent 2, Lighter 40% (column 6, row 4) with a stop position of 100%. Change the Type of Linear and Direction to Linear Up.

6. Move the Good 4 U logo onto the white part of the subtitle placeholder.

7. Draw a seven-point star on slide 1 in the lower right corner of the slide, and insert the picture **employee1** from your student files. Position and size it appropriately, and adjust the offsets as needed so that the employee's head is not cut off.

8. On slide 5, draw a 16-point star at the bottom right of the slide. Key the text **Substantial!** inside the star. Format the star as follows:

   a. make it 1.75 inches high and 4 inches wide.

   b. change the text size to 22 points, change the text color to Brown, Text 2, and make the text bold.

   c. rotate it slightly to the left.

   d. change the shape fill to the texture Cork with transparency of 25%.

   e. adjust the star's position as necessary to make a pleasing composition.

9. From the Insert tab, in the Illustrations group, click the Shapes button 🄿; then click the Arrow button ◥, and draw an arrow pointing from the star to the text "Annual profit sharing." Change the arrow's line thickness to 4.5 pt and the color to Brown, Accent 4, Darker 50% (column 8, row 6).

10. Check spelling in the presentation.

11. Create a handout header and footer: Include the date, your name as the header, the page number, and *[your initials]*8-23 as the footer.

12. Move to slide 1, and save the presentation as *[your initials]*8-23 in your Lesson 8 folder.

13. Close the presentation and submit your work.

Exercise 8-24

Apply outlines and fills, use custom colors, draw an arrow, and apply shape effects.

1. Open the file **Franchise2**.

2. Key the text **Good 4 U** in the subtitle placeholder on slide 1.

3. Move to slide 2, draw a rectangle slightly larger than the body text placeholder, and position it on top of the placeholder. Use the Fill, Line Style, and Line Color options in the Format Shape dialog box to format the rectangle as shown in Figure 8-24. Follow these steps:

   a. use Green, Accent 1 as the solid fill color; then modify this color in custom colors, and make it a little darker than the current color.

   b. change the transparency to 75%.

   c. under Line Style, change the width to 6 pt, and change the Compound type to triple.

   d. for Color of the line, use Black, Text 1.

   e. copy the rectangle, move to slide 3, and paste it.

Figure 8-24
Slide with formatted
rectangle

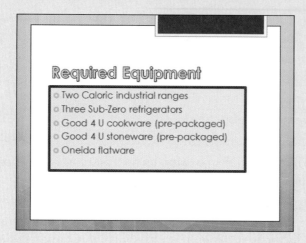

4. Search for an appropriate image, and position it to the left of the title and subtitle on slide 1. Recolor the picture to match the theme colors.

5. After slide 5, insert a new slide with a blank layout. Insert a WordArt using Fill - Green, Accent 1, Metal Bevel, Reflection (column 5, row 6), and key the text **Welcome!**.

6. Resize and reposition the WordArt for a pleasing appearance.

7. Move to slide 4, and draw a left block arrow from the right edge of the slide down to quarter 4. Rotate the arrow as necessary.

8. Format the arrow to include the White Marble texture fill.

9. Apply the Glow shape effect to the arrow using the Olive Green, 11 pt glow, Accent color 4.

10. Move to slide 1, and apply a Reflection picture effect to the picture. Choose the Half Reflection, 4 pt offset.

11. View the presentation as a slide show.

12. Check spelling in the presentation.

13. Create a handout header and footer: Include the date, your name as the header, the page number, and *[your initials]*8-24 as the footer.

14. Move to slide 1, and save the presentation as *[your initials]*8-24 in your Lesson 8 folder.

15. Close the presentation and submit your work.

Exercise 8-25

Change outline colors, styles, and fills of objects; add an arrowhead; and adjust grayscale settings.

1. Open the file **Franchise3**.

2. On slide 1, insert the date to replace the words "current date."

3. On slide 2, color the dollar sign illustration to a green to better blend with the slide theme color.

4. On slide 3, insert a text box near the upper right corner of the graph.

↔ **REVIEW**

To change the text box to a callout shape, select the shape and then, from the Drawing Tools Format tab, in the Insert Shapes group, click the Edit Shape button and choose Change Shape. Select the Oval Callout shape.

5. Key **Estimating over $89,000!** on two lines.

6. Change the font to Arial at 16 points and Bold.

7. Add a three-point green accent outline to the text box and use a lighter-shade green accent fill; then change its shape to an Oval Callout.

8. Use the callout shape's yellow adjustment handles to make the callout line point to the tallest column on the graph. Adjust the callout on the right without overlapping the title.

9. On slide 4, in the body text placeholder, key **10% discount off the lunch menu, Monday through Thursday!** Remove the bullet.

10. Format the text box as follows to give it a blackboard effect:

    a. change the fill color to Black, Background 1.

    b. center the text.

    c. change the font to Harlow Solid Italic at 32 points.

    d. apply a White outline at 8 pt with the compound type Thin Thick.

    e. apply a Divot Bevel effect using Soft Edge material.

11. Resize and reposition the body text placeholder to fit the text and to create a pleasing composition.

12. On slide 4, change the grayscale setting for the shape to Light Grayscale. Review all the slides in Grayscale view, and make any other necessary adjustments.

13. Check spelling in the presentation.

14. Create a handout header and footer: Include the date, your name as the header, the page number, and *[your initials]*8-25 as the footer.

15. Move to slide 1, and save the presentation as *[your initials]*8-25 in your Lesson 8 folder.

16. Close the presentation and submit your work.

Exercise 8-26 ◆ Challenge Yourself

Apply and format fills, outlines, effects, and grayscale settings.

1. Open the file **Market3**.

2. Select the title on slide 1, and center the text; then change the title placeholder to an oval shape.

3. Apply a fill, an outline, and shape effects to the selected oval with the following properties:

   - Fill: White, Text 1, Darker 25%.
   - Outline: Gray-25%, Accent 4, Darker 90%.
   - Outline width: 6 pt.
   - Shadow effect: Perspective Diagonal Upper Right.
   - Bevel effect: Divot.

4. Apply a two-stop gradient fill to the title text placeholder on slide 2 with the following properties, as shown in Figure 8-25:
   - Stop 1: Gray-25%, Accent 4, Darker 50% with a stop position of 25% and Transparency of 100%.
   - Stop 2: White, Text 1, Darker 15% with a stop position of 100%.
   - Direction: Linear Up.

Figure 8-25
Gradient title placeholder

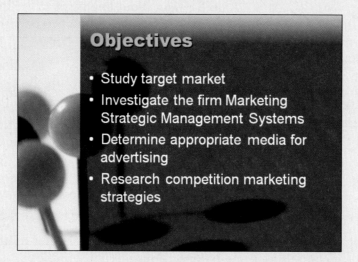

5. Apply the same gradient fill to the title text placeholders on slides 3 and 4.

6. Add a Title Only slide after slide 4.

7. Key **Summary** in the title text placeholder, and format it the same as you did for the other title text placeholders.

8. Draw an Explosion 2 shape in the middle of slide 6, and format it with the following properties:
   - Gradient fill: Chrome Preset with Path type.
   - Bevel effect: Convex.
   - 3-D Rotation: Perspective Contrasting Right.

9. Create a WordArt Gradient Fill - Blue-Gray, Accent 1, Outline - White, and key **Good 4 U!** Resize and rotate the WordArt to fit onto the Explosion shape. You may also resize the shape if necessary.

10. Review the presentation in Grayscale view, and make any necessary adjustments including changing several items to Light Grayscale.

11. View the presentation as a slide show.

12. Check spelling in the presentation.

13. Create a handout header and footer: Include the date, your name as the header, the page number, and *[your initials]*8-26 as the footer.

14. Move to slide 1, and save the presentation as *[your initials]*8-26 in your Lesson 8 folder.

15. Close the presentation and submit your work.

On Your Own

In these exercises you work on your own, as you would in a real-life work environment. Use the skills you've learned to accomplish the task—and be creative.

Exercise 8-27

As the event planner at your civic center, plan a birthday party for a group of young people, a church group, or an elementary school class. Prepare a presentation to help promote the event. Using a design theme with your choice of theme colors, create a title slide and separate slides listing activities or games and the rules or instructions for each one. For example, you could plan activities at the civic center pool and playground, or you could schedule seasonal activities or a trip to a local place of interest.

If you have access to a scanner or digital camera, include digital pictures that relate to the activities. Otherwise, find clip art pictures to illustrate your presentation. Use your own creativity to format an attractive presentation that uses many of the outlines, fills, and effects presented in this lesson. Modify the grayscale settings as needed to print the presentation in grayscale. Save the presentation as *[your initials]*8-27. Close the presentation and submit your work.

Exercise 8-28

You are a travel agent for Regency Travel. A customer has recently contracted with you to organize a weekend family reunion for a large family at a location where they can enjoy tourist activities together (not at someone's house). For example, they could travel to South Dakota and explore Mount Rushmore and other local attractions, or they could go to Gatlinburg, Tennessee, and see local shows, the Great Smoky Mountains National Park, and other local attractions and shopping.

Create a presentation describing the reunion, including location, planned activities, estimated costs, and a slide encouraging them to attend. Apply a design theme and color theme of your choice. Format the presentation by using outline, fill, and shape effects. Add clip art and photographs. Modify the grayscale settings as needed to print the presentation in grayscale. Save the presentation as *[your initials]*8-28. Close the presentation and submit your work.

Exercise 8-29

Open the file **SanFran** used in this lesson. Change to a different theme and colors of your choice. Change all the slide titles to WordArt, and apply fill effects, outlines, and shape effects to all shapes and body text placeholders in the presentation. Be careful to keep the look and style of each slide uniform throughout the presentation, and use good judgment to keep the design from looking too busy. Save the presentation as *[your initials]*8-29. Close the presentation and submit your work.

Layering and Grouping Techniques

OBJECTIVES | *After completing this lesson, you will be able to:*

1. Work with multiple objects.
2. Align, distribute, and flip objects.
3. Work with layers of objects.
4. Group, ungroup, and regroup objects.
5. Edit images.

Estimated Time: 1½ hours

Objects on a slide can be aligned and layered in interesting ways. Multiple objects can be grouped so that they can be repositioned as one group. These techniques enable you to quickly make unique changes to your slide design to match your presentation message. As you design, consider how slide objects align with each other and continue some unifying characteristics throughout your presentation.

Roy Olafsen has requested your assistance to enhance a marketing strategy presentation for Good 4 U employees. He is meeting with them to discuss some new promotion ideas and wants to have their input.

Working with Multiple Objects

When you want to treat multiple objects on a slide the same way, such as making them all the same color, you can select the objects at the same time. Several different selection techniques can be used:

- Select one object, hold down Shift, and click each additional object you want to select.
- Draw a selection rectangle around the objects you want to select by holding down your left mouse button while you drag the pointer to create a rectangle around all the objects.

- From the Home tab, in the Editing group, click the Select button ; then choose Select All, Select Objects, or the Selection Pane to select object shapes from a list.
- Press Ctrl+A to select all objects.

To deselect all items, simply click a blank area of the slide or press Esc.

Exercise 9-1 SELECT MULTIPLE OBJECTS USING THE SHIFT KEY

To select multiple objects one at a time, first click an object to select it and then add objects to the selection by pressing Shift as you click another object.

1. Open the file **Strategy1**.
2. With slide 1 displayed, press Ctrl+A. Notice the multiple sets of sizing handles. Every item on slide 1 is selected, as shown in Figure 9-1.

Figure 9-1
Multiple selected objects

3. Click a blank area on the slide (or press Esc) to deselect the items.
4. Click the top line of the four horizontal lines. Notice its sizing handles.
5. Hold down Shift, and click the next line. Notice that there are sizing handles around both objects, indicating that they are both selected.
6. With the two lines selected, from the Drawing Tools Format tab, in the Shape Styles group, click the Shape Outline button, and change their color to Brown, Background 2, Lighter 90%. Both selected lines change to a very light tan color.

> **TIP**
>
> You can also select multiple lines by pressing Ctrl while you click, just as you select noncontiguous slides in the Slide tab.

7. With the two tan lines selected, press Shift and click the next two lines. Now all four horizontal lines are selected.
8. Change the shape outline color to Brown, Background 2, Lighter 50% so that the lines are more noticeable.

Exercise 9-2 SELECT MULTIPLE OBJECTS BY DRAWING A SELECTION RECTANGLE

To draw a selection rectangle, start at a blank area of the slide, click the left mouse button, and hold while you drag your pointer diagonally to create a rectangle surrounding the objects that you want to select. Only objects completely enclosed in the selection rectangle are selected.

It takes a little practice to learn where to start a selection rectangle, and it's easy to miss an object. If that happens, try drawing the selection rectangle again, or add a missed object to the selection by using the [Shift]+click method.

1. On slide 2, from the View tab, in the Zoom group, click the Fit to Window button ⊞ to be sure that your entire slide fits on your screen.

2. Point to the left above the first shape with text.

3. Click and hold the left mouse button while you drag your pointer diagonally to the lower right of the slide. As you drag, you will see a temporary rectangle, as shown in Figure 9-2, with a blue border and semitransparent blue fill—a selection rectangle—that shows the area you are attempting to select.

Figure 9-2
Selection rectangle

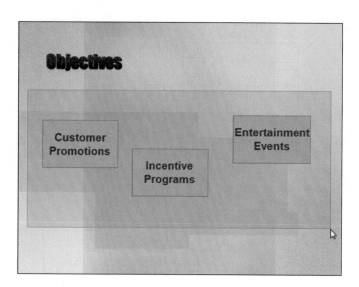

4. Release the left mouse button. Notice the sizing handles surrounding each of the shapes with text.

5. If one or more of the shapes is not selected, try again, making sure that all shapes are completely inside the selection rectangle.

6. With the shapes selected, change the shape outline to Brown, Background 2, Lighter 10%, and change the weight to 3 pt.

Exercise 9-3 REMOVE AN OBJECT FROM A GROUP OF SELECTED OBJECTS

To remove one object from a group of selected objects, hold down Shift and click the object to deselect it, leaving the remaining items in the group selected.

1. Move back to slide 1, and select all four lines using a selection rectangle. Drag from right to left so that you do not select the large brown rectangle on the left.

2. To deselect the line at the top and leave the other three lines selected, hold Shift and click the top line. The remaining three lines are still selected.

3. Hold Shift and click the bottom line. The bottom line is deselected, leaving only the two center lines selected.

4. With the shapes selected, change the shape outline to Brown, Background 2, Lighter 25%.

Exercise 9-4 CREATE A DIAGRAM WITH SHAPES AND CONNECTOR LINES

You may need to visually show a process or relationship that is not available through SmartArt. To do so, you can create a diagram using shapes and connector lines. As you learned previously, *connector lines* are straight, curved, or angled lines with special endpoints that can lock onto an object's *connection sites*—handles on an object that indicate where connector lines can be attached. When you rearrange objects joined with connector lines, the lines stay attached and adjust to the new position of the shapes they connect.

In this exercise the diagram is a very simple one, but the same concepts apply to very complex diagrams.

1. On slide 2, select the shape "Customer Promotions."

2. From the Drawing Tools Format tab, in the Insert Shapes group, click the More button ⬇. From the Lines category, click the Arrow button ↘, and notice that your pointer changes to a crosshair.

3. As you move the crosshair over the shapes, a red connection site appears on each side of the shapes, as shown in Figure 9-3.

Figure 9-3
Drawing a connector
line

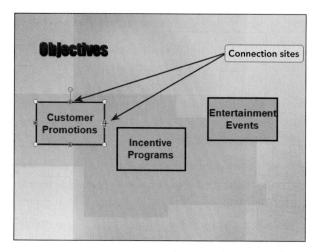

4. Click the connection site on the right side of the first shape ("Customer Promotions"), and drag to the left connection site of the second shape ("Incentive Programs"). When the arrow is selected, the endpoints will be red, showing that it is connected to the shapes. The arrow is thin right now, but you will change the line color and thickness later.

5. Select the first shape, and change its position slightly. Notice that the two shapes stay connected when you move one.

6. From the Insert Shapes gallery, click the Arrow button ⬊; then repeat step 3 to connect the middle shape to the right shape, "Entertainment Events."

7. Select the right shape, and from the Insert Shapes gallery, click the Elbow Arrow Connector button ⅂. Connect the bottom of the third shape to the bottom of the first shape. Use the yellow adjustment handle to move the line as needed to make sure your arrows point in the directions shown in Figure 9-4, creating a looping pattern.

8. Select all the arrow connectors; then from the Drawing Tools Format tab, in the Shape Styles group, click the Shape Outline button ▱, choose Brown, Background 2, Lighter 10%, and change the Weight to 3 pt so that the line is more visible.

Figure 9-4
Finished connector
lines

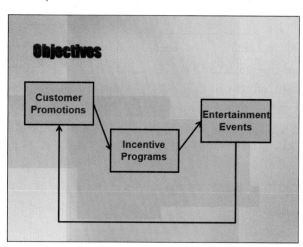

9. Create a new folder for Lesson 9, and save the presentation as *[your initials]*9-4 in the new folder.

Aligning, Distributing, and Flipping Objects

The commands available in the Arrange group on the contextual (Drawing or Picture) Tools Format tab can help with object positioning on the slide. Selected objects can be aligned with each other or spaced evenly across the slide either vertically or horizontally. You can rotate or flip objects to create mirror images of the originals.

Exercise 9-5 ALIGN OBJECTS HORIZONTALLY AND VERTICALLY

 TIP

The align and rotate options are also available from the Home tab or the contextual Format tab, in the Arrange group.

Table 9-1 lists the various alignment options. Vertical alignment appears at the top of the **Align** list, followed by horizontal options.

TABLE 9-1 Alignment Options

Option	Purpose
Align Bottom	Horizontally aligns the bottom edges of objects.
Align Center	Vertically aligns the centers of objects.
Align Left	Vertically aligns the left edges of objects.
Align Middle	Horizontally aligns the center points of objects.
Align Right	Vertically aligns the right edges of objects.
Align Selected Objects	A toggle button. When selected, aligns or spaces objects relative to other selected objects on the slide. When not selected, aligns or spaces objects relative to the slide.
Align to Slide	A toggle button. When selected, aligns or spaces objects relative to the slide. When not selected, aligns or spaces objects relative to each other.
Align Top	Horizontally aligns the top edges of objects.
Distribute Horizontally	Spaces objects evenly in a horizontal direction.
Distribute Vertically	Spaces objects evenly in a vertical direction.
View Gridlines	Turns on gridlines to which you can align objects in the document.

1. On slide 2, select the three rectangles.

2. From the Drawing Tools Format tab, in the Arrange Group, click the Align button to view the Alignment options.

3. Check Align to Slide if it is not already checked.

4. From the Drawing Tools Format tab, in the Arrange Group, click the Align button , and choose the Align Middle option. The objects line up across the middle of the slide.

5. Deselect the objects. From the View tab, in the Show group, click the check box beside Ruler (if it is not already selected) and the check box beside Gridlines.

6. Drag the shape that is farthest to the right up about 1 inch; use the ruler to help you position the shape. Drag the shape that is farthest to the left down to the bottom of the slide, leaving enough room to still view the connector line.

7. Draw a selection rectangle around all three shapes and their connector lines.

8. From the Drawing Tools Format tab, in the Arrange group, click the Align button, and choose Align Selected Objects; then repeat to choose Align Bottom. The objects align horizontally again, but this time they align with the bottom of the slide.

9. Click the Undo button several times to return the shapes to their previous position, where they are evenly aligned in the middle of the slide.

10. Select the three rectangles. From the Drawing Tools Format tab, in the Arrange group, click the Align button, and then choose Align Left. The objects are all aligned at the left, but two of the shapes are hidden because they are under one shape.

11. Click the Undo button to return to the middle alignment again.

Exercise 9-6   DISTRIBUTE OBJECTS HORIZONTALLY AND VERTICALLY

1. Still working on slide 2, deselect the shapes. Select only the right shape, and drag it up about 1.5 inches. Select the left shape, and drag it down about 1 inch.

2. Reselect the three rectangles and not the connector lines.

TIP

You can align objects very quickly by establishing one object in the left position and one in the right position and other objects between them. You don't have to worry about precise positioning because the Distribute Horizontally option takes care of that. Then, while the objects are selected, click the top, middle, or bottom alignment option so that all objects are evenly aligned from both directions.

3. From the Drawing Tools Format tab, click the Align button, and choose Distribute Vertically. Now the shapes are evenly spaced vertically based on the positions of the highest and lowest shapes—the extra space is divided evenly between the shapes.

4. Using the gridline to keep the same height on the slide, select the top shape and move it to the right; then select the bottom shape, and move it to the left.

5. Select all three shapes; then click the Align button and choose Distribute Horizontally so that the shapes are spaced evenly.

6. Adjust the arrow connectors as needed.

Exercise 9-7 FLIP AND ROTATE OBJECTS

Use the Rotate and Flip commands on a single object or a group of objects. You can rotate and flip any PowerPoint object, including text placeholders.

1. Move to slide 1, and select the picture.

Figure 9-5
Rotate options

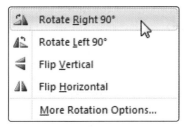

2. From the Picture Tools Format tab, in the Arrange group, click the Rotate button, and choose the Flip Horizontal option. The arrow is now pointing in the other direction.

3. From the Drawing Tools Format tab, in the Arrange group, click the Rotate button, and choose Rotate Right 90°, as shown in Figure 9-5. Complete this three more times. The picture rotates around and ends up in the original position.

4. Move to slide 5, and select both the WordArt title "Teamwork" and the banner behind it. With the objects selected, use the arrow keys on the keyboard to move the objects so they are centered above the illustrated image.

5. Select all the objects on the slide. From the Drawing Tools Format tab, in the Arrange group, click the Align button, and choose Align to Slide; then repeat to choose Align Center.

6. From the View tab, remove the check in front of Gridlines to turn off gridlines.

7. Save the presentation as *[your initials]*9-7 in your Lesson 9 folder.

Working with Layers of Objects

Although objects appear to be drawn on one surface, each of a slide's objects actually exists as a separate layer. Imagine that the objects are drawn on individual sheets of transparent plastic stacked on top of one another. When you rearrange the sheets, different objects appear on the top, sometimes hiding parts of the objects beneath them. The most recently drawn object is added to the top of the stack.

Within a stack of objects, you can move an individual object backward and forward as listed in Table 9-2.

TABLE 9-2 Order Options

Option	Purpose
Bring Forward	Brings an object up one layer in the stack.
Bring to Front	Brings an object to the top of the stack.
Send Backward	Moves an object down one layer in the stack.
Send to Back	Moves an object to the bottom of the stack.

Exercise 9-8   BRING OBJECTS FORWARD OR BACKWARD

If several objects are already layered on a slide and you draw a new object, it automatically becomes the top object on the stack. To change its layer, select it and then, from the Drawing Tools Format tab, in the Arrange group, choose from among the order options.

When you are working with layered objects, sometimes you want to change the stacking order by just one level to make one object appear on top of another object. The Bring Forward and Send Backward commands move the selected object one layer at a time. If the selected object is not visible, you can press Tab several times until the desired object is selected and then you can move it.

The Bring to Front and Send to Back commands move a selected object to the front of all other objects or behind all other objects.

1. Move to slide 4. From the Home tab, in the Drawing group, click the Shapes button 📷, and choose the Rectangle. Press Shift while you click and drag to draw a square larger than the circle to cover it.

2. With the shape selected, from the Home tab, in the Drawing group, click the Shape Fill button 🎨 to change the fill color to Brown, Background 1, Lighter 40%. Click the Shape Fill button 🎨 again, and choose More Fill Colors; then change Transparency to 25%.

3. With the shape selected, from the Home tab, in the Drawing group, click the Shape Outline button 🎨, and remove the outline. Now you can see the circle faintly behind the rectangle.

4. Press Tab, and notice that selection handles appear around the circle. Pressing Tab is a good technique to use when layering because it is difficult to select an object with your pointer when it is under another object.

5. From the Home tab, in the Drawing group, click the Arrange button 🖳. Under the Order Objects heading, choose Bring Forward to move the circle on top of the square, as shown in Figure 9-6.

Figure 9-6
Rectangle and circle

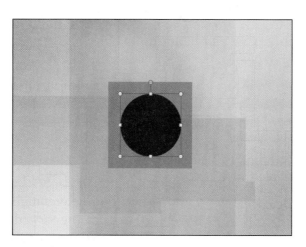

6. From the Home tab, in the Drawing group, click the Shapes button 📄; then from the Basic Shapes category, click the Diamond. Click and drag to draw a diamond about the size of the square, and then change the shape fill to Tan, Text 2 and the shape outline to No Outline.

7. With the diamond shape selected, from the Home tab, in the Drawing group, click the Arrange button 🖳, and choose Send Backward. The diamond moves behind the circle but is in front of the square.

8. Repeat this step to make the diamond go behind the square.

Exercise 9-9 BRING OBJECTS TO THE FRONT OR SEND TO THE BACK

To manipulate an object that is located behind several other objects, you can send the top objects to the back, one at a time, until the desired object is on top.

1. Still working on slide 4, draw a square to cover the existing shapes on the slide, and change the shape fill to Brown, Background 1.

2. From the Home tab, in the Drawing group, click the Arrange button 🖳. Choose the Send to Back option. The new square moves behind all the other objects.

3. Select the diamond by clicking on one object and pressing ⟨Tab⟩ until the diamond is selected. Remember that it was sent behind the first square.

4. From the Home tab, in the Drawing group, click the Arrange button 🖳.

5. Under the Order Objects heading, choose the Bring to Front option. The diamond moves to the top of the object stack.

Exercise 9-10   USE THE SELECTION AND VISIBILITY PANE TO CHANGE THE STACKING ORDER

When you are planning to change the order of multiple objects, the Selection and Visibility pane can be a productivity booster. Because this pane stays open, you can change the order of all objects quickly.

Figure 9-7
Selection and
Visibility pane

1. Still working on slide 4, from the Home tab, in the Editing group, click the Select button, and choose Selection Pane. The Selection and Visibility pane opens on the right side of your screen, as shown in Figure 9-7.

2. Click Rectangle 1 in the Selection and Visibility pane. Notice that the rectangle is now selected in Normal view. Click the Re-order Bring Forward (upward-pointing) arrow at the bottom of the Selection pane twice. The tan transparent rectangle is now on top of the stack.

3. Click Oval 2 in the Selection and Visibility pane, and click the Re-order Bring Forward (upward-pointing) arrow twice. The circle is now back on top, as shown in Figure 9-8.

4. Key **Increased Profits!** on two lines in the oval. Change the font color to Tan, Text 2, and make the text bold, centered, and shadowed.

Figure 9-8
Completed stack
of objects

5. Click the Close button ☒ on the Selection and Visibility pane.

6. Save the presentation as *[your initials]*9-10 in your Lesson 9 folder.

Grouping, Ungrouping, and Regrouping Objects

When you group objects, you combine two or more objects so that they behave as one. If you then move one object in the group, all the other objects move with it. Grouping ensures that objects meant to stay together don't accidentally get moved individually or deleted. When you apply formatting to a group, all the objects of the group receive the same formatting.

Exercise 9-11   GROUP OBJECTS

To create a group of objects, first select the objects and then, from the Home tab, in the Drawing group, click the Arrange button 🖿 and choose Group.

1. On slide 1, select the four lines in the middle of the slide. Notice the four sets of sizing handles.

2. From the Home tab, in the Drawing group, click the Arrange button 🖿, and choose Group. Now only one set of sizing handles appears, indicating that all four lines are grouped as a single object, as shown in Figure 9-9.

Figure 9-9
Objects after grouping

3. Drag the top resizing handle up, just below the title text. Notice that it creates more space between the lines and the top line moves up.

4. Drag the top resizing handle back down to the previous setting so that the lines are positioned closer together.

5. Move the group up, close to the bottom of the title, and nudge it into position using the arrow keys if necessary. Notice that the group moved to the new position without creating extra space between the lines.

Exercise 9-12   UNGROUP AND REGROUP OBJECTS

If you want to delete an object in a group, change its position relative to the other objects, or change its size, you must first ungroup the objects. When the objects are ungrouped, they once again become individual objects.

After working on individual objects in an ungrouped object, you can easily regroup the objects by selecting any one of the group's original members. The Regroup command finds all the objects of the original group that remain on the slide and groups them again.

1. Right-click any of the grouped lines; then choose Group from the shortcut menu and Ungroup. Each line now has its own set of sizing handles.

2. Click a blank area of the slide to deselect all the lines.

3. Click the third line to select it (the other lines should not be selected), and then press Delete. One line is deleted from the slide.

4. Move the last line up under the second line, and select all three lines by using a selection rectangle.

5. With the three lines selected, from the Home tab, in the Drawing group, click the Arrange button 🗗, choose Align, verify that Align Selected Objects is selected, and then choose Distribute Vertically.

6. Select one of the remaining lines; then from the Home tab, in the Drawing group, click the Arrange button 🗗, and choose Regroup. The three remaining lines are grouped again.

Exercise 9-13   FORMAT PART OF A GROUPED OBJECT

You can easily select one member of a group of objects to make individual changes. First select the group; then click an object within the group. The group remains selected, but the object also displays selection handles, indicating that you can change its shape fill, outline, and orientation without affecting the other objects in the group.

1. Move to slide 2, and select the three rectangles only.

2. With the shapes selected, right-click on one of the shape outlines, choose Group, and then choose Group from the shortcut menu to make the shapes behave as one object. A set of white sizing handles appears, and the whole group can be moved or resized.

3. Click the outline of the middle shape. Selection handles surround the rectangle, as shown in Figure 9-10. Text can be edited in each of the grouped shapes, and the shapes can still be resized or moved individually within the group even though they are contained in the group.

Figure 9-10
Selecting a single
object in a group

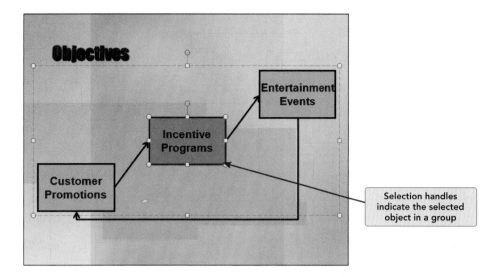

4. From the Home tab, in the Drawing group, click the Arrange button 🔲, and choose **Rotate** and the **Flip Vertical** option. The selected rectangle turns upside down.

5. Repeat the previous step again to make the rectangle return to its previous position.

6. For the selected rectangle, click the Shape Fill button 🔲, and then click **Tan, Text 2, Darker 25%**.

7. Move to slide 1, and save the presentation as *[your initials]*9-13 in your Lesson 9 folder.

Editing Images

PowerPoint enables you to customize pictures and illustrations in a variety of ways. Illustrated images can be recolored, ungrouped with parts removed, or rearranged as needed for unique illustrations. Pictures can be made more vivid or more subtle, styles can be applied for creating framing, and pictures can be compressed to reduce a presentation's file size.

Exercise 9-14 MODIFY ILLUSTRATION COLORS

The *Color* feature may be applied to illustrated images or pictures to blend them with the theme colors. When the Color feature is chosen, the whole image is changed to shades of the chosen variation.

1. Move to slide 5, and select the illustrated image on the slide.

2. From the Picture Tools Format tab, in the Adjust group, click the Color button 🔲.

3. From the Light Variations listed in the bottom row, choose **Brown, Accent color 2 Light** (column 3, row 3). Notice how the whole illustration is changed to match this variation, as shown in Figure 9-11.

Figure 9-11
Changing the color
of an illustrated
image

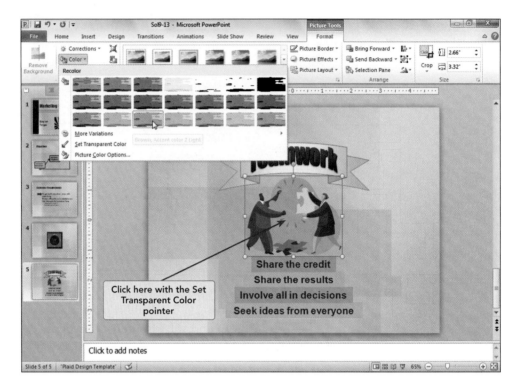

4. Select the illustration; then from the Picture Tools Format tab, in the Adjust group, click the Color button, and choose **No Recolor** (the first option) to return the image to its original colors.

5. From the Picture Tools Format tab, in the Adjust group, click the Color button, and choose **Set Transparent Color**. Your pointer changes.

6. Click the area of the illustration as shown in Figure 9-11. The background green color will be removed; however, an outline will remain, since only one color can be removed in this way.

Exercise 9-15 UNGROUP AND CHANGE THE FILL COLOR FOR PARTS OF AN ILLUSTRATED IMAGE

When you insert a Microsoft Windows Metafile (a vector graphics format used commonly as an illustration format), from the Clip Organizer, you can ungroup and change colors in an illustration to match the color theme of your presentation.

When a vector-based image is ungrouped, it is converted into a collection of PowerPoint shapes that you can delete, resize, and reposition, just like any shapes that you draw. You can also change the fill color and outline for parts of an illustration that has been converted.

1. Still working on slide 5, select the illustrated image.

2. With the image selected, from the View tab, change the Zoom setting to **100%** so that you can see the details better.

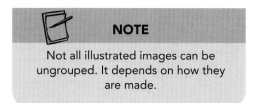

NOTE

Not all illustrated images can be ungrouped. It depends on how they are made.

3. Right-click the image, and choose Group from the shortcut menu and then Ungroup. A dialog box asks whether you want to convert this picture (referring to the image) to a Microsoft Office drawing object, as shown in Figure 9-12.

Figure 9-12
Converting an illustrated image to a Microsoft Office drawing object

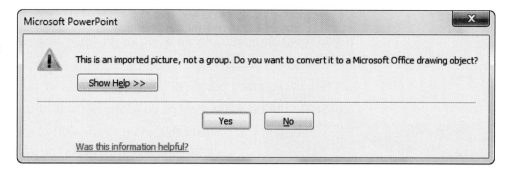

4. Click Yes to agree to the conversion. Notice that when you ungroup, the picture resets to the original background color, overriding the color changes that were applied in the previous activity.

Figure 9-13
Ungrouped illustration

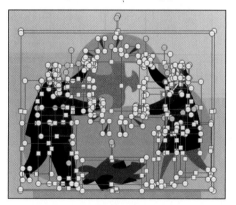

5. Right-click the image, and choose Group from the shortcut menu and Ungroup again. You will see many sets of selection handles, as shown in Figure 9-13. Notice that on this particular image you have two rotation handles and two corner selection handles at the top of the image. One of these sets is for the green background shape; the other is for a square behind the green shape that isn't needed. You'll remove these shapes in the next exercise.

Figure 9-14
Selecting a part of an ungrouped illustration

6. Press [Esc] (or click any blank area of the slide) to deselect all the pieces of the illustration.

7. Select the puzzle piece that the woman is holding, as shown in Figure 9-14, and change the color. From the Drawing Tools Format tab, in the Shape Styles group, click Shape Fill button [icon]; then choose More Fill colors. On the Standard tab, click the dark-red color on the bottom of the honeycomb of colors, one color swatch to the left from the right corner.

8. Hold down the Shift key while you carefully select the four small, pointed shapes above and below the puzzle pieces and change their shape fill to dark red, now available from the **Recent Colors** category. Be careful not to select the green background shape.

Exercise 9-16 DELETE PARTS OF AN ILLUSTRATED IMAGE

If you want to delete pieces of an ungrouped image, you must select them and then press Delete.

1. Select the green puzzle piece at the bottom of the image. Press Delete.

2. Select the brown puzzle piece at the bottom of the image. Press Delete.

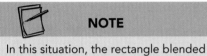

NOTE

In this situation, the rectangle blended with the background, so it would have been OK to leave it on the slide. However, a background can affect the design you are trying to achieve when it is not colored with one of the design theme colors, so you need to know how to remove it if necessary.

3. Select the green shape that creates the background of the image. Because of its rounded shape, the selection handles seem far away from the image. Press Delete.

4. This image has a rectangle behind it that is transparent. Click above the woman's head, and you will see selection handles in a position similar to the shape you just removed. To confirm this, apply a different shape fill color, and you can see where the rectangle is located. Press Delete.

5. Compare your image with Figure 9-15. If too much of the illustration was deleted, click the Undo button 🔄 and try again.

6. Draw a selection rectangle around the remaining parts of the picture. From the Drawing Tools Format tab, in the Arrange group, click the Group button 🔠, and choose **Group**. (Do not use the Regroup command.)

7. From the View tab, click the Fit to Window button 🔲.

Figure 9-15
Modified illustration

8. If the ruler is displayed, hide it by clicking the **View** tab, in the Show/Hide group, and removing the check beside **Ruler**.

Exercise 9-17 FRAMING A PICTURE WITH SOFT EDGES

Soft edges can be applied to a picture, but then no color shows around the picture. If a picture border is applied to add color, then the edges are not soft. To achieve the effect of a soft-edge image framed with color having soft edges, a rectangle can be placed behind the image.

1. Move to slide 1, and select the picture.

2. From the Picture Tools Format tab, change the picture height to 3″, and the width will change to 4.47″ automatically.

3. From the Home tab, in the Drawing group, click the Shapes button , and select the oval shape. Draw the oval to cover the picture. From the Format tab, adjust its size to a height of 4″ and a width of 5.5″, and center it over the picture (the picture corners will still be showing for now).

4. With the shape selected, use the Drawing Tools Format tab to change its appearance by following these steps:

    a. Click the Shape Fill button ; then click Brown, Background 2, Lighter 50%.

    b. Click the Shape Outline button , and choose No Outline.

    c. Click the Shape Effects button , and choose Soft Edges and then 10 Point.

    d. From the Arrange group, choose Send to Back so that the rectangle is behind the picture. This creates a soft frame around the picture.

5. Select the picture, and make a similar change to soften the edges:

    a. From the Picture Tools Format tab, in the Picture Styles group, select the Picture Styles More button to view the Style Gallery.

    b. Choose Soft Edge Oval from the Style Gallery, as shown in Figure 9-16.

Figure 9-16
Changing picture styles

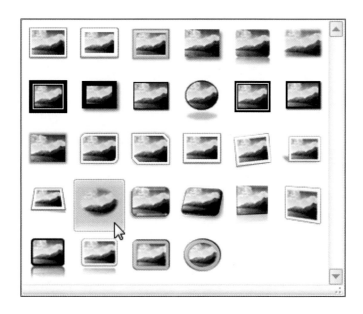

6. Select both the picture and the rectangle, right-click one of the object outlines, and choose Group and then Group to make them behave as one object.

7. Save the presentation as *[your initials]*9-17 in your Lesson 9 folder.

Exercise 9-18   COMPRESS PICTURES

When you use many photographic images, your presentation's file size can increase dramatically. Optimizing your pictures (illustrations and photographs) will usually reduce your presentation's file size. However, you will want to do this only if the presentation is for viewing as a slide show or on the Web. A reduction in image quality will usually not be noticeable for on-screen viewing, but it will make a difference in printed output. You will also have the option of deleting cropped areas of pictures.

When a presentation is saved, the file sizes of newly inserted images are decreased to 220 ppi by default. You have the opportunity to decrease to smaller sizes through the Compress Pictures options. If a file size is smaller than 220 ppi when it is inserted, only the smaller available options will display.

1. On slide 1, select the illustration.

2. From the Picture Tools Format tab, in the Adjust group, click the Compress Pictures button 🔳.

3. Be sure both boxes at the top of the dialog box are checked for Compression options. Leave the Target output set for E-mail, as shown in Figure 9-17. This will compress all images in the document and make them good quality for sharing the files via e-mail or other Web sharing features.

Figure 9-17
Compressing
pictures

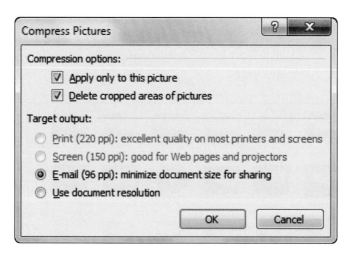

4. Click OK.

5. Check spelling in the presentation.

6. View the presentation in grayscale to be sure all slides will be readable for printing. Make any changes if necessary.

7. Create a handout header and footer: Include the date, your name as the header, the page number, and *[your initials]*9-18 as the footer.

8. Save the presentation as *[your initials]*9-18 in your Lesson 9 folder. Close the presentation and submit your work.

9. To test the difference in file sizes, access the storage location where your exercise files are saved and compare the file sizes of Exercise 17 and Exercise 18. In this case, you may not see a dramatic reduction because of the particular picture used. However, a file size can be reduced by one half or even more depending on the type of images you are using and how many you have compressed.

TIP

In presentations that have a lot of photographs, especially high-resolution images, you will see a dramatic difference in file size.

Lesson 9 Summary

- Select multiple objects when you want to perform the same operation on all of them, such as making them all the same color or moving all of them at the same time.

- Select multiple objects one at a time by holding down ⏵Shift⏴ while clicking each object.

- Select multiple objects all at once by drawing a selection rectangle around them (click and drag the pointer). Be sure to start dragging on a blank area of the slide.

- Add items to a selection by using the ⏵Shift⏴+click method. Remove an item from a group of selected items by pressing ⏵Shift⏴ and clicking the item.

- Selected objects can be aligned horizontally or vertically to the whole slide or to other selected objects. They can be aligned by the top, bottom, middle, right side, left side, or center. They can be aligned relative to the edges of a slide when the Align to Slide option is selected.

- Selected objects can be evenly spaced by using the Distribute Horizontally or Distribute Vertically options. Objects can also be evenly distributed across the width or height of a slide when the Align to Slide option is turned on.

- Flipping an object creates a mirror image of it. The Rotate Left and Rotate Right options rotate objects in 90-degree increments.

- When objects overlap, use the order options or the Selection and Visibility pane to control which object appears on the top. The most recently drawn object will be on top until you change its order.

- Grouping two or more objects combines them so that they behave as if they were one object.

- After you group objects, an individual object within the group can be selected without ungrouping all the objects. First click the group to select it; then click an object in the group. The selection handles indicate which object is selected. The selected group object can have its shape fill and outline formatted and can be flipped, but it cannot be deleted, resized, or rotated.

- To delete, resize, or rotate an individual object within a group, first ungroup the objects. After you are finished working on individual objects in a group, regroup them.
- Vector-based illustrations (for example, images with the **.wmf** file extension) can be converted into a group of PowerPoint shapes by using the Ungroup command. Once ungrouped, the individual shapes can be formatted and manipulated like any PowerPoint shape.
- To reduce the file size of a presentation containing pictures, the Compress Pictures command can reduce the resolution of one or more pictures and omit cropped areas.

LESSON 9		Command Summary	
Feature	**Button**	**Menu**	**Keyboard**
Add to a selection of objects			Shift + click
Align or distribute objects		Home, Drawing group, Arrange, Align; or Contextual Format tab, Arrange group, Align	
Change the order of objects		Home, Drawing group, Arrange, Order Objects; or Contextual Format tab, Arrange group	
Color illustration		Picture Tools Format, Adjust group, Color	
Compress pictures		Picture Tools Format, Adjust group, Compress Pictures	
Deselect all selected objects			Esc
Deselect one object from a group of selected objects			Shift + click
Display the gridlines		View, Show group, Gridlines	
Display the ruler		View, Show group, Ruler	
Flip or rotate objects		Home, Drawing group, Arrange, Rotate; or Contextual Format tab, Arrange group, Rotate	
Group objects		Home, Drawing group, Arrange, Group; or Contextual Format tab, Arrange group, Group	Ctrl + G
Regroup objects		Home, Drawing group, Arrange, Regroup; or Contextual Format tab, Arrange group, Group, Regroup	
Select all objects		Home, Drawing group, Select; or Contextual Format tab, Arrange group, Group, Regroup	Ctrl + A
Ungroup objects		Home, Drawing group, Arrange, Ungroup; or Contextual Format tab, Arrange group, Group, Ungroup	Ctrl + H

Concepts Review

True/False Questions

Each of the following statements is either true or false. Indicate your choice by circling T or F.

T   F   1.   You cannot use selection rectangles to select multiple objects.

T   F   2.   Flipping an object makes it appear at a 45-degree angle.

T   F   3.   If you click the Rotate Left option several times while an object is selected, the object eventually returns to its original position.

T   F   4.   To select multiple objects, press [Shift] while clicking each object.

T   F   5.   You can align objects relative to other selected objects or relative to the slide.

T   F   6.   Vector-based illustrations can be converted into a group of PowerPoint shapes by using the Ungroup command.

T   F   7.   You cannot change the order of objects using the Selection and Visibility pane.

T   F   8.   The keyboard command to select all objects on a slide is [Ctrl]+[A].

Short Answer Questions

Write the correct answer in the space provided.

1.   To select multiple objects, which key do you press while clicking?

_____

2.   What appears when you drag the pointer to select multiple objects?

_____

3.   Which align options are used to line up objects side by side along the bottom of the slide?

_____

4.   Which button flips an object from left to right?

_____

5.   Which order places an object at the top of all the other objects on a slide?

_____

6.   On what layer does the most recently drawn object appear?

_____

7. What appears when you ungroup an illustrated image?

_____

8. What can you do to reduce the file size of a presentation that contains illustrations and photographs?

_____

Critical Thinking

Answer these questions on a separate page. Support your answers with examples from your own experience, if possible.

1. In this lesson you learned different ways to select objects. Which method do you prefer to use, and why?

2. Think of how you have layered multiple objects. How could you use this technique to design an interesting title slide?

Skills Review

Exercise 9-19

Select multiple objects; and align, distribute, and group objects.

1. Open the file **Staffing**.

2. From the Drawing Tools Format tab, change the color of multiple objects:

    a. On slide 1, click one of the small orange circles below the title; then press [Shift] while clicking the remaining two circles.

    b. With all three circles selected, change the shape fill to Green, Accent 1.

3. From the Drawing Tools Format tab, in the Arrange group, click the Align button to make the following adjustments so that the circles are even and touching each other:

    a. Align Selected Objects.

    b. Align Top.

4. From the Drawing Tools Format tab, in the Shape Styles group, click the Shape Effects button, and choose Bevel and Circle.

5. With all three circles selected, from the Drawing Tools Format tab, in the Arrange group, click the Group button, and choose Group. Move the grouped circles below the green horizontal line, lined up with the right of the line and approximately even with the current date.

6. Copy the circle group, and paste it on slide 4. Move the group below the text box. Select both the rectangle and the circle group. From the Drawing Tools Format tab, in the Arrange group, click the Align button 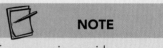, and choose Align Right.

7. On slide 1, click one of the small white circles on the upper left. From the Drawing Tools Format tab, notice that the square has a height and width of .33 inches, which is the same size as the circles you have already adjusted.

8. Use a selection rectangle to select all the white circles.

9. Align and distribute the circles relative to the slide. From the Drawing Tools Format tab, in the Arrange group, click the Align button to make these adjustments:

    a. Align to Slide.

    b. Align Top.

    c. Distribute Horizontally.

10. From the Drawing Tools Format tab, in the Shape Styles group, click the Shape Fill button, and choose Green, Accent 1.

11. Still working on the Drawing Tools Format tab, in the Shape Styles group, click the Shape Effects button, and choose Bevel and Circle.

12. You should now have a row of beveled, green circles in the green area across the top of your slide, similar to Figure 9-18.

NOTE

If you are using a wide-screen monitor, your circles may be spread apart, and that is acceptable. If you wish, you could duplicate additional circles and then redistribute them until you achieve the look of a solid row of circles across the top of the slide.

Figure 9-18
Green circles distributed and aligned to slide

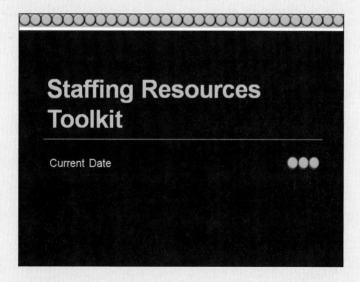

13. Select all the green circles at the top of slide 1, and copy them. Move to slide 2, and paste. With all of them selected, use the down arrow to move them below the slide title.

14. From the Drawing Tools Format tab, in the Size group, change the height and width of the green circles to .1". In the Arrange group, click the Group button ⊞▾, and choose Group.

15. Copy the grouped circles, and paste them in the same position on slide 3.

16. Create a handout header and footer: Include the date, your name as the header, the page number, and *[your initials]*9-19 as the footer.

17. Move to slide 1, and save the presentation as *[your initials]*9-19 in your Lesson 9 folder.

18. Close the presentation and submit your work.

Exercise 9-20

Align and distribute objects relative to selected objects and to the slide, and layer objects.

1. Open the file **Social media**.

2. On slide 1, from the Home tab, in the Drawing group, click the Shapes button 🗗, and choose Explosion 1. Draw the object on slide 1, making the height and width 7 inches. Position it on top of the title text and extending off the left and top edges of the slide.

3. With the shape selected, from the Drawing Tools Format tab, click the Shape Fill button 🖌, and choose Blue-Gray, Accent 4, Darker 25% (column 8). Click the Shape Outline button ✐, and choose Blue-Gray, Accent 4, Darker 50%.

4. With the explosion shape selected, from the Drawing Tools Format tab, in the Arrange group, click the Send Backward button ⬓, and choose Send to Back.

5. Select the "smiley-face" shape, and press Ctrl+D three times to duplicate it. Position the first and last shapes in their approximate positions as shown in Figure 9-19, with the middle two shapes between them.

6. Select the four smiley-face shapes; then from the Drawing Tools Format tab, in the Arrange group, click the Align button ⬓▾ to make these adjustments:

   a. Align Selected Objects.

   b. Align Bottom.

   c. Distribute Horizontally.

7. Change the colors on three of these shapes to different light-blue theme colors.

Figure 9-19
Objects layered and
aligned

8. Copy the explosion shape from slide 1, and paste it on slide 2.

9. From the Drawing Tools Format tab, in the Size group, resize the explosion on slide 2 so that the height and width are both 2".

 TIP

To fine-tune the explosion's position, hold down Ctrl while pressing the arrow keys on your keyboard, or hold down Alt and drag the explosion with your pointer.

10. Move the explosion so that it covers the word "Social"; then from the Drawing Tools Format tab, click the Send Backward button 🔲. Fine-tune the explosion's position as needed.

11. On slide 3, from the Home tab, in the Drawing group, click the Shapes button 🔳; then from the Basic Shapes category, insert a Cloud.

12. With the cloud selected, from the Drawing Tools Format tab, in the Size group, change the height to 1.5" and the width to 2.3".

13. Duplicate the cloud three times by using Ctrl+D, and then select all four clouds. From the Drawing Tools Format tab, in the Arrange group, click the Align button 📄, making these adjustments:

    a. Align to Slide.

    b. Align Middle.

    c. Distribute Horizontally.

14. Key the following text inside the clouds:

    a. Twitter.

    b. Facebook.

    c. YouTube.

    d. MySpace.

15. Select all the clouds, and change the font to 20 pt and bold.

16. From the Insert tab, in the Text group, click the Text Box button 🄰, insert a text box below the last cloud, and key **And Many More!** in 20 points and bold.

17. Create a handout header and footer: Include the date, your name as the header, the page number, and *[your initials]*9-20 as the footer.

18. Move to slide 1, and save the presentation as *[your initials]*9-20 in your Lesson 9 folder.

19. Close the presentation and submit your work.

Exercise 9-21

Select multiple objects; align, distribute, and group objects; and work with layers.

1. Open the file **AdMedia**.

2. Move to slide 2, and select the four rectangles using the Shift+click method.

3. Align and distribute the rectangles. From the Home tab, in the Drawing group, click the Arrange button 🔳; then click Align to make these adjustments:

   a. Align Selected Objects.

   b. Align Center.

   c. Distribute Vertically.

4. Key the following text inside the rectangles:
   Rectangle 1: **Quality**
   Rectangle 2: **Frequency**
   Rectangle 3: **Effectiveness**
   Rectangle 4: **Cost**

5. Select all four rectangles using a selection rectangle. From the Home tab, in the Drawing group, click the Arrange button 🔳, and choose Group.

6. Edit the rectangles by following these steps:

   a. Select the group.

   b. From the Drawing Tools Format tab, in the Shape Styles group, click the Shape Effects button 🔲, and choose Bevel.

   c. Choose Cool Slant.

7. Change the order of the objects to reveal a hidden logo:

   a. Move to slide 1.

   b. Select the diamond shape.

   c. Right-click the diamond shape, and choose Send to Back from the shortcut menu.

8. Move to slide 4, and select the four bright-red circles. From the Drawing Tools Format tab, in the Arrange group, Click the Align button 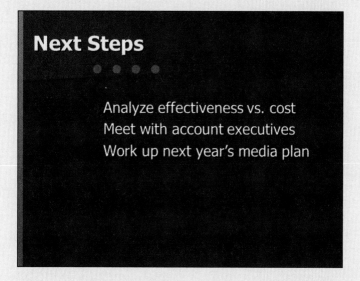, and choose:
    a. Align Selected Objects.
    b. Align Top.
    c. Distribute Horizontally.

9. With the red circles selected, from the Home tab, in the Drawing group, click the Arrange button, and choose Group.

10. Position the grouped red circles under the word "Steps" so that they help to separate the slide title from other text on the slide, as in Figure 9-20.

Figure 9-20
Circles grouped and repositioned

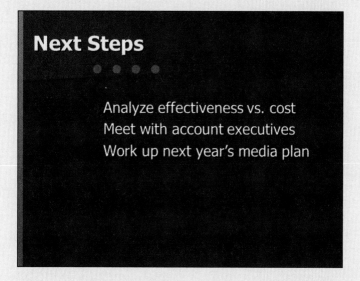

11. Copy the grouped circles, and paste them on slides 1, 2, and 3.
    a. On slides 2 and 3, paste them in the same position as that on slide 4.
    b. On slide 1, reposition them to appear below the title on the left.

12. On slide 1, select the diamond shape. From the Drawing Tools Format tab, in the Shape Styles group, click the Shape Effects button, and choose Bevel and then Cool Slant.

13. On slide 2, move the grouped rectangles to the right of the circles on the slide.

14. Check the presentation in Grayscale view. Change the grayscale setting for the diamond shape on slide 1 and the rectangles on slide 2 to Light Grayscale.

15. Create a handout header and footer: Include the date, your name as the header, the page number, and *[your initials]*9-21 as the footer.

16. Move to slide 1, and save the presentation as *[your initials]*9-21 in your Lesson 9 folder.

17. Close the presentation and submit your work.

Exercise 9-22

Select multiple objects; layer, align, and distribute objects; flip and group objects; and use image editing tools.

1. Open the file **Welcome**.

2. On slide 1, select the beach umbrella illustration, and color parts of it by following these steps:

   a. From the Home tab, in the Drawing group, click the Arrange button 🔳, and choose Ungroup. When asked about converting to a drawing object, click Yes.

   b. Click the Arrange button 🔳 again, and choose Ungroup again.

   c. Zoom to 200%. Click off the picture once so that the selection handles disappear.

   d. Click one of the white sections of the beach ball; then change its color to bright yellow. Select each of the remaining white sections of the beach ball, and change them to bright yellow. One section has two pieces to change.

   e. For the remaining alternating sections, including the circle on the ball, change the color to red.

   f. Right-click any piece of the illustration, and choose Group from the shortcut menu and then Regroup.

   g. From the View tab, in the Zoom group, click the Fit to Window button 🔳.

3. Now resize and reposition the beach umbrella using the Drawing Tools Format tab:

   a. Temporarily move the beach umbrella to the center of the slide so that you can see the entire image as you change its height to 5 inches and width to 4.8 inches.

   b. In the Arrange group, click the Rotate button 🔳; then select Flip Horizontal.

   c. In the Arrange group, click the Align button 🔳; then select Align to Slide, Align Right, and Align Bottom.

4. On slide 1, select the sun, and move it to the upper left of the slide with part of the sun rays extending off the edge of the slide as shown in Figure 9-21.

5. On slide 1, select the title text. Right-click, and from the Floating Font group change the font color to the Standard Dark Red.

6. Select the title text placeholder, and make these changes using the Drawing Tools Format tab:

   a. In the Arrange group, click the Bring Forward button 🔳 drop-down arrow, and choose Bring to Front.

   b. Move the title text so that the first letter is close to the middle of the sun.

7. On slide 1, select the subtitle text, and move it so that it appears at the bottom of the slide near the umbrella image.

Figure 9-21
Completed slide 1

8. On slide 1, copy the umbrella illustration, and paste it on slide 2; then make these changes using the Drawing Tools Format tab:

   a. In the Size group, change the height to 1.5 inches and width to 1.3 inches.

   b. In the Arrange group, click the Align button ⊟▾, and choose Align Right and Align Bottom.

9. On slide 2, select the title, and change the text color to dark red.

10. On slide 2, select both the small sun and the text box, and make these changes using the Drawing Tools Format tab:

    a. In the Arrange group, click the Align button ⊟▾; then select Align Selected Objects and Align Middle.

    b. In the Arrange group, click the Group button ⊞▾, and choose Group.

11. Press Ctrl + D three times to duplicate the sun-and-text group three times.

12. Now position the lowest item by dragging down one sun-and-text group to position it slightly above the top of the umbrella. Drag another copy up, so that it is approximately an inch below the title (use the ruler and gridlines as needed to position the objects).

13. Select all the sun-and-text groups, being careful not to select the umbrella. Make these changes using the Drawing Tools Format tab:

    a. In the Arrange group, click the Align button ⊟▾, and choose Distribute Vertically and Align Center.

    b. If the spacing doesn't look correct, move the top or bottom group up or down a small amount and then vertically redistribute the groups again.

    c. Edit groups 2 through 4 as shown in Figure 9-22.

    d. Group the four sun-and-text groups.

Figure 9-22
Completed slide 2

14. In the Slides tab, select slide 2, and press Ctrl+D to duplicate it; then make these changes to the duplicated slide:

    a. Edit the title text by keying **A Unique Setting**.

    b. Edit the first three sun-and-text groups by keying:

    Beachfront
    Patio juice bar
    Boardwalk

    c. Select the group, and then from the Drawing Tools Format tab, in the Arrange group, click the Group button, and choose Ungroup.

    d. Delete the last sun-and-text group. Draw a selection rectangle around the three items; from the Drawing Tools Format tab, in the Arrange group, click the Group button, and choose Group.

    e. With the group selected, from the Drawing Tools Format tab, in the Arrange group, click the Align button, and choose Align to Slide and Align Center.

15. From the Slides and Outline pane, copy slide 1, and paste the copy after slide 3.

16. On slide 4, edit the title text by keying **Come Visit!**.

17. On slide 4, edit the subtitle text by keying **Healthy dining in the sun**; adjust the size of the text box so that the text fits on two lines, and move it beside the umbrella.

18. Check spelling in the presentation.

19. Create a handout header and footer: Include the date, your name as the header, the page number, and **[your initials]9-22** as the footer.

20. Move to slide 1, and save the presentation as **[your initials]9-22** in your Lesson 9 folder.

21. Close the presentation and submit your work.

Lesson Applications

Exercise 9-23

Select, align, and layer multiple objects; and group objects.

1. Open the file **Personnel**.

2. On slide 1, select all the tiny diamonds, and make these changes:

   a. Align to Slide, Align Top, and Distribute Horizontally.

   b. Select all the small diamonds and group them. Move the row of diamonds down on the slide, below the title.

3. Copy the group of diamonds, and paste them below the titles on slides 2 and 3.

4. On slide 4, select the large diamond, and make these changes:

   a. Send the large diamond shape behind the title text.

   b. Select the large diamond and the title text; then choose Align Middle.

   c. Center those two items horizontally by choosing Align to Slide and then Align Center.

   d. Change the title placeholder to center alignment.

   e. Apply an Angle Bevel shape effect to the diamond.

   f. Duplicate the diamond, and increase its size proportionally so that the height and width are both 6.7 inches.

   g. Change its shape fill to Blue, Accent 1, Darker 25%; then send it to the back.

   h. Select the text box and both diamonds, and choose Align Middle and Align Center.

5. Check spelling.

6. View the presentation in Grayscale view, and make any necessary adjustments to the grayscale settings.

7. Create a handout header and footer: Include the date, your name as the header, the page number, and *[your initials]*9-23 as the footer.

8. Move to slide 1, and save the presentation as *[your initials]*9-23 in your Lesson 9 folder.

9. Close the presentation and submit your work.

UNIT 3 LESSON 9

Exercise 9-24

Align, distribute, layer, and group objects.

1. Open the file **Fine dining**.

2. On slide 1, create a group of three lines:

   a. Draw a 10-inch constrained 6-point horizontal line in the lower part of the slide. By default, the color is Gray-50%, Accent 1 (column 5).

   b. Duplicate this line twice, and change the color of the second line to Tan, Accent 3, Darker 25% and of the third line to Black, Background 1. Move the three lines together without overlapping them, and align them on the left.

   c. Group the lines, and move them over the middle of the title text placeholder.

3. On slide 1, instead of using the title placeholder, draw a rectangle 4.5 inches high and 7 inches wide with a 6-point shape outline using Gray-50%, Accent 1 and the shape fill of White, Text 1. Align the rectangle in the middle and center of the slide.

4. Key the text shown in Figure 9-23 using the font Lucida Calligraphy, black, bold, and 44 points. Increase the line spacing to 1.5.

Figure 9-23
Slide 1 completed

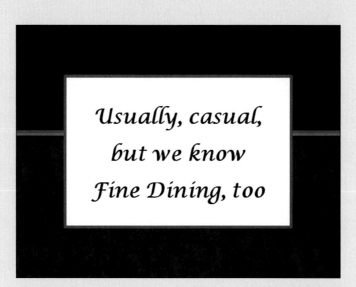

5. On slide 2, increase the width of the picture to 8 inches (height will be 5.33 inches), and move it up to cover the white title area. Use Align Center to center it horizontally on the slide.

6. On slide 3, make these changes to the title:

   a. Change the font to Lucida Calligraphy in bold, 36 points.

   b. Increase the size of the white title placeholder so that the text fits on one line.

   c. Change the title case to capitalize each word.

7. On slide 3, make these changes to the body text:

   a. Change the font to Lucida Calligraphy in bold, 24 points.

   b. Increase the line spacing to 2.0.

   c. Use Align Center for body text and the title on the slide.

8. On slide 4, text is hidden behind the picture. Select the picture, press Tab to select the text, and then move it down. Make these changes:

   a. Change the font to Lucida Calligraphy in bold, 24 points.

   b. Change the line spacing to 2.0.

   c. If necessary, move the picture up so that the vertical position is about 0.50.

   d. Adjust the position of the text so that it is balanced in the black area below the picture.

   e. Use Align Center for the picture and the text on the slide.

9. On slide 5, text is hidden behind the tuxedo picture. Select the picture; then make these changes and Send Backward.

   a. Select the text and change the font to Lucida Calligraphy in bold, 24 points.

   b. Use Align Center for the text, and position it just above the bottom shirt button.

10. On slide 2, change the picture border to Gray-50%, Accent 1 with a weight of 6 pt so that it matches the rectangle treatment on the first slide.

11. Use the Format Painter to apply the same border to the picture on slide 4.

12. On slide 1, copy the grouped lines, and paste them on slide 5. Send the lines to the back so that the picture is on the top of the grouped lines.

13. Apply the Glitter transition to all slides in the presentation.

14. Compress the pictures to Screen output.

15. Create a handout header and footer: Include the date, your name as the header, the page number, and *[your initials]*9-24 as the footer.

16. Move to slide 1, and save the presentation as *[your initials]*9-24 in your Lesson 9 folder.

17. Close the presentation and submit your work.

Exercise 9-25

Modify an illustrated image, and align, distribute, layer, and group objects.

1. Open the file **Branding**.

2. On slide 4, select the three long arrows, center-align them on the slide, and distribute them vertically on the slide. "Competitive Environment" should be at the top.

3. Move to slide 5. Copy one of the short arrows, and paste it once on slide 5 and three times on slide 6.

4. Make these adjustments on slide 5:

   a. Position each short arrow in front of a text box (but not touching the box).

   b. Select the three arrows, and align them on the left in relation to selected objects.

   c. Select the first arrow and the text box, middle-align them, and then group them. Repeat for the second and third arrows and text boxes.

   d. Select the three groups, and distribute vertically relative to selected objects so that the spacing is even.

   e. If necessary for even spacing, move the bulleted list down slightly.

5. On slide 5, ungroup to convert the newspaper image to a Microsoft Office drawing object. Then select the pink background parts, and remove them. Group the image then position it on the upper right, as shown on Figure 9-24.

Figure 9-24
Slide 5 completed

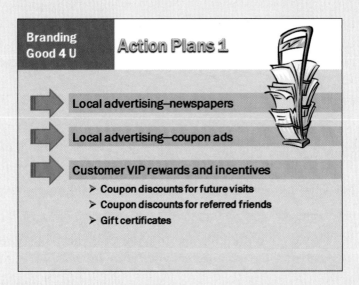

6. Repeat step 4 to align the arrows, group the text, and adjust the list on slide 6.

7. On slide 6, ungroup the mouse image to convert it to a Microsoft Office drawing object. Then select the pink background, and remove it. Group the image then position it on the upper right of the slide.

8. Review the presentation in Grayscale view, and make adjustments where needed.

9. Create a handout header and footer: Include the date, your name as the header, the page number, and *[your initials]*9-25 as the footer.

10. Move to slide 1, and save the presentation as *[your initials]*9-25 in your Lesson 9 folder.

11. Close the presentation and submit your work.

Exercise 9-26 ◆ Challenge Yourself

Work with multiple objects; align, rotate, and flip objects; work with layers; and use image editing tools.

1. Open the file **WhoWeAre**.

2. Change to the Urban design theme with the Verve colors.

3. For slide 1, search for an illustration that is appropriate to the content of the presentation, and insert it in the lower right corner of the slide. Size the image appropriately, and change its color to Pink, Accent color 2 Dark. Rotate or flip the image, if needed, to create better positioning, and adjust the contrast and brightness as necessary.

4. On slide 2, add rectangles at the bottom by following these steps:

   a. Draw a rectangle with a height of .40 inches and a width of 10 inches. Change the shape fill color to Gray 50%, Text 2 with no outline. Align the rectangle on the bottom of the slide.

   b. Duplicate this rectangle, and change the height to .10 inch and the fill color to Pink, Accent 2 with no outline. Align this rectangle directly above the first one.

   c. Duplicate the pink rectangle, and change the shape fill to Pink, Accent 2, Lighter 40%. Align it directly above the other pink line.

   d. Select the three rectangles, and group them.

5. Copy the group of rectangles, and paste the group on slides 3 through 5.

6. On slide 1, select the title placeholder, change the font to Arial, 60 points, bold, and apply the WordArt Quick Style of Fill - Pink, Accent 2, Warm Matte Bevel (column 3, row 5).

7. On slide 2, resize the body text placeholder to fit the text, and then center- and middle-align it on the slide.

8. On slide 2, draw a constrained diamond shape with a height and width of 4.5 inches. Change the fill color to a light shade of gray. Remove the outline.

9. Select both the diamond and the body text placeholder, and align their middles and centers relative to each other. Send the diamond behind the text.

10. Copy the diamond, and paste it to slide 4. Resize the text placeholder to fit the text, select both the diamond and the body text placeholder, and align their middles and centers relative to each other. Send the diamond behind the text.

11. Copy the diamond, and paste it to slide 3. Send the diamond to the back, and then position it behind the picture of people. Align the centers and middles of the picture and diamond relative to each other; then move them slightly to the left.

12. Still working on slide 3, adjust the body text placeholder by increasing the font size to 30 points. Adjust its vertical position so that it is balanced with the image.

13. Format slide 5 in the same style as slide 3, but make the diamond narrower to better fit the picture.

14. Review the presentation in Grayscale view, and make adjustments where needed.

15. View the presentation as a slide show.

16. Compress the pictures to screen output.

17. Create a handout header and footer: Include the date, your name as the header, the page number, and *[your initials]*9-26 as the footer.

18. Move to slide 1, and save the presentation as *[your initials]*9-26 in your Lesson 9 folder.

19. Close the presentation and submit your work.

On Your Own

In these exercises you work on your own, as you would in a real-life work environment. Use the skills you've learned to accomplish the task—and be creative.

Exercise 9-27

Imagine that you have invented a new product: a vacuum that runs itself, heated pants, a new type of breathable waterproof fabric, a new type of golf ball, or whatever else you choose. Create a persuasive presentation targeted at possible financial backers for the product. Explain the product's features and the benefits of its use. Identify its potential market. Include at least five slides in your presentation. Use the tools and features presented in this lesson and in previous lessons to create an attractive presentation. Be sure to group multiple objects together and have a combination of layered objects. Save the presentation as *[your initials]*9-27. Close the presentation and submit your work.

Exercise 9-28

Create a presentation that will be used to solicit donations for a charity event sponsored by a community organization. The event could be a blood drive, an adopt-a-family project, a heart walk, a bowl for kids' sake, or an event of your choosing. In your presentation, describe the organization and the event activities, including dates and times. Also include one or two slides explaining to people why they should donate. Use the tools and features presented in this lesson and in previous lessons to create an attractive presentation. Be sure to have a slide with multiple objects that you can align and distribute or flip. Save the presentation as *[your initials]*9-28. Close the presentation and submit your work.

Exercise 9-29

Imagine that you are organizing a chili cook-off in a local community. Create a presentation describing the contest, rules, location, and categories. Recognize winners from the previous year. Format your presentation attractively and in keeping with the theme of your idea. Use the concepts for working with layers and multiple objects on at least one slide. Save the presentation as *[your initials]*9-29. Close the presentation and submit your work.

Lesson 10
Animating and Using Multimedia Effects

OBJECTIVES *After completing this lesson, you will be able to:*

1. Apply animation.
2. Modify and enhance animations.
3. Add audio.
4. Add video.
5. Insert hyperlinks.

Estimated Time: 2 hours

While PowerPoint's transitions are used to add movement between slides, *animations* create interesting visual effects for objects on a slide. Commands on the Animations tab are used to control the timing, speed, audio, and other aspects of movement. These effects can be applied to control how an object appears, how it is emphasized on a slide, or how it leaves the slide. Video and audio can be inserted to help convey the message in the presentation.

Gus Irvinelli is preparing this presentation for a talk he is giving about Good 4 U at the local Chamber of Commerce. He plans to include information about an upcoming cooking contest. He has asked you to add some animation effects and insert multimedia elements to enhance the presentation.

Applying Animation

To *animate* means to apply movement and audio effects that control how objects, text or images, behave during a slide show. For example, an object can:

- Fly into the center of the screen accompanied by an audio effect.
- Fade into the background when another object appears.
- Blink when you click your mouse button.
- Leave the screen in a spiral path.

When objects on a slide are selected, commands on the Animations tab enable you to add movement and other effects as well as control their animation settings and order of appearance. If you enjoy using these tools, you will want to spend time on your own experimenting with endless possibilities for animation.

But remember to use animation carefully to enhance—not distract from—the message your presentation needs to deliver.

Exercise 10-1 ADD ENTRANCE EFFECTS AND CHANGE EFFECT OPTIONS

To apply an animation to a selected object, click an animation effect from the gallery on the Animations tab or click the Add Animation button and choose an effect. The four types of effects are:

- *Entrance*. Controls how an object first appears on a slide.
- *Emphasis*. Draws attention to an object that is already displayed on a slide.
- *Exit*. Controls how an object leaves (or disappears from) a slide.
- *Motion Path*. Defines the line of travel that an object can follow as part of an animation effect.

After you apply an effect, an animation tag—a small, numbered box—appears on the slide next to the animated object. This number correlates with the effects listed in the Animation pane as you apply them. Items in this list can be reordered.

Once an animation effect is applied, then additional effect options can customize the movement even more. The number of effect options varies on the basis of each particular animation.

Figure 10-1
Choosing an entrance effect

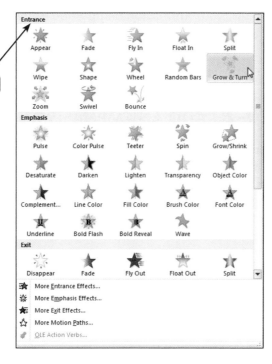

1. Open **Motion1**, the Healthy Food presentation.

2. On slide 1, select the "Healthy Food" object.

3. From the Animations tab, in the Advanced Animation group, click the Add Animation button to see the gallery of effects. As you point to effects in the gallery, a live preview will display on your selected object.

4. From the Entrance category, click Grow & Turn, as shown in Figure 10-1.

5. The animation tag "1" appears next to the object.

6. Still working on slide 1, select the text "for the Athlete in You." From the Animations tab, in the Animation group, click the More button ⊽, and choose More Entrance Effects.

7. The Change Entrance Effect dialog box opens. Scroll through the complete list of entrance effects in the categories of Basic, Subtle, Moderate, and Exciting, as shown in Figure 10-2.

8. From the Change Entrance Effect dialog box, in the Basic category, choose Wheel, and then click OK. The animation tag "2" appears next to the animated object.

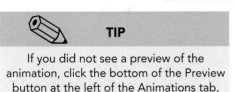

TIP

If you did not see a preview of the animation, click the bottom of the Preview button at the left of the Animations tab, in the Preview group, and be sure AutoPreview is checked.

Figure 10-2
Click and drag slider bar to view more entrance effects

More entrance effects

9. Select the text "for the Athlete in You"; then from the Animations tab, in the Animation group, click the Effect Options button ▊. The available effect options vary on the basis of each different effect. For this particular effect, choose 8 Spokes, and repeat to choose All at Once.

10. From the Animations tab, in the Preview group, click ⭐ to view your animations.

11. From the Animations tab, in the Advanced Animation group, click the Animation Pane button 🎞. Your two animation effects are listed in the order you applied them. To see the effects on your slide, click the Play button ▶ Play at the top of the pane.

12. You can also test your animation using Slide Show view. Click the Slide Show View button 🖵, and slide 1 appears; then click two times to activate the entrance effects so that the remaining objects appear. Press Esc to return to Normal view.

Exercise 10-2 ADD AN EMPHASIS AND EXIT EFFECT

In addition to entrance animation effects, you can use interesting emphasis effects to draw your audience's attention to an object on your slide. Or you can use exit effects to make objects leave. Effects can be combined too. While you are learning about animation, it is fun to try different combinations. However, you ultimately want to select movements that seem logical and contribute to the audience's understanding of your information.

1. On slide 2, select the gold star to the left of the text "Gus Irvinelli."

2. From the Animations tab, in the Advanced Animation group, click the Add Animation button 🌟, and choose Appear from the Entrance category.

TIP

The Add Animation button and More button provide access to the same animation effects. If you see the effect you want in either animation gallery, you can select it from the list. Choose more effects only when the effect you want is not on the gallery.

3. Select the star, and click the Add Animation button again; then choose More Emphasis Effects. From the Moderate category, choose Color Pulse, and click OK.

4. Select the star, and click the Add Animation button again; then choose Disappear from the Exit category.

5. From the Animations tab, in the Preview group, click the Preview button to see the star pulse and then disappear.

Exercise 10-3 APPLY A MOTION PATH TO AN OBJECT AND REMOVE ANIMATIONS

Depending on the particular effect you choose, different directions of movement are available. However, with a *motion path* effect, you can make an object enter a slide from any point and travel across the slide in a variety of paths, including diagonal, zigzag, or spiral paths. You can even draw your own path to customize the movement.

If you want to remove an animation effect from an object, select it in the animation tag number on the slide or select the animation in the list in the Animation pane and press Delete. You can remove multiple items from the list in the same way that you select and delete multiple slide thumbnails.

Figure 10-3
Choosing a preset motion path

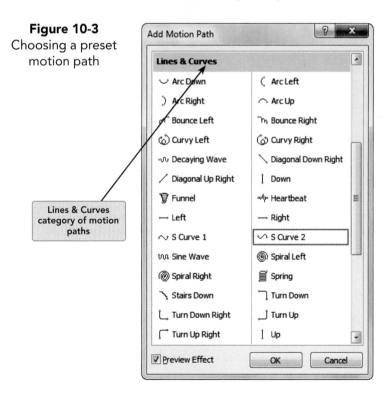

1. Change the zoom to a low setting, for example, 40%, so that you can see a large blank area around the slide.

2. On slide 1, select the illustrated runner, and move him off the slide to the blank area on the left of the title.

3. With the runner selected, from the Animations tab, in the Advanced Animation group, click the Add Animation button, and choose More Motion Paths. The Add Motion Path dialog box offers a large number of choices, as shown in Figure 10-3. You can add motion paths to any object, including text.

4. In the Lines and Curves category, scroll down to choose S Curve 2, and click OK.

5. A curving line extends from the runner to the right, with triangles at each end of the line. The green triangle indicates the start of the path, and the red triangle indicates the end, as shown in Figure 10-4.

Figure 10-4
Working with a
preset motion path

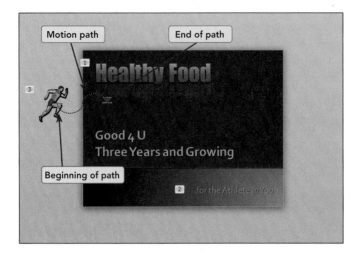

6. Select the motion path only; then drag its right sizing handle to extend it across to the right of the slide. Drag the center sizing handle down, and use the rotation handle to adjust the angle slightly, as shown in Figure 10-5, so that the animation ends lower on the slide than where it starts. Even if the rotation causes the green beginning triangle to move away from the runner, he will begin movement from the triangle position.

Figure 10-5
Final motion path

7. Click **Play** in the Animation pane to test these movements on the slide. The animations will occur in numerical order from 1 to 3.

8. After viewing the animations for slide 1, it seems there is too much movement.

9. Working on slide 1, from the Animation pane, select "Rectangle 1: Healthy Food," and press (Delete).

10. Now only two numbered items appear in the list, and they are renumbered, as are the animation tags on the slide.

Exercise 10-4 ANIMATE CHART ELEMENTS

Animation effects for charts can add movement to the whole chart or make the chart appear by series or category data. Effects that work well with charts are Dissolve In, Split, Random Bars, Blinds, and Wipe.

1. On slide 3, select the chart. From the Animations tab, in the Advanced Animation group, click the Add Animation button ⭐, and choose Wipe from the Entrance category.

2. In the Animation pane, click the list box arrow for the animation; then choose Effect Options.

3. On the Wipe dialog box, from the Chart Animation tab, click the Group chart list box arrow, and choose By Category, as shown in Figure 10-6.

Figure 10-6
Chart animation options

4. Clear the check box for Start animation by drawing the chart background. By turning off this option, the chart layout will appear when the slide is displayed. Click OK.

5. Preview this animation, and notice how the columns come in by category.

6. In the Animation pane, click the list box arrow for animation 1 again, and choose Effect Options.

7. From the Chart Animation tab, click the Group chart list box arrow, and choose By Series. Click OK.

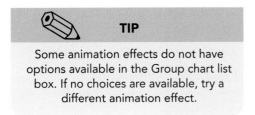

TIP

Some animation effects do not have options available in the Group chart list box. If no choices are available, try a different animation effect.

8. View the presentation as a slide show, starting with slide 3. When you get to the animated chart, click the mouse to make each series of columns appear, one after the other.

9. Create a Lesson 10 folder. Save the presentation as *[your initials]*10-4 in your new Lesson 10 folder.

Modifying and Enhancing Animations

Animations can be modified in many ways. They can be made to appear faster or slower, move in different ways, be activated by a mouse click, or play automatically. In addition, you can attach audio effects to animations.

Exercise 10-5 MODIFY ANIMATIONS

The animations you have created up to this point appear during a slide show when you click your mouse, which triggers the animation to begin. In this exercise, you will modify an animation so that it appears automatically, change the animation speed, and adjust what triggers the animation.

1. If the Animation pane is not visible, from the Animations tab, in the Advanced Animation group, click the Animation Pane button .

2. On slide 1, click anywhere on the text "for the Athlete in You," and the Wheel entrance effect 1 applied earlier is selected in the Animation pane.

3. In the Animation pane, click the list box arrow, and choose Start After Previous. The animation items are renumbered.

4. With this item still selected, click the list box arrow, and choose Timing. From the Timing tab, change the Duration to 3 seconds (Slow), and click OK.

5. Click the image of the runner. In the Animation pane, notice that the Group 7 animation effect is selected.

6. From the Animations tab, in the Advanced Animation group, click the Trigger button ⚡, and choose On Click of and then Rectangle 1. This makes clicking the "Healthy Food" title the trigger for bringing in the runner.

7. With this item still selected, click the list box arrow, and choose Timing. From the Timing tab, change the Duration to 3 seconds (Slow), and click OK.

8. Notice that the animation tags now contain a lightning bolt or the number 0. The 0 indicates that the animation sequence will start automatically when the slide appears, while the lightning bolt indicates that there is a trigger that will start the animation.

9. View the slide show, starting with slide 1. Click the "Healthy Food" title to bring in the runner after the subtitle has appeared. Press Esc to return to the presentation.

10. Move to slide 2, and select the star. To make the star pulse more than one time, in the Animation pane click the list box arrow for animation item 2 and choose Timing. The Timing tab for the Color Pulse dialog box appears.

11. From the Repeat list box, choose 3, and click OK. The star will now pulse three times.

12. In the Animation pane, click the list box arrow for the first item, "5-Point Star 1," which has the Appear effect. Choose Start After Previous. Notice that the animation tag changes to 0.

13. For the second item, which has the Color Pulse effect, change to Start After Previous.

14. For the third item, which has the Disappear effect, change to Start After Previous. Now the star will appear, flicker, and then disappear without the need for additional mouse clicks.

15. Click Play in the Animation pane to test the animations on the slide.

TIP

When listed items move to a different position, timing and start settings sometimes need to be changed. You will need to experiment to determine the best settings for the effect you want.

TIP

Choosing Start After Previous when there is no previous event makes the animation start as soon as the slide is displayed. The previous event is the display of the slide, before any animation occurs. The animation tag will show 0.

Exercise 10-6 ADD AUDIO EFFECTS TO ANIMATIONS

Be sure to use audio carefully so that it does not distract from the presentation. Use it to draw attention to an object or to provide a subtle background effect, such as playing soft music before a presentation begins. It is very difficult to talk while music is playing.

Always test audio effects on the equipment you plan to use when presenting a slide show. You might need to adjust the volume for the size of the room in which you will present the slide show, or you might need to add external speakers to amplify the audio if you will be speaking in a large room.

In this exercise, you will add audio effects as part of an object's animation by using the Animation pane.

 TIP

If you have trouble adjusting the volume the way you want, click the speaker icon on the right side of the Windows task bar to adjust your system's sound. Some speakers have volume knobs as well.

1. Move to slide 1, and select the text "Healthy Food." On the Animations tab, click the Add Animation button; then choose the Bounce effect.

2. In the Animation pane, click the list box arrow, and choose Effect Options. The Bounce dialog box opens. Each animation effect has its own dialog box. The options vary, depending on the animation.

Figure 10-7
Adding a sound effect

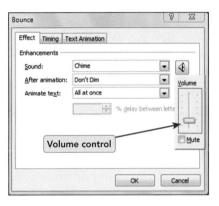

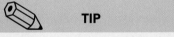
Volume control

3. Click the Sound list box arrow; then scroll down the list of sounds, and select Chime.

4. Click the Speaker button to the right of the Sound list box. Move the Volume slider down, near the bottom, to lower the sound level, as shown in Figure 10-7. Click OK. The chime sound plays.

5. If necessary, access Effect Options again to adjust the sound volume up or down as needed to create a quiet sound.

 TIP

Audio clips that you have recorded can be inserted using the same dialog box.

6. Use the steps outlined above to add the same chime sound to the other text animation.

7. Click Play at the bottom of the Animation pane to preview the animations and sounds.

Exercise 10-7 REORDER AND SEQUENCE ANIMATIONS

To make an animation appear at the same time as another animation, reposition its listing in the Animation pane so that it is directly below the other animation, and change its Start setting to With Previous.

When animating a body text placeholder, you can control the order of how the text appears by controlling the sequence:

- *As One Object.* The selection appears and is animated as one object.

- *All at Once.* All items appear at once, but the animation effect is applied to each part individually.

- *By Paragraph.* Each bullet and subset of bullets are brought in together.

NOTE

The difference between As One Object and All at Once is very subtle when working with text. If you apply either effect option to a SmartArt diagram where objects are set to grow or rotate, the effect becomes much more evident.

1. Move to slide 4, and select the bulleted text placeholder. From the Animations tab, in the Advanced Animation group, click the Add Animation button 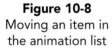, and from the Entrance category, choose Fly In.

2. From the Animations tab, in the Animation group, click the Effect Options button , and change the Direction to From Left and the Sequence to By Paragraph.

3. Preview this animation.

4. On slide 5, select the three arrows.

5. From the Animations tab, in the Advanced Animation group, click the Add Animation button , and from the Entrance category, choose Wipe. (Because a title and four bulleted items are on the slide, these arrows are numbered 6, 7, and 8.)

6. Select all three arrows again, and in the Animation pane, click the list box arrow for the three, and choose Effect Options. Be sure the Direction is From Bottom.

7. Select all three arrows. On the Animations tab, in the Timing group, click the Start list box, and choose After Previous.

8. Click Play to preview this effect. The list appears with the slide, since it has no animation; then the arrows appear after the listed text.

Figure 10-8

Moving an item in the animation list

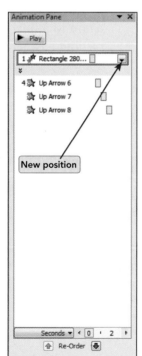

9. Still working on slide 5, select the bulleted list placeholder, and select the Fly In entrance effect from the gallery on the Animations tab, in the Animation group.

10. From the Animations tab, in the Animation group, click the Effect Options button , and change the Direction to From Bottom-Right.

11. In the Animation pane, click the listing for this animation, "Rectangle," and click the Re-Order up arrow until it is at the top of the list.

12. Move to slide 1, select "Rectangle 1," and reorder the animations so that "Healthy Food" appears first, "for the Athlete in You" appears second, and the runner appears last after you click the "Healthy Food" title.

13. View the entire presentation as a slide show.

Exercise 10-8 MODIFY AN ANIMATION'S DURATION

You have already seen that you can make an animation start automatically with the display of a slide, start immediately after another animation has completed, or wait until you click your mouse. You can fine-tune the timing of an animation by specifying a delay before the animation begins. These settings can be controlled with commands on the Animations tab or in the Animation pane.

1. On slide 1, select the second item in the Animation list, "for the Athlete in You". From the Animations tab, in the Timing group, click in the Delay spin box, and key **2** (for 2 seconds—this will show as 02:00). This delays the current animation 2 seconds so that the previous one has time to take effect.

2. Repeat step 1 to add a 2-second delay to the first list item, "Healthy Food."

3. With the first item, "Healthy Food," selected, click the Start list box, and choose After Previous.

4. On slide 2, select the star listed in the Animation pane, click its list box arrow, and choose Timing. Key **0.5** (for 0.5 second) in the Delay box. Click OK. Notice that when you set the timing this way, it appears just as before in the Delay list box.

5. Starting on slide 1, view your presentation as a slide show to see the effect of the delayed starts. When the animations are complete on slides 1 and 2, press [Esc] to end the show.

Exercise 10-9 COPY AN ANIMATION USING ANIMATION PAINTER

When you copy and paste an animated object, on the same slide or on a different slide, the animations are copied along with the object. The *Animation Painter* enables you to copy the animation effects from one object and apply them to a different object.

1. Working on slide 2, select the star on the slide, copy it, and then paste it on the same slide.

2. Use your arrow keys to nudge the copied star to the right of the name "Julie Wolfe," as shown in Figure 10-9. Select both stars, and align them on the left. Preview the animation.

Figure 10-9
Slide 2 with the completed star animation

3. On slide 5, select one of the arrows. From the Animations tab, in the Advanced Animation group, click the Animation Painter button 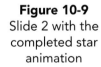.

4. On slide 7, click the text placeholder. The same animation is applied, so the text will appear as one object.

5. From the Animations tab, in the Animation group, click the Effect Options button ⬛, and choose By Paragraph to change the sequence.

6. Preview the animation. Close the Animation pane.

7. Save the presentation as *[your initials]*10-9 in your Lesson 10 folder.

Adding Audio

Besides attaching audio effects to animations, you can add audio objects that stand on their own. Like most animations, audio objects can be set to play automatically when a slide appears or to wait for a mouse click. Like the chime sound you used with an animation, many of the audio files in Microsoft's collection are short "event" sounds, such as a door closing or glass clinking, that are small files with the extension of **.wav**. However, some of the files are music sounds with the extension of **.mid**. In the following exercises you will distinguish between these file types and look at the file properties.

Exercise 10-10   INSERT CLIP ART AUDIO

Audio effects, like other effects, should be chosen carefully to make sure that they enhance—not distract from—your presentation's message. You can play a short burst of music to accompany an effect, or you can set music to play for an entire slide or an entire presentation.

1. Move to slide 1 in Normal view.

2. From the Insert tab, in the Media group, click the bottom of the Audio button 🔊, and select Clip Art Audio.

3. The Clip Art pane opens, displaying audio files. All the thumbnails have an icon with a musical note and the letters "WAV" (Windows Audio File). When you move the pointer over the audio thumbnail, information about the file appears. You can see the number of seconds the file will play, its file size, and the type of file. Those showing WAV are usually short audio effects, such as a drumroll, chimes, or applause. Others showing MID (or MIDI, Musical Instrument Digital Interface) are music files that are usually longer in length.

4. In the Search for box, key **sports**.

5. Click the Results should be list box arrow, and make sure Audio is checked. Clear any other check boxes that might be selected. Click the list arrow again to close the list box; then click Go. If Microsoft media content was installed on your computer or if your computer is connected to the Internet, audio files relating to sports themes will appear as shown in Figure 10-10.

Figure 10-10
Audio files in the
Clip Art pane

6. Right-click any audio file icon, and choose Preview/Properties from the shortcut menu. The current audio file begins to play.

7. In the Preview/Properties dialog box, click the Next button [Next >] to preview the next audio. Most (if not all) the audio clips are short audio effects. Click Close to close the Preview/Properties dialog box.

8. Locate the audio file **Sports Drive** on the Clip Art pane, and click it to insert.

9. By default, the audio clip is indicated by a speaker that appears with a control panel in the center of the slide. See Figure 10-11.

Figure 10-11
Audio file object and
play controls

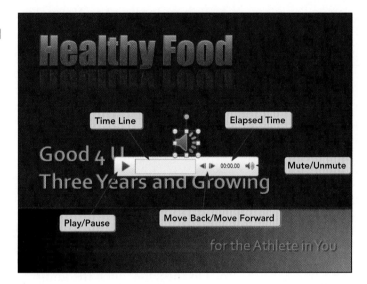

 TIP

By default, the audio speaker icon and control panel will also display during a slide show but in a more subtle design. You can move the control panel to the lower portion of the slide for ease of use during a presentation, or you can hide it, as you do in the next exercise.

10. The playback control has Play/Pause, a Time Line, Move Back/Move Forward, elapsed time in seconds, and a volume control.

11. Drag the speaker icon down so that it is just below the red line on the slide in the empty section on the left of the slide.

12. View this slide as a slide show, and move the mouse over the speaker icon so that you can see the control panel.

13. By default, the audio will play When Clicked. Click the speaker icon or Play/Pause on the control panel and the music will play. Click a blank area of the screen to turn off the music. Press [Esc] to end the slide show.

14. Close the Clip Art pane.

Exercise 10-11 CONTROL START AND PLAYBACK OPTIONS

By using the Audio Tools Playback tab, you can control an audio clip so that it plays automatically when a slide starts, when you click the mouse, or while several slides are displayed. If the clip is set to play automatically, the audio speaker can be hidden in one of two ways—by checking Hide During Show on the Audio Tools Playback tab or by dragging the audio object off your slide onto the gray desktop area of the Slide pane. Bookmarks can be added to mark a specific point in the audio, and both the beginning and the end of the clip can be trimmed. You also have the choice of removing the control panel but leaving the speaker icon. On the Slide Show tab, remove the check in front of Show Media Controls.

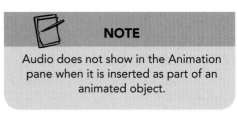

NOTE

Audio does not show in the Animation pane when it is inserted as part of an animated object.

Figure 10-12
Animation list showing four items including two with triggers

Music object name

1. Return to slide 1 in Normal view. Click the audio speaker.

2. From the Animations tab, in the Animations group, click the Animation Pane button 📊. The audio clip now appears in the list.

3. If your animation list contains items not shown in Figure 10-12, delete the extra list items.

4. Select the music object name in the Animation pane (it may display as Sports Drive.mid), and click the Re-Order up arrow to move the item to the top of the animation list.

5. On the Animations tab, in the Timing group, click the Start list box, and choose With Previous.

6. On the slide, click the audio speaker; then click the Audio Tools Playback tab. Figure 10-13 shows the Audio Tools Playback tab.

Figure 10-13
Audio Tools Playback tab

7. Working on the Audio Tools Playback tab, in the Audio Options group, make the following changes:

   a. For Start, the list box should show Automatically.

   b. Click the Volume button 🔊, and choose Low.

   c. Place a check for Hide During Show so that the speaker icon will not be displayed.

TIP

This change is necessary because the After Previous setting would cause this event to wait until the music stops playing. By adding the 2-second delay, the animation gives the appearance of starting after the music starts.

TIP

To make an audio file play for the duration of an entire presentation, from the Audio Tools Playback tab, check Loop until Stopped.

8. Select the second item in the animation list, "Healthy Food." On the Animations tab, in the Timing group, click the Start list box, choose With Previous, and then reset the Delay to 2 seconds. Repeat these modifications for the third item in the animation list, "for the Athlete in You."

9. Since there is an audio clip on slide 1, the chimes seem out of place. From the Animation task pane, access the Effect Options, and choose No Sound for both the title, "Healthy Food," and subtitle, "for the Athlete in You," animations.

10. View the presentation as a slide show, starting on slide 1; then return to Normal view.

Exercise 10-12   BOOKMARK AND TRIM AN AUDIO CLIP

Using the audio playback panel, you can add a *bookmark* so that you can jump to a specific location in the clip if you need to begin playing it from a certain point. If you need to play only a portion of the entire clip, you can *trim* the audio clip to shorten it from the beginning or end.

1. On slide 1, select the speaker; then notice that, as you move your pointer over the audio control time line, the elapsed seconds appear.

2. Click the time line at about 10 seconds; then from the Audio Tools Playback tab, in the Bookmarks group, click the Add Bookmark button. A circle appears on the time line showing the bookmark location.

3. To see how this looks during a slide show, remove the check for Hide During Show.

4. View your presentation as a slide show, starting on this slide. Point to the speaker, and the time line will appear showing the circle of the bookmark.

5. On the control panel, click Play ▶, if necessary, to start the audio; then click in different positions on the time line to see how to move around. Practice working with pause ❙❙ and play ▶ so that you can see how to pause the audio, go back to a previous position, and then play the audio.

6. Press Esc to end the slide show.

7. Still working on slide 1, select the speaker. On the Audio Tools Playback tab, in the Editing group, click Trim Audio.

8. In the Trim Audio dialog box, locate the start and end points.

Figure 10-14
Trim Audio dialog box

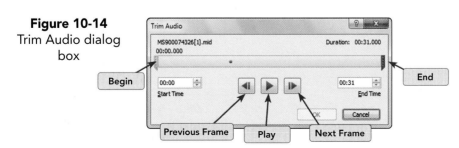

9. A green marker indicates the starting point, and a red marker indicates the ending point. The bookmark you made shows as a blue dot. Start and end times are shown, as well as controls for play, previous frame, and next frame.

TIP

Changing an audio clip in this way affects how it is played in your presentation but does not affect the original file. You will need to test carefully to achieve the exact duration you need in your presentation.

10. Click the Next Frame button ▶ several times, and notice that the start time changes. You can also click the spin box arrows or drag each marker to a different position on the time line.

11. Drag the Start marker to about 00:02; then use the spin box arrows at Start Time to adjust if necessary.

12. Drag the End marker to about 00:22; then use the spin box arrows at End Time to adjust if necessary.

13. Click OK.

Exercise 10-13 INSERT AN AUDIO CLIP FROM A FILE

Audio file formats that will play in PowerPoint include:

- *AIFF.* Audio Interchange File Format (extension **.aiff**)
- *AU.* Unix Audio (extension **.au**)
- *MIDI.* Musical Instrument Digital Interface (extension **.mid** or **.midi**)
- *MP3.* MPEG Audio Layer 3 (extension **.mp3**)
- *WAV.* Wave Form (extension **.wav**)
- *WMA.* Windows Media Audio (extension **.wma**)

Additional file types can be made compatible by using a program to convert them.

1. Move to slide 7.

2. From the Insert tab, in the Media group, click the bottom half of the Audio button 🔊, and select Audio from File.

3. Select the WAV file **BackgroundMusic1** from your Lesson 10 student files, and click Insert, as shown in Figure 10-15.

Figure 10-15
Insert audio clip from file

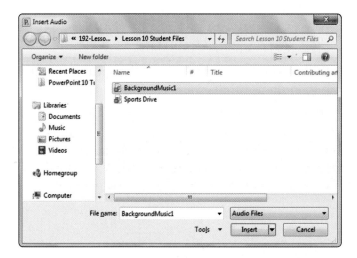

4. From the Audio Tools Playback tab, in the Audio Options group, click the Start list box, choose Automatically, and check Hide During Show.

5. View slide 7 in Slide Show view, clicking through the animations until you reach the audio file; then press [Esc] to end the show.

Exercise 10-14   RECORD AUDIO

PowerPoint has the ability to record audio input. For example, a microphone connected to the computer may be used to record your own voice to create an audio clip. The *Record Audio* feature should be used for short audio clips and not for narrating, which is covered later in this book. You may skip this exercise if a microphone is not available.

1. Move to slide 3, the financial growth chart.

2. From the Insert tab, in the Media group, click the arrow on the Audio button 🔊, and select Record Audio to open the Record Sound dialog box, as shown in Figure 10-16.

Figure 10-16
Recording audio

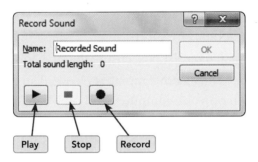

3. In the Name box, key this title for the audio recording:
Financial Growth.

4. Click the Record button ● to begin your recording, and then speak into the microphone "Wow! Look at the third-year profit jump!" or provide a different comment of your own about the chart.

5. When finished, click the Stop button ■ to stop the recording.

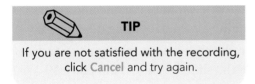

TIP

If you are not satisfied with the recording, click Cancel and try again.

6. Click the Play button ▶ to review your recording. If you are satisfied, click OK to insert the new recording into your slide.

7. Move the audio icon over to the right side of the slide, beside the chart.

8. View the slide in Slide Show view. Click the audio icon when you are ready to listen to your recording. Click [Esc] to return to Normal view.

9. Save the presentation as *[your initials]*10-14 in your Lesson 10 folder.

Adding Video

In PowerPoint, the term *video* refers to any motion file. Microsoft provides animated files (sometimes called animated GIFs) within Office 2010. Additional material is available on the Web at Microsoft Office Online. You can also insert video files from other sources. Video file formats that will play in PowerPoint include:

- *Adobe Flash Media.* Flash Video (extension **.swf**)
- *Windows Media file.* Advanced Streaming Format (extension **.asf**)

- *Windows Video file.* Audio Video Interleave (extension **.avi**)
- *Movie file.* Moving Picture Experts Group (extension **.mpg**)
- *Windows Media Video file.* Windows Media Video (extension **.wmv**)

Additional formats will play but may require installation of the Apple QuickTime player.

Exercise 10-15   INSERT CLIP ART VIDEO

Inserting a video (or animated file) onto a slide is similar to inserting an audio object. Once it's on the slide, you can add animation effects to control when and how it appears. Such videos are all small in size—usually 100 pixels in height and width. Be careful when increasing their size, because the image can become quite distorted.

1. On slide 7, from the Insert tab, in the Media group, click the bottom of the Video button 📹, and select Clip Art Video. In the Clip Art pane, an animation icon 🌟 (a small yellow star) in the lower right corner of the thumbnails identifies video files.

2. In the Search for box, key **sports**.

3. In the Results should be: list box, ensure that the only box checked is Videos.

4. Be sure Include Office.com content is checked so that the search will be performed both on your computer and on Microsoft Online if you are currently connected to the Internet.

TIP

The size dimensions of most animated videos cannot be increased without distorting them, so be careful when you are trying to make these images larger.

5. Click Go.

6. Right-click one of the animation thumbnails, and choose Preview/Properties to preview the animation; then click Close. Insert a video, with a suitable theme and colors, that represents reaching a goal or coming a long way.

7. Once the video is on the slide, resize it proportionately to fit below the text on the slide, as shown in Figure 10-17.

Figure 10-17
Insert a video clip

8. On the Animations tab, click the Preview button to view all the slide animations and videos.

9. Close the Clip Art pane.

Exercise 10-16   INSERT A VIDEO FROM A FILE

Video files can be inserted using the same method used to insert audio files.

1. On slide 6, from the Insert tab, in the Media group, click the bottom of the Video button 🎞, and select Video from File.

2. Select the file **TestKitchen** from your Lesson 10 student files, as shown in Figure 10-18. Click Insert.

Figure 10-18
Insert video from file

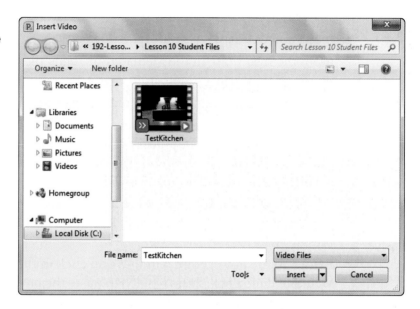

TIP

The Compress Media feature is similar to Compress Pictures. The feature is available from the File tab, in the Info category. It can be used to save disk space and improve playback performance; however, media quality may be affected. There are three choices for compression: Presentation Quality, which maintains audio and video quality; Internet Quality, which is similar to streamed media on the Web; and Low Quality, which is appropriate when space is limited, such as in e-mail messages.

3. From the Video Tools Playback tab, in the Video Options group, click the Start list box, and choose Automatically.

4. From the Video Tools Playback tab, in the Preview group, click the Play button ▶ to test the video.

5. View slide 6 in Slide Show view. Press Esc to end the show after slide 6.

6. From the Video Tools Playback tab, in the Video Options group, check Play Full Screen; then test this slide in Slide Show view. You will notice jagged edges of the objects in the kitchen because the video quality is not high enough to show at this size.

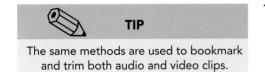

TIP

The same methods are used to bookmark and trim both audio and video clips.

7. Only a small size increase would be appropriate, so remove the check from **Play Full Screen** to return to the size at insertion. Resize the video: From the Video Tools Format tab, in the Size group, choose **3** inches for the height and **4** inches for the width.

Exercise 10-17 INSERT A VIDEO FROM A WEB SITE

Video files can be inserted into a presentation from a Web site by using embed codes. Video-sharing sites, such as Youtube.com, provide embed codes to enable easy access to videos. Make sure that you have the owner's approval before you link to, use, or distribute content that is copyrighted.

In a computer lab you may be restricted from using this feature, so read the exercise steps to understand the concept without actually embedding a video.

1. Insert a new **Title Only** slide after slide 6.

2. From the Insert tab, in the Media group, click the bottom of the Video button 🎞, and select **Video From Web Site**.

3. The Insert Video From Web Site dialog box appears.

4. Open a browser, and go to the Web site www.youtube.com. Search for a **continuous improvement process** video. When you identify a video that describes the continuous improvement process applicable to any business, click the video image to view it.

5. On the right of the Web site, there are two boxes. One is labeled URL, and the other is labeled Embed. Select the code in the Embed box, and press Ctrl+C to copy the code.

6. Return to the PowerPoint window, and click in the Insert Video From Web Site dialog box. Press Ctrl+V to paste the embed code into the dialog box, as shown in Figure 10-19.

Figure 10-19
Insert video from Web site

Insert Video From Web Site

To insert a link to a video you've uploaded to a Web site, copy the embed code from that Web site and paste it into the text box below:

```
<object width="425" height="344"><param name="movie"
value="http://www.youtube.com/v/5CkkcI_QmZM&hl=en_US&fs=1&"></param><param
name="allowFullScreen" value="true"></param><param name="allowscriptaccess" value="always">
</param><embed src="http://www.youtube.com/v/5CkkcI_QmZM&hl=en_US&fs=1&"
type="application/x-shockwave-flash" allowscriptaccess="always" allowfullscreen="true" width="425"
height="344"></embed></object>
```

Help and examples

Insert   Cancel

TIP

Most Web sites that contain videos include an embed code, yet the locations of embed codes will differ depending on each Web site. If there is not an embed code, you cannot use this feature to link to the video.

7. Click Insert to insert the video.

8. From the Video Tools Playback tab, in the Preview group, click the Play button ▶ to test the video.

9. Key the slide title **Continuous Improvement Process**.

10. Save the presentation as *[your initials]***10-17** in your Lesson 10 folder.

Inserting Hyperlinks

Hyperlinks are links from a particular place in your presentation to other slides, other PowerPoint presentations, other application files, or Web sites. Hyperlinks can be created from text, action buttons, or objects. They provide a way to integrate information from other sources or to navigate in a presentation by using a menu.

To create a hyperlink from selected text or objects, from the Insert tab, in the Links group, click the Hyperlink button 🌐. You may also press Ctrl+K to open the Insert Hyperlink dialog box. Action buttons are in the Shapes gallery. Action settings can be applied to any shape or object that will control what happens when you click it or point to it.

Exercise 10-18   ADD HYPERLINKS TO SELECTED SLIDES BY USING TEXT

By default, PowerPoint displays a slide show in sequential order. Creating hyperlinks to other slides is a convenient way to move to certain slides within your presentation. For instance, if you are discussing five major points, you could create a menu with the text of each major point linked to the first slide in a series that explains each point. The menu could be used as an agenda slide or a table-of-contents slide. It could also be used to wrap up or summarize at the end of a presentation.

1. Insert a new Title and Content slide between current slides 1 and 2. The new slide 2 will be a menu linking to other slides in the presentation.

2. For the slide title, key **Discussion Points**.

3. Key this text for bulleted items:

Where We Began
Financial History
Continuous Improvement
Where We're Now Growing
Michele's Test Kitchen
We've Come a Long Way

4. Select the text for the first bulleted item, and press Ctrl+K.

5. In the Insert Hyperlink dialog box, under Link to on the left side, choose Place in This Document, as shown in Figure 10-20. In the Select a place in this document list box, choose 3. Where We Began. Click OK.

Figure 10-20
Inserting a hyperlink
on a menu slide

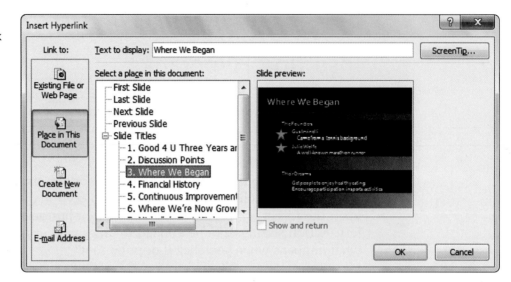

6. Using steps 4 and 5 as a guide, create additional hyperlinks for the remaining bulleted items, linking to their respective slides. Notice that the text changes to a different color and an underline is applied, indicating a hyperlink.

Exercise 10-19 CREATE ACTION BUTTONS FOR MENU OPTIONS

Setting up links on a menu slide enables you to jump to different slides in a presentation as you complete discussion on each topic. Usually, after you get to a linked slide, you'll want to return to the menu slide and then link to another topic. This requires an action button or hyperlink on the appropriate slides that jumps back to the menu slide.

1. Move to slide 3. From the Insert Tab, in the Illustrations group, click the Shapes button 🔲 to create an action button to return to the menu slide.

2. Select the third action button, Action Button: Beginning, as shown in Figure 10-21, and draw a small rectangle in the lower right of the slide. The Action Settings dialog box will automatically open.

Figure 10-21
Inserting an action
button

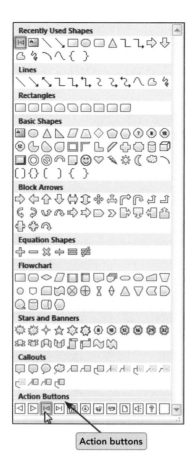

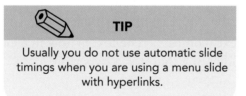

Action buttons

3. Click the Hyperlink to list box arrow, and choose Slide.

4. In the Hyperlink to Slide dialog box, choose Slide 2, Discussion Points. Click OK. Click OK again to close the Action Settings dialog box.

5. Copy the action button and paste this button in the same place for slides 4 through 6 to create action buttons that will link to the menu slide.

6. Beginning with slide 2, "Discussion Points," view the presentation as a slide show.

7. Click Financial History. The show jumps to that slide. Click the action button that you created to return to the discussion points slide.

8. Test the remaining links and action buttons to be sure they work correctly.

9. Press [Esc] to end the slide show.

10. Save the presentation as *[your initials]*10-19 in your Lesson 10 folder.

TIP

Usually you do not use automatic slide timings when you are using a menu slide with hyperlinks.

TIP

When creating hyperlinks for a menu slide, be sure the slide to which you link matches the text at the top of the Insert Hyperlink dialog box.

Exercise 10-20 ADD HYPERLINKS TO OTHER PRESENTATIONS

When you want to create a hyperlink to another file (for example, to another PowerPoint presentation), it is a good idea to first copy or save the file to the same folder as the presentation containing the hyperlink. If you move the presentation to another location, be sure to move the hyperlinked file as well. Otherwise, the hyperlink will no longer work after the move.

1. Move to slide 5, "Continuous Improvement," and select the word "contests" in the first bulleted item under "New initiatives."

2. From the Insert tab, in the Links group, choose the Hyperlink button  (or press [Ctrl]+[K]). The Insert Hyperlink dialog box opens.

3. Under the Link to heading on the left side, choose Existing File or Web Page.

4. In the Look in box, navigate to your Lesson 10 student files.

5. From the list of files, select **Contest**. Notice the PowerPoint icon 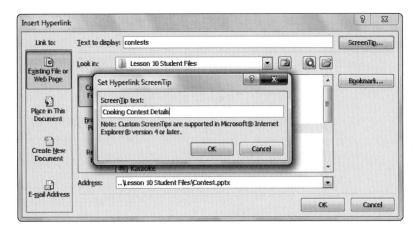 to the left of the file name.

6. Click the ScreenTip button ScreenTip... in the upper right corner of the dialog box. The Set Hyperlink ScreenTip dialog box opens, as shown in Figure 10-22.

7. For the ScreenTip text, key **Cooking Contest Details**. This text will be the ScreenTip that appears when you point to the hyperlink during a slide show.

Figure 10-22
Setting the hyperlink
ScreenTip

8. Click OK to close the Set Hyperlink ScreenTip dialog box; then click OK again to close the Insert Hyperlink dialog box.

9. Deselect the text "contests." The text is now in a contrasting color and underlined, indicating that it is a hyperlink.

Exercise 10-21　ADD HYPERLINKS TO OTHER FILES

Hyperlinks can be created for any file type by using the same method as used for linking to a presentation file. As you learned for linking to presentation files, it is a good idea to save the file you will be linking to in the same folder as the presentation containing the hyperlink.

1. Working again on slide 5, "Continuous Improvement," select the text "vendors" in the last bulleted item.

2. Press Ctrl+K to open the Insert Hyperlink dialog box.

3. Under the Link to heading on the left, click Existing File or Web Page.

4. Navigate to your Lesson 10 student files, and select the Excel spreadsheet Vendor Expenses from the list of files. Notice the Excel icon to the left of the **file name**.

5. Click the ScreenTip button ScreenTip... , and then key **Major Vendors Chart**. Click OK to close the Set Hyperlink ScreenTip dialog box.

6. Click OK again to close the Insert Hyperlink dialog box.

7. View the slide show from slide 5, and test the hyperlinks. The Contests slide show will open automatically, and when it is finished, you will automatically return to slide 5. After viewing the Excel file, use the PowerPoint button on the taskbar to return to your slide show.

8. Press [Esc] to end the slide show. Close the other files opened in this exercise, but leave your presentation open.

Exercise 10-22 ADD HYPERLINKS TO WEB PAGES

Hyperlinks to Web pages open a Web site from within PowerPoint. A Web browser will automatically load, and the page will appear.

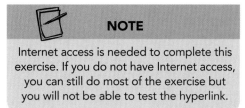

NOTE

Internet access is needed to complete this exercise. If you do not have Internet access, you can still do most of the exercise but you will not be able to test the hyperlink.

1. Open a browser, and search for a Web site related to sports activities or exercise. Make a note of the Web address (or copy it to the Clipboard), and then close your browser. If this is not possible, use the Web address provided in step 4 below or one provided by your instructor.

2. At the bottom of slide 3, select the text "sports activities," and then press [Ctrl]+[K] to open the Insert Hyperlink dialog box.

3. Under the Link to heading on the left, click Existing File or Web Page, as shown in Figure 10-23.

4. In the Address list box, key the address for the Web site you found in step 2 above (or paste it from the Clipboard). For example, key **http://www.fitness.gov**.

Figure 10-23
Insert Hyperlink
dialog box

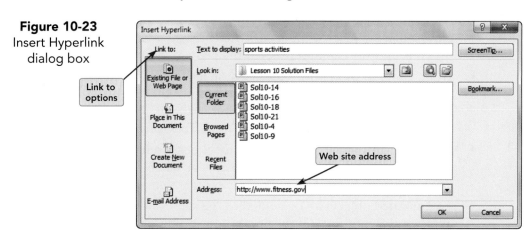

5. Click the ScreenTip button [ScreenTip...], and key descriptive text appropriate to the Web site you are using—for example, "The President's Council on Physical Fitness and Sports." Click OK to close the Set Hyperlink ScreenTip dialog box. Click OK again to close the Insert Hyperlink dialog box.

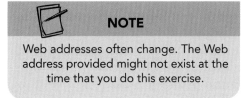

NOTE

Web addresses often change. The Web address provided might not exist at the time that you do this exercise.

6. View slide 3 in Slide Show view, and test the hyperlink to the Web site. Use the taskbar PowerPoint button to return to your slide show. Press [Esc] to return to Normal view.

7. Close the browser.

8. Create a handout header and footer: Include the date, your name as the header, the page number, and *[your initials]*10-22 as the footer.

9. Save the presentation as *[your initials]*10-22 in your Lesson 10 folder.

10. Close the presentation and submit your work.

Lesson 10   Summary

- Animation enables you to control the timing, speed, audio, trigger, and other aspects of how and when a slide's elements appear on the screen.

- To animate an object means to apply visual and audio effects that control how an object behaves during a slide show. You can apply several animation effects to a single object.

- All animation effects are available from the Animation pane. You can choose from entrance, emphasis, and exit effects and vary the direction, timing, speed, and other options.

- A motion path can be used to control how an object moves across the screen. PowerPoint provides a large variety of predefined paths that you can resize, rotate, and reposition to suit your needs.

- To remove an animation from a slide, select its list arrow in the animation list and then click Remove or press [Delete].

- Audio effects can be added to individual animations. The audio effect plays when the animation occurs. Be careful with audio, making sure that it is appropriate and plays at the proper volume.

- When multiple animations are used on a slide, the order of their appearance is determined by the order in which they are listed in the Animation pane. You change the order in the list by selecting the item and then using the Reorder arrows to move within the list.

- As part of the timing options, you can choose to have an animation appear when you click your mouse, appear when a previous animation appears, or be delayed a number of seconds that you specify.

- An animated object can be copied to the same slide, another slide, or another presentation. All the animation settings are copied along with the object.

- The Animation Painter can be used to copy all animation settings from one object to another.

- Besides attaching audio effects to individual animations, you can also add audio objects that stand on their own in presentations. Audio objects can be set to play for the duration of a single slide, for an entire presentation, or until you click your mouse.

- Audio and video effects can be trimmed and options customized to fit your presentation.
- Animated clip art or videos can be inserted on a slide. Once on a slide, they can be animated in the same way as any other object.
- Videos can be inserted from a file, from the Clip Art pane, or from a Web site.
- Creating action buttons or hyperlinks to presentation slides makes it easy to jump to preplanned locations within your presentation.
- Another way to manage a slide show is to create a menu slide listing the titles of each slide, each with hyperlinks to the actual slide.
- Hyperlinks enable you to jump to supplemental material during a presentation. Hyperlinks can link to other slides in your slide shows, other presentations, documents created in other programs, and Web sites on the Internet.
- To use a hyperlink, start a slide show and then click the hyperlinked text. You can distinguish hyperlinked text by its contrasting color and its underline.

LESSON 10		Command Summary	
Feature	**Button**	**Ribbon**	**Keyboard**
Action button		Insert, Illustrations group, Shapes, Action Buttons	
Add audio effects		Animation pane, Select item, list arrow, Effect Options	
Add music		Insert, Media Clips group, Audio	
Add videos		Insert, Media Clips group, Video	
Animation		Animations tab, Animations group, Add Animation	
Animation Painter		Animations tab, Advanced Animation group, Animation Painter	
Bookmark audio or video		Audio or Video Tools Playback tab, Bookmarks group, Add Bookmark	
Hyperlink		Insert, Links group, Hyperlink	Ctrl + K
Modify an effect		Animations tab, Animation group, Effect Options	
Modify timings		Animations tab, Timing group	
Remove animation		Animation pane, Select item, list arrow, Remove	
Reorder animation effects		Animation pane, Select item, Reorder up or down arrow	
Trim audio or video		Audio or Video Tools Playback tab, Editing group, Trim Audio or Trim Video	

UNIT 3 · LESSON 10

Concepts Review

True/False Questions

Each of the following statements is either true or false. Indicate your choice by circling T or F.

T F 1. An emphasis effect controls how an animated object first appears on a slide.

T F 2. Before adding a different animation effect to an object, you can delete its existing animations by selecting the object on the slide and pressing Delete.

T F 3. You add audio effects to animated objects by using the Insert tab.

T F 4. You can change the order of animations on a slide.

T F 5. You can insert videos and audio clips in your presentation from the Clip Art pane.

T F 6. You can set different timings for each animated object in a slide show.

T F 7. Audio recordings can be added to slides without animating objects.

T F 8. You can insert a hyperlink on a slide by pressing Ctrl + M.

Short Answer Questions

Write the correct answer in the space provided.

1. How do you add an animation effect?

_____

2. How do you change the order in which animations occur on a slide?

_____

3. How do you copy animations from one object to another?

_____

4. What do you call an object that, when clicked, displays another slide, a new presentation, a Web site, or another file?

_____

5. How do you set an animation effect to start automatically without a mouse click?

_____

6. How do you insert an action button?

_____

7. What effect applies animation as an object leaves the slide?

_____

8. What happens to hyperlink text after you click it during a slide show?

_____

Critical Thinking

Answer these questions on a separate page. Support your answers with examples from your own experience, if possible.

1. Describe a scenario in which you might want to insert a video from a Web site into a slide presentation.

2. Adding audio effects, text and object animations, and slide transitions to a slide show provides a great deal of variety. How can you avoid distracting from the presentation's message?

Skills Review

Exercise 10-23

Add entrance, emphasis, and exit animation effects; add an animation audio effect; and change animation timing.

1. Open the file **Promotion**.

2. On slide 1, select the hat, and animate it by following these steps:

   a. From the Animations tab, in the Animation group, click the More button ⬇ to open the gallery.

   b. In the Entrance category, choose Zoom.

   c. On the Animations tab, in the Timing group, click the Start list box, and choose With Previous.

   d. On the Animations tab, in the Timing group, change Duration to 02:00.

3. On slide 1, select the hat, and apply an audio effect:

   a. From the Animations tab, in the Advanced Animation group, click the Animation Pane button 🔲.

   b. In the Animation pane, click the list box arrow for the animated item, labeled Group 6.

   c. Choose Effect Options.

   d. Click the Sound list box arrow, and choose Wind.

   e. Click the Speaker button 🔊, and move the slider down slightly to lower the volume.

   f. Click the Timing tab in the dialog box.

   g. In the Delay spin box, key **1** (for 1 second). Click OK.

4. Move to slide 3, and animate the star on the T-shirt by following these steps:

   a. Zoom to 100%, and select the star on the T-shirt.

   b. From the Animations tab, in the Advanced Animation group, click the Add Animation button ⭐; then click More Entrance Effects. Scroll down to the Moderate category, and choose Spinner. Click OK.

5. Change the timing for the star's animation by following these steps:

   a. In the Animation pane, click the list box arrow for this animation, and choose Timing. Set the following timing options:

Start	With Previous
Duration	0.5 seconds (Very Fast)
Repeat	3

   b. Click OK.

6. Add an emphasis effect to the star by following these steps:

   a. With the star selected, from the Animations tab, click the Add Animation button ⭐; then from the Emphasis category choose Grow and Shrink.

   b. Select the second item in the animation pane, click its list box arrow, and apply the same timing options as those in step 5a.

   c. Change the zoom setting back to Fit.

7. On slide 1, select the title, and add an entrance effect:

   a. From the Animations tab, in the Animation group, click the More button ▾, and choose Shape. Click the Effect Options button ◩, and choose Out and then Circle.

   b. Click the Start list box, and choose With Previous.

   c. In the Animation pane, select the last item (Rectangle 55), and reorder it to appear at the top of the list so that it will play first.

   d. Test the animation.

8. Create a handout header and footer: Include the date, your name as the header, the page number, and *[your initials]*10-23 as the footer.

9. Save the presentation as *[your initials]*10-23 in your Lesson 10 folder.

10. Move to slide 1, and view the presentation as a slide show to check all of the animations.

11. Close the presentation and submit your work.

Exercise 10-24

Add animation effects, animate a chart, and add an audio clip.

1. Open the file **Beverages**.

2. Add an entrance effect to the slide 1 title:

   a. Select the title text on slide 1.

   b. From the Animations tab, in the Advanced Animations group, click the Add Animation button 🌟.

   c. In the Entrance category, click Wipe.

   d. From the Animation group, click the Effect Options button ◤, and choose the From Left effect.

   e. In the Timing group, click the Start list box, and choose With Previous.

   f. In the Timing group, change Duration to 02.00.

3. Using step 2 as a guide, apply an entrance effect to the subtitle text on slide 1:

   a. Use the Float In entrance effect.

   b. In the Timing group, start After Previous, and change the Delay to 03:00.

4. Insert a music file that plays throughout the entire slide show; follow these steps:

   a. On slide 1, from the Insert tab, in the Media group, click the bottom of the Audio button 🔊, and choose Audio from File.

   b. Select the WAV file **BackgroundMusic2** from your Lesson 10 student files. Click Insert. Drag the speaker and play control below the subtitle.

   c. From the Audio Tools Playback tab, in the Audio Options group, make these changes:

   • Click the Start list box, and choose Automatically.

   • Check Hide During Show.

   • Click the Volume button 🔊, and choose Medium.

   d. From the Animations tab, in the Advanced Animation group, click the Animation pane button 🔂.

   e. From the Animation pane, click the list box for the audio animation, and choose Effect Options.

   • On the Effect tab, and under Start playing, make sure that From beginning is selected.

   • Under Stop playing, key **5** slides in the After spin box.

   • On the Timing tab, under Start, click the list box arrow, and choose With Previous.

   • Check the box for Rewind when done playing.

   • Click the Repeat list box arrow, and choose Until End of Slide.

   • Click OK.

   f. In the Animation pane, reorder the audio clip item to the top of the animation list.

5. Select the chart on slide 3, and apply these effects:

    a. From the Animations tab, in the Advanced Animation group, click the Add Animation button 🟊; then choose More Entrance Effects.

    b. From the Basic category, choose the Wipe effect, and click OK.

    c. From the Animations tab, in the Animation group, click the Effect Options button ◼, and choose By Series.

    d. From the Animations tab, in the Timing group, change the Duration to 02:00.

    e. In the Animation pane, click the list box for this animation, and choose Effect Options.

    f. On the Chart Animation tab, clear the check box for Start animation by drawing the chart background. Turning off this option ensures that the chart layout will appear when the slide is displayed. Click OK.

6. Animate an object to appear and then disappear; follow these steps:

    a. Move to slide 4, and select the illustration in the lower right corner, which is an animated image.

    b. From the Animations tab, in the Advanced Animation group, click the Add Animation button 🟊, and choose Wheel.

    c. In the Timing group, click the Start list box, and choose After Previous.

    d. With the illustration still selected, click the Add Animation button 🟊 again, and choose More Exit Effects.

    e. In the Basic category, choose the Wheel, and click OK.

    f. In the Timing group, click the Start list box, and choose After Previous.

    g. In the Timing group, change the Duration to 03:00 and change the Delay to 03:00 to delay the effect's start for 3 seconds.

    h. Test the animation.

7. Create a handout header and footer: Include the date, your name as the header, the page number, and *[your initials]*10-24 as the footer.

8. Save the presentation as *[your initials]*10-24 in your Lesson 10 folder.

9. View the presentation as a slide show.

10. Close the presentation and submit your work.

Exercise 10-25

Change animation settings, insert a video from a Web site, and create action buttons and hyperlinks.

1. Open the file **Equipment**.

2. View the presentation as a slide show to view the text animation. As you can see, too much clicking is required to advance through the slides. In this exercise, you will change animation settings to streamline the animation and improve the effects.

3. From the Animations tab, in the Advanced Animation group, click the Animation pane button 🔂 to display the Animation pane.

4. On slide 1, from the Animation pane, select the animated object. From the Animations tab, in the Timing group, click the Start list box, and choose With Previous.

5. On slide 2, select the animated object, and make the following changes using the Animations tab:

   a. In the Timing group, click the Start list box, and choose With Previous.

   b. In the Animation group, click the Effect Options button 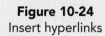, and choose As One Object.

   c. In the Advanced Animation group, click the Add Animation button , and choose More Emphasis Effects and then Line Color; click OK.

6. Select the animated object on slide 2; then from the Animations tab, in the Advanced Animation group, click the Animation Painter . Move to slide 7, and click the text box to apply the same animation effects.

7. On slide 3, select the animated object, and make the following changes using the Animations tab:

   a. In the Timing group, click the Start list box, choose With Previous, and change the Duration to 02:00.

   b. In the Animation group, click Effect Options , and choose As One Object.

8. Select the list on slide 3, and double-click the Animation Painter . Using the Animation Painter, click on the lists on slides 4, 5, and 6 to apply the animation effects. Press Esc to turn off the Animation Painter.

9. On slide 2, change the height of the text box to 3 inches and the width to 4 inches; then move it to the left of the slide. Duplicate the text box, position it on the right, and edit the text as shown in Figure 10-24.

10. Using the text in the duplicated box, create three hyperlinks to other slides:

    a. Select the first item, "The big stuff," and press Ctrl+K.

    b. In the Insert Hyperlink dialog box, under Link to, click Place in This Document.

    c. From the list of slides in the presentation, select slide 3.

    d. Click OK.

    e. Repeat step 10 for the remaining items, linking them to the slides with the corresponding titles.

Figure 10-24
Insert hyperlinks

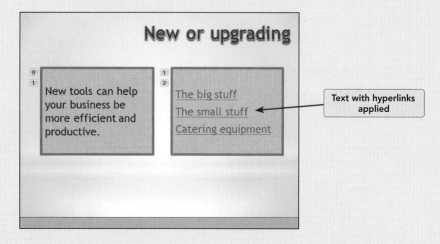

11. On slide 3, create an action button to return to slide 2; follow these steps:

   a. From the Insert tab, in the Illustrations group, click the Shapes button .

   b. Under the Action Buttons category, select the third button, Action Button: Beginning, and draw a small rectangle in the lower right of the slide.

   c. In the Action Settings dialog box, click the Hyperlink to list box arrow, and choose Slide.

   d. In the Hyperlink to Slide dialog box, choose 2. New or Upgrading. Click OK. Click OK again to close the Action Settings dialog box.

12. Copy the action button on slide 3, and paste it in the same location on slides 5 and 6.

13. Test your animation changes.

14. Insert a Title Only slide after slide 7. Key the title **Equipment video**.

> **NOTE**
>
> If you are restricted from downloading a video from a web site, then skip step 15.

15. Insert a video from a Web site by following these steps:

   a. Working on slide 8, from the Insert tab, in the Media group, click the bottom of the Video button , and choose Video From Web Site.

   b. Open a browser, and visit www.youtube.com. Search for a video by keying **Commercial Kitchen Equipment**.

   c. When you identify an appropriate video that concerns commercial kitchen equipment, click the video image to view it.

   d. On the right of the Web site, there are two boxes. One is labeled URL, and the other is labeled Embed. Select the code in the embed box, and press Ctrl+C to copy the code.

   e. Return to the PowerPoint window, and click in the Insert Video from Web Site dialog box. Press Ctrl+V to paste the embed code into the dialog box.

   f. Click Insert to insert the video.

   g. From the Video Tools Playback tab, in the Preview group, click the Play button ▷ to test the video.

16. Create a handout header and footer: Include the date, your name as the header, the page number, and *[your initials]*10-25 as the footer.

17. Save the presentation as *[your initials]*10-25 in your Lesson 10 folder.

18. Close the presentation and submit your work.

Exercise 10-26

Create hyperlinks to other files, and insert a clip art video.

1. Copy the presentations **Market3** and **Market4**, and paste them in your Lesson 10 folder.

2. Open the file **AdMedia2**. On slide 4, create hyperlinks to the other presentations:

    a. Select "Business," and then right-click and choose Hyperlink (or press Ctrl + K).

    b. In the Insert Hyperlink dialog box, under Link to, choose Existing File or Web Page.

    c. Navigate to your Lesson 10 folder, and select the presentation **Market3**.

    d. Click ScreenTip, and then key **Marketing Our Business** as the ScreenTip text. Click OK, and then click OK again to close the Insert Hyperlink dialog box.

    e. Still working on slide 4, select "Services," and create a hyperlink to the presentation **Market4** by following steps 2a to 2d. Use the ScreenTip **Marketing Our Services**.

3. On slide 2, insert a clip art video:

    a. From the Insert tab, in the Media Clips group, click the bottom of the Video button 🎞, and choose Clip Art Video.

    b. In the Search for box, key **dollar sign**, and click Go.

    c. Click an appropriate video to insert it on slide 2 in the upper right. Increase the size slightly if you can do so without distorting the video.

    d. Close the Clip Art pane.

4. Create a handout header and footer: Include the date, your name as the header, the page number, and *[your initials]*10-26 as the footer.

5. Save the presentation as *[your initials]*10-26 in your Lesson 10 folder.

6. View the presentation as a slide show. When you come to slide 4, click each of the hyperlinks to jump to the linked presentations. Press Esc to return to the main presentation.

7. Close the presentation and submit your work.

Lesson Applications

Exercise 10-27

Animate text and objects.

1. Open the file **Competition**.

2. On slide 4, apply these animation effects to the bread image:

   a. Entrance effect Zoom, start After Previous, and delay of 01:00.

   b. Exit effect Wheel, start After Previous, and duration and delay of 02:00.

3. In the animation list, select both of the bread animation items (Picture 422), and use Reorder to move them up so that they follow item 1, "Best bread."

4. Use the Animation Painter to apply the two bread effects to the plate of spaghetti and meatballs. Move these effects below item 3, "Power-packed pasta."

5. Repeat this process for the remaining three images so that the image animation follows each corresponding bulleted item.

6. On slide 5, use the Animation Painter to apply the same animation effects to the four clip art images, reordering them so that one clip art appears after each of the bullets.

7. On slide 1, move the prize ribbon to the top left, just off the edge of the slide; then choose a motion path to animate it going diagonally down to the right. Adjust the position as needed, and adjust the length of the motion path as needed.

8. Move to slide 3, and make the picture of people Wipe, From Top, on a mouse click. Apply animation on the text at the bottom using the options As One Object, Wipe, and From Bottom.

9. Run the show, making sure all animations are correct, and then stop it by pressing [Esc].

10. Create a handout header and footer: Include the date, your name as the header, the page number, and *[your initials]*10-27 as the footer.

11. Save the presentation as *[your initials]*10-27 in your Lesson 10 folder.

12. Close the presentation and submit your work.

Exercise 10-28

Create animations, add a video clip and audio clip, and add action buttons.

1. Open the file **Special Event1**.

2. On slide 1, select the "Scheduling Events" title, and apply the Split entrance effect; for Direction, choose Vertical Out, and for the Start setting, choose On Click.

3. Draw a long, thin, right-pointing block arrow with a Dark Teal, Text 2, Lighter 60% (column 4) fill. Send the arrow behind the text, and adjust its size as shown in Figure 10-25.

Figure 10-25
Arrow size and placement

4. Group the arrow and the text. Apply the Fly In effect, and change Direction to From Left, Start to With Previous, and Duration to 01.30.

5. Select the arrow and text combination, and apply the Drum Roll sound effect at an appropriate volume.

6. On slide 1, find an appropriate clip art video using the search word "gymnastics," and insert it at the bottom left of the slide. Recolor the video to match the theme colors.

7. Insert an audio clip of your choice on slide 2, and use the display options to hide the audio icon during the slide show. Make the clip play automatically for the duration of slide 2. Adjust its sound level to an appropriate volume.

8. On slide 2, create an action button that links to slide 4. Use Action Button: Information.

9. On slide 4, create an action button that links back to slide 2. Use Action Button: Return.

10. Create a handout header and footer: Include the date, your name as the header, the page number, and *[your initials]*10-28 as the footer.

11. Save the presentation as *[your initials]*10-28 in your Lesson 10 folder.

12. View the presentation as a slide show. On slide 2, click the action button to display slide 4. Use the action button on slide 4 to return to slide 2, and then continue viewing the slide show.

13. Close the presentation and submit your work.

Exercise 10-29

Add and modify animations, use the Animation Painter, and insert a hyperlink to a Word document.

1. Copy the Word document **Foods1** to your Lesson 10 student files folder. Open the file **Honey Products**.

2. On slide 1, apply an entrance and exit animation effect to the title text, "Natural Honey Products."

3. On slide 2, apply an entrance animation effect to the bulleted list by paragraphs.

4. Use the Animation Painter to apply the same entrance effect to slides 3 and 4.

5. On slide 3, find an appropriate illustrated image to place below the text, apply animation, and include an audio effect with the animation.

6. On slide 2, create a hyperlink that will display the Word file **Foods1** when you click the text "Products made with honey." Give it the ScreenTip **Foods and Beverages Made with Honey**.

7. Create a handout header and footer: Include the date, your name as the header, the page number, and *[your initials]***10-29** as the footer.

8. Save the presentation as *[your initials]***10-29** in your Lesson 10 folder.

9. View the presentation as a slide show, and click the hyperlink on slide 2 to be sure it works correctly.

10. Close the presentation and submit your work.

Exercise 10-30 ◆ Challenge Yourself

Apply entrance, emphasis, and exit effects to objects; animate text; and add audio to animations.

1. Open the file **Karaoke**.

2. On slide 1, make each of the rounded rectangles with words Fly In with a Duration of 00.50. Use these directions and timings then apply the sound Push to each rectangle.
   - *Kid's:* From Bottom-Right, With Previous
   - *Karaoke:* From Right, After Previous
   - *Night:* From Top-Right, After Previous

3. On slide 3, apply a Zoom entrance effect to the "Congratulations" image from Slide Center; start On Click, with a duration of 03:00.

4. Insert a star shape with a red fill. Rotate it, and make it large enough to cover the largest star in the image. Duplicate this star, make it slightly smaller, and rotate it to cover another star in the image. Repeat this process two more times for the remaining stars.

5. Select all the stars, and apply a Shape entrance effect and a Spin emphasis effect After Previous.

6. Animate the body text on slide 2 by using any effect of your choice, making sure that the bullets appear one at a time on a mouse click.

7. Create a handout header and footer: Include the date, your name as the header, the page number, and *[your initials]***10-30** as the footer.

8. Save the presentation as *[your initials]*10-30 in your Lesson 10 folder.

9. View as a slide show, watching all the animation.

10. Close the presentation and submit your work.

On Your Own

In these exercises you work on your own, as you would in a real-life work environment. Use the skills you've learned to accomplish the task—and be creative.

Exercise 10-31

Assume you are on a committee sponsoring a summer night movie event in a large outdoor area on campus. You will be talking to various student organizations to promote the event. Create a presentation with at least six slides that describes the movie to be shown that night. Identify the main characters, quotable lines, and the main idea of the movie. Animate the presentation to draw attention to key points. The slide show should advance by mouse clicks. Insert audio clips, videos, and hyperlinks to create interest in your presentation. Add a slide footer with your name and *[your initials]*10-31. Save the presentation as *[your initials]*10-31. Close the presentation and submit your work.

Exercise 10-32

Create a presentation of at least six slides that could be used as a self-running slide show for a car dealership. The presentation should promote new models and features of vehicles. It could focus on a new SUV, car, truck, or the like that might draw the interest of people entering the dealership. Apply eye-catching animations to the presentation, including audio, but make sure the animations do not obscure the presentation's message. Test and refine the presentation's animations as needed to make the show run smoothly and professionally. Check spelling and grayscale settings. Add a slide footer with your name and *[your initials]*10-32. Save the presentation as *[your initials]*10-32. Close the presentation and submit your work.

Exercise 10-33

Imagine that you are an artist or someone marketing the work of an artist. Choose an artistic theme, and then design a four-slide presentation by using several animation sequences, making objects and text appear and disappear as you please, and adding music, videos, and other audio effects. Play the animation, and then fine-tune it. Be prepared to run your presentation for your instructor and your classmates. Add a slide footer with your name and *[your initials]*10-33. Save the presentation as *[your initials]*10-33. Close the presentation and submit your work.

Lesson 11
Customizing Themes and Slide Masters

OBJECTIVES *After completing this lesson, you will be able to:*

1. Customize an existing theme.

2. Format background styles.

3. Work with slide masters for a custom design theme.

4. Apply themes and templates from Microsoft's Office.com.

5. Customize handout and notes masters.

Estimated Time: 1½ hours

PowerPoint *themes* give presentations a unified appearance. Each theme provides a completely different "look" because of the built-in effects applied to backgrounds, text, tables, charts, SmartArt, and other objects.

PowerPoint provides consistency through the use of themes, with backgrounds, fonts, and colors that work well together. The term "template" refers to a presentation that provides content to help you get started in composing the presentation. *Slide masters* with a variety of *slide layouts* store this information.

Themes can be used across applications in Microsoft Office. They can be customized and new themes saved for use in PowerPoint and other applications. Additional themes and templates are available at Microsoft's Office.com.

Julie Wolfe is scheduled to present a manager recruiting session at a local career exposition to recent college graduates. You will be assisting Julie in updating and preparing for this vital presentation. Before you begin working on the manager recruiting presentation, you will practice some of the new features in a blank presentation.

NOTE

The procedures outlined here will work when you are using your own computer and a new custom theme will be available to use again. However, in computer lab classrooms, the new theme may not remain on the computer when it is rebooted. Some labs use routine maintenance procedures in which the computer is restored to its original state each day; therefore, changes to default settings or files that have been saved will be removed.

Customizing an Existing Theme

In previous lessons you have selected colors from existing themes. In this lesson you learn more about how these colors work and how to customize them by making your own color selections to create new themes. Changes made to theme components immediately affect the active presentation.

Exercise 11-1 EXAMINE BUILT-IN COLOR THEMES

This exercise will develop your understanding of *theme colors*. You will create three slides with sample text and graphics so that you can see how the default colors are affected when the theme colors change.

On the Design tab, in the Themes group, the Colors button ▣ displays four colors of the current theme; the colors on the button change as you select different themes. When you click this button, you will see all colors listed alphabetically by the name for each group. It appears as though each theme consists of eight colors. However, you can actually change twelve different theme colors: four text and background, six accent, and two hyperlink colors.

1. Start a new, blank presentation, and from the Design tab, in the Themes group, click the Colors button ▣. Notice that the "Office" theme is selected. The words "Office Theme" also appear in the status bar on the lower left to define this particular group of colors.

2. Refer to Figure 11-1 as you complete the next steps.

Figure 11-1
Sample slides

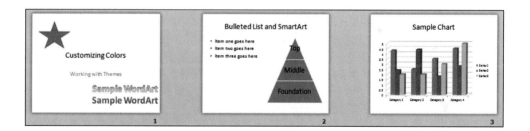

3. On slide 1, use the Title Slide layout:
   a. For the slide title key **Customizing Colors**, and for the subtitle key **Working with Themes**.
   b. Insert a star in the upper left corner.
   c. Insert WordArt, and choose Fill - White, Gradient Outline - Accent 1 (first column, third row). Key **Sample WordArt**. Move the WordArt below the subtitle and to the right.
   d. Duplicate the WordArt, and position the copy below the original WordArt. Change the WordArt style to Fill - Red, Accent 2, Warm Matte Bevel (third column, fifth row).

4. Create a new slide 2 using the Two Content layout:

   a. For the slide title, key **Bulleted List and SmartArt**.

   b. For the bulleted items, use the left content placeholder to key sample text for three items, such as **Item one goes here**, and so on.

   c. In the right content placeholder, insert a Basic Pyramid SmartArt graphic from the Pyramid category, and click OK.

   d. On the pyramid shapes, key three words: **Foundation** (on the bottom), **Middle**, and **Top**.

5. Create a new slide 3 using the Title and Content layout:

   a. For the slide title, key **Sample Chart**.

   b. Insert a 3-D Clustered Column chart from the Column category, and click OK. Excel will appear, showing sample data.

   c. Close Excel to accept the sample data.

6. Now you have a short presentation with a variety of graphics, so you can see how theme colors affect them.

7. Create a new folder for Lesson 11, and save this presentation as *[your initials]***11-1** in your new Lesson 11 folder.

Exercise 11-2 CREATE AND SAVE CUSTOM THEME COLORS

To create custom theme colors, from the Design tab, in the Themes group, click the Colors button ◼; then choose Create New Theme Colors at the bottom of the built-in colors list. A dialog box will open in which the theme colors can be changed individually.

After the dialog box is open, click the button of a color you want to change and select from other theme colors or standard colors. If you choose More Colors, you can choose colors from the Standard tab or click the Custom tab to mix your own color. The color changes will be illustrated in the Sample area on the right of the Create New Theme Colors dialog box. If you don't like the changes, you can click the Reset button ▭Reset▭. If you want to use the new colors in the future, save the new colors as new theme colors.

1. Expand your Slides and Outline pane so that you can see color changes on all three slides at the same time.

2. From the Design tab, in the Themes group, click the Colors button ◼; then choose Create New Theme Colors. Notice the theme colors that are displayed in the Create New Theme Colors dialog box and displayed in Figure 11-2.

Figure 11-2
Create New Theme
Colors dialog box

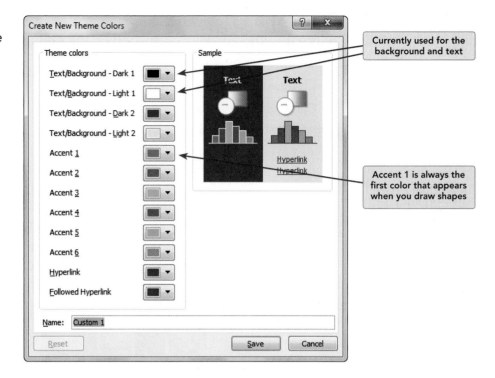

3. Position this dialog box on your screen so that you can see it as well as your Slides and Outline pane. The different theme colors are shown on the left and a sample of the colors is shown on the right. Notice that you have both light and dark versions of text and background colors. Right now the presentation is using Light 1 for the white background and Dark 1 for the text color for slide titles and other text.

4. Six accent colors are shown. Notice these applications:

   a. Accent 1 color is used on the star shape, on the SmartArt diagram, and on the first series on the chart.

   b. Accent 2 and Accent 3 are used on the chart for the second and third series. Charts or diagrams may use more colors depending on how they are constructed.

   c. The WordArt colors are Accent 1 and Accent 2. All the styles you see when you access the WordArt Styles gallery are displayed in theme colors.

   d. The Hyperlink and Followed Hyperlink colors are not being used because the presentation does not include these features. The two hyperlink colors are used to control the color when a text hyperlink is first displayed and after it has been clicked during a presentation.

5. From the Create New Theme Colors dialog box, choose the Accent 1 color, and your color choices will appear in color swatches. Notice that the different theme colors span the top of this window and that variations of those colors, which represent shades (percentages) of the theme colors, are below. Standard color swatches are arranged almost like a rainbow at the bottom of this window.

6. Use the standard colors to change the first three accent colors, and notice the different colors displayed on the sample:

   a. Change Accent 1 to Yellow.

   b. Change Accent 2 to Light Blue.

   c. Change Accent 3 to Purple.

NOTE

If you change theme colors and the WordArt colors do not automatically update, go to the Drawing Tools Format tab, in the WordArt Styles group, click ⬇, and reapply the same effect.

7. At the bottom of this dialog box, key **Color Practice** as the name of this new theme, and then click Save. Changes are immediately made to your slides, the Colors button ▪ shows different colors, and this new theme name is added to your Custom Theme Colors list.

8. These colors can be edited, as shown in Figure 11-3. Click the Colors button ▪, right-click the Color Practice theme, and then choose Edit.

Figure 11-3
Editing a custom color theme

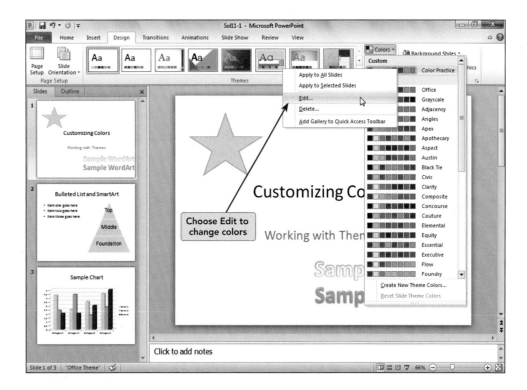

NOTE

From the Theme Colors gallery, you can choose More Colors and then select additional colors from the Standard swatches or mix your own color from the Custom tab, just as you have changed fill colors for shapes.

9. From the dialog box, change the Accent 3 color to the standard color Orange. Click Save.

10. From the Design tab, in the Background group, click the Background Styles button 🖼 to select a different background color. The four variations of light and dark colors are shown across the Background Styles gallery with gradient variations for each color, as shown in Figure 11-4.

Figure 11-4
Changing the
background style

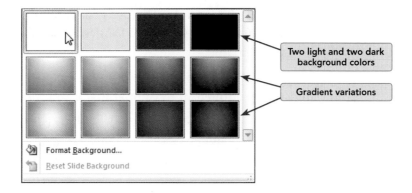

Two light and two dark
background colors

Gradient variations

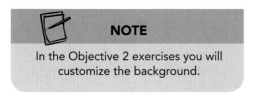

NOTE

In the Objective 2 exercises you will
customize the background.

11. Choose Style 11 (third column, third row) to place the darkest area of the gradient background around the edges of the slide.

12. Because this style uses a dark background, the theme font color changes to white; however, this causes a problem with the yellow accent color that was earlier applied because white text does not have sufficient contrast to be readable on top of yellow.

13. Click the Colors button ▮; then right-click the Color Practice theme, and choose Edit. Change the yellow Accent 1 color to the standard color Dark Blue. Click Save to change your custom theme. Be sure you are resaving it with the same name.

14. Move to slide 1, and select the star. Even though the star was colored using the first accent color in the theme, it can be recolored independently, just as you have been coloring shapes in the last several lessons. From the Home tab, in the Drawing group, click the Shape Fill button ⬛, and choose the standard orange that you used in the color theme for a unified look.

Exercise 11-3 CHANGE THEME FONTS AND EXAMINE BUILT-IN EFFECTS

Remember that text must be easy to read. When you change text placeholder font colors, be sure to have a high contrast between the slide background colors and the text colors. For many fonts, a bold attribute will make the text easier to read. Sometimes a shadow can help to define letter forms, but, again, contrast is needed so that the shadow outlines the text and does not make it look blurred.

The fonts you use affect the tone of your presentation. Some look very formal or traditional, while others seem more modern. Some fonts seem casual and resemble handwriting. Use one or perhaps two fonts in a presentation. Be sure that slide titles are emphasized more than the text in the body of the slides.

Theme fonts in PowerPoint control the heading font and the body text font. For many of the themes, the same font is used in both places; however, some themes use two fonts.

1. From the Design tab, in the Themes group, click the Theme Fonts button 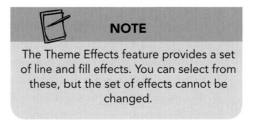 to access the gallery of font combinations organized by a built-in theme name.

2. At the bottom of the gallery, choose Create New Theme Fonts.

3. Change the Heading font to Cooper Black and the Body font to Arial.

4. At the bottom of this dialog box, key **Font Practice** as the name of this new theme; then click Save.

Figure 11-5
Creating New Theme
Fonts

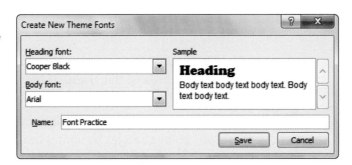

5. Notice that the text is automatically updated to these fonts. In this font and size, the titles stand out more from other information on the slides. However, no adjustments have been made to the positions of the slide elements. The different font makes the WordArt samples larger; move them to the left slightly so that they are completely on the slide.

> **NOTE**
>
> The Theme Effects feature provides a set of line and fill effects. You can select from these, but the set of effects cannot be changed.

Exercise 11-4 SAVE A CUSTOM THEME

In this lesson, you started with a blank slide and then added some sample text and shapes. You changed colors and saved and edited a theme color. You also saved a new theme font and applied a background style with a gradient effect. All of these settings can be saved in a theme that will be available for use again.

1. From the Design tab, in the Themes group, click the More button ⬇. Click Save Current Theme, and a dialog box will appear. Notice that this new theme will, by default, go into your Document Themes folder, as shown in Figure 11-6.

Figure 11-6
Saving a current
theme

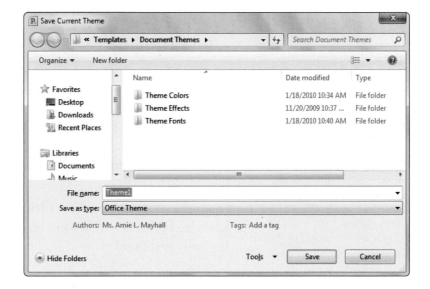

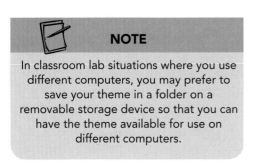

NOTE

In classroom lab situations where you use different computers, you may prefer to save your theme in a folder on a removable storage device so that you can have the theme available for use on different computers.

2. For the file name, key **Practice theme**. The Save as type should remain Office Theme because this new theme will be available to use across Microsoft Office applications. Click **Save**. If you already have a Practice theme, click **Yes** to replace.

3. Save this presentation as *[your initials]***11-4** in your Lesson 11 folder.

4. Now consider what happens to all your color selections if you choose a different built-in theme. From the Design tab, in the Themes group, click the More button ⬇. Choose the **Median** theme to apply it.

5. Notice that, when the new theme is applied, placeholder positioning has changed as well as the colors and fonts for title text and bulleted lists. The WordArt samples overlap where the title and subtitle information is in this theme design.

6. Notice that the star has retained its orange color because it was changed as a separate shape after the theme colors were saved.

7. When you need to control placeholder positioning, you need to adjust slide layouts by using the Slide Master feature, which you will learn about in this lesson. Close this presentation without saving the theme change.

Formatting Background Styles

In the previous exercise, you changed the appearance of the background by choosing one of the preset styles that uses theme colors. Many more changes are possible. You can change background effects for an entire presentation or for just one slide. Just as shapes can have a variety of fill types applied, backgrounds can be solid colors, gradient fills, patterns, textures, or pictures.

Exercise 11-5   APPLY SOLID FILL AND GRADIENT BACKGROUNDS

The Background dialog box lets you choose from the theme colors, other colors, or fill effects.

In this exercise, you will work with a presentation that has a very simple background so that you can concentrate on the impact that backgrounds have on slides. Later, you will insert graphics and adjust backgrounds in different ways.

1. Open the presentation **Recruiting**. This presentation has a background with a solid fill color. The placeholders for body text (subtitle and bulleted lists) have been filled with a color that blends with the background color.

2. On slide 1, from the Design tab, in the Background group, click the Background Styles button 🖾. The current theme colors show with solid and gradient colors. On the bottom of this gallery click Format Background.

3. From the dialog box that appears, choose Solid fill, and then change the Fill Color to Tan, Background 2, Darker 50%, as shown in Figure 11-7. Immediately the background color changes on the slide, and the title text has better color contrast on this darker color.

Figure 11-7
Format Background
dialog box

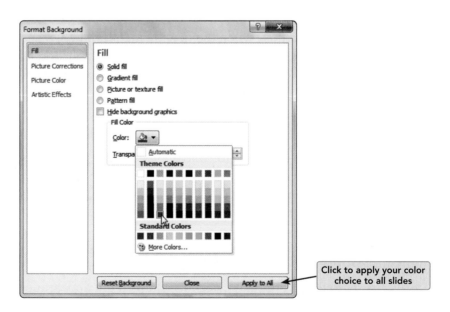

4. Choose Apply to All so that this color is placed on all slides in the presentation. Click Close.

5. Still working on slide 1, repeat this process but apply a gradient fill. From the Design tab, in the Background group, click the Dialog Box Launcher ⬛, and choose Gradient fill. Make the following adjustments, as shown in Figure 11-8:

a. For Preset colors choose Gold.

b. For Type choose Radial.

c. For Direction choose From Bottom Right Corner.

d. Click Close to apply this gradient to the background on the title slide only.

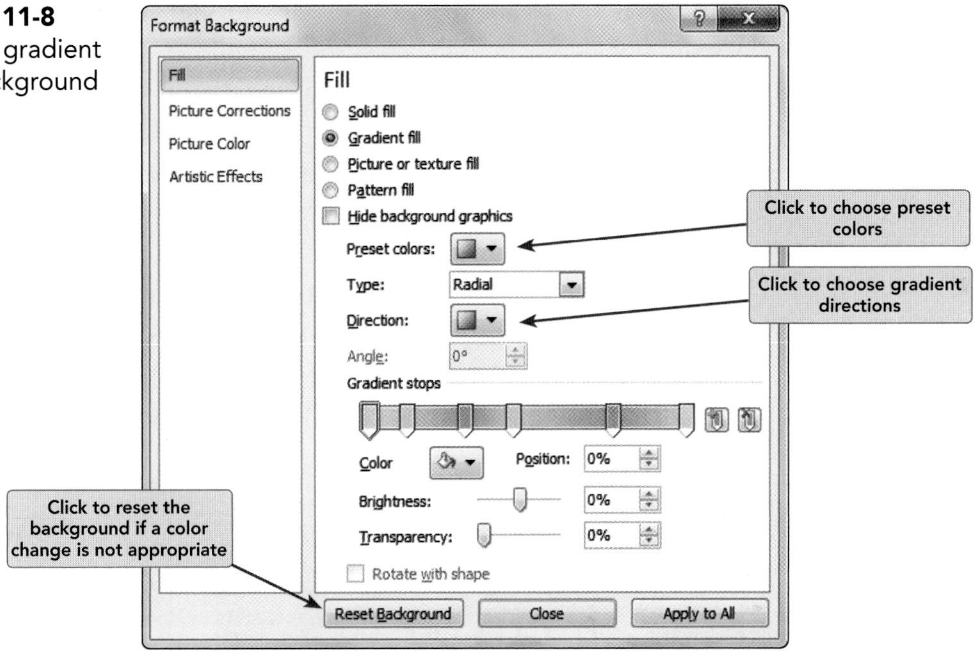

Figure 11-8
Applying a gradient fill to a background

Exercise 11-6   APPLY PATTERNED AND TEXTURED BACKGROUNDS

In addition to solid and gradient colors, patterned and textured effects can be used for backgrounds. For patterned effects two colors are available—foreground and background. When the two colors are similar, the effect will be subtle. When they are very different, the pattern will be very noticeable. Use subtle effects when filling an entire slide background, and reserve the more dramatic effects for smaller areas.

Choose these effects carefully so that your text will remain easy to read with the colors and fonts that you are using.

1. Move to slide 3, and from the Design tab, in the Background group, click the Dialog Box Launcher ⬛.

2. Choose Pattern fill. Choose 90% (column 2, row 6).

3. Click Close to apply the changes only to slide 3.

4. Move to slide 1; from the Design tab, in the Background group, click the Background Styles button 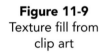, and choose Format Background.

5. Choose Picture or texture fill. Choose Texture, and you will see a limited number of textures. Choose the Walnut texture that looks like dark wood.

6. Choose Apply to All and then Close. Scroll through the presentation to verify that the dark wood is on all the slides. Click the Undo button to remove the walnut texture from slides 2 through 7.

7. Still working on slide 1, from the Design tab, in the Background group, click the Dialog Box Launcher.

8. Choose Picture or texture fill. Under Insert from, click Clip Art; for the Search text, key **texture**.

9. Be sure you have a check at the top of the dialog box to Include content from Office.com; then click Go.

10. Find a texture that goes well with the theme colors, such as a linen or other light texture as shown in Figure 11-9. Click OK, and the single image fills the screen.

11. Choose the option Tile picture as texture, and then additional tiling options appear (to control how the image repeats). For Alignment, choose Center, and for Mirror type, choose Both.

12. Click Close to apply this texture to the title slide only.

Figure 11-9
Texture fill from clip art

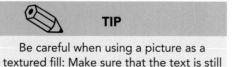
TIP

Be careful when using a picture as a textured fill: Make sure that the text is still easy to read on top of the picture.

Exercise 11-7 CREATE A PICTURE BACKGROUND FROM A FILE

Using a picture as a slide background is an interesting technique, but it provides some design challenges. Because pictures are made up of so many colors, it is difficult to select text colors and fonts that are easily readable over all areas of a picture. In this exercise you will apply a picture of vegetables and consider how the solid color of the text placeholders keeps the text easy to read.

Although background consistency is important for a unified presentation theme, at times you will want a different background for one or more slides in a presentation. For example, slide 7 in the current presentation already displays several pictures, so the background should have a different effect. From the Format Background dialog box you can adjust the transparency setting or even choose to hide the background. It is important to be sure that the colors you choose blend with the overall theme colors and the tone of the presentation.

1. On slide 4, from the Design tab, in the Background group, click the Background Styles button ▨, and then choose Format Background.

2. For Fill, select Picture or texture fill, and then choose File. On the Insert Picture dialog box, locate your student files, and choose **dollars**; then click Insert. The picture immediately appears on slide 1.

3. Choose the option Tile picture as texture. For Alignment, choose Center, and for Mirror type, choose Both.

4. From the Artistic Effects options on the left of the dialog box, choose Artistic Effects and Line Drawing (column 5, row 1) to apply an artistic effect and transparency settings. Now the picture is faded to de-emphasize the background, as shown in Figure 11-10.

5. Click Close.

6. Select the title, and change the font color to Brown, Accent 1 so that it is legible on the image.

Figure 11-10
Background picture fill

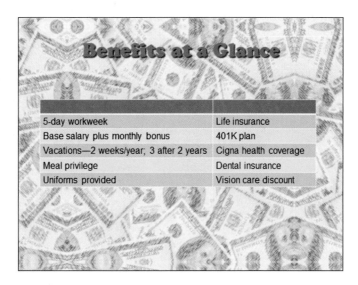

7. Save the presentation as *[your initials]*11-7.

Working with Slide Masters for a Custom Design Theme

Presentation themes can be used to control fonts and colors, but PowerPoint's *Slide Master* feature enables you to design a custom background and position graphics to be displayed on all slides. Using slide masters, you can adjust *slide layouts* to control placeholder positioning for titles, subtitles, bulleted lists, charts, SmartArt, and so on, in addition to storing color and font information.

When combined, these features can create a theme so that you apply design elements consistently throughout a presentation for a unified appearance. Any design element that appears on all slides should be controlled on a slide master.

You can create a theme from a blank presentation or from an existing theme. Themes can be customized for a topic or designed with specific needs in mind such as matching university colors or including a company logo on all slides. Themes can be saved for future use. A wide variety of predesigned themes exist at Microsoft's Office.com that you can download, apply to your presentation, and customize if necessary.

Exercise 11-8 REARRANGE BACKGROUND GRAPHICS

To customize the look of a theme, you can modify or delete existing objects (lines, shapes, images) plus add your own objects suitable for your particular topic. Remember to keep the design changes you make professional and suitable for the presentation topic. These changes are made using a slide master.

1. On slide 1, from the View tab, in the Master Views group, click the Slide Master button . In Slide Master view, you see all the possible predesigned layouts that are available to use, as shown on the left in Figure 11-11. Each of these can be customized. You should have the second slide layout selected in Slide Master view.

Figure 11-11
Slide Master view

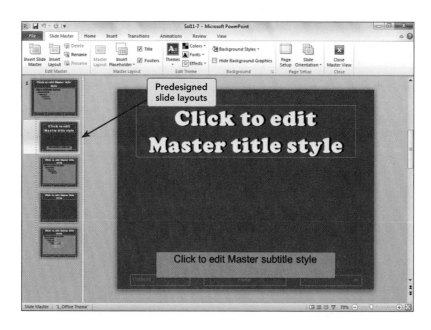

2. The first layout controls the background for all slides; other layouts can be made to look different if you wish. So move to the first layout, and begin with your changes on this layout; then change additional layouts as needed. No work is required on the ones you do not use in your presentation.

3. From the Slide Master tab, in the Edit Theme group, click the Colors button 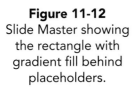, and choose the Technic colors.

4. From the Slide Master tab, in the Background group, click the Background Styles button 🔯, and then choose Format Background. From the Format Background dialog box, click Gradient fill. From the Preset colors, choose Moss.

5. For Type choose Rectangular, and for Direction choose From Bottom Right Corner.

6. Click Apply to All. This step removes the picture that you applied in the last exercise and applies the same gradient coloring to all slides. Click Close.

7. On the first layout, from the Home tab, in the Drawing group, choose the Rectangle shape, and draw a rectangle extending from the top to the bottom, as shown in Figure 11-12. Apply the following settings using the Drawing Tools Format tab:

    •   *Size.* Height is 7.5 inches, and width is 1.5 inches.

    •   *Shape Fill.* Choose Gradient and More Gradients, and then choose the same preset color, Moss. Choose the Direction of Linear Down. This applies the same colors as those on the slide background, but the light green is now on the top.

    •   *Shape Outline.* Choose No Outline.

    •   *Arrange.* Choose Send to Back so that the rectangle is behind the text placeholders on the slide.

Figure 11-12
Slide Master showing the rectangle with gradient fill behind placeholders.

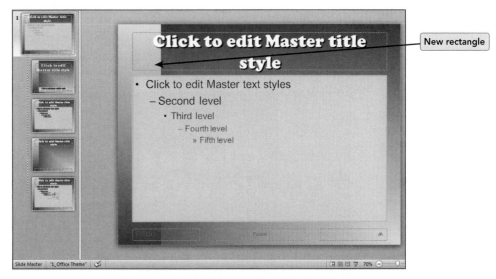

8. Select the rectangle, and copy it. Move to the first layout master below the one you have just changed. This is the Title Slide master. The rectangle you positioned previously now appears here; however, it is not wide enough for this slide.

9. Paste the copied rectangle, and from the Drawing Tools Format tab, in the Size group, increase its width to 2.5 inches. The height remains the same. Be sure to align this rectangle with the left of the slide. Choose Send to Back so that the rectangle is behind the text placeholders.

Exercise 11-9   CHANGE AND REPOSITION PLACEHOLDERS

When you change the layout of the graphics and the backgrounds of a theme, you often must reposition the theme placeholders for all objects to fit attractively on the slide. Previously the slide titles were centered, but in this exercise the added shape at the left calls for a left-alignment pattern. Also, the positioning and fill of the placeholders should be changed to fit this new design.

1. Still working in Slide Master view, select the first master at the top left. Select the title placeholder, and apply Left Alignment. Resize the title placeholder from the left so that the text starts beside the rectangle and not on it.

2. Select the body placeholder, and apply No Fill and No Outline. Resize the placeholder from the left to left-align it with the title placeholder beside the newly inserted rectangle.

3. Select the placeholder text, and from the Drawing Tools Format tab, in the WordArt Styles group, click the Text Outline button 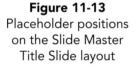, and choose No Text Outline.

4. Select the second layout master for the title slide. Resize the title placeholder from the left so that the text fits on three lines. Move it down and to the right, as shown in Figure 11-13.

5. Select the subtitle placeholder, and move it up and to the right. Remove the fill and outline color, and change to left alignment. Select the text, and apply bold. Resize and reposition to match Figure 11-13.

Figure 11-13
Placeholder positions on the Slide Master Title Slide layout

Exercise 11-10 CHANGE BULLETS

Bullets can be updated in Slide Master view. For this design, you will use a picture bullet.

1. On the first Slide Master layout, select the bulleted list placeholder, and click within the first-level bulleted text. From the Home tab, in the Paragraph group, click the down arrow on the Bullets button 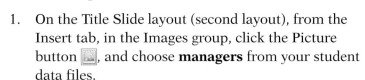 to open the gallery, and then choose Bullets and Numbering.

2. From the Bullets and Numbering dialog box, click Picture. From the Picture Bullet dialog box, select a black picture bullet of your choice. Click OK. Now the picture bullet will be applied to all the bullets in this presentation because they are all level 1 bullets.

Exercise 11-11 INSERT AN IMAGE

To add interest to your design theme and help to establish your presentation's meaning, insert an illustrated image on the Slide Master Title layout. Repeat the same image in a smaller size on the slide master for all the slides in the presentation.

TIP

One or more images can be added to slide masters. You can recolor these images if they are Windows Metafile pictures (file name extension **.wmf**) to harmonize with your theme's color scheme. Also, you can ungroup images, rearrange some or all parts of them, and use these modified images in your design. You can include other objects such as shapes or photograph images. The effects for your background should be rather subtle so that your audience will focus on the information each slide contains.

1. On the Title Slide layout (second layout), from the Insert tab, in the Images group, click the Picture button, and choose **managers** from your student data files.

2. From the Picture Tools Format tab, in the Size group, resize the image to make the height 2.4 inches and the width 2.41 inches.

3. In the Picture Styles group, click the More button, and choose Reflected Perspective Right (column 5, row 4). Position the image within the rectangle at the left beside the title text, as shown in Figure 11-14.

Figure 11-14
Completed slide master for the Title Slide layout

4. Copy the image, paste it on the first Slide Master layout, resize it to a height and width of 1.3 inches, and position it on top of the rectangle beside the title placeholder.

Exercise 11-12   ADJUST FOOTER POSITIONING AND ADD FOOTER TEXT

By default, the objects that appear in a footer (date, footer text, and slide numbering) appear across the bottom of the slide. In this exercise, you will change the position and color of the text on the Slide Master layout to better fit your background design and then add footer text so that it will show on the slides.

1. On the first Slide Master layout, select the footer placeholders for the date, footer text, and page number. From the Home tab, in the Font group, change the font size to 14 points; apply bold, white text color, and left alignment.

2. Select only the date text placeholder, and move it to the left and down just a little so that it fits within the rectangle at the left. Move the footer text placeholder above the date placeholder. Move the page number placeholder above the footer, and align all three items on the left.

3. On the Slide Master tab, click the Close Master View button ⊠.

4. Create a footer: Include the date, the page number, and *[your initials]*11-12. Click Apply to All.

Exercise 11-13   ADJUST SLIDE ELEMENTS TO FIT A NEW THEME

After a new design is complete, the positioning of images and other graphics already used in the presentation may need adjusting. This presentation has several items that need to be adjusted to go with the new theme. After new themes are modified and applied, the layouts may also need resetting to apply the changes.

1. Select all the slides in the Slides and Outline pane.

2. From the Home tab, in the Slides group, reset the layouts.

3. On slide 1, delete the image in the middle of the slide, and move the logo up under the title.

4. On slide 3, select the SmartArt diagram, and apply the Subtle Effect SmartArt Style and Colored Fill - Accent 2.

5. On slide 4, resize the table and reposition it to the right of the rectangle. Apply the Table Style Medium Style 2.

6. On slide 5, select the rectangle with text at the bottom of the slide, and apply the Shape Style Intense Effect - Black, Dark 1.

7. On slide 8, delete the title placeholder, and resize the body text placeholder to go from top to bottom of the slide and fit beside the pictures to the right.

8. Update your footer text to *[your initials]*11-13.

9. Save your presentation as *[your initials]***11-13**.

10. Save this customized theme by following these steps:

   a. From the Design tab, in the Themes group, click the More button ⤓, and choose Save Current Theme.

   b. In the Save Current Theme dialog box, name the file **Green background**. Because this file is an Office Theme, it will have the file extension of **.thmx** and will automatically be saved in the Document Themes directory. Click Save.

   c. Notice that the new theme appears in your Themes gallery in the Custom category and can be used for other presentations.

Exercise 11-14   SAVE A NEW POWERPOINT TEMPLATE

For situations in which you have customized a theme and developed presentation content that you may need to use again in another way, you can save the file as a PowerPoint template. Save the template in a location that is convenient: in the default template directory, on your student disk, in your lesson folder, or in any other place that provides convenient access.

1. On the File tab, choose Save As to open the Save As dialog box.

2. In the Save as type drop-down list, choose PowerPoint Template. Automatically, the Templates folder on the computer you are using will be selected as the destination. However, you need to save this file with your other files.

3. In the Save in box, navigate to your Lesson 11 folder.

4. In the File name box, key the file name **Green gradient**. Click Save. Your template is now ready to use. You can tell it is a template file because the file extension is **.potx** instead of the presentation extension of **.pptx** if your computer is set up to show extensions with file names.

5. Close the template.

Applying Themes and Templates from Microsoft's Office.com

Many professionally designed themes and templates are available from Microsoft's Office.com. These themes can be used as is, or you can customize them. Downloading these files requires ActiveX control for downloads on your computer.

Exercise 11-15   SEARCH MICROSOFT'S OFFICE.COM

From the File tab, choose New:

- From the Available Templates and Themes area, you have options to search Office.com by keyword or to choose from categories of Office.com templates.

- Take a few moments to explore the available options. Some of them have simple backgrounds, while others include a lot of artwork that is very specific to a particular topic. Some of these are made available for use by companies other than Microsoft.

- In the Presentations folder, templates are organized by categories, but these templates also include suggested content to help you get started developing a presentation.

- In the More Categories folder, several categories are listed as well as an Office Themes folder.

- Once you have located something you would like to download, select it and then choose Download.

By default, themes and templates are downloaded to specific locations on your computer unless you specify other locations. Here are some concepts to remember:

- Themes will download into the Document Themes folder within the Office program files on your computer.

- If additional color or font themes are used in a design theme, they will be placed in the related folders within the Document Themes folder.

- Templates are downloaded into the Templates folder.

- Themes and templates that you download may be saved in an earlier version of PowerPoint.

1. Using any of the methods described above, download at least three themes or templates that you find attractive. As you download them, each will open in a new window. Close these windows.

2. You will apply one of these designs in the next exercise.

Exercise 11-16   BROWSE FOR THEMES

Once themes or templates have been downloaded, they are available for future use.

1. Create a four-slide presentation using Figure 11-15 as a guide.

2. From the Design tab, in the Themes group, click the More button ⬇. The new themes you have downloaded will be displayed in the Custom category.

3. To look for additional themes that may have been downloaded in a previous work session, click the More button ⬇ again and choose Browse for Themes to locate the folder in which you saved them.

4. Select the theme, and click Open so that it will be applied to your current presentation. The **Fresh** theme is provided with your student files in case you are unable to download from Office.com. Be aware that your colors, layouts, and presentation may look totally different from the figure if you choose a different theme.

5. Insert a nutrition-related image on slide 1.

Figure 11-15
Content for
presentation

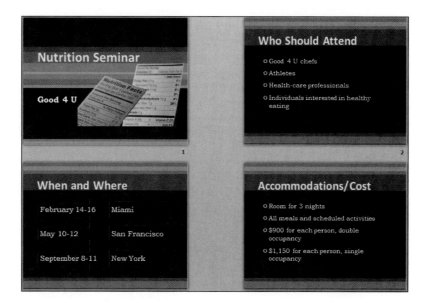

6. Insert a slide footer with the date and *[your initials]***11-16**. Save the presentation as *[your initials]***11-16**.

7. Close the presentation.

Customizing Handout and Notes Masters

Just as the Slide Master feature controls the appearance of the slides in your presentation, the Notes Master and Handout Master features control the overall look and formatting of notes and handouts.

Exercise 11-17 WORK WITH THE NOTES MASTER

The main purpose of a notes page is to provide detailed information about a slide that a speaker might need as a reference when delivering a presentation. On a notes master, you can format, resize, and reposition the body text placeholder, the slide image placeholder, and the header and footer placeholders in the same way as you do on a slide master. You can also add pictures, text boxes, and other shapes. All of these options are available on the Notes Master Ribbon.

1. Reopen the file you saved as *[your initials]***11-13**.

2. From the View tab, in the Master Views group, click the Notes Master button . Note the portrait orientation of the Notes Master page.

3. Click the Page Setup button , and select **Letter Paper** from the Slides Sized For drop-down list. Click **OK**.

4. Now from the Home tab, make these adjustments:

a. Select the slide image, and apply an outline in black with 3-point weight.

b. Select the note text placeholder, and increase the font size to 18 points.

c. Select the header placeholder, and change the font to 24 points, bold.

d. Select the date placeholder, and reduce its width so that the date fits perfectly in the placeholder.

e. Increase the width of the header placeholder so that the end of it reaches the beginning of the date placeholder.

f. Change the text alignment to bottom for both the title and date placeholders, as shown in Figure 11-16.

Figure 11-16
Notes master with adjustments

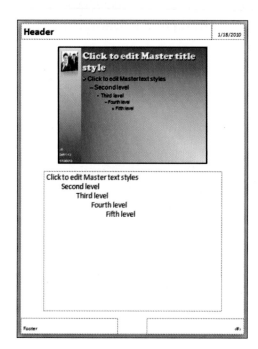

5. From the Notes Master tab, click the Close Master View button ☒. From the View tab, in the Presentation Views group, click the Normal View button 🖳.

6. Add the following notes to the slides indicated. You may need to increase the size of the Notes pane so that you can easily key the text below each slide.

a. Slide 2: **Remind potential recruits that they can also find more information about openings at each location at the Good 4 U Web site.**

b. Slide 7: **For a list of accredited restaurant management programs, visit the Good 4 U Web site under the heading "Employment."**

7. Update the slide footer to read *[your initials]***11-17**.

8. Create a handout header and footer: Include the date, **Management Recruitment** as the header, the page number, and *[your initials]***11-17** as the footer. Click Apply to All.

Exercise 11-18 WORK WITH THE HANDOUT MASTER

On a handout master, you can make the same kinds of changes as you do on a notes master, except that you cannot alter the size or position of the slide image placeholders that show where the slides will fit when the page is printed. Handout masters come with six different prearranged layouts, ranging from one to nine slides per page. When placing pictures or other objects on a handout master, you must be careful to size and position them so that that they do not overlap the slide placeholders.

1. From slide 1, copy the Good 4 U logo.

2. From the View tab, in Master Views group, click the Handout Master button ▦.

3. Notice the portrait orientation of this page. In the Page Setup group, click the Handout Orientation button 🖺, and choose Landscape. The slides are represented by dotted outlines.

4. Press Ctrl+V to paste the logo. Make it slightly smaller, and then move it to the lower center under the middle slide in the bottom row.

5. From the Home tab, make these adjustments:

   a. Use a shape tool to draw a rectangle across the top of the page. Click the Quick Styles button ▣ (or choose from the Quick Styles gallery if it is displayed), and choose Subtle Effect - Olive Green, Accent 3.

   b. Click the Arrange button ▦; then choose Send to Back to position the rectangle behind the header and date placeholders. Adjust the placeholder size and position as shown in Figure 11-17.

   c. Change the header placeholder text to 28 points in bold, and align the text in both placeholders in the middle.

6. From the Handout Master tab, in the Placeholders group, remove the check before Footer.

Figure 11-17
Handout master with adjustments

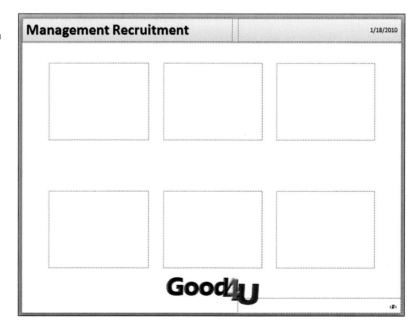

7. Click the Close Master View button ⊠.

8. Update the slide footer and the note and handout footer to read *[your initials]*11-18.

9. Save the presentation as *[your initials]*11-18 in your Lesson 11 folder.

10. Close the presentation and submit your work.

Lesson 11   Summary

- You can customize presentation theme colors to suit individual needs. From the Design tab, in the Themes group, click the Colors button, and then choose from the available themes. Click Create New Theme Colors to change individual colors, and save them as a new theme. You can choose colors from the Colors dialog box by using the Standard tab or create a color by using the Custom tab.

- On the Design tab, in the Background Styles group, use the Background Styles button to apply a background effect to one or more slides in a presentation. Backgrounds can be solid colors, gradient fills, patterns, textures, or pictures.

- The Apply to All command on the Background dialog box applies a background effect to all slides in a presentation. The Close command applies a background effect only to slides that are currently selected.

- Customize a predesigned theme by rearranging graphics, changing the background, repositioning placeholders, and changing font treatments.

- Create a new design theme by changing and adding elements on the slide and title masters of an existing theme or a blank presentation.

- Save a presentation as a template by choosing PowerPoint Template in the Save as type list box.

- Additional themes and templates can be downloaded from Office.com.

- Notes and handout masters can be customized in a way similar to customizing slide master layouts. Slide placeholders on a handout master cannot be moved or resized.

- When placing text boxes or pictures on a handout master, take care to make sure that the objects do not conflict with the slide placeholder layouts.

LESSON 11		Command Summary
Feature	**Button**	**Ribbon**
Change background		Design tab, Background group, Background Styles
Change theme fonts		Design tab, Themes group, Theme Fonts
Create themes/templates		View tab, Master Views group, Slide Master
Customize a color theme		Design tab, Theme group, Colors
Customize a handout master		View tab, Master Views group, Handout Master
Customize a notes master		View tab, Master Views group, Notes Master
Download a template or theme from Microsoft's Office.com		File tab, New, choose a theme or template, Download
Save a custom theme		Design tab, Themes group, More, Save Current Theme
Save a PowerPoint template		File tab, Save As, choose PowerPoint Template from Save as type box

Concepts Review

True/False Questions

Each of the following statements is either true or false. Indicate your choice by circling T or F.

T F 1. You can create gradient fills for slide backgrounds.

T F 2. Gradient fills are available in preset colors only.

T F 3. PowerPoint themes give presentations a unified appearance.

T F 4. If you choose a picture for a background, it must be applied to only one slide.

T F 5. You can use both theme colors and standard colors in a custom theme color.

T F 6. It is possible to modify an existing design theme to fit a unique presentation topic.

T F 7. You can save a PowerPoint template that you create on your computer or a removable storage device.

T F 8. If you want to apply a theme from Microsoft's Office.com, you must complete the presentation before applying the design theme.

Short Answer Questions

Write the correct answer in the space provided.

1. How do you change slide background styles?

2. What kinds of fill effects can you apply to backgrounds?

3. Which option will apply a background to only a selected slide?

4. How do you create new theme colors?

5. When customizing a presentation's theme colors, what is the maximum number of accent colors that you can change?

6. How do you apply a theme that does not appear on the Design tab in the Themes group?

_____

7. Where can you make changes to an entire theme, such as rearranging the graphics?

_____

8. How can you customize a handout master to complement a presentation's design?

_____

Critical Thinking

Answer these questions on a separate page. Support your answers with examples from your own experience, if possible.

1. Discuss the benefits of customizing a background for your presentation's content. Briefly describe a business, and explain how the business could use graphics to help establish the tone of a presentation or convey the identity of the company.

2. Many themes and templates are available at Office.com. Why might someone who uses PowerPoint regularly choose to find themes online rather than using the themes available within the software?

Skills Review

Exercise 11-19

Change colors and fonts in an existing theme.

1. Open the presentation **Investors**. This presentation uses the Median theme.

2. Change the background for the entire presentation. Make the following changes from the Design tab:

   a. In the Themes group, click the Colors button ■, and choose Origin.

   b. In the Background group, click the Background Styles button ▨, and from the gallery that appears, choose Style 11, which applies a horizontal pinstripe effect.

3. Change the background for just one slide by following these steps:

   a. On slide 1, from the Design tab, in the Background group, click the Dialog Box Launcher.

   b. For the Fill option, choose a Solid fill, and change the color to Indigo, Background 2, Darker 50% (column 3).

   c. Click Close.

4. From the Design tab, in the Themes group, click the Theme Fonts button $\boxed{A}$, and choose the Trek theme, which applies the font Franklin Gothic Book.

5. Make these changes to slide 1:

   a. Select the title placeholder, and move it up and to the left. From the Home tab, in the Font group, increase the text size to 54 points, and change the case to capitalize each word.

   b. From the Insert tab, in the Images group, search for and insert a picture of money. Resize the picture to 5.5 inches wide. Apply a picture border in white at 6 points to blend with the other white lines on the slide. Change the color as necessary to blend with the theme.

   c. Adjust the positioning of the picture and title as shown in Figure 11-18.

Figure 11-18
Title slide completed

6. Create a handout header and footer: Include the date, your name as the header, the page number, and *[your initials]*11-19 as the footer.

7. Save the presentation as *[your initials]*11-19 in your Lesson 11 folder.

8. Close the presentation and submit your work.

Exercise 11-20

Apply gradient and a picture fill to create a custom theme.

1. Open the presentation file **RaceParty**.

2. From the Design tab, in the Background group, click the Background Styles button $\boxed{\text{🎨}}$, and select Style 12.

3. From the View tab, in the Master Views group, click the Slide Master button 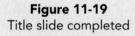. On the Title Slide layout, delete the clip art image and the red line. From the Slide Master tab, click the Close Master View button ⊠.

4. On slide 1, make these changes:

   a. Select "Post-Race Party." From the Home tab, change the font to Impact, remove bold, and change the size to 54 points. Resize the placeholder so that the text fits on one line, and then move this text below "New York Marathon."

   b. Move the flag picture down to the lower right of the slide. From the Insert tab, in the Illustrations group, click the Shapes button 📄, and choose the Oval tool. Draw an oval large enough to cover all the white area of the flag picture. Make the oval white with a black outline, 4.5 points. Send it behind the flag picture, and be sure that no corners of the flag picture extend beyond the edge of the oval.

   c. Group the flag and the oval. Position these grouped shapes on the right of the slide.

   d. From the Insert tab, in the Images group, click the Clip Art button ▓; then search for a picture image of runners, and insert it.

   e. With the picture selected, from the Picture Format tab, in the Picture Styles group, choose the picture style Beveled Oval, Black. Resize as shown in Figure 11-19.

Figure 11-19
Title slide completed

5. Create a new slide 4 with a blank layout. On slide 4, make these changes:

   a. On the Design tab, in the Background group, click the Dialog Box Launcher. In the Format Background dialog box, for the Fill, choose Picture or texture fill. For Insert From, click Clip Art. From the Select Picture dialog box, search for runners. Select the picture that you used on slide 1. Click OK to accept the picture. Click Close to place it only on slide 4.

   b. From the Insert tab, in the Text group, click the Text box button 🄰, and key the text **Congratulations!**.

c. Right-click, and from the floating font group change the font to Impact at 54 points. Apply a black fill, bold, and center alignment.

d. From the Drawing Tools Format tab, in the WordArt Styles group, click the More button ⟱; then from the gallery select the Fill - Red, Accent 2, Warm Matte Bevel (column 3, row 5) style.

e. Increase the width of the text box to 7 inches so that the text is emphasized a little more by the black fill color behind it. Position this text box as shown in Figure 11-20.

Figure 11-20
Slide 4 completed

6. Create a handout header and footer: Include the date, your name as the header, the page number, and *[your initials]*11-20 as the footer.

7. Move to slide 1, and save the presentation as *[your initials]*11-20 in your Lesson 11 folder.

8. Close the presentation and submit your work.

Exercise 11-21

Use slide masters to create and save a new PowerPoint template.

1. Start a new, blank presentation.

2. From the View tab, in the Master Views group, click the Slide Master button 🖽.

3. From the Slide Master tab, in the Edit Theme group, click the Colors button ◼, and make these changes:

a. Choose the Opulent color theme.

b. From the Theme Colors gallery, choose Create New Theme Colors.

c. Notice the setting for Accent 1 in the fifth column of color swatches.

d. Change the Text/Background - Dark 2 to a darker variation of that accent color, Pink - Accent 1, Darker 25%.

e. Name the new color theme **Boxes Colors**, and save it.

4. Select the first Slide Master layout; then from the Slide Master tab, in the Background group, click the Background styles button 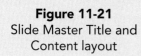, and choose Style 3.

5. Select the third Slide Master layout (Title and Content). From the Insert tab, in the Illustrations group, click the Shapes button, and draw a rectangle 2.85 inches high by 3.95 inches wide. Use the Drawing Tools Format tab to make these changes:

   a. For the fill color choose Gradient; then from the Dark Variations gallery click Linear Diagonal - Top Left to Bottom Right.

   b. From the Gradient gallery, click More Gradients; then set stop 1 Transparency to 50%.

   c. Choose No Outline.

6. Duplicate the rectangle three times (for a total of four rectangles); then make these changes:

   a. Select all four rectangles.

   b. From the Drawing Tools Format tab, in the Arrange group, click the Align button, and choose Align to Slide, Distribute Horizontally, and Distribute Vertically. Notice how the rectangles are positioned evenly across the slide, going from the upper left corner to the lower right corner as shown in Figure 11-21.

   c. Group the rectangles, and send them to the back behind the text placeholders.

7. Copy the grouped rectangles; then move to the Title Slide Master layout, and paste them. (Do not send the rectangles to the back on the Title Slide Master layout yet.)

8. On the Title and Content Master layout, make the following changes to the placeholders, as shown in Figure 11-21:

   a. Change the title placeholder to left alignment.

   b. Choose the Fill - White, Drop Shadow WordArt style to match the treatment used on the title slide.

   c. Change the first-level bullet to a square.

   d. Reduce the text by one font size.

Figure 11-21
Slide Master Title and
Content layout

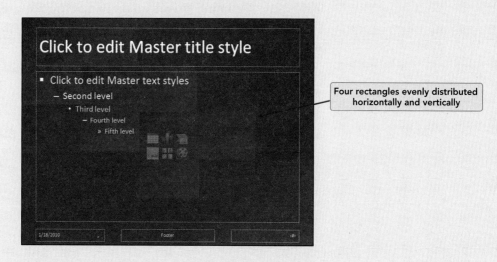

9. On the Title Slide Master layout, make these changes:

   a. Ungroup the rectangles, delete the third one from the top, and make the second rectangle larger by dragging its lower right corner down and to the right, as shown in Figure 11-22.

   b. Group the three rectangles, and send them to the back.

   c. Select the title placeholder, and from the Drawing Tools Format tab, in the WordArt Styles group, click the More button ⏷. From the gallery that appears, choose the Fill - White, Drop Shadow style.

   d. Increase the font size to 54 points; then adjust the position of the title placeholder so that it is horizontally centered in the large rectangle.

   e. Select the subtitle placeholder, and move it below the title placeholder and slightly to the right. Make this text bold.

   f. From the Slide Master tab, in the Close group, click the Close Master View button ⊠.

Figure 11-22
Slide Master Title
Slide layout

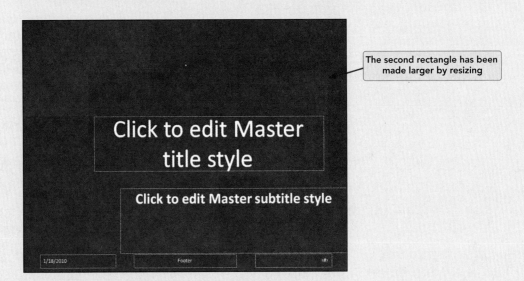

The second rectangle has been made larger by resizing

10. Save the presentation as a template in your Lesson 11 folder by following these steps:

    a. Click the File tab; then choose Save As.

    b. Key the file name **Boxes**, and change the Save as type to PowerPoint Template. Save this file in your Lesson 11 folder.

    c. Close the presentation.

11. Open the file **Reservations**, and then apply the **Boxes** template that you just created. Follow these steps:

    a. From the Design tab, in the Themes group, click the More button ⏷.

    b. From the gallery that appears, choose Browse for Themes, and locate the folder in which you saved your new template.

    c. Select the template **Boxes**, and choose Apply.

12. On the title slide, reduce the size of the subtitle placeholder, and move it to the right so that the word "Operations" fits on the rectangle there.

13. Notice that the gradient boxes are not showing on slides 2 to 4. These slides were created using a different layout from the one you have prepared. So change the layout following these steps:

    a. In the Slides and Outline pane, select slides 2 to 4.

    b. From the Home tab, choose the Title and Content layout.

14. Create a handout header and footer: Include the date, your name as the header, the page number, and *[your initials]*11-21 as the footer.

15. Save the presentation with the file name *[your initials]*11-21 in your Lesson 11 folder.

16. Close the presentation and submit your work.

Exercise 11-22

Apply a template from Microsoft's Office.com.

1. Open the file **Training3**.

2. From the File tab, choose New, in the search box key **Blue Green Cave**, and press Enter.

3. Choose Download to add this template to the computer you are using. Close the presentation that automatically opens.

4. A thumbnail for this design now shows in the Themes gallery. Click the thumbnail to apply this design to the current presentation.

5. Check placeholder and image positioning to see whether all slide elements adjusted effectively.

6. Select the chart on slide 3; then from the Chart Tools Design tab, in the Chart Styles group, change the style to Style 44 so that the chart labeling is easier to read.

7. Create a handout header and footer: Include the date, your name as the header, the page number, and *[your initials]*11-22 as the footer.

8. Save the presentation as *[your initials]*11-22 in your Lesson 11 folder.

9. Close the presentation and submit your work.

Lesson Applications

Exercise 11-23

Change colors, fonts, and backgrounds in an existing theme.

1.　Open the presentation **Specials**.

2.　From the Design tab, make these changes:

　　a. Change Theme colors to Solstice.

　　b. Format the background for a Gradient Fill, and choose the preset color Wheat. The Type should be set to Linear and the Angle to 45°. Click Apply to All; then click Close.

3.　On slide 1, access the Slide Master, and make these changes to the Slide Master Title layout:

　　a. For the teal-colored rectangle, increase its size vertically to 2 inches and send it to the back so that it is behind the title text.

　　b. Select the title placeholder, and move it slightly so that it is evenly spaced within the rectangle.

　　c. Move the title placeholder and rectangle so that the top starts approximately 1 inch from the top of the slide.

　　d. From the Home tab, change the font to Arial Black at 60 points.

　　e. From the Drawing Tools Format tab, in the WordArt Styles group, choose Gradient Fill - Black, Outline - White, Outer Shadow (column 3, row 4). Adjust positioning if necessary so that the text is centered over the rectangle.

　　f. Close the Slide Master view.

4.　On slide 1, delete the subtitle placeholder, and reset the layout if necessary so that the title appears in the rectangle.

5.　Make these changes to the illustration on slide 1:

　　a. Change the width to 5 inches, and the height will automatically increase to 3.97 inches.

　　b. Adjust its position to fit on the right of the slide. Refer to the finished slide shown in Figure 11-23.

Figure 11-23
Title slide completed

6. On slide 2, access the Slide Master, and make these changes to the Slide Master Two Content layout:

   a. Select the rectangle at the top of the slide, and make it large enough to cover the title text. Send the rectangle to the back so that it is behind the slide title placeholder.

   b. Change the title text to Arial Black at 36 points; then apply the same WordArt style, Gradient Fill - Black, Outline - White, Outer Shadow.

   c. Click the first-level bulleted item on the left, and apply bold. Repeat this step for the list on the right.

   d. For both bulleted lists, change the first-level bullet to a square in Aqua, Accent 1, Darker 50%.

   e. Close the Slide Master view.

7. Create a handout header and footer: Include the date, your name as the header, the page number, and *[your initials]*11-23 as the footer.

8. Move to slide 1, and save the presentation as *[your initials]*11-23 in your Lesson 11 folder.

9. Close the presentation and submit your work.

Exercise 11-24

Create a custom theme, and add picture backgrounds.

1. Open the file **Software**.

2. From the Design tab, choose the Opulent theme color; then make these custom changes:

   a. Open the Slide Master first layout.

   b. Insert the **perspective** picture background from your Lesson 11 student file folder, and apply it to all slides.

3. On the Title Slide layout, draw a rectangle to cover both the title and subtitle placeholders. Make these changes:

   a. Change the shape fill color to Lavender, Background 2, Darker 90% (column 3, row 6); then set the transparency to 30%.

   b. Remove the outline.

   c. Send this rectangle behind the placeholders.

   d. Copy the rectangle.

4. On the Title and Content layout, make these changes:

   a. Paste the rectangle; then resize it to fit across the slide, from below the title placeholder to the bottom of the slide.

   b. Send this rectangle behind the content placeholder.

   c. Draw a line as an accent below the title placeholder. Use the theme color Orange, Accent 6 (column 10, row 1), and make the line width 10 points.

   d. Select the title placeholder, and choose the WordArt style Fill - Orange, Accent 6, Warm Matte Bevel (column 2, row 6).

e. Select the content placeholder, and move it down slightly. Make the text white.

f. Change the first-level bullet to the color Orange, Accent 6.

5. On the Title Slide layout, make these changes:

a. Select the rectangle, and add the same line color and weight for the shape outline.

b. Select the title placeholder; apply the same WordArt style, and increase the font size to 54 points.

c. Select the subtitle placeholder, and change the font color to white.

d. Close the Slide Master view.

6. When you look now at the Slides and Outline pane, you can see that your new design has been applied to the title slide but not the other slides. This is because the others were prepared with a Title and Text layout.

7. Select slides 2 to 5, and change the layout to Title and Content. Now all of your changes appear as shown in Figure 11-24.

Figure 11-24
Custom theme slides

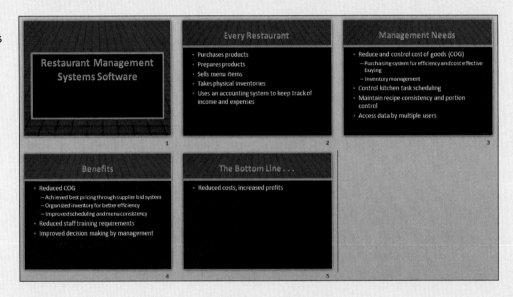

8. Create a handout header and footer: Include the date, your name as the header, the page number, and *[your initials]*11-24 as the footer.

9. Save the presentation as *[your initials]*11-24 in your Lesson 11 folder.

10. Close the presentation and submit your work.

Exercise 11-25

Apply a template from Microsoft's Office.com, and adjust placeholders.

1. Open the file **Retreat**.

2. Download the Botanical extract design template (found under the Design Slides folder, and in the Nature folder) to the computer you are using, and apply it to your current presentation.

3. This attractive background uses soft colors that work well for the background. However, the text colors are too soft for easy reading. Also, the title slide text is not as bold as the slide text. The text appearance can be improved.

4. From the Design tab, create new theme fonts for the heading and body, and use Segoe Print for a more casual appearance. (If you do not have this font, then substitute a different font with a similar appearance. See Figure 11-25.) Name the theme font Nature.

5. Use the Slide Master Title Slide layout, and make these changes to the text placeholders:

   a. Select both placeholders, make the text bold, and nudge them slightly up and to the right.

   b. Select the title placeholder, and apply the bevel effect Cool Slant and the shadow effect Offset Diagonal Bottom Left.

   c. Adjust the shadow settings to Transparency 30%, Size 100%, Blur 4 points, Angle 135°, and Distance 3 points. Change the shadow color to Gray 50%, Background 2, Darker 50%.

   d. Increase the size of the title text to 60 points.

   e. Move the title placeholder up so that it is not overlapping the subtitle placeholder.

6. On the first Slide Master layout, make these changes to the text placeholders:

   a. On the title placeholder, use the same text effects, but make the text 44 points and top-align the text in the placeholder.

   b. On the bulleted list, change the text color to Gray 50%, Background 2, Darker 50%.

   c. Change the first-level bullet to a check mark Pink, Text 2, Darker 50%, and increase the size to 120%.

   d. Reposition the text placeholders as shown in Figure 11-25.

Figure 11-25
Customized
template

7. Adjust slide elements as necessary, including resizing and repositioning the subtitle text placeholder.

8. Create a handout header and footer: Include the date, your name as the header, the page number, and *[your initials]*11-25 as the footer.

9. Save the presentation as *[your initials]*11-25 in your Lesson 11 folder.

10. Close the presentation and submit your work.

Exercise 11-26 ◆ Challenge Yourself

Apply a design theme, and then modify it for a new theme with customized handouts.

1. Open the file **Wellness**, and apply the Oriel design theme.

2. Choose the Flow theme color, and change the theme font to Cooper Black for headings and Arial for the body.

3. Right-click the background, and choose Format Background. Choose Gradient fill; then choose the preset color Sapphire. Change the Type to Linear and the Direction to Linear Left, and apply these changes to all slides.

4. Change placeholder treatments to fit in with the new background. On the Slide Master first layout, make the following changes:

   a. Delete the circle on the lower right behind the slide number placeholder.

   b. Change the title placeholder text to white and 40 points. Apply the Text Effect of Circle bevel.

   c. Change the bulleted text to white and bold. Move the placeholder down slightly.

5. On the Title Slide layout, make the following changes:

   a. Delete the circles on the left, and move the slide number placeholder to the lower left.

   b. Increase the size of the title placeholder to 54 points, and move it up slightly. Apply the Text Effect of Circle bevel.

   c. Increase the size of the subtitle placeholder to 32 points, and make the color white.

   d. Search for a picture image using the word "fitness," and insert it to the left of the title. Apply the Picture Style of Rotated White.

   e. Move the title and subtitle placeholders to the right slightly to leave room for the rotated image.

6. From the View tab, in the Presentation Views group, click the Handout Master button ▦ and make these changes:

   a. Adjust the header and footer placeholders by reducing their height.

   b. Move the header placeholder down to the bottom of the page, above the footer.

   c. Move the date down to the bottom of the page, above the page number.

   d. Add a rectangle across the top of the page, and apply a gradient fill to match the one used in the presentation, Sapphire. Change the gradient to Linear Down because this direction works better for this shape.

   e. Add WordArt, and choose a WordArt style with a white fill. Key the text **Wellness Program**, and position it on top of the blue shape.

7. Close the Slide Master view.

8. Check each of the slides to be sure that slide 1 uses the Title Slide layout and the other slides use the Title and Content layout.

9. Create a handout header and footer: Include the date, your name as the header, the page number, and *[your initials]*11-26 as the footer.

10. Save the presentation as *[your initials]*11-26 in your Lesson 11 folder.

11. Close the presentation and submit your work.

On Your Own

In these exercises you work on your own, as you would in a real-life work environment. Use the skills you've learned to accomplish the task—and be creative.

Exercise 11-27

Open the file **Fitness**. Change the design theme and graphics. Use any tools you have learned about up to this point to create a unique design theme expressing your own taste, but remember to keep a uniform look throughout that harmonizes with the presentation's subject matter. Customize the handout master to blend with your template design. Save the presentation as *[your initials]*11-27. Close the presentation and submit your work.

Exercise 11-28

Create a new design theme, and use your own creativity to make it interesting and attractive. You can develop a design that would be suitable for a wide range of topics or a design appropriate for a specific topic, depending on the graphics you choose to use. Be sure to customize the Slide Master Title Slide layout and Content Slide layout so that you have two background variations that blend together. Key text on at least two slides so that your placeholder positioning is evident. Customize the handout master to blend with your template design. Save the template as *[your initials]*11-28. Close the presentation and submit your work.

Exercise 11-29

Search the Web for information on your favorite music group or singer. Imagine that you are the public relations manager for this group or singer and will be presenting this information to potential venues that are interested in hiring performers. Condense the information into major points, and use these points to create a presentation of at least six slides. Using the tools you learned about in this lesson and in previous lessons, create a custom theme and format your presentation attractively and in keeping with your topic. Save the presentation as *[your initials]*11-29. Customize the handout master to blend with your theme. Close the presentation and submit your work.

Unit 3 Applications

Unit Application 3-1

Work with WordArt effects; modify illustrations to group and ungroup; apply gradient fills; and align, rotate, and flip.

1. Open the file **Franchise4**.

2. On slide 1, select the title text, and apply these effects:

   a. Change the font to Arial Black, 48 points.

   b. Choose the WordArt style Gradient Fill - Light Yellow, Accent 1 (column 4, row 3).

   c. Change the WordArt gradient fill to the preset color Fire, Type Linear, Direction Linear Down, and Angle 90°.

   d. Change the text outline to 1½ pt, Red, Background 2, Darker 50%.

   e. Apply the shadow Offset Bottom, and change the shadow options to Black, Background 1 with no transparency.

   f. Move the text up to the top of the yellow rectangle, and keep it centered.

3. For the subtitle placeholder, key **Good 4 U**. Remove the shadow, and change the color to Black, Background 1. Move the placeholder to the bottom of the yellow rectangle.

4. Insert two new slides with the Title and Content layout. Select the title placeholder, and apply text effects with the same settings as those for the title on slide 1. Reduce the font size to 40 points, and adjust the WordArt shadow settings to match slide 1 if necessary.

5. Key this text for slides 2 and 3:

   Advantages

   - **Fast-growing market**
   - **Excellent income potential**
   - **Expert training and support**

   Objectives

   - **Help people achieve a healthy lifestyle**
   - **Help you grow a healthy business**

6. On slide 1, ungroup and convert the picture of the knife, fork, and spoon to Microsoft Office objects. Ungroup the objects again; then delete all the parts that make up the spoon. Delete the transparent rectangle that is behind the objects.

7. Arrange the remaining knife and fork parts as follows:

   a. Select all the parts of the knife, and group them; then select all the fork parts, and group them as a second group.

   b. Rotate the fork to the right and the knife to the left.

   c. Align the knife and fork middles and centers relative to each other; then group them to form one object.

   d. Position the knife and fork in the middle of the yellow rectangle.

   e. Increase the subtitle placeholder size so that it fits on one line, and move it up slightly, as shown in Figure U3-1.

Figure U3-1
Completed title slide

8. Review each slide to be sure all elements are positioned effectively.

9. Change the grayscale settings for all three WordArt objects to Light Grayscale.

10. Check spelling in the presentation.

11. Create a handout header and footer: Include the date, your name, and the page number as the header and *[your initials]*U3-1 as the footer.

12. Create a new folder for Unit 3 applications. Save the presentation with the file name *[your initials]*U3-1 in this folder.

13. View the presentation as a slide show.

14. Submit your work.

Unit Application 3-2

Work with effects, modify an illustration, align and group objects, and modify a Slide Master layout.

1. Open the file **Training**.

2. On slide 1, select the illustration, and change its width to 2.6 inches. Make these changes:

a. Ungroup the illustration until handles appear on all the shapes in the image.

b. Select just the people at the bottom, and drag them away from the rest of the image. Delete all other parts of the image, keeping only the people.

c. Duplicate the people three times, and distribute the four images horizontally and align the bottom of the images relative to the slide. Group the images, and move the group about 0.5 inch from the bottom of the slide.

3. Move the subtitle near the top of the slide, and make the text bold. Resize the placeholder to 10 inches wide, and apply a Black, Background 1 fill.

4. Make the following changes to the title text:

a. Change the font to 60 points. Make the placeholder 9 inches wide and 3 inches high.

b. Apply the WordArt Quick Style Fill - Red, Accent 2, Matte Bevel (column 3, row 6). Change the text fill color to Orange, Accent 1 (column 5, row 1).

c. From Text Effects choose Transform; then apply the Deflate Bottom shape.

5. Horizontally center all objects on the slide. Refer to Figure U3-2 for the final arrangement of the slide.

Figure U3-2
Object placement
guide

6. Copy the group of people, and then view the slide master. Make these changes to the Title and Content layout:

a. Paste the people in the same position, near the bottom of the slide.

b. Select the title placeholder, and apply the same WordArt style: Fill - Red, Accent 2, Matte Bevel. Change the text fill color to Orange, Accent 1.

c. Close the Slide Master view.

7. On slide 2, select the SmartArt, and move it up for even spacing. Apply the SmartArt style Polished.

8. On slide 3, select the table, and apply the Circle Cell Bevel effect.

9. Check spelling in the presentation.

10. Create a handout header and footer: Include the date, your name, and the page number as the header and *[your initials]*U3-2 as the footer.

11. Save the presentation as *[your initials]*U3-2 in your Unit 3 Applications folder.

12. Submit your work.

Unit Application 3-3

Customize a design theme using masters, use tabs, insert an audio clip, and add animations and transitions.

1. Open the file **JobFair**. Change the color theme to Verve. Customize the theme colors with these changes:
   a. *Text/Background - Dark 2:* Standard Dark Blue.
   b. *Text/Background - Light 1:* White.
   c. *Accent 4:* Standard Light Green.

2. On the first slide master, make these changes:
   a. Increase all text in the title placeholder and the body text placeholder by one increment.
   b. Change the font for all text to Arial Narrow, and make all text bold.
   c. Select the title placeholder, and use Change Case to choose Capitalize Each Word.
   d. Change the first-level bullet to a slightly larger Wingdings 2 round bullet, and make the color Lime - Accent 4.

3. On the Slide Master Title Slide layout, increase the title placeholder text to 60 points and the subtitle placeholder text to 40 points.

4. Close the Slide Master view.

5. On slide 1, reset the layout. Resize the logo to make it slightly smaller; then adjust its position to align with the other text.

6. On slide 2, replace the text "waiters and waitresses" with **servers**.

7. After slide 2, insert a new slide with the Title Only layout. Key the title **Salary Ranges**, and insert a text box to create a tabbed table. Use a decimal tab for the wage and a right-aligned tab for the last item. Key the following text:

Wait staff	$8.25	plus tips
Assistant chefs	$15.50	to start
Experienced chefs	$19.00	and up

8. Size and position the text box so that it is more balanced. Apply a Gray-25%, Background 2 fill and a Dark Blue, Text 2 outline with a 3 pt weight.

9. To the table, apply the Entrance animation effect Fade, making it start on click.

10. On slide 1, select the title; apply the Entrance animation effect Fly In, and choose the effect option From Bottom Left. Change the Start to With Previous and the Duration to 01:00.

11. Use the Animation Painter to apply the same treatment to the word "at" and the logo.

12. For the second and third objects, change the Start to After Previous so that the title enters first and the logo last.

13. Insert a clip art audio of music on slide 1, and reorder it to be at the top of the list on the Animation pane. On the Audio Tools Playback tab, change Start to Play across slides. Select Hide During Show, Loop until Stopped, and Rewind after Playing.

14. On slide 4, change the slide layout to Title Slide.

15. Still working on slide 4, search for a picture of a server, and insert it. Apply the Metal Frame picture effect.

16. Apply the Wipe slide transition effect to all the slides in the presentation, using the From Left effect option and No Sound.

17. Run the slide show to test the slides' timing and animation effects.

18. Customize the handout master by deleting the page number placeholder and keying the text **Job Fair Presentation** in the footer placeholder. Resize the footer placeholder, and center it horizontally; center-align the footer text, and change the font to Arial Narrow, 18 points. Move the placeholder up slightly. Close the Slide Master view.

19. Create a handout header and footer: Include the date, your name, and the text *[your initials]*U3-3 as the header. The footer text was already entered on the master. Delete the check beside page number.

20. Save the presentation as *[your initials]*U3-3 in your Unit 3 Applications folder.

21. Submit your work.

Unit Application 3-4 ◆ Using the Internet

Add an image to a slide master, apply custom animation, add music or sound effects, add 3-D effects, and create action buttons.

Imagine you are a travel agent planning a trip for a client to a vacation destination such as Orlando, Florida; San Diego, California; Billings, Montana; Williamsburg, Virginia; or some other location. Use the Internet to gather information about places to visit, unique restaurants, accommodations, and any other information that would be helpful to your client.

Use the information you gathered to create a presentation. Select a design theme, and create a new theme color scheme that complements your material. Add an image that relates to the presentation on the slide master, and apply picture effects as well as an artistic effect. Include at least six slides. Include text and object animations and audio effects where appropriate.

Insert an appropriate YouTube video about the destination, if possible. Create a slide that lists the title of each slide presenting a change of topic, and create an action button to each of those slides. Include a "Home" action button on the Slide Master Title and Content layout so that each slide will have a link back to the original slide. Check spelling, and review all the slides in Grayscale view, making grayscale adjustments if needed.

In the slide footer, include the text **Prepared by**, followed by your name. Include the slide number on all slides but not the date. In the handout footer, include the completed file name *[your initials]*U3-4. In the handout header, key **Presented to**, and then identify to whom you would be giving this presentation. Include in the handout the date you would be delivering the presentation.

Save the presentation as *[your initials]*U3-4 in your Unit 3 Applications folder. Practice delivering the presentation. Submit your work.

Unit 4

DEVELOPMENT AND DISTRIBUTION

Integrating with Other Programs

OBJECTIVES *After completing this lesson, you will be able to:*

1. Use content from other sources.

2. Create screenshots and pictures.

3. Work with multiple open presentations.

4. Collaborate with others.

5. Use language tools.

Estimated Time: 1½ hours

The illustrations or other content you need for a presentation may be from other Microsoft applications; therefore, PowerPoint can integrate content from other sources, such as outlines, images, slides, and worksheets. Another application window can be displayed within a presentation, too, and artwork developed in PowerPoint can be used in other applications.

Working with multiple presentations can make development more efficient as you integrate content. You can collaborate with other people by having them insert comments within your presentation file. All the techniques explained in this lesson can help you be more productive.

Roy Olafsen is working with the marketing department to develop poster ideas for a promotional campaign to increase public awareness of Good 4 U events. In this lesson, you will create images and integrate content from other applications to help complete his presentation.

Using Content from Other Sources

PowerPoint is very user-friendly when you need to integrate content from other Office applications. You can create slides from Word content, display other documents, and link to other applications or Web sites.

Exercise 12-1 IMPORT AN OUTLINE FROM WORD

When writing the text for a presentation, some people prefer to develop their outline using a word-processing program, such as Microsoft Word, and then import the outline file into PowerPoint to create slides instead of keying in PowerPoint.

To import a Word outline into PowerPoint, use one of these methods:

- From the File tab, choose Open to open the outline file from within PowerPoint.

- From the Home tab, in the Slides group, click the down arrow on the New Slide button , and choose Slides from Outline.

1. From the PowerPoint File tab, choose Open.

2. Navigate to the Lesson 12 student data files. Click the Files of type list box (All PowerPoint Presentations), and choose All Files.

3. Notice that **Poster Ideas.docx** has a Word file icon 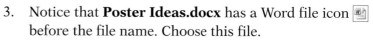 before the file name. Choose this file.

> **NOTE**
>
> In this lesson, file names other than PowerPoint will be shown with their extension to indicate the file type.

4. Click Open. PowerPoint interprets the structure of your outline and creates new slides, creating titles from the Word level 1 headings and body text from the level 2 and level 3 headings. All the slides use the Title and Text layout.

5. Change the layout of the new slide 1, "Poster Ideas," to the Title Slide layout.

6. Apply the design theme Civic, and use the color theme Median.

Exercise 12-2 INSERT A MICROSOFT WORD DOCUMENT

You can insert documents from other Office applications as objects. For example, if you have created a flyer or other document in Word, you can insert it as an object into PowerPoint. However, a full-page document displayed on a PowerPoint slide is usually too small to be readable during a presentation. So use this technique when you need to speak in general terms about the document and you don't need to feature detailed information.

1. Move to slide 4.

2. From the Insert tab, in the Text group, click the Object button 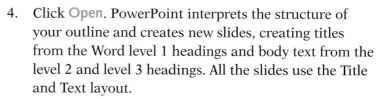.

3. In the Insert Object dialog box, choose the Create from File option.

4. Click the Browse button ⌷ Browse... ⌷, navigate to your student files for Lesson 12, and choose **July4.docx**, as shown in Figure 12-1.

5. Click OK.

Figure 12-1
Insert Object
dialog box

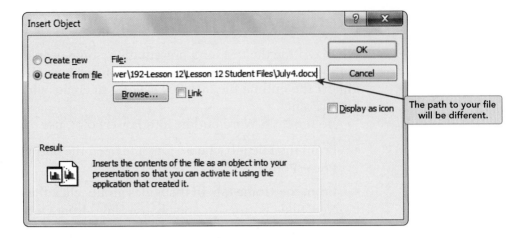

6. From the Insert Object dialog box, click OK again. The Fourth of July Celebration flyer is now inserted on slide 4.

7. With the flyer selected, from the Drawing Tools Format tab, in the Shape Styles group, click the Shape Outline button 🖊, and change the Weight to 1½ pt so that a line appears around the edge of the flyer to distinguish it from the slide background.

8. Resize or reposition the flyer as needed to match Figure 12-2.

Figure 12-2
Flyer displayed on
a slide

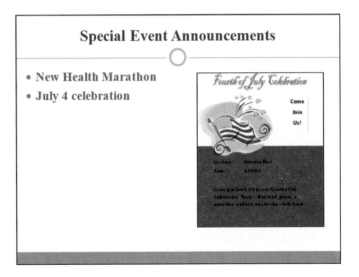

9. Double-click the flyer. Notice that a Word screen opens from which you can edit the file.

10. Change the time to **4:30 PM**; then press ⎋Esc to return to PowerPoint.

Exercise 12-3 REUSE SLIDES FROM A DIFFERENT PRESENTATION

Combining slides from multiple presentations is a common task in PowerPoint. For example, you could reuse a particular diagram or drawing from one presentation in another. The *Reuse Slides* command provides a quick way to integrate one or more slides from a different presentation into your current presentation.

Figure 12-3
The Reuse Slides
pane

1. Move to slide 1.

2. From the Home tab, in the Slides group, click the down arrow on the New Slide button, and choose Reuse Slides. The Reuse Slide pane opens.

3. Click the Browse button Browse ▾, and choose Browse File.

4. Navigate to your student files for Lesson 12, and choose the **Public Relations1** file.

5. Click Open. The slides that are in the public relations presentation are displayed in the Reuse Slides pane, as shown in Figure 12-3.

6. When you point to the slide thumbnail, the size temporarily increases so that you can read the slide title. Click the second slide in the list to insert it after the current slide.

7. Click the Close button ✕ on the Reuse Slides pane. Notice that the inserted slide took on the Slide Master formatting from the current presentation.

TIP

If you want to keep the formatting of the source presentation, check Keep source formatting at the bottom of the Reuse Slides pane.

Exercise 12-4 LINK AN EXCEL WORKSHEET

Another integration technique is to *link* files from other Office programs, such as Excel. When a file is *linked,* any changes that are made in the source document or the destination document are reflected in both documents.

Follow these steps to link to an Excel worksheet: Open the Excel worksheet, select the range you want to link, and click the Copy button. Within PowerPoint, from the Home tab, in the Clipboard group, click the down arrow on the Paste button, and choose Paste Special.

1. Open Excel, and navigate to your student files for Lesson 12.

2. Open the **Menu items by category.xlsx** file.

Figure 12-4
Selected range
in Excel

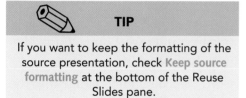

3. Select cells A1:B7 by clicking on the title "Menu Items by Category" and dragging the pointer down through row 7, as shown in Figure 12-4.

4. Working in Excel, from the Home tab, in the Clipboard group, click the Copy button.

5. Return to your PowerPoint file, and move to slide 3.

6. From the Home tab, in the Clipboard group, click the down arrow on the Paste button, and choose Paste Special below the icons.

7. From the Paste Special dialog box, choose Paste link and Microsoft Excel Worksheet Object, as shown in Figure 12-5.

Figure 12-5
Paste Special
dialog box

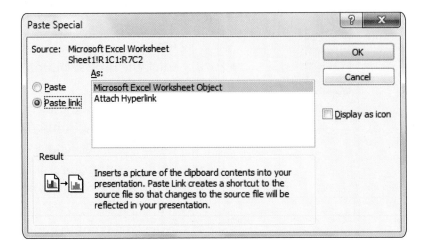

8. Click OK. PowerPoint inserts a small Excel worksheet into your presentation.

9. Double-click the worksheet in PowerPoint. Notice that doing so returns you to Excel to edit.

TIP

Because the Excel file is read only, when you close out of the PowerPoint file and reenter, you will receive a warning of a potential security concern about accessing linked files. Click Cancel to avoid updating the links. If you were working on your own files, you would want to save changes and update the links when entering and exiting the files.

TIP

If you would like the source file to open within the source application, create a hyperlink to the file.

10. In Excel, click the word "Snacks," and change it to the word **Salads**. In the taskbar, click the PowerPoint file to return to your presentation, and notice that the word has also been changed in the small worksheet. This happens because of the link between PowerPoint and Excel.

11. Close Excel without saving your changes.

12. In PowerPoint, select the table, and from the Drawing Tools Format tab change the width to 5 inches so that the text is easy to read. Reposition as necessary for a balanced appearance.

13. Create a Lesson 12 folder. Save the presentation as *[your initials]*12-4 in your new Lesson 12 folder.

Creating Screenshots and Pictures

PowerPoint provides many tools for creating original illustrations, pictures, and logos within the PowerPoint application.

While PowerPoint's illustration tools provide a wide array of ways to visually arrange your slide content, you can also use PowerPoint to create artwork and save it for other applications or to create files of individual slides.

Exercise 12-5   CREATE AND INSERT A SCREENSHOT

In some situations, such as a training session, it may be important to show an image of another application to discuss its features. For example, this book shows you images of what your screen should look like to help you understand the concept of the task you are completing. In other situations, you might need to show a Web page when you are presenting in a location that does not have Internet access.

PowerPoint's *Screenshot* command makes a capture of an entire window of any application, and you can insert this image into the current presentation. *Screen Clipping* allows you to click and drag to select a portion of a screen to capture. The Screenshot tool is available from the Insert tab, in the Images group.

TIP

In previous versions of Office, or in programs that do not contain the Screenshot feature, pressing Print Screen on your keyboard captures the entire screen and saves it to the Clipboard. Pressing Alt + Print Screen on your keyboard captures the active window only. Press Ctrl + V to paste the capture on the current slide.

NOTE

If you cannot locate an appropriate Web site, open **Fishy.jpg** from your student files and capture the image.

NOTE

The Screenshot command captures an entire window, while Screen Clipping allows you to choose what portion of the screen is captured.

1. Move to slide 4.

2. Open your Internet browser, and search for "fish hatchery" to find a Web site about this type of business.

3. Have your browser open with the first page of the Web site you will capture. Go to PowerPoint; then from the Insert tab, in the Images group, click the Screenshot button, and choose Screen Clipping.

4. Click and drag the mouse to select only the main content of the page, and then release the mouse button. Notice that the portion of the screen that you selected comes into PowerPoint.

5. If your selection area was not precise and you need to adjust the edges, from the Picture Tools Format tab, in the Size group, click the Crop button to remove excess areas.

6. Resize and position the Web page image as shown in Figure 12-6.

Figure 12-6
Screen clip of a
Web page

Vendor Profiles

- **Local organic farmers**
- **Herb farms**
- **Fish hatcheries**

FISHY, FISHY, FISHY

Welcome to Olney, IL Fish Hatchery!

We have several species of fish that are raised here at the hatchery. We are located in a small town in rural Illinois, and welcome visitors to the hatchery.

For details on how to order these wonderful fish, click the link on the left "How to Order".

Contact us for any questions you may have.

7. Now capture an image of just an active window by following these steps:

    a. Right-click the picture, and choose Format Picture from the shortcut menu.

    b. With the Format Picture dialog box open, from the Insert tab, in the Images group, click the Screenshot button [image]. Notice that the dialog box is in the list of available windows to capture.

    c. Click the dialog box from the list. This takes a screenshot of just the active window.

    d. Click Close on the dialog box, and notice that your image is inserted into the PowerPoint presentation. Note that you have a picture of only what was the current window, the Format Picture dialog box.

8. Click the Undo button [image] to remove this screen capture.

Exercise 12-6   DESIGN A LOGO AND SAVE AS A PICTURE

One example of artwork that you could create in PowerPoint for use in other programs is a logo. Logos are symbols of the organizations they stand for. Many of the presentations in this book include a Good 4 U logo. In this exercise you will create a Good 4 U logo that is a little different by combining text with an image.

Olafsen has requested that you save the logo in different file formats so that he can compare the quality of each one.

1. Move to slide 1. As you create the parts of the logo, position them randomly across the top of the slide; then arrange all the parts when they are complete.

2. Create the logo text using three different WordArt objects with different effects from the WordArt gallery as follows:

    Good   Fill - Olive Green, Accent 3, Powder Bevel (column 4, row 5).
    4   Fill - White, Background 1, Metal Bevel (column 2, row 5).
    U   Fill - Olive Green, Accent 3, Powder Bevel (column 4, row 5). Change the text fill color to Olive Green, Accent 3, Darker 50% (column 7, row 6).

3. Insert the **Apple2.jpg** picture from your student files.

4. From the Picture Tools Format tab, make these adjustments to the apple image:

    a. In the Adjust group, click the Remove Background button [image]. Increase the selection area so the stem at the top of the apple and the bottom of the apple is included. From the Background Removal tab, click the Mark Areas to Keep button [image] and click the blank area of the apple until the color reappears. Click the Keep Changes button [image].

    b. Resize the apple to a width of 2.3 inches.

    c. Right-click the apple, and choose Send to Back to put the apple behind the WordArt text.

Figure 12-7
Create a logo

5. Rearrange the WordArt text and the apple as shown in Figure 12-7.

6. Select the text "Good 4 U" and the apple, and group them to form one object.

7. Save this grouped object in three different graphic file types so that you can compare the results of using different graphic file types. Each different format can be used in other Microsoft applications or even in designing a Web site.

   a. Right-click the grouped object, and choose Save as Picture from the shortcut menu.

   b. In the Save as type list box, select JPEG File Interchange Format.

   c. Name the picture **Logo1**, and save it in your Lesson 12 folder. It will have the file extension **.jpg**.

   d. Repeat this process using the file name **Logo2** and the Save as type GIF Graphics Interchange Format. The picture will have the file extension **.gif**.

   e. Repeat this process using the file name **Logo3** and the Save as type PNG Portable Network Graphics Format. The picture will have the file extension **.png**.

TIP

You can save other objects such as SmartArt graphics using this process.

8. After slide 1, insert a new slide with a Title and Content layout. Key the title **Graphic Formats Compared** and delete the content placeholder.

9. From the Insert tab, in the Images group, click the Picture button 🖾 to insert each of these logos so that you can examine the quality of each image on the same slide. Position them on the slide as shown in Figure 12-8; then click the Slide Show button 🖳 so that you can compare them in a larger size while considering the comments below. This slide will show Olafsen the difference between each file type.

   a. **Logo1.jpg.** This image has excellent photo quality because the JPEG file format is well suited for photographs. However, a white background is automatically added, so this format will work best when your slide background is white.

   b. **Logo2.gif.** This image preserves the transparent areas of the logo, but the apple and text look "grainy" and the edges of the letters are not smooth. The GIF format works best for simple line art and drawings with solid colors. It typically does not work well for photographs.

   c. **Logo3.png.** This image preserves the transparent areas of the logo, and the image quality is similar to that of the **.jpg** image. The PNG format works well when you want to create transparent areas of a photograph. However, the file size of this image is much larger than that of the other two.

Figure 12-8
Graphic formats
compared

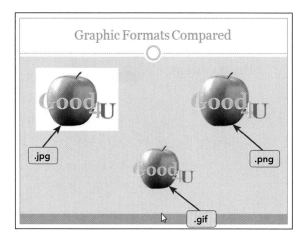

Exercise 12-7   SAVE A SLIDE AS A PICTURE

Slides can be saved as pictures and inserted into other presentations or documents. For example, you might need to refer to slide content for training materials or reports. This capability can be especially helpful if you need to show a SmartArt graphic or other artwork you have created.

1.   Move to slide 1.

2.   From the File tab, choose Save As.

3.   From the Save As dialog box, select your Lesson 12 folder. Name the file as **Slide1**.

4.   In the Save as type list box, select JPEG File Interchange Format; then click Save.

5.   In the message box that appears, as shown in Figure 12-9, click Current Slide Only. The slide is now saved as a picture that can be inserted.

Figure 12-9
Save current slide
only

6.   To test this process of saving a slide, create a new slide with a blank layout after slide 6.

7.   From the Insert tab, in the Images group, click the Picture button ⬛; then locate your Lesson 12 folder, and select the image **Slide1**. Click Insert. The complete slide will appear.

8.   Resize the image just as you would any other illustration; make the width 5 inches, and center the image.

9.   Save the presentation as *[your initials]*12-7 in your Lesson 12 folder.

Working with Multiple Open Presentations

Information from an existing presentation can be added to a new presentation by copying from one presentation and pasting in another. With two presentations open, you can layer them or you can arrange them in small sizes so that you can see more than one presentation at the same time. These different views allow you to more easily work with multiple files.

Exercise 12-8   USE CASCADE TO LAYER MULTIPLE PRESENTATION WINDOWS

The *Cascade* command allows you to display open presentations in separate windows that can be resized. If you click the window title bar, you can drag the window to reposition it on your screen.

1. Still working in PowerPoint, navigate to your student files for Lesson 12, and open the file **Public Relations2**. You should now have two presentations open.

2. In either presentation, from the View tab, in the Window group, click the Cascade button ⊞. Notice how the two presentations are layered, with the names of the presentations viewable on the title bars, as shown in Figure 12-10.

Figure 12-10
Presentations layered using Cascade

3. The active presentation window is on top. To switch windows, from the View tab, in the Window group, click the Switch Windows button ⊞ and choose the other presentation name from the list that appears. You can also switch between presentations by clicking the separate presentation windows or using the taskbar.

Exercise 12-9 USE ARRANGE ALL TO SEE MULTIPLE PRESENTATION WINDOWS

The *Arrange All* command allows you to view multiple files at the same time. This is an excellent feature to use when copying and pasting from one presentation to another because the separate windows for each presentation are displayed side by side on the screen.

1. In either presentation, from the View tab, in the Window group, click the Arrange All button ▤.

2. The presentations are now side by side, making it easy to compare and change both presentations, as shown in Figure 12-11. Your presentations may be reversed.

Figure 12-11
Presentations displayed using Arrange All

Exercise 12-10 COPY AND PASTE BETWEEN PRESENTATIONS

You have used Copy and Paste for many of the individual presentations you have completed. In this exercise you will copy and paste between two presentations.

1. In the file **Public Relations2**, select slide 2 in the Slides tab.

2. From the Home tab, in the Clipboard group, click the Copy button ▣.

3. Click anywhere in the presentation *[your initials]*12-7 to make it active, and click after slide 7. Notice how convenient it is to work with the two presentations using the Arrange All command.

4. From the Home tab, in the Clipboard group, click the Paste button ▣. The slide takes on the characteristics of the design theme of the presentation that you pasted it into, as shown in Figure 12-12.

Figure 12-12
Pasted slide

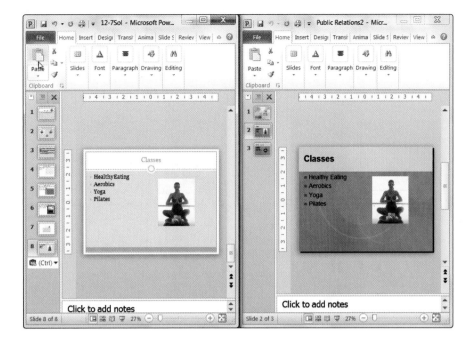

5. In the file **Public Relations2**, select slide 3 in the Slides tab.

6. From the Home tab, in the Clipboard group, click the Copy button.

7. Return to the presentation *[your initials]***12-7**, and click after slide 8.

8. From the Home tab, in the Clipboard group, click the Paste button.

Exercise 12-11 USE FORMAT PAINTER TO COPY FORMATTING BETWEEN PRESENTATIONS

The Format Painter can be used to copy formatting from slides in one presentation to slides in another presentation. It is easiest to complete this task if the presentations are arranged, using Arrange All, so that you can see multiple presentations.

1. In the file **Public Relations2**, select slide 1 in the Slides tab.

2. From the Home tab, in the Clipboard group, click the Format Painter button.

3. In the presentation *[your initials]***12-7**, click slide 1 in the Slides tab to make this presentation active; then click slide 1 again to apply the formatting from the other presentation.

4. In the file **Public Relations2**, select slide 2 in the Slides tab.

5. From the Home tab, in the Clipboard group, double-click the Format Painter button so that the Format Painter remains on.

6. In the presentation *[your initials]***12-7**, click slide 2 to make the presentation active; then click again to apply the formatting. Continue clicking on the remaining slides to apply the formatting from the other presentation, as shown in Figure 12-13.

7. Click the Format Painter button to turn off the Format Painter.

Figure 12-13
Using Format Painter
to format slide
backgrounds

8. Close the file **Public Relations2** without saving any changes, and maximize the screen for the open presentation.

9. Select all slides in the Slides tab, and from the Home tab, in the Slides group, click the Reset button to change all text to black with the different font that is used in this design theme.

10. Reposition the logo on slide 1 so that it is centered on the slide and "resting" on the green rectangle. Reposition any other graphics as needed after the theme and text changes.

11. Scroll through the presentation, and notice that the Word flyer that was inserted on slide 6 has changed to match the theme colors. The top of the flyer now looks transparent. Make a white rectangle with no outline, and send it to the back so that the rectangle is behind the flyer. Adjust the width of the flyer and that of the rectangle to the exact same size. Click the Slide Show button to test your alignment on the full screen.

12. Create another rectangle to cover the flyer. Change the fill color to no fill and the outline to black at 6 points. Adjust the edges of this rectangle to fit the flyer and act as a border covering any uneven edges where the flyer and white rectangle meet. When you are satisfied that the appearance is correct, group these three objects.

13. On slide 8, add a black, 6-point picture border to match the flyer on slide 6.

14. Save the presentation as *[your initials]*12-11 in your Lesson 12 folder.

Collaborating with Others

Before delivering a presentation, you might want others to review it and perhaps contribute to it. PowerPoint makes this an easy and convenient task. The reviewer can make comments on the presentations for you to view and consider. If you have access to available network space, PowerPoint can create a Document Workspace for sharing files with others. This feature may not be available in computer classrooms.

Exercise 12-12 INSERT AND EDIT COMMENTS IN A PRESENTATION

Comments are similar to the comments you add when working with a word-processing program. When the Show Markup button 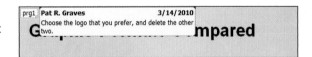 is active, comments are indicated on the slide by a *comment marker,* a small colored rectangle in the upper left corner of a slide. You might use this feature to make notes to yourself as you fine-tune a presentation, or you might ask others to review the presentation and use this feature so that you can obtain their feedback as you are developing the presentation.

Comments are identified by the reviewer's initials. You can read the comment by double-clicking the comment marker, but comments will not print on the slides or display during a slide show.

1. Move to slide 2.

2. From the Review tab, in the Comments group, click the New Comment button . A colored box appears in which you can key a comment.

3. Key the following in the comment box: **Please check out these logos and let me know which you prefer**.

4. Click outside the comment box to close it. Notice the comment marker (the small colored box in the upper left corner) with the reviewer's initials and the number 1, indicating the first comment inserted by this reviewer.

5. To edit the comment you keyed, double-click the comment marker and then edit the comment to read: **Choose the logo that you prefer, and delete the other two.**

6. The complete comment is shown in Figure 12-14.

Figure 12-14
Inserting a comment

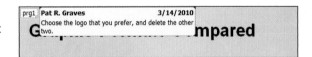

7. From the Review tab, in the Comments group, click the Show Markup button , and notice that the comment marker disappears. This feature can be used so that others do not see the comments in the presentation. Click the Show Markup button again to make the comment marker appear.

8. Move to slide 3; then click the New Comment button , and key the following comment: **This slide is great since many people do not understand public relations.**

9. Click anywhere on slide 3. On the Review tab, in the Comments group, click the Delete button , and choose Delete All Markup on the Current Slide.

Exercise 12-13   PRINT SLIDE COMMENTS

As you saw in Exercise 12-12, *Show Markup* enables you to see the comments within a presentation and you can turn off this feature so that the comments do not display on the slide. However, you may need a printed copy of all comments that have been made. For printing, PowerPoint organizes the comments together on a page following your last presentation slide. For example, you can print handouts showing the comment markers and a sheet listing the related slide comments.

1. Create a handout header and footer: Include the date, your name as the header, the page number, and *[your initials]*12-13 as the footer.

2. Save the presentation as *[your initials]*12-13 in your Lesson 12 folder.

3. From the File tab, choose Print to open Print Backstage View.

4. Choose the following options: handouts, nine slides per page horizontal, grayscale, scale to fit paper, and framed.

5. In the handout list, ensure that there is a check beside Print Comments and Ink Markup.

6. Click the next arrow to view page 2 of the handouts. Here you can see the comments, as shown in Figure 12-15. Adjust the scroll bars and zoom slider as needed to see the comments.

Figure 12-15
Printing slide comments

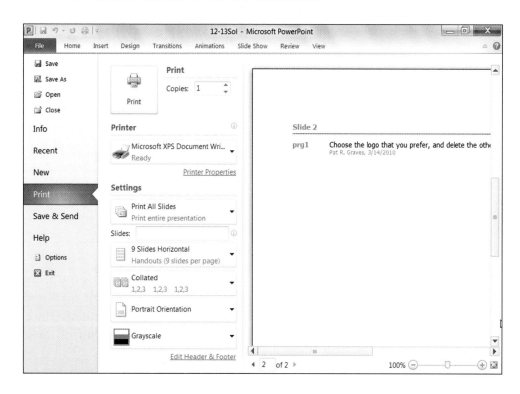

7. Click Print.

Using Language Tools

NOTE

To use a different input keyboard, you must install the corresponding language pack in your operating system.

PowerPoint has language tools that provide easy access for changing the proofing language. Changing the proofing language allows you to key in a different language and use the corresponding language file to check spelling and grammar.

Exercise 12-14 CHANGE THE PROOFING LANGUAGE FOR A TEXT BOX

The proofing language in PowerPoint controls which language file will be used during a spelling and grammar check.

1. Insert a slide after slide 9, using the Title and Content layout.
2. Click in the title text box on slide 10. From the Review tab, in the Language group, click the Language button 🌐, and choose Set Proofing Language. From the list, choose Spanish (United States), and click OK.
3. Key **Thank You**. Notice that the two words are marked as spelling errors since they are not words in the Spanish (United States) language file dictionary.
4. Select "Thank You," and key **Gracias**. Notice that the marks are removed since this is a word found in the language file.

Exercise 12-15 TRANSLATE A WORD INTO A DIFFERENT LANGUAGE

The *Translate* command can convert a word or group of words to a different language. This feature is not meant to translate an entire presentation; if it is used for a large block of text, the translation should be checked for accuracy. In this exercise you will create a list of how to say "Thank You" in four different languages.

1. Still working on slide 10, click in the body placeholder and key **Thank You**.
2. From the Review tab, in the Language group, click the Translate button 🔤, and choose Choose Translation Language.
3. Click the drop-down arrow, choose French (France), and click OK.
4. From the Review tab, in the Language group, click the Translate button 🔤, and choose Mini Translator.
5. Move your mouse pointer over "Thank You," and the Bilingual Dictionary displays. Notice that the word beside "thank you" is "merci." This means that in French the word for "thank you" is "merci."

6. Create a second bullet, and key **Merci**.

7. Repeat steps 2 to 6 for German (Germany) and again for Italian (Italy).

8. Increase the font size of the bulleted items to 44 points.

9. To double-check the accuracy of the translation, select "Merci." From the Review tab, in the Language group, click the Translate button ⓐあ, and choose Translate Selected Text.

10. In the Research pane, translate from French (France) to English (U.S.). Notice that the translation of "merci" is "thank you." You have successfully translated the word.

11. Close the Research pane.

12. Update the handout header and footer to include *[your initials]***12-15** as the footer.

13. Save the presentation as *[your initials]***12-15** in your Lesson 12 folder. Close the presentation and submit your work.

Lesson 12   Summary

- Outlines can be created in Word and imported into PowerPoint as presentation slides by using the Slides from Outline command.

- A flyer or another Word document can be inserted into PowerPoint as a PowerPoint object using the Object button on the Insert tab.

- Slides from other presentations can be placed in a current presentation with the Reuse Slides command.

- When reusing slides, you can choose whether to keep the source formatting or use the current slide formatting.

- Files from other Microsoft applications can be linked using the Paste Special feature. When either the source document or the destination document is edited, both documents are changed.

- Screenshots can be taken of any application and inserted in a presentation.

- Objects in PowerPoint can be saved as pictures to be inserted into other applications or used at a later date. Some examples include logos, WordArt, SmartArt graphics, and slides.

- From the View tab, the Window options make working with multiple open presentations more convenient because you can see more than one presentation at the same time.

- Use the Cascade button to layer presentation windows.

- Use the Arrange All button to view presentations side by side.

- Use Copy and Paste to share information between multiple open presentations, and use the Format Painter to copy formatting between presentations.

- On the Review tab, the Comments feature enables you to communicate with others who are reviewing your presentation and to receive feedback from them. Comments can be edited, deleted, shown or hidden, and printed to make collaborating with others easy.
- Use the Language command to translate a word or group of words to another language.

LESSON 12		Command Summary	
Feature	**Button**	**Ribbon**	**Keyboard**
Arrange presentation windows		View tab, Window group, Arrange All	
Capture a full screen		Insert tab, Images group, Screenshot	Print Screen
Cascade presentation windows		View tab, Window group, Cascade	
Change proofing language		Review tab, Language group, Language, Set Proofing Language	
Import a Word outline		File tab and Open; or Home tab, Slides group, New slide down arrow, Slides from Outline	
Insert a document		Insert tab, Text group, Object	
Insert comments		Review tab, Comments group, New Comment	
Link to a document		Home tab, Clipboard group, Paste down arrow, Paste Special	
Reuse slides		Home tab, Slides group, New Slide down arrow, Reuse Slides	
Save a slide as a picture		File tab, Save As, Save as type	
Switch windows		View tab, Window group, Switch Windows	
Translate a word		Review tab, Language group, Translate	

Concepts Review

True/False Questions

Each of the following statements is either true or false. Indicate your choice by circling T or F.

T F 1. A Word outline can be imported into PowerPoint as a presentation.

T F 2. Objects in PowerPoint can be linked to Microsoft Office files.

T F 3. PowerPoint slides cannot be reused in different presentations.

T F 4. Comments can be viewed in a presentation or be hidden.

T F 5. Comments can be printed on a sheet following the last presentation slide.

T F 6. Screenshots of Web pages or other applications can be inserted in PowerPoint.

T F 7. Arrange All makes it convenient to work with multiple open presentations.

T F 8. Original illustrations cannot be saved as images within PowerPoint.

Short Answer Questions

Write the correct answer in the space provided.

1. How do you insert a Microsoft Word document into a presentation?

2. What does it mean to link to an Excel worksheet?

3. How do you capture the active window for a screen capture?

4. How do you delete a comment?

5. How do you print reviewer comments?

6. What are the steps for saving a created logo as a picture?

7. How can you copy formatting from one presentation to another?

_____

8. How can you get a slide from one presentation into another?

_____

Critical Thinking

Answer these questions on a separate page. Support your answers with examples from your own experience, if possible.

1. Think about the type of applications in which you could use artwork or drawings. Now that you know how to save objects as pictures, list one way you might use the Save as Picture feature.

2. Discuss ways that screenshots can be used to enhance training materials.

Skills Review

Exercise 12-16

Import an outline from Word, and reuse slides.

1. Open PowerPoint, and start a new, blank presentation.

2. Import an outline from Word following these steps:
   a. From the File tab, choose Open.
   b. Choose All Files, navigate to your student files for Lesson 12, and choose **Catering Outline.docx**; then click Open.
   c. Change the layout for the new slide 1 to a title slide.

3. Choose the Hardcover design theme and Concourse color theme for the presentation.

4. Reuse slides from another presentation by following these steps:
   a. Click after slide 4 in the presentation.
   b. From the Home tab, in the Slides group, click the down arrow on the New Slide button.
   c. Choose Reuse Slides.
   d. From the Reuse Slides pane, choose Browse and Browse File.
   e. Navigate to your student files for Lesson 12, choose **Catering Services**, and click Open.
   f. Click slide 2 to add it to the current presentation.
   g. Close the Reuse Slides pane.
   h. Working in the Slides and Outline pane, select all slides.
   i. From the Home tab, in the Slides group, click the Reset button to reset the layouts to the new theme.

5. Create a handout header and footer: Include the date, your name as the header, the page number, and *[your initials]*12-16 as the footer.

6. Save the presentation as *[your initials]*12-16 in your Lesson 12 folder.

7. Close the presentation and submit your work.

Exercise 12-17

Insert a Word document, insert a Screenshot, use Arrange All to see multiple presentation windows, and copy formatting from one presentation to another.

1. Open the file **One Stop**.

2. Move to slide 5.

3. Insert a Microsoft Word document by following these steps:

   a. Delete the content placeholder on the right.

   b. From the Insert tab, in the Text group, click the Object button 📖.

   c. Choose Create from File.

   d. Click Browse; then navigate to your student files.

   e. Select **Cater Wedding.docx**; then click OK to close the Browse dialog box. Click OK to close the Insert Object dialog box.

   f. The document is inserted into the presentation. Resize to an appropriate size, and position as needed, as shown in Figure 12-16. From the Drawing Tools Format tab, in the Shape Styles group, click the Shape Outline button 🖊, and choose the weight of 3 points in Black, Text 1. This outline will define the flyer, since white is used on both the flyer and the slide background.

Figure 12-16
Slide with flyer

4. Insert a slide after slide 5 using the Title and Content layout.

   a. Key the title text **Other Services**.

   b. Key the body text **Good 4 U computer operators can design a PowerPoint presentation including pictures of you and your spouse growing up through the years.**

   c. Press Esc twice to turn off the body text selection.

5. Insert a screenshot by following these steps:

   a. Open the file **Sample Presentation**, and display slide 1.

   b. Move back to slide 6 in the **One Stop** presentation. From the Insert tab, in the Images group, click the Screenshot button 🖼️; from the available windows, choose the presentation with slide 1 displayed.

   c. Crop the screen capture so that only the slide is showing. After cropping, click off the image to remove the excess cropped areas.

   d. The image of slide 1 may be so large that you cannot see the corner sizing handles to make it smaller. Set the height to about 2 inches.

   e. Position this image under the text on the lower portion of the slide.

   f. Add a 3-point picture border in Black, Text 1.

6. Working in **One Stop**, from the View tab, in the Window group, click the Arrange All button 🗗.

7. With the presentations side by side, copy the formatting from **Sample Presentation** to **One Stop** by following these steps:

   a. On the **Sample Presentation** Slides tab, select slide 1.

   b. From the Home tab, in the Clipboard group, click the Format Painter button 🖌️.

   c. On the **One Stop** Slides tab, click slide 1 twice to copy the formatting.

   d. Move to slide 2 in **Sample Presentation**, and double-click the Format Painter to keep it active.

   e. In the **One Stop** Slides tab, click slide 2 twice to copy the formatting, and then click each remaining slide to apply the same formatting.

   f. Close **Sample Presentation**.

   g. Check the position of objects on each slide and reset layouts. Resize, or reposition objects as necessary to fit with the new formatting.

8. On slide 6, select the inserted screen capture image; then use the Format Painter to apply the same border to the pictures on slides 2, 3, and 4.

9. Create a handout header and footer: Include the date, your name as the header, the page number, and *[your initials]*12-17 as the footer.

10. Save the presentation as *[your initials]*12-17 in your Lesson 12 folder. Close the presentation and submit your work.

Exercise 12-18

Link an Excel worksheet, use Cascade to layer multiple presentations, and copy and paste between presentations.

1. Open the file **Healthy Living**.

2. Open the file **Poster Ideas**.

3. Layer the two presentations by following these steps:

   a. Make the **Poster Ideas** file your active file.

   b. From the View tab, in the Window group, click the Cascade button ⊡.

4. Copy and paste between presentations by following these steps:

   a. Still working in the **Poster Ideas** file, select slide 6 on the Slides tab.

   b. From the Home tab, in the Clipboard group, click the Copy button ⊡.

   c. Click the title bar of the **Healthy Living** presentation to make it active.

   d. Click after slide 2 in the Slides tab, and press [Ctrl]+[V]. Notice that the slide is copied to the new location and changed to the destination design theme.

   e. Close the **Poster Ideas** PowerPoint presentation and maximize the **Healthy Living** window.

5. Insert a new slide after slide 3 using the Title Only layout. Key the title **Cost Analysis of the Classes**.

6. Link an Excel worksheet by following these steps:

   a. Open Excel; then navigate to your student files for Lesson 12, and open the Excel file **Cost for Classes.xlsx**.

   b. Select from A1:F8 by clicking in cell A1 and dragging the pointer through F8.

   c. Press [Ctrl]+[C] to copy.

   d. Move back to slide 4 in the **Healthy Living** presentation.

   e. From the Home tab, in the Clipboard group, click the down arrow on the Paste button ⊡, and choose Paste Special.

   f. Choose Paste Link.

   g. Choose Microsoft Excel Worksheet Object.

   h. Click OK.

   i. Enlarge and reposition the worksheet as needed to fit the slide.

   j. Double-click the worksheet to edit it. Increase the size of "Community Classes" to 18 points; then check the presentation slide to be sure the change appears there too.

   k. Close the Excel worksheet without saving.

7. Create a handout header and footer: Include the date, your name as the header, the page number, and *[your initials]*12-18 as the footer.

8. Save the presentation as *[your initials]*12-18 in your Lesson 12 folder. Close the presentation and submit your work.

Exercise 12-19

Save grouped objects as a picture, insert comments, print comments and markup, and edit language.

1. Open the file **Menu**, and select slide 1.

2. Create a logo for Good 4 U with a font size of 44 points using three different WordArt objects with different effects from the WordArt gallery as follows:

Good	Gradient Fill - Gray - 25%, Accent 1, Outline - White (column 4, row 4)
4	Fill - Black, Accent 4, Outer Shadow - Accent 4, Soft Edge Bevel (column 4, row 6)
U	Fill - Green, Accent 6, Warm Matte Bevel (column 2, row 6)

3. Insert a shape using a five-point star. For the Fill color, click Gradient and then choose More Gradients. For the Gradient fill, use the preset color Fire; for the Type, use Path. Click Close.

4. Position the star behind the WordArt. Resize and reposition the WordArt and shape to appear similar to Figure 12-17. Group these objects together, and position the group with even spacing below the subtitle.

5. Right-click the object, and choose Save as Picture; name the file **Logo-star**, and use the PNG format.

Figure 12-17
Logo

6. On slide 3, delete the "Chicken and Potato Salad" entrée. Insert your own idea of a healthy entrée in its place.

7. Insert a comment on slide 3 by following these instructions:

   a. From the Review tab, in the Comments group, click anywhere in the new entrée you inserted, and click the New Comment button 🖿.

   b. In the colored comment box, key **I removed the Chicken and Potato Salad entrée because it got poor reviews from the taste testers.**

   c. Click outside the comment box to close it.

   d. On slide 4, change "Rice Pudding" to **Julie's Cherry Jubilee Pudding.**

   e. Insert a comment explaining why you changed the name of the rice pudding dessert: **The rice pudding needed a jazzier name.**

8. Since papaya originated in Mexico, rename "Papaya Dessert" with a Spanish name. From the Review tab, in the Language group, click the Translate button 🔤, and choose Choose Translation Language. From the list, choose Spanish (International Sort).

9. From the Review tab, in the Language group, click the Translate button 🔤, and choose Mini Translator.

10. Move your pointer over the word "Dessert," and notice that the translation is "postre." Delete the text "Dessert," and key **Postre**.

11. Create a handout header and footer: Include the date, your name as the header, the page number, and **[your initials]12-19** as the footer.

12. Save the presentation as **[your initials]12-19** in your Lesson 12 folder.

13. Print comment pages by following these steps:

   a. From the File tab, choose Print.

   b. Set up the print options so that all slides will print as handouts, four slides per page, grayscale, framed.

   c. Check to be sure that Print Comments and Ink Markup is checked.

   d. Move to the second page, and then zoom to 100%. The comments appear, identified by the slide on which they appear and by the initials of the reviewer.

   e. Click Print, and then click OK.

14. Close the presentation and submit your work.

Lesson Applications

Exercise 12-20

Import an outline from Word, insert a Word document, and link an Excel file.

1. Start a new blank presentation.

2. Create a presentation from the Word file **Yoga.docx** included with your student files.

3. If you have a blank slide 1, delete it. Change the layout of the new slide 1, "Yoga Classes," to a Title slide.

4. Move to slide 3, and change to the Two Content layout. Cut the text from "Head to Knee" through "The Corpse," and paste these items in the second column. Change the font size to 28 points if necessary.

5. Change the body text size on slides 2 and 5 to 28 points.

6. On slide 1, select the title text, and apply a WordArt style that will make the title easier to read.

7. Change slide 4 to Title Only layout.

8. Insert appropriate images on slides 4 and 5.

9. Apply a design theme and theme color of your choice.

10. On slide 2, resize the text placeholder, and insert the Word document **Yoga Flyer.docx**. Resize and position attractively. Add an outline color if needed.

11. Open the Excel file **Yoga Budget.xlsx**, and link the range A1:B4 to slide 5 of your presentation. Resize and position attractively with your picture and text on the slide. See Figure 12-18 for an example.

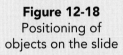

Figure 12-18
Positioning of objects on the slide

12. Create a handout header and footer: Include the current date, your name as the header, the page number, and *[your initials]***12-20** as the footer.

13. Save the file as *[your initials]***12-20**. Close the presentation and submit your work.

Exercise 12-21

Insert Screenshots, use Arrange All to view multiple presentations, and copy and paste from another presentation.

1. Open the presentation **Healthy Eating**.

2. Add a slide after slide 3, using the Title and Content layout.

3. Key the information from Figure 12-19.

Figure 12-19
Slide 4

Heart Healthy Snacks

- Apples
- Broccoli & Cauliflower
- Celery
- Grapes
- Pretzels
- Low-Fat Yogurt

4. After slide 5, add a slide using the Title and Content layout. Key the title **Upcoming Classes**, and key the text **Don't miss out on our Nutrition Myth class coming up Saturday, August 19!**

5. Open the presentation **Nutrition**.

6. Make a screen clipping of slide 1 (just the slide), and place it on slide 6 of the **Healthy Eating** presentation. Resize and reposition as appropriate.

7. Use the Arrange All feature to view the presentations side by side.

8. Select slides 2 and 3 in the **Nutrition** presentation, and copy them.

9. Paste them into the **Healthy Eating** presentation after slide 5.

10. Close the **Nutrition** file, and maximize the screen of the **Healthy Eating** presentation.

11. Use the Format Painter to copy the formatting from the title text on slide 5 to slides 6 and 7.

12. Add slide transitions to the whole presentation.

13. Create a handout header and footer: Include the current date, your name as the header, the page number, and *[your initials]*12-21 as the footer.

14. Save the file as *[your initials]*12-21. Close the presentation and submit your work.

Exercise 12-22

Insert comments, and print slide markup.

1. Open the presentation **July Fun2**.

2. Correct all the spelling errors in the presentation, and create a comment for each spelling correction noting that you corrected it, as shown in Figure 12-20.

Figure 12-20
Comment

3. On slide 1, move the title down so that it is on the black rectangle, and create a comment stating that you changed its position. Select and reposition each comment about spelling on slide 1 so that they are with the title.

4. On slide 3, remove the comma and the words "and no seeds to spoil the fun," and create a comment stating the change that you made.

5. On slide 5, change the slide title from uppercase to capitalize only the "E." Create a comment describing this change.

6. Add animation to all text in the presentation. Choose an effect similar to fireworks, such as the entrance effect Zoom.

7. Add a party horn sound to slide 1, and hide the icon during the slide show.

8. Create a handout header and footer: Include the current date, your name as the header, the page number, and *[your initials]*12-22 as the footer.

9. Save the file as *[your initials]*12-22. Close the presentation and submit your work.

Exercise 12-23 ◆ Challenge Yourself

Import slides from an outline, create a logo and save it as a picture, insert comments, and print slide markup.

1. Open the presentation **Nutrition**.

2. Using the Home tab and New Slide button 🖼, insert all slides from the **Nutrition Myths.docx** outline after **Nutrition** slide 1 and before slide 2.

3. Select slides 2 to 9, and apply the Quote layout. With slides 2 to 9 still selected, use the Reset button 🖼 to update the fonts to the new formatting.

4. Insert a clapping sound on slide 1, and hide the icon.

5. Create a Good 4 U logo matching the slide theme and topic, group it, and save it as **picture2**.

6. Insert the logo picture on the first Slide Master layout, in an appropriate place such as the bottom right corner, so that it is applied to all layouts.

7. Adjust your text and content as needed so that the logo can be seen on each slide.

8. Insert at least two comments into the presentation.

9. Create a handout header and footer: Include the current date, your name as the header, the page number, and *[your initials]*12-23 as the footer.

10. Save the file as *[your initials]*12-23. Print it as handouts—grayscale, framed, six slides per page—and include the slide markup pages.

On Your Own

In these exercises you work on your own, as you would in a real-life work environment. Use the skills you've learned to accomplish the task—and be creative.

Exercise 12-24

Create a biography presentation of your favorite sports player. Imagine you are the player's manager and must use this presentation to build goodwill and positive feelings toward the player. Create at least six slides. Use tables, charts, and/or diagrams to show the player's statistics. Create an attractive and lively presentation. Write a script that you could use if presenting your presentation to an audience, and use the script to create suitable note pages. Insert a screenshot of something you find on the Web about this player, and create a reference slide listing all the resources you used. Use the concepts learned in this lesson to enhance your presentation.

Insert a handout header and footer: Include the current date, your name as the header, the page number, and *[your initials]*12-24 as the footer. Save your presentation as *[your initials]*12-24. Close the presentation and submit your work.

Exercise 12-25

Imagine you are a party/event planner. Create a presentation that lists and organizes tasks that need to be completed to have a successful book fair fund-raising event. Include content from other sources, and copy formatting from another presentation that you have completed. Have another student in your class evaluate the presentation and give you comments using the Comment feature in PowerPoint. Based on this evaluation, make any needed corrections.

Insert a handout header and footer: Include the current date, your name as the header, the page number, and *[your initials]*12-25 as the footer. Print the comment pages with a copy of the handouts. Save the presentation as *[your initials]*12-25. Close the presentation and submit your work.

Exercise 12-26

Imagine that you are starting your own business. Create a presentation that presents reasons for a bank to give you a start-up loan for the business. Create your own logo, and save it as a picture. Create at least six slides describing the business, the major tasks necessary to open the business, and the people who will be responsible. Provide estimated earnings for the first few years of the business. Use data from other sources as necessary to develop your content.

Insert a handout header and footer: Include the current date, your name as the header, the page number, and *[your initials]*12-26 as the footer. Save the presentation as *[your initials]*12-26. Close the presentation and submit your work.

Lesson 13

Preparing a Presentation for Delivery

OBJECTIVES   *After completing this lesson, you will be able to:*

1. Control a slide show.

2. Adjust screen dimensions and use two monitors.

3. Present with projection equipment.

4. Prepare presentations for delivery in other formats.

5. Create an interactive kiosk presentation.

Estimated Time: 2 hours

The features presented in this lesson will prepare you to deliver a "live" presentation to a group of people. An on-screen slide show is the most commonly used method for visually supporting a presentation. This method can be used with a projector for larger groups or a computer monitor for smaller groups. Some of the advantages are that the presenter controls the slide show and that the use of animation, video, and audio effects is possible.

To help prepare for your delivery, you can use PowerPoint to rehearse your presentation and record timings. You can use these timings to create a self-running slide show so that the animations and slides advance automatically. A self-running sequential approach would be appropriate for a show displayed continuously, such as one at an open-house event. An interactive approach would be appropriate for a trade show kiosk, a Web-based presentation, or a presentation distributed via CD in which "visitors" choose the content they want to see from menu selections by using either a mouse click or touch screen.

When you are presenting with an on-screen show, equipment must be available for projection and it must be compatible with the slide show being presented. You may need to adjust screen resolution for different screen sizes. Annotation pens allow you to mark up slides or make notes on your slides during a presentation.

For situations where projection equipment is not available, different types of media are needed. The tried-and-true 35-mm slides and overhead transparencies can be prepared and used just as effectively today as they were many years ago, and a variety of methods for electronic distribution of presentations are available and presented in Lesson 14.

Roy Olafsen is presenting a Good 4 U marketing analysis to co-owners Julie Wolfe and Gus Irvinelli. Because Julie is out of town, Roy will prepare a kiosk presentation so that she can review it the day after she returns. In this lesson you will help him get prepared for this presentation.

Controlling a Slide Show

Presentation slide shows can be used in different ways. By using PowerPoint's *Rehearse Timings* feature, you can practice the delivery of your presentation. You can set up a show to display only selected slides in your presentation, or you can make your presentation free-running with automatic looping to repeat continuously.

Exercise 13-1   USE REHEARSE TIMINGS TO SET AUTOMATIC SLIDE TIMINGS

PowerPoint's *Rehearse Timings* feature offers a convenient way to set slide timings. When you start the Rehearse Timings procedure, the slide show begins with the Rehearsal toolbar displayed, as shown in Figure 13-1. You use its buttons to advance animations and slides, to pause, or to repeat a slide. Slides can be advanced, too, by using the [Spacebar] or clicking the left mouse button.

The time it takes to advance from one animation or one slide to another is automatically recorded. These times are used when the slide show is set to run automatically. During a rehearsal procedure, make sure to allow enough time for each animation so that your viewer can read and absorb the information before moving on.

1. Open the file **Ads**.
2. From the Slide Show tab, in the Set Up group, choose the Rehearse Timings button ![button]. A slide show begins, starting on slide 1. The Rehearsal toolbar appears in the upper left corner of your screen.
3. When all the animation on slide 1 is complete, wait 2 or 3 seconds; then click the Next button ![button] on the Rehearsal toolbar to move to slide 2. Don't worry about the exact timing because you will adjust the seconds in the next exercise.

Figure 13-1
Rehearsal toolbar

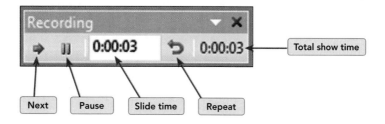

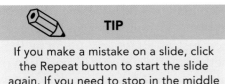

TIP

If you make a mistake on a slide, click the Repeat button to start the slide again. If you need to stop in the middle of a rehearsal for any reason, click the Pause button to stop the timer temporarily. Click Pause again to continue with the rehearsal.

4. Wait for the title text and pie chart to appear, and then allow a few seconds to analyze the chart; then click the Next button ➡ again. Repeat through the next animations to:

   a. Advance to slide 3, where a SmartArt diagram will appear. Wait for all three shapes to appear, and allow enough time to read the text.

   b. Advance through the rest of the slides in the presentation, allowing time for each slide to be read and comprehended.

5. When the last slide has displayed, an information box appears, informing you of the show's total time, as shown in Figure 13-2. Click **Yes** to keep the slide timings that were recorded during the rehearsal. Slide Sorter view is displayed, showing the timings below each slide.

Figure 13-2
Save slide timings

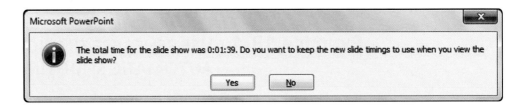

6. Select slide 1, and then click the Slide Show view button 🖵 on the Status bar. The show progresses automatically, without any mouse clicks, according to the times recorded during rehearsal.

7. When the show is complete, press Esc to return to Slide Sorter view.

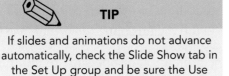

TIP

If slides and animations do not advance automatically, check the Slide Show tab in the Set Up group and be sure the Use Timings box is checked.

8. If you need more practice with the timings, you can repeat the process to rehearse timings again. The timings are not permanently recorded until you save your presentation, and if they are recorded multiple times, PowerPoint will ask if you want to keep the new slide timings. If you choose **Yes**, they will replace the old timings.

Exercise 13-2   SET TIMINGS MANUALLY

It is also possible to set timings manually if you can estimate how long each slide must be displayed. You can set the timing on each slide individually, or you can use Rehearse Timings first and then edit the time as necessary for selected slides.

1. From the Slide Sorter view, select slide 2. From the Transitions tab, in the Timing group, in the Advance Slide section, change the Automatically After number to **15** seconds.

2. Select slide 3, and change the Automatically After number to **10** seconds.

3. Select slides 4 to 9, and change the Automatically After number to **8** seconds.

4. Move to slide 1, and view the presentation as a slide show. Notice that the slide timings are set a little differently than they were before. Click [Esc] to return to Slide Sorter view.

5. Create a new Lesson 13 folder, and save the presentation as *[your initials]***13-2** in your Lesson 13 folder.

Exercise 13-3   SET UP A SLIDE SHOW

A slide show can run in several different ways. Before this lesson, you viewed all slide shows as full-screen shows, advancing manually from one slide to the next. PowerPoint gives you tools to fine-tune the way you run a show. For example, you can:

- Run a show in a window or use the full screen.
- Advance slides by using the mouse and keyboard or have slides advance automatically by using preset slide timings as you did in Exercises 13-1 and 13-2.
- Run a show with or without preset animations.
- Run a show with or without prerecorded voice narration.
- Display a show on one or two monitors.
- Adjust slide show resolution.

The Slide Show tab gives you access to the various options you can use to customize your show. If your slide show does not run as expected, chances are that changing a setting in the Set Up Show dialog box will fix the problem.

1. From the Slide Show tab, in the Set Up group, click the Set Up Slide Show button . Notice the many options in this dialog box, as shown in Figure 13-3.

Figure 13-3
Set Up Show dialog box

Set Up Show	? X
Show type	**Show slides**
◉ Presented by a speaker (full screen)	◉ All
○ Browsed by an individual (window)	○ From: 1 To:
○ Browsed at a kiosk (full screen)	○ Custom show:
Show options	**Advance slides**
☐ Loop continuously until 'Esc'	○ Manually
☐ Show without narration	◉ Using timings, if present
☐ Show without animation	**Multiple monitors**
Pen color: ▬	Display slide show on:
Laser pointer color: ▬	Primary Monitor
	☐ Show Presenter View

To show a laser pointer during slide show, hold down the Ctrl key and press the left mouse button.

OK   Cancel

2. Under Show type, the first option is selected by default. Presented by a speaker (full screen) is the most common way to use PowerPoint when giving a presentation.

3. Click the Show type Browsed at a kiosk (full screen). This option makes a show loop continuously until you press Esc to stop it.

4. Click OK. The kiosk option is useful for a presentation that is set up to run unattended in a public place where visitors can interact with the presentation.

5. Select slide 8, click the Slide Show view button ▣, and then start the slide show on this slide. Slide 9 will appear, and then the slide show will automatically repeat. After slide 1 appears, press Esc to stop the slide show.

6. From the Slide Show tab, in the Set Up group, click the Set Up Slide Show button ▣. Under Show type, choose Presented by a speaker (full screen).

7. Under Advance slides, choose Manually. This option will override any slide timings that have been set. It gives the speaker flexibility in deciding when it's time to display the next animation or the next slide. It's also the best choice if you plan to use hyperlinks during a show or if you have a discussion-based presentation.

8. Click OK. Then view the slide show starting with slide 1 so that you can see the difference in how much mouse clicking is required.

Exercise 13-4 CREATE AND RUN CUSTOM SHOWS

A *custom show* is a presentation within a presentation. It displays only specially selected slides instead of all the slides in a show. This is convenient if you have a large presentation that deals with several different topics. You can create a custom show for each topic that includes only related slides, but the entire presentation is still available to you if you want to switch to another topic.

You create a custom show by selecting related slides within a presentation and giving the selected group a name.

1. From the Slide Show tab, in the Start Slide Show group, click the Custom Slide Show button ▣; then choose Custom Shows. The Custom Shows dialog box opens.

2. Click New. The Define Custom Show dialog box appears. The slide titles from the current presentation are listed in the Slides in presentation list box.

3. In the Slide show name box, key **Advertising**.

4. Using Ctrl+click, select slides 1, 2, 4, 5, 6, and 7. Click Add. The selected slides are added to the Slides in custom show list box on the right, as shown in Figure 13-4.

Figure 13-4
Define Custom Show
dialog box

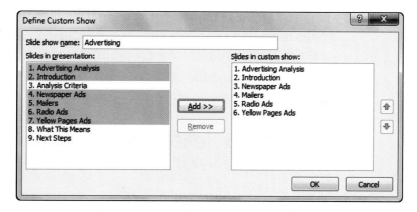

5. In the Slides in custom show list box, select slide 2, "Introduction." Click Remove. Slide 2 is removed from the custom show list. Click OK. You have defined a custom show containing five slides.

6. With the Custom Shows dialog box still open, click New again to create a second show.

7. For the slide show name, key **Planning**.

8. Select slides 3, 8, and 9. Click Add.

9. Select slide 1 from the Slides in presentation list box, and click Add again. Slide 1 is added to the bottom of the Slides in custom show list, meaning that it will be the last slide displayed in the custom show.

10. Select the last slide in the Slides in custom show list, and then click the Re-Order Up button 🔼 three times until the slide is at the top of the list, as shown in Figure 13-5.

Figure 13-5
Repositioning a slide
in the custom show
list

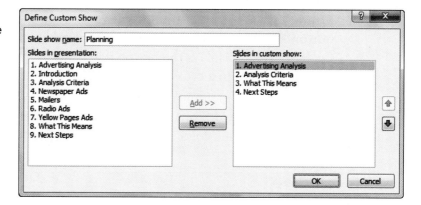

11. Click OK. The Custom Shows dialog box is once again displayed, and two shows are listed in the Custom shows list box.

12. Select "Advertising" from the list, and then click Show. A slide show with five slides displays on the screen; move forward through the entire presentation.

13. When the show ends, return to Normal view. From the Slide Show tab, in the Start Slide Show group, click the Custom Slide Show button 🖳, and notice that both custom shows are listed.

14. Click Planning, and the slide show will start automatically. Press Esc to end the slide show.

Exercise 13-5 CREATE ACTION BUTTONS FOR CUSTOM SHOWS

Using the Custom Shows dialog box to start a presentation is not very professional-looking when you are delivering your presentation. Instead, when you prepare your slide show, you can create an action button—an object with a link associated with it—for each show that you can click to discreetly choose the show that's right for your audience.

The action buttons you create in this exercise will be placed on slide 1. Because both custom shows start on slide 1 as well, this will create a conflict unless the custom show lists are edited.

1. From the Slide Show tab, in the Start Slide Show group, click the Custom Slide Show button 🖳; then choose Custom Shows.

2. Select "Advertising," and then click Edit. In the Slides in custom show list box on the right, select the first item, "Advertising Analysis," and click Remove. Click OK.

3. Using step 2 above as a guide, remove the first slide from the "Planning" custom show.

4. Click Close to close the Custom Shows dialog box.

5. Display slide 1 in Normal view.

6. From the Insert tab, in the Illustrations group, click the Shapes button 🗊; then in the Action Buttons category select Action Button: Custom, which displays the button you draw as an empty box. Your pointer changes to a crosshair.

7. Use this pointer to draw a rectangle with an approximate height of 0.5 inch and width of 1.5 inches in the lower left corner of slide 1, above the Good 4 U logo. The Action Settings dialog box automatically opens.

Figure 13-6
Link to Custom Show
dialog box

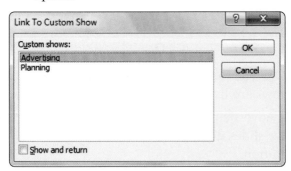

8. On the Mouse Click tab, under Action on click, choose Hyperlink to.

9. In the Hyperlink to list box, scroll to the bottom of the list, and choose Custom Show.

10. In the Link to Custom Show dialog box, as shown in Figure 13-6, select "Advertising" and click OK. Click OK again to close the Action Settings dialog box.

11. In the Slide pane, with the Action Button shape selected, key **Advertising** to identify the button.

12. To make the button less obvious on the slide, from the Drawing Tools Format tab, in the Shape Styles group, click the Shape Styles More button ⬇, and choose Moderate Effect – Gray – 50%, Accent 6. Adjust the button size, if needed, so that the text fits inside the button.

13. Duplicate the button, and move the duplicate above the original, but keep the two buttons close together and align them on the left.

14. Select the bottom button, and change the text to **Planning**. Press Esc to select the button and not the text.

15. From the Insert tab, in the Links group, click the Hyperlink button 🖼. Working on the Mouse Click tab, from the Hyperlink to drop-down list, choose Custom Show and then "Planning." Click OK. Click OK again to close the Action Settings dialog box.

16. Move to slide 1, and view the presentation as a slide show. As soon as all the animated text placeholders and the picture appear, click one of the action buttons. The custom show you selected should run automatically. Run the show again to test the other action button.

17. On slide 1, delete "Student Name" and key your name.

18. Save the presentation as *[your initials]***13-5** in your Lesson 13 folder.

Adjusting Screen Dimensions and Using Two Monitors

Computer screens come in a variety of sizes. The 17-inch or 19-inch computer screen that has been popular for many years has a 4:3 *aspect ratio*, which is the relationship (ratio) of width to height. This is the rectangular shape used for the slide images in this book.

However, just as televisions have evolved into wide-screen displays, both desktop and notebook computers have wide screens too. A 16:9 or 16:10 aspect ratio displays a more panoramic view—the screen size is almost twice as wide as it is high.

So understanding the particular screen ratio being used for development and for presentation is important. Designs that fit well at a 4:3 aspect ratio will look stretched out at the 16:9 ratio. Conversely, wide-screen designs will look crowded when displayed at a 4:3 ratio.

Exercise 13-6 ADJUST THE ON-SCREEN SHOW ASPECT RATIO

Changing the aspect ratio is very simple. This is a Page Setup function.

1. Move to slide 1. From the Design tab, in the Page Setup group, click the Page Setup button ▦. Notice that the **Slides sized for** setting displays **On-screen Show (4:3)** with a width of 10 inches and a height of 7.5 inches, as shown in Figure 13-7.

Figure 13-7
Page Setup dialog box

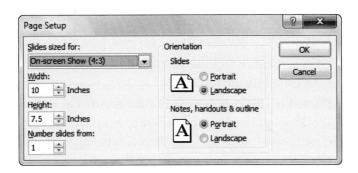

2. Open the Slides sized for list box to see additional sizes available, and choose **On-screen Show (16:9)**. The width is still 10 inches but the height changes to 5.63 inches. Click **OK**, and the result of this change will be very apparent.

3. Click the Slide Show view button ▤ to see how all the layouts have changed. View the entire presentation, and note the adjustments that would be needed if this screen size was used. The slides with only bulleted lists are affected the least; however, the images are stretched horizontally. The diagram would require several adjustments to work at this screen size.

4. On slide 1, notice what an image looks like when it is distorted due to the aspect ratio. Select the image, and from the Picture Tools Format tab, in the Size group, click the Dialog Box Launcher ▣. On the Format Picture dialog box, choose **Size**. Both **Lock aspect ratio** and **Relative to original picture size** should be checked; then click the Reset button ▧ so that the picture returns to its original dimensions.

5. Resize the image proportionally to fit on the slide.

6. This process can become very time-consuming if you have a lot of pictures; if you change back to your original aspect ratio, the pictures will require the same adjustments again.

7. Click the Undo button ↩ several times until you return to the 4:3 aspect ratio.

Exercise 13-7 ADJUST SCREEN RESOLUTION

The image on your computer screen is made up of small elements called *pixels*, which display closely spaced colors of red, green, and blue. All the colors that we see are created from a blending of those colors. Image clarity, or sharpness, is directly related to the number of pixels that are available to create the image. This sharpness is generally described as *resolution*. Pixels are arranged in horizontal lines that fill the screen; therefore, with a resolution of 1,024 × 768, the horizontal axis has 1,024 pixels and the vertical axis has 768 pixels.

For the best projected image, the resolution of your computer screen should be set to the highest-possible resolution. However, you may have a situation in which your output device is an older data/video projector or another type of projector that cannot handle the highest resolution. Therefore, you can adjust this setting in PowerPoint.

1. From the Slide Show tab, in the Monitors group, click the Resolution list box to see your options. Click the option that shows (Fastest, Lowest Fidelity) beside it.

2. On slide 1, click the Slide Show view button 🖳; then advance through several slides, and notice that the text looks blurred and the edges of letters look jagged.

3. Now change the resolution to the option that shows (Slowest, Highest Fidelity) beside it.

4. On slide 1, click the Slide Show view button 🖳, and notice the difference in clarity as you advance through several slides.

Exercise 13-8 SHOW PRESENTER VIEW

PowerPoint's *Presenter view* enables you to display your presentation on the screens of two computer monitors or one monitor and a projector. Therefore, this option may not be available for you to test if you are working at home or in a computer lab. To use two monitors, a desktop computer requires either two video cards or a dual-output video card; most notebook computers have multiple-monitor capability built in.

Presenter view provides several benefits for speakers. It enables you to:

- Preview slides to see what is displayed on upcoming slides before you display them to your audience.

- View speaker notes in a large size for easy reading.

- Blank a screen and still have notes available.

- Select slides out of sequence to create a customized show as you present.

- Easily change pointer options and use buttons to advance.

NOTE

If the computer you are working on has one monitor and you click Use Presenter View, an error message will display asking you to check whether the computer can display on multiple monitors.

In Presenter view, buttons for advancing through your presentation appear in a larger size that is easier to use when you are presenting. Slide numbers and the elapsed time since the start of your presentation are displayed.

First you must set up your computer to use two monitors. If you have two monitors, you can complete the following steps. If you do not, then continue to the next exercise.

1. Click the Windows Start button 🌐, click Control Panel, and then choose Appearance and Personalization. Under Display, click Connect to an external display.

2. Monitor 1 should be your main monitor that will display Presenter view; monitor 2 should display the presentation slide show. Click Identify Monitors to confirm the location of each one. In Figure 13-8, monitor 1 is selected, and a wide-screen monitor is shown for monitor 2.

Figure 13-8
Multiple monitor displays

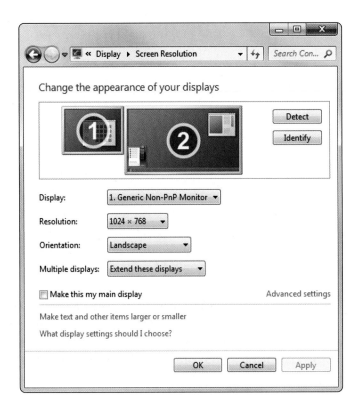

3. Select each monitor, and apply an appropriate resolution.

4. For the Multiple displays list box, choose Extend these displays.

5. Select the monitor that you need to use during the presentation with the Presenter view, and check Make this my main display. Click OK. Close the Appearance and Personalization dialog box.

6. In PowerPoint, from the Slide Show tab, in the Monitors group, notice that the Show On list box now indicates monitor 2. Check Use Presenter View.

7. Click the Slide Show view button 🖥; the Presenter view is displayed on monitor 1, and the slide show will display on monitor 2.

8. View your presentation, and practice using the different features of Presenter view. See Figure 13-9.

Figure 13-9
Presenter view
showing slide 2

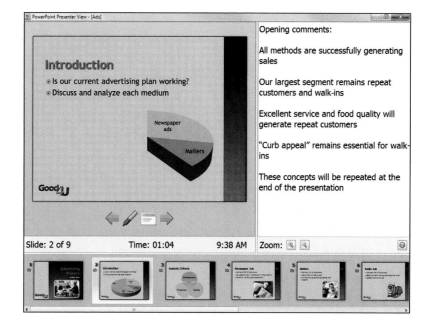

9. When you have finished practicing, close Presenter view. On the Slide Show tab, click the Show On list box, and select Primary Monitor; then remove the check for Use Presenter View.

10. Save the presentation as *[your initials]*13-8 in your Lesson 13 folder.

Presenting with Projection Equipment

When you are presenting with PowerPoint and projection equipment, set up your equipment well in advance of your presentation and test the equipment and your slide show. Be sure your equipment is arranged in an effective manner so that your computer monitor is visible to you while you are talking. It is better to glance at the monitor than to look at the projected image on a large screen while you are talking. For safety, arrange any necessary cables or electrical cords so that they will not trip you.

The following exercises will introduce you to several PowerPoint features that can be very helpful during your delivery of a presentation.

Exercise 13-9   USE ON-SCREEN NAVIGATION TOOLS

During a slide show, you can navigate from slide to slide or to a specific slide by using a shortcut menu.

TIP

If you're going to be presenting to a group of people at a meeting, slide timings are usually not appropriate because you'll want to be flexible with the amount of time spent on individual slides to encourage discussion. Slide timings are most appropriate for self-running presentations.

1. From the Slide Show tab, in the Set Up group, click the Set Up Slide Show button.

2. In the Set Up Show dialog box, under Show type, choose Presented by a speaker (full screen). Under Show options, choose Show without animation. Under Advance slides, choose Manually. Click OK. This turns off any slide animations and timings that might have been set.

3. Run the presentation as a slide show, starting with slide 1. Imagine that you are presenting this at a meeting and that the group is commenting and making decisions as you move from slide to slide. You will move back and forth between the slides as your discussion progresses.

Figure 13-10
Shortcut menu for slide show navigation

4. With slide 1 displayed, right-click anywhere on the screen to display the shortcut menu, as shown in Figure 13-10.

5. The shortcut menu provides a variety of options related to the slide show. Notice that you can click Next or Previous (when you have slides available before or after your current slide) to move forward or backward in the slide show.

6. Point to Go to Slide on the shortcut menu. Notice that slides are listed in order with their titles displayed. Click "3 Analysis Criteria" to go to slide 3.

7. Click the left mouse button twice to advance through slide 4 and slide 5 to display each slide.

8. Another way to move between your slides is to use the menu options that are displayed when you move your mouse over them on the lower left of the slide during a slide show. This area of the screen is shown in Figure 13-11.

Figure 13-11
Menu options for slide show navigation

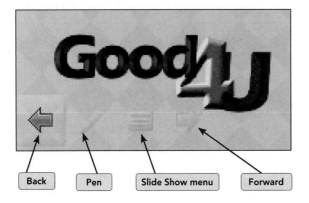

Back   Pen   Slide Show menu   Forward

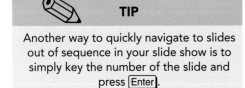
TIP

Another way to quickly navigate to slides out of sequence in your slide show is to simply key the number of the slide and press Enter.

9. Click the Slide Show menu button ▤; then point to Go to Slide on the menu. Click slide 2.

10. Click the left mouse button one time to advance to slide 3.

Exercise 13-10 USE ANNOTATION PENS AND THE LASER POINTER

During a slide show you can use your pointer to direct your audience's attention to something on a slide. When using the pointer, be deliberate with movements so your audience has time to look where you are pointing. Too many movements or movements that are too quick may be seen as nervous mannerisms. The *annotation pens* are useful for "drawing" on your slides during a slide show, and you have two different tools. For example, you can use the pen to draw a circle around an important number or underline a word. You can use the highlighter to draw a wider mark that makes something stand out on the slide.

You could even use the pen to add a simple handwritten note to a slide. During a meeting it might be very helpful to draw a quick diagram or to make a sketch about something. At the end of a slide show, you have the option of saving annotations, so anything you draw or write can be saved with your presentation.

To point to objects on your slide and highlight them as though you were actually pointing to them with a laser pointer, hold down Ctrl and press your left mouse button. A dot (red by default) will replace your pointer on the screen.

1. With slide 3 displayed in Slide Show view, right-click the screen; choose Pointer Options and then Pen from the shortcut menu, as shown in Figure 13-12. The pointer changes to a pen shape.

Figure 13-12
Using the pen during a slide show

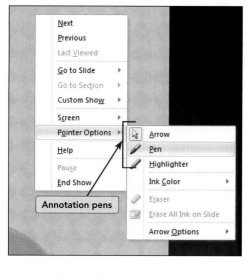

2. Using the pen pointer, draw an oval around the title word "Criteria" to emphasize this word. The current pen color may vary on your computer.

3. Right-click the screen, and choose Pointer Options and then Eraser from the shortcut menu. Your pointer changes to an eraser, so click on the oval to erase it. You can also press E on your keyboard to activate the eraser, and then click on lines you have drawn to remove these annotations.

4. Right-click the screen, choose Pointer Options, and then choose Pen.

5. Right-click the screen, choose Pointer Options, and then choose Ink Color. Choose Accent 6 for the pen color.

6. Draw an oval around the word "Criteria," and notice the different color.

7. Right-click the screen, and choose Pointer Options and then Highlighter. Right-click the screen again, choose Pointer Options, and then choose Ink Color. Choose Accent 3 for the highlighter color. Highlight through "Frequency," as shown in Figure 13-13.

TIP

You don't have to draw precisely when using the annotation pen. Pen marks remain on one slide when you advance to another. You will be given the option at the end of the slide show to retain the marks. Then you can use drawing tools to modify them or delete the ones you don't want to keep.

Figure 13-13
Annotation pen
sample marks

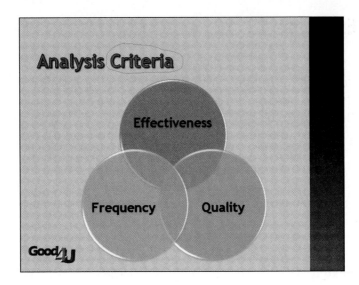

8. Open the shortcut menu again, choose Pointer Options, and then choose Arrow to restore the arrow pointer. (Or press the keyboard shortcut Ctrl+A.)

9. On slide 4, hold down Ctrl, and press the left mouse button. A dot (red by default) will replace your pointer on the screen, and you can move it around. Two other colors, green and blue, are available on the Set Up Show dialog box.

10. Using the laser pointer, point to "28%" on the slide.

11. Advance through the last slide. When you reach the end of the presentation, click once more to exit the presentation. A message box will automatically appear, as shown in Figure 13-14.

Figure 13-14
Dialog box
concerning ink
annotations

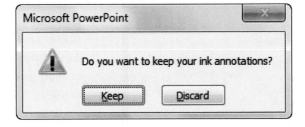

12. Click Keep to retain the annotation pen marks.

13. Now look at the slides on which you used annotation pens. You will see your drawings, which can be recolored or resized with line tools. Even though you might have drawn a rectangle shape, you cannot apply fill colors.

14. Create a blank slide after slide 3. View this slide as a presentation, and practice with these tools a little more. The keyboard shortcut to activate the pen is Ctrl+P; press Esc to turn off the pen.

15. Practice using the laser pointer.

16. When you have finished practicing, delete this slide.

Exercise 13-11 BLANK SLIDES

During a slide show you can blank your computer screen without closing your slide show. You might want to digress from your original topic or simply have a discussion without an image being projected so that audience attention is focused on you, the speaker.

Two letters on the keyboard, B and W, will *blank slides* during a slide show. This feature works with uppercase or lowercase letters, and it does not require any advance setup. It provides an excellent means for managing when your slides are displayed, and after slides have been blank, the transitions you use can make their appearance dramatic.

1. Move to slide 4, and view the presentation as a slide show.

2. With slide 4 displayed in Slide Show view, press B on your keyboard to blank the screen to black; press B again to return to this slide in your slide show.

3. With slide 4 displayed in Slide Show view, press W on your keyboard to blank the screen to white; press W again to return to this slide in your slide show. A white screen can be glaring, however, so blanking to white might not be the best choice to use.

4. Press Esc to return to Normal view.

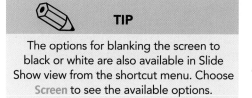

TIP

The options for blanking the screen to black or white are also available in Slide Show view from the shortcut menu. Choose Screen to see the available options.

Exercise 13-12 HIDE AND REVEAL SLIDES

You may decide to include in your presentation a few extra slides about additional concepts in case someone in the audience has a question about these concepts, or you may want to include slides about supplemental content you may or may not have time to cover. You can include these slides as part of your presentation but use the *Hide Slides* option and *reveal* them only if you choose to.

1. Click the Slide Sorter view button 🔲, and select slide 8, with the title "What This Means."

2. With slide 8 selected, from the Slide Show tab, in the Set Up group, click the Hide Slide button 🔲.

Figure 13-15
Hiding a slide

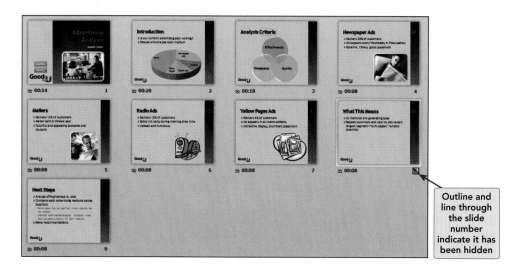

Outline and line through the slide number indicate it has been hidden

3. Still in Slide Sorter view, select slide 7. Click the Slide Show view button ⬚, and then advance to the next slide. Slide 9 appears.

4. Still on slide 9 in Slide Show view, key **8**; then press [Enter]. The hidden slide is then revealed. The technique of displaying a slide by keying its number works from any slide in your presentation during a slide show.

5. Press [Esc] to return to Slide Sorter view.

6. Move to slide 1 in Normal view, and save the presentation as *[your initials]*13-12 in your Lesson 13 folder.

Preparing Presentations for Delivery in Other Formats

Throughout this book, you have viewed presentations on your computer screen and printed them on paper. You have used the Page Setup dialog box to change slide orientation from landscape to portrait and to change the sizes of slides for different monitor sizes. In the same dialog box, you can resize presentation slides for other formats such as 35-mm slides, overheads, letter paper, or custom paper sizes. These different formats have different aspect ratios.

Exercise 13-13   PREPARE A PRESENTATION IN 35-MM FORMAT

Quality color with high color saturation is possible with 35-mm slides displayed using a slide projector. Advance preparation is required, usually by sending your presentation file (on a CD or as a file attachment through e-mail) to a service company that supports printing and slide production. Before the days of computer projection, this was the highest-quality projection medium. However, because this is an old technology, equipment may not be readily available to display the slides.

To prepare 35-mm slides, you need to change the slide size by using the Page Setup dialog box. The aspect ratio of 35-mm slides differs from that of on-screen slides or overheads.

1. From the Design tab, in the Page Setup group, click the Page Setup button ⬚ to open the Page Setup dialog box. Notice that the slides are sized for On-screen Show (4:3 aspect ratio)—they have a 10-inch width and 7.5 inch height with a landscape orientation.

2. Click the Slides sized for list box drop-down arrow to display the available choices.

3. Choose 35mm Slides. Notice that the width has changed to 11.25 inches but the height remains the same as that for an On-screen Show, as shown in Figure 13-16.

Figure 13-16
Page Setup dialog
box

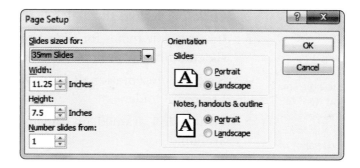

4.   Click OK to close the dialog box. Notice that the 35-mm format is slightly wider than the on-screen format.

5.   Scroll through all the slides, and observe any changes in proportions to individual objects. In this case, the body placeholders have simply become wider.

6.   Move to slide 1, and save the presentation as *[your initials]*13-13 in your Lesson 13 folder. Your presentation is now ready to be translated into 35-mm slides for use with a slide projector. You can send the presentation file as an e-mail attachment to a printing service company, or you can use the Package for CD feature (covered in Lesson 14) to copy the presentation to a CD-R and then mail or hand-deliver it to a service bureau for 35-mm slide production.

TIP

It is best to choose the output format of a presentation (on-screen, letter paper, 35-mm slides, overhead, and so on) and the orientation (landscape or portrait) before creating the presentation. However, you might have to change the output format after the presentation is complete. In that case, review each slide because a change in the aspect ratio will change objects too. You may need to change object proportions, positions, and font sizes.

Exercise 13-14 PREPARE A PRESENTATION FOR USE AS OVERHEADS

NOTE

PowerPoint's default orientation is landscape because that dimension fits computer screens and provides more horizontal space on each slide. Also, this orientation is better for audience viewing than portrait orientation, in which some of the information would be too low on a projection screen for an audience to see. However, you may encounter a situation in which portrait orientation will work better than landscape. If you know you will need portrait orientation, it is best to change the orientation before creating any slides. Because this setting changes the slide aspect ratio, it can affect a lot of slide elements if you change orientation after your development work has been done.

Overheads are printed on special film and displayed with an overhead projector. They are inexpensive to create but require advance preparation. Overheads have been available for many years, and they are still commonly used for "low-tech" situations today when computer projection is not available. Full-color overheads can be prepared with desktop printers, with copiers, or through service companies.

1.   From the Design tab, in the Page Setup group, click the Page Setup button ☐, and change the Slides sized for setting to Overhead. This changes the width to 10 inches, keeping the height at 7.5 inches (the same as for an on-screen show), which works well for most overhead projectors.

TIP

It is important to understand the capabilities of your printer and the type of output it generates. If you are using a small ink-jet printer, then you might want to conserve ink and print as fast as possible. Large areas of dark or intense colors will take a long time to print and use a lot of ink. It is best to choose light background colors and use dark or intense colors for accent colors. With color laser printing, you do not have these limitations.

2. Click OK to close the dialog box.

3. Insert a slide footer for slide 1 only, containing the slide number, your name, and *[your initials]***13-14**.

4. Save the presentation as *[your initials]***13-14** in your Lesson 13 folder.

5. Print slide 1, framed, on transparency film if it is available.

6. Change Page Setup to return to On-screen Show with a 4:3 aspect ratio.

Creating an Interactive Kiosk Presentation

A *kiosk* presentation is a self-running slide show or one that can be controlled by the person viewing it. This type of presentation can be used for trade shows or open-house events where people might walk up to a computer and decide what portion of the slide show they want to see. A menu with *hyperlinks* to certain slides makes it easy to view portions of the presentation.

Exercise 13-15   PROVIDE NAVIGATION OPTIONS

A menu slide with a list of topics that are hyperlinked in some way, either as text or as labeled shapes, enables the person viewing the presentation to jump to the first slide that begins each topic. At the end of each topic, a hyperlink is needed to return to the menu slide. In this exercise you will create a menu slide using shapes made to look like actual buttons with a linking action associated with each one.

1. Move to slide 1, and insert a new slide with a Title Only layout.

2. On the new slide 2, key the title **Menu**.

3. From the Insert tab, in the Illustrations group, click the Shapes button, and then select the Rounded Rectangle button.

4. Draw a rectangle with a height of 0.6 inch and a width of 2.75 inches.

5. Change the Shape Style to Intense Effect - Gold, Accent 4. Click on the yellow adjustment handle, and drag it in to add dimension and make the shape edges more rounded like an actual button.

6. From the Home tab, in the Font group, change the font size to 28 points, with left alignment, and key the text **Introduction**.

7. Select the text, and apply the WordArt style of Fill – White, Drop Shadow.

8. Select the shape, and then from the Insert tab, in the Links group, click the Action button. In the Action Settings dialog box, select Hyperlink to:, and from the list box choose Slide. Choose 3. Introduction. Click OK. Click OK again to close the Action Settings dialog box.

9. Now with the shape selected, press Ctrl+D twice; then position the duplicated rectangles below the first one.

10. Change the text on the second shape to **Options** and on the third shape to **Next Steps**.

11. Select the "Options" shape, and then from the Insert tab, in the Links group, click the Action button ⊞. Follow the procedure of step 8, but change the hyperlink to slide 5.

12. Repeat this process for the "Next Steps" shape so that it is linked to slide 10.

13. Position the three action shapes as shown in Figure 13-17.

14. For a decorative effect, add a star on the left of the "Introduction" shape. Use Intense Effect – Ice Blue, Accent 1, and rotate the star slightly, as shown in Figure 13-17.

15. Duplicate the star twice, and position the copies on the left of the "Options" and "Next Steps" shapes.

16. Adjust any positioning and alignment of objects as needed, and your menu slide is complete.

Figure 13-17
Menu options

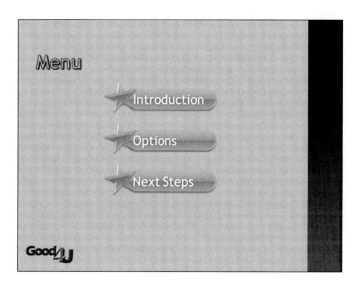

17. Move to slide 3. Draw a right block arrow on the lower right of the slide using the Intense Effect - Ice Blue, Accent 1 color. Key the text **Next**.

18. With this shape selected (not the text), from the Insert tab, in the Links group, click the Action button ⊞. Click Hyperlink to:, and then choose Next Slide. Click OK.

19. Copy this "Next" shape now that it contains the linked setting, and paste it on the slides that need to advance: slides 1, 5, 6, and 7.

20. Draw a left block arrow on slide 10 using the same formatting and size as the right block arrows, and key **Menu**. From the Insert tab, in the Links group, click the Action button ⊞, select Hyperlink to: and Slide...; then choose 2. Menu, and click OK and OK.

21. Copy this "Menu" shape, and paste a copy on slides 4 and 8.

Exercise 13-16   USE SET UP SHOW TO CREATE A KIOSK PRESENTATION

For a kiosk presentation in which the slides are shown in sequence, the slide show should be set up to loop continuously so that the show automatically repeats. This exercise illustrates the steps in doing this. However, because a menu is being used for navigation in this slide show, the navigation made possible by the menu and other action settings controls the movement through the slides.

1. From the Slide Show tab, in the Set Up group, click the Set Up Slide Show button ⊞.

2. In the Set Up Show dialog box, under Show type, choose Browsed at a kiosk (full screen). Under Show options, notice that Loop continuously until 'Esc' is selected and gray, which indicates that you may not deselect this option. If Show without animation is not selected, check the box.

3. For Advance slides, choose Manually if not selected, and then click OK.

4. Move to slide 1, and view your slide show using your action buttons to be sure that all slides advance or return to the menu as you planned. Click Esc to return to Normal view.

5. Create a handout header and footer: Include the current date, your name as the header, the page number, and *[your initials]*13-16 as the footer.

6. Update the slide footer on slide 1 to reflect the file name *[your initials]*13-16.

7. Save the presentation as *[your initials]*13-16 in your Lesson 13 folder.

8. Close the presentation and submit your work.

Lesson 13   Summary

- Use the Rehearse Timings feature to practice the timing of a presentation or record the timing for how long slides are displayed as you advance through a presentation. These timings can be edited and also used for a self-running slide show.

- Use the Transitions tab to set timings manually.

- Using the Set Up Show dialog box, you can set slide shows to run continuously with no manual intervention, to run only on mouse clicks, or to be modified in many other ways.

- Another way to make a presentation adaptable to varying audiences is to create custom shows. Custom shows are subsets of a complete show, displaying only preselected slides.

- Creating action buttons or hyperlinks to custom shows makes it easy to access them during a presentation.

- One way to organize a slide show is to create a menu slide listing presentation topics, each with a hyperlink to the slide that begins that topic.

- Slide size can be adjusted for different computer screen sizes and different types of output.

- Resolution can be adjusted to be the appropriate quality for the computer you are using.

- Presenter view enables you to display your presentation on two monitors while the audience can see only what is displayed on one of them.
- Use the annotation pens and laser pointer during a slide show to call attention to something on a slide, draw an impromptu diagram, or record audience feedback.
- During a slide show, you can blank the screen to black by pressing B; press B again to return to the slide show. To blank to a white screen, press W.
- Slides can be hidden so that they will not be displayed during a slide show. To reveal hidden slides, key the slide number and press Enter.
- The page size and orientation of presentation slides can be changed to fit your needs. Use the Page Setup dialog box to choose landscape or portrait orientation, different sizes for on-screen shows, or sizes such as letter paper, 35-mm slides, overhead, and custom sizes.
- Presentations prepared for 35-mm format or for overhead format can be sent to a service company on a CD or as an e-mail attachment to be created as 35-mm color slides, color transparencies, or color prints. Overheads (also called overhead transparencies) can be created by using transparency film in a standard printer.

LESSON 13		Command Summary	
Feature	**Button**	**Ribbon**	**Keyboard**
Action		Insert tab, Links group, Action	
Action buttons		Insert tab, Illustrations group, Shapes, Action Buttons	
Adjust page setup		Design tab, Page Setup group, Page Setup	
Blank slides			B or W in Slide Show view
Create a custom show		Slide Show tab, Start Slide Show group, Custom Slide Show	
Hide Slide		Slide Show tab, Set Up group, Hide Slide	
Pointer Options		Slide Show view, Shortcut menu, Pointer Options	Ctrl + P, turn off with Esc
Rehearse Timings		Slide Show tab, Set Up group, Rehearse Timings	
Screen resolution		Slide Show tab, Monitors group, Resolution	
Set timings manually		Transitions tab, Timing group, After	
Set Up Slide Show		Slide Show tab, Set Up group, Set Up Slide Show	
Show Presenter view		Slide Show tab, Monitors group, Use Presenter View	

Concepts Review

True/False Questions

Each of the following statements is either true or false. Indicate your choice by circling T or F.

T F 1. You can set different timings for each slide in a presentation.

T F 2. Only one custom show is possible in a presentation.

T F 3. Action buttons provide the ability to hyperlink within a presentation.

T F 4. The aspect ratio is determined by comparing the number of slides that are illustrated to the number that contain only text.

T F 5. Resolution is a measurement of the number of pixels on a computer screen; fewer pixels keep the image less cluttered and more sharp.

T F 6. The pen tool makes a wider mark on a slide than the highlighter when you use it to annotate a slide.

T F 7. Files can be sent via e-mail to a service company for printing as 35-mm slides or overhead transparencies.

T F 8. A kiosk presentation is one that is speaker-independent because it will usually be designed as a self-running slide show.

Short Answer Questions

Write the correct answer in the space provided.

1. How do you display the action button shapes?

_____

2. What do you call an object that, when clicked, displays another slide?

_____

3. Without using a hyperlink, an action button, or the Set Up Show dialog box, how can you run a custom show?

_____

4. What is the aspect ratio for wide-screen monitors?

_____

5. When you are viewing a presentation, what is the keyboard shortcut that activates the annotation pen and what key stops its use?

_____

6. When you are viewing a presentation, what is the keyboard shortcut that blanks the screen?

_____

7. How can you hide a slide so that it does not display during a presentation?

_____

8. Why might a presenter use a menu with action buttons?

_____

Critical Thinking

Answer these questions on a separate page. Support your answers with examples from your own experience, if possible.

1. Imagine you are preparing for a presentation to be given at a conference in the near future. List the items you need to consider about the equipment, setup of the room, and use of PowerPoint to ensure a smooth presentation.

2. Discuss ways that annotating slides during a presentation would be useful for you during a meeting to plan a future event.

Skills Review

Exercise 13-17

Rehearse timings, adjust timings manually, and set up a show.

1. Open the presentation **Power Walk**.

2. Apply the Grow and Turn entrance animation effect to the title and subtitle text on slide 1 and the illustration on slide 4.

3. Apply the Vortex transition effect From Bottom, change the Duration to 02:00, and apply these changes to all the slides in the presentation.

4. Check the presentation for spelling errors. Correct the word "Consideratons" to "Considerations," and correct any other spelling errors that appear.

5. Move to slide 1.

6. Use Rehearse Timings to set timings for the presentation by following these steps:

    a. From the Slide Show tab, in the Set Up group, click the Rehearse Timings button 🖳.

    b. Click the Next button ⬀ on the Rehearsal toolbar to begin making objects appear on the slides and to advance slides.

    c. Continue clicking the Next button ⬀ each time you are ready for another object or a new slide to appear. If you need to redo a slide, press the Repeat button ↺ and fix the timing.

    d. When you have completed the slide timings, a dialog box will appear and ask you if you want to keep the timings. Click Yes.

7. Change the timings manually by following these steps:

   a. Working in Slide Sorter view, click slide 2.

   b. From the Transitions tab, in the Timings group, change the Automatically After time to 5 seconds for slide 2.

   c. Move to slide 3, and change the After time to 5 seconds.

   d. Move to slide 4, and change the After time to 10 seconds.

   e. Return to Normal view, and move to slide 1.

8. Set up the presentation for browsing at a kiosk by following these steps:

   a. From the Slide Show tab, in the Set Up group, click the Set Up Slide Show button 📑.

   b. In the Set Up Show dialog box, choose Browsed at a Kiosk (Full Screen). The Show options will then automatically select Loop Continuously until 'Esc,' and the option will be grayed out.

   c. Click OK to exit the dialog box.

9. Create a handout header and footer: Include the current date, your name as the header, the page number, and *[your initials]*13-17 as the footer.

10. View the presentation as a slide show, pressing Esc at the end to exit Slide Show view.

11. Save the presentation as *[your initials]*13-17 in your Lesson 13 folder.

12. Close the presentation and submit your work.

Exercise 13-18

Change screen size and screen resolution, and use annotation tools.

1. Open the presentation **Walk Promotion**.

2. Change the theme colors to Flow.

3. Adjust the aspect ratio of the presentation to a wide-screen format by following these steps:

   a. From the Design tab, in the Page Setup group, click the Page Setup button 🔲.

   b. In the Slides sized for drop-down list, choose On-screen Show 16:9.

   c. Click OK. Notice that the slides have changed size.

4. Move to slide 2.

5. Decrease the size of the diagram to better match the size of the tables on slides 3 and 4. Move it down slightly.

6. Move to slide 1, and resize the illustration so that it does not appear distorted.

7. Use annotation tools to make annotations in the presentation by following these steps:

   a. View the presentation as a slide show.

   b. Move to slide 2. Right-click, choose Pointer Options, and then click Pen. Draw an arrow pointing at the dates of the walk on the right side of the SmartArt diagram.

   c. Press [Spacebar] to move to slide 3. Right-click, choose Pointer Options, and then click Pen. Circle the number 6.

   d. Right-click the slide, choose Pointer Options, and select Arrow.

   e. Finish viewing the presentation, and choose to Keep the annotations.

8. Assume the computer you plan on presenting with goes to only an 800 × 600 screen resolution. Modify the screen resolution by following these steps:

   a. From the Slide Show tab, in the Monitors group, click the drop-down list arrow for Resolution.

   b. Choose 800 × 600 resolution.

   c. View the presentation as a slide show to ensure that all objects appear clearly.

9. Create a handout header and footer: Include the current date, your name as the header, the page number, and *[your initials]*13-18 as the footer.

10. Save the presentation as *[your initials]*13-18 in your Lesson 13 folder.

11. Close the presentation and submit your work.

Exercise 13-19

Change a presentation to 35-mm slide format, and use on-screen navigation tools.

1. Open the presentation **Lunch Specials**.

2. Format the presentation for output as 35-mm slides by following these steps:

   a. From the Design tab, in the Page Setup group, click the Page Setup button ▢.

   b. In the Slides sized for list box, choose 35mm Slides.

   c. Click OK. Notice that the slides have changed size.

3. Review each slide individually, and make adjustments to tabs so that all meal prices align evenly. Resize the picture so that it is not distorted.

4. Copy the picture from slide 1, and paste it to slide 2. Make it smaller to fit in the upper part of the slide.

5. Cut the picture from slide 2, and paste it onto the slide master so that it appears in the upper right part of the slide on all content slides.

6. View the presentation as a slide show, and use the on-screen navigation tools to move throughout the presentation.

7. Create a handout header and footer: Include the date, your name as the header, the page number, and *[your initials]*13-19 as the footer.

8. Save the presentation as *[your initials]*13-19 in your Lesson 13 folder.

9. Close the presentation and submit your work.

Lesson Applications

Exercise 13-20

Create a custom show, adjust the screen resolution, and set up the show for browsing at a kiosk.

1. From the File tab, select New, and from Office.com Templates, click Presentations and then Healthcare. Download the **Food Pyramid Presentation**. If you are not connected to the Internet, open the **Food Pyramid** file from your student files for Lesson 13.

2. Apply the Cube transition From Bottom with a Chime sound to all the slides in the presentation.

3. Create a custom show called **Portions**, using slides 4 to 9 of the original presentation.

4. Create another custom show, called **Final Thoughts**, using slides 11 to 13 of the original presentation.

5. Create custom action buttons on slide 2 with the title of each custom show on a button, and link to each custom show. Use a shape style to improve the appearance of the button.

6. On slide 9 and slide 13 create a custom action button that matches the previous action buttons, with the text **Menu**, that will return the viewer to slide 2, which contains the link to the other custom show.

7. Test the presentation action buttons to ensure that they all work correctly.

8. Set up the slide show for browsing at a kiosk, and choose to advance slides manually.

9. Assume the kiosk that you will be using can display a presentation only up to 800 × 600; therefore, update the presentation resolution to 800 × 600.

10. Create a handout header and footer: Include the date, your name as the header, the page number, and *[your initials]*13-20 as the footer.

11. Save the presentation as *[your initials]*13-20 in your Lesson 13 folder.

12. Close the presentation and submit your work.

Exercise 13-21

Prepare a presentation slide as a flyer in letter paper size.

1. Create a new presentation.

2. Delete the two placeholders.

3. Change the orientation to portrait and the slide size to letter paper (8.5 × 11 inches).

4. Create a Black, Text 1 rectangle covering all but 0.25 inch around the edge of the slide. Create a Blue, Accent 1, Darker 50% triangle shape on top of the rectangle, and use the adjustment handle to size as shown in Figure 13-18.

Figure 13-18
Flyer background

5. Group the two background shapes.

6. Use the font Calibri for all text that you arrange in different ways, as described in the next steps.

7. Create a text box with left alignment over the top of the black area of the background, and key:

   PowerWalk
   with
   Enter Enter
   November 11!

8. Make all the text bold, and apply White, Background 1 with "PowerWalk" in italic at 60 points and the other text at 40 points.

9. Create a Good 4 U logo using WordArt, and position it in the blank space above the date in the text box you created in step 7.

10. Insert a picture showing someone power walking, and position it on the right. Apply a Blue, Accent 1, Darker 50% border to match the color of the triangle.

11. Create another text box with a White, Background 1 fill and no outline. Make the left edge of the box align with the text above as shown in Figure 13-19. Key **Fitness counts...** in 36 points, bold, left alignment.

Figure 13-19
Completed flyer

12. Create a black oval shape with an Orange, Accent 6 outline. Use center alignment, and key **Community** in White, Background 1, 18 points, bold.

13. Duplicate the object three times, and replace the text with **Contribution**, **Promotions**, and **Fun**.

14. Use alignment tools to align the ovals as shown in Figure 13-19; then draw a straight line to connect them. Select the four ovals, and bring them to the front.

15. Save the presentation as *[your initials]*13-21 in your Lesson 13 folder.

16. Close the presentation and submit your work.

Exercise 13-22 ◆ Challenge Yourself

Create a menu-based kiosk presentation using action buttons.

1. Open the file **Walk Sponsor**.

2. After slide 1, insert a new slide with a Title Only layout. Key the title **Menu**.

3. Draw a rounded rectangle shape, and change the shape style to Intense Effect – Indigo, Accent 6.

4. Key **Purpose** on the rectangle. Make the font 20 points and bold.

5. Duplicate the rectangle four times, and replace the text on each one as follows:

   Overview
   Advertising
   Training Seminars
   Sponsors

6. Use alignment and distribute features to position these shapes in a vertical arrangement to create a menu as shown in Figure 13-20.

7. From the Insert tab, in the Links group, click the Action button 🔲, and link each button to the correct slide.

Figure 13-20
Menu slide

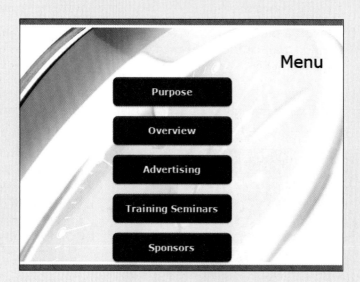

8. Move to slide 3, draw a left arrow, and key **Menu** in the bottom left corner of the presentation.

9. Change the arrow to the Intense Effect - Indigo, Accent 6 shape style to match the other menu items.

10. From the Insert tab, in the Links group, click the Action button 🔲 to link to the menu slide.

11. Copy the menu button, and paste it in the same position on slides 4 to 7.

12. Set up the slide show for viewing at a kiosk and advancing slides manually.

13. Check the spelling in the presentation, and correct any spelling errors; change "Clientel" to "Clientele."

14. Create a handout header and footer: Include the date, your name as the header, the page number, and *[your initials]*13-22 as the footer.

15. Save the presentation as *[your initials]*13-22 in your Lesson 13 folder.

16. Close the presentation and submit your work.

On Your Own

In these exercises you work on your own, as you would in a real-life work environment. Use the skills you've learned to accomplish the task—and be creative.

Exercise 13-23

Create a presentation that will be viewed at a collector's convention and that describes the different types of products on display. Examples include figurines, baseball gloves, bears, and antiques. Describe the elements of a good collection of these items, inserting images and diagrams as appropriate. Using Rehearse Timings, set transition timings allowing enough time for a viewer to read the content on each slide. Modify the timings as necessary. Create a menu-based presentation that will be viewed at a kiosk and will loop continuously as the collectors pass.

    Insert a handout header and footer: Include the date, your name as the header, the page number, and *[your initials]*13-23 as the footer. Save the presentation as *[your initials]*13-23. Close the presentation and submit your work.

Exercise 13-24

Research and compare the different types of computer file storage. Compare the storage devices by price, reliability, compatibility, durability, and amount of information that they can hold.

    Create a presentation summarizing your findings. Size the presentation for overheads that could be used in a classroom where computer projection equipment is not available. Add appropriate graphics and charts as necessary. On the final slide in the presentation, recommend the storage device that you believe is the best choice for students in computer classes today.

    Insert a handout header and footer: Include the date, your name as the header, the page number, and *[your initials]*13-24 as the footer. Save the presentation as *[your initials]*13-24. Close the presentation and submit your work.

Exercise 13-25

Create a presentation describing the major tasks in buying and selling real estate. Make it a menu-based presentation, using action buttons, that you will present at an upcoming meeting. Use appropriate images and other graphics to illustrate the home-buying and home-selling process. Create a custom show for the buying process, and one for the selling process. If possible, set up the presentation for the Presenter view. After completing the presentation, view it as a slide show using on-screen tools to circle, draw, and emphasize objects in the presentation. Keep the ink annotations at the end.

    Insert a handout header and footer: Include the date, your name as the header, the page number, and *[your initials]*13-25 as the footer. Save the presentation as *[your initials]*13-25. Close the presentation and submit your work.

Lesson 14

Preparing for Electronic Distribution

OBJECTIVES   *After completing this lesson, you will be able to:*

1. Record a slide show.

2. Prepare and protect a presentation.

3. Prepare and share a presentation.

4. Share in different file types.

5. Convert between PowerPoint versions.

> Estimated Time: 2 hours

For situations in which people cannot meet in person, presentations can be distributed electronically using various methods. You might e-mail a presentation when you are working collaboratively with other people to develop the presentation or to follow up on details after the presentation has been delivered. Also, you could prepare a presentation for broadcasting if people need to view it from different locations. If your audience needs to hear you discuss the slide content, you can record the slide show including timings and narration so that people can hear your voice when you cannot meet them face-to-face.

In this lesson you will use these features plus learn ways to make the file copy of your presentation more secure and to identify your presentation using document properties.

In the first exercise of this lesson, Roy Olafsen has requested that you add narration and timing to his presentation on the upcoming company picnic. This presentation will be saved for electronic review, so it is important that the details of the picnic be recorded with the presentation so employees can hear Roy's comments when they view the presentation.

Recording a Slide Show

Recording a slide show can add value to a presentation designed to be shown at a kiosk or through a Web site because people watching the presentation can hear your comments as well as have slide and animation timings that will move them through the presentation. The laser pointer can also be recorded to emphasize major points during the presentation. You will need a microphone connected to your computer to record your narration.

Exercise 14-1 PLAN RECORDING FOR EACH PRESENTATION SLIDE

Recording can take place before or during a presentation. Recording can be started from the beginning or from the current slide in a presentation. If narration is recorded and you decide you don't want to use it, you can turn off narration.

1. Open the file **Picnic**.
2. Before actually recording, spend a few minutes thinking about which slides in the presentation you will want to narrate.
3. Suggested text is provided in the Notes pane for slide 2. Add your thoughts to the notes page of each slide for use as guidelines when speaking to record your narration.
4. When finished, print a copy of the notes pages to use as a script:
   a. From the File tab, click Print, and choose Notes Pages.
   b. Click Print.
5. Create a new Lesson 14 folder, and save the presentation as *[your initials]*14-1.

Exercise 14-2 RECORD A SLIDE SHOW

When recording a slide show, you choose the slide to start on and then begin recording your voice as you speak. You can pause if necessary. Depending on your preference, the narration can be either embedded (default) or linked to the presentation. Slide and animation timings as well as laser pointer movements can be saved along with slide narration.

1. Move to slide 1 in the presentation.
2. On the Slide Show tab, in the Set Up group, click the bottom of the Record Slide Show button ⓢ, and choose Start Recording from Beginning.
3. In the Record Slide Show dialog box, ensure that both boxes are checked so that the recording will include your timings and your narration and laser pointer, as shown in Figure 14-1.

Figure 14-1
Record Slide Show
dialog box

4. From the Record Slide Show dialog box, click Start Recording to begin recording on slide 1. The screen will switch to the Slide Show view.

5. Use the notes pages printed in the first exercise to explain the content of the slides as you advance them.

6. Use the Next button to move forward within the presentation.

7. Use the laser pointer on slide 2 (Ctrl+left mouse click) to point out the time of the picnic.

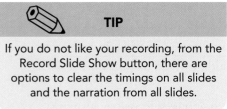

TIP

If you do not like your recording, from the Record Slide Show button, there are options to clear the timings on all slides and the narration from all slides.

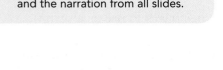

NOTE

Be sure that you are using your notes for reference and ideas but not reading them directly. Audiences appreciate an interactive and dynamic speaker who talks rather than reads.

8. If you need to pause for a moment, right-click in the slide show and choose Pause Recording. To continue, right-click in the slide show again and choose Resume Recording.

9. At the end of the slide show, you will return to Slide Sorter view, and PowerPoint will embed the narration in your presentation file as audio files on each slide and will save the slide timings.

10. Notice the sound icons that appear on each slide as a result of saving the narration. You can make changes to the audio clip on each slide, such as changing the volume, trimming the audio clip, and hiding the icon during the presentation.

11. View your slide show, and listen to the narration.

12. Return to Normal view, and save the presentation as *[your initials]*14-2. Close the presentation.

Preparing and Protecting a Presentation

Before you share a file copy of your presentation, you can test your presentation to be sure that objects are identified and ordered within the presentation so that they are as accessible as possible for people with special needs or disabilities. You can also check it for hidden or personal information that other people should not see. You may want to identify the presentation in some way or protect it so that the presentation cannot be changed.

In the following exercises you will learn several different techniques using the **Kitchen** presentation. Chef Michele is giving a presentation about kitchen planning at a home improvement expo. She will use PowerPoint's Package Presentation for CD feature to prepare a CD of her presentation for all attendees.

Exercise 14-3 CHECK FOR ACCESSIBILITY

Viewing presentations and hearing audio recordings can be difficult for people who have special needs or disabilities. These issues become increasingly important when a presentation is self-guided and distributed on a CD or made available for viewing over the Internet. Assistive technologies aid people in many ways. For example, computer screen images can be enlarged for people with limited vision, and screen readers convert on-screen text to audio words. Limited motor skills can make using a mouse difficult or even impossible; therefore, keyboard shortcuts can replace mouse movements.

To address these issues, government and standards groups have developed guidelines to ensure that everyone can access information. These guidelines continuously evolve as technology changes. In Office 2010, Microsoft provides features that help to make documents and presentations more accessible. By using the *Accessibility Checker,* you can identify potential problems so that you can fix as many as possible before a presentation is distributed. You might need to identify pictures by adding a name and descriptive text, called *Alt Text.* Or you may need to adjust the order in which objects will be read from the slide. You must decide whether or not to make changes.

On the basis of the difficulty that users with disabilities might have, the issues identified by the Accessibility Checker are classified as follows:

- *Error.* The content would be very difficult or impossible to understand.

- *Warning.* The content would, in most cases, be difficult to understand.

- *Tip.* The content could be understood, but better organization would be helpful.

Figure 14-2
Accessibility Checker

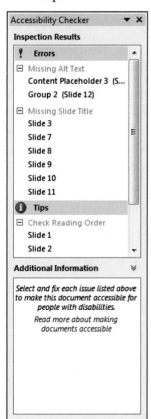

1. Open the **Kitchen** presentation. From the File tab, in the Info section, under Prepare for Sharing, a comment shows that this presentation has content that people with disabilities will find difficult to read.

2. Click Check for Issues, and then click Check Accessibility. The Accessibility Checker pane will open on the right, showing a list of inspection results, as shown in Figure 14-2.

3. The first error shown is Missing Alt Text on two slides. To understand what this means, look at the Alt Text that has been applied on three slides.

   a. On slide 2, select the picture, right-click, and choose Format Picture. On the left of the dialog box, click Alt Text, and notice that both a title and a description have been entered for this picture. These provide text-based information to represent the picture for people who cannot see it. Click Close.

   b. All pictures in this presentation have Alt Text. Repeat this process to read the Alt Text for the picture on slide 3.

   c. On slide 1, select the logo, right-click, and choose Format Shape. Click Alt Text, and notice the title wording. Select the description text, and copy it. Click Close.

4. On slide 12, select the logo, right-click, and choose Format Shape. Click Alt Text, and paste the description text. For the title, key **Good 4 U logo**. Click Close.

5. On slide 5, select the SmartArt; then right-click and choose Format Object. Using step 4 as an example, key a title and descriptive text for the SmartArt diagram.

6. The second error on the Accessibility Checker pane is Missing Slide Title for six slides. Five of these slides have only a picture with Alt Text describing the picture, so nothing needs to be changed. However, slide 8 should be corrected.

7. On slide 8, from the Home tab, in the Slides group, click Layout, and select the Title Only layout. In the title placeholder, key the text currently shown on this slide in the text box at the bottom, and make the title placeholder 10 inches wide. Delete the text box, and move the title placeholder to the bottom of the slide in the same position.

8. The Accessibility Checker pane shows a Tip to Check for Reading Order. All the slides have the correct reading order except slide 1. While the order on slide 1 does not affect the way the slide looks, it determines the order in which a viewer hears the content when it is read with a screen reader.

9. On slide 1, from the Home tab, in the Drawing group, click the Arrange button, and choose Selection Pane.

10. In the Selection and Visibility pane, select Title 1, and click the Re-order button (Bring Forward) twice to reorder the sequence so that the title is first. Reorder subtitle 2 so that it is second in the list in the Selection and Visibility pane.

11. Close the Selection and Visibility pane and the Accessibility Checker pane.

Exercise 14-4   USE THE DOCUMENT INSPECTOR TO IDENTIFY HIDDEN INFORMATION

When preparing presentations, you routinely check the arrangement of all slide content and check spelling. However, when you distribute electronic versions of your presentation, you should check for hidden data that may be confidential or personal.

Electronic files contain *metadata*, which are data that describe data. Metadata consist of hidden information that is placed in files automatically, such as the author's name and the subject of the presentation. Metadata can also include e-mail addresses or file information you may not want to share publicly. Microsoft's *Document Inspector* can identify and remove such hidden data and personal information.

1. Click the File tab; in the Info section, choose Check for Issues and then Inspect Document. If you get a warning message that you have not saved, click No. While you may save at this time, it is not essential for this particular exercise.

2. From the Document Inspector dialog box, check all the options except Off-Slide Content, as shown in Figure 14-3.

Figure 14-3
Document Inspector

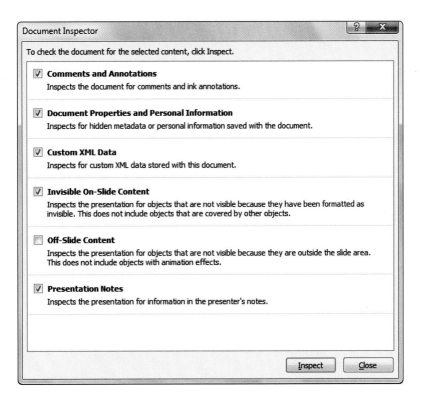

3. Click Inspect. The results are displayed with a check before each of the options for which nothing is found. For Document Properties and Personal Information, information was found.

4. Click Close.

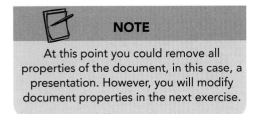

NOTE

At this point you could remove all properties of the document, in this case, a presentation. However, you will modify document properties in the next exercise.

Exercise 14-5   EDIT PRESENTATION PROPERTIES

The *Document Properties* feature records metadata about the presentation file. The information is stored automatically and can be customized. In lesson 1, you learned how to view document properties, and in this lesson you will learn how to make the document properties your own.

1. From the File tab, in the Info section, click Properties and then Show Document Panel. The Document Information panel opens between the Ribbon and the slide area. It shows the title and other information about the presentation.

2.   Key the following information as shown in Figure 14-4.

Author:	*[Your Name]*
Title:	**Kitchen Planning Seminar**
Subject:	**Kitchen Planning**
Keywords:	**Training, Kitchen**
Category:	**Community Service Event**
Status:	**In progress**
Comments:	**This training event will be held as needed based on community interest.**

Figure 14-4
Document Properties

3.   At the top of this area, click Document Properties, and select Advanced Properties. From the dialog box that appears, click the tabs at the top, and notice the type of information that appears in each tab, as shown in Figure 14-5.

General. The type of file, location of storage, file size, and file dates.
Summary. The information you entered, which can be edited.
Statistics. File dates, revisions, editing time, and other statistics.
Contents. Fonts, themes, and slide titles.
Custom. Name options, type, and value that can be added or deleted.

Figure 14-5
Advanced document
properties

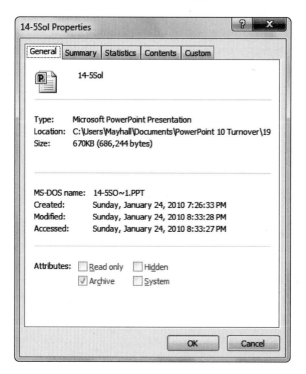

4.   No changes are necessary now, so click OK. On the Document Information panel, click the Close button [×].

5.   Save the presentation as *[your initials]*14-5 in your Lesson 14 folder.

Exercise 14-6 ADD A DIGITAL SIGNATURE

A *digital signature* can help verify a document's integrity. However, Microsoft does not warrant the legality of such a signature because laws affecting evidence vary. To use a digital signature, you must create your own *digital ID* or purchase one from a certificate authority. A digital ID is necessary because it provides a means of authenticating digital information. Once a presentation has been digitally signed, it becomes read-only to prevent modifications.

1. Still working with the presentation *[your initials]*14-5, save it now as *[your initials]*14-6 in your Lesson 14 folder. A presentation cannot be resaved once a signature has been added because any changes to the presentation invalidate the signature.

2. From the File tab, in the Info section, click Protect Presentation and Add a Digital Signature. A warning box appears that briefly explains Microsoft's position, as shown in Figure 14-6.

Figure 14-6
Digital signature legality statement

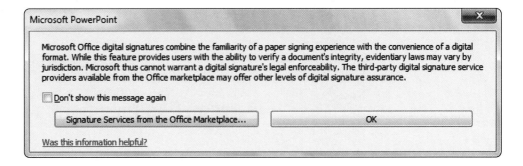

3. Click OK.

4. In the Get a Digital ID dialog box, click Create your own digital ID, and notice the statement explaining that you will be able to authenticate your digital signature only on the computer you are using.

5. Click OK.

6. In the Create a Digital ID dialog box, key your personal information for Name, E-mail address, Organization, and Location.

7. Click Create.

8. In the Sign dialog box, for the Purpose for signing this document, key **Presentation Security**, as shown in Figure 14-7.

Figure 14-7
Sign dialog box

9. Click **Sign**. You will receive a Signature Confirmation message indicating that your signature has been successfully saved with this document.

10. Click **OK**. On the File tab, the Info section now indicates that this presentation has been signed.

11. Two more changes appear. A yellow information bar at the top of the screen shows Marked as Final and a Signature button 🔳 is displayed in the status bar.

12. Click the Signature button 🔳 to open the Signature pane, as shown in Figure 14-8, that shows the document is signed. Any edits to the document will invalidate the signature.

Figure 14-8
Signature pane and
Signature button

13. Close the Signature pane. Close the presentation.

Exercise 14-7 CHANGE PERMISSION LEVELS

An important aspect of collaborating electronically in today's workplace is making sure that only the people authorized to receive information are the ones who can view the files, thereby protecting sensitive information. Through *Information Rights Management (IRM)*, Microsoft has provided a way to control access and restrict usage no matter where the information is because the permission is stored in the document file itself. However, you must sign up for this service from Microsoft; therefore, this exercise will help you understand this service, but you will not be able to complete the exercise if you are using a computer in a computer classroom.

IRM was designed to help individuals protect personal and private information as well as to help organizations enforce policies about the control and distribution of their information. The level of permission can vary from very limited to full control:

- *Read.* Users can read a presentation but cannot edit, copy, or print it.
- *Change.* Users can read, edit, and save a presentation, but they cannot print it.
- *Full control.* Users have full privileges to modify the presentation and also to set expiration dates and give others permission to modify the presentation.

Different permission levels can be assigned to different people allowed to access the presentation. However, after a permission expires, the presentation can be opened only by the author or by users with full control.

NOTE

It is possible to set a password for protection of the file without enrolling in the IRM program. From the File tab, in the Info section, click Protect Presentation, and choose Encrypt with Password. Key a password, and confirm the same password. Anyone who chooses to open this file will be required to have this password. If you lose the password, you will not be able to access the file.

1. Open the presentation *[your initials]***14-5** from your Lesson 14 folder. (You need to use this file and not the one from the previous exercise because *[your initials]***14-6** has a signature.)

2. From the File tab, in the Info section, click Protect Presentation and Restrict Permission by People, and then choose Restricted Access.

3. As you can see from the information in the Service Sign-Up dialog box in Figure 14-9, you must have a Windows Live ID to use this service.

Figure 14-9
Information Rights
Management Service
Sign-Up

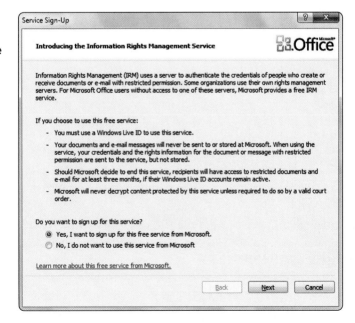

4. If you have your own computer and want to participate in this service, select Yes, click Next, and then complete the necessary steps. If you are using a computer in a computer classroom, select No, and then click Cancel. Click OK to the error message that displays.

Exercise 14-8   MARK THE PRESENTATION AS FINAL

To prevent changes to a presentation when you distribute an electronic copy to other people, you can use the *Mark as Final* command to create a read-only file. This action helps to communicate that the presentation is complete, and it prevents inadvertent or intentional changes from being made. Mark as Final is automatically applied when you add a signature, but a signature is not required to use Mark as Final.

However, this command is not considered a security feature because the Mark as Final status can be removed by people receiving the file.

1. Because the process of marking the presentation as final saves the presentation, you need to save your presentation now as *[your initials]*14-8 in your Lesson 14 folder.

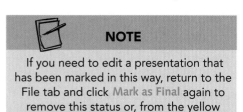

NOTE

If you need to edit a presentation that has been marked in this way, return to the File tab and click Mark as Final again to remove this status or, from the yellow information bar, choose Edit Anyway.

2. From the File tab, in the Info section, click Protect Presentation and then Mark as Final.

3. A confirmation message appears. Click OK and OK.

4. Click the File tab to return to the presentation.

5. Notice the yellow information bar at the top of the screen and the Marked as Final button now displayed in the status bar, as shown in Figure 14-10.

Figure 14-10
Marked as Final Information bar and button in status bar

6. Close the presentation so that it will remain marked as final.

Preparing and Sharing a Presentation

The *Package Presentation for CD* feature conveniently saves your presentation file and any linked files to a CD or to a folder that you designate to contain the files. This is especially helpful when you need to present with a computer that is not the one you used to develop your presentation. You can include a viewer program that makes it possible to display the slide show without PowerPoint.

When you deliver your presentation using a different computer from the one you used to develop the presentation, the same fonts may not be available. Fortunately, you can embed, or save, the fonts used in your presentation so that they will be available wherever your presentation is displayed.

Exercise 14-9 SAVE EMBEDDED FONTS IN A PRESENTATION

You can *embed* any TrueType font included with the Microsoft Windows or PowerPoint installation. A TrueType font is one that can be sized to any size and that prints looking exactly the same as it appears on your screen.

1. Open the file *[your initials]***14-5** that you saved before signatures or other restrictions were added to the file.

Figure 14-11
Font types

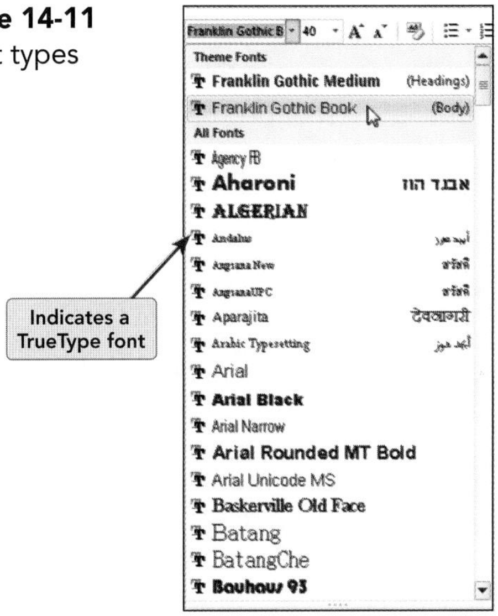

Indicates a TrueType font

2. Select some text on slide 2. From the Home tab, in the Font group, click to open the Font list box. Notice that the font used in this presentation, Franklin Gothic Book, is a TrueType font. Most of the fonts available on your computer are likely to be TrueType fonts, indicated by the TrueType logo 🅣 to the left of the font name, as shown in Figure 14-11.

3. Press Esc to close the Font list box.

4. From the File tab, click Options.

5. From the PowerPoint Options dialog box, click the Save option on the left, as shown in Figure 14-12. Check the option Embed fonts in the file, and then select the option Embed all characters (best for editing by other people).

Figure 14-12
Embedding fonts in
the presentation file

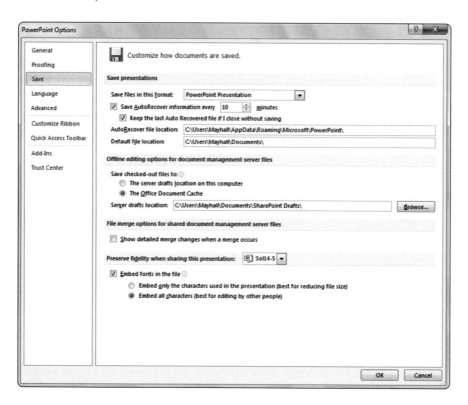

TIP

If you are concerned about file size and
disk space, don't embed TrueType fonts
unless necessary. Embedding fonts
increases the size of your presentation files.

6. Click **OK** to close the PowerPoint Options dialog box.

7. Save the presentation as *[your initials]*14-9 in your Lesson 14 folder. The presentation is now saved with the embedded TrueType font Franklin Gothic Book (the only font used in this presentation).

Exercise 14-10 SAVE WITH PACKAGE PRESENTATION FOR CD TO MAINTAIN MEDIA LINKS

The *Package Presentation for CD* feature allows you to copy your presentation to a CD, a folder on the hard drive of your computer, or a network location. This feature also copies any linked files, such as movies and sounds, too, which is very important when you are using media files and presenting with a computer different from the one on which you developed the presentation.

Before using the Package Presentation for CD feature, decide how you want to store your presentation. You can copy to a blank recordable CD (CD-R) or a blank rewritable CD (CD-RW). If you do not have a CD available, you can save the presentation to a folder on your hard drive. If you save it to a hard drive folder, you can later copy the contents of the folder to the type of removable media you are using, such as a flash drive or a CD-R, a CD-RW, or even a DVD-R.

In this exercise you will save a presentation to a CD-R or to a different location that your instructor specifies. Make sure you have a blank CD-R on hand before beginning.

1. With the file *[your initials]*14-9 open, move to slide 1. Resave the presentation as *[your initials]*14-10.

2. From the Insert tab, in the Media group, click the Audio button 🔊, and then choose Audio from File. Navigate to your student files, and choose the file **Maple Leaf Rag.mid**, which is a brief music clip. Set it to start automatically as the slide show starts.

3. From the Audio Tools Playback tab, in the Audio Options group, click Hide During Show so that the speaker icon will not be displayed and Loop until Stopped so that the clip will repeat itself until it is stopped.

4. From the Animations tab, in the Timing group, click the Start list box, and choose With Previous.

5. From the Animations tab, in the Advanced Animation group, click the Animation Pane button 🎞️.

6. Select "Maple Leaf Rag" from the list, click the list box arrow, and choose Effect Options.

7. On the Play Audio dialog box Effect tab, for Stop Playing select After; then key **12** slides so that the music will end with the last slide. Click OK.

8. From the Transition tab, in the Transitions to this Slide group, click the More button ⏷; then from the gallery of transitions choose Push and From Left. Change the Duration to 01.50. Remove the check for On Mouse Click, check After, and key **00:03** for 3 seconds. Click Apply to All.

9. For slides 1 and 5, increase the After time to 6 seconds.

10. From the Slide Show tab, in the Set Up group, click the Set Up Slide Show button 🖥️. For Show type click Presented by a speaker (full screen), and for Show options click Loop continuously until 'Esc'; then click OK.

11. Move to slide 1, and view the presentation as a slide show to test the timings and music.

12. From the File tab, click Save & Send, choose Package Presentation for CD, and click the Package for CD option on the right. The Package for CD dialog box appears, as shown in Figure 14-13.

Figure 14-13
Package for CD
dialog box

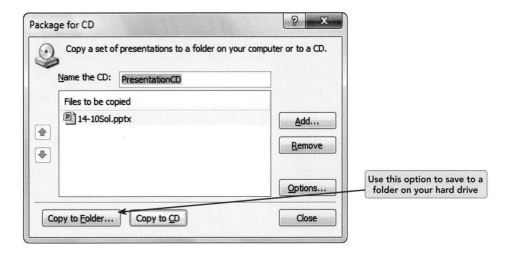

13. Give the CD a name that will identify its content; in the Name the CD box, key **Kitchen Planning**.

14. Click **Options**.

15. From the Options dialog box, check both **Linked files** and **Embedded TrueType fonts**, as shown in Figure 14-14. As you learned in the previous exercise, embedding fonts will save the fonts you used with your presentation. Saving linked files will copy the necessary files and maintain all the links to sound or movie files you may have used.

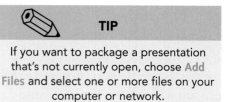

TIP

If you want to package a presentation that's not currently open, choose **Add Files** and select one or more files on your computer or network.

Figure 14-14
Options dialog box

16. Click **OK** to close this dialog box.

17. Click the Copy to CD button [Copy to CD], and the tray for the default CD burner will open if you have not already inserted a CD.

18. Insert a blank CD-R in your CD drive.

19. The CD will be detected automatically by PowerPoint, and CD burning will begin. If you are asked whether to trust the links, click **Yes**.

20. If you do not have a CD available, you can click the Copy to Folder button [Copy to Folder...] and create a folder to hold the files in your Lesson 14 folder. If you have included linked files, a dialog box will open asking you to be sure that the linked files are from a trusted source.

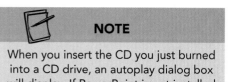

NOTE

When you insert the CD you just burned into a CD drive, an autoplay dialog box will display. If PowerPoint is not installed on the computer, the CD will direct you to the Microsoft Web site to download PowerPoint Viewer. You can also open the presentation by using Windows Explorer or the Open feature from PowerPoint.

21. When the Package Presentation for CD process is complete, your presentation file plus linked files and PowerPoint Viewer files are saved in the location you specified.

22. A dialog box appears stating that the files were successfully copied to CD and asking if you want to copy the same files to another CD. Click **No**.

23. Click **Close** to close the Package for CD dialog box.

24. Close the Animation pane, save the presentation (it is already named), and close the presentation. Remove your CD-R, and label it appropriately.

Sharing in Different File Types

Sharing presentations can happen in various formats. PowerPoint provides many different file types to meet the needs of sharing through the Web, e-mail, printed copy, and face-to-face meetings.

Roy Olafsen will use several of these techniques to announce company picnic details. His presentation will be saved as a video and posted to an employee section of the Good 4 U Web site so that employees can review it at their convenience. For alternative viewing methods, the file will also be saved as a PDF and as handouts in Word.

> **NOTE**
>
> Add-ins provide access to supplemental programs that extend the functionality of Microsoft Office. Customized features are rarely available to users in computer classroom situations; however, you can explore these options on a personal computer from the File tab and the Options button. Choose Add-ins to explore the available Active Application, Inactive Application, Document Related, and Disabled Application add-ins.

Exercise 14-11   SAVE AS PDF OR XPS FILES

Microsoft provides two popular file types that are designed to save files in a fixed-layout format that is easy to share and print but difficult to modify. They are:

- *PDF (Portable Document Format).* Preserves document formatting for viewing online or printing as originally designed. This format is useful for commercial printing too.

- *XPS (XML Paper Specification).* Preserves document formatting for viewing online or printing as originally designed.

1. Open the file *[your initials]*14-2.

2. From the File tab, click Save & Send; then click Create PDF/XPS Document and Create PDF/XPS Document at the right.

3. The Save As dialog box opens. Key *[your initials]*14-11 as the file name. Check to be sure PDF is displayed in the Save as type box, as shown in Figure 14-15.

Figure 14-15
Save as PDF

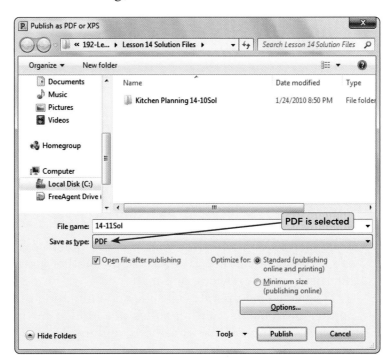

4. Click **Publish**. The PDF document opens for viewing. Close the PDF, but leave the PowerPoint presentation open.

Exercise 14-12 CREATE HANDOUTS IN WORD

Previously, you learned to create and print handouts from PowerPoint. The Save & Send feature in PowerPoint also provides a quick and simple method for creating handouts for formatting and editing in Word.

1. Continue working in *[your initials]***14-2**. From the File tab, click **Save & Send**; then click **Create Handouts** and **Create Handouts** on the right.

2. From the Send To Microsoft Word dialog box, choose **Blank lines next to slides** and **Paste link**, as shown in Figure 14-16.

Figure 14-16
Create handouts

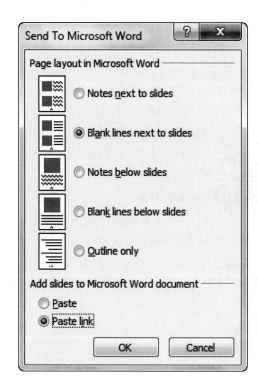

3. Click **OK**.

4. Save the handouts in Word as *[your initials]***14-12** in your Lesson 14 folder. Close Word, but keep the PowerPoint presentation open.

Exercise 14-13 CREATE A VIDEO FROM A PRESENTATION

Creating a video transforms your presentation into a full-fidelity video that can be distributed via a DVD, a CD, or another storage medium or via the Internet, portable devices, or e-mail.

The video incorporates all slide and animation timings, narrations, laser pointer movements, and all slides not hidden in the presentation, and it preserves all animations, transitions, and media.

The time it takes to create a video varies depending on the length of the presentation and the complexity of the slides and media.

1. With the presentation *[your initials]*14-2 still open, move to slide 1.

2. From the File tab, click Save & Send; then click Create a Video, and view the options for output of the video and for including recorded timings and narration.

3. Choose Computer & HD Displays and Use Recorded Timings and Narration, as shown in Figure 14-17.

Figure 14-17
Options for creating a video

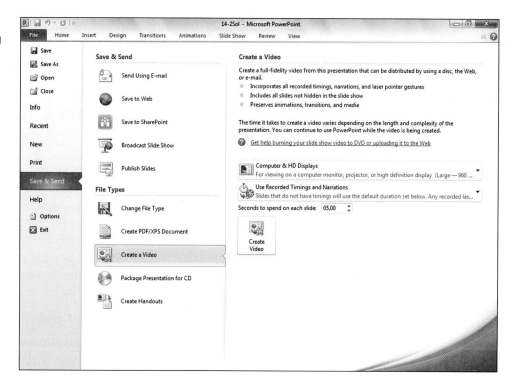

4. Click Create Video.

5. Navigate to your Lesson 14 folder, and create the file name *[your initials]*14-13. The video is saved in the Windows Media Player format. Windows Media Player must be installed to view the video.

6. Click Save. The process of creating a video takes time, depending on the length and complexity of the presentation. Be patient.

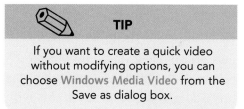

TIP

If you want to create a quick video without modifying options, you can choose Windows Media Video from the Save as dialog box.

7. Close the *[your initials]*14-2 file.

8. Now play your video. Navigate to your student files, and double-click the file named *[your initials]*14-13.

9. The presentation will open in Windows Media Player. Click Play if necessary to start the presentation. Notice that the timings, narration, and laser pointer gestures, if present, are all included in the video.

Converting between PowerPoint Versions

Opening a presentation in PowerPoint 2010 or PowerPoint 2007 that was saved in PowerPoint 97-2003, which represents several earlier versions, is very simple because the file will open automatically. You can preserve this version or upgrade it to 2010. However, a PowerPoint 2010 presentation cannot automatically be opened in a version earlier than PowerPoint 2007.

A PowerPoint 2010 presentation can be saved in a format for viewing with a previous version of PowerPoint; however, some of the graphics and visual effects may be displayed differently or not at all in an earlier version. The exercises in this section will guide you through the processes of converting between PowerPoint versions and help you identify which features of PowerPoint 2010 are not supported by PowerPoint 97-2003. These concepts can be very important for you to understand if you are collaborating with people who have not yet upgraded to the current software version.

Exercise 14-14 CONVERT FROM A PREVIOUS POWERPOINT VERSION

Presentations created in 97-2003 versions of PowerPoint have the file extension **.ppt**. When you open one of these presentations, you can work on it in *compatibility mode* in case you need to open it again in the earlier PowerPoint version. If you want to upgrade the presentation to use 2010 capabilities, you can resave it with the file extension **.pptx**.

Chef Michele is reporting to the Good 4 U staff in New York about her research on the new menu. She will present her conclusions and recommend some menu changes.

> **NOTE**
>
> If you are using a computer that has other versions of PowerPoint, be sure to launch PowerPoint 2010 and then open the file to operate in compatibility mode. If you attempt to open the file from Windows Explorer, it will automatically open in the earlier version of PowerPoint instead.

1. Open the file **NewMenu1.ppt**.

2. Notice in the title bar that the words "Compatibility Mode" follow the file name. This indicates that you are using a file from a 97-2003 version of PowerPoint.

3. From the File tab, choose **Save As**; then choose **PowerPoint Presentation** in the Save as type list box. Save the presentation as *[your initials]***14-14** so that you can use effects available in the current software.

4. From the Design tab, in the Themes group, change the design theme to **Solstice**.

5. On slide 1, delete the lower rectangle that now has the green border.

6. From the View tab, in the Master Views group, click the Slide Master button . On the left, scroll up to the top of the Slide Master layouts, and delete the first layout with the gray and green background; this will delete all the layouts in that design that are no longer being used.

7. On the first Slide Master layout, delete the rectangle that has the green border.

8. Change the theme fonts to the **Trek** combination of Franklin Gothic.

9. Select the title text on the first slide layout, and apply the text effects of **Bevel, Circle**, and **Aqua, 5 pt Glow, Accent Color 1**. Add a Reflection effect of **Tight Reflection, Touching**.

10. Select the bulleted list placeholder, make it bold, and resize it down slightly from the top.

11. From the Slide Master tab, click Close Master View.

12. On slide 1, change the font size for the title to 66 points; reposition the title placeholder up slightly toward the top of the slide.

13. On slide 1, search for a photograph using the keyword "menu" that would be appropriate for this presentation. Position this image on the right, and add the picture style Reflected Bevel, Black. Now both the title and the picture have a reflection effect.

14. Resize the subtitle placeholder, right-align the text, and reposition the text below the picture, as shown in Figure 14-18.

Figure 14-18
Completed title slide

15. On slide 2, select the bulleted text, and convert to a Nondirectional Cycle SmartArt diagram.

16. Choose a primary theme color of Dark 2 Fill and the Polished style, as shown in Figure 14-19.

Figure 14-19
Completed SmartArt graphic

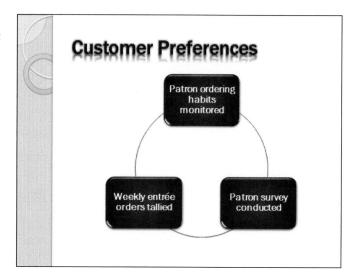

17. After slide 3, insert a new slide using the Title and Content layout with the title "Number of Menu Items." Click the Table button 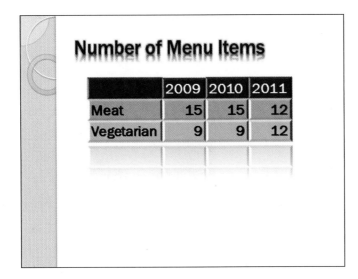 to insert a four-column, three-row table. Enter the text shown in Figure 14-20.

18. Reformat the table to blend with other effects used in the presentation:

- Use Medium Style 2 - Accent 5.
- Apply a Cell Bevel, Circle effect.
- Add a reflection: Half Reflection, 4 pt offset.
- Change the font to 32 points, bold.
- Change the number cell alignment to Right.
- Adjust the cell width and reposition the table as needed to match Figure 14-20.

Figure 14-20
Completed table

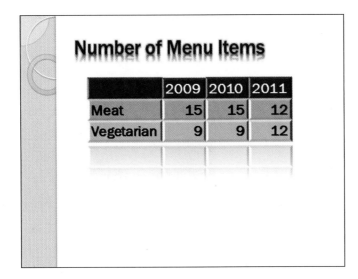

19. Save your changes to the presentation.

Exercise 14-15   IDENTIFY FEATURES NOT SUPPORTED BY PREVIOUS POWERPOINT VERSIONS

If you know that you will need to save your presentation in a 97-2003 version of PowerPoint, you can run the *Compatibility Checker* to see what features used are not supported by the earlier versions. While PowerPoint 2010 files can be saved to be compatible with PowerPoint 97-2003 versions, some of the features will change when the presentation is opened in an earlier version. The following list is not all-inclusive, but it will give you an idea of the type of changes that will be made:

- *Charts.* Charts are converted to OLE (Object Linking and Embedding) objects that can be edited; however, they may appear differently.
- *Drop shadows.* Soft shadows are converted to hard shadows that can be edited.
- *PowerPoint 2010 effects.* The objects to which new effects were applied are converted to uneditable pictures.
- *SmartArt graphics.* The graphics are converted to uneditable pictures.

Once you understand these limitations, you could choose not to use those particular effects when you develop a presentation using PowerPoint 2010 that must be displayed using a PowerPoint 97-2003 version.

1. From the File tab, in the Info section, click Check for Issues and then Check Compatibility.

2. A dialog box will appear, similar to the one shown in Figure 14-21, indicating the features used in this presentation that may be lost or degraded when you save it in an earlier format.

Figure 14-21
Compatibility
Checker dialog box

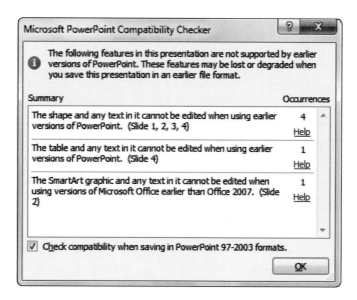

3. Click OK to indicate that you are aware of these features.

Exercise 14-16 SAVE AS COMPATIBLE WITH POWERPOINT 97-2003

When you work in compatibility mode, some of the PowerPoint 2010 features will not be available to you. The Compatibility Checker runs automatically when you save your presentation. While the list that is generated will give you a good indication of what will change, you should still open your file in the earlier version of PowerPoint that you will be using to test the impact of these changes. The results could be minor changes, or you may need to redo some of the slides.

1. From the File tab, click Save As, and then choose PowerPoint 97-2003 Presentation in the Save as type list box. Save the presentation as *[your initials]***14-16**. When the Compatibility Checker list appears showing the features that are not supported, click Continue.

2. If an earlier version of PowerPoint is available, open this file and test it to see how the slides have changed. The slides look very similar in PowerPoint 2003, but the SmartArt graphic and table are now images that cannot be edited.

3. Close your presentation and submit your work.

Lesson 14   Summary

- Recording a slide show allows you to save the audio portion of a presentation, using a microphone attached to your computer, along with slide and animation timings as well as laser pointer gestures.

- You can record narration on all slides in a presentation or only on selected slides.

- Presentation properties contain file metadata.

- The Accessibility Checker inspects the document for issues that can be difficult for people who have special needs or disabilities.

- The Document Inspector can remove hidden data and personal data that are stored as metadata with a file.

- A digital signature can help verify a document's integrity through the use of a digital ID to authenticate the signature.

- Information Rights Management is a service provided by Microsoft so that subscribers can control file access and restrict usage to protect personal and private information. The necessary permission is stored in the file itself.

- The Mark as Final command creates a read-only file that prevents changes in files distributed electronically.

- When preparing presentations that will be displayed on other computers, you should embed the fonts you use. Your presentation will be displayed with the fonts you used to create it.

- The Package Presentation for CD feature saves a presentation with all its linked files on a CD or another removable medium for use on another computer. When using Package Presentation for CD, you have the option of embedding fonts.

- Presentations can be saved as PDF or XPS for easy sharing of content.

- Handouts can be created in Word to allow formatting changes of the handouts.

- A video of a presentation can be created with options for intended output and what to include in the video.

- Presentation files created in previous versions of PowerPoint will open in PowerPoint 2010 in compatibility mode. You can continue to work with these files in compatibility mode or can upgrade the file to the 2010 version so that all of PowerPoint's new features can be used.

- Before saving a PowerPoint 2010 file in a PowerPoint 97-2003 version, it is a good idea to check compatibility to identify the features used that are not supported by the older software.

- When a file is converted from PowerPoint 2010 to a PowerPoint 97-2003 version, some content will remain editable in the older versions while other content will not. For example, text in bulleted lists will still be editable, while text used in SmartArt graphics or tables will not be editable. Graphics made possible only in the newer software will be converted to images that cannot be edited.

LESSON 14		Command Summary
Feature	Button	Ribbon
Add a digital signature		File tab, Info, Protect Presentation, Add Digital Signature
Change PowerPoint options		File tab, Options
Check for accessibility		File tab, Info, Check for Issues, Check Accessibility
Check for compatibility		File tab, Info, Check for Issues, Check Compatibility
Create a video		File tab, Save & Send, Create a Video
Create handouts in Word		File tab, Save & Send, Create Handouts
Embed fonts		File tab, Options, Save As, Embed fonts in the file
Inspect a document		File tab, Info, Check for Issues, Inspect Document
Mark as Final		File tab, Info, Protect Presentation, Mark as Final
Package a presentation for CD		File tab, Save & Send, Package Presentation for CD
Record a slide show		Slide Show tab, Set Up group, Record Slide Show
Restrict permissions		File tab, Info, Protect Presentation, Restrict Permission by People, Restricted Access
Save as PDF or XPS		File tab, Save & Send, Create PDF/XPS Document
View document properties		File tab, Info, Properties

Concepts Review

True/False Questions

Each of the following statements is either true or false. Indicate your choice by circling T or F.

T   F   1. Narration can be included with all slides in a presentation or only some slides.

T   F   2. Information saved in the Document Information panel is there for security reasons and cannot be changed.

T   F   3. A digital signature can help verify a document's integrity.

T   F   4. A read-only file is created when you use the Mark as Final command.

T   F   5. The Package Presentation for CD feature will work with CD-Rs only.

T   F   6. The Package Presentation for CD feature can be used to maintain links to media files.

T   F   7. Presentations can be converted into videos.

T   F   8. PowerPoint 2010 presentations cannot be viewed in earlier versions of PowerPoint.

Short Answer Questions

Write the correct answer in the space provided.

1. List the steps in checking for accessibility.

2. Can a presentation marked as final be changed? If so, how?

3. How do you embed a font in a presentation?

4. Why is it important to use the Package Presentation for CD feature when you will be presenting using a computer different from the one you used to develop your presentation?

5. What are the three options for output of a video created in PowerPoint?

6. How can you create handouts in Word?

_____

7. What happens to features unique to PowerPoint 2010, such as SmartArt and reflection effects, when you convert the file to a 97-2003 presentation?

_____

Critical Thinking

Answer these questions on a separate page. Support your answers with examples from your own experience, if possible.

1. Discuss techniques for getting organized before recording a slide show. How might a slide show that includes audio be useful where you work, for organizations to which you belong, or for your volunteer activities?

2. Describe why an individual might need to add a digital signature to a presentation distributed electronically.

Skills Review

Exercise 14-17

Record a slide show.

1. Open the file **Beverage**.

2. Notice that information is provided in the Notes pane for four of the five slides.

3. To make recording easier, make a copy of this text by either printing note pages or copying the text and pasting it into a Word document so that it will fit on one page. If you wish, revise the wording slightly.

4. On slide 3, make plans to point out that soft drinks and fruit juices account for the largest number of sales. Use the laser pointer to point out the soft-drink and fruit-juice bars on the chart ([Ctrl]+left mouse click).

5. Move to slide 1. From the Slide Show tab, in the Set Up group, click the Record Slide Show button 🖰, and choose Start Recording from Beginning. Click Start Recording, and then begin recording the information for this slide.

6. Advance through all five slides, and record the appropriate text for each slide.

7. Return to Normal view, and save the presentation as *[your initials]*14-17 in your Lesson 14 folder. View the presentation as a slide show to test your recordings.

8. Close the presentation and submit your work.

Exercise 14-18

Use the Document Inspector, edit presentation properties, and use Mark as Final.

1. Open the file **Event**.
2. From the File tab, in the Info section, click Check for Issues and Inspect Document. Choose all selected content to inspect except Off-Slide Content. Click Inspect.
3. Document Properties and Personal Information is found. Click Remove All, and click Close.
4. From the File tab, in the Info section, click Properties and Show Document Panel. In the Document Information panel, key the following information:

Author:	**[Your Name]**
Title:	**Special Event Revenue**
Subject:	**Financial Analysis**
Keywords:	**New York**
Category:	**Income**
Status:	**Year-end summary report**
Comments:	**This summary represents New York only; additional reports will be made for other locations.**

5. Close the Document Information panel.
6. Save the presentation as *[your initials]***14-18** in your Lesson 14 folder.
7. From the File tab, in the Info group, click Protect Presentation, and then choose Mark as Final. On the message box that appears, click OK and OK again on the next dialog box. The Marked as Final button 📝 should be displayed in the status bar, and the yellow information bar should be at the top of the document.
8. Close the presentation and submit your work.

Exercise 14-19

Embed fonts using the Package Presentation for CD option, and save a presentation to a folder.

1. Open the file **Apply**.
2. From the File tab, click Save & Send, and then choose Package Presentation for CD and the Package for CD option on the right.
3. Name the CD **Apply Wait Staff**.
4. Click Options, and check Embedded TrueType fonts and Linked Files. Click OK.
5. Click the Copy to Folder button Copy to Folder... , and create a folder called Wait Staff 14-19 to hold the presentation within your Lesson 14 folder.
6. Click OK.
7. In the dialog box that appears, click Yes to trust links.
8. From the Package for CD dialog box, click Close.
9. Close the presentation and submit your work.

Lesson Applications

Exercise 14-20

Convert a presentation, apply chart styles, and record a slide show.

1. Open the file **Apparel.ppt**, which is a PowerPoint 2003 file.

2. From the File tab, click Save As. Save the presentation as *[your initials]*14-20 with the Save as type PowerPoint Presentation (a PowerPoint 2010 file) in your Lesson 14 folder.

3. For the pie chart on slide 5, double-click the chart and click Convert so you can use features in PowerPoint 2010. Change the chart style to Style 26.

4. For the column chart on slide 4, double-click the chart and click Convert. Change the chart style to Style 26.

5. Print the note pages to use as a script while recording the slide show, or copy the text and paste it on a single page using Word.

6. Move to slide 1, and go through the presentation to rehearse how you will say the information for each slide. After you have practiced, then begin your recording.

7. Return to Normal view, and save your changes.

8. Close the presentation and submit your work.

Exercise 14-21

Save a presentation as a video.

1. Open the presentation **InfoPak**.

2. Add transition effects of your choice.

3. Use Rehearse Timings to set timings for the presentation.

4. From the File tab, click Save & Send, and then choose Create a Video. Keep the default options checked.

5. Name the file *[your initials]*14-21.

6. Test the video using Windows Media Player to be sure that it displays correctly.

7. Close the presentation and submit your work.

Exercise 14-22

Identify effects not supported in earlier PowerPoint versions, and save a presentation in a PowerPoint 97-2003 format.

1. Open the file **Wait Staff**.

2. From the File tab, in the Info section, click Check for Issues; then choose Check Compatibility to see what features will not be supported in earlier versions of PowerPoint. The SmartArt graphics on slides 2 and 3 will be identified.

3. Click OK.

4. From the File tab, click Save As and then PowerPoint 97-2003 Presentation. Name the file *[your initials]***14-22** in your Lesson 14 folder.

5. Close the presentation and submit your work.

On Your Own

In these exercises you work on your own, as you would in a real-life work environment. Use the skills you've learned to accomplish the task—and be creative.

Exercise 14-23

What will you do in an emergency such as a severe storm or burglary? Assume you are a restaurant manager and you are faced with this question. Identify three different scenarios that would be dangerous to the patrons of your business. Develop a presentation for shift managers and wait staff at your restaurant with discussion points and guidelines for emergency preparedness to promote safety for your employees and patrons. Create a unique background design by customizing a design theme. Check for compatibility and accessibility issues. Add a digital signature and use Package Presentation for CD to make a copy of the presentation for each employee to review at home. Save the presentation as *[your initials]***14-23**. Close the presentation and submit your work.

Exercise 14-24

Assume you are a member of the National Restaurant Association and you want to make employees in restaurants such as Good 4 U aware of services the organization provides for the restaurant and food service industry. Review the two Web sites for the association and its foundation, www.restaurant.org and www.nraef.org, to learn about what is available, and then develop a presentation based on the concepts you think would be most helpful.

Customize a design theme for this topic. Mark the presentation as a final, and use the Package Presentation for CD feature to copy it to a CD that can be distributed to restaurants when you speak about the association. Save the presentation as *[your initials]*14-24. Close the presentation and submit your work.

Exercise 14-25

Prepare a presentation to promote family-oriented events and seasonal activities for your restaurant. You might plan a frightful Halloween dinner with special entrées, a breakfast with Santa, or a New Year's Eve extravaganza. Prepare a presentation, including recorded narrations and timings, to announce and explain this event, and then save it as a video. Assume that you will place the finished video presentation on your restaurant's Web site in an area where you feature seasonal events. Create a custom design theme for your topic. Check for compatibility and accessibility issues. Save the presentation as *[your initials]*14-25, and then save it again as a video. Preview it in a Windows Media Player to be sure that everything works correctly. Close the presentation and submit your work.

Unit 4 Applications

Unit Application 4-1

Insert slides from another presentation and copy formatting; save a picture file, use navigation tools, blank a slide, and change presentation properties.

1. Open the file **Fish1**, and apply the Flow design theme.

2. After slide 2, insert slides 2 through 5 from the file **Fish2** using the Reuse Slides command with the box checked to Keep source formatting. Close the Reuse Slides pane.

3. View the changes to the presentation.

4. Open **Fish2**.

5. With both presentations open, use the Arrange All command to see both presentations at once.

6. On **Fish1**, using the Format Painter, copy the new formatting from slide 3 to slide 2.

7. Use the Format Painter to copy the formatting for the first slide from **Fish2** to **Fish1**.

8. Close the **Fish2** file.

9. Maximize your PowerPoint window. Working in the Slide Sorter, rearrange slides 3 through 6 so that they are in the following order:

Slide number	Title
3	Saltwater Fish
4	Freshwater Fish
5	Shellfish
6	Specialties

10. On slide 5, "Shellfish," promote all the bulleted text one level to first-level bullets.

11. Create a logo for Good 4 U with a seafood theme, including images and colors to match the design theme as shown in Figure U4-1. Group the logo, and position it at the bottom of the title slide.

12. Create a new Unit 4 Applications folder. Using the PNG file format, save the logo as **logo-fish** in your Unit 4 Applications folder.

13. Insert the **logo-fish** picture on the first Slide Master layout so that the logo is in the bottom center of all slides. Close the Slide Master view.

14. Add images to liven up the presentation, and apply appropriate picture effects and/or styles to the images to make them look professional.

15. Add animation to the objects and transitions to the slides of the presentation.

Figure U4-1
Title slide with logo

16. From the File tab, choose Info and then Advanced Properties. On the Summary tab change the author name to your name. Delete the company name, or replace it with your college or university name.

17. Create a handout header and footer: Include the date, your name as the header, the page number, and *[your initials]*U4-1 as the footer.

18. Save the presentation as *[your initials]*U4-1 in your Unit 4 Applications folder.

19. View the presentation as a slide show, using the navigation tools, and blank a slide.

20. Submit your work.

Unit Application 4-2

Create slides from a Word outline, add speaker's notes, create an Excel chart screenshot, link an Excel worksheet, add transitions with automatic timing, and save the presentation as a video.

1. Create a new presentation from the Word outline file **Power Walk4. docx** using the Slides from Outline command. You should have five slides. If you have more, delete the blank slides.

2. Apply the design theme Solstice with the Civic theme color.

3. Apply the Title Slide layout to slide 1. Reset the layout on all other slides.

4. On slide 2, promote the third-level bullets under "Healthy diet" to second-level bullets.

5. Reverse the positions of slide 4 and slide 5.

6. On slide 1, delete the word "Restaurant," and add the following speaker's note to slide 1: **Read first paragraph from mayor's press release on Power Walk event.**

7. On slide 2, change the case of the body text placeholder to sentence case.

8. Insert two new slides with the Title Only layout after slide 5.

9. Open the Excel file **Calories.xlsx**, and save it in your Unit 4 Applications folder.

10. On the Excel bottom tab Calories chart, make a screen clipping of the chart with its title and blue rectangle behind it, and paste it on slide 6.

11. On the Excel bottom tab Calories table, copy from A1:H10, and create a link to the Excel worksheet on slide 7. Resize the pasted link as necessary for a balanced appearance.

12. Key **Why Walk?** as the title of slide 6 and slide 7. Increase the size of the Excel objects slightly to fit well on the slide, and center them horizontally in the white part of the slide.

13. Create a text box on the lower part of slide 5. Key the text **We hope to see you here!** Make the text Verdana, 28 points, bold, and italic. Rotate the text box slightly. Move slide 5 below slide 7 so that it is the last slide in the presentation.

14. For Advanced Properties, enter your name as the author and your college or university as the company.

15. Apply slide transitions. Use Rehearse Timings to record the time that each slide should be displayed (from 2 to 5 seconds for this situation). Make the slides advance automatically.

16. Create a handout header and footer: Include the date, your name as the header, the page number, and *[your initials]***U4-2** as the footer.

17. Save the presentation with the file name *[your initials]***U4-2** in your Unit 4 Applications folder.

18. Create a video of the presentation.

19. Submit your work.

Unit Application 4-3

Draw a timeline, insert comments, insert images, insert Alt Text, use the annotation pen, and mark the presentation as final.

1. Open **Summertime**.

2. After slide 1, insert a slide with the Title Only layout, and key **Timeline for New Products** as the title.

3. Draw a timeline using constrained lines, text boxes for the months, and callout boxes labeling each major event as shown in Figure U4-2.

Figure U4-2
Completed timeline

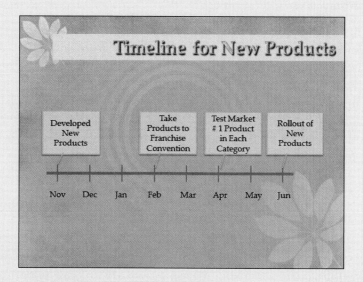

4. Insert a comment on slide 4 about the Tex-Mex Tofu, and key **The Tex-Mex Tofu was a hit, but the crowd overwhelmingly chose the Swordfish as number 1. This could be a great start for next summer!**

5. Insert a comment on slide 5 about the Grilled Bananas and Peaches, and key **The combination of bananas and peaches was not favored.**

6. Insert appropriate images on slides 3, 4, and 5. Apply the Beveled Oval, Black picture style, and make the images smaller to fit on the right side of each slide. You may need to adjust text word-wraps so that the pictures do not overlap the text.

7. On slide 6, add Alt Text to the diagram. For the title key **Taste Test Results**, and for the description key **The top three items in the taste test were Mango Supreme, Grilled Swordfish, and Papaya Sundae.**

8. Add slide transitions to the presentation, and apply appropriate animations to some objects.

9. For Advanced Properties, update the presentation title, and enter your name as the author and your college or university as the company.

10. Create a handout header and footer: Include the date, your name as the header, the page number, and *[your initials]***U4-3** as the footer.

11. Move to slide 1, and save the presentation with the file name *[your initials]***U4-3** in your Unit 4 Applications folder.

12. View the presentation as a slide show, and use the annotation pen to write **WOW!** on slide 6. Finish the presentation, and choose to Keep the annotations.

13. Mark the presentation as final, and close the presentation.

Unit Application 4-4 ◆ Using the Internet

Create a presentation, prepare speaker's notes, record narration, and create a video.

Use the Internet to research the most prevalent types of manufacturing industries in the state where you live or go to school.

Create a presentation with at least six slides describing these industries, including historical information and what the future holds for them. Include at least one chart or diagram and at least one table.

Add visual interest to your presentation by choosing an appropriate design theme and theme colors. Customize the theme as you see fit, and add graphic elements to enhance it.

Compose a script for your presentation, and use the script to create suitable note pages for each slide.

In the slide footer, include the text **Prepared by**, followed by your name. Include the slide number on all slides but not the date. In the handout footer, include *[your initials]* **U4-4**. In the handout header, key **Presented to**, and then identify to whom you would be giving this presentation. Include in the handout the date you would be delivering the presentation and the page number.

Preview your presentation, and then print it as handouts. Print the note pages for each slide and refer to these notes as necessary when you explain your presentation. Make sure that the microphone is turned on and correctly recording before you start.

Save this presentation with the file name *[your initials]* **U4-4** in your Unit 4 Applications folder. Create a video of the presentation.

Submit your work.

Parenthesis ( ) denotes lesson number where term can be found.

Accessibility Checker   Identifies potential problems for people with special needs so that you can fix as many as possible before a presentation is distributed. (14)

Action button   Button drawn on a slide that has a link associated with it. Although special shapes are used for action buttons, any shape or other object can be set up to act as an action button. Action buttons serve the same purpose as hyperlinks. (10) (13)

Activate   To select a placeholder by clicking it. An activated text placeholder can accept text that you key, or it can be moved or resized. (1)

Adjustment handle   Yellow diamond-shaped handle used to change a prominent feature of a shape. For example, you can change the size of an arrowhead relative to the body of the arrow. (4)

Album layout   Used to change how pictures are positioned in a photo album. (4)

Alignment   Left, center, right, and justify attributes available for text positioning in various objects. Also refers to how objects are positioned on a slide. (5)

Alt Text   Descriptive text added to pictures that can be read by screen readers, for people with vision problems. (14)

Animate   To apply movement and audio effects to slide text or objects. (10)

Animation effects   Visual effects that control how text, pictures, movies, and other objects move on a slide during a slide show. May include audio. (1) (10)

Animation Painter   Tool used to copy animation effects from one object and apply them to a different object. (10)

Animation pane   Displays all the animation effects applied to objects on the current slide. Items are listed in the order that they will occur during a slide show. (10)

Animation tag   Small, numbered box that appears on a slide next to an animated object. The number indicates the animation order and correlates with the item numbers in the Animation pane. (10)

Animations   See **Animation effects.**

Annotation pen   Pointer used to draw on the screen during a slide show presentation. Annotation pen marks can be saved with the presentation. (13)

Arrange all   Displays multiple open files at the same time in windows resized to fit side-by-side. (12)

Arrowheads   Lines with tips on either end that can be changed to arrowheads, dots, and diamonds. (8)

Artistic Effect   Effect that applies photo filters to pictures. Effects include Painting, Blur, Cement, Light Screen, Plastic Wrap, Pastels, and other effects. (4)

Aspect ratio   Relationship (ratio) of the width to height of a computer screen or images. (13)

Assistant shape   Shape in an organization chart that is usually placed below a superior shape and above subordinate shapes. Usually, an assistant shape has no subordinates. (7)

AutoCorrect   Feature that automatically corrects commonly misspelled words as you key text. (2)

Autofit options   Options for fitting text into placeholders. (2)

Axis   Line that borders one side of the chart plot area. The Vertical (Value) Axis displays a range of numbers, and the Horizontal (Category) Axis displays category names. (6)

Background Removal   Allows for the removal of the background of a picture to help the audience focus on the important part of that picture. (4)

Backstage view   Contains quick commands that include file management and printing options such as print settings and a preview area so that you can review slides before printing. (1)

Backward   Used to adjust object stacking order and move a selected object behind another object. (9)

Banded Columns   Table style option that provides columns in alternating colors. (5)

Banded Rows   Table style option that provides rows in alternating colors. (5)

Bar chart   Chart that compares one data element with another data element using horizontal bars. (6)

Bevel   Effect that makes a picture or some other shape look dimensional; has several different options available. (4) (8)

Bitmap pictures   Made up of tiny colored pixels (picture elements). The more you enlarge a bitmap, the more blurred it becomes. Examples of bitmaps are pictures created in a paint program, photographs and other images that come from a scanner, and images that come from a digital camera. (4)

Black and White   View that converts all colors to either black or white, eliminating shades of gray. Generally used for printing. (1)

Blank presentation   Empty presentation. May be used to start a new presentation with no design elements such as colors, text, or other content. (2)

Blank slide   During a slide show the display screen can blank to black by pressing B or it can blank to white by pressing W. Pressing the same key will redisplay the current slide. (13)

Body text   Text on a slide, excluding titles. On a PowerPoint slide, body text placeholders usually display bulleted text. (1)

Bookmark   Allows you to jump to a specific location in an audio or video clip to begin playing. (10)

Brightness   Adjusts the overall lightness of the colors in a picture. (4)

Bullet   Small dot, square, or other symbol placed at the left of each item in a list. (1)

Cascade   Displays multiple open files in separate windows, layered to show each title bar. (12)

Cell   Intersection of a row and a column in a table or a worksheet. (5) (6)

Cell Bevel   Dimensional effect to make cells look raised and rounded or pressed in. (5)

Cell margin   Space between the text in a cell and its borders. (5)

Cell pointer   Pointer in the shape of a white cross used to select cells in a Microsoft Excel worksheet or Microsoft Graph datasheet. (6)

Chart   Displays numbers in pictorial format, such as slices of a pie or columns in varying heights. Charts are sometimes called *graphs*. (6)

Chart Layouts   Controls the position in which different chart elements appear on a chart. (6)

Chart Styles   Preset styles that can be applied to a chart to enhance its appearance through colors matching the document theme colors. (6)

Clip art   Ready-to-use media files including illustration, photograph, video, and audio files that you can insert in a presentation. Also called *clips*. (4)

Clipboard   Temporary storage area in the computer's memory, used to hold text or objects that are cut or copied. (3)

Clipboard options   Allow the control of settings of the Clipboard task pane. (3)

Clips   See **Clip art.**

Collate   To print all the pages of a document before starting to print the first page of the next copy. (1)

Color   View that displays the presentation in full color for slide shows and printing. (4) (9)

Color saturation   Controls the intensity of colors, making an image less or more vivid as the percentage changes from 100 percent. (4)

Color tone   Creates cool or warm tones by changing the temperature of image colors on a scale of 4,700 to 11,200. The low end of this scale has cool tones, and the high end has warm tones. (4)

Column chart   Chart that compares one data element with another data element using vertical bars. (6)

Columns   Individual cells aligned vertically in a table or worksheet. (5)

Command buttons   Buttons designed to perform a function or display a gallery of options. (1)

Comment marker   Small rectangle appearing on a slide that indicates the presence of a reviewer comment. You read a comment by pointing to the comment marker. (12)

Comments   Notes to yourself or others made during the review of a presentation. Comments are identified by comment markers. (12)

Compatibility Checker   Identifies features that are not supported in PowerPoint 97-2003. (14)

Compatibility mode   Allows a file created with current software to be opened in PowerPoint 97-2003. (14)

Connection sites   Red handles on an object that indicate where connector lines can be attached. (4) (9)

Connector line   Straight, curved, or angled line with special endpoints that can lock onto connection sites on a shape or other PowerPoint object. (4) (9)

Constrain   Used to draw objects in precise increments or proportions. For example, a line will be straight or angled in precise amounts, a rectangle will be square, and an oval will be round. When resizing an object, the correct size ratio is maintained. (2) (4)

Contiguous slides   Slides that follow one after another, such as slides numbered 2, 3, and 4. (3) See also **Noncontiguous slides.**

Continuous Picture List   SmartArt graphic that contains round placeholders for pictures and a horizontal arrow to communicate that the items shown represent interconnected information. (7)

Contrast   Adjusts the intensity of the colors in a picture by adjusting the difference between the lightest and darkest areas. (4)

Copy   Reproduces a selected object or text and stores it on the Clipboard without removing the selection from its original place. (3)

Corrections   Modifies the brightness and/or contrast of a picture. (4)

Coworker shape   Shape in an organization chart that is connected to the same superior shape as another shape. (7)

Crop   To trim the vertical or horizontal edges of a picture. (4)

Cropping handles   Short black markers on the sides and corners of a picture selected for cropping. When you drag one of these handles with the cropping tool, an edge of the picture is cut away (trimmed). (4)

Crosshair pointer   Shape of your pointer when drawing objects. (4)

Custom show   Presentation within a presentation. It displays only specially selected slides instead of all the slides in a slide show. (13)

Cut   Removes a selected object or text from a presentation and stores it on the Clipboard. (3)

Cycle SmartArt graphic   Diagram that illustrates a continuous process. (7)

Dash style   Patterns of dashes and dots that can be applied to shape outlines, lines, and arrows. (8)

Data series   Group of data that relates to a common object or category such as a product, geographic area, or year. A single chart may display more than one data series. (6)

Datasheet   Table that is part of Microsoft Graph and in which you enter numbers and labels that are used to create a chart if you do not have Microsoft Excel installed on your computer. When you start a new chart, the datasheet appears automatically, containing sample data that you can delete or overwrite. (6)

Date and time   Option that displays the current date and time to be updated automatically or keyed as a fixed date. (3)

Decrease list level   To move text to a lower outline or heading level. (2)

Demote   To decrease the level of a shape in a SmartArt graphic. (2)

Design theme   Predesigned background graphics, theme colors, theme fonts, theme effects, and other formatting options that can be applied to presentations for a consistent appearance. These can be customized for a particular topic or unique design. (2) (3) (11)

Destination   When working with Clipboard objects, the presentation or other document in which the objects are pasted. (3)

Diagram   Visual representation of information that can help an audience understand a presenter's message. (7)

Digital ID   Provides a means to authenticate digital information and is necessary to add a digital signature. (14)

Digital signature   Helps to verify a document's integrity by using a digital ID to sign a document and save it as a read-only copy. (14)

Distribute   To evenly space selected objects, either in relation to one another or across the length or width of a slide. Objects can be distributed either horizontally or vertically. (9)

Distribute columns   To evenly space columns in a table using the current width of the table. (9)

Distribute rows   To evenly space rows in a table using the current height of the table. (9)

Document Inspector   Identifies and removes hidden metadata (data or personal information). (14)

Document Properties   Records metadata about the presentation file. (14)

Drag   To move a selected object from one location to another by holding down the left mouse button while moving the pointer. (1)

Draw Table   Method of inserting a table by using the pencil pointer to control the height and width as well as the vertical and horizontal lines within the table. (5)

Duplicate   To make a copy of a selected object on the same slide or to reproduce slides. The duplicate is stored on the Clipboard without removing the selection from its original place. (3) (4)

Embed fonts   To save any TrueType font with the presentation. (14)

Emphasis effect   Animation effect applied to draw attention to an object that is already displayed on a slide. (10)

Entrance effect   Animation effect applied to text or an object to control how it first appears on a slide. (10)

Eraser   Used to erase table cell borders. (5)

Exit effect   Animation effect applied to control how an object leaves (or disappears from) a slide. (10)

Explode   To move a pie slice away from other slices in a pie chart to add emphasis. (6)

File name   Unique name given to a PowerPoint presentation file, a Word document file, or files created by other applications. (1)

File tab   Tab that provides access to opening, saving, printing, and sharing your PowerPoint file with others. (1)

Find   Locates text in a presentation. (3)

First Column   Table style option that emphasizes the first column of the table. (5)

First-line indent   Indent in which the first line of the paragraph is indented farther to the right than the other lines in the paragraph. (2)

Fit to Window   Changes from the current zoom settings so that the slide will fit in the window that is open. (1)

Flip   To reverse an object either horizontally or vertically; can be used to create a mirror image of the original object. (9)

Font face   Set of characters with a specific design such as Times New Roman or Arial. (2)

Font size   Point measurement of characters in a font. (2)

Footer   Text that usually appears at the bottom of a slide, notes page, or handout page. (3)

Format Painter   Used to copy formatting from one object to another. (3)

Forward   Used to adjust object stacking order and move a selected object in front of another object. (9)

Four-pointed arrow   Used to move placeholders and other objects without resizing them; can also be used to select text in a bulleted list by clicking the bullet. (2)

Gallery   Collection of thumbnails displaying different effect options. (1)

Gear SmartArt graphic   Diagram that illustrates interlocking ideas. (7)

Glow   Effect that adds a soft color around the object's edges, making the object stand out from the background. (4) (8)

Go to Slide   Feature available using the shortcut menu during a slide show. Used to skip forward or backward in a presentation or to display a particular slide. (13)

Gradient fill   Consists of one color blending to black, two colors that blend to each other, or a preset combination of multiple colors. (8)

Graph   See **Chart.**

Grayscale   View that displays slides in shades of gray for printing on a black-and-white printer. (1)

Gridlines   On a slide, evenly spaced vertical and horizontal lines that can be shown to help with alignment. On a chart, the background lines that aid interpretation of data quantities. (4) (6)

Group   To combine selected objects so that they behave as one object. On the Ribbon, a set of related command buttons. (1) (4)

Guides   Horizontal and vertical lines used to align objects. Guides do not display in a slide show or when printed. (4)

Handout   Printout that contains one, two, three, four, six, or nine PowerPoint slides on a page. (1)

Handout master   Used to control how objects are positioned on printed handout pages. Often includes header or footer text, date, and page numbers; graphic elements such as a company logo can be included. (11)

Hanging indent   Indentation of the second and subsequent lines of a paragraph. Also, an organization chart format in which subordinate shapes are displayed under a superior shape. (2) (7)

Header   Text that usually appears at the top of a slide, notes page, or handout page. (3)

Header Row   Table style option that emphasizes the first row of the table. (5)

Help   Reference tool for getting assistance with PowerPoint. (1)

Hide Slides   Slides can remain in a presentation file but be hidden when you run the presentation. This feature is available from the Slide Show tab. (13)

Hue   Name of a color. (8)

Hyperlink   Text or object that you click to move to other slides, other PowerPoint presentations, other application files, or a Web site. For text hyperlinks, an underline is added. (10) (13)

I-beam   Shape of the pointer when positioned in a text area; used to select text or mark the location at which you can insert text. (1)

Increase list level   To move text to a higher outline or heading level. (2)

Indent marker   On the horizontal ruler, a small triangle or rectangle that controls indent positions. (2)

Information Rights Management (IRM)   Service that controls access and restricts usage because permission is stored in the document file itself. (14)

Insertion point   Blinking line that indicates where text will be inserted. (1)

Keyword(s)   Word (or words) that describe the subject matter of your clip art search. (4)

Kiosk   Self-running slide show or one that can be controlled by the person viewing it. (13)

Landscape   Horizontal orientation for slides or printed pages in which the width is greater than the height; the opposite of portrait. (1)

Last Column   Table style option that emphasizes the last column of the table. (5)

Layout   See **Slide layouts.**

Legend   Used to identify by color or pattern the data series or categories in a chart. (6)

Level   In organization charts, the position in the hierarchy of the organization being diagrammed. (7)

Line spacing   Amount of vertical space between lines of text and between paragraphs. (2)

Line weight   Thickness of a line measured in points. (4) (8)

Linked object   Object, such as an Excel chart or a Word table, that is displayed within PowerPoint (the destination). When you make changes to a linked object, you are making changes to the actual file (the source) that was used to create the object. (12)

List SmartArt graphic   Diagram that illustrates information in groups and subgroups. (7)

Live Preview   Feature that shows the result of applying an effect as you point to the effect thumbnail in a gallery before selecting the effect. (1)

Lock aspect ratio   Keeps the vertical and horizontal dimensions in the same proportions when an object is resized. (8)

Lock Drawing Mode   Enables drawing the same shape multiple times without having to reactivate the shape tool. (4)

Luminance   Brightness of a color. (8)

Mark as Final   Creates a read-only file to communicate that the presentation is complete and to prevent changes from being made. (14)

Merge cells   To combine two or more table cells into one larger cell. (5)

Metadata   Data that describe data, such as the author's name and subject of the presentation, that are automatically placed in a presentation. (14)

Motion path   Path that an object follows as part of an animation effect. (10)

Noncontiguous slides   Slides that do not follow one after another, such as slides numbered 1, 3, 5, and 7. (3) See also **Contiguous slides.**

Normal indent   Indent in which all lines are indented the same amount from the left margin. (2)

Normal view   Displays the three parts of the PowerPoint window: the Slides and Outline pane, the Slide pane, and the Notes pane. (1)

Notes master   Used to control how objects are positioned on printed notes pages. Often includes header or footer text, date, and page numbers; graphic elements such as a company logo can be included. (11)

Notes page   Feature that prints a slide image on the top half of a page, with speaker notes on the lower half of the page. (1)

Notes Page view   Displays speaker notes as they will appear when printed. (1)

Notes pane   Area below the Slide pane where you can add speaker notes for a slide. (1)

Nudge   To move an object in very small increments by using the arrow keys. (4)

Offsets   Used to scale the size of a picture within a shape or to reposition a picture within a shape. (8)

OpenType fonts   Provide more detailed letter shapes and more variations of character sets than do TrueType fonts. (2)

Optimize   To reduce a presentation's file size by compressing pictures. (9)

Organization chart   SmartArt graphic that shows hierarchical relationships of an organization. (7)

Outline   Presentation content in a text format showing slide titles and listed information. (1)

Overheads   Output format to print slides on individual transparency sheets for projecting with an overhead projector when computer projection is not available. Overheads can be prepared with an ink-jet printer, a laser printer, or a photocopier. (13)

Package Presentation for CD   Saves a presentation and all the files that link to it for display on a different computer. (14)

Page number   Placed in the lower right corner of notes and handout pages by default. (3)

Paste   Inserts an item stored on the Clipboard at the current location. (3)

Paste Options   Button showing options that appears near a pasted item when the source formatting is different from the formatting of the destination presentation. (3)

Pencil pointer   Used to draw and recolor table borders. (5)

Photo Album   Creates a presentation consisting mostly of pictures that can be formatted to create electronic scrapbooks or photo albums. (4)

Picture Border   Line that surrounds pictures. (4)

Picture effects   Customizable special effects for pictures such as shadows, glow, bevel effects, and soft edges. (4)

Picture style   Selection of preset effects to enhance the appearance of pictures. (4)

Pie chart   Chart that shows the proportions of individual components compared to the whole. (6)

Pixels   Small elements that display closely spaced colors of red, green, and blue to make up the image on your computer screen. Also used as a measurement for image sizing. (13)

Placeholder   Box that can contain title text, body text, pictures, or other objects. Most slide layouts contain placeholders. A placeholder's formatting, size, and position is set on a master slide and can be customized. (1)

Plot area   Area of a chart that displays the shapes, such as columns or pie slices, that represent data. (6)

Points   Measure of font size; 1 inch has 72 points. (2)

Portrait   Vertical orientation for slides or printed pages in which the height is greater than the width; the opposite of landscape. (1)

Presenter view   Displays your presentation on the screens of two computer monitors or one monitor and a projector. (13)

Preset   Effects or settings that are automatically available. (4)

Process SmartArt graphic   Diagram that illustrates sequential concepts or events. (7)

Promote   To increase the level of a shape in a SmartArt graphic. (2)

Proofreaders' marks   Handwritten notations used to mark corrections on printed text. (1)

Proportions   Relationships between the height and the width of an object. When resizing an object, its proportions will be preserved if both the height and the width of the object change at the same rate or percentage. An object that is out of proportion is either too tall and skinny or too short and wide. (4)

Pyramid SmartArt graphic   Diagram that illustrates relationships based on foundational concepts. (7)

Quick Access Toolbar   Toolbar located at the top of the PowerPoint window that provides access to frequently used commands. (1)

Quick Styles   Preset effects that are displayed in a gallery and used to enhance the appearance of shapes. (7)

Radial SmartArt graphic   Diagram that illustrates relationships focused on or directed at a central element. (7)

Reading view   Displays the presentation in a view with the title bar showing that is easy to browse. (1)

Record Audio   Feature used for recording short audio clips and not for narrating entire presentations. (10)

Record Slide Show   Records narration, slide timings, and laser pointer gestures for viewers of the presentation. (14)

Redo   Reverses a previous action such as an editing change. Up to 20 actions can be reversed if the Save feature has not been used. (3)

Reflection   Illusion of an object being reflected off another surface by displaying a semitransparent copy of the object as a mirror image. (4) (5)

Regroup   Recombines objects that were at one time part of the same group. (4)

Rehearse Timings   Feature used to record the amount of time spent on each slide as you practice a presentation. It could also be used to control the speed of advancing slides when audio is recorded to support a self-running presentation. (13)

Replace   Locates text in a presentation and replaces it with different text that you specify. (3)

Research   Searches reference materials such as dictionaries, encyclopedias, and translation services to find information you need. (3)

Reset Picture   Used to return a picture to its original state after its colors have been changed. (4)

Resolution   Number of pixels on the horizontal axis by the number of pixels on the vertical axis, such as 1,024 × 768. Image clarity is directly related to the number of pixels available to create the image. (13)

Reveal   Show slides that have been hidden. (13)

Ribbon   Consists of task-oriented tabs arranged at the top of the PowerPoint window that each contain commands organized in logical groups. (1)

Rotate   Change the angle of an object. (2)

Rotation handle   Green handle appearing above a selected object that you can drag to change the angle of the object. (4)

Rows   Individual cells arranged horizontally across the table or worksheet. (5)

Ruler   Measurement shown at the top and left side of the slide pane to help with object positioning, sizing, and tabs. (5)

Saturation   Intensity of a color. (8)

Scale   Specifies the range of values on a chart's value axis and the interval between values. (6)

Screen clipping   Capture of a portion of the window of any application that can be inserted into the current presentation. (12)

Screenshot   Capture of an entire window of any application that can be inserted into the current presentation. (12)

ScreenTip   Identifying information displayed in a small box that appears when you point to an on-screen item such as a command. (1)

Scroll bars   Used to move what you see on the screen right or left and up or down. For example, you can use the vertical scroll bar to move from slide to slide. (1)

Service company   Business that translates computer files into high-quality output such as slide transparencies, high-resolution full-color prints, and large-format prints. (13)

Shadow   Effect that gives the illusion of light shining on an object, producing a dark area behind it. (4) (5) (8)

Shape   One of a group of predefined shapes that are easy to draw. Available shapes include rectangles, circles, arrows, flowchart symbols, stars, banners, callouts, lines, and connectors. (6)

Shape outline   Border of a shape. (8)

Show Markup   Enables users to see the comments or turn off viewing the comments within a presentation. (12)

Sizing handles   Small circles and squares on the border of a selected object that are used to resize the object. (2)

Slide layouts   Contain placeholders for slide content such as titles, bulleted lists, charts, tables, and SmartArt. (1) (2) (11)

Slide Master   Used to control how objects are positioned on slides. Users can design a custom background to be displayed on all slides for presentation consistency. (11)

Slide number   Placed on slides, usually in the lower right corner, depending on the theme. (3)

Slide pane   Area where you create and edit presentation slides. (1)

Slide Show view   View that displays slides sequentially in full-screen size. Slides can advance manually or automatically with slide timings, using a variety of transition effects. Slide shows can display movies and animated elements. (1)

Slide Sorter view   Displays several thumbnails of slides, making it easy to reorder, add, delete, or duplicate slides and set transition effects. (1) (3)

Slide transitions   Visual effects that enhance the way slides change during a slide show as you move from one slide to another. May include audio. (3)

Slides and Outline pane   Area that can display either an outline of the presentation's text or thumbnails of the presentation's slides. You choose either Outline or Slides by clicking the appropriate tab. (1)

SmartArt graphics   Shapes arranged in a diagram format to visually communicate information. (7)

Soft Edges   Effect that changes a picture's normal hard edges to a soft, feathered appearance that gradually fades into the background color. (4) (8)

Source   When working with Clipboard objects, the presentation or other document from which the objects were cut or copied. (3)

Spelling   Feature that corrects spelling by comparing words to an internal dictionary file. (3)

Split cells   To divide a table cell into two smaller cells. (5)

Standard   Layout for displaying an organization chart; also, can refer to standard colors such as red, blue, green, or yellow. (7)

Status bar   Horizontal bar at the bottom of the PowerPoint window that displays information about the current presentation on the left and viewing commands on the right. (1)

Subordinate shape   Shape in an organization chart that is connected to a superior shape reflecting a higher level. (7)

Table   Arrangement of information in rows and columns. (5)

Table borders   Lines forming the edges of cells, columns, and rows and the outline of the table. (5)

Table style   Combination of formatting options based on theme colors. (5)

Tabs   On the Ribbon, task-oriented groups of commands. Used with Tab, tabs can be used to indent text. Tab stops appear on the horizontal ruler. (1)

Template   Preformatted presentation with a background design, font settings, and suggested content that is ready for input. (2)

Text box   Free-form text object used to add text to slides. (2)

Text fill   WordArt fill effect that can be a solid color, gradient fill, pattern, texture, or picture fill. (4)

Text outline   WordArt outline effect that can be modified by color, width, and line style. (4)

Theme   See **Design Theme.**

Theme colors   Preset groups of colors for text, background, accent, and hyperlinks that can be applied to a presentation. (2) (3) (11)

Theme effects   Selection of built-in effects that can be applied to a presentation. (3)

Theme fonts   Selection of fonts that can be applied to a presentation. (3) (11)

Thesaurus   Finds words with similar meanings. (3)

35-mm slides   Output format that creates individual 35-millimeter slides from each slide in a presentation. These slides are usually prepared by a service bureau and then arranged in a slide carousel tray to project with a 35-mm projector. (13)

3-D   Orientation that adds a perspective dimension to create the illusion of depth. (7)

3-D Rotation   Effect that enables an object to be displayed in a variety of dimensional treatments. (4) (8)

Thumbnail   Miniature version of a graphic image. In PowerPoint, a miniature version of a slide is often referred to as a "thumbnail." (1)

Tick marks   Small measurement marks on a chart's value or category axis. (6)

Title text   Text that usually appears at the top of a PowerPoint slide. Title text is usually placed in a title text placeholder. (1)

Toggle button   Switches between on and off when clicked. (2)

Total Row   Table style option that emphasizes the last row of the table. (5)

Transform   Effect that changes text into different shapes. (4)

Transition effects   Visual or sound effects used when changing between slides during a slide show. (1)

Transitions   See **Slide transitions.**

Translate   Used to convert a word or group of words to a different language. (12)

Transparency   Allows the color behind an object to show through the object. (8)

Trim   Feature used to shorten an audio clip from the beginning or the end. (10)

TrueType font   Most common font format. (2) (14)

2-D   Orientation in which you see the shapes in dimensions of height (up/down measurement) and width (left/right measurement). (7)

Undo   Reverses the last action, such as an editing change. PowerPoint can undo up to 20 actions if the Save feature has not been used. (3)

Ungroup   To separate a group of objects. When an object is ungrouped, each of its parts behaves as an individual object. (4)

Vector drawing   Illustration made up of lines and shapes that can be scaled to any size or aspect ratio without blurring. Vector drawings can be modified in PowerPoint by recoloring and by adding, removing, and rearranging individual elements. (4)

Video   Any motion file that will play during a slide show. May include animated video clips. (10)

View buttons   Four buttons located on the lower right corner of the PowerPoint window. You use these buttons to switch between Normal view (the default), Slide Sorter view, Reading view, and Slide Show view. (1)

Word wrap   Text automatically continues to the next line in a placeholder or text box when a line is full. (2)

WordArt   Text objects with fill and line colors plus special effects such as Shadow, Reflection, Glow, Bevel, 3-D Rotation, and Transform. (4)

Worksheet   Area in Microsoft Excel in which you enter numbers and labels that are used to create a chart. When you create a new chart in PowerPoint, an Excel worksheet automatically appears containing sample data that you can delete or overwrite. (6)

Zoom   Used to change the size at which you view an area of the screen. (1)